Martin Frobisher

Martin Frobisher

Elizabethan Privateer

James McDermott

Yale University Press
New Haven and London

For information about this and other Yale University Press publications, please contact:
U.S. Office: sales.press@yale.edu   www.yale.edu/yup
Europe Office: sales@yaleup.co.uk   www.yaleup.co.uk

Set in Adobe Garamond by Best-set Typesetter Ltd, Hong Kong
Printed in Great Britain by St Edmundsbury Press, Suffolk

Library of Congress Cataloging-in-Publication Data
McDermott, James, 1956–
Sir Martin Frobisher : Elizabethan privateer / James McDermott.
p.   cm.
Includes bibliographical references and index.
ISBN 0-300-08380-7 (cloth : alk. paper)
1. Frobisher, Martin, Sir, ca. 1535-1594.   2. Great Britain—History—Elizabeth, 1558-1603—Biography.   3. Privateering—Great Britain—History—16th century. 4. Great Britain—History, Naval—Tudors, 1485-1603.   5. Ship captains—Great Britain—Biography.   6. Explorers—Great Britain—Biography.   7. Pirates—Great Britain—Biography.   8. Northwest Passage.   9. Armada, 1588.   I. Title.

DA66.1.F76 M37   2001   910.4'5'092—dc21   [B]   00-049948

A catalogue record for this book is available from the British Library.

10 9 8 7 6 5 4 3 2 1

Published with assistance from the foundation established in memory of Oliver Baty Cunningham of the Class of 1917, Yale College.

O Frobusher, thy brute and name
shalbe enroled in bookes,
That whosoever after coms
and on thy labor lookes
Shall muse and marvell at thyne actes,
and greatness of thy minde . . .

Thomas Churchyard, 1578

He is . . . so full of lyenge talke as no man maye
credytt hym in anye thinge that he doethe speake.

Michael Lok, 1579

Contents

List of Illustrations

Note on Editorial Policy

All primary source material has been presented utilizing original grammar, punctuation and spelling, with elisions therein expanded and shown in parenthesis. Common sixteenth-century usages, such as the random transpositions of 'u' and 'v', 'i' and 'j', have been retained, though the Old English thorn is represented as 'th' throughout. Documents reproduced in important secondary collections such as Laughton, Oppenheim and Corbett, who followed the modernizing conventions of their day, have been quoted verbatim unless the author has considered it necessary, due to the relevance (or dubious transcription) of a particular piece, to return to the original manuscript. All passages with modernized spelling are so noted.

Most of the original documents cited in this work are of English origin and, therefore, dated in the Julian style; this has been retained for the purpose of consistency (it is unsatisfactory, for example, to refer to the 'war of 21 July' – the contemporary English name for the Armada campaign – as having commenced on 31 July). The relatively few dates cited in Spanish and French documents post-1582 are of the Gregorian style with the Julian equivalent given, if necessary, in parenthesis. The New Year has been taken as 1 January throughout and date-years corrected where necessary.

Personal names are reproduced in the preferred contemporary forms, insofar as any consistency was observed. Frobisher himself presents particular difficulties, having never decided upon a definitive version of his family name. In his case, the author uses the accepted modern form.

Finally, a brief apology. The term 'Englishmen' is employed throughout this work for want of a suitably gender-neutral term (Spaniards, Italians and Germans are well provided for in this respect; the English and French races are not). In certain contexts, the phrase is appropriate; in others, it implicitly renders inconsequential half the population of contemporary England. The author's hope that offence will not be taken may be optimistic, but it is sincere nevertheless.

Acknowledgements

The genesis of the present work may be traced to a conversation with David Beers Quinn, with whom the author was associated in the work of the Archival Research Task Force (ARTAF), the UK-based arm of the Canadian Museum of Civilization's *Meta Incognita* project. From 1990 to 1999, scholars working with the project drew upon existing and newly researched documentary, archaeological and sociological data to re-examine Martin Frobisher's three north-west voyages of 1576–8, the first recorded contacts between Europeans and the Inuit culture of Baffin Island. Much of the author's own research is recalled in the relevant parts of the present work, which unashamedly seeks to complement, and to promote further interest in, the project and its findings.

In addition to Professor Quinn (to whom further thanks are owed for his generous offer to read and criticize a first draft of this work), the author wishes to express his gratitude to other members of, and associate advisors to, ARTAF, whose work has been an invaluable source of material on the northwest voyages – not least, to Sir Ian Gourlay, ARTAF chairman and one of nature's least-lay laymen; to Mr George Frobisher, descendant of Martin Frobisher and family genealogist; to Stephanie Le Gall for translations of contemporary Spanish documents; to the staffs of the British Library, the Public Record Office, the Pepys Library, Magdalene College, Cambridge, the Bodleian Library, Oxford, the New York Public Library and the Henry E. Huntington Library, San Marino, California, and to the archivists of Mercers' and Stationers' Halls, London. Finally, the author owes his deepest gratitude to his wife, Julia: a rigorous healer of split infinitives, scourge of meandering sentences and enduring font of common sense.

Introduction

Martin Frobisher died at or about the age of fifty-nine, from an injury sustained in a hand-to-hand maul. Leading a force of Englishmen through the gateway of a Spanish fortress on French soil, he suffered a pistol shot to his thigh 'alongst the huckell bonne'. The fortress – *El Leon* – was overrun, and a bloody massacre ensued; in the early evening, hard-pressed English survivors tended their wounded and ignored those of their French allies, who had sustained many more casualties. The English army, of some 2,000–3,000 soldiers and mariners, had a staff comprising just two field-surgeons and six assistants; inevitably, medical attention on the battlefield was at best cursory, and many of those lying in and around the fort who had survived the immediate battle were to die within the next few hours. Frobisher believed his own wound to be a trifling matter – no doubt he was forced to lie still by the anonymous butcher who examined him – but it appeared, superficially, that the injury was not serious. The ball was prised from his thigh, the wound dressed, and the surgeon moved on thereafter to other, less august causes. Had more comprehensive treatment been available immediately, it is likely that the diagnosis of the commander of the French forces, Marshal Aumont – who wrote solicitously to Queen Elizabeth a few days later to inform her that her admiral had been slightly wounded, 'mais ce ne sera rien' – would have been accurate. But Frobisher's assailant had been so close to him that the wadding from the charge had impacted with the ball, and at least part of this remained within his thigh. Two weeks after the fall of *El Leon*, on 22 November 1594, Frobisher died at Plymouth, poisoned by a gangrenous infection that had spread throughout his lower parts.

For almost six years, England had been engaged in a war against the widest-flung empire on earth: one that, in the span of its irruptions, may be regarded as the first global conflict. In the grip of that struggle, the outcome of which threatened the very independence of the English nation, the death of one man created no great stir of popular emotion. Frobisher's innards were removed and buried at Plymouth – for reasons of hygiene, rather than as a sop to the town's civic pride – and the hollowed body was carried to London thereafter to be buried in the church of St Giles Without-the-Walls, Cripplegate. If the terms of his will were honoured, there was also a solemn memorial service held at the parish church of All Saints, Normanton in West Yorkshire, close to the estate that had served his family for more than a century. These brief tokens of esteem being discharged, the memory of Martin Frobisher, like that of a generation of his fellow adventurers, faded swiftly into the charnel anonymity of war. Richard Grenville was dead already, struck down upon the deck of the *Revenge* during a lunatic joust against an entire Spanish fleet. Francis Drake and John Hawkins were to die little more than a year hence, their hearts and bowels sacrificed to that perennial icon of English longing, the Panama Isthmus. The struggle against Spain dragged out its course, and the age was divested one by one of those who had defined it. In Frobisher's case, reputation had been given its barest due: a swaddling of death-linen put around a corpse that, even in death, was too large to be managed discreetly, and the small privilege of a grave beneath the roof of a church allowed to it. Much later, a mural depicting the most memorable episodes in Frobisher's career was placed upon the church wall above his tomb, but this was destroyed during another human conflagration, the Blitz.

There is only one known idiosyncratic portrait of Frobisher. Now held in the Bodleian Library, Oxford, it was painted by Cornelius Ketel in the early months of 1577. He portrayed a man of impressive height and build, dressed in best which is nevertheless sober by contemporary standards. In the background, partially obscured by the subject's body, stands a globe: the symbol of a recent, imagined achievement. In his right hand, he holds a pistol; the other rests upon the hilt of a sword. His eyes are hard and seem to express impatience; his mouth turns slightly downwards in a bad-tempered *moue* that may have been his habitual expression or a hint that the painter had very little time before either the pistol or sword was tested. The image is not one of a man at ease, either with himself or the world about him, and as such it is a fine testament to Ketel's artistic perception. A likeness that reflected more of the inner man is hardly to be imagined.

The turbulence of Martin Frobisher's temperament mirrored that of his career, and to a great extent obfuscated it. He was, and is, remembered principally for a disastrous three-year commercial venture and an heroic but flawed role in that classically ambiguous English achievement, the 1588 Armada campaign. The rest of his life has been largely passed over, or rendered in the broadest strokes. He remains the least known of that generation of Elizabethan adventurers whose exploits have long fed posterity's need for heavily coloured heroes, though there is more of prudence than indolence in this oversight. Conflicting contemporary opinions regarding the man and his achievements – few of which could be regarded as remotely impartial – had begun to harden even before his death, and provide little from which to reflesh an elusive character. Frobisher, it seems, did not encourage impartial perspectives. The positive assessments of certain episodes in his career have outweighed the negative, but that balance is hardly conclusive. The poor opinions tend to be of those who had actually met him.

The loquacity of Frobisher's critics was in no way matched by that of his intimates – an imbalance for which he must take much of the blame. His passions, if profligate, were spent entirely in the service of his own ends; though married twice, he devoted neither time nor affection to domestic commitments which seem to have been made for the sake of convention only. No children – who might best have provided a warmer posterity – resulted from these associations. His blood-kin provided no better memorial; they remained dutifully anonymous throughout his lifetime, inherited and squandered his painfully acquired estate and fled thereafter into oblivion. As for his friends, none is known to us as more than a name, and his sparse surviving correspondence does nothing to fill out this emptiness. Martin Frobisher was, in effect, his only close witness; yet even at the end of his life, surrounded by those tokens of honour and wealth that he had sought so assiduously, he remained only semi-literate, with little ability – or, probably, inclination – to set out his version of events that seemed often to overwhelm his capacity to determine them.

Having failed to provide or arrange for his own defence, Frobisher hardly attempted to confound the criticisms of others. He imposed himself in a strikingly physical manner, carrying habitually prudent men into ill-founded speculation and sometimes outright banditry by the force of his presence, will and conviction; yet despite these superficial tokens of an inner strength, his career was defined by an abiding inability to subdue or disguise his manifold weaknesses of character. The present author is aware that he makes a very poor argument for a biography of such a man; but within the discrepant aspects of this troubled nature lie strong clues to a *Zeitgeist* that is often disregarded in favour of the more palatable tokens of the Elizabethan age. Frobisher never considered himself as 'of the people' (the suggestion would have outraged him); nevertheless, he conformed precisely to the common man's idea of the popular hero: at once the antithesis of all that courtly culture held dear and an exemplary product of the fractures that pervaded contemporary English society.

This study is, inevitably, a portrait of that society, if only in setting a context for the dislocations that informed much of Frobisher's life and career. It will not be an Elizabethan pageant, though mention of familiar names and events will be unavoidable. The emphasis will lie rather upon the peculiar possibilities and pitfalls that determined the nature of what was slowly emerging as a fledgling sense of 'Englishness', and how, particularly, they affected one man. In all ages, nations ask the same questions of their nature and identity, but these were never more urgently posed by Englishmen than during the years that approximately coincided with Frobisher's life – years riven by upheaval, disharmony and the failure of old certainties to provide new answers. To Frobisher himself, such questions were at most irrelevances, and more likely incomprehensible; nevertheless, the course of his life was moulded by their every implication. His failure to understand this probably helped to preserve what little peace of mind he was able to achieve, but that merciful disengagement has since served only to obscure further what is already opaque. If, as the author intends, the present work places this furious mind, life and career in a rounder perspective, the least-known of Elizabeth's first-rank of 'sea-dogs' may emerge as something more than a footnote upon a spurious roll-call of derring-do.

Prologue

In the early hours of 7 June 1578, an east wind carried strongly off Cape Clear, one of the western-most points of Ireland. A few miles seaward of that timeless sailors' landmark, a small bark, the *Grechwinde* of Bristol, struggled to keep a south-easterly course towards her home port, and deliverance.

On that morning, the *Grechwinde* was a dying ship. Several days earlier, returning from Spain with a cargo of olives and wine-sack, she had been attacked and overwhelmed off Cape St Vincent by a French privateer. For years past, the coastal waters of western Europe had teemed with such free-booters, set loose against their princes' enemies under commissions that were interpreted loosely, if heeded at all. The privateers are likely to have been Protestants, as were many, if not most, of their victims in the *Grechwinde*; they may have paid lip service to the alliance of Englishman and Huguenot against the surging tide of the Counter Reformation (though little that was not self-serving ever came from that association); they may, most likely, have thought of their prize money and cared nothing for whom or what they attacked. For men such as these, war was a livelihood rather than a human disaster; and depredation, as always, provided the readiest means of securing a profit.

Several of the *Grechwinde*'s mariners had been killed outright in the fight to save her cargoes. Others lay too severely wounded to assist those few of their able comrades who still attempted to set their bark against contrary winds and currents. Their increasingly desperate labours were unavailing, and the small vessel had been swept far to the north and west, past the Scillies and into the ocean proper. By now, their strength was almost spent; for several days past, their only sustenance had been rank water and a few olives spilled by the victorious Frenchmen as they stripped the vessel of anything that seemed remotely valuable. The morning of 7 June was, probably, the last in which their failing efforts would count for anything: another small ship, like dozens before it – too many of them from Bristol – seemed set to disappear into the enormity of the Ocean Sea.

It may have been the sound of gulls, following a human detritus which they themselves could no longer spare, that made the few uninjured mariners pause in their labours and search the sea before them. From the south, an unimaginable salvation emerged swiftly through low, driving rain: fifteen ships, possibly the largest English fleet to put into the Atlantic since the Hundred Years' War, bore down directly upon the *Grechwinde*. Their flag-ship, one of the Queen's own vessels, came up to the stricken bark and heaved to; the other vessels, faithful to their precise instructions, lowered their sails also.

It is unlikely that anyone in the fleet had any prior acquaintance with the Bristol men or their bark, but to assist distressed compatriots upon the seas was an abiding obligation. One of the flagship's two surgeons was lowered into the bark to treat her wounded; men bringing barrels of fresh water, biscuit, cheese, butter and peas followed him, to replace necessities stolen by the freebooters. The entire transaction would have been discharged in less than an half-an-hour; barely time to hear the woeful victims' tale, or to warn them of the likelihood of further freebooters ahead and wish them 'God Speed'. One of the Bristol men, looking up from his cup, may have asked the fleet's business before his deliverers returned to their ship. If so, what he heard was almost beyond belief; but salvation breeds politeness, and almost certainly he would not have laughed aloud.

The brief act of mercy done, the ships set sail once more and veered away, north and westwards. For them, this was as a fair and prosperous a wind as it had been deadly to the *Grechwinde* sweeping them rapidly out into the ocean. Within minutes, they must have been invisible once more, cloaked by the low clouds and haar that lay unseasonably upon the western approaches that summer. So swiftly had their saviours come and gone that the men of the *Grechwinde* might have mistrusted their senses, had they not the proof of their full bellies and – a small *quid pro quo* – letters they had undertaken to deliver to a man who waited anxiously for news of the fleet's progress.

This was not a military expedition, for all that war pressed upon many of the nations of Europe. It had an admiral whose interest in peaceful purposes was at best peripheral, and guns, and orders to defend itself if necessary; but in its ships' holds were pickaxes and shovels, and great, prefabricated frames to build a home in a land in which no known white man had ever dwelt. The ballast of two of the ships consisted of 10,000 bricks, because the great house was intended to have walls that would endure, the vagaries of fate, weather and a new enemy permitting. In it would dwell carpenters, miners, shoemakers, fishermen and bakers; all of whose skills would provide for this, the first English colony in the New World – a colony without women, or children, and with but a single, impossibly optimistic purpose.

The holds of the other ships held further supplies and provisions, but these were for pioneers who would labour alongside the colonists and then return to England thereafter, their ships now laden with a different, more precious ballast: one that was intended to enrich England as the plunder of the Aztec and Incan empires had enriched Spain only a few decades earlier. The Queen herself had set out this enterprise, having seized and then turned the original intentions of its architects. To remind them of this unpalatable truth, she had given a commission to her admiral under the Broad Seal of England, and this represented more than a token of her faith in his abilities. It represented money – her money – and she expected a large return upon it.

We do not know if the surviving mariners of the bark *Grechwinde* reached their home port before exhaustion finished the job that the French privateers had started; but if they did so, their gratitude to the commander of the strange, ghostly fleet would have been intense. Even then, they could have had little understanding of the true magnitude of their good fortune. Despoiled by privateers, they had been saved thereafter by another; one of the most persistent of the breed. They had been fed from the pockets of merchants, courtiers and the Queen herself, all of whom were coming to rue the burden they had assumed whilst hoping, with waning enthusiasm, that something worthwhile might yet come of it. Their wounds and thirst had been eased by men who were as yet uncertain of their own recompense for passing beyond the sensible bounds of the world, though the coming ordeal was all too clearly anticipated. The stricken mariners of the *Grechwinde* had thought themselves cursed by the direst misfortune, but it was they alone who were to derive the slightest benefit from this voyage.

PART ONE

To Serve His Owne Turne:
c. 1535–74

Of honest parentage, Jentlemen of a good house and antiquity[1]

ONE

Early Life

Like much else in Martin Frobisher's life, its beginning is a matter of some uncertainty. He was born at his family's ancestral home of Altofts: a small manor in the parish of Normanton, near Wakefield in the West Riding of Yorkshire, the name of which suggests pre-Danelaw origins.[2] Much later, he implied his birth-year to have been 1539, but recent research casts doubt upon this. In 1538, Thomas Cromwell instituted a national system of parish registration of births and deaths, to replace *ad hoc* arrangements that had relied entirely upon the varying diligence of individual parish priests. As a member of a prominent local family, Martin's name would have appeared in the new Normanton parish register had he been born in that year or later. Since it did not, he was almost certainly born earlier, perhaps as early as 1535/6, given the chronology of later events.[3]

No record of the manorial properties which comprised Altofts has survived. Its possession brought a local magistracy and, no doubt, a seat at the sheriff's peripatetic table; but the estate has long vanished, having been partitioned and sold off very soon after Martin's death. The hamlet of Altofts is now a large village, half-lost among the motorways and sprawling conurbations of West Yorkshire, its discreet identity preserved only by a fortuitous loop in the river Calder that almost surrounds it. Upon the most detailed maps of the area, symbols commemorate dismantled railways, disused opencast scourings and other tokens of a recent, industrial past, but of Altoft's more distant manorial dignity there is not the slightest memorial. 'What's past, and what's to come is strewn with husks and formless ruin of oblivion' is a truth that reasserted itself with particular swiftness upon the house of

Frobisher, perhaps even before the sentiment itself was set down, barely six years after this story closes.[4]

The provenance of the name Frobisher has not been established definitively, but it has been suggested that the persistence of the form 'Furbisher' into the sixteenth century may commemorate the French *fourbisseur*, or sword-cutler. As the earliest known ancestor of Martin Frobisher was a professional soldier, this remains a plausible assumption.[5] The family first settled in West Yorkshire sometime during the fifteenth century; prior to that, it had resided in lands around Chirke in the Welsh Border country, the gift of Edward I to John Frobisher (b. *circa* 1260), a Scot who had served in the English army during the Welsh campaigns. Thurstan Frobisher (b. 1420), was the first of the family to cross the Pennines eastwards; his son, John, married Joan, the daughter of Sir William Scargill, steward of Pontefract Castle, through whom the manor of Altofts appears to have devolved upon the Frobisher family. Since that time, successive generations of the family had held it continuously in fee from the Crown, and cemented the foundations of their estate by further judicious marriages – most notably, that of Martin's uncle, Francis Frobisher, to Christiana, daughter of Sir Brian Hastings, Sheriff of Yorkshire; a man who included among his acquaintances William Fitzwilliam, Earl of Southampton and Lord Admiral of England.[6]

Martin Frobisher's mother was Margaret, *née* Yorke, of Gowthwaite. She bore at least five children who survived into adulthood; these were, in probable order of birth, John, David, Martin, Jane and Margaret. Her father, Sir John Yorke, was either the father or uncle of his name sake, Sir John Yorke of London: the notable merchant-taylor, financier and Iberian trader.[7] Of Martin's own father, Bernard Frobisher, there is little extant information. He died prematurely in August 1542, leaving no known obligations but the care of his wife and children to his elder brother, Francis: farmer of the manor of Altofts, Recorder of Doncaster and Mayor of that borough in 1535.[8]

Thus the path of the Frobishers' advancement to solid second- or third-string county stock had been unremarkably steady. By the early decades of the sixteenth century their pretensions to gentility required a coat of arms, described much later as 'ermine on a fesie ingrayled between three griffons heads erased, sable, a greyhound cursant, argent, colared ules lyned or';[9] but this minor – and entirely conventional – self-indulgence apart, it does not seem that they had ever aspired to more than local prominence. There is no evidence that they were a particularly well-travelled clan, nor even that their interests habitually extended beyond the bounds of the West and South Ridings (though Francis Frobisher himself – perhaps by right of his judicious marriage – was to be appointed to the Council of the North at Elizabeth's accession, and would serve upon it at least until 1562).[10] Had Bernard Frobisher not died as a relatively young man, there is no reason to assume that any of his sons would have pushed their horizons out beyond those of their forefathers. Nor does the traumatic occasion of his death appear to have brought any immediate dislocation in his immediate family's circumstances; for several years thereafter, Altofts remained the centre – perhaps the entirety – of the young Martin's world: a place in which, probably, he was happy. He left it at a relatively early age, but there is no evidence that he did so willingly. His later marriage to a local girl, and his acquisition of properties thereabouts, suggest that the memories and associations of his childhood continued to exert a powerfully centripetal effect, even across oceanic distances.

Without a witness to these formative years at Altofts, we may only speculate upon their nature. The ward of a country gentleman – even one who enjoyed a substantial local reputation – would not have been placed too often in the path of great men or events, though the family's social status would have required its boys to be raised to a certain standard. It is reasonable to assume that Martin acquired the most basic skills of the rural gentleman: horse-riding, elementary sword-play and the minor degree of literacy that compulsory attendance at divine service encouraged were all requirements that preceeded – even obviated – the need for a more formal education. Perhaps, had he remained at Altofts, he would have begun to understand the rudiments of estate management also; but not upon an estate that was ever intended to be his own. Francis Frobisher was clearly a man of some means, yet as fond or as dutiful a surrogate for his brother as he tried to be, it is unlikely that either his purse or estate could stretch to accommodate indefinitely the needs of six extra mouths. His guardianship of his dead brother's family was a Christian duty and he obliged it, but only until provision could be made for them elsewhere. What that provision was for Martin's siblings is, and will probably remain, unclear: their lives are almost entirely obscure, save where they briefly converge upon that of their famous brother. In the case of Martin himself, there seems to have been little agonizing on Francis's part. He quickly used the occasion of his sister's death in 1549 to transfer responsibility for the boy to the maternal line. Martin was packed off to London, probably at some time during the same year, to learn a trade in the household of his mother's kinsman, Sir John Yorke.[11]

Many years later, it was claimed that a lack of suitable schools around Altofts had forced this removal.[12] This is plausible, but not entirely convincing. The dissolution of monastic foundations did not appreciably reduce the number of school places; most of the abolished chantry establishments were immediately reinstituted as grammar schools under Edward VI's patronage, and West Yorkshire did not otherwise suffer unduly from a lack of resources.[13] The claim may have been intended retrospectively to address and absolve a different issue – that of Martin Frobisher's abiding semi-literacy. The sparse surviving examples of his written style indicates that whatever schooling he received was to make very little mark upon him. Conversely, the weighty evidence of his fiery and unpredictable temperament makes it very likely that the true reason for his translation to the Yorke household was Francis Frobisher's urgent need to place his nephew where his robust and unintellectual energies could be diverted into practical channels. Whether the choice of London was one of several options or a final resort cannot be determined; what is clear is that opportunities for advancement for a willing young man were much more plentiful there than in the West Riding of Yorkshire, and that the London Yorkes were well placed to identify them.

To any fourteen-year-old country boy, removal to London would have been a daunting prospect. As the kingdom's premier urban sprawl and the focus of almost all political, social and economic vitality, the city did not so much eclipse other centres of population as provide an entirely different form of social continuity. It was – though successive kings had struggled to prevent it – the closest English equivalent to the semi-independent urban polities of the European mainland. Those who lived within its walls, or in the proto-suburbs that had begun to spread north and west from the medieval heart, regarded themselves as citizens first and subjects only a distant thereafter. This was a community of self-belief that was not diluted by the extreme social and economic disparities endured by almost 150,000 souls inhabiting an area of less than two square miles. To be of the city was to enjoy rights of ancient liberties – ephemeral in fact but vital in presumption – that had been secured over centuries of alternating struggle and accommodation with the Crown, and defended more than once with the blood of its beneficiaries. The peculiar polity that had grown from such ancient strifes was unique in English society. Londoners owed their loyalties to the king no less than any rural swineherd, yet they had a civic government that was as often a creditor upon royal resources and goodwill as it was the corporate expression of their fealty. What this exceptionalist state represented to individual Londoners depended entirely upon personal circumstances: at one extreme, it meant nothing more than the right to dwell in the gutter of one's choosing; for a few, as we shall see, it provided the possibility for collaborations in which new and frightening opportunities for advancement or ruin might be tested. For one recent addition to the City's population in 1549 – the young Martin Frobisher – the translation represented a sea-change in circumstances so profound that his time in Yorkshire seems almost inconsequential in shaping his future nature and ambitions. It is only in London – or rather, from London – that we begin to understand something of that process.

The means by which the boy came to the City are not known. He may have shipped in one of the hundreds of tiny vessels that plied their coastal trade between the rivers Humber and Thames, if his uncle Francis was willing to pay the relatively expensive fare for excess cargo. If not, the slower, more dangerous but cheaper three-day passage along the great North Road would have brought him south, with overnight stops, probably at two or more of the venerable coaching towns – Grantham, Huntingdon, Biggleswade or Ware – *en route*. At the City walls, no doubt he would have needed to have been directed to Walbrook, the riverside ward in which Sir John Yorke's home was situated.[14] The prior arrangements concluded between Francis Frobisher and Yorke in respect of the boy remained a private family matter, as did the nature of his welcome at his new home; but it is unlikely that either offered false reassurance of easy times to come. His uncle, it will become clear, was not a man to indulge the idle pursuits of the would-be gentleman; nor was he over-burdened with sentimental affections, least of all to those come upon the charity that kinship demanded. As a poor cousin, the boy was at best a burden; as a resource, he had at least the potential to repay the outlay upon his daily bread. How that resource was realized in the short term is, again, a matter for speculation. Martin may have received further schooling – though to little effect, given his lack of aptitude. Some attempt may have been made to teach him the rudiments of book-keeping (his later accounts for disbursements of money during the north-west enterprise suggest he was familiar with, though not competent in, its techniques). Perhaps he also received a cursory introduction to the protocols and subtleties of merchandising, if only in watching his patron and associates at their business. Most probably, however, he was immediately put to those physical tasks which required minimum of initiative or supervision – loading and unloading goods or running errands for his uncle – until some better use could be made of him. For almost four years, the boy served the house of Yorke in this modest way, and left no account of the experience. There can be little doubt, however, that like many Londoners of widely divergent talents, he was waiting upon something more. It may be too convenient to assume, as has often been the case, that he was always intended for the sea;

but human beings, like liquids, usually find their own level. The brashness and aggression that he displayed all too frequently in later life suggest that even as a youth, he entertained few of the normal fears and uncertainties that provide a necessary balance to more introspective natures. His final recorded statement, set down some forty-five years later, recalled the imminent dread of battle (and, possibly, his own death) with no more fearful anticipation than 'it was tyme for vs to goa through with it'.[15] This quality of imperturbability, as it became apparent to his uncle, may have rendered any further estimation of his character and talents entirely unnecessary. To go to sea required a modicum of courage and little else; station and presumption deferred to ability in its egalitarian vastness and in turn were marked by it. For those seeking fame, or fortune, or placement for a superfluous nephew, it had always been an attractive recourse; but during these years, it would prove to be a particularly felicitous highway. In the absence of a more voluble witness to Martin's early life, we cannot know precisely where his own ambitions lay (if indeed he ever rationalized them); yet whatever he anticipated, circumstance and possibility strongly converged at the water side to which he had been brought by necessity. At that moment, there was a young king upon the English throne, an old certainty of profit dissolving and new occasions – dimly perceived but palpable nevertheless – to lay out some money to good effect. Here, upon London's principal artery, the means and will to realize such opportunities had begun to gather.

TWO

London and Yorke

At what time our Marchants perceived the commodities and wares of England to bee in small request with the countreys and people about us, and neere unto us, and that those Marchandizes which strangers in the time and memorie of our auncestors did earnestly seeke and desire, were nowe neglected, and the price thereof abated, although by us carried to their owne portes, and all forreine Marchandizes in great accompt, and their prises wonderfully raised: certeine grave Citizens of London, and men of great wisedome, and carefull for the good of their Countrey, begane to thinke with themselves, howe this mischiefe might bee remedied.[1]

During the mid-sixteenth century, much of the English nation felt itself to be at, or approaching, a portentous crossroads. The so-called 'mid-Tudor crisis' was, and has remained, an opaque beast. Whether in fact there was a crisis at all is still a matter of considerable debate, but perhaps the question of its actuality is less relevant than the widespread (if diffuse) appreciation held by many thoughtful English men and women, that theirs was an increasingly unfortunate age. The breakdown of religious consensus, the emerging crises of succession and the subsequent factionalism fostered, the apparently omnipresent threat of invasion or rebellion – all were problems whose seeming intractability unnerved a race that by nature remained innately conservative, notwithstanding its readiness to endure abstract novelty for practical peace. And if these several discontents, real and perceived, were not occupation enough for troubled minds, they were supplemented by a further and far more immediate problem from the year 1550.

The English merchant, whether before his God or his ledger, was a pragmatic creature. For him, the stewardship and increase of his physical estate remained an overwhelming priority, despite his readiness to co-opt the Deity as its sole foundation or sustainer. At the precise mid-point of the century, this admirably practical perspective was both tested and sharpened by an equally practical problem. The English economy, having long enjoyed relative stability, entered an intensely unsettled phase. The conditions that brought this upheaval had been ripening for a number of years; but their implications, as always, struck with little forewarning, and with particular virulence upon the most sensitive yardstick of the nation's health: its overseas trade.

For almost a century, the exemplar of that trade had been the merchant adventurer who carried his broadcloths and, more recently, his kerseys to one or more of the four great trade fairs in the Low Countries – 'Pask' (Easter), 'Synxon' (St John's day), 'Bamas' (early autumn) and 'Cold' (winter) – held annually at the towns of Antwerp and, fifty miles to the north-west, Bergen-op-Zoom ('Barrow' to lazy English tongues).[2] As the sixteenth century progressed, these month-long occasions proved increasingly inadequate for the growing number of transactions in English cloths, and the market gradually expanded to become a continuous activity, based almost entirely at Antwerp alone.[3] The volume of business contracted there, and the regulations which governed it, set benchmarks of price and quality for much of the northern and central European markets. For fifty years prior to 1550, these markets had drawn in an ever greater proportion of London capital, disinclining its cloth merchants (whose number and influence had increased commensurately with the growth of the trade) to look elsewhere for their profits. From the 1540s, their business was given a huge boost by successive devaluations of the English coinage, initiated by Henry VIII to subsidize a vainglorious foreign policy, which both increased the saleability of English cloths abroad and further narrowed the scope for, or interest in, diversification.

The speculative element was not entirely lacking, even so. Prominent merchant adventurer families such as the Greshams, Bondes and Loks, whilst principally committed to trade in the Low Countries, did business as far afield as the Greek islands and the Levant, bringing Candian wines, dried fruits and other luxury comestibles directly to English tables, thus avoiding an Antwerp 'turn' on their importation.[4] However, commercial traffic with the eastern Mediterranean was fraught with the incremental risks of distance in an uncertain age, and was never to represent more than a small proportion of English overseas trade in the sixteenth century. It was in any case to be disrupted

by the decline of the Venetian sea-routes and corresponding expansion of
Ottoman sea-power from the 1530s onward – a process which, inevitably, concentrated even more of western Europe's trade with the East through its
Antwerp entrepôt.[5] In other directions, as we shall see, English merchants had
begun to tap the riches of the New World via the Iberian ports of Seville,
San Lucar and Lisbon; but direct London trade to Spain and Portugal,
though valuable in terms of the volume of transactions, was not statistically
significant. The Iberian countries took many English cloths, but they did so
principally via the Antwerp market or, in the case of Spain, via Portuguese
middle-men.[6]

In English ports outside London, merchants needed markets more distant
than Antwerp to allow them to survive (if never to challenge) the commercial supremacy of the capital. From Bristol, Southampton and Exeter, ships
had long been set out to trade with Gascony and the Basque country
(Southampton continued to maintain a monopoly on the importation of
sweet wines), or to voyage beyond the continental shelf to Iceland, where,
since 1413 at the latest, they had traded cloths and other commodities for
stockfish.[7] As we shall see, a number of enterprising Southampton merchants
had ventured further still during the 1540s, but these were highly individualistic episodes that had little precedent and even less future. Though
resourceful, the merchants of the provincial ports disposed of too little capital
to control more than a small proportion of England's external commerce.[8]
Respectively, Bristol (the kingdom's second port) and Exeter had accounted
for approximately eleven and seven per cent of official English cloth exports
at the beginning of the century, and since then they had been in relative
decline.[9] Of the southern English ports outside London, only Portsmouth
and Plymouth, standing upon the threshold of a golden age fuelled by their
busy privateers and the needs of war, prospered as, elsewhere, the long and
growing demand in Europe for English finished cloths diverted more and
more resources into satisfying its voracity. The volume of this trade, centred
upon the capital, had come to eclipse all other forms of international commerce. English overseas business had become, effectively, London business;
and until 1550, London's merchant adventurers had little incentive to change
the manner in which they managed their affairs.

Yet all booms, however protracted, eventually create the conditions for
their own destruction. The same forces that had brought so much new trade
to London had, inescapably, placed too much pressure upon established infrastructures elsewhere. An explosion of wool-producing centres in the English
countryside, new enclosures of land and the wholesale eviction of non-sheep

livestock from pastures were all symptoms of the drive to satisfy this market; all, in turn, contributed to the dangerous loading of the English economy. Furthermore, the median quality of English cloths began to fall as the number of domestic cloth-producers rose to meet demand, thereby partially undermining the reputation that had given them such a great proportion of the European market.[10] In 1550, that market finally overheated. For the first time in living memory, merchant adventurers taking their wares to the Low Countries found that they had too much produce to satisfy too few customers. Cloth prices plummeted just as the effects of the most recent devaluation of the English coinage – to pay for expensive military campaigns in Scotland – fed into the home economy. London merchants, long used to – and cushioned by – favourable trading conditions, found themselves with unwanted stock on their hands and a currency that could buy far less foreign goods than previously. It was not to be a fatal shock to English commerce – the market recovered somewhat during the early part of 1551 (though it fell again in the following year), and the purity of English silver currency was eventually re-established under Elizabeth – but subsequent exchange-rate fluctuations, continuing over-production in England and the first stirrings of the coming, century-long revolt in the Low Countries meant that old assumptions of market stability had gone forever. Between 1500 and 1550, though subject to occasional, short-term slumps, English cloth exports had risen three-fold. In that latter year, over 130,000 short-cloths went abroad, bound principally for the Low Countries. By 1552, the total had fallen to less than 85,000.[11] For many merchants – those very many whose imaginations were incapable of innovation – the times brought new hardships and even ruin; but for others they provided a strong purgative effect upon the manner in which they did business. A significant number of London's mercantile families took the lesson of the trade crisis to look for new, more distant outlets for their goods, and in the process – whether by design or circumstance – they became intensely speculative, ready to ride the uncertainty of their age rather than place their capital in the traditionally secure havens of land and property. The economic conservatism formerly prevalent among English overseas merchants was beginning to give way, like their confessional tastes, to something that was heavy with promise both of increase and disaster.

In fact, the Reformation was by no means irrelevant to the trend. Though a profoundly spiritual upheaval, it provided a further impetus for practical change. It is hardly appropriate to examine its vast and complex implications here, but it is indisputable that no part of English society escaped them, once a momentum for reform had gathered strength. The precise extent of what that reform might or should be remained unclear for many years – one might argue that it was never to be determined – yet the precise degree of dislocation created by a very diffuse and uncoordinated 'Reformation' (a quantity that historians continue to debate) was a less profound engine for new thinking than the quality of uncertainty it engendered. During Henry's lifetime, its disruptions were largely structural – other than to the edifice of monastic life – and did little more than remove the more intrusive, ceremonial tokens of Roman Catholicism. With Henry's death in 1547, however, the uneasy consensus that had allowed such limited revolution broke down definitively. Though the mass of the population outside London remained relatively comfortable with traditional forms minus direct Papal authority, the accession of a new king brought to political power several men whose attitude to change *per se* was far less constrained by long-held values.

For more than five years thereafter, Lord Protector Somerset and Lord President Northumberland – successive guardians of the government of the sickly Edward VI – relied upon the political support of the City of London to maintain their programme of government. That they were able to do so owed much to the powerful reformist element among the City's mercantile community. Many of the men whose business activities had taken them to the European centres of spiritual revolution in the 1520s had returned as humanist critics of the established order, and, eventually, as standard bearers of the struggle against Rome.[12] Without political power, their influence had been necessarily peripheral, but from 1547, an economically powerful and radical community of interest acquired a government whose partialities and preoccupations almost precisely reflected their own.

However, even ambitions sustained both by spiritual conviction and practical necessity required the physical means to achieve them. Opportunities to break free from established economic conditions – particularly from the increasingly unsatisfactory reliance upon the Antwerp trade – could be forged for over-abundant English cloths only in entirely new markets: a truth that brought its own peculiar problems. Though England was a nation with a centuries-old sea-going tradition, she had little home-grown experience of oceanic travel.[13] In 1509, long before the significance of the new discoveries was fully appreciated, Sebastian Brant had prematurely dismissed the ambitions of Spain as little more than human vanity:

Ferdynandus that late was kynge of spayne
Of londe and people hath founde plenty and store
Of whome the bydynge to us was uncertayne

No christen man of them harde tell before
Thus it is foly to tende unto the lore
And unsure science of vayne geometry
Syns none can knowe all the worlde perfytely.[14]

Knowing the world 'perfytely' was an accomplishment to which Englishmen, even several decades after Brant wrote, could lay particularly little claim. English goods that passed further overseas than the coasts of western Europe were carried largely in foreign ships, piloted by men whose experience of long-range voyages eclipsed those of relatively parochial Englishmen.[15] This historical disparity had less to do with innate temperament or talent than with geographical reality. Upon the north-western fringe of Europe, swept by currents that drove ships north and eastwards, ships putting to sea from England were encouraged by nature towards regions that provided fish but little else of value. English voyages to the south were on the whole coast-hugging affairs, with a brief fraught dash out of sight of land across the deep, stormy waters of the Bay of Biscay. Upon such courses, the ancient skills of pilotage – of knowing one's coastlines, reefs, seabeds, approximate landfalls and the locations of ports – were all that the English master required to bring his ship to market and return it home safely again.

In contrast, the oceanic currents off the Iberian Peninsula were far more conducive to longer range voyaging, carrying vessels easily to the north-west coast of Africa and to its exotic and unfamiliar produce. Such a striking geographical advantage made it natural that Spain and Portugal should have led the rest of Europe in expanding their physical and conceptual borders beyond the immediate horizon. Yet these nations were not blessed with any peculiar aptitude in the art of following a course at sea. Their skills in oceanic navigation had developed slowly, upon the back of the same imperatives that had forced back the tide of Islamic Europe from the Pyrenees – a process that was almost half a millennium old by the turn of the sixteenth century. When schools of navigation were established in Portugal and Spain, it was not to initiate a conscious, pre-planned agenda of exploration, but to address new problems that a venerable tradition of expansion had moved out to encounter.

Upon that accretion of ocean-faring lore, new empires had been built swiftly. Brant's unconvincing criticisms apart, Englishmen looked enviously upon its achievement, but did not seek immediately to emulate it. Apart from a brief, if spectacular, surge of pioneering Atlantic voyages made by Bristol men (native and adopted) in the late fifteenth century – one of which may have brought an English ship to the American coastline several years before Columbus sailed – English long-range activities were minimal.[16] Indeed, for almost twenty years following Columbus's 'discovery' of the West Indies, its implications were hardly understood in England. Until 1519, when Hernán Cortés overthrew the Aztec empire and returned to Spain dripping with golden booty, it was principally the closer Spanish trade of the Canaries and Portugal's African commerce that occupied English attention. The lessons derived from the practice of this trade, for so long as it followed legitimate paths, brought no further significant development of English sea-faring skills or technology. Henry VIII built a strong navy, and established the Corporation of Trinity House in 1514 to produce a supply of domestically trained pilots, but his were largely structural improvements intended to support a defensive, home-waters policy; in themselves, they did not provide the means by which England might become an oceanic power. For several decades after the establishment of new trades to Africa, Brazil and the East Indies – even after the first permanent Spanish settlements were laid out in New Spain and the Main – Englishmen crossed oceans very rarely. Bristol fishermen continued to sail to the Newfoundland Banks, but like John and Sebastian Cabot before them, they utilized little more science than did the sea-gulls in their wake: their 'technique' consisted entirely of maintaining a due-west course until their deep-sea sounding lines told them that it was time to cast their nets. The employees of more enterprising Englishmen, who had long made voyages to Spain, Portugal and the Mediterranean countries, continued to rely upon skills that were both venerable and basic; sight of land was rarely lost, and so celestial observation was largely irrelevant. Those very few Englishmen who had gone further still had done so either in Spanish ships – Roger Barlow and Henry Latimer had sailed with Sebastian Cabot (then an employee of the Spanish Crown) to the River Plate in 1526 – or with the assistance of Portuguese or French pilots, such as those employed by William Hawkins in voyages to the Brazil coast in the 1530s and 1540/1, or the Southampton merchants Reniger, Pudsey and Borey in similar enterprises 'below the equinoctiall' in 1540 and 1542.[17] Englishmen, however adventurous, continued to rely upon the skills and knowledge of other nations, because they had neither the means – nor, on the whole, the inclination – to do otherwise.

In the mid-sixteenth century, this relative backwardness began to be addressed precisely because unfamiliar economic problems were demanding, and the philosophical upheavals of the Reformation were encouraging, the changes we have noted above. The practical repercussions of these pressures were soon apparent. In 1548, the Pilot-Major of Spain, Sebastian Cabot, had been enticed back to England as a royal pensioner (though this was initially described to his Spanish employers as a temporary leave of absence).[18] In addition to divulging the latest intelligences from the *Casa de Contratación* in Seville, Cabot most vitally conferred his experience of the minutiae of organizing, outfitting and despatching long-range voyages, a talent that was almost completely lacking among his renewed English acquaintances.

In the meantime, English scholars responded to the enthusiasms of their new, overtly Protestant Lords, and to the patronage they delivered.[19] An elementary text on geometry and the use of the quadrant – *The Pathway to Knowledge* – was produced in 1551 by Robert Recorde, a London physician who also gave public lectures on mathematics (and who, in 1553, succeeded Sir John Yorke as master of the Tower Mint). Two years later, Richard Eden translated Sebastian Munster's *A Treatyse of the Newe India etc*, the first detailed description of the known (and assumed) Americas to appear in English. With the death of Edward VI and accession of the Catholic Mary Tudor, this self-improving trend did not abate. In 1555, Recorde added to his accomplishments a treatise on the sphere, *The Castle of Knowledge*, specifically at the request of the Russia Company, an entity that had come into being in the meantime to exploit the first, formally established new trade to a distant market. In the following year, Eden published a translation of Peter Martyr's *Decades of the New World*, to which he added narratives of the English Guinea voyages of 1553–4: effectively providing the first English 'rutter' for the Atlantic Ocean.[20] Five years later, he also gave Englishmen the first vernacular edition of Martin Cortés's *Arte de Navegar* – a compendium of the latest navigational data and instruction. As *The Art of Navigation*, this was to be one of the most influential books on oceanic navigation ever to appear in the English language.[21] Perhaps of even more immediate practical value to pilots, the first English compendium of cosmographical data – the *Cosmographical Glasse* – was produced before the end of the 1550s by William Cuningham.[22]

How quickly these works became known and available to English navigators is hard to assess precisely, but as propagandist instruments for the aims of Lords, merchants and seamen they were invaluable in maintaining a momentum for change. Meanwhile, in the first flush of enthusiasm to seek out the world beyond the continental shelf, Sebastian Cabot had been put to work on a supremely practical project: to assist in preparations for a voyage which was – and was intended – to provide the first corpus of English long-range maritime expertise. This was the voyage of the bark *Aucher*: ostensibly a trading expedition to the Ottoman Levant, it was in fact a maritime school training for a generation of English oceanic voyagers. The *Aucher* sailed in 1550, carrying a crew of seventy men and boys, most of whom, according to the testimony of her master, Roger Bodenham, were to qualify as masters in their own right within six years of the voyage.[23] No such project had ever been conceived – let alone undertaken – by Englishmen; but perhaps even more important than the relative novelty of its destination (and certainly the meagre profit it generated for its backers), the voyage began the process of instilling the practical experience and mind-set necessary to traverse large distances out of sight of land. Men and boys of the crew (amongst them Richard Chancellor, the Borough brothers, Stephen and William, and the later master-shipwright, Matthew Baker) were the first of many who would acquire the empirical knowledge and skills to allow laggardly Englishmen to follow, emulate and, ultimately, challenge the wealth and power of those who had passed across the oceans before them.

Here, then, in the overgrown market town of London, as the half century turned, the pressures and consequences of these novel economic and spiritual uncertainties began to work their changes upon men whose fathers had been among the most conservative-minded of her citizens. They had come to live with a newly insecure throne, a disturbingly imprecise God and, worst of all, severely fluctuating profits in a world whose boundaries (in every sense) were falling away into the dimly perceived distance. In his new home in Walbrook, the young Martin Frobisher would have understood little of the subtleties of these trends but experienced all of their implications; indeed, his future career, though not yet remotely discernible, was already being shaped by the striking manner in which these changes impinged upon the circumstances of his foster family. Had his uncle been a bookseller or a bishop, life might have continued to unfold at the pace that had seemed habitual at Altofts, and ambition directed or crushed accordingly; but Sir John Yorke's preoccupations lay at and across the most unsettled nexes of his age, and as these turned towards as yet unknown resolutions, his young nephew – however unwittingly – would be obliged to follow. Frobisher's time with his London relatives would be brief and end with a degree of bitterness on both sides; but the significance of the experience in shaping his peculiar view of the world can hardly be overstated. His relationship with Sir John Yorke in particular was to provide several striking lessons. Some of these would be beneficial, providing the grounding for a life spent largely upon the deck of a ship; but others were to fix in Frobisher's mind hard opinions regarding merchants as a breed. Many of their occupation, though almost entirely innocent of Yorke's cupidities – and certainly of any prior acquaintance with his nephew – would come to regret the implications of that over-rigorous education.

Nevertheless, if Francis Frobisher had wanted the best start for his nephew, he certainly did not stint in his choice of mentor. Even by the exacting standards set by his contemporaries in the City, Yorke appears to have been an extremely industrious man – so much so that one marvels at the time and effort he was able to devote to siring a family of ten sons and three daughters (the even greater industry of his wife, Anne, in this respect, must remain an entirely anonymous achievement). Early details of his career are obscure, but by the 1530s he had been entered into the livery of the Merchant-Taylors' Company and was trading to Antwerp and the English wool-staple town of Calais. From there, like many of his contemporaries, he despatched occasional, clandestine correspondence to Thomas Cromwell, repeating rumours of wars, plots and stratagems that were potentially of profit or danger to England.[24] It may have been partly in recognition of these early labours that he was appointed as assay-master at the Tower Mint in 1544, though the nature of the appointment suggests that he already had experience of the mechanics of English fiscal policy – perhaps of the same foreign loan-raising activities he is known to have undertaken on his king's behalf after 1550.[25] In the following year, he headed a team of five men who crossed the river to open the new Southwark Mint, though he maintained strong links (and, it seems, direction of much minting activity) at the Tower. Cromwell's fall, and the death of Henry VIII, hardly slowed the smooth, upward progress of Yorke's career. By 1547 he was under-treasurer at Southwark; two years later, approximately at the time that his nephew came to live at Walbrook, he recrossed the river to become under-treasurer at the Tower Mint, and was elected as Sheriff of London at about the same time.[26] Within weeks of this latter appointment, a stream of civic and political dignitaries made their way to Walbrook, eager to use Yorke's good offices in the City to further their own causes – contacts, new and old, whose society had been cultivated by a man who knew precisely how to use his rising wealth to buy far more than mere commodities. As he took his place in the first rank of London's merchants, this fusion of commercial success and political influence had attained an almost organic quality, its fruits gathered from the very pinnacle of English society: even Lord Protector Somerset himself, at his first temporary disgrace in October 1549, was known to be personally beholden to Yorke for a huge loan of £2,500, advanced to cover his household expenses.

It may have been the immediate burden of this obligation, or the growing suspicion that Yorke was beginning to side with the more radical elements in the Privy Council gathering around John Dudley, Earl of Warwick, that turned Somerset against his former financier during the summer of 1549 – most obviously when he tried to block Yorke's election as Sheriff.[27] It was a singular mistake for a man whose other friends were abandoning him or choosing to sit out the political game that was unfolding. Yorke's political loyalties – or rather, the politics of his loyalties – were remarkably fluid and more than capable of being stirred by new, even antagonistic possibilities. He may also have been nervous of Somerset's capacity to implicate him in previous decisions to debase the coinage, a hugely unpopular policy both in the city and countryside.[28] Within weeks, he had switched his previous affections so decisively that he was reported by the Spanish Ambassador in London to be leading the City's support for Warwick against Somerset.[29] On 6 October, even before the Lord Protector was committed to the Tower, Warwick had taken up residence in Yorke's house to coordinate and strengthen these vital links, and was careful to associate his host closely with the new regime; indeed, it seems that the Privy Council met there officially upon several occasions to transact its state business.[30] On 17 October, Edward VI also came to dine at Yorke's table; that afternoon, perhaps seduced by the excellence of the fare, or prompted by his new Lord President, the young King knighted his host. Thereafter, Yorke was the most consistent supporter of the new government, if only in fulfilment of the Faustian pact to which he and Warwick had committed themselves. In the meantime, his home continued to accommodate some of the pivotal events in the struggle for power between Somerset and Warwick. When the former Lord Protector was released from the Tower in February 1550, he was brought to Yorke's house on the merchant's personal parole 'without grete garde or busynis';[31] when, briefly, he threatened to reassume his former pre-eminence, Warwick in turn fled to Walbrook once more to raise the City in his own defence. With Somerset's second fall and subsequent execution, both Warwick (now Duke of Northumberland) and Yorke were secure, but they were also indelibly linked as conspirators in the public eye. How close that link was in reality was amply illustrated following Somerset's death, when Yorke, using Northumberland's good offices, persuaded the Privy Council to honour fully the (now-missing) promissory notes the former Lord Protector had given for his loans.

Other rewards for Yorke's shifting loyalties followed swiftly. At the end of 1549, he had been given the sinecure of officer of the King's woods (his enthusiasm for felling trees in the Bishop of London's woods at Dartford resulted in repeated – and ineffectual – warnings from the Privy Council); from 1550 onwards, he acted as one of the King's principal financial agents in the

Netherlands, raising and repaying loans on the Antwerp money markets and organizing clandestine purchases of munitions; and, most lucratively, he received unprecedented terms to supply the Tower Mint with silver bullion from Flanders. Granted a turn of between 7sh. 2d. and 10sh. per ounce on such transactions, he thus concentrated in his own hands much of the responsibility for determining the cost of the nation's money, its purity and rate of distribution.[32]

With these manifold tokens of favour, Yorke's personal wealth, already substantial, was increasing rapidly in the years during which Martin Frobisher lived at his house. Like many of his contemporaries, he had begun to transfer a proportion of this into the traditionally secure havens of land and property. One of his most substantial acquisitions was Whitby Abbey in Yorkshire, a former major monastic foundation that had fallen to Northumberland as part of his share of the spoils of the Henrician Reformation. The abbey enjoyed considerable rental income from its tied estates which Yorke immediately set about exploiting with a thorough and unattractive industry. As profitable as this and other peripheral acquisitions proved, however, his principal business seems to have remained the export of 'woollen-cloths', though the commodities he took in return varied across the enterprises with which he was associated. As late as 1568, for example, even as English merchant adventurers were preparing – albeit reluctantly – to abandon their cloth-mart there, he was importing pepper, mace, nutmeg and aniseed from Antwerp.[33]

The practicalities of Yorke's day-to-day activities are obscure, but certain broad assumptions may be made. Like many of his contemporaries in business, he would have had access to a plot of land abutting the Thames – possibly shared with several of his peers – with a warehouse and jetty or water-stairs to allow the ships they hired (or, in many cases, owned) to lade and unlade their wares. Its precise location is unknown, but it was undoubtedly of a style that was repeated along both banks of the Thames eastwards from Barnard's Castle.[34] Upon a long, narrow site, with one short boundary on the waterfront, its warehouse would have stood back from, or above, a lading area at the water's edge. Here, goods purchased for export and those brought back into England would be stacked, awaiting their removal or assignment into the hands of Yorke's factor, John Beryn (Yorke himself was by now sufficiently wealthy to put his foreign transactions – and the arduous months of voyaging they entailed – into the hands of his trusted employee).[35] Bills of exchange and promissory notes from the Low Countries, Spain, Portugal and the eastern Mediterranean would record the dozens of transactions that Yorke himself or Beryn painstakingly set down in the memorial or waste book, to await more formal posting to the 'great book of merchandize', the most comprehensive manifest of the merchant's estate. Other, less formal arrangements – layings-out, takings-up and unofficial 'government' loans – would have been recorded elsewhere; probably in a book to which neither Beryn nor any other employee had access. The fruits of its entries must have been substantial, but success brought its own disadvantages. In an age that knew no secure banking arrangements, and allowing for his growing portfolio of land and properties, a large proportion of Yorke's wealth would have remained in his cellars in Walbrook; no doubt causing him the same occasional anxieties that Samuel Pepys was to experience a century later in Seething Lane, just a few streets to the east.

With that preoccupation, Yorke must have been acutely aware that the safest place for money was in transactions – as many as could be sustained simultaneously. Nothing stood still because stationary commerce was, by definition, no commerce. 'The diligent Merchant runneth to the furthest Indies, flying poverty by Roks, by Seas, by fyers': goods were insured, risks were spread as far as the market would allow, but the way of the world being extremely harsh, any man who did not handle his business in a timely fashion watched it sink thereafter.[36] However unattractive Yorke's personal qualities may have been (and we will find much evidence to that effect), there can be little doubt that he generated and maintained a striking momentum in the business of using money to make more money during these years.

Inevitably, Yorke's commercial activities were strongly affected by the upheavals in England's cloth trade and the money markets, and he had followed – if not jumped some way ahead of – the resulting trend towards diversification. As under-treasurer of the Tower Mint overseeing successive debasements of the coinage, he could not have been unaware of the potentially disastrous repercussions of inflation; nor of the dictum, most famously expressed by Thomas Gresham, that 'bad money drives good money overseas'. Indeed, as the man most immediately responsible for several tranches of bad money passing into circulation (including the most debased issue of all – that of 14 April 1551), he was probably only too sensitive to the need to minimize its effects upon his own business.[37] Accordingly, for some years prior to 1550, he had been sending a proportion of his wares to the ports of the Iberian Peninsula and to Madeira, to tap directly into the trade of the Portuguese and Spanish sea-empires. His business links with Antwerp probably continued to constitute the major part of his mercantile activities for a few years following the trade crisis of that year, but in responding to pressures for which he was in part responsible, Yorke's ambitions were already passing beyond the bounds of the world known to Englishmen. In 1552, he re-ordered his existing preoccupations to allow their fulfillment. That year, he retired from his duties at the Tower Mint, no doubt as a very wealthy man. Thus freed from one of his principal commitments, he wholeheartedly joined the growing search for alternatives to the Antwerp stranglehold. In the following twelve months – a strikingly consequential year for England – he was to risk his capital in equally speculative ventures to beyond the opposite known ends of the world: ventures in which English mariners, almost simultaneously, were having their first taste of Arctic squalls and fever-laden African swamps.

However, investments in risk-heavy projects to find new markets for English cloths required large purses – larger, even, than Sir John's. His existing Iberian activities probably required him to be a member of a small syndicate, whose collective wealth could absorb the additional risks of doing business across the Bay of Biscay. For even more speculative ventures, requiring several ships and the very real prospect of lost cargoes, such pooling of resources was obligatory. It has been estimated that up to 240 merchants and speculators invested in the 1553 voyage of Willoughby and Chancellor that was to establish English commerce with Muscovy, and Yorke was almost certainly amongst them.[38] The first Barbary voyages, though on a smaller scale, were never set out by less than four merchants, and often by many more. The principles behind such arrangements were not new – for centuries, merchants had collaborated to dilute their individual risk – but the turbulent years of the mid-sixteenth century saw London's commercial community embarking upon an unprecedented series of novel and highly speculative ventures. If England and the near coasts of Europe were not world enough to secure a profit, other places had to hold the means and provision, and they lay across greater seas than most Englishmen had yet encountered. Enterprises conceived to realize these half-formed ambitions required organization, which in turn required the discussion of possibilities, potential and resources. From these loose, informal beginnings of small intimate communities of interest joining forces to find ways to take a profit from uncertainty and speculation, the first long-range trading entities – the Russia, Barbary, Guinea, Eastland, Levant and, eventually, the East India and Hudson Bay Companies – were to gather the world's exotic produce and bring it into English homes. Their genesis lay in London at the dawn of the 1550s in the houses and warehouses of substantial men of business such as Sir John Yorke: men for whom no single commodity or market was a sufficient safeguard against the spectre of ruin.

We cannot say precisely how the young Martin Frobisher, newly arrived in one of the most active of these households, was marked by such upheavals; but their novelty must have made a profound impression. In particular, the prospect of Lord Protectors, Kings, Lord Presidents and Privy Councillors, flying through the front door in turn like the cast of a political farce to seek favour or finance, was not one that the West Riding of Yorkshire could habitually provide. It was a new world, in every sense; and a young man at its busy heart, running errands for his principals, bending to the strange disciplines of the ledger or simply gawping idly at the spectacle before him, had little chance of avoiding its consequences even had he wished to do so. In Frobisher's case, his new circumstances made any prior expectations – whatever they were – superfluous. He had no skills, prospects or other faculty to recommend him to his wealthier cousins; but when new horizons beckon, obscure qualities often come to the fore. Given his impulsive and restless nature, it is very likely that he was keen to prove himself to his uncle; it is probable that Sir John Yorke felt obliged to provide some sort of means by which he could do so; and it is beyond doubt that the boy possessed one, indisputably valuable quality in an age of growing dislocation and opportunity – that of being entirely expendable.

THREE

The Guinea Coast: 1553–58

Some English merchants – amongst them Sir John Yorke and his factor Beryn – had long been familiar with the quaysides of Spanish and Portuguese ports. Looking around at the strange and precious bounty stacked so abundantly there, they saw much more than the immediate fruits of the business they had come to transact. The produce that had raised two near-impoverished Iberian nations to empire in less than half a century came from somewhere else; somewhere across the Ocean Sea before them. As guileless as they may have tried to appear to their hosts, these men were precisely aware of how much more expensive their purchases became in passing through the warehouses of Seville and Lisbon, and a growing number were moved to do something about it.

The Anglo-Iberian trade, even in the mid-sixteenth century, had a venerable record. Many Englishmen had maintained a commercial presence in Seville, the administrative centre of the Spanish overseas trade, since the late fifteenth century. They had established a factory at San Lucar de Barrameda, at the furthest reach of the river Guadalquivir navigable by sea-going vessels, and had been allowed a chapel there at the waterside, dedicated to St George.[1] Gradually, as the English community built houses around their place of worship, they organized their presence under quasi-formal arrangements, with a consul to oversee their local activities and adjudicate in disputes between individual merchants. They had a charter, granted by the Duke of Medina Sidonia, to whom San Lucar's port levies were due under long-held seigneurial privileges. This was the fundament of their identity as 'the brotherhood of St George' – for many years the only corporate manifestation of English trade with the Iberian Peninsula.[2]

In 1530, Henry VIII belatedly granted a very limited form of recognition to the Anglo-Iberian trade when he allowed the incorporation of the English 'Andalusian Company', but in doing so he merely recognized the *de facto* practices of the existing structures in Spain and, to a lesser extent, in Portugal. Though relatively small, and subject to periodic upheavals, the trade was a profitable one, drawing strength from links that grew at more personal levels. Some of the early Anglo-Iberian traders bought homes in the neighbourhood and remained as Spanish subjects; a few went out to the New World in Spanish ships and became colonists in Santo Domingo and Hispaniola;[3] still more had travelled to the Canaries, established factories there and brought the produce of the islands into England. Madeiran sugar was being sold in Bristol as early as the 1450s; to establish a partial hold upon this valuable commodity at its source, Englishmen were settling in the island as plantation owners and subjects of the Portuguese Crown by 1510.[4] For some years at least, despite occasional problems between England and Spain at a diplomatic level, there was little official hindrance to these activities. However, the Spanish and Portuguese authorities drew a fundamental distinction between the pursuit of trade between English and Iberian ports and unauthorized English attempts to circumvent the official channels through which that trade was conducted. In particular, the Spanish advance from their new Antilles possessions on to the coast of mainland America resulted in a crucial change in the Spanish Crown's attitude towards foreign traders. The conquests of Central America and Peru brought a huge leap in the economic potential of Spain's overseas empire, and the Spanish Crown was not slow to impose its heavy hand upon all aspects of their exploitation. From the first years of Spain's mainland empire in Central America, Anglo-Iberian traders found the cornucopia gathered at New Spain and the Main much more difficult to access than that of the older territories. The latter continued to be open to direct English trade, but America was clearly labelled a forbidden area for non-Iberian ships, even to those of such loyal foreign traders as the Brotherhood of St George.[5]

A further limiting factor for Englishmen trading to the Iberian countries – and to Spain in particular – was the uncertainty of their rights and privileges. The trade was sanctioned under treaty but not always precisely defined in practice, particularly in ports where the English presence was less welcome than at San Lucar. Naturally, where it had no legal identity, there was no adequate recourse to law to protect the rights of its participants. With no consistency or forewarning, local officials often supplemented their income by the arbitrary seizure of English cargoes on flimsy pretexts. In 1553, John Lok, a pilgrim halting briefly at Cadiz *en route* to the Holy Land, recorded his experience: '. . . the Spaniardes, according to their accustomed manner with all shippes of extraordinarie goodnes and burden, picked a quarrell against the company, meaning to have forfeited, or at the least to have arrested the said shippe.'[6] To remove their trade from such endemic abuses whilst maintaining or even enhancing their profits was a goal that must have recommended itself greatly to the Anglo-Iberian merchants. However, when finally they attempted to realize it, their first objective was not a part of the Spanish sphere of interest (most of which was exploited as the fruits of conquest, and therefore rigorously policed), but of the more loosely protected Portuguese 'possessions'.

The principle of exclusion from direct trade with the host's overseas territories was no less strongly applied by Portugal. Indeed, the Portuguese government had been attempting to keep Englishmen out of their African markets for many years prior to the Spanish conquests in America. Though the Barbary and Guinea Coasts were as yet physically unfamiliar to Englishmen, their merchants had been interested in African produce for almost a century, from the time when Portuguese intercourse with the Moors and Negroes of Saharan Africa, Senegambia and Benin had first begun to fill Lisbon warehouses with strange and precious commodities. From their plantations on Madeira, Englishmen would have seen – and envied – the traffic of wealth from the African coast as it plied its way northwards towards Europe; in Lisbon itself, English merchants at their factory would have laid their hands upon samples of this traffic as they haggled to secure a reasonably regular supply; and at Antwerp – where, finally, they could deal at arm's length at the official Portuguese entrepôt in northern Europe – they would have been fully aware of the striking appreciation that brought unprecedented profits for their suppliers. Almost from the point of acquisition, opportunities for Englishmen to covet their neighbours' goods and markets were plentiful, and growing.

The Portuguese themselves introduced English cloths to Africa, lading their ships with the product at Antwerp and, much less frequently, at London and Bristol. It may have been these transactions that gave English suppliers first occasion to think seriously about following their cloths to the new markets. Anecdotal evidence suggests that as early as the reign of Edward IV, the Portuguese King was intervening in London to prevent the despatch of ships owned by two Englishmen, John Tintam and William Fabian, that were intended to encroach upon the Guinea trade.[7] In succeeding decades, Portuguese diplomatic activity to nip in the bud any further English interest was largely successful. There is no documentary evidence that English ships reached the Guinea coast before 1530, when William Hawkins made the first of three voyages in the ship *Paul* to Brazil, via Guinea.[8] That the principal focus of Hawkins' interest was Brazil seems evident from the lack of information regarding his brief stay in Guinea. All we know is that he avoided contact with the Portuguese ships that policed the coast, and traded ivory and 'other commodities which that place yeeldeth' with the inhabitants. Portuguese interest in the region centred upon the trade in spices and, to a lesser extent, gold; but it is unlikely that Hawkins managed to pass sufficiently eastwards along the Gold Coast to tap into this commerce. Had he done so, Brazil might have slipped a little in his preoccupations, and Portuguese efforts to stop him almost certainly would have been much more assiduous.

In the following decade, English privateers followed on after their more enterprising French counterparts, and began to prey upon Portuguese and Moorish vessels as they left the Barbary coast laden with its produce; but documented English trade with the region did not begin until the reign of Edward VI. In 1551, Thomas Wyndham – a Norfolk man, sometime naval captain, former Barbary pirate and Master of the Ordnance at the Tower – departed from England with two ships and a brief to test the possibilities of legitimate trade with Portugal's existing clients. He visited Santa Cruz (the present-day Agadir) on the Saharan coast of West Africa, and acquired unspecified goods there before returning to England.[9] The precise identities of his backers in this voyage are not known, though speculation has dwelt upon the names of the London merchants William Chester, William Garrard and Thomas Lodge.[10] All three men were future Muscovy, Barbary and Guinea traders, as was a fourth – whom we may, for the same reasons, add as a further possibility: Sir John Yorke.

No known eye-witness accounts of the voyage have survived, but it appears to have provided a modest profit (or at least the promise of one), and was swiftly followed up. In 1552 Wyndham commanded a second expedition to the region, financed by a new syndicate of London merchants that definitely included Yorke.[11] It comprised three ships – the *Lion of London*, the *Buttolfe* and a former Portuguese caravel – heavily laden with goods from the warehouses of their owners. Once more, the expedition put in at Santa Cruz, and after convincing the local authorities that the voyage had been authorized by their king (a bold, if necessary lie), the Englishmen did brisk business there. There is some evidence that they took weapons to trade with the Moors, but the principal wares they carried were English cloths, baltic amber, coral and jet.[12] In return, Wyndham obtained molasses, sugar, dates and almonds – all high-value commodities in England. Furthermore, whilst at the coastal town of Safi, he despatched some of his cloths inland to the entrepôt of Marrakesh, thus priming the market there for English goods carried in subsequent voyages.

The Portuguese were of course aggrieved at this intrusion into what they considered to be their sphere of economic interest, and made it clear to English travellers to the region that 'if they tooke us in those partes, they would use us as their mortall enemies, with greate threates and menaces'.[13] In reality, however, they had little effective power to intervene. Until 1541, they had maintained small forts at Safi and Santa Cruz, but the demolition of these strongholds by the Moor Muley Mohammed, who had recently established an independent kingdom in Morocco, ended their presence on that coast. It was their evacuation that allowed Englishmen to make their first, tentative visits to the region, and to establish a regular trade there by the end of the decade. In contrast, the continuing Portuguese establishments on the Guinea and Gold coasts were to provide a real obstacle – one that was almost as great an impediment as the appalling climate – to the establishment of a regular English trade in the region.

In England, the official attitude to encroachments upon existing Spanish or Portuguese trades was conditioned by how these monopolies were justified in law – and, indeed, by what constituted 'law' as such. In 1493, Pope Alexander VI's bull, *Inter caetaera*, had divided the non-European world and gifted its respective parts to the Iberian nations by reason of their oceanic explorations and conquests. However, other European nations – particularly those who would come to care little how or what the Bishop of Rome disposed – strongly distinguished between the two achievements. Later, during the 1560s, Elizabeth answered the Portuguese Ambassador's protests against English interloping in Guinea by setting out her opinion of such claims for monopoly, having just been provided with information on the region by one Martin Frobisher. She protested that she did not understand what conquests had been made by the Portuguese King that the negro nations of the region should be regarded as bound to Portugal. She could not, she wrote, forbid Englishmen to go to these countries unless their inhabitants were forbidden in turn to come to England. Nor, particularly, could she see reason to forbid them to trade where the Portuguese King had neither dominion, obedience or tribute: 'as amongst all Princes and countries the use of intercourse of merchandise is the chief exercise of amity'.[14]

So this was not a matter of challenging rival political or even papal authorities, but of economic reality. To encroach overtly upon the territories of other states was one thing – no one would argue that a prince did not have the absolute right to protect his subjects from outright depredation – but to allow just one or two nations to dominate the entire non-European world's traffic of commerce was inconceivable to all but Spaniards and 'Portingals'. Richard Eden had succinctly stated this principle in his *Decades of the New World*, even as a Spanish monarch sat as king-consort upon the English throne: '. . . it may seeme somewhat rigorous, and against good reason and conscience, or rather against the charitie that ought to be among Christian men, that such as violently invade the dominions of other, should not permit other friendly to vse the trade of merchandise . . .'.[15] Convinced of the justice of this, Englishmen continued to press further into areas where nations with existing interests would look unkindly upon competition. In 1554, their Catholic Queen, urged on by her husband Prince Philip (whose defence of Portuguese interests was made wholly with their Spanish equivalents in mind), attempted to ban all English voyages to Guinea – a proscription that was entirely ignored.[16] If, of necessity, English merchants were careful not to interlope too overtly upon existing Spanish interests, the explicit rejection of papal determination nevertheless continued to be made, and increasingly blatantly.

In the early 1550s, the Barbary voyages were the first officially sanctioned English challenges to this supposed world-order. The Guinea expeditions followed almost immediately thereafter; there is some debate as to whether one was a direct consequence of the other. Their respective organizations were dissimilar; the Guinea voyages were a series of terminable joint-stock ventures in which trade was conducted on behalf of the adventurers as a whole, whereas the Barbary trade quickly developed into a 'regulated' arrangement in which individual merchants traded solely on their own accounts or in small partnerships. This distinction alone is not conclusive, however. The very different conditions under which business was done in these two regions probably made such technical dissimilarities inevitable, and there can be little doubt that the men who ventured their money in the first Guinea voyages were influenced by the experience of – and returns from – Wyndham's two Barbary expeditions.[17] In many cases, the same merchants were to invest in both trades. The apparent popularity of English cloths in this formerly unknown region, first hinted at by the purchases and on-sales of the Portuguese themselves and now confirmed by Wyndham, was bound to excite the interest of wealthy merchant adventurers whose established markets for cloths were shrinking. Africa was unknown, but it was very large, dripping with unfamiliar commodities and – vitally – unconquered by potential rivals (despite

Portuguese pretensions to the contrary). In the face of such vast potential, the question was not whether trade should be attempted, but how far it might practically be extended.

The fact that English understanding of the region was – to say the least – blurred was in many respects more of an advantage than a hindrance to their efforts. Portuguese ships had been sailing down the African coast to Benin and beyond for a century. Latterly, the French had followed, and were beginning to build their own empirical knowledge of the region. However, all that Englishmen knew of Guinea came from French and Portuguese rutters, or directly from disaffected Portuguese pilots. Men such as Yorke and Garrard, informed at best by a half-sight of the problems they faced, probably believed that voyages past the Barbary Coast to the Guinea region required only an incremental effort (almost certainly, they had little if any access to William Hawkins's data). They were very wrong in that assumption: the further passage would prove to be a devastating experience to men who had little inkling of the extreme heat and strange maladies that swept the east West African coast from the Malaguetta region (modern-day Liberia) to the Bight of Benin. Whether a better understanding of this would have inclined Englishmen to greater caution is difficult to assess, but unlikely nevertheless. What they had a reasonable certainty of was that the potential return on Guinea gold, ivory and spices, set against those of the previously mentioned Barbary wares, was anything *but* incremental.

The half-understood voyages of William Hawkins apart, the first direct English contact with the bounty of the Guinea coast may have occurred in 1552, when a Portuguese pilot, Simão Pires, made a voyage to the port of Mina and returned to England (possibly unintentionally) with a cargo of gold and spices.[18] The evidence is anecdotal, but English interest was certainly aroused by the beginning of the following year. A small syndicate of men who were already involved in the Iberian and Barbary trades – Sir John Yorke amongst them – organized an expedition that was to pass far beyond those that they had previously financed. One vessel – the *Lion of London* once more – was provided by the syndicate, whilst two more, the *Primrose* and a large pinnance, the *Moon*, were royal ships, hired for the voyage.[19] As his experience made him the overwhelming – that is, the only – English authority on African voyages, Thomas Wyndham was engaged to command the expedition, and he in turn hired two renegade Portuguese pilots to lead it to the Guinea coast.[20] The vessels required a total complement of 140 seamen, excluding the merchants who were to sail as the factors of those who had financed the voyage. Amongst this latter group was an eighteen-year-old apprentice merchant named Martin Frobisher, carried under the charge and supervision of his uncle's representative, John Beryn.

Frobisher's role in the second, 1554, Guinea voyage is documented, but the only evidence of his presence on the first expedition is from a rare source – his own testimony. Much later, on 27 May 1562, he made a deposition to the Privy Council (themselves still trying to understand the bounds of Portuguese power in the Guinea region), to allow the Queen to formulate her opinion upon the sovereign rights of the Portuguese King as recalled above. It is entitled *The declaracion of Martyne Frubishere, who was (on) the first and second viages in the parties of Guinea. . . .*[21] The statement itself is the sole reference to his participation in the 1553 voyage, and his precise role therein remains unknown. His participation may have been part of the normal commercial education of a young man in the Yorke family; alternatively, he may actively have pressed his uncle to allow him to go with Beryn upon a journey that few Englishmen could have as yet anticipated, much less experienced. In turn, Yorke's apparent appreciation of Martin's 'great spirit and bould courage, and naturall hardnes of body'[22] may be read equally as praise of the boy's potential or a hint of the desire to be rid of a boisterous and unpromising element of his household. Whatever circumstances brought about Frobisher's inclusion in the ships' complement, we may be certain that he did not sail as a passenger. When time permitted, he probably received instruction and more practical advice from Beryn on the mysteries of merchant-factoring; when it did not, he was doubtless put to work with the common mariners upon those onerous tasks that often made life at sea a short and brutal option. If rumours of his 'hardnes' were accurate, he probably enjoyed a robust constitution, and unless John Beryn showed far more tender concern for his young charge than their mutual employer (which is highly unlikely), it was this hardiness alone that preserved him from the singular ordeal that he and his shipmates were about to endure.

Novel as the aims of this voyage were, there was nothing new or unexpected in the problems encountered in getting the ships away from their English quay-side. As was their habit, Portuguese diplomats in London attempted to detain the voyage: by offering inducements to the two Portuguese pilots not to assist the English and, when these proved unresponsive, by plotting to kidnap them. They failed, not least because the ailing Edward VI and his mentor Northumberland were enthusiastic supporters of any and all private English initiatives to break free from their Antwerp stranglehold. Wyndham swiftly secured the intervention of a sympathetic Admiralty Court, who, on 3 March, had two Portuguese *agents-provocateurs* thrown into prison.

They were released twelve days later, but the Portuguese King took the hint and recalled them soon afterwards.

Even without such distractions, arrangements for the voyage proceeded slowly. This was no doubt due in part to the repercussions of Yorke's close association with Northumberland; particularly with the latter's suicidal attempt, following Edward VI's death on 6 July 1553, to overthrow the order of succession by placing his daughter-in-law Jane Grey upon the English throne against the claims of Mary Tudor. Yorke himself was lucky to keep his head. On 19 July, the day that Mary was proclaimed Queen, he only just escaped a lynching at the hands of a patriotic mob as he returned to his Walbrook home (he was on horseback, and may have managed to force his way through to the doubtful sanctuary of his cash-filled cellars).[23] Placed under house-arrest four days later, his former status at the Tower was somewhat modified when, on 27 July, he was incarcerated there for his implicit association with Northumberland. He remained in confinement for three months thereafter; fortunately, his fellow Guinea adventurers had his prior investment safely spent, and were able to proceed with their arrangements in the meantime.[24] On 12 August 1553, Wyndham's three ships finally sailed from the Thames with his promoters' wares.

As an achievement, the voyage may be considered either as a modest success or a near apocalyptic disaster, and its repercussions were to be felt for years thereafter. Wherever Wyndham and his men touched upon Portuguese territory and interests, it was in a manner not unlike a hot needle thrust into sensitive skin. Wyndham himself seems to have taken to heart the Portuguese threats and subterfuges intended to prevent him sailing, and responded by treating any and all of their possessions as legitimate targets. He sailed first for Madeira, putting in there with the ostensible intention of buying wines. Piero Gonçalves, one of the agents of John III who had failed to halt the expedition in London, was already on the island waiting for the Englishmen. He offered Wyndham his hospitality, but again sought to detain the renegade pilots the English ships carried with them. All his approaches were brusquely rejected. After a few days, Wyndham obtained his wine (inevitably, from locals who were less fastidious about whom they did business with than their king), but when his ships sailed, they immediately attacked and plundered two Portuguese merchantmen bringing goods into Madeira from other islands in the group.

The expedition then made for the island of Deserta, where Wyndham carried out a full-blown raid to secure supplies. His men were beaten off in an ambush, but they managed to seize other ships and their goods at sea. By the time that the English expedition passed on to the Malaguetta coast, it had laid up trouble for almost every subsequent sixteenth-century English voyage to Guinea, and confirmed the Portuguese prejudice – not entirely unjust – that when Englishmen pretended trade they really looked for plunder.

These depredations, however profitable, had delayed the English ships' schedule. The tropical summer was coming to its oppressive climax, a debilitating season for Europeans – even for those with prior experience of its dangers. With the stubbornness typical of their race, the Englishmen were not only oblivious to their peril but dismissive of any attempt to cure that ignorance. On the Mina coast, Wyndham managed to barter some of his English wares for approximately 150lbs of gold: a transaction that probably put the expedition into profit, but which also whetted his appetite for further returns. One of his Portuguese pilots, Antonio Anes Pinteado, urgently argued against going further: '. . . for the safegard of the men and their lives, which they should put in danger, if they came too late, for the Rossia, which is their winter, not for cold but for smothering heate with close and cloudie aire and storming weather of such putrifying qualitie that it rotted the coates of their backs. . . .'[25] The warning could not have been less equivocal, but Wyndham had gold in his hands and a prospect of more to come. Dismissing Pinteado as a 'whoreson Jew', he decided to pass on eastwards to the Bight of Benin – a further distance of almost one thousand miles, into a region that no Englishman had yet visited.

At Benin, the local ruler was initially reluctant to deal with the Englishmen (possibly fearing Portuguese reprisals if he did business with these new interlopers), but when he was told that their own king had blessed their efforts he swiftly relented. Members of the expedition, led by Pinteado, went into the hinterland to supervise the collection of pepper. Eventually, about eighty tons of the commodity were gathered, ready for transportation to the coast; but in the meantime many of the Englishmen, both on-shore and at the mouth of the Benin river, had begun to fall sick, most probably having contracted one of the many viral infections of the region. Knowing nothing either of their affliction or the compromises in lifestyle that its proper treatment demanded, the English sailors persisted with their heavy, protein-rich diet and over-consumption of beer (much of which, inevitably, was sour; thus adding the burden of acute enteritis to the tally of their woes). Wyndham was one of the first to die, followed by a host of his men. Naturally, Pinteado was blamed for their predicament, but he managed to die also before his shipmates' ire could be fully directed his way. Very soon, not enough of the crews remained alive to man all three English ships, and a decision was made to abandon the *Lion* at the mouth of the Benin river. So swiftly did the survivors re-embark in the *Primrose* and *Moon* that several of their unfortunate countrymen who had remained in Benin City – including Nicholas Lambert, brother of one of the principal backers of the voyage – were abandoned there, as were several tons of pepper that had awaited lading.[26] Neither the men nor the pepper were seen again by European eyes.

The return voyage brought further, heavy mortality among a crew already weakened by fever. The prevailing currents and winds off the West African coast made a due west course extremely difficult to follow under sail alone. For those who did not know the optimum manoeuvre – that which the Portuguese named the *volta da Mina*: to sail south-westwards into the mid-Atlantic and then north-west to catch the Gulf Stream – the only option was to tack laboriously against contrary winds and the push of the South Equatorial current. Speaking of his own experience during the second Guinea voyage (in which far more able-bodied mariners survived to work their vessels), Robert Gaynsh, master of the ship *John Evangelist*, was to observe that 'whereas they sailed thither in seven weekes, they coulde returne in no lesse space then twentie weekes'.[27] For Wyndham's enfeebled mariners, this back-bending toil was a ferocious reaper of sickly constitutions; by the time that the two ships returned to England – probably some time during May or June 1554 – they carried barely forty survivors, several of whom died within days of their return. Their cargoes, however, remained intact. These included several tons of pepper and, much more importantly, the gold traded on the Mina coast. For the backers of the venture, this was entirely satisfactory: a clear profit, even with the loss of the *Lion* and ruin of the *Primrose*, to men who not only did not regard the deaths of hired men as their own misfortune, but who also refused to pay the survivors, or their next of kin, more than twelve and a half months' wages for sixteen months' employment in the voyage.[28]

What mark such an arduous experience had left upon the young, untested Martin Frobisher is unclear. No narrative – not even his own brief declaration – mentions his reactions to it. To have watched so many of his shipmates die would have been intensely traumatic, particularly as the disease which took them was both voracious and unfamiliar; ironically, it may only have been the chronic mortality in the two remaining ships that prevented the survivors from dwelling too deeply upon it – with so few hands to work their vessels, there can be little doubt that the expedition's 'safe' return was as much a matter of unremitting toil and blind luck as of brilliant seamanship. Sir

Hugh Willoughby's doomed Arctic voyage of that same year aside, no other English expedition of the period was to suffer such extreme ill-fortune, and if Sir John Yorke had intended his nephew to be blooded by the experience, he could hardly have been disappointed. Yet as brutal as this first taste of life and death at sea must have been, Frobisher seems to have weathered it well. Indeed, the seaman's life and its extraordinary hardships appear to have appealed immediately and strongly to the robust and adventurous boy who, until then, may not have voyaged further than the end of an English quay. Were it otherwise, it is hardly likely that he would have been preparing to set out on a second Guinea voyage within months of his fortunate return.

Of the previous year's promoters, Yorke and Sir George Barne, exercised by the promise of that magical, optimum transaction of gold for English cloths, had swiftly put together a new syndicate of five London merchants to finance a further voyage. Other than themselves, this comprised Edward Castelyn, Anthony Hickman and Thomas Lok – men who had also traded for a number of years as an Anglo-Iberian syndicate (Hickman and Castelyn jointly maintained a factory in the Canaries, from where they imported sugar into England).[29] It may have been upon a visit of these men to Sir John Yorke's house that Martin Frobisher first became known to the Lok family; an unremarkable event in itself, but one that, eventually, was to be of profound consequence for the Loks, for Frobisher himself, and even for a monarch who was as yet supremely uncertain of assuming her throne.

Thomas Lok was the eldest of five brothers, of a family that had long been associated with the Mercers' and Merchant Adventurers' companies. Their father, Sir William Lok, had been Sheriff of London in 1548 (immediately prior to Sir John Yorke). He was a devoutly Protestant merchant who had acted formerly as personal supplier of fine cloths to Henry VIII and the princesses Elizabeth and Mary, and – a personal service offered *gratis* – of vernacular French psalm books to Anne Boleyn.[30] In addition to his trade in merceries, he had for many years sent ships to the Greek islands of Chios and Zante, purchasing currants, wine and other valuable comestibles with English cloths, horse harnesses and beer.[31] However, like Sir John Yorke, the export of English broadcloths and import of luxury goods had been his staple, and it was that of his sons also. The disruptions to the Antwerp mart – and, to a lesser degree, the virtual extinction of the English Levant trade during the 1550s – had therefore hit the Loks hard. So, no less, had the accession of Mary Tudor. Among the leading merchant families in London, the Loks had been early converts to a particularly enthusiastic variety of non-conformity which had since shaded to outright Calvinism – a dangerous affliction to which the

Lok womenfolk were particularly prone. Unlike the supremely unprincipled Yorke (who promptly took to attending Mass following his release from the Tower),[32] the Loks bore their persecution and largely refused to bend before prevailing confessional winds. For them, the powerful lure of new overseas markets was supplemented by equally urgent devotional considerations, to make foreign climes – the more foreign the better – seem increasingly attractive from 1553 onwards.

Sir William had died in 1550, probably only just missing a tenure as Lord Mayor of London.[33] His son Thomas, now patriarch of the family, had formed particularly strong business links with Anthony Hickman, which they cemented in marriage – each man had married the other's sister – and would soon strengthen further in adversity, when, during the Marian persecutions, they would be imprisoned together for assisting other poorer Protestants to flee from England.[34] It may have been through Hickman that Lok was brought into the new venture, though the coincidence of his business activities with those of Yorke (Lok, too, was to be a charter member of the Russia Company in 1555) does not require us to search too far for potential connections. In the slightly incestuous society of sixteenth-century mercantile London, men set about the same occupations could not avoid each others' society, much less their company.

The new syndicate began its preparations in some haste, hoping to miss the worst of the tropical summer season. Inconveniently, Thomas Wyndham had died, and so a new man was needed to command the expedition. The adventurers of 1554 chose John Lok, younger brother of Thomas. His qualifications for assuming this role are not entirely obvious. In 1553 he had made a personal pilgrimage to Jerusalem,[35] but he had shipped in other men's vessels, not his own. This relatively novel experience alone would not therefore have been sufficient to convince his brother's partners of his aptness for the new venture. However, it is likely that he had also commanded or at least sailed in previous voyages to the eastern Mediterranean carrying his father's goods, during which he would also have performed the function of factor, negotiating terms with his foreign customers (the Lok brothers, as we shall see from the career of their youngest sibling, had been brought up to be men of flexible talents). Certainly, John Lok's record in the coming voyage, both as a seaman and merchant, was to justify the faith of men who had put good money into an enterprise that was clearly fraught with potential disaster.

In fact, the lessons of the arduous 1553 voyage had been well absorbed. Lok sailed from Dartmouth on 1 November 1554 with three ships – the *Trinity of*

London, John Evangelist and *Bartholemew* – and two small pinnaces. The expedition did not put in at Madeira or any other Portuguese possession; nor did it pass as far as the fever-swept Benin coast. Seven weeks after departing from England, Lok's ships made their first landfall somewhere near the mouth of the river Sestos (the latter day Sess or Cess, on the Liberian coast), where they paused only to acquire a quantity of Malaguetta pepper. When members of the expedition next went on-shore, it was at their intended destination: upon what was to become known as the Gold Coast, the hub of the West African gold trade.

The Negro traders of the region proved to be not nearly as obliging as those of Benin in the previous year. Understanding something of the value of their principal commodity, they drove hard bargains. Somewhat outraged, Robert Gaynsh complained that the local traders were so brazenly adept at trade that they actually used weights and measures, and 'will not lose one sparke of golde of any value'.[36] Furthermore, the Portuguese, keen to preserve their hold on the fabulously lucrative gold and spice trades, maintained forts at Mina and Axim, and policed the coast between the two effectively. When Lok anchored at the town of Shamma, the local governor, fearing either white men's sharp practices or hostile Portuguese intervention, demanded a hostage as a pre-condition of doing business. When one was duly sent ashore, negotiations began. Before trading could commence, however, a Portuguese brigantine appeared and opened fire on the English ships. The Englishmen fled, leaving their hostage with the governor who, anxious to preserve the good offices of his best customers, immediately handed him over to the furious Portuguese. The interlopers, apparently not too devastated by the loss of one of their company, sailed eastwards into the territory of the Fetu people where they did further brisk business. Their absent colleague, the young Martin Frobisher, passed into Portuguese custody.

The only extant reference to the event states that 'Martine, by his owne desire and assent of some of the commissioners that were in the pinnesse, went ashoare to the towne'.[37] Why his shipmates should have assented so readily is not made explicit, but the choice seems to have been the logical one. It may have been the first inkling of a tendency to fearlessness, much evident in subsequent years, that inclined Frobisher to volunteer to be a hostage. It is also likely that he was regarded as the most expendable option: less adept at the mariner's art than his more experienced colleagues, and, with the presence in the voyage of John Beryn also, a superfluous resource in trade negotiations. If the logic seems callous, someone had to be put at risk if any trade was to be done, and more experienced men were otherwise employed.

In a voyage in which everyone – including John Lok himself – was regarded
as expendable in the pursuit of profit, there would have been little hesitation
in providing the required collateral.

The expedition returned to England successfully, without putting in again
at Shamma or otherwise attempting to recover its missing hostage. Only
twenty-four men were lost, a remarkable improvement upon the previous
year. The adventurers made a huge profit on their investment, the ships being
laden with pepper, ivory and approximately 400 lbs of gold. No doubt Yorke's
own share of this booty softened the pain of his presumed bereavement, and
he further distracted himself by immediately taking in hand preparations for
a further Guinea voyage. It need hardly be stated that no time was wasted
in making representations – diplomatic or otherwise – on behalf of Martin
Frobisher.

In fact, his captivity seems to have been a relatively comfortable affair, with
few of the 'greate threates and menaces' previously promised. His captors took
him to their fort or castle, *São Jorge da Mina*, where, according to his future
testimony, he remained for about nine months. Apparently, the local inhabitants of the lands around the fort were disinclined to be compliant hosts, so
the Portuguese, regarding Frobisher to be no less expendable than had his
supposed shipmates, fell into the habit of arming him with their best wishes
and sending him off to obtain provisions from among these supposedly savage
folk.[38]

Clearly, the young Englishman managed to engage his suppliers' goodwill
sufficiently to escape harm. The 'perill' may have been overstated (perhaps
his captors had sent him out to gauge it), though there were intermittent
bouts of conflict throughout the period in which the Portuguese maintained
their tenuous presence on the Guinea coast. Perhaps, if the locals appeared
to be hostile, Frobisher kept the peace by paying more than the going rate
for foodstuffs he obtained; if not, his relatively great height and build may
have made them more circumspect. Whichever is the case, it is unlikely that
he kept any ruder company with his victuallers than with his gaolers – many
of whom, apparently, had been posted to the Guinea coast as a punishment
for crimes that otherwise merited the death sentence in Portugal.[39]

It is difficult to assess how gravely the Portuguese regarded the offence in
which Frobisher had been so obviously implicated. Despite their strenuous
efforts to discourage or hinder interlopers, it was a fact of life that any valuable trade, absent the protection of prior conquest, was open to challenge.
Absent also a state of outright war, Portuguese measures to curb the problem
tended to fall short of brutality (except when visited upon their own coun-

trymen). In Frobisher's case, the extreme penalty seems not to have been considered, and, failing that convenient means of disposing of an embarrassing guest, the fort at Mina was otherwise entirely unsuitable as a gaol. The nine months' captivity he suffered there probably represented the time his captors required to arrange for his transfer back to Portugal. Certainly, he was to spend some months thereafter in Lisbon. Writing over twenty years later to publicize the north-west voyages, Richard Willes claimed that Frobisher's interest in the possibility of a navigable north-west passage had first been aroused in conversations with a Portuguese seaman, held in a Lisbon gaol, who claimed to have made that voyage.[40] Whether these conversations ever took place as reported remains doubtful, as we shall see, though the incarceration undoubtedly occurred. The circumstances in which Frobisher regained his freedom are similarly obscure. It is possible that Sir John Yorke, who was well known to the Portuguese authorities, may have sought the Privy Council's intercession; but his obvious indifference to his nephew's fate, his own bad standing with the current English regime and his deserved reputation as an interloper in the Guinea trade all make this seem unlikely. It is far more probable that Frobisher eventually came to be regarded by his captors as not worth the expense of feeding. A young Englishman with few connections would have constituted no great bargaining counter in Portuguese attempts to stifle the English Guinea trade in its crib. Conversely, a cheap but timely humanitarian gesture might have been seen as an encouragement to a fellow Catholic monarch to use her far greater influence to that end. Whether Frobisher was released in time for that gesture to have any appreciable effect before Mary died is doubtful, even had a solitary, troublesome young man been considered a good swap for an embryonic but lucrative trade. It is safe to assume that neither the Queen nor Sir John Yorke and his colleagues were asked to make that difficult choice.

How Frobisher returned to England – if, indeed, he did so directly – is not known, though it is likely that he was obliged to throw himself upon the charity of Anglo-Iberian traders going about their business in Lisbon, many of whom must have been known to the Yorke family. Whatever the precise circumstances that permitted it, his does not seem to have been a happy return. There is no evidence that he took up residence once more in Sir John's household, or even that he continued to be associated in Yorke's business ventures. He was far too late to secure a share of the profits from the second Guinea voyage, and it is possible that he missed his wages, too. Yorke was famously parsimonious, and it may have been upon a matter of money that their relationship was now severed. Both men, it is clear, had good reasons to draw a line under their association. For Frobisher, two perilous voyages to Guinea and a sojourn in Portuguese gaols without even the comforting weight of a full purse to ease the pain did not auger well for his future prospects as a Yorke. For Sir John's part, it must have become apparent that his nephew possessed not the slightest interest in, nor aptitude for, trade; nor, without investing further time and money, was there likelihood of recouping several years' expenditure upon this poor and inconvenient cousin. With such mutually strong grounds for separation, the break that now took place seems to have been definitive. There is some evidence that Frobisher was involved with a number of Sir John's sons in subsequent projects, but not, it seems, as part of a larger family compact.[41]

Without the Yorke connection, Frobisher must have addressed his future prospects with some urgency. His qualifications to date comprised an untypical experience of long-range voyages, a certain natural hardiness, a unique understanding (for an Englishman) of the techniques of purchasing victuals from the Infidel and an inclination – of inestimable value in an age of dissolving certainties – towards rootlessness. Freed from Yorke's cold and somewhat shabby stewardship, he had neither family nor other exemplar to check or otherwise bend these qualities to the service of useful employment. Perhaps here, both in the cause and consequences of this necessitous state, lay the germ of his future antipathy towards men of business. The unremitting misfortune of his exposure to the merchant's world had provided a hard schooling, its most striking lesson being that the lawful acquisition of profit need not be a uniformly benign or godly process. In comparison to the value of those commodities he had been charged to obtain on his uncle's behalf, his own worth – as a cousin, an employee and, indeed, as a human being – had been pegged in a particularly callous manner. The revelation may have been a cathartic one; it was certainly to have lasting implications.

However, the only two extant references to Frobisher's activities immediately following his release do little to further clarify the circumstances that were to shape his future character and intentions. An Admiralty Court exemplification, set down in 1604, infers that one Anthony Hammond was brought back to England from Barbary by Frobisher sometime during the year 1559.[42] The statement is nowhere corroborated, but if accurate it suggests two things: that Frobisher was in command of an African expedition by the age of twenty-four, and that his contacts with Yorke's circle of Barbary colleagues may not have been entirely severed by the unfortunate experiences of the 1554 Guinea expedition. Whilst Yorke himself is not known to have financed any Barbary voyages in 1558–9, others undoubtedly did. As the trade became more established towards the end of the 1550s, individual voyages became unremarkable events, and often entirely anonymous. Frobisher was certainly known to two of Yorke's long-time business associates, Sir Thomas White and Arthur Dawbeney, who remained so engaged in the Barbary commerce as to maintain a resident factor at the port of Safi.[43] It is likely that his experiences on the 1553–4 voyages, and his subsequent relationship with the Portuguese authorities, made him an obvious candidate to take command of an expedition that – if not yet actually routine – was no longer considered rigorous. The episode is obscure but interesting, if true, in providing the earliest evidence of Frobisher's role as a sea-commander. Whether he was employed in this business long enough for it to become a familiar occupation is impossible to judge, as indeed is the very nature of that business. It is equally possible, as we shall see, that the voyage had a much darker purpose than lawful trade. Whatever its precise circumstances, the apparent favour done for the family of the anonymous Hammond child is the final reference to Frobisher's African activities – to any legitimate occupation – for more than a decade thereafter.

The only other piece of information regarding his preoccupations during this period refers to the slight matter of his marriage, on 30 September 1559, to Isobel, widow of Thomas Rigatt, of Snaith.[44] The fact is stated, and that is all. Efforts to determine Frobisher's attitude to Isobel, to romantic attachments in general, or to any other circumstance of domesticity are doomed to failure. His life appears to have been singularly free of amorous adventures, even by the rigorous standards of Elizabeth's other 'sea-dogs' (the incorrigibly romantic Walter Ralegh excepted). Admittedly, our perception is shaped by an utter dearth of information; in the years in which a more conventional relationship might have been attested by the arrival of children, or by the manner in which it impacted upon other adjacent lives, Martin and Isobel Frobisher enjoyed at best a titular estate: a concommitant feature, inevitably, of the lifestyle of a man who was to remain at sea almost continuously during the years of their marriage. Whether this circumstance reflected or deflected the reality of their relationship is, and will remain, unclear. They were to be estranged, eventually, in a striking manner; but whether this occurred within months or years of their marriage we cannot say. We know only that Isobel brought children and a settlement of indeterminable value from her first marriage, had the latter squandered by her new husband, and ended her days in abject poverty: abandoned by a man for whom the remorseless quest for wealth and reputation would leave little time to observe such niggling distractions as marital duty and human compassion.

Nevertheless, the bare details of the arrangement are revealing. The reference to Snaith, barely fifteen miles from Frobisher's place of birth, suggests either that Isobel had been known to him for a number of years – perhaps even before he left Altofts as a teenager – or that he had sent to his family to arrange a suitable match from amongst suitable local stock. It is also the first indication (later supported by the many local properties he acquired) that Frobisher's links with West Yorkshire had not only survived his translation to London, but strengthened *in absentia*.

Isobel was not to bear any children by Frobisher. Her own fertility is not in doubt, and given the much later evidence of her husband's will – particularly its preoccupation with preserving his estate through a male line – it is inconceivable that he regarded the production of an heir as unimportant. It is possible then that Frobisher was infertile – perhaps even impotent – or that his home visits may have been too fleeting to facilitate the hoped-for event. His apparently callous attitude to his wife and her children suggests that this was never a relationship built upon affection; perhaps Isobel had been enticed into the match by the promise of a security that the estate of widowhood palpably lacked, the *quid pro quo* for which was a dutiful career as a brood-mare. Her failure to oblige in this respect may have been the catalyst in removing any vestigial sense of responsibility that Frobisher may have entertained; and he, no less than his contemporary biographers (none of whom was to give the slightest hint that their hero ever possessed a wife), washed his hands of the commitment thereafter. Having welcomed Isobel Frobisher to this story, we may – with two later, unfortunate asides – bid her farewell.

Regarding Frobisher's life in its entirety, there is much that seems incongruous about his activities during this period, with their emphasis upon legitimate commercial employment and growing domestic entanglements. It is tempting to see in their relative brevity and abrupt ending a side to his nature that made their perpetuation an impossibility: that the pressures and preoccupations which shaped his character were entirely antipathetic to commitments that had been thrust upon him by convention alone. We shall find much and varied evidence that his violent, impulsive nature was in large part a manifestation of an inner frustration: most palpably, with the due processes of living in conformity with society. What were, for most of its component souls, the necessary foundations upon which that society was raised often materialized in Frobisher's path as obstacles – as he saw them – to his advancement. Whether this was solely a consequence of his temperament, or of unlucky circumstance also, remains open to question; but his inability to follow the role of good husband, the trade of the merchant or the discipline of the master mariner plying a lawful trade appears to have been a symptom, rather than the cause, of disruptions in his character that formed early and decisively.

At this point, having evidence of some faint inclinations towards conformity, we lose sight of Frobisher for almost four years. Such obscurity is always frustrating; often it hints at no more than a quiet period in the life of the subject – at activities too mundane or unworthy of note to have found their way into the various media of record. In Frobisher's case, our frustration is heightened by the near-certainty that he was *not* enjoying or suffering a quiet phase in his career during these years. On the contrary, it was rapidly evolving – apparently seamlessly – from a shaky but salutary apprenticeship in the legitimate trade of his adopted family to one that balanced precariously on the very edge of banditry. Unless this resulted from a *volte face* of Pauline proportions, influences about which we have no information were working vigorously upon him. Only one thing is clear: at some point between 1556 and 1560 he make a conscious decision to abandon all attempts to forge a career in the company of merchants. A young man in need of a fortune requires abilities, and the nature of those abilities invariably determines the path upon which that fortune is sought. For Martin Frobisher – needful yet lacking patronage, semi-literate and almost certainly innumerate – it seems that there were only two realistic alternatives: to starve, or to enrich himself from the purses, rather than in the employment, of those men of business who had been content to regard his death as one of the more acceptable costs of securing a lawful profit.

FOUR

Divers and Sundrye Pyracies: 1559–71

In September 1559, a frequently imprisoned pirate named Henry Stranguishe (known more commonly as Strangways) was brought before the Admiralty Court on a charge of intended piracy. He was accused of planning a raid on the Guinea coast, specifically to capture and plunder the Portuguese fortress at Mina where Martin Frobisher had been held captive some five years earlier. The offence had been prevented by his arrest; but the intention, if proven, had serious implications. To interlope upon Portuguese economic interests was one thing – as we have seen, if commerce is a form of economic warfare, then English tastes were extremely sanguinary in that respect – but to prey aggressively upon the possessions of a nation not at war with England was to deny the Queen the right to make policy at her own pace. The gravity of the offence was further aggravated by Stranguishe's previous 'form'. As early as 1552, the Admiralty had set out ships to apprehend him for acts of piracy.[1] The effort appears to have been successful; in the following year, he was imprisoned for seizing vessels of the Biscayan fleet (some of his men, not sharing his influential connections, had been hanged for the offence). Remarkably, having somehow escaped this confinement and fled to Cork, Stranguishe had been pursued thereafter by an entire fleet, set out by the Admiralty specifically to recapture him. In 1555, he was in prison once more, though he appears to have been released soon afterwards – through the good offices, apparently, of one of the Princess Elizabeth's ladies-in-waiting. In 1557, he was again before the Admiralty Court on charges of preying upon Spanish ships off Fowey, and in the following year he was bound over in the sum of £500 to keep the peace. This new, alleged transgression, set upon such a pedigree, was one that promised to deliver up Stranguishe to the fate he had so narrowly escaped in 1553; particularly as Elizabeth herself – now Queen of England – had come to the opinion that he was overdue an appointment with the gibbet.[2]

The accused must have been well aware of the delicacy of his situation. Instead of denying everything (a risky ploy before an Admiralty Court that had his record to hand), he fell back upon the time-honoured technique of farming out the blame. In his declaration to the court, he stated that one Martin Frobisher was involved in the project and had also originally intended to sail, though subsequently he had withdrawn. For good measure, Stranguishe also attempted to implicate John Lok, claiming he had spoken directly to him of the matter.[3]

This is the first known reference to Frobisher's involvement with men whose ideas on personal advancement involved something less onerous than the practice of commerce. Stranguishe's accusations, unsupported by hard evidence as far as we know, were intended to deflect the court's attention from his own culpability – or at least to dilute the judge's interest in it. The accusation against John Lok was almost certainly an outright lie; no member of the Lok family is known ever to have been involved in privateering ventures, much less outright piracy; and John Lok seems, upon other evidence, to have been a relatively fastidious man.[4] Frobisher's alleged involvement, however, is not so easily dismissed. He knew the fort at Mina better than any of his countrymen   indeed, he was probably the only Englishman ever to have been within its walls. He had also sailed in two of only five documented English voyages to Guinea prior to that time, and was well placed to advise upon the sea-routes that would avoid premature trouble (and, if the later claims of the near anonymous Anthony Hammond are true, he had been developing his knowledge of the African coast in the very year that Stranguishe made his accusations). If expertise in local conditions was required (and it almost certainly was), then Martin Frobisher would have been able to provide it. Even so, Stranguishe's evidence was entirely circumstantial; standing alone, it would and should have deserved little attention, particularly when we consider the character of the man from whom it came. However, other evidence of Frobisher's activities during these years, and of the connections which he and Stranguishe are known to have shared, makes it seem wholly plausible. By the year 1560, it is almost certain that Frobisher was an active privateer, and possibly also a pirate. Thereafter, all doubt vanishes.

Privateering – the setting out of privately owned vessels under letters of marque or reprisal – was ostensibly a means by which 'private' wrongs were redressed. A merchant whose property had been illegally seized at sea could apply for a licence from the Admiralty, to recover by force goods or monies to a specified value from the fellow countrymen of the offending party. The licence was issued for a finite period – usually six months – but only after the case had been examined by the High Court of Admiralty, where witnesses to the alleged incident would be heard and judgment given. The important point was that privateering activities were intended to result from a legal proccss in which their scope was precisely defined: a process that represented the only legal sanction in an era before international treaties allowed recourse to a mechanism transcending national boundaries.[5]

This was the intention under law. The reality, in contrast, was that many privateers were engaged in their trade by professional inclination, and sought merely to enrich themselves at the expense of innocent foreigners. Private warfare, legally authorized and waged in search of recompense, was a good excuse to put to sea; but inevitably it evolved into something more as the profit motive took hold. Once out of sight of land, the precise terms of letters of reprisal became something of a moot point. Whether an amount of plunder was in excess of that permitted by their terms was hard to determine accurately; in any case, surpluses could be set down upon a coast far from the eyes of Admiralty agents, or a portion set aside with the honourable intention of bribing them. Nor was it always clear or considered worth determining whose letters of reprisal were being carried by whom – there was, it seems, a strong and profitable trade in the letters themselves. Men whose reputations made it impossible to secure licences under their own names were frequently willing to acquire them from merchants with legitimate grievances. With a little creative arbitrage, the man of business might receive a risk-free measure of recompense whilst the freebooter could put to sea with *carte blanche* to determine his own profit. It was, in practice, one of the purest forms of free enterprise.

From the Crown's perspective, the wholesale issue of letters of reprisal usually foreshadowed or reflected a wider conflict – one whose burden upon the Exchequer could be considerably relieved by the efforts of men setting out ships at their own expense. Inevitably, excesses committed during privately organized expeditions sometimes had a deleterious effect. If sufficiently conspicuous, they could undermine official government policy by encouraging economic sanctions or, worse, exacerbating the potential for outright warfare. How often such depredations occurred cannot be established (it would be impossible to estimate with any accuracy the proportion of vessels belonging to neutral or friendly nations that were taken by English privateers during Elizabeth's reign), but it will become all too apparent that foreign plaintiffs' applications for redress provided constant and onerous work for the Admiralty Court. Under such provocation, the Queen's officials periodically acted to curb the freebooters, but a consistent or rational policy was never to be formulated, much less implemented.

Therefore, whereas the precise circumstances that led Frobisher to become a privateer are not known, the reasons are easily understood. The practice of lawful commerce required patience, aptitude and credit: for none of which, to date, he had provided much evidence. Privateering, on the other hand, required a ship – as often as not, one could be supplied or partly financed by a gentleman or merchant for a slice of the expected bounty – and the enthusiasm to chase God-sent opportunities to despoil the commerce of others. For a young man of slim prospects and boundless energy, it was an option that did not so much recommend itself as render inconsequential any more legitimate alternative.

It was Frobisher's good fortune – and, perhaps, a determining factor – that he took to the profession at a particularly auspicious moment. Had he been active at this pastime in the years prior to the early 1560s, his unruly energies might have led him to an entirely less happy end. Outright piracy had been a favoured occupation among such unscrupulous Englishmen as the voluble Stranguishe for several decades, but it had been a business that demanded a large degree of circumspection. During Mary's reign, when the brief Anglo-French war of 1557–8 had provided English privateers with legitimate commissions to attack French vessels, they had devoted much – perhaps most – of their attention to neutral Spanish and Netherlander ships; but they had also been sufficiently prudent (given that they were, in effect, despoiling the subjects of their own king) to use the safe havens of 'foreign' ports – usually Irish – to unload their wares.[6] With the end of the war, the activities of such men became entirely unacceptable once more, and active measures were taken to curb them – as master Stranguishe, preying upon Spanish ships off Fowey, had discovered. However, their persecution was brief. From almost the beginning of Elizabeth's reign, the evolving circumstances which dictated her foreign policy also allowed for – indeed, demanded – privateering activity on a scale which made its effective policing impossible. It was an industry that would bring much work for her ambassadors at the courts of princes whose subjects had been unlawfully despoiled; though initially at least, it rose admirably to meet the needs of a government that had neither the economic nor military means to hold the initiative. War, to Elizabeth even more than to the apocryphal Good Prince, was a final resort; but the circumstances and timing of her succession meant that calls upon her war-chest were immediately heavy and insistent, and incurred particularly against the threat of foreign intervention in English affairs.

That intervention, in the early 1560s, was universally expected to be of French origin. At the time, Spain presented little discernible threat to the English nation. Until very recently, Philip II had been King of England; and though never well loved by his English subjects (and despite his near certainty that Elizabeth would entirely reverse her half-sister's religious policies), he had few reasons for disturbing the cautious yet profitable amity that existed between his present and former kingdoms.[7] Indeed, in 1560, when Francis II covertly urged that France and Spain, the two foremost Catholic powers, collaborate to further God's cause by invading England, Philip secretly ordered his army in the Netherlands to prepare to assist Elizabeth if French troops crossed the Channel.[8] In their mutual distrust of France (particularly, of the ambitions of Francis II and his young wife Mary Stuart), and in the benefits accruing from the historic Anglo-Burgundian trade in the Netherlands, Spain and England shared a self-interest in maintaining good relations which dampened – if it did not render inconsequential – the problem of Elizabeth's heretical leanings.

In contrast, France posed a threat that was both immediate and enduring. England and France remained technically at war at Elizabeth's accession; the old wool-staple town of Calais, the last vestige of England's once mighty French empire, had been lost as recently as 1557, and there were many Frenchmen who believed that an early invasion of England was the logical next step in this advance of arms. French troops had already passed in strength northwards through the Narrow Seas to support the Catholic Scottish Crown against the Protestant Lords of the Congregation; in 1558 they remained on British soil as a threat, just across England's troubled northern border. The regent of the Scottish throne, Mary of Guise, was a member of the noble house that exemplified French ambitions for English conquests; ambitions that were both strengthened and legitimized by the accession of an heretic to the English throne. To Mary and her powerful relations, Elizabeth's rule – even her existence – was intolerable. Her brother Francis, Duke of Guise, conqueror of Calais and uncle of Mary Stuart, strongly supported his niece's claim to the English throne – which, it could be argued, was every bit as firm as Elizabeth's (Mary was Henry VII's great grand-daughter through a 'legitimate' line; Elizabeth's mother Anne Boleyn was, in Catholic eyes, a whore). In addition to being a fond uncle, Guise was also the virtual ruler of France until the death of Francis II in 1561 severed his direct influence over the throne.

The accession of the young Charles IX brought a new regent, Catherine de' Medici; but Guise and his party remained a formidable power within the state, and continued to control the royal army and its artillery train. It was the person and ambitions of Guise, rather than the French Crown, that represented the most persistent foreign policy issue of the English Queen's early reign; and it was no less a threat for being a semi-private vendetta.

Fortunately for Elizabeth, Guise was soon too busy to devote his attention to the invasion of England. At the beginning of 1562, Catherine de' Medici's proclamation of what became known as the January Edict, ostensibly providing for freedom of worship for Protestant congregations throughout France, put a match to the tinder of France's unresolved confessional crises. As the foremost champion of the Catholic party, Guise gleefully accepted its challenge. On 1 March 1562, he expressed his righteous ire in an entirely practical manner, by allowing his followers to slaughter seventy-four Huguenots at worship in their church at Vassy, Champagne. With this atrocity, the first of the wars of religion that were to wrack France for almost half a century commenced, and both sides, Catholic and Huguenot, set about finding allies.

For Philip II, who was still struggling to resolve the political implications of his father's death and the subsequent sundering of the Hapsburg inheritance, the conflict removed at a stroke the greatest potential threat to his European possessions outside Spain. The latter years of Charles V's rule had been dogged by a growing French power that was perfectly placed to disrupt the commercial and political intercourse between the widely dispersed Hapsburg core territories. The onset of civil war in France, and corresponding collapse of the French Crown's ability to do anything other than ensure its own survival, should therefore have been considered an unmitigated blessing. It was not, however. Setting aside the unfeigned horror with which Philip II regarded any outbreak of heresy (no matter how personally convenient), the prospect of a vast new source of confessional strife so close to the Netherlands, where his father had already experienced much difficulty in imposing effective counter-measures against the rise of the Protestant faith in urban areas, promised only further potential for huge discord.

For Elizabeth also, French civil strife provided as many problems as opportunities. Guise's open opposition to the regency, and the support he received from the moderate Catholic Bourbon and Montmorency families, once more effectively placed the reins of government into his hands. His involvement in the civil war prevented him from attempting to realize his English ambitions directly, but the prospects for a Huguenot victory remained extremely poor – indeed, it seemed that without some urgent expression of external support, the Protestant cause in France was doomed. It was the first of many occasions upon which Elizabeth found herself obliged to champion her co-religionists for entirely selfish reasons. It was also, in the manner of many learning experiences, to be the most disastrously conceived.

Initially, the total inadequacy of England's military resources inclined her to prudence (she had not even the means to fortify Portsmouth adequately against a prospective French attack).[9] The Prince of Condé, desperate to reverse a series of early Huguenot setbacks, sought English intervention and a loan of 100,000 crowns to prosecute the war. Both pleas fell upon deaf ears, but Elizabeth was happy to offer a cheaper alternative. The only realistic gesture that might be made at little or no cost to her was to offer the services of her eager subjects. Disappointed in his other requests, the desperate Condé promptly took the hint and issued letters of marque to English privateers to harry the French Catholic sea-trade. Many Englishmen took up these commissions, which were supplemented in the following year by English letters of marque when Elizabeth, momentarily blinded to the reality of her resources, succumbed to the siren prospect of recovering Calais and took England openly into the war.[10]

Her first decision – to set loose English privateers in the Channel and off the Atlantic coast of France – was theoretically sound. It placed a screen of ships between Guise's forces and the English coast, giving Elizabeth a measure of cost-free security and, on paper at least, an opportunity to weaken the seaborne economy of the enemy. The English 'invasion' of northern France during 1563 was, in contrast, to be the single most disastrous foreign policy decision of her reign; achieving nothing but the emptying of her purse, the humiliation of her armed forces and the irrevocable ending of English claims to any foothold upon French soil. Its only positive result was the harsh lesson that Elizabeth was to absorb and apply for the rest of her life in resisting almost all subsequent temptations to indulge in continental adventures.

Having very briefly made a useful contribution, the swarm of English privateers at sea also proved to be a mixed blessing. Even before the end of 1563, it was estimated that up to 400 English ships and 25,000 seamen were already in the Channel and western approaches, looking for the vessels of their new enemy.[11] In such a saturated market, there were not nearly enough legitimate prizes to go around, and commissions – whether issued by Condé or the Admiralty Court – were abused almost from the first. More often than not, any French vessel was considered to be Catholic, and any foreign vessel a Frenchman. As in 1557–8, Spanish and Netherlander vessels were particularly favoured, being on the whole laded with richer goods than those of the northern French sea-trade. Having been brought into the war as the surrogate means of conducting an official foreign policy, the Queen's subjects went their own way, with no thought for the larger consequences of their actions.

Margaret of Parma, sister-in-law of Philip II and his regent in the Nether-lands, protested vehemently at the growing number of English depredations against her subjects' vessels. However, having set loose her privateers, Eliza-beth could do little to curb them; nor – at least initially – does she seem to have tried too assiduously. She issued a proclamation on 1 September 1563 which ordered 'proper' English ships to defend the King of Spain's subjects against English despoilations.[12] Nevertheless, the increasing incidence of English attacks upon Spanish ships resulted in the brief detention of all English vessels in northern Spanish ports in January 1564. Meanwhile in the Channel, seizures of Netherlander ships rose to the point where Margaret's government retaliated with an embargo upon English ships trading with the Low Countries (her desire to reduce or remove English export duties on cloths exported to Antwerp appears to have provided an equally robust motive).[13] This latter act proved to be a costly error. Elizabeth was obliged to defend English dignity by imposing her own embargo in return; though she subse-quently also issued a further proclamation forbidding the seizure of Nether-lander vessels, claiming that she had 'no manner of intention to impair the amity betwixt her and the King of Spain her good brother but rather to fortify and increase it'.[14]

Having temporarily lost their principal bourse, English cloth merchants extemporized by switching their mart to Emden, immediately across the German boundary of Margaret's domains. They barely managed to off-load that year's surplus of finished cloths in the same north German markets that usually took their commodities via Antwerp; whilst Antwerp itself and other centres of trade in the Netherlands, deprived of their middle-men's cut, underwent a minor depression.[15] Weighing the relative merits of his kingly dignity and a looming economic recession (and, it seems, being misled by his sister as to the true extent of English remorse), Philip II ordered the reopen-ing of his ports in the Low Countries to English ships before the end of the year; but these episodes were the first serious testing of the old Anglo-Burgundian amity. Privateers had proved a clumsy device to set loose upon the fragile firmament of diplomacy, being entirely self-serving and almost impos-sible to fine-tune to the needs of the state. Former pirates had discovered that they could be handsomely rewarded for doing what came naturally, whilst others who had formerly plied a legal trade had seen how much more readily

their wealth could be supplemented by taking that of 'Frenchmen'. Martin
Frobisher, it will become apparent, was not to be counted among those for
whom the benefits of privateering had come as a recent revelation. The timing
of his own conversion to the cause of other men's cargoes is obscure; but
almost certainly it had anticipated official English policy by some years.

Nothing more is known of his involvement with Stranguishe and the supposed Guinea project. The precise circumstances under which he first became
involved in the privateering profession are similarly obscure; perhaps, in the
brief but promising Anglo-French war of 1557–8, he had signed on in one of
the numerous English vessels that had descended upon the coast of France,
and – if his future predeliction for taking the 'wrong' vessels was symptomatic
of the lessons of his apprenticeship – upon the neutral trade that attempted
to pass through that dangerous screen on its passage to the Low Countries
and beyond. If so, it was probably in these years that he first nurtured what
would become life-long connections with the West Country's burgeoning
stock of privateers; of whom Henry Stranguishe was only the most voluble,
if not the most trustworthy. However, the first unequivocal evidence regarding this new career does not arise until the year 1563 (though the same evidence offers strong hints of earlier misdeeds), when Frobisher returned to
Yorkshire to go into partnership with his blood-kin. At some time prior to
this, his brother John had obtained the patronage of Sir Henry Percy, future
eighth Earl of Northumberland (and, incidentally, one of history's least convincing suicides),[16] and had become a ship-owner in partnership with a fellow
Yorkshireman, John Appleyard. In 1553, Appleyard took up letters of commission from Condé in his own name; under their licence he set out three
ships, the *John Appleyard* (also known as the *Bark Frobisher*; probably owned
jointly with John Frobisher), the *Anne Appleyard* and the *Elizabeth Appleyard*:
commanded respectively by John Frobisher, Martin Frobisher and Peter
Killigrew of Cornwall – the latter, significantly, being also a known privateering partner of Henry Stranguishe.[17] On 6 March 1553, the Frobishers and
Killigrew gave bonds of £50 each for their good conduct – specifically undertaking not to despoil Spanish or Portuguese ships – and then put to sea
with their small fleet.[18] Initially, they seem to have been both industrious and
relatively well behaved. By May 1563, they had already taken five vessels, all
apparently owned by French Catholics, and brought them into Plymouth as
prizes. Almost as soon as their feet touched dry land, however, these spoils
were seized.

This, Martin Frobisher's first known brush with English law, seems to have
constituted a genuine miscarriage of justice. According to extant Admiralty

Court records, the Frobisher brothers had not contravened the letter of John Appleyard's commission. However, the *Anne Appleyard* had become involved – possibly unwittingly – in the final stages of a sea-fight between a Spanish ship, the *Katherine*, and that of another English privateer, Thomas Cobham. Cobham, a once and future pirate, clearly took little notice of the detail of his own commission. His later deposition to the authorities stated that he had mistaken the *Katherine* for a French vessel, an error which surely would have been resolved as he closed to engage her. Certainly, his subsequent actions blatantly belied his claims. His attack upon the *Katherine* was brutally protracted, with the English fatalities alone numbering above forty. Frobisher's assistance was therefore timely and, by contemporary lights, entirely proper, no matter what Cobham's own offence.

Unfortunately, once the fight had been won and the Spanish ship captured, Frobisher succumbed to temptation and accepted Cobham's offer of a portion of her cargo of wines and tapestries (no doubt Cobham was exercised more by the need to implicate Frobisher in his own offence than by any surge of gratitude). The *Anne Appleyard* accompanied Cobham's ship and his Spanish prize to Baltimore in Ireland, a notorious resort of English privateers 'fencing' their illicitly seized goods. There, the swiftly emptied *Katherine* was scuttled, her cargoes divided into parcels and transported thereafter in small boats via St Ives in Cornwall to Plymouth, where Peter Killigrew waited to arrange for their dispersal. Unfortunately, Arthur Champernowne, vice-admiral of Devon, waited there also, to seize both the goods and their purloiners.[19] He was acting on the orders of the Privy Council, who had been pointedly apprised of the *Katherine's* seizure by the Spanish Ambassador in London, Guzman da Silva (his principal concern was the restoration of rich tapestries she had been carrying, which were to have been presented to Philip II himself). Martin Frobisher's culpability, if indirect, is clear; but his brother John's involvement is difficult to determine. It may have been his misfortune merely to have rendezvoused with Martin just prior to reaching Plymouth, thus implicating himself by association. He is not known to have had any part in taking the *Katherine*, but when examples needed to be made, the Admiralty seems to have been no more assiduous in establishing innocence than they were in proving guilt at other times.

Martin and John Frobisher rode to London. There they successfully petitioned the Privy Council to order the release of their French prizes, and also of the *Katherine's* wines to John Appleyard, who had protested his ignorance of the incident and may have undertaken to deliver them to the Spanish Ambassador.[20] However, Appleyard's agent, Thomas Bowes (son of Sir Martin

Bowes, a former Lord Mayor of London), using the Privy Council's licence, took possession of the booty from the mayor of Plymouth and disappeared somewhere between the West Country and London. The Spanish Ambassador may or may not have recovered the tapestries, but the wines had gone. It is possible that some of the profit from these was claimed by Appleyard, but given the evidence of Bowes's subsequent abandonment of Appleyard and close association with Martin Frobisher, it is more probable that the booty fell wholly to the benefit of Bowes and his privateering partners.[21]

Appleyard emerged from the episode with his reputation unscathed, but he did so in part by casting Martin and John Frobisher to the wolves. It was he, it seems, who initiated a lawsuit against both men for the recovery of the lost wines.[22] On 15 July 1564, the Frobisher brothers were arrested and confined in Launceston gaol; they remained there until September, when the Privy Council ordered that they be sent up to London to answer charges laid against them.[23] Having given their testimony, they appear to have been freed immediately.

The Frobishers may have felt aggrieved at their treatment (certainly, it had given Martin in particular further strong reason to fear the duplicity of merchants), but they had been relatively fortunate. However tardily the Privy Council's clemency had been granted, it contrasted strongly with the severity of the punishment threatened upon Cobham when he was brought to book for his offence. Such was his infamy that a royal proclamation had been issued on 15 July 1564 – the very day that the Frobisher brothers entered Launceston gaol – that commanded 'all persons, of what condition soever they be, to do their uttermost to apprehend by sea or by land the said Thomas or any of his accomplices'.[24] It seems that he was captured soon afterwards; a year and a day later, the Spanish Ambassador wrote to his king, informing him that Cobham had been adjudged guilty of despoiling the *Katherine* (despite his refusal to enter a plea before the Admiralty Court) and sentence pronounced. He was to be returned to the Tower, stripped naked and his head shaved, and thereafter hung upside down to be beaten upon the soles of the feet (the *bastinado*). Following this, he was to be laid upon the floor with his arms and legs stretched out, a sharp stone to be placed under his back and a large piece of ordnance – too heavy to bear but not sufficient to kill him outright – placed upon his belly. Having been thus arranged, Cobham was to enjoy a full three grains' weight of barley per day, with filthy water to still his thirst, until he died.[25] A week later, da Silva wrote once more to Philip II, informing him that Cobham's relatives had begged for his timely intervention with the Queen to commute this harsh sentence (Lord Thomas Cobham, perhaps the most exalted of these kinsmen, was not amongst the supplicants; he considered the Court's decision to be perfectly appropriate). Even the Earl of Sussex had interceded, asking the Spanish Ambassador to use what offices he thought fit; which suggests that Cobham had enjoyed some influential patronage during his illicit career. Da Silva himself expressed the opinion that the sentence was unlikely to be carried out and hinted that, if asked, he would opt for mercy (though, like Lord Thomas, he thought the judgment sound enough).[26] There is no evidence that Cobham was subsequently subjected to the full rigour of the Court's decision; in 1565, before the activities of Hawkins, Drake and others brought a more consistent, salutary policy, Philip II was still minded to forgive occasional acts of English piracy.

Yet the seizure of the *Katherine* was typical of many such infractions of the commissions under which men of doubtful reputation sailed. Redress for foreign ship-owners through English courts was slow and uncertain, even where the culprits could be identified unequivocally. Often, as in the case of the *Katherine*, the loot simply disappeared before effective action to arrest its loss could be taken, presenting the plaintiffs with a *fait accompli* that discouraged their making any further effort on principle alone. Nor could they always rely upon their own governments to make effective representation on their behalf, even – or particularly – if relations between the respective states were amicable. For Philip II, still keen to maintain the profitable Anglo-Spanish amity, the loss of small vessels to privateers was an irritation that could be borne in the greater interest (albeit with the occasional 'warning-shot', such as his seizure of English ships, when the phenomenon threatened to become onerous). Elizabeth, for her part, maintained an ambiguous attitude towards the privateers. The well-worn, cinematic image of a Queen excoriating her 'sea-dogs' in public whilst lauding their daring in private has long been discredited as simplistic. As we have seen, their depredations were more often a source of contention than a useful tool of policy. However, Elizabeth's options were always limited. Her often lawless subjects were undoubtedly an enthusiastic and, as we have seen, a cheap resource; they fulfilled part of her commitment to the Huguenot cause whilst obviating the need for costly – and certainly, more portentous – military adventures. It is probably fair to assume that whilst no privateer had *carte blanche* to conduct unlimited warfare upon a prey of choice, his crimes had to be major, protracted and, above all, an embarrassment to the Crown before the Admiralty Court applied the full weight of its authority in a condign manner. If he was taken at an inopportune moment in the cycle of amity or hostility that marked Elizabeth's relationships with foreign princes, an example might be made to discourage others; otherwise, the letter of the law was entirely subordinated to more pressing concerns. In the cases of Thomas Cobham and Henry Stranguishe, their respective prior connections with respectable figures such as the Earl of Sussex and Sir Nicholas Throckmorton ensured that pleas for clemency made on their behalf were heard. Other, similarly heartfelt pleas were by no means universally successful, but enough felons escaped the noose for a distinct strategy to be discerned: one which attempted to impose a degree of conformity to the Queen's will whilst preserving a reservoir of highly trained and motivated English mariners. Frobisher's own career as a privateer will provide ample evidence of this pragmatic policy.

In 1564, he and his brother had been released because their collusion with Cobham was seen to have been unpremeditated. However, if innocent of the specific deed, Frobisher was hardly blameless in a wider sense. An officer of the Admiralty Court who had attempted to detain the *Anne Appleyard* whilst she lay off Kinsale later stated that he had been resisted at sword-point by her entire crew – hardly the response of respectable, law-abiding mariners mistaken for felons.[27] Indeed, as early as the following year, Frobisher was beginning to be regarded as a persistent troublemaker. A Spanish petition, dated 27 May 1565, named him as one of several known despoilers of Spanish vessels: in this instance, of the ship *Flying Spirit*, out of Andalusia with a cargo of cochineal.[28] We have suggested that this tendency not to read the terms of his commissions was to become a habit; undoubtedly, it was one that was nurtured by the undeniable truth that such transgressions were rarely witnessed, and even more rarely punished. Indeed, it seems that Frobisher made an early, if modest, profit from such depredations. It was at about this time that he accumulated sufficient funds to purchase his own vessel, the *Mary Flower*. His former association with John Appleyard seems to have ended; legal warring had undoubtedly soured their relationship, though there could also have been a further, more direct professional clash when, during 1564, Appleyard apparently underwent a Pauline conversion as a result of his experience with the Frobisher brothers and Thomas Bowes, and may have been authorized to set out ships to intercept privateers.[29]

Whether the funds that enabled Frobisher to purchase the *Mary Flower* had been derived solely from the practice of seizing other men's cargoes is unclear, though the absence of evidence may indicate only that he and his brother had been successful in their trade; Admiralty records are a rich source of information, but only upon felons who had been caught in the act of despoiling friendly vessels. Apparently, Martin and John Frobisher had avoided trouble during the previous year, yet it seems that the Admiralty

Court had taken note of Spanish complaints. The manner in which its officials were to deal with the brothers in respect of their latest enterprise indicates that they were regarded as two of the usual suspects, though it is fair to say also that they obliged the Court handsomely by providing a salutary foil to the image of privateers as cool and ruthless men of war. From the moment that the *Mary Flower* slipped her anchor at Tynemouth, the voyage was a farcical affair in which the weather, human circumstance and Martin Frobisher's already poor reputation conspired to deliver him up as surely as if he had walked into gaol of his own free will.

There are two surviving depositions concerning the voyage of the *Mary Flower* given by Frobisher himself and one Walter Darbie, described therein as a 'gentleman' of Barnard's Inn, London.[30] These were made to Dr David Lewes, judge of the Admiralty Court: a man whom Frobisher would come to know more closely than many of his own kin, though hardly by choice. As opaque as their testimony was (and was meant to be), it is nevertheless extremely revealing of arrangements under which many of the small-scale English voyages were set out during the period, and hints also at relationships and connections which, nurtured out of sight of posterity, cannot be reconstructed with any certainty.

Early in September 1565, Frobisher rode into north-east England in the company of John Frobisher, Walter Darbie, Sir Henry Percy and an unnamed son of Sir Anthony Cooke.[31] The *Mary Flower* lay at Tynemouth already, where she was being re-caulked, rigged and victualled. Frobisher had purchased her in London the previous Easter from one John Baxter, described in testimony as yet another 'gentilman', but who was also the town bailiff of Scarborough. She was a vessel of approximately 100 tons, 'a black shipp', previously named the *Matthew*. The name *Mary Flower* was therefore the choice of John or Martin; many men named ships after their loved ones as a surety of good fortune, and Mary may have been John's wife – clearly, Isobel Frobisher was as unlucky in this as in every other aspect of her marriage.

As will become clear, the intentions of the voyagers were supremely well masked, but their ostensible goal was *Buiney*, or the Guinea coast – where, apparently, the Frobisher brothers intended to trade. Lack of funds meant that the victualling of the *Mary Flower* was a protracted affair, however, and the ship was able to depart from Tynemouth only a few days before Christmas 1565. She carried some thirty-six men, including – suspiciously – her former owner, John Baxter, and several other, unnamed 'gentlemen'. Three further backers – George Claxton, Ralph Hazelby and Robert Layton, all of whom were also characterized as gentlemen – were due to join the expedition in the West Country, having been recommended by Frobisher to Richard Erisey of Falmouth (a cousin of the Grenvilles, who, with Peter Killigrew, had previously acted as the Frobisher brothers' agent in Plymouth for the planned dispersal of the *Katherine*'s cargoes).[32]

The *Mary Flower* had passed only as far south as the Humber estuary when a great storm arose, driving the ship northwards once more. All her masts and sails were ruined or lost, and Frobisher was forced to beach her, at or near the port of Scarborough, on Christmas Day. This proved to be more than a minor inconvenience. For almost five months thereafter, the *Mary Flower* remained on the sands, buffeted by successive tides and bad weather, whilst the Frobisher brothers attempted to raise sufficient money to replace her lost fittings. According to Martin's own testimony, this first setback was a decisive one: 'becawse he sawe his evill luck and lacked money to furnishe the said voyadge in such sorthe as was requisit he left of the same, and mindid either to sell the said shipp, or elles to make some shorter voyadge therewithe'.

It appears that the brothers' penury had resulted from another clash with the law. At Tynemouth, Frobisher had boarded the *Mary Flower* with £50 of his own money and a further £100 ventured by George Claxton, with an equal amount to be provided once they reached the West Country. Whilst not a fortune, it was undoubtedly sufficient to take them as far as their first rendezvous in the West Country; however, as soon as the adventurers washed up at Scarborough, Admiralty bailiffs pounced and arrested the *Mary Flower* at the suit of one Kinge of Essex, to whom John Frobisher apparently owed money. Kinge's warrant was examined and rejected by the town's bailiff, John Baxter; though it was only when John Frobisher turned over what funds he and his brother carried with them, and a certain Edward Rye – servant of Thomas, Lord Darcy of Chiche – made the sum up to £200 that the bailiffs released the ship. Rye seems to have made his largesse conditional upon his being taken into France, but the Frobishers refused to oblige him thereafter; he then abandoned the company, though leaving a servant, Richard Ogden, to sail in the proposed voyage in his place.

The *Mary Flower* was released, but without money to refit her she remained beached at Scarborough. Clearly, the Frobisher brothers' credit was poor in the town (even though – or, perhaps, because – its bailiff was associated with their venture); but eventually they managed to raise sufficient funds locally to repair their ship and victual her for a further month. Three tons of beer were found – or scavenged – in Hull, as well as hogsheads of beef, butter, cheese and fish. Before they could depart from Scarborough, however, Martin Frobisher was taken by Admiralty officers to be examined at York. There he was detained, pending his removal to London to appear before the Privy Council. Taking his earlier experience in the *Katherine* episode to heart, John Frobisher immediately put to sea in the *Mary Flower*, probably on 5 or 6 May 1566.

The intrepid voyagers sailed another ten miles and put in at Burlington. John went ashore to the house of an acquaintance named Boynton, where he begged further victuals, returning to the ship the next day with 'a shepe, capons, fishe, and bread'.[33] Thereafter, the *Mary Flower* put to sea again, and, once more, contrary winds drove her north almost to Newcastle. By 10 May, however, she had beaten south as far as Yarmouth. When the master of the *Mary Flower* (one Wolfall) went ashore there, yet another bailiff appeared, and attempted to arrest him – this time for alleged piracy – but was persuaded of his innocence and allowed him to leave.

The ship came into the Thames estuary on 14 May. By now, several of the voyagers had become heartily sick of their sad showing and abandoned the expedition (including Walter Darbie, who went to London to seek out Martin Frobisher and apprise him of their progress, or lack of it). Nevertheless, John Frobisher made a decision to press on with his remaining crew, at which point the *Mary Flower* disappears from official records. There is no extant information on whether she did indeed take on further supplies in the West Country, though on 5 June, the mayor of Saltash in Devon wrote to the Privy Council regarding instructions he had been given to detain the ship, informing them that she had not arrived.[34] Yet as we shall see, if posterity heard no more of the *Mary Flower*, it was hardly because she was unemployed during the following months.

These are the bare facts of the voyage, as related to Dr Lewes by Frobisher and Walter Darbie. Behind their curious sequence lies a wealth of ambiguity, however. The pertinence of the questions asked of Frobisher by Lewes makes it obvious that there was a typical *modus operandi* observed by privateers putting to sea without lawful commission, and that he strongly suspected the Frobisher brothers of observing it. The first and most suspicious circumstance was that although Martin Frobisher claimed to have set out a voyage to Guinea for trading purposes, he had sailed without wares with which to trade. Also, the ship had been provisioned for a month only, and if this was possibly due to a shortage of funds, it was equally likely that the *Mary Flower* was never intended to pass much further than the English Channel. It is also the case – as Dr Lewes must have been aware – that any ship of 100 tons, carry-ing a crew of just thirty-six 'mariners' (few of whom actually *were* mariners), was seriously undermanned for a long voyage: particularly one to a destination which promised a heavy rate of mortality *en route*.

Frobisher answered the Court's justifiable suspicions by claiming that he had been intending to lade his ship both with victuals and – as merchandise – linens and waxed kerseys in the West Country. It was a fair alibi, difficult to prove either way. It is likely that any number of would-be privateers, taken by officers of the Admiralty, were making similar claims during these years. Without being unduly gullible, Lewes might have given Frobisher the benefit of the doubt – had he carried with him a single person who was habitually involved in trade. Of merchants there was none, however. The company Frobisher had assembled looked fit for many eventualities, but not for lawful trade. John Baxter was on board, having sold his ship to Frobisher and joined his complement thereafter at Tynemouth. Meanwhile, Frobisher's backer, George Claxton, awaited the *Mary Flower* in Cornwall with the balance of his funds and several other so-called gentlemen. They may have been intending to sail also – in which case Frobisher's West Country alibi might have stood up – or they may have waited there to dispose of illicitly seized cargoes. The three men – Frobisher, Baxter and Claxton – had stood bonds (of £1,200) against their good behaviour before setting out to sea, which indicates that they held some sort of commission – probably of Huguenot origin – which usually required the recipients' service in the Channel or Western Approaches. Once at his home town of Scarborough, John Baxter had abused his authority as town bailiff to protect the Frobisher brothers from Admiralty officers, though there is no suggestion that their warrant was incorrectly or erroneously drafted. Then there was the mysterious and generous Edward Rye, servant of Lord Darcy, who had come to Scarborough with the express purpose of giving £50 to the penurious John Frobisher, apparently to be carried clandestinely into France thereafter (at a time when the Huguenot armies – the usual resort of martially inclined Protestant Englishmen entering France – had virtually stood down, pending the outcome of Catherine de' Medici's latest peace initiative).[35]

These facts add up to little that could condemn a man, but cumulatively they suggest that lawful commerce was not the intended business of the voyagers – or that it was seen to be so. Assorted gentlemen did not go on trading ventures without merchants or merchants' factors; indeed, the term 'gentleman', when applied to a voyager, usually indicated surplus cargo of the fighting variety, rather than someone who might have made himself useful about a ship. Furthermore, it is highly unlikely that men of the calibre and preoccupations of Percy, Darcy and Sir Anthony Cooke would have involved themselves in a trading project that had been so cursorily planned and under-provisioned for success (had it sailed as financed, this would have been by far the smallest 'Guinea' expedition of the sixteenth century). Nor, incidentally, would a purely commercial venture usually carry a sacre, two quarter-slings, six bases, two falcons (all deck-clearing ordnance), twenty corselets, ten bows and two to three dozen pikes, merely as a prudent measure of self-protection.[36] The crew of the *Mary Flower*, it seems, was expecting – or expecting to cause – trouble: an assumption that was amply confirmed before the end of the year, when the Privy Council was obliged to write to the Earl of Desmond at the behest of a group of Antwerp merchants, requesting him to assist in the recovery of cargoes seized and taken into Irish ports by John Frobisher and others.[37] The vessel in which Frobisher made these seizures was almost certainly the *Mary Flower*.

His brother Martin had probably added to the Court's suspicions with a performance that resounds across the centuries as a model of hurt innocence. The well-worn West Country alibi, reinforced by the apparently spontaneous change of mind brought on by his 'evill luck' at Scarborough, was hardly water-tight. Nevertheless, Frobisher rose to his part. He claimed that he was as surprised as anyone when the *Mary Flower* had gone south after he left her; that he had told his brother to go back to Newcastle to lade coal there and take to La Rochelle, where he was to pick up a cargo of salt in return. Superficially, this seems a supremely optimistic claim; but it has some extant, if very oblique, corroboration in a strange, fragmentary petition for letters patent to be issued to Frobisher and one Richard Morley of London, to have charge over the measurement of sea-coals at Newcastle.[38] Whether Frobisher ever took up this licence is doubtful; but again, its threadbare veil of legitimacy was yet another, hopefully blurring, circumstance to set against the weight of Admiralty Court suspicions.

Listening to this richly imaginative testimony, Dr Lewes was probably not concerned with Guinea, La Rochelle or Frobisher's apparent ambition to be a coal exporter and/or salt importer. He was exercised rather by a Flemish ship, possibly the *White Unicorn*,[39] and precisely who had despoiled her at the mouth of the Thames – as, coincidentally, the *Mary Flower* had been beating south towards her alleged West Country appointment. In his own testimony, Walter Darbie claimed that they had only come to the North Foreland on or around 14 May. A margin note to this statement, in Secretary William Cecil's hand, noted 'the Flemynges were spoyled as they say ye vjth of Maii'.[40] If this was true, Martin Frobisher's detention upon suspicion of abetting the crime was unjust, whoever else was responsible – the Flemish ship was 'spoyled' on the very day that the Admiralty Court convened at York.

Perhaps the case against him only went so far because his brother John – a more likely suspect – was already at sea, well out of Dr Lewes's grasp.

Darbie claimed that the *Mary Flower* had been the victim of mistaken identity; that it had been another 'black ship', commanded by a Scot, that had taken the Flemish prize.[41] His testimony, uncorroborated, was hardly more convincing than that with which Frobisher had been entertaining his examiners; but the known movements of the Flemish ship (by her crews' own testimony) simply could not be reconciled with those of the *Mary Flower*. This, it seems, was the circumstance which broke any case against the prisoner. Just twelve days after Frobisher appeared before Admiralty Court, the Privy Council ordered the keeper of the counter at Great Wood Street gaol to set him free. He was merely required to give sureties against his parole not to go to sea without licence.[42]

The precise motives that had set out the *Mary Flower* will never be known. That Frobisher really did intend a peaceful trading voyage to Guinea is almost inconceivable; nevertheless, the circumstances behind his arrest and examination are puzzling. As ambiguous as his own testimony and intentions had been, they were more than matched by the ambivalence of a court that was faithfully implementing official policy. The manner in which Frobisher had been taken *before* the offence in question had been committed might have seemed somewhat suspicious, even in isolation; but there were other, seemingly irreconcilable facts which remained carefully unaired in court – for example, that many of the *Mary Flower*'s guns had been provided by the master of the Queen's ordnance at Newcastle.[43] Whilst Martin Frobisher himself could not have been involved in the capture of the *White Unicorn*, it is apparent nevertheless that the Admiralty Court had strong suspicions concerning his intentions, the provenance of which it did not care to reveal; perhaps because to have done so would have incriminated men whose reputations were not as expendable as that of an habitual privateer. The whole episode has the air of a finely judged process being enacted: in this case, for an audience that sat across the English Channel. Margaret of Parma, it seems, was being sent a message that the Queen of England was finally acting against her troublesome subjects.

For Frobisher, the timing of the *Mary Flower*'s alleged Guinea voyage had been particularly unfortunate. In the period between the conclusion of peace with France in June 1563 and the destruction of Nassau's rebel army by Alva in 1568 (which required the hasty licensing of English privateers to interrupt Alva's supply chain and shore up a crumbling Netherlander resistance), Elizabeth was less inclined to humour the private depredations that complemented her policies in time of war. The continuing seizure of French Catholic vessels was probably not a matter of great concern to her – though she did not offi-cially sanction it – but attacks upon Spanish and Netherlander vessels had begun to have a real impact upon her foreign policy. The interruption of trade in 1563–4 had been only a temporary setback, but the behaviour of English privateers continued to cause diplomatic ill-will that affected far more impor-tant matters of policy. Throughout 1565–6, the Queen was involved in rene-gotiating the terms of the *Magnus Intercursus* (or Intercourse) with Margaret of Parma. This treaty, first entered into by Henry VII, determined the respec-tive official 'take' from the Anglo-Netherlands trade in setting the respective customs tariffs imposed upon their commercial traffic in cloths.[44] Activities of privateers which slowed or spoiled the progress of these negotiations directly affected Elizabeth's purse, the most tender part of her sovereign anatomy. In light of this threat, she had committed herself, however briefly, to curbing her subject's depredations. On 25 June 1564, Guzman de Silva had written to Philip, saying that the Queen was definitely set on ridding herself of pirates.[45] Probably this represented a rare flash of over-optimism on his part; but Frobisher's arrest the following year may have been one of the many repercussions of a temporary but much needed policy adjustment.

The example having been made, Frobisher was set free in London, but with neither licence to go to sea nor ship to make the attempt. Though his brother John was still at large in the *Mary Flower*, industriously upholding his side of their unlucky partnership, more immediate prospects were not entirely lacking. Martin's unemployed status appears to have endured the span of a short walk from the City to Hackney, to the rented home of Cardinal Châtillon, brother of the new Huguenot leader, Admiral Coligny. There, Châtillon obligingly provided the necessary commission for Frobisher to seize any French Catholic vessels in the service of their enemies. Within weeks, he was at sea once more, commanding the ship *Robert* in consort with five other ships, three of which were captained by John Chichester, Joseph Harrys and Ralph Hazelby (the latter had been one of the 'gentlemen' who had sailed in the *Mary Flower*).[46]

Many men of respectable reputation sailed under Châtillon's commissions. Members of the Hawkins family, for example, were among the most enthu-siastic of his employees, enriching both themselves and their home town Ply-mouth with proceeds from the seizures – illicit or otherwise – that they made under Huguenot licence. However, the question of reputation does not appear to have exercised Frobisher in making his own choice of company. Nothing more is known of Hazelby, though Harrys may have been that

Joseph Harrys who commanded the *Conclude of Plymouth* in Watts' 1590 West Indies raid.[47] There is no such doubt as to Chichester's identity, however. He was an unregenerate pirate who almost certainly ended his life on the gallows after a career in taking English cargoes.[48]

There is no reason to suppose, moreover, that in consorting with these men Frobisher was moving below either his station or his inclinations. Indeed, by the following year he had acquired a number of even less reputable associates. Now based near Rye in command of two vessels (one of which was the *Robert*) he was sailing in the company of John Vaughan, one of the more infamous English pirates of the age. The partnership appears to have been an attractive one for other privateers; within weeks, John Chichester and one Christopher Conway had joined them with their ships – as, once more, had Thomas Bowes, now in partnership with a London mercer and merchant adventurer, John Foxall, with whom he had set out the *Bark Bowes*.[49]

John Vaughan, like Frobisher, held letters of marque from Châtillon that authorized him to intercept and seize French Catholic vessels.[50] However, by this time, neither man appears to have cared about the source or purpose of their commissions. The vessels they took qualified for seizure solely on the basis of their suspected cargoes, not the identity of their owners. Indeed, they seemed much less interested in the vessels of French Catholics than those of their co-religionists – even their compatriots. The merchants of Rye – who themselves were not above setting out privateers – complained to the Privy Council about Frobisher's depredations upon Protestant vessels carrying their goods. They obtained permission to set out ships to deal with the problem, but then claimed they were unable to find six ships sufficient to out-fight Frobisher's two.[51] Ostensibly, such a claim, made in anger to powerful men, could only have dealt further damage to an already dark reputation; but in measuring this young man's abilities – however lamentable – it constituted the genesis of a more useful fame: one that would recommend him, eventually, to a Queen who needed effective sea-commanders in moments when the more delicate questions regarding their prior experience had become superflous, and even frivolous.

In March 1569, the *Robert* and *Roe*, cruising off Guernsey, were joined by a Weymouth ship, the *Salomon*, and a large, armed pinnace.[52] On 23 March, the small fleet chased and took the *Mary* (or *Mari*) of Mortaigne, laden with Bordeaux wines and resin. She was brought into Newport on the Isle of Wight, a thriving haven for English and, since the previous year, Dutch privateers; there, her cargo was sold off. In June, Frobisher was detained onshore by the Queen's officers and called before his old friend Dr Lewes to answer the accusations of Robert Friar, an English merchant who had proved good title to part of the *Mary*'s cargo.[53] In the meantime, Vaughan had managed to evade the law and put to sea; standing alone before the court, Frobisher took good advantage of his colleague's inability to put across his own side of the story, claiming that it was Vaughan who had taken the *Mary*; that he himself 'knewe not certenlye what she was vntill he him selfe was put from the seas to the said Rode of Newport iij dayes after'.[54] Though he admitted taking a single hogshead of wine from the seized vessel, he had done so, he told his interrogator, out of consideration for his thirsty crew. Unfortunately for Frobisher, the *Robert* does not seem to have been an entirely happy ship, and his touching testimony was immediately contradicted by the supposed recipients of his largesse: '. . . some of the Companye of the foresaid Frobisher declared and tolde this examinant that they had neither half pennye nor pennye worthe of the said wines'. Obligingly, they also revealed that whilst Vaughan himself had taken 10 tons of wine out of the *Mary*, Frobisher, one Strowbridge (master of the *Salomon*) and the pinnace's captain had shared the rest of what Robert Friar claimed had been a haul of 60 tons of wine and thirty pieces (or cakes) of resin.[55]

The case was held over, pending further testimony, and Frobisher was allowed to return to sea for the moment (presumably having first replaced the dissident element of the *Robert*'s crew). His luck was decidedly lacking during these months, however. The *Mary*'s seizure was but one of several involving the *Robert*, and most appear to have come to the attention of the Admiralty Court. In April, Frobisher and Vaughan had taken a ship named the *Saint John* of Bordeaux and disposed of her cargoes in Portsmouth;[56] in consort with Chichester, Harrys and Conway, they had also seized the *Swallow*, an English ship carrying cottons, kerseys, wax and lead;[57] in June, at large once more after his court appearance and cruising with the *Bark Bowes* and *Roe*, Frobisher's *Robert* took the *Magdalene* of Cherbourg, returning from Cape Verde and Bordeaux with a cargo of lead, ivory and wine.[58] This last seizure generated an unusually weighty body of correspondence. The *Magdalene* was owned by one Gilbert Cassellier of Rouen, and freighted by a syndicate of the city's merchants (including Anthony Toque, an Englishman resident there), all of whom promptly petitioned the Privy Council for restitution.[59]

For all of this undoubted industry, Frobisher does not seem to have generated much in the way of ready income from his depredations. On 22 May 1569, he gave bonds for a loan of just £13 8sh. 8d. from Richard Bromley, a London butcher, to be repaid at the following feast of Pentecost.[60] Bromley may have been one of the London merchants who financed privateering ventures long before the Spanish war made it a respectable business activity (certainly, Frobisher had spent little time cultivating the acquaintance of law-abiding merchants in the previous decade); possibly, he was that Richard 'Morley' named as Frobisher's co-licensee in the strange patent to measure Newcastle coals that we have noted above. However, what is most significant is not the source of the loan, but its paltry value. Unless it had been procured to overcome a temporary interruption of a cash-flow usually secured upon stolen cargoes, or obtained for the benefit of Isobel Frobisher and her children until their 'provider' returned from sea, its modesty hardly suggests that a successful career had been built upon the proceeds of these many illicit seizures.

In fact, the prospect of that success was about to recede even further beyond the horizon. The case of the *Mary* had been dragging on through the Admiralty Court. Her stolen wine's persistent owner, Robert Friar, had obtained a warrant to arrest his property; armed with this, he went off to Portsmouth, Chichester and other towns on the south coast to trace the wine through numerous on-sales. Eventually, he found six hogsheads carrying his mark in the cellars of William Overton, a wine-merchant of Chichester. Overton refused to restore them until he recovered his outlay, but he was willing enough in the meantime to betray his suppliers, *gratis*. He told Friar (who subsequently testified the same to Dr Lewes) that the wine had been sold to him directly by Vaughan and Frobisher; and alleged, furthermore, that they often disposed of seized cargoes – particularly wines – before they reached port: holding auctions 'in open rode by the shipps side'.[61] It is not clear whether it was this particular episode or the cumulative effect of a catalogue of similar depredations that finally broke the patience of the Admiralty Court, but when in July or August 1569 Frobisher sailed into the Suffolk port of Aldburgh with his new ship, the *Magdalene*, he was promptly arrested.[62]

This time, there was to be no sham trial. The *Magdalene* and her remaining cargoes were immediately restored to her rightful owners. On 26 August, the Privy Council wrote to Dr Lewes:

We sende vnto you by this bearer, one of the knight Marshall(e)s men, Martyn Furbusher, against whome you knowe what grevous complayntes have ben made of diuers and sundrye pyracies by him com(m)itted / We pray you theirfore, to sende him to the Marshallsie where he maye remaine in sure and safe custodie, till you send for him agayne and maye vppon suche informac(i)ons as he is to be charged withall, proceede agaynste him withall severitie . . .[63]

Lewes obliged his masters, particularly in their desire for severity. Frobisher was kept in the Marshalsea in lieu of payment of a fine of £900; a huge sum that was almost certainly intended to be far beyond his means to pay. What he had learned, if a little belatedly, was that there was a limit to even the Queen's patience.

However, having been prepared to see him punished condignly for his crimes, Elizabeth herself may have played a significant part in easing his plight. Almost as soon as the ink upon Frobisher's committal papers was dry, the busy Thomas Bowes asserted his right of possession over the ship *Robert* (though this was probably with the connivance of his imprisoned associate, who was not likely to find useful employment for it in his present condition). Equally swiftly, Elizabeth Fiennes, the shrewd wife of the Lord Admiral, Baron Clinton, wrote to the Admiralty Court offering to buy the *Robert* from Bowes if he could show good title.[64] The speed with which the deal was concluded does not suggest that the parties were unknown to each other, nor that the coincidence of their interests was a matter of blind good fortune. Like Thomas Cobham and Henry Stranguishe, it seems that Frobisher had been making a number of important connections (probably amongst those who had provided the market for his ill-gotten wares) for which we have no firm information. Unfortunately (though Frobisher himself would not have considered it so) he was never quite to reach the extremity of circumstance that required an outright appeal for clemency from one of his patrons; nevertheless, he was undoubtedly obliged to redeem whatever moral promissory notes that he still held. Certainly, if the Lord Admiral could be counted among his acquaintances, he had access to circles more rarefied than his own antecedents alone might have brought him to. There was also the tenuous link provided by his previous association with Cecil's father-in-law, Sir Anthony Cooke: one which might first have brought him to the attention of Cecil himself. One of the aspects of privateering that made it so difficult to curb, once permitted, was that everyone from the Queen downwards took some profit from it, and almost always clandestinely. Despite the upward mobility allowed by the acquisition of wealth, boundaries between social classes remained strong; yet the traffic in illicit goods undoubtedly created points of contact which circumvented the social norms, particularly as the middle-men excluded from its transactions – the merchants involved in legitimate trade – comprised the 'middle' classes through whom most commercial intercourse necessarily flowed. These contacts, once established, did not dissipate with a handshake or the delivery of stolen goods; they remained, if dormant, ready to be resurrected when other, greater causes required. Even allowing for the excellent work done to date, there is much that may yet be written about this great, black economy and the wider social and political implications that grew from its anonymous processes.

In Frobisher's case, the non-pecuniary fruits of his illegal activities proved to be substantial. No sooner had the doors of the Marshalsea slammed upon him than a minor diplomatic offensive commenced to have him released. It seems that the Clintons were enjoying the particular favour of the Queen at that time (setting aside Lord Clinton's role as the nation's premier naval commander, the two Elizabeths were long-standing friends), and she is known to have dined at their house upon a number of occasions. It is possible that at one such dinner the matter of the privateer and his plight was raised, perhaps as part of the earlier bargain concluded upon the *Robert*. Meanwhile, Cardinal Châtillon was also doing his bit for a valued employee; on 24 February 1570, he wrote to Cecil to draw attention to a plea of a certain female supplicant that her husband, 'Capne fourbisour', be released to provide for his family.[65] Whether unrequited love proved more effective than the Lord Admiral's wife's dinners cannot be determined; but clearly, Frobisher – again, like Stranguishe, Cobham and a host of similarly ill-favoured reprobates – had benefited from the voracious need of fine English homes for illicit wares.

Whatever their provenance, these clandestine contacts swiftly proved to be of supremely practical value. An order issued by the Council in February directed that Frobisher be transferred to the Fleet prison, to be kept there until 'he shall satisfye & pay the same [i.e., the fine of £900], or otherwise take order for the same'.[66] The wording seems unrelenting, but the latter qualification was erased by Cecil personally, and replaced by the words 'or otherwise be released by us'. The Queen's principal secretary of state was hardly a man to be swayed by the predicament of an incorrigible freebooter; yet unless Elizabeth herself had intervened, we must assume he was acting upon his own initiative. Someone – Lady Clinton, the good Cardinal, Sir Anthony Cooke or perhaps even Cecil himself – moved by the potential of the prisoner for some other, as yet secret purpose, had exercised an influence that transcended the authority of the Admiralty Court's writ. Ultimately, Dr Lewes's industry and perseverance were to prove rather pointless; less than a month after altering the Council's order, Cecil saw fit to exercise the clemency he had provided for, and the prisoner walked free.

Again, the apparent inconsistency of the official response to Frobisher's

crimes, reflected in many similar Admiralty Court proceedings and judg-
ments throughout the period, revealed a wider condition of uncertainty. The
years 1569–71 were perhaps the most dangerous to Elizabeth personally. A
deepening (though subsequently healed) rift with Philip II; her excommuni-
cation by the Pope in February 1570; the Northern Rising with its associated
plots to assassinate her and place Mary Stuart on the English throne – these
problems descended almost simultaneously, but each required a separate and
commensurate response. If Elizabeth has a deserved reputation for equivoca-
tion, it was forged in adversities whose dangers were never capable of being
assessed precisely, until the final, irrevocable sundering of Anglo-Spanish
amity in the 1580s removed all doubts. Though a supremely ambiguous tool
of policy, privateers provided a relatively convenient response to short-term
external problems; upon occasion, they constituted her principal – perhaps
her only – military resource. Such men could no more be dispensed with than
allowed a free rein in their depredations, and in trying to avoid these extremities, the Queen inevitably prevaricated. Many freebooters – men more, less
or as virtuous as Frobisher – benefited from this. There can be little doubt
that at other times, in different situations, he might have suffered the fate
that the ultimately fortunate Thomas Cobham had briefly faced. Neither man
in fact ended his life upon the gallows or pinned beneath a piece of ordnance;
but that good fortune was almost entirely the result of political necessity and,
certainly, the right connections.

So the consequences of Frobisher's 'sundrye pyracies' were to be remarkably light. No fines were paid, no known sureties offered; the sudden and
seemingly absolute reversal of his fortunes is startling, even acknowledging the capricious record of official policy. Cecil was not in the habit of
bestowing his mercies on a whim, however. Conversations may have taken
place in the Marshalsea: unrecorded, deniable offers or threats which hinted
at something new and unexpected to a man who had deserved only the most
seasonable punishment. Perhaps there was something in Frobisher's character, invisible to posterity, that made him seem less of a recidivist (or more
pliable) than others who had suffered more severely at the hands of the Admiralty judges. He may have had the sense of a change in the wind: a half-
understanding that having been caught upon so many occasions, his reputation and credibility were compromised so badly that to continue as before
was impossible. How sincerely he agreed to the terms of his release cannot
be determined; he may, even now, have harboured expectations of returning
immediately to sea, perhaps having first dusted off his commission from the
ever-grateful Châtillon and obtained the assistance of a shipowner who was

himself either too principled or circumspect to take his own prizes. If so, he was to be swiftly disabused. Having been a persistent and irritating component of a problem, Frobisher was about to offer his services – however unwillingly – as part of its cure.

Ironically, it was during the same years that privateering was proving so useful to the Crown that the repercussions of its excesses approached their unwelcome peak. In 1568, English privateers had begun to coordinate their efforts with those of the men of La Rochelle, and the Netherlander 'sea-beggars' had come out also, to join their Protestant brethren. The latter made the Isle of Wight their base, from which they attacked shipping with a lack of discrimination at which even Frobisher might have jibed. Their leader, William de la Marck, as much as admitted that he was powerless to curb his crews' enthusiasm; by 1571, the Queen was sufficiently irritated by this abuse of her hospitality – and its increasingly negative influence upon the course of Anglo–Spanish relations – to consider active steps to deal with the privateering problem in its entirety. In the following year, she banned all foreign freebooters from English ports 'upon pain of forfeiture of their ships and goods', and set out the Controller of the Queen's ships, William Holstocke, in two navy vessels to sweep them from the Channel.[67] The campaign began, however, with Elizabeth's habitual opening gambit: the cheap option.

Freebooters, set loose with a commission to chase their former associates, were far less of a drain upon the public purse than any officially organized expedition. Minimal Crown investment was required, and that largely took the form of faith in faithless men. In any case, given the nature and depth of the privateering problem by 1571, the use of men who were intimately familiar with the tactics of the 'enemy' was superficially appealing. There was nothing new in the strategy; many privateers, even without the occasion of war to legitimize their activities, had been obliged to perform Crown service between less salubrious employments. John Chichester and Peter Killigrew, both former associates of Frobisher, had served their time in this manner.[68] Precisely who now proposed Frobisher for a similar role is not known; it may have been Cecil, reminded of a possibility by a letter he had received from Cardinal Châtillon; perhaps his name was now familiar to Elizabeth herself, recalled from a recent dinner at the Clintons' home. What is clear, however, despite the apparent leniency that had been exercised to his advantage, is that Frobisher emerged from the Marshalsea at a price. In the eighteen months following that fortunate deliverance, he had avoided the attention of the Admiralty Court; a remarkable achievement in itself but also, possibly, the fruits of a probationary period: one in which he may have done some small services for Cecil or others that were not considered worthy of record.[69] They are hinted at, if only obliquely, in a letter dated 20 August 1571, written by Edward Horsey to Cecil. Horsey himself had been an enthusiastic privateer during the reign of Mary; now, as Captain of the Isle of Wight, he was overseeing much of the illicit importation industry that Frobisher, Vaughan and others had generated. His letter mentioned that a hulk in the Queen's shipyard at Portsmouth was being repaired and refitted at royal expense for Frobisher's use. Almost incidentally, he noted also that Frobisher 'hathe receyved the more favor at my hand(e)s for that I finde in your L. last l(ett)res that yo(u) do conceive well of him of late'.[70] This suggests more than a fleeting manifestation of good behaviour. Whilst Frobisher's newly discovered habit of not taking friendly vessels at sea was an improvement upon past conduct, it was an insufficient inactivity, alone, to have so raised his stock in Cecil's eyes. Perhaps we need not search too hard for reasons for this 'conceiving well' of an ex-pirate. Whatever honour lay between thieves, it could not be allowed to survive the clemency of the Queen's principal secretary, nor remain untested by him. It is likely, perhaps even probable, that Frobisher had been obliged to provide a more convincing token of his new loyalties by identifying the vessels and traffic of his former associates in the privateering trade: at once providing invaluable insider information whilst lessening the prospect of recidivism on his part. In October 1571, however, he was given the opportunity to repay his moral debt in a more palpable manner. Commanding the newly refurbished *Carrack Lane* and three other vessels, he set sail from Portsmouth with orders from the Privy Council itself: to intercept known privateers and search their ships for illicitly seized goods.

Though this new commission had an exemplary provenance, it does not seem that Frobisher now sought to keep less ill-favoured company than previously. On 18 September, Sir Henry Radcliffe wrote to Cecil from Portsmouth to inform him that the town was filling unpleasantly with seamen: 'the most part dependers of one forbusher who hath here the carigke Sedney & saith he hath speciall comyssion to goe to see . . .'.[71] Radcliffe also mentioned that another ship, the *Griffon of Essex*, had come to Portsmouth carrying gentlemen and mariners intending to join Frobisher; apparently, they had somewhat undermined their putative role in the coming expedition by seizing a prize *en route*, and stealing her cargo of sugar loaves and fish. Nervously, he complained that 'as yett I have seene noe sufficient comyssion from forbussher . . .'. At that time, Radcliffe seems to have had little trust in the motives of men putting to sea under such ambiguous arrangements (though he was himself to be implicated in later privateering ventures);[72] but his fears for the reputation and trustworthiness of Frobisher and his men were probably well founded. In recruiting crews for his ships, the ex-privateer almost certainly would have given preference to men he knew from his previous career; men who habitually formed a pool of labour for precisely those ships that he now intended to intercept. Fortunately for Sir Henry's peace of mind, neither this rabble nor their commander remained long at Portsmouth.

The Privy Council's new faith in Frobisher was not so robust as to render the usual precautions unnecessary. The *Carrick Lane*'s owners, Thomas Lane and Richard West, were required to place bonds of £1,000 with the Admiralty Court against their captain's good behaviour under his commission; though she had been at sea for almost a month before the bonds were taken. The Spanish Ambassador, writing to his king, noted tartly that the bonds had been taken for form's sake only; an understandably cynical reaction, perhaps, but such sureties rarely provided much in the way of insurance (and if Frobisher had previously risked losing his own bonds in the pursuit of other men's money, he was hardly likely to regard this latest commitment as sacrosanct).[73] Nevertheless, in the weeks following his departure from Portsmouth, the Queen's newest officer appears not to have disturbed the tremulous faith that had set him loose upon the seas. In fact, he was only too well behaved.

In the annals of maritime endeavour, there can have been few projects undertaken with less determination or commitment than Frobisher now displayed in chasing his former colleagues. Not a single privateer appears to have been sighted by his small fleet, much less chased, in the months that followed its departure from Portsmouth, despite his intimate knowledge of the practices and resorts of men with whom he had only recently enjoyed a close working association. The threat that William Holstocke brought against English privateers in the following year was clearly intended to improve upon Frobisher's efforts. In truth, it could hardly have failed to do so. Contemporary records do not show evidence of any traffic through the Admiralty Court having been generated by Frobisher, in a period in which depredations against neutral vessels rose to a new high. This, his first taste of gainful employment in a decade, revealed where his partialities lay no less clearly than had the ship-side auctions of stolen goods he had overseen during years of banditry. With warrants for his arrest still in force against his performance in this duty, it would have required an iron nerve to dismiss the majesty of consequence so readily.

Yet Elizabeth's new policy, whether implemented sincerely or merely as a sop to Philip II, was bound to fail, whatever resources were provided. The English navy of the period had no capacity to operate as an effective policing force. A hundred or more ships, acting singly or in tiny fleets to seize, strip and sink foreign merchantmen, were beyond the power of the most industrious pursuer to curb. If, as Oppenheim claimed, piracy 'almost attained the dignity of a recognised profession' during the reign of Elizabeth,[74] it was during these years that the many apprenticeships begun during the first French wars of religion matured into something more permanent, with pro-found implications for the future of Anglo-Spanish relationships. Under such circumstances, even official policies became mere gestures – though a worse choice of gesture than Frobisher could hardly be conceived.

The particularly poor showing of his little fleet was not his fault alone, however. Other, privately organized expeditions against pirates had been set out before (those of the Rye merchants and – possibly – of John Appleyard were by no means isolated incidents);[75] but ships equipped at government expense almost always suffered from the curse of under-funding. Those which Frobisher commanded were no exception. During the weeks in which his small fleet lay at Portsmouth, word of his commission must have circulated freely around the town and carried across the Solent to the Isle of Wight, where the greater number of his intended victims were based. By the time that Frobisher put to sea, virtually every inlet on the south coast would have been primed as alternative dropping-off points for illicitly seized cargoes, using ships that were almost certainly faster, more weatherly and manned by a more motivated class of reprobate than were Frobisher's own hulks.[76] Given these handicaps, it is hardly surprising that he was so ineffective; though the fact that he hardly attempted to be otherwise undoubtedly made his failure seem even more abject.

The famously comprehensive working notes of Cecil (from January 1572 Baron Burghley) do not record his feelings at having exercised his clemency to such little effect. Though not an intrinsically callous man, he did not often intervene in the due process of justice to free felons – particularly those with such well-proven records in their chosen careers. Nor, however, did he now use the obvious fact of Frobisher's indifference to his commission to rescind the conditional pardon that had prised him from the Marshalsea. Fortunately for this pale nemesis of freebooters, there were other uses to which a com-petent sea-commander could be put: indeed, the palpably short return upon the Queen's anti-privateering investment to date made the small fleet he commanded both superfluous in its present role and a continuing expense against which other, more profitable employment had to be found, urgently. This need to squeeze value from every Exchequer coin may have been all that saved the remiss Frobisher from another, and certainly longer, spell in gaol.

In the event, his new employment was designed to place him under much tighter supervision than before. Still in command of his anti-privateering fleet, he was diverted from virtual non-employment in the Channel into outright naval service, when early in 1572 his ships were assigned to the transportation of men and materials to Ireland, to assist in quelling the rebellion of James Fitzmaurice.

FIVE

The Ambiguous Papist: 1572–74

The 'problem' of Ireland during the latter part of the sixteenth century would require several volumes to address adequately. For the purposes of examining Frobisher's role in the so-called pacification, we need only recall the wider matters. The first and most relevant of these may be put succinctly: that nothing was, or appeared to be, straightforward. As so often during the course of their turbulent history, the relationship between Irish magnates and their ostensible English overlords was pregnant with unresolved problems. Locally, dynastic vendettas, religious disharmonies and the English habit of treating the population with overweening (if absent-minded) brutality made not so much for unrest as a permanent state of semi-anarchy in the provinces outside the Pale and Leinster. Attempts to impose an early-modern system of government upon a feudal society, and the English failure to understand their evil consequences, made good order impossible to achieve, let alone maintain. In those few areas where Englishmen could not oblige in the process of making life unbearable, the local nobility acted cheerfully as surrogate oppressors. The tortured course of malice and betrayal that constituted their habitual intercourse may have been intended as no more than self-serving; nevertheless, its most pronounced effect was to heap further misery upon the disastrously deprived folk who formed the vast majority of the population. For these wretches, particularly in Connaught and Munster, the quality of their lives had deteriorated to a state unparalleled even in their own, brutal experience.

The English occupiers, to give them very little credit, were not always entirely indifferent to the repercussions of their policies. The Lord Deputy of

Ireland, Sir Henry Sydney, touring Munster upon returning to his duties in 1568, commented of the land:

> ... as I never was in a more pleasant country in all my life, so never saw I a more waste and desolate land, no, not in the confines of other countries where actual war hath continually been kept by the greatest princes of Christendom; and never heard I such lamentable cries and doleful complaints made by that small remain of people which yet are left.[1]

However, having made this concerned and timely reflection, Sir Henry took the same measures to alleviate the problem as his predecessors – that is, none whatsoever. If Irish rebels were content to regard the suffering of their people as a necessary consequence of conflict, the enemy was doubly so.

The latest rebellion had commenced in 1568, but spluttered irregularly since. Fired with a genuine hatred of the English oppressors (an emotion that most of his kinsmen managed to generate as their interests demanded), James Fitzmaurice had sacked the countryside around Cork, burned the town of Kilmallock and raised the greater part of counties Mayo and Munster against the Queen's officers. Yet even with a rich and bitter vein of unrest upon which to draw, his rebellion was sporadic and ineffectual. He was – or considered himself to be – hampered from the start by a lack of promised Spanish resources for his cause. On 4 May 1570, he and his 'parliament' had written to their agent in Spain, Maurice Reagh Fitzgibbon, Archbishop of Cashiel, with considerable bitterness on this point: 'No words can express our astonishment that in all this time Your Grace has received no decision from his Majesty about the business for which you were sent. . . . we trust that if you have been negligent in carrying out this business retribution will fall upon you and you will not escape the divine wrath.'[2]

The exhortation was heartfelt, but it was hardly just. Philip II had listened to Fitzgibbon with feigned sympathy, but he was far from ready to challenge Elizabeth's sovereign right to further spoil Ireland. Indeed, he had a particular reason not to upset her at that time. In London, his ambassador was engaged in sensitive negotiations with the Privy Council concerning the hoped-for return of Netherlander ships and goods seized by English privateers (who had been typically assiduous in mis-identifying all vessels they encountered as being of French Catholic origin).[3] For once – though absolutely involuntarily – Frobisher and his fellow privateers had contributed something worthwhile to the implementation of England's foreign policy: by so wilfully contravening the letter of the licences under which they had sailed, the potential reinforcement or succour of an enemy of their Queen had been averted. Their efforts, conscious or otherwise, would rarely prove so felicitous.

Throughout 1572, the rebellion in Munster and then Connaught proceeded desultorily. English efforts decisively to defeat the rebels were hampered by the Queen's refusal to pay for a resolution to the crisis; whilst Fitzmaurice, permanently short of funds himself, had the resources only to march upon and sack small districts at a time. Finally, in November, Sir Edward Butler's modest but effective force fell upon the rebel camp near Kilkenny and scattered Fitzmaurice's men. By February 1572, disheartened and abandoned by most of his followers, the rebel leader was keen to take advantage of the clemency that the Queen had hinted at, and the rebellion came to an inglorious end.

For Frobisher, his new duties – plying the waters between the West Country and the Irish coast to bring supplies to the English forces – lasted only as long as Fitzmaurice's rebellion. His command of the ship *Carrick Lane* seems to have survived the conclusion of this official employment by some weeks, though he soon reverted to doing business on his own account, upon the (by now threadbare) authority of a commission from the Prince of Orange.[4] His first victims were not, however, the most obvious enemies of the rebel provinces. Even as he returned to England from Ireland, he seized a number of French ships in the western Channel. They were taken into Plymouth, where he claimed title to their cargoes. Soon afterwards, he attacked and seized an overtly friendly vessel, a Hamburg munitions ship bound for the assistance of the beleaguered States-General at Flushing (Hamburg, from 1569 replacing Antwerp as the bourse for English merchant adventurers, also – reluctantly – acquired much of the corresponding privateering trade). One or both of these infractions proved to be beyond the Admiralty's whim to overlook, and once more, warrants for Frobisher's arrest were issued.[5]

Superficially, it seems that his piracies were becoming intolerable. To go beyond the bounds of privateering whilst sailing with letters of reprisal was one thing – an undoubted offence but one which might be mitigated by the circumstances of official policy – but to commit acts of outright depredation whilst under the threat of several existing warrants was to flaunt the authority of the Queen herself. Yet whilst it is almost certain that these warrants were intended to be enforced, some mitigation held back the Admiralty's officers at Plymouth – at least, for the moment. A new business had arisen; one in which a man with elastic scruples might prove useful or – as in Guinea, some two decades earlier – expendable. The threat of imprisonment or worse did not recede; but piracy no longer provided the only career-path to the gibbet. Frobisher, it seems, had by now descended a further level through the strata of social exclusion, and taken up with traitors – this time in the cause, rather than the suppression, of Irish liberties.

In such muddy waters, precisely what constituted a traitor was often difficult to determine. The principle of Elizabeth's overlordship was – very loosely – recognized by local magnates when it suited them, and irreparable religious differences between the mass of the population and the English were not always an immediate *casus belli*. There remained many passive Catholics and disaffected Protestants, even after years of brutal English pacification; but race and religion were always ready combustibles to add conviction and legitimacy to a particular cause. A declaration that one was fighting for Irish liberties and/or the True Faith was always an effective recruiting ploy for exiled troublemakers, loitering upon the docksides of Lisbon and Cadiz in the hope of putting together another rebellion. In attempting to deal with her potential enemies, the Queen's most intractable problem was that the discernible gap between disaffected subject and outright traitor was often a thin one. Many of the Irish nobility passed between the two states with blurring inconsistency, abetted in part by Elizabeth's uncanny readiness to forgive any act of disloyalty that was not directed maliciously against her own person. Following the crushing of Fitzmaurice's uprising, these endemic problems of duty and loyalty were neither more nor less pronounced than at any other time but, as always, they offered opportunities both for profit and ruin. In a period of thin prospects, and with the weight of Admiralty attention pressing heavily upon him once more, Martin Frobisher now joined this potentially deadly game.

Though his recent employment against the errant Fitzmaurice had been of a logistical nature only, it is highly unlikely that Frobisher was a stranger to the troublesome magnates of western Ireland. By 1572 he was known – either personally or by reputation – to friends of Gerald Fitzgerald, Earl of Desmond and first cousin of James Fitzmaurice. It is possible that this was a relatively recent acquaintance, but given the necessarily constrictive nature of Crown service, it is more likely to have had a relatively venerable provenance among the several (and, possibly, many) occasions upon which both Martin and John Frobisher had revisited the Irish coast to unload illegally seized goods in the years following the capture of the *Katherine* and their first taste of Irish hospitality.[6] Baltimore and Cork were far more than handy places to set down an illicit cargo; they had become freebooters' entrepôts in which an entire sub-economy thrived, safe from sporadic (and personally risky) attempts by

Admiralty Court officers to interrupt its intercourse. It is almost inconceivable that the Frobisher brothers had not followed the practice of their fellow privateers in the years since the *Katherine*'s capture: men such as they needed recourse to these places as much as the merchants they despoiled needed an Antwerp, an Emden or a Hamburg.

Stolen Spanish wine, landed at Baltimore, had been the cause of Frobisher's first English imprisonment; it is a curious coincidence that an argument over the sharing of quantities of the same commodity, landed at Kinsale by anonymous privateers, had provided the seed for the feud between Desmond and his former son-in-law, the Earl of Ormond: an apparently niggling matter that had grown since to become one of Ireland's most enduring grudge-matches.[7] Desmond, a powerful but troublesome vassal of the Queen, had long been an exemplar of that Irish nobleman whose ambiguous loyalties shifted with the wind. He had conducted his vendetta against Ormond with scant respect for (and even less attention to) the wishes of Elizabeth, and subsequently had been confined for a time in London before being allowed to return to Ireland in 1564 (where he and Ormond had promptly fought out what was to be the last 'private' battle between subjects of an English monarch). By the early 1570s their feud remained active still, though Ormond – strikingly handsome and therefore a personal favourite of the Queen – had the sense to keep his sovereign well apprised of his loyalty to her. Desmond, insofar as he was ever to make a firm commitment to any position, inclined towards disaffection. He and his three brothers grew increasingly disruptive in Munster, until Sir Henry Sydney arrested him once more and despatched him to London. For a while he resided in the Tower, but then Elizabeth, perhaps acknowledging the bias she had shown to Ormond, eased his confinement. He was given lodgings at Crosby Hall in Bishopgate Street, the magnificent home of alderman Sir William Bonde, a leading City haberdasher who was soon to become one of Frobisher's principal backers in the north-west enterprise. Though chaffing even at this soft restraint, Desmond seems to have been resigned to his lot, until discovering that his wife (who shared his confinement) was pregnant. Thereafter, he became increasingly desperate to remove them both from England, possibly to prevent the child becoming another English hostage.

In the third week in August 1572, a servant of Desmond named Ralph Whaley approached Frobisher at rooms he had taken in Lambeth, to ask him to assist in smuggling the Earl out of England. For Frobisher, the repercussions of his recent depredations at sea may have provided a rare incentive to re-acquaint himself with a drier environment (the Lambeth address is the only known land-based accommodation occupied by him since his time in Sir John Yorke's house in Walbrook, some eighteen years earlier); any likelihood of gain – lawful or otherwise – that kept him from the attention of the Admiralty Court must therefore have been tempting. According to testimony that he later provided to the Queen's commissioners, Frobisher offered at least the appearance of being willing to consider the proposal.[8] For a fortnight thereafter, the faithful Whaley passed between alderman Bonde's house and Frobisher's rooms, bringing news and suggestions for getting Desmond out of England. He also revealed that the Earl of Ormond had apparently offered to use his good offices with the Queen to have Lady Desmond (Ormond's mother's successor in Desmond's bed) removed perfectly legally to Ireland; an offer that Desmond must have viewed with intense suspicion.

Of the various plans considered, the one which appealed most to Desmond was for him to be carried out of the Thames in an oyster boat, to rendezvous with a bark in the Channel and go from thence either to Ireland, France or Flanders: 'w(hi)che he helde to be the best & soundest way for hymself for that he was an ill horsman and not able to get a horsback w(i)thowte helpe'. Unfortunately for his prospects of deliverance, Desmond was also 'very Sick on the sea, and not able to bide at length' (one wonders why Elizabeth bothered to confine him at all). Having decided broadly upon the method of his deliverance, however, he repeatedly postponed his own escape until he could ensure that his wife was safely conveyed out of England.

Several weeks passed, during which Whaley repeatedly pressed Frobisher to accept this illicit commission. The latter remained noncommittal, but pointedly warned that he had too little money to remain for much longer in London. Eventually, a meeting was arranged between Desmond and his potential deliverer. This was at 'Sent-leger' house in Southwark, adjacent to St Olave's Church; the former London home of the Abbots of St Augustine's Abbey, Canterbury. At the Dissolution, the property had been bestowed upon the St Leger family, whose collective – and expensive – habits of losing legal actions and drinking themselves to the point of death had created financial difficulties which their relative by marriage, Richard Grenville, had eased by purchasing large parts of their estate, including this ancient, rambling pile overhanging the Thames.[9] Grenville himself does not appear to have used it as his own residence in the city, and as a ferocious chaser of real and imagined Catholic plots, it is unlikely that he would willingly have allowed his hospitality to be thus defiled by Desmond's stratagems.

At their first meeting there, Desmond offered Frobisher a ship worth £500 and the lordship of the island of Valentia, off the Kerry coast, if he would assist the Earl's proposed escape from England. Frobisher gave some form of encouraging, if ambiguous, response, and in subsequent days they continued to meet; either at St Leger House or walking abroad in Ratcliffe fields. Upon these occasions, Desmond took great care not provide hard evidence of his intentions, saying nothing that was incriminating in the hearing of more than one man. He was ill served, however, by someone close to him – perhaps even by Frobisher himself. In November, both Desmond and Whaley were seized by order of the Privy Council and placed in the Tower.

Throughout this affair, Frobisher had kept his motives admirably cloudy. If he truly was short of money and thinking of leaving London – no doubt to put to sea once more – the offer he had received was almost certainly tempting, and a sound excuse for the Queen's commissioners to have him arrested. However, as he was required to face no more than an inquiry which took down his statement and dismissed him thereafter, it seems that he managed to convey himself with sufficient aplomb (or ambiguity) to convince them of his loyalty.

For a few months thereafter, Frobisher returned to the safer environment of the sea, and his old practice of privateering. He is cited as having been in Munster at some point during the winter months of 1572, selling goods which almost certainly had been taken as prize cargoes; and in January 1573, in the company of the ship *Mary Graynfelde*, he was involved in the seizure of a French ship laden with Portuguese goods.[10] Such pastimes were almost certainly insufficient in themselves to cure a penury nurtured over almost three years of semi-respectability, but a further opportunity was to arise during these months: one that Englishmen of widely diverse reputations were to seize. Their motives were as varied as their stations; some would be moved by high principle, others by greed alone. Frobisher himself would in turn exhibit remarkably consistent symptoms of treachery, cupidity and double-dealing that even now can hardly be resolved into a half-glimpse of his true intentions. The episode remains curious; yet more than any other in his career, it illustrates perfectly his capacity for inconstancy.

On the night of 24 August 1572 – St Bartholemew's Day – almost the entire hierarchy of the Huguenot cause was slaughtered in Paris amidst the more general massacre of their co-religionists. Only Henry of Navarre, the vidame of Chartres and count Montgomery had escaped; the latter, switching horses as each in turn fell exhausted, reached the French coast and escaped to Jersey. For several months thereafter, he attempted to persuade Elizabeth to finance an expedition to relieve the now besieged city of La Rochelle. To have acquiesced would have constituted an overt act of war against the French

Crown; but she tacitly encouraged a private response from those among her subjects who had been outraged by the events of 24 August. Approximately four hundred Englishmen, moved by sincere principle or sensing a hint of plunder in the air, subsequently responded to Montgomery's recruitment drive and volunteered to fight for his cause. Among them was Martin Frobisher.

On 1 June 1573, following the failure of Montgomery's expedition before La Rochelle, Antonio de Guaras – a Spanish merchant resident in London and tireless agent of the Spanish Crown – informed the Duke of Alva that Frobisher had approached him, offering to recruit up to three hundred English soldiers for Alva's army from unpaid English mercenaries returning from La Rochelle. Guaras claimed that Frobisher had accompanied the recent expedition as an agent of the French Ambassador in London, Archbishop de la Mothe Fénelon, and that he had spoken personally to Montgomery's son, who revealed that the returning Huguenot fleet was to go on to Flushing to relieve La Marck's besieged sea-beggars. Apparently, Frobisher had rounded off this remarkable manifest of ill-faith by offering his own services also, to act as an on-going agent of Spain in Montgomery's camp.[11]

The Spanish Court, apprised in turn by Alva, acted swiftly to test this and other proposed treacheries. Orders were issued (to be conveyed verbally) to instruct an agent named Zubiar to contact Frobisher and captains John Morgan, Ralph Lane, one Olivier and an unnamed German.[12] Zubiar was to 'press the business home with the one that appears to be most attached to his Majesty's interests and is best fitted for the execution of the business'. Specifically, it was envisaged that one or more of these men would carry approximately one thousand loyal Walloons into Flushing to seize one of the city gates. Should they succeed in taking the city outright, they would be richly rewarded; if not, or even if the attempt upon Flushing were to prove entirely fruitless, the rogue Englishmen were to be put into contact with the governor-general, Don Luis de Requeséns, to test what other service they might provide. Significantly, this business was to be so secret that the instructions explicitly forbade Zubiar from informing Guaras or any other Spaniard in London of it; a hint that the Spanish intelligence service already suspected its network to be compromised by Walsingham's agents.

Somewhat in the dark, the industrious Guaras continued his correspondence with Alva in the following months. On 26 June, he reported Frobisher's return to London and their discussions to turn 300 English mariners to the Spanish cause; four days later, he wrote again, saying that these disaffected men would land at Dunkirk or Ostend within twenty-three days. By now, it seems, the immediate plot had grown to encompass several, unnamed Englishmen, and Guaras at least was enthusiastic about their potential: 'This Frobisher is a man very helpful and of great courage, and so is his lieutenant, and two gentlemen of good reputation . . .'. He had rewarded his new English traitor with £20 for his efforts to date, and in turn was able to assure the Duke that Frobisher 'with much gratitude . . . kisses the hands of your Excellency'.[13]

However, it seems that by 26 August the Privy Council had been made at least partly aware of these clandestine negotiations. On that day, Guaras informed Alva that Frobisher had been detained at Dover, and that there seemed little hope he would be released. However, he was definitely at large once more by 15 November, when he sent word to Guaras that he would be in Dunkirk within a few days with some men of his company. This appears to have been their last contact during 1573; nine days later, Guaras wrote to Alva, complaining that he had heard nothing further, though one of Frobisher's companions had given him hope 'that he will go and serve without failing.'[14]

What were Frobisher's true intentions in initiating this dangerous game? That he had in fact discussed any meaningful stratagem with disloyal English soldiers is unlikely (unless it was of the sort to be mooted over tankards in a port-side tavern); however, there was undoubtedly an air of disaffection amongst those Englishmen who had volunteered their services for Mont-gomery's cause only to see it fail so cravenly, and Frobisher was hardly making unrealistic promises regarding their willingness to abandon their present employment. Also, his claim to have been in contact with Montgomery and his son seems convincing. Certainly, he was able to provide very accurate information on the size of the Huguenot forces (if not their intentions),[15] and his own capacity for duplicity was a proven quality – not least, to have simul-taneously juggled the affections of Archbishop La Mothe Fénelon and his opposite number Cardinal Châtillon spoke of a serious talent for artfulness. To Guaras, the motives of such a man were both transparent and plausible; as a privateer whose career had entered a relatively unprofitable phase, and who was now 'marked' by the Privy Council, his sense of duty could be expected to be vestigial at best. Even so, with his travelling expenses covered and the prospect of significant rewards to come, Frobisher did not dare – or desire – to take the further step of actually going to Dunkirk: a prudence which, even without further evidence, seems to clear him of the taint of treachery.

Probably, he had been looking for a lucrative opportunity and promising the earth to someone who was willing to be duped by a man of rigorously ambiguous morals. We need not search too industriously to find the provenance for such a dangerous association. Hawkins's famous and successful offer to Philip II was fresh in English minds; he had secured the release of his men from Spanish prisons and, far more importantly, the promise of a Spanish estate and its commensurate income.[16] For Englishmen whose experience at sea was as great as that of Hawkins, the temptation to tout for business in the hope that Philip's gullibility was inexhaustible must have been overwhelming. From his privateering activities, Frobisher was already known in the Netherlands – he held an open-ended commission from the Prince of Orange to harry Spanish shipping, dating either from 1568–9 or 1572 – so his approach and offer were hardly implausible.[17] Yet the suspicious brevity of his detention in August indicates that he had informed the Privy Council at an early stage in his discussions with Guaras. It may be (though we have no evidence to confirm this) that the entire episode had been cleared with, or planned by, Walsingham himself. As with his involvement in Desmond's botched escape from England, Frobisher suffered no consequences of his supposed treachery. However, if he believed he was merely emulating an honourable example, he was mistaken. There was a small matter of reputation once more. Hawkins had also been careful to keep the Council well informed of his intentions, but since 1568 he had been generally known as an enemy of Spain, against whom few accusations of treachery would seem credible. In contrast, Frobisher's known loyalties were to himself alone, and no suspicion regarding his integrity could be dismissed out of hand. As late as September 1575, when, as we shall see, he had recently been disappointed in an expectation of gainful employment, Guaras was to report once more from London:

> Captain Martin Frobisher has decided to go to Flanders to see his Excellency about the great services which he hopes to render, and he will leave in a week. He is the best seaman and the bravest in this country, and his great name and valour will be already known in Flanders. I have promised him a safe conduct to go and come free of debt and the consequences of past events, if no arrangement is made there.[18]

Guaras was wrong; but his judgement was based upon fairly sound evidence. At the time of his active contact with Frobisher, the Englishman had been in danger of becoming a professional double-agent: a universally unloved creature whose career rarely progressed to a happy or prosperous retirement. Privy Councillors, in the manner of all great officers of state, used such men with scant regard for their safety (the high proportion of convicted felons who habitually filled the role was indicative both of its requirements and prospects), and regarded a job well done as no reason to further their interests beyond the next, equally fraught employment. Frobisher had proved himself twice in such business, in the process of which he seems to have acquired a talent for artifice that made him dangerously qualified for more of the same. Accordingly, his association with Guaras was hardly over before he was utilized in another, even more dangerous plot – indeed, the two may briefly have been concurrent duplicities.

At some time during the latter part of 1573, Sir Warrham St Leger and Jeremy Brett 'allured to them Martin Furbisher, with the Promes of 20 li by the year or with the vallew of it in ready money, to transport them over to their cousin Stukely'.[19] Thomas Stukely (yet another cousin of the Grenvilles) was an English Catholic and sometime pirate; a plausible rogue whose flair and bravado periodically excited the admiration of the less discerning members of Philip II's court. As early as 1563, he had betrayed his putative plans to assist the Huguenot colony in Florida to the Spanish Ambassador;[20] a decade later, he was in Spain, straining his hosts' hospitality with his profligacy whilst openly attempting to raise troops for an invasion of Ireland on behalf of its oppressed Catholic population. Clearly, the man was parlous company for anyone wishing to keep his head; yet it seems that far from offering a poisoned chalice to Frobisher, St Leger was acting merely as a messenger between old acquaintances. The origin of their association is obscure. There is a possible – though somewhat unlikely – link through Sir John Yorke: on 2 April 1556, the Privy Council had ordered Stukely (who was briefly residing in Aldgate at that time) to 'keepe the peace and be of good abearinge' towards Yorke.[21] We have no further details of their quarrel (if it could be put so strongly), and in any case Frobisher himself was almost certainly in a Lisbon gaol at the time. A far more likely connection occurs through his later privateering activities, and again, the dark presences of Henry Stranguishe and Peter Killigrew loom. Both men had been partners with Stukely in taking ships off Fowey in 1557;[22] being a known associate of Killigrew at least (and formerly implicated with Stranguishe, if only by the man himself), it is unlikely that Frobisher had escaped the infection of association with Stukely also.[23] If St Leger and Brett – who are not known to have had any prior acquaintance with Frobisher – approached him as a safe option, it is because they knew already that he could be trusted in a palpably untrustworthy business.

Had this new scheme proceeded as its ostensible intentions demanded, Frobisher might well have seen his unlovely career brought to a swift conclusion; but the danger to his reputation and neck appears, once more, to have been illusory. The proposed arrangement was probably part of a complicated plot to lure Stukely back into Ireland, where he could be taken and no doubt despatched with the minimum of effort. In another example of the treacheries which seem to have informed almost every privateer's career, St Leger was in close contact with the Privy Council, and acting to betray his cousin. Whether Frobisher himself was fully aware of the scheme cannot be determined; Wheater, quoting an unattributed source, claimed that Isobel Frobisher (from whom, presumably, Frobisher was not yet entirely estranged), formed an instant dislike for St Leger and urged her husband to have nothing to do with him.[24] If so, she was not heeded. On 23 November 1573, Frobisher and one Richard Yorke (possibly one of Sir John Yorke's sons), 'beinge in a shippe called the Clocke on the Downe', were summoned to appear before the Council.[25] Five days later, a safe conduct was provided to Frobisher to allow him to pass to London unmolested. The same Privy Council order also noted that

> Upon informacion that the shippe called the Clocke, pretended to be set forth by Sir Warrham St Leger for service in Ireland, shold take in hand some enterprise not to be sufferid, letters were sent to Sir Warrham to take order that the said ship shuld not go forthe untill sureties were put into the Courte of the Admiraltie.

That there was even a chance that St Leger was involved in an enterprise 'not to be sufferid' suggests that the Privy Council were not entirely convinced either of his plans or his fidelity. The demand for sureties was common enough, as we have seen, but these would hardly have been required had the voyage been entirely under official auspices and control. It is probable that St Leger's loyalties were considered to have been strained by his unwilling removal from the office of President of Munster two years earlier – and indeed, by his very exposure to the treacherous sink of Irish politics.[26] The plot, whatever its provenance, was stifled, and the fortunate Stukely survived the consequences of his actions for a few more years.

Once more, Frobisher's role in an ambiguous enterprise was probably held to be blameless. The matter that had detained him and brought him before the Council had more to it of prior reputations than rebellion: the part-owner of the *Clock*, one John Lane (a member of the Fishmongers' Company), had previously stood bonds that Frobisher and Yorke should not go to sea in that particular vessel (possibly it had been the *Clock* in which Frobisher had intended – or proposed – to visit Dunkirk on his 'Spanish' business only thirteen days earlier). In other words, sworn to serve some secret design of St Leger (and still embroiled in supposedly treasonous correspondence with the Duke of Alva), the accomplished conspirator had attempted to put to sea in a 'hot' ship.

There is no evidence that the Council subsequently interrogated Frobisher on the matters of Alva and Stukely and, certainly, he was not further taken to task for his involvement in either plot. Nevertheless, there is little doubt that in these and the earlier Desmond businesses, he had been – to use an apt metaphor – sailing far too close to a lee shore. His reputation, poor before he entered the Marshalsea in 1569, had since accumulated a significant further taint of perfidy that even his former privateering colleagues might have considered unseemly. And as the year 1574 turned, the matter of reputation had become paramount. By now thirty-eight years old – well into early middle-age by the harsh yardstick of contemporary mortality – Frobisher was known principally as a privateer whose inability to leave friendly shipping unmolested (and undoubted ability to be caught in the act of failing to do so), had been amply proven in the Admiralty Court. Even so, with several warrants hanging by the thinnest of threads above his head, he still carried valid letters of reprisal. He had probably not even consulted their terms, though undoubtedly he had exercised their writ with alarming liberality. His implied if pretended involvement with Irish Catholic rebels marked him out as untrustworthy, even to those who had used him in that business (though it is probable that Philip II and his agents deluded themselves as to his potential for treachery), and there can be little doubt that his only known legitimate connections – those arising from his time with the Yorkes of London – had by now been totally squandered.

In his favour, there is some evidence that Frobisher was regarded in a better light by certain members of the Privy Council. Burghley's 'conceiving well of him', and the Earl of Warwick's patronage (which was to arise, seemingly from nowhere, in the following months), hint at past employments, satisfactorily discharged, that prudence ensured were never set to paper. Frobisher was not trustworthy, but his endearingly loose understanding of the bounds of legality appears to have been found useful by men whose own characters had to be seen to be above reproach. This at least indicates that he had continued to nurture the contacts that had preserved him from the worst that his privateering felonies might otherwise have ensured.

Nevertheless, these small mitigations aside, any honest appraisal of his career to date must have left Frobisher with an uneasy feeling that time and circumstance were running contrary to his interests. He was known to the right people, but not in a promising context. He was courageous, bold and, probably, persuasive; but he was also ill-disciplined and of palpably elastic morals. There is a strong sense of drift to his ambitions, or at least an inability on his part to resolve them into something worthwhile. If he had the intelligence to see this, the burden of his past reputation might, even now, be lifted. What the precise catalyst for this sea-change in attitude was to be, we cannot say. The temporarily declining prospects in the privateering trade, his regrettably high profile as a potential traitor or the inertial drag of several existing warrants for his arrest – any or all of these problems might have inclined him to look at alternative employments. All that we know with any certainty is that sometime during the course of 1574 Frobisher turned himself – apparently decisively – from his previous lawlessness. With the backing of a man he may first have met twenty years before, but whose own career since could hardly have been more dissimilar, he was to return to the Privy Council with a remarkable and seemingly uncharacteristic proposition: one which was to bring him greater fame than infamy, but greater misfortune than either.

PART TWO

The Glittering Fleece That He Doth Bring . . .[1] *1574–79*

SIX

The North-west Passage

... All which learned men and painefull travellers have affirmed with one consent and voice, that America was an Island: and that there lyeth a great Sea betweene it, Cataia and Grondland, by the which any man of our countrey, that will give the attempt, may with small danger passe to Cataia, the Moluccae, India, and all other places in the East, in much shorter time, than either the Spaniard, or Portugal doeth, or may doe, from the neerest parte of any of their countreys within Europe.[2]

English interest in the possibility of a navigable north-west passage into the Pacific Ocean was already strong by 1566, when Humphrey Gilbert set down these lines of his *Discourse*, soon after appearing before the Privy Council to debate its possibilities against the great proponent of a north-eastern route, Anthony Jenkinson.[3] The concept was mentioned in print as early as 1517 by John Rastell, brother-in-law of Sir Thomas More. Rastell, disappointed in his ambition to make an American voyage, comforted himself by writing a play, *A new interlude and a mery of the nature of the iiii elements*, in which he speculated, albeit obliquely, upon the possibility of an unexploited route to Asia:

But these newe landis by all cosmografye
Frome the Cane of Catous lande cannot lye
Lytell paste a thousande myle;
But from those newe landis men may sayle playne
Eastwarde, and com to Englande againe,
Where we began ere whyle.[4]

The earliest known Englishman actively to lobby for a project to find the passage was Robert Thorne the younger, a Bristol merchant sometime resident in Seville (Thorne had invested in Sebastian Cabot's 1526 voyage to the River Plate, on which his future partner, Roger Barlowe – another Bristol merchant – had sailed). In 1527, Thorne addressed a long letter to Henry VIII, via Robert Ley, English Ambassador to the Spanish Court. Following the obligatory protracted introduction, Thorne began by reiterating the unpleasant truth of the world: '. . . for out of Spaine they haue discouered all the Indies and Seas Occidental, and out of Portugale all the Indies and Seas Oriental: so that by this part of the Orient and Occident, they haue encompassed the worlde.'[5] In light of these indisputable obstacles, Thorne argued that it was only to the northwards that Englishmen would find their own increase: that, decisively, 'the coste heerein will bee nothing, in comparison to the great profite'.

Thorne's ambitious solution – an English transpolar voyage to the East – was subsequently promoted by himself and Barlowe in partnership, though without engaging sufficient attention from potential investors. Following Thorne's early death in 1532, Barlowe wrote his *Brief Summe of Geographie* to resurrect the scheme (which was considered by the Privy Council as late as 1541).[6] It was never to be attempted, though as we shall see, Sebastian Cabot may have been thinking of a similar venture in 1551. The fact that such a route – if it existed – must be far shorter than those dominated by Spain and Portugal was undoubtedly its principal attraction, but claims for the north-west passage and its feasibility were from the first clouded by misrepresentations, hearsay and outright falsehoods. Sometime before 1550, Cabot wrote to the Venetian John Baptista Ramusio, stating that he himself had entered the eastern entrance of the passage as early as 1507–9. Whether he actually made a voyage between those years was long disputed by scholars, though recent research has established the bare verity of his claim, if not its detail.[7] Ramusio, later quoted by Richard Hakluyt, claimed that Cabot

. . . sayled along and beyonde this lande of New Fraunce [i.e., Labrador.] at the charges of king Henrie the seventh king of Englande: And hee tolde mee that hauing sayled a long time West and by Northe beyonde these Ilandes vnto the latitude of 67. degrees and an halfe vnder the North Pole, and at the 11. day of June finding still the open sea without any manner of impediment, he thought verily by that way to haue passed on still the way to Cathaio, which is in the East, and woulde haue done it, if the

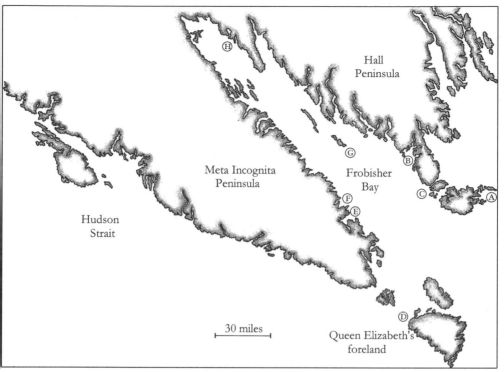

A. Hall Island, B. Countess of Warwick Sound, C. Beare Sound, D. Gabriel Strait, E. Jackman Sound, F. Yorke Sound, G. Gabriel Island, H. Five Men's Sound (conjectural)

1. South Baffin Island and Frobisher Bay. Author's collection.

mutinie of the shipmaster and marriners had not rebelled and made him to returne homewardes from that place.[8]

If Cabot did indeed reach a latitude of 67°–30′N, he would have been off Baffin Island, perhaps as high as Cape Dyer and across the Arctic Circle. There is no open expanse of water to the west at that point; had he been a little further south, he may have mistaken the entrance to Home Bay for the mouth of a passage. Neither option seems entirely plausible, however. Other accounts of this voyage variously place the highest latitude he reached at 55° and 52°, either of which seems more likely.[9] What is certain, however, is that this voyage, like other Bristol-based attempts which followed, was an isolated example of individual enterprise, rather than part of a concerted 'push' to find a navigable route to the East.

The next, and certainly the most accomplished effort was made in 1527 by John Rut. With Henry VIII's backing, Rut left England with two ships, the *Mary Guildford* (a naval vessel) and the *Sampson*; they reached the coast of Labrador, where the latter vessel was lost. Moving southwards (possibly to search for the isthmus rumoured to have been discovered by Verrezzano), Rut reached Santo Domingo before returning to England.[10] He made no further attempt to find an 'English' route into the Pacific, though another Englishman, Richard Hore, subsequently commanded a voyage to Labrador during 1536: a disastrous episode whose only palpable achievement was to give Englishmen a first taste of other Englishmen.[11]

Whatever the precise achievements of these men, the significant point is that knowledge of the voyages they undertook, and of the exact nature of the land or lands they descried, was no more widespread in the mid-sixteenth century than it is today. The continental mass across the Ocean Sea remained a dark and abiding mystery, notwithstanding infrequent news of Spanish advances in its southern regions. When Ramusio prophetically concluded his account of Sebastian Cabot's voyage with the statement: 'But it seemeth that God doth yet still reserve this great enterprise for some great Prince, to discover this voyage to Cathaio . . .', he succinctly stated both the case and its abiding disincentive. Englishmen, exercised by the fabulous example of the Spanish and Portuguese empires – and frustrated by the brake to their ambitions that it represented – needed a possibility that was as yet untested: one that might allow them to tap the riches of the East without overtly challenging the existing claims of empire. Yet such a possibility, by definition, was one that was intrinsically unattractive to rival powers. Spanish and Portuguese navigators had been industrious, and their comprehensive claims of discovery and possession, confirmed by no less an authority than papal bull, had swept up all the known 'easy' options. For those who followed, the only feasible routes lay to the north-east or north-west – in climates far too severe to excite Mediterranean temperaments – or via the politically risky seizure and exploitation of 'Terra Australis', the mythical continent that supposedly spanned the southern extremity of the Pacific Ocean. The inevitable dangers in attempting to realize one of these options, and the undoubted backwardness of English maritime skills, were deterrents which for many years discouraged more active English attempts to follow their Iberian examplars.

The little-known voyages of Cabot, Rut and Hore apart, the first practical English efforts to find a 'new' passage to the Far East were in a north-easterly direction. Cabot himself, having returned from Spain to take up his English pension, was reported to have been working during 1551 with Jean Ribault, the enterprising Huguenot navigator, to resurrect the Thorne/Barlow transpolar scheme; but any palpable progress they may have made was soon subsumed into preparations for the seminal 1553 north-east voyage of Sir Hugh Willoughby and Richard Chancellor.[12] This expedition, in which merchants, courtiers, cosmographers and men of letters invested such high hopes, did not establish the feasibility of the route; but it did open up a new English trade with Russia – one that, from 1555 under the aegis of the newly incorporated Russia Company, allowed the search for a north-eastern route to Cathay to continue. However, the subsequent failure of the company to establish the existence (or otherwise) of a passage in that direction, and, more particularly, to realize a significant or consistent profit for its long-suffering investors, was almost certainly one of the principal factors in intensifying interest in an alternative, north-western route from the 1560s onwards.[13]

Existing cosmographical data on the region, uncritically accepted by propagandists for a north-west passage, added weight to its perceived potential. As new discoveries had been made northwards along the eastern seaboard of North America, cosmographers had added such data as they possessed. 'Labrador' and 'Baccalaos' (the terms were interchangeable, their imagined location broadly corresponding to the coast of present day Labrador) had begun to appear on maps during the 1530s, crudely represented yet confirmed, nevertheless, by the brief landings of Basque and French fishermen on their shores. What might lie to the north of this region was the subject of much speculation, and little else. As always, lack of reliable information was not merely an impediment: it also encouraged error, hearsay, legend and outright deception to be presented as 'fact' until specifically proved otherwise. One spurious claim enjoyed a particularly long and influential currency, and had profound implications for future English voyages to the north-west Atlantic. In 1558, a map appeared in Venice which purported to show discoveries made during the fourteenth century by two Venetian brothers, Niccolo and Antonio Zeno, who allegedly had sailed to the region. The map itself was an invention, perpetrated by a direct descendant of the brothers, also named Niccolo; it depicted Greenland as attached to Scandinavia, its southern-most tip lying as far north as 66°N. To the south, the islands of 'Icaria' and 'Friesland' (the latter descending to 60°N) lay in mid-Atlantic, whilst to the west, almost precisely in the true location of southern Baffin Island, was the coastline of 'Estotiland', supposedly first discovered by the intrepid brothers. This data, which seemed to open up the geography of the region, challenged previous speculation that the north-eastern American seaboard might be a continuous land mass. Not surprisingly, it was accepted almost immediately by influential Venetian cartographers: firstly by Giacomo Gastaldi in his world map of 1561, and then by Bolognini Zaltieri (1566) and Giovanni Francesco Cammocio (1567).[14]

Alone, these features might not have excited significant wider interest; however, as early as 1532, Francesco Rosselli had portrayed a speculative passage of water that carried through to the Pacific, a feature that was repeated on the Gemma Frisius–Mercator globe of 1537.[15] In 1546, Gastaldi had speculated further, increasing the dimensions of the passage to make it a vast body of water, separating America (to the south) from Asia (to the north). Now, transposing the Zeno information, it seemed that the easternmost extremity of this navigation, previously represented as closing so as almost to prevent ingress from the Atlantic, might remain extremely wide throughout. Abraham Ortelius (1564) and Cammocio (1567) produced maps which married these features for the first time. In 1569, the data received much more widespread dissemination when Mercator published his vastly influential world map, with this feature – by now known as the 'Strait of Anian' – prominent upon it.[16] Mercator's map (the first to use his now famous projection) was immediately popular amongst contemporary cartographers, and widely copied. Ortelius produced his compendium of existing cartographical knowledge, *Theatrum Orbis Terrarum* in 1570, and this largely reproduced his own and Mercator's work on the Strait. In the light of such august support, what had commenced as a forgery in 1558 had become orthodoxy less than fifteen years later; and with this supposed evidence of an easy navigation to the Far East so palpably laid before them, English promoters of a north-west passage had begun to argue its potential with great conviction.

Gilbert's *Discourse*, finally published in 1576, presented a cogent and seductive argument for the passage, citing as its authorities such diverse sources as Plato, Aristotle, Pliny, Gemma Frisius, Ortelius, Coronado and Urdaneta. Yet there were dissenting voices also. Another, unpublished discourse – written in 1573–4 by Gilbert's cousin, Richard Grenville – accepted that the passage probably existed, but made the dissenting case in a more practical manner:

> The distanse of the Straightes of Anian to the north-weste course being 200 grades (i.e., degrees) in longitude maketh 6,000 myles, alowinge 30 miles to a grade, for suche is the quantitie of a grade in 60 of latitude. Herto if we maye adioyne 1,200 myles, which is the quantitie of 10 grades ascendinge and 10 descendinge (here)tofore mencioned, there amounteth 7,200 myles. Nowe consideringe the seas and ayre vnder the Artike circle are so congeled that they are navigable only 3 monethes in the yeare, wherof it is requisite to reserve at leaste one monethe to retorne, if the said passadge sholde not be mette withall. Then examyne howe farr in the moyetie

of that quarter a man maie passe, and the possibilitie of the voiadge will soone apeare.[17]

In other words, even if the passage existed, no ship could pass through it swiftly enough to avoid being entombed when ice reformed at the end of the brief northern summer. The discourse concluded that any attempt to force the passage would be 'vtterly impossible or not without extreme perills of liefe and expence of victualles, without any advauntage in the meane'.

However, Grenville had a strong ulterior motive for discouraging any attempt to prove the passage navigable from its eastern entrance. He had presented a petition to the Queen on 22 March 1574, requesting permission to make a voyage to discover and take in her name the lands of 'Terra Australis', and – possibly – to discover the western extremity of the north-west passage, which was portrayed by some cartographers to lie much further south than its eastern opening.[18] As it transpired, the recent patching up of relations between England and Spain, underlined by the 1574 Treaty of Bristol, made Grenville's project – or *any* southern project – far too provocative for the Queen's tastes, and in so doing provided a new spur to the 'northern' propagandists. Indeed, almost as soon as it had been stated, Grenville's refutation of pro-north-west passage theories was itself in turn refuted by an anonymous author, who pointed out that the sea-route to Muscovy via the White Sea lay in 72° at its northernmost point, yet remained navigable for up to five months in most years.[19]

The truth was that despite the assurance with which the protagonists made their respective claims, no one could cite more definitive evidence than that of men who themselves had speculated, lied or leaned upon their own partialities. The world remained an uncertain place, and the desire to find within it the means of enrichment or glory meant that supposition and 'fact' often became inextricably compounded. The very goal of the propagandists, whether for the north-west or north-east passages, was a myth; 'Cathay' was not strictly synonymous with China, as many commentators have since assumed, but with a wishful, flawed composite of the dreams of commodities and markets which Englishmen had only ever touched through the intermediary activities of other nations.

Such ignorance and half-sight, fuelled by the imperfections of contemporary science, could only be goaded to further excesses by the English longing to emulate Iberian achievements. All sixteenth-century English commentators who addressed the future and nature of their nation's economic potential returned, again and again, to the prising of some part of this bonanza

from foreign hands – not by means of war, for which England was perpetu-
ally ill-prepared, but in the pursuit and practice of trade; trade which required
new, secure and exclusive routes. It was precisely because such routes existed
beyond the present boundaries of European experience that English attention
was now turning towards regions for which the only intelligence lay in imagination and speculation.

With such wide and indistinct parameters before them, Englishmen with
even a little experience of long-range voyaging were presented with opportunities whose rewards, if ephemeral, were potentially staggering. Most did not
choose to seek them. For such as they, the unspectacular business of carrying
commodities to existing foreign markets was labour enough; its modest
recompense sufficient to provide for families who saw little enough of their
menfolk. For others, however, such considerations were at best peripheral,
and more likely irrelevant. It is hardly necessary to observe that most of the
men who extended the physical horizons of the known world made bad hus-
bands and fathers, and often poor companions, too. When fabulous success
attended their efforts, their misanthropic tendencies were played down, or
even presented as symptoms of a lonely genius – to Englishmen, Francis
Drake is perhaps the greatest exemplar of this happy type. However, for those
who did not share Drake's great abilities (or his even greater good fortune),
the consequences of the gulf between ambition and achievement only served
to emphasize the self-exclusion that defined their lives and careers. Whether
bound for glory or oblivion, however, these men shared a near instinctive perception: that the sea – particularly the far, unknown sea – was a blank sheet
upon which past disappointments and weak prospects could be rewritten.

SEVEN

Michael Lok

To the quickening English debate upon potential routes to new markets, an unlikely voice was added late in 1574, when Martin Frobisher – failed Guinea trader, over-zealous privateer and ambiguous consort of traitors – approached the Privy Council with a petition. He sought their permission and assistance to set out an attempt to find a sea-passage towards the north-west, to sail through it to Cathay and return via the same route; establishing a *de facto* and, eventually, a *de jure* English right to its exploitation.

It has since been suggested this somewhat surprising proposal had an Irish provenance; that Frobisher and Humphrey Gilbert had met, and perhaps become friends, whilst upon their recent (and concurrent) military service there: at which Gilbert, disappointed in his own ambitions, had passed the torch of his obsession to a new and vigorous hand.[1] Tidy as this seems, however, there is not the slightest documentary evidence that the two men were acquainted prior to 1576; indeed, Frobisher's initiative was unavoidably antagonistic to Gilbert's scheme, which, though moribund in 1574, was not yet dead. Martin Frobisher – visionary, explorer and propagandist for maritime expansion – was a re-invention for which there is no easy explanation.

Certain members of the Privy Council were intrigued by Frobisher's proposal, but wary; they referred him to the Russia Company, whose charter, providing exclusive rights of exploration and exploitation of all routes to the East via northern seas, had been the legal bulwark against which Gilbert's hopes had been dashed almost nine years earlier.[2] The outcome of that episode had irritated certain members of the Council; particularly the Dudley brothers, the Earls Warwick and Leicester, who, like their late father the Duke of Northumberland, were enthusiastic promoters of speculative ventures. For this new attempt, Frobisher was provided with stronger ammunition when the Council gave him a letter of introduction to the Russia Company, suggesting that if it were not inclined to set out its own attempt, a licence might be granted to 'others which are desyrous now to attempt the same'.[3]

The following month, the court of the Russia Company – George Barne, William Towerson, Steven Borough and Michael Lok – dutifully considered the petition and promptly refused it. Lok, writing of the incident some years later, claimed that: '. . . we purceving the purpose to be to the North-westward, & no good evidence shewed by the parties for proof of the matter: vpon our relation therof made to the company, they suspected some other matter to be meant by the parties . . .'[4]. Whatever other matters were suspected, the company jealously guarded its existing rights, even if it had no immediate intention of exercising them. As almost a decade earlier, their discouraging decision was notified to the Privy Council, and the matter – a brief, possibly troublesome aside to the company's habitual business – seemed to be closed. Yet just two months later, on 3 February 1575, the company issued a licence which effectively overrode its own rights to explore and take possession of a north-west passage, and to enjoy the possible fruits of its discovery.[5] The permit was made out in the names of Martin Frobisher, Michael Lok and whomsoever would join with them, and the sum of £1 (the cost of setting down the document) was paid to Thomas Nichols, clerk of the Russia Company. Hopefully, the charge was satisfied in good coin, as it represented the company's entire compensation for having relinquished its right to exploit the riches of almost a quarter of the planet.[6]

The Russia Company's abandonment of its former policy had little to do with sage reflection. Most persuasively, the Privy Council had continued to put considerable pressure upon the company either to search for the passage themselves or get out of the manger. At the same time, Michael Lok – youngest of the Lok brothers and London Agent of the company – had been busily encouraging resistance from the inside. He was well aware that there existed a strong, discontented element therein, among men who had committed their money to the trade for years without seeing much of a return upon it. Some of them, almost certainly, were those who had been loosely identified as 'others which are now desyrous' of a new, north-west enterprise.

The Muscovy trade, by now just twenty years old, had come about incidentally; its activities a small compensation for the English failure to reach the Far East via a north-eastern route. It was, potentially, a lucrative trade;

but it bore heavy overheads, even into the 1570s. The passage to Russia via the White Sea remained a hazardous one, and the trade itself was fraught with local economic and political difficulties. The English company's privileges in Russia were enjoyed wholly at the whim of the Tsar, and though these had been granted under charter, there was no effective legal system to which the company could refer, should its trade be interrupted or penalized – for example, in the period October 1570 to May 1572, when its goods were temporarily subject to swingeing Russian customs duties. Nor was this an unchallenged market. A great deal of the Muscovy traders' efforts were devoted to protecting their monopoly from interlopers of other nations; some of whom also, if briefly, gained preferential terms from Ivan IV.

In addition to these structural problems, there was also the occasional tectonic upheaval. In 1571, the destruction of the company's warehouse during the Tartar sack of Moscow had resulted in the loss of approximately £6,600 of uninsured goods. Fortunately, such setbacks were uncommon; but dividends from the trade were rarely substantial, and would never come to represent a significant part of the portfolio of England's foreign earnings.[7] At the height of its sixteenth-century activities, the company despatched at most some twelve to sixteen ships to Russia annually. They returned with furs, timber and other naval supplies and, occasionally, silks acquired from Persia. The first and last commodities apart, these were necessities, rather than high value goods of the sort that had tempted Englishmen southwards on to the Guinea and Benin coasts. The Muscovy trade, though undoubtedly worthy of the attempt – and increasingly vital to the English navy – represented a relatively uneven and risk-heavy return on private capital.[8]

Faced with these endemic discouragements to their habitual business, there was much sympathy for the new, north-west proposal amongst men whose very membership of the Russia Company indicated an abiding interest in the markets of the seemingly unattainable East. Of the eventual investors in Frobisher's 1576 voyage, all but two would be members of either the Russia or Mercers' Companies, and Michael Lok was a member of both.[9] In following his own priorities he undoubtedly played upon the general dissatisfaction with the existing trade; but that he was able to do so without antagonizing his employers suggests that their resistance was both desultory and ready to be undermined. Objections based upon old charter privileges that had never been exercised were not likely to stand in the way of a determined effort to seize the initiative.

Worthy as it had the potential to be, why should this proposal have come from Frobisher, and at this precise time? He himself did not leave any

declaration of his prior interest, but in retrospect strong claims were made on
his behalf. Writing in 1578 to provide a provenance (or, perhaps, a mythol-
ogy) for the north-west voyages, George Best – a gentleman-soldier who sailed
with Frobisher in 1577 and 1578 – claimed for his commander a near-
obsession in the matter:

> He began first with himselfe to deuise, and then with his friendes to con-
> ferre, and layde a playne platte vnto them, that that voyage was not onely
> possible by the Northweast, but also as he coulde proue, easie to be per-
> formed. And further, he determined and resolued with himselfe, to go
> make full proofe therof, & to accomplishe, or bring true certificat of the
> truth, or else neuer to returne againe, knowing this to be the onely thing
> of the Worlde that was left yet undone, whereby a notable mind mighte
> be made famous and fortunate . . . Long tyme he conferred with his priuate
> friendes of these secretes, and made also manye offers for the performing
> of the same in effect, vnto sundry Merchants of our Countery, aboue xv.
> yeares before he attempted the same . . . [10]

The identity of these seemingly short-sighted 'sundry Merchants' is hardly
a mystery. It was most of them. Frobisher had been busy during those same
fifteen years in employments that would have inclined few men of legitimate
business to do more than report him to the nearest Admiralty officer. Indeed,
Best may have inadvertently admitted as much in protesting too strongly of
their breed '. . . whiche neuer regard Vertue, withoute sure, certayne, and
present gaynes . . .' (omitting to mention, of course, that Frobisher had been
an enthusiastic pursuer of the very same gains by more immediate methods).
In fact, a number of merchants were to prove themselves very receptive to
the idea of the north-west passage; the only reservation they were to express,
at least initially, was regarding Frobisher's involvement in finding it.

As we have seen, another uncritical source for Frobisher's interest in the
north-west passage was Richard Willes, who supplied the anecdote regarding
its alleged provenance during a discussion in a Lisbon gaol in the mid-1550s
– an encounter which, had it actually occurred, would have made Frobisher's
'obsession' even more venerable. To the extent that the claims of Best and
Willes are broadly corroborative, it seems we should treat them seriously; but
the strength and focus of Frobisher's interest in such a project, prior to 1574,
is questionable to say the least. Willes produced his preface to the new edition
of Eden's *History* at the behest of the Countess of Warwick (to whom it was
also dedicated): like her husband, she was an early and keen supporter of the

north-west project. The temptation to rewrite history to suit the moment was therefore a powerful one. That Frobisher should have triumphed after decades of striving provided an admirable context for the north-west voyages and their apparent success; yet his career prior to this time had been marked above all by the very absence of a discernible direction to his ambitions. The only pursuit to which he had devoted any sustained effort was privateering, for which he had earned only a parlous reputation and a reserved seat in the dock of the Admiralty Court; and even if the claims of Best and Willes for his enthusiasm had some substance – that he had indeed harboured a longing to set out across the Ocean Sea – his known practical experience was hardly apposite. The Guinea voyages of 1553–4 and a possible Barbary expedition in 1559 apart, Frobisher seems to have spent his entire career to date in northern European waters, doing very little in the way of preparing for a life of oceanic exploration. He was, to be sure, a known quality as a leader of men (albeit down paths which were better untrodden); but there were many others who had far greater intellectual sympathy with – and true under-standing of – the aims and aspirations of the expansionists. In fact, it would be difficult to imagine a man less exercised by the prospects of initiating a new trade-route, or more indifferent to the perceived economic problems that would be ameliorated by it, than Martin Frobisher.

Yet he was now, apparently, the leading proponent of an attempt to exploit a north-west passage; though the precise sequence of events that brought him before the Russia Company is no less obscure than his conversion to the cause of England's foreign markets. We are told that he first managed to secure the interest of Warwick, who then secured further backing within the Privy Council. This is of course possible; it should be recalled that several of these men enjoyed far more intimate, day-to-day relationships than those fostered by their roles as Privy Councillors and courtiers.[11] However, it is equally likely that men such as the Earl of Leicester, Burghley and Walsingham – all long-standing members of the Russia Company – had a far more obvious connection through which they came to hear of the project.[12] Certainly, the provenance of Frobisher's relationship with Warwick – if it may be put so strongly – is unclear. It has been suggested that they became known to each other through Sir Henry Sydney (Warwick's brother-in-law, Lord Deputy and commander of English land forces in Ireland during Frobisher's service there).[13] Again, however, there is no extant evidence to support this. Frobisher's earliest unequivocal connection with the Sydney family arose in 1575, when Henry's son Philip became a prospective investor in the north-west enterprise (and again, the younger Sydney's relationship with his uncles

Warwick and Leicester offers a far firmer provenance than any assumed prior acquaintance arising during Frobisher's extremely brief Irish duties).

In attempting to establish and defend the likelihood of such relationships upon flimsy or non-existent evidence, the most germane issue remains that of credibility – specifically, of Frobisher's personal credibility. We have seen that by 1574 he was known to men such as Burghley, Edward Horsey (an intimate of Leicester's) and Sir Henry Radcliffe; any of whom might have provided valuable introductions to others who were known to be promoters of new, speculative ventures. However, whether these connections amounted to relationships that Frobisher could actively exploit in this manner is very doubtful. The fact that he had been employed by Burghley – and, indirectly, by the rest of the Privy Council – in a number of ambiguous schemes hardly suggests that he was trusted by them. Indeed, it might equally be argued that his very faithlessness was the quality that had recommended him to their service. It was a quality that had proved valuable in the sink of Irish subterfuges, but it was not necessarily one upon which men of high affairs would risk their money.

On balance, Best's claims – both for Frobisher's motives and his connections in the latter part of 1574 – are weak, and rely upon extremely doubtful assumptions. It is far more probable that during this period, Frobisher was willing to be exercised by any project that promised to make him 'famous and fortunate'; and that some opaque sequence of events brought him to the Cheapside home of Michael Lok in the latter months of 1574 with at most a half-formed idea, and at least the need to find that idea and exploit it. For once, however, his luck was kind. If it is the name of Martin Frobisher with which the north-west voyages of 1576–8 are indelibly associated, it was in the mind, character and preoccupations of Lok that their intellectual genesis undoubtedly lay.[14]

The association of Thomas and John Lok with the second Guinea voyage offers the possibility that Frobisher and Michael Lok had met as early as 1554, but this is unlikely.[15] Though Thomas Lok himself remained in England during the reign of Mary (where according to his half-sister Rose, 'for feare of further trouble to fashion himself outwardly to the popish religion, in some sort was so greeved in mynd thereat . . . he died shortly after, with seven of his children'),[16] Michael was travelling in Europe throughout those dangerous years.[17] By the time of his return at the accession of Elizabeth, Frobisher had probably begun his career as a privateer; an occupation which would have set him entirely at odds with the interests and livelihoods of the surviving Lok brothers. We know that both men had been in Portugal during the same approximate period in the mid-1550s, and from this it is tempting to speculate that Lok had been the anonymous Samaritan who had assisted Frobisher's passage from a Lisbon gaol to England sometime between 1556 and 1558. Seductive though this possibility seems, however, we search vainly for evidence of it. Until the early 1570s – perhaps until the year 1574 itself – it is more likely that the two men were strangers; that Frobisher approached Lok as someone with whom he had mutual connections, rather than as an active acquaintance.

Lok's own prior interest in cosmography, cartography and their practical application to the furtherance of English trade are indisputable, unlike Frobisher's. By his own reckoning, he had amassed a library of relevant literature worth some £500: a huge commitment, and far in excess of that required by mere intellectual curiosity.[18] Later, when his name and purse had paid the heavy price of his association with Frobisher, Richard Hakluyt was to make much use of this material in compiling his *Divers Voyages*, in the preface of which he gave his opinion of its provider: '. . . a man for his knowledge in diuers languages & especially in Cosmographie, able to doe his country good, & worthie in my judgment for the manifold partes in him, of good reputation & better fortune.'

Lok's 'manifold partes' were the products of an unusually peripatetic career. His extraordinary expertise in languages – Spanish, French, Italian, Latin, Greek and, probably, Arabic[19] – had derived from a professional odyssey that had taken him as a boy to the Low Countries (he had served an apprenticeship there under William Lok and then, possibly, as the factor of his elder brother Thomas), and thereafter to France, Spain and Portugal – where the sight of ships unloading the wealth of the Indies upon the dockside had, by his own admission, provided the germ of his future obsession with foreign markets – to Venice, the Greek islands and, eventually, to the Levant: to the latter of which he claimed to have voyaged as captain of a great ship of 1,000 tons.[20] These travels, and the lessons they instilled, had filled the young Lok with an urgent, and possibly obsessive desire to see England's relative backwardness in the pursuit of international trade corrected. Perhaps he was presumptuous in regarding himself as capable of providing part of the cure, but he promoted his ideas tirelessly following his return to England at the accession of Elizabeth. Within a year, he and his fellow exile and brother-in-law Richard Springham had addressed a pamphlet to the Privy Council, entitled 'A note of the purpose of vs Richard springham and mighell Lok m(ar)chantt(e)s to be furder considered of Your honors/then we can brefly declare touching the making of silkes yn yngland'.[21] Its proposal was the creation of a domestic industry in both the manufacturing and finishing of silks – and, by implication, the utter undermining of his own company's decaying monopoly over their importation. From a man who had spent over half of his life to date outside England, the proposal exhibited a self-confidence bordering upon insolence; a quality that Lok was to exhibit several times in his subsequent career, and almost always at precisely the wrong moment.

Since that early pamphlet (whose recommendations, apparently, were neither answered nor acted upon by the Privy Council), Lok had penned further notes on preventing interlopers in the trade to Russia, on the benefits of a closer political alliance between Elizabeth and Ivan IV, and on the expansion of direct English trade with Persia, by which the interests of the Turks and Venetians would be undermined and those of the Portuguese spice trade in India 'utterly overthrowne'.[22] To a modern eye, the breadth of his vision suggests a certain intellectual indiscipline (and more than a little optimism), but Lok's preoccupations can be seen as a microcosm of the pressures and expectations that set out dozens of speculative voyages in search of new trades during these years, all of which were informed by a readiness to seize any number of opportunities in the hope of one success. The preface to his later account of Frobisher's 1576 voyage provided a striking rationale for this procreative urge:

> But of the matters that chiefly moved me to enterprise and avance this new voyage and to venture my Mony therein so largely: I will say briefly that three things chiefly moved me thereto. First the great hope to fy(nde) o(u)r English seas open into the Seas of East India by that way, which I con-ceved by the great likelyhood therof which I found by reading the his-tories of many mens travailes toward that parte of the world. Whereby we might have passage by Sea to those rich Cuntries for Traffik of Merchan-dize, which was the thing I chiefly desyred. Secondly, I was assured by manifolde goode proofs of dyvers Travailers & histories that the Cuntries of Baccaleaw, Canada, & the new fownd Lands thereto adioining were full of people, & full of such Commodities & Merchandize, as are in the Cuntries of Lappia, Russia, Moscovia, Permia, Pechora, Samoietza, & the Cuntries thereto adioyning. Which are Furres, Hydes, Wax, Tallow, Oyle, & other. Whereby yf yt should happen those new Lands to stretch to the North Pole, so that we could not have passage by Sea that way which we sought to the North-westward to pas into East India, yet in those same new Lands to the North-westward might be established the like Trade of

Merchandize, as is now in the other sayd Cuntries of the (world. Thirdly, it is well known) that on the Sea Coasts (that lie) to the North-westwards is (great abundan)ce of fish of many kyndes, & of wh(ales and other gre)at fisshes wherof the trane Oyle is had (& the best pl)ace for fisshing therof, that is any place (in the wor)ld, whereby would allso grow to the Realm, & (to such) followers therof great Riches & Benefit.[23]

This was the very manifest of the mind of a diligent and enterprising merchant. Clearly, despite the keenness of his intellectual interests, Lok was no idle scholar. The aspect of the world, its strangeness and novelty, interested him enormously; but only insofar as it might be turned to profit — principally, his own. Nor should his appreciation of abstract concepts disguise the fact that he was in other ways an extremely industrious man, a typical scion of the devout, hard-working Lok family. Whilst composing vastly ambitious proposals to open new markets to English merchants, his trade in merceries, though relatively modest in scale, seems to have thrived. Throughout the 1560s, he set himself assiduously to the task of building an estate, not least in the arrangements he made for his posterity. At the start of the decade, he married Jane Wilkinson, daughter of the Sheriff of London and herself of sterling Protestant pedigree — indeed, in making this match, Lok convincingly confirmed his own credentials. Jane's mother, Joan — formerly Anne Boleyn's silk seamstress — had openly visited Bishops Cranmer, Hooper, Latimer and Ridley in their Oxford gaol during the Marian persecutions, and Jane herself had been a friend both of Cranmer and Hooper.[24] In her (1556) will, Joan directed that her daughter should be disinherited if she did not marry 'a man fearing God . . . in religion of godly conversation utterly abhorring papistry': a qualification that Lok appears to have fulfilled precisely.[25]

From the start of their marriage, he and Jane bred copiously, forging a dynasty that would, if time and fortune permitted, provide a new generation of names to be entered at Mercers' Hall. During the same years, he may have continued to go abroad when necessary – he maintained contacts in Germany (probably Hamburg), Ireland and Scotland – but evidently these connections loosened as the demands of his family grew.[26] In 1571, the untimely death of Jane (due in no small part to the rigours of near continuous pregnancy, one suspects) brought a domestic crisis that required him to modify his business activities considerably. He was by now the father of eight young children, and no longer had either parents or willing siblings to act as surrogate parents whilst he was overseas.[27] It seems more than coincidence, therefore, that in the year in which Jane died, Lok accepted the post of London Agent of the Russia Company: an appointment that brought a salary and associated benefits (including rent-free housing) worth some £400 per year. Though brought about by necessity, this was hardly a retrograde step in his career. The company's London Agent has been described as 'a sort of general manager' supervising the English end of the company's business.[28] One of three principal salaried officers (in addition to the Treasurer and the Secretary), his pivotal role reflected the manner in which the Russia Company was organized. As a joint-stock entity, its London Agent acted, in effect, as the resident 'English' factor for the company, arranging the purchase of domestic wares to be traded in Muscovy and supervising the receipt of Russian cargoes in England. Many of the company's shareholders were merchants in their own right of course, and their wares were often carried in company ships (an opportunity for some incremental profit upon a sometimes shaky investment). The London Agent would have been virtuous indeed had he not allowed himself to be persuaded by his fellow company men of the excellence of their wares, whether for a small percentage of their value or a less overt but equally useful *quid pro quo* elsewhere. Discharged conscientiously (and discreetly), the role would have presented Lok with a fine opportunity to make money, keep many of London's foremost men of business obliged for his efforts, and indulge his passionate interest in the markets of far-off lands: an employment that must have seemed tailor-made for his altered circumstances. Few opportunities are entirely without potential for ill-fortune, however; and as Lok built himself a reputation in the City and rose in the regard of his professional colleagues, it was as the Russia Company's London Agent that his preoccupations and Martin Frobisher's needs began to converge.

Despite his impeccable credentials as a man of business, Lok's initial part in undermining his employers' charter rights was hardly less ambiguous than that of Frobisher. The Russia Company had failed to establish a stable and profitable trade, yet Lok was on record as firmly proclaiming the sanctity of its charter privileges – indeed, one of the principal roles of the London Agent was to formulate and implement company strategy against interlopers upon its trade.[29] Like most of his peers, he appreciated that any commercial activity unprotected by the letter of the law was at best fraught with uncertainty; at worst, an intercourse of freebooters. But the fact that he was always to believe in (and seek to operate under) legal forms did not prevent him from using all lawful means to overturn them to his own advantage. Alone, he had neither the resources nor standing within the company to attempt this; at the turn of 1574, however, with the implicit backing of several members of the Privy Council, Lok was presented with a chance to channel his obsessions into a realizable project. The moment at which he turned irrevocably from the service of his employers to that of his own ends was a discreet one, and remains obscure; but it was profoundly portentous nevertheless. His life until then had followed the track upon which he had been set by family tradition, circumstance and, probably, temperament. It had provided a gentle though discernible upward path to a station within the second-rank of London's mercantile community, and an employment that might have continued to keep the large Lok brood in an enviably comfortable estate.[30] However, the second-rank, for Lok, may have represented a personal failure, particularly in light of the illustrious example set by previous generations of his family. His father William had stood almost at the pinnacle of their community. Known as the 'King's mercer' (he was given sole rights to supply Court revels from 1527 onwards), he had received and dined Henry VIII at his Cheapside home upon at least one occasion.[31] Rising among his peers to become an alderman and then Sheriff of London in 1548, William had died at the apogee of his career. His funeral had been a civic occasion, with forty poor men of their parish preceding his coffin, followed by mourners, clerks and priests; on that day, all of Cheapside – the major London thoroughfare upon which the family's principal residence stood – had been hung with black flags carrying his coat of arms.[32] Michael's great-grandfather John Lok had been no less prominent. He, too, had been Sheriff of London, and in 1461, had ridden as one of twenty-four Notables of the City in the honour guard sent to escort the victorious Edward IV into London.[33]

With such antecedents, perhaps Michael Lok regarded his achievements by 1574 as falling short of his potential; certainly, the self-assurance evident in his written proposals and defences of trade suggests that he regarded his voice – that of a Lok – as an important one. His association with Frobisher may now have provided the means to marry unfulfilled ambition with palpable achievement – to be the mover and founder of a new trade to the East would have raised him, at a stroke, to pre-eminence amongst his peers, bringing the wealth and civic recognition that he so clearly craved. Though the respective characters of Michael Lok and Martin Frobisher were entirely antipathetic (and would prove to be so in a spectacular manner), their mutual need for a reputation – whatever its nature – transcended the oddity of their brief collaboration.

As London Agent, Lok had been one of the men appointed by the Russia Company to consider Frobisher's first approach in December 1574; and it was he, together with one of the Company's two Governors, Roland Hayward, who then informed the Privy Council of the Company's refusal to relinquish its charter rights. Lok's explanation of his subsequent, absolute conversion to Frobisher's cause is superficially plausible, but hardly more convincing than his partner's claimed obsession to find a north-west passage:

> . . . althoughe (accordinge to my dutie towardes the Company of Muscovie, knowinge the inconveniences that therby might growe unto their trade of Merchandiz) I did also dislyke of this motion for a tyme/yet afterwardes, uppon consideracion of my dutye towardes my contrye, and knowinge by myne owne knowledge (as my manifold writtinges therof wille witnes) the great benyfitte that therby might growe to the same . . . I did so enterelie joyne with him therein, that through my frindshippe with the company I obtayned of them a previledge and lycens to followe that attempt . . .[34]

Here, Lok performs an unconvincing feat of legerdemain: claiming that Frobisher had initiated the project, but thereafter portraying himself as its primary moving force. This is hardly credible. The alacrity with which he 'so enterelie' joined Frobisher – so much so that within two months of being a party to refusing the licence he was being named as co-licensee in the new venture – suggests a certain premeditation, to say the least; certainly, its timing casts serious doubts upon the implication, made both by Lok and Frobisher's contemporary biographers, that their first meeting occurred across a table at Muscovy House. Similarly, though we have no evidence of wider collusion, the immediate readiness of other members of the Company to join with Lok strongly suggests that he had begun to discuss the matter informally with them even before Frobisher came to Muscovy House for the first time.

The Russia Company's refusal to grant the licence, once stated, was swiftly shown to be untenable. Whatever their prior connection with Frobisher or Lok, the Privy Councillors who were to participate in the north-west enterprise were avid promoters of new reconnaissances, and impatient with protectionist obstacles (other, of course, than those that were conceived for the direct benefit of the Exchequer). Once such men as these had become enthused by the possibilities of the new scheme, its implementation in some form was inevitable. There was probably no active conspiracy, but what appeared to be a privateer's presumptuous and unsolicited proposal was in reality the most transparent step in a contrived process to secure the licence that Humphrey Gilbert had failed to obtain.

When Lok ceases to be coy, his claims regarding his role during the early stages of the new project are convincing, unlike those made on Frobisher's behalf. He was a respected officer of one of the City's most active new companies, and had many valuable connections within the wider mercantile community. Frobisher, in contrast, was an unemployed privateer in dire financial straits. At the time he approached Lok, he was living in cheap lodgings in Fleet Street (it is not known whether his wife Isobel was with him there). He seems to have been evicted soon after, and Lok was obliged to find and pay for new lodgings, at one Mrs Hancockes's house in Mark Lane.[35] Much later, when Frobisher allowed this early charity to slip his memory, his one-time benefactor was not minded to do likewise:

And hereuppon I used M(aster) Furbusher as my fellow and frinde, and opened vnto him all myne owne private studies and labores passed in twenty yeares continuans befor, for knowledge of the state of the worlde, and shewed him all my bookes, cartes, mappes, instrument(e)s, so many as cost me vc poundes of mony, and writtinges, and my nottes collected therof. And dalye instructid him therin to my skyll, and lent him the same to his owne lodginge at his will for his better defence in talke thereof w(i)th other men. And to be short, dalye increased my good will towardes him, makinge my howse his howse and my purse his purse at his neede, and my credite to his credite to my powre, when he was vtterlye destitute boath of mony and credite and of frindes . . .[36]

Allowing for his slightly injured hyperbole, Lok's recollections are plausible. If Frobisher's reputation and fortunes were at a low point in late 1574, his credit – moral or financial – could hardly have been much higher. Lok's contribution to the project must therefore have constituted more than the frequent loosening of his purse strings. Being entirely speculative, it required an expression of confidence to attract further interest. The confidence of a penniless adventurer – however expressed – counted for little. The balance of probability suggests that it was Frobisher's partner who provided the weight of opinion, arguments and resources in securing financial backing for the enterprise, notwithstanding Best's claims to the contrary.[37]

In fact, Lok himself contradicted Best in some detail:

. . . whereuppon to begine the matter I made a writtinge dated the 9 of Februarie 1574 (1575), for the venturars to sett downe their some of monye w(i)th their owne handes, and for the better incorraginge of others I first sett doune my selfe for one hundreth poundes, whereuppon divers others followid in the cittie to the some of v^cli, and afterwards M. Furbusher carried that in writtinge to the court (for befor that tyme no handes would be hade there) . . .[38]

As the man whose enthusiasm for, and investment in, the enterprise would eclipse that of any other investor (the Queen excepted), Lok hardly overstates his commitment. His immediate willingness to venture the equivalent of six months' salary in the project was undoubtedly a timely example; having made it, his first recourse thereafter was to those with whom he had already discussed the possibility of the new project – his associates in the Russia Company. The extent of the canker within that body was made immediately apparent when he secured the participation of one of the Company's two Governors, Lionel Duckett; an original charter member, William Bonde; the Company's former Ambassador to the Russian Court, Thomas Randolphe; and Anthony Jenkinson, the outstanding Anglo-Russian trader of the sixteenth century and, formerly, a principal propagandist for the north-eastern route – ironically, the very man whose arguments had told so decisively against those of Humphrey Gilbert.[39]

Despite having secured these august recruits to his cause, Lok's industry and powers of persuasion were not entirely sufficient. His contacts within the Russia Company were soon exploited to the full, but their investment – and that secured from those members of the Privy Council who were not also Muscovy men – was not nearly enough to set out a voyage. In the meantime, however, he had also turned to his connections in the Mercers' Company.[40] Two leading mercers – William Burde (then Customer of London) and Thomas Gresham – agreed to invest in the new venture, with major shares of £100 each: double that of the most enthusiastic Privy Councillors. Both men had long-standing commercial ties with the Lok family as co-shippers of goods to Chios and Zante in the eastern Mediterranean. Two 'lesser' investors, Matthew Field and Edmund Hogan, ventured £25 each; both men were mercers, but also, respectively, Lok's brother-in-law and occasional partner in business.[41]

With the considerable moral (but financially modest) backing of Burghley, Warwick, Leicester, Sussex and Walsingham, the number of would-be investors who set down their names in 1575 was just eighteen, with a total ventured stock of £875.[42] By any measure this was a disappointing effort, but in view of the underlying intentions of the promoters – particularly those of Lok and his Russia Company colleagues – it was also a predictable one. In contrast to the early Barbary and Guinea voyages, wherein a small number of merchants utilized their own ships and merchandise with the aim of real-izing a quick profit, the new scheme's objectives were less immediate. It was, in the manner of the first Muscovy voyages before it, an attempt to establish a new trade, not one that would interlope upon existing commercial activity (whose benefits, by definition, were either known already or strongly sus-pected). The disadvantage of such a far-sighted goal was that it was both extremely speculative and unlikely to generate quick returns: a disincentive that the Russia Company's experience had highlighted only too clearly. Most men of business, then as now, preferred to put their capital where the risk was smallest – and certainly, where it was calculable. The obvious exposures inherent in testing this new scheme proved decisive. For all of Lok's efforts to interest his associates in the City, he was unable to widen the base of investment in the enterprise by even a single investor. The season in which the voyage should have been despatched came and went; and, reluctantly, Lok and Frobisher accepted that their project would be postponed for that year.

Such enthusiasm as had been exhibited by those who had promised funds for the proposed 1575 voyage (and would do so again in the following year) was to some extent a corollary of their relatively substantial worth. Members of the Privy Council, and merchants such as Gresham, Burde and Bonde, were willing to risk sums which represented little in the balance of their total wealth, because the potential rewards – however long-term – might be deci-sive. If a new trade were established, they would have bought a preferential position at its heart; if the venture failed, they could afford to shrug off the losses – it was important above all that the opportunity or risk be covered. For men whose circumstances fell short of outright wealth, such a venture was fraught with possibilities of the worst sort, and they treated it accord-ingly. Only Lok, a man who was already beginning to part with the acumen that had sustained him in business, would be prepared to commit the larger part of his own resources to see its goals realized.

This general sense of reservation did not ease as the enterprise progressed. In 1577 and 1578 there were to be other individuals who would allow enthu-siasm to override prudence when the seemingly limitless promise of new gold-mines was laid before them; but this was to remain a relatively discreet phenomenon. Even with the lure of a seemingly inexhaustible vein of New

World wealth in prospect, a grand total of just sixty investors was to be secured (of whom fourteen were from Lok's immediate family). When funds – or rather, their shortfall – became a serious problem from mid-1577, further attempts to widen the base of investment, even with the authority of the Queen herself underwriting them, were to be entirely unsuccessful.[43]

For lack of ready money, therefore, the 1575 voyage was not set out, though it seems that as late as 15 July it was still considered viable (on that day Elizabeth licensed Frobisher to depart out of the realm).[44] However, there had been a further problem, which Lok was only too happy to recall:

> . . . but now the greatest matter remayned still in doubt, and not satisfied amongest the venturares, w(hi)ch was who should take charge of conducte and commaundement of the shipps being alreadie at the see; for that M(aster) Furbusher had verie littell credite at home and muche lesse to be credited w(i)th the shippes abroad: this matter was the cause of the over-throw of the voyage . . .[45]

By 1575, Frobisher's reputation was one of almost unremitting black-guardry, principally directed against men who set their goods to sea in ships – men such as Duckett, Randolphe, Bonde, Burde and Gresham, whose purses he had now opened by more legitimate means. It is hardly surprising that they had reservations concerning the choice of sea-commander for the project, notwithstanding his claims for having conceived it. The prospect of Frobisher simply disappearing over the horizon with their money may not have been considered a serious risk (though not entirely beyond the bounds of possibility), but his qualifications for discovering the north-west passage were, as we have seen, almost non-existent. Their investment required some surety – not against loss (which was a legitimate and half-expected risk in such ventures), but against bad faith, or incompetence. In the following year, when the enterprise was resurrected, Lok desperately sought to provide such reassurance: firstly by offering his own credit on Frobisher's behalf, and then in drawing up a commission to commit Frobisher to consulting his officers upon all major decisions whilst at sea. What Frobisher himself thought of such an intended curb to his authority has not been recorded; but as we shall see, his resistance to the concept of taking good counsel (however notional) upon other occasions makes it clear that this commission could only be a sop to the more nervous investors. Nevertheless, the fact that Lok needed to devote his precious time to such diversions during the business of setting out the voyage is perhaps the most obvious evidence of Frobisher's lack of credibility in 1575. The issue was embarrassing, and could hardly have improved his opinion of merchants, but having worked so industriously for more than a decade to acquire a reputation that was anything but ambiguous, he had little right to expect more.

EIGHT

The 1576 Voyage

Having tried and failed to raise sufficient funds to set out an Atlantic voyage in 1575, Lok returned for the moment to his Russia Company chores (he seems to have retained his position as London Agent until at least mid-1576); principally to oversee the purchase of Manchester cottons, paper, wine-sack, flax, cotton-wool, lead, pewter, tin and brazil wood that constituted the cargoes of the fleet of six company ships which sailed for Muscovy early in May 1576.[1] Frobisher's activities during these months are obscure; there is no record of his being at sea, but this may suggest only the worst, given the nature of his habitual employment (he was certainly at his old pastime of inviting potentially fatal associations, with the Spanish spy Antonio de Guaras waxing enthusiastically about his capacity for double-dealing).[2] Prospects for his further, legitimate employment appear to have been conspicuously absent.

Nevertheless, to have come so close, and in such exalted company, to realizing the most promising opportunity of his life to date must have kept his appetite for the north-west project alive. We do not know if he had already abandoned Isobel Frobisher by 1575 (certainly, there is no reference to her in Lok's recollections of the period), but the continuing spectre of penury, even a penury uncomplicated by family obligations, would have given a sharp edge to that ambition. Furthermore, in Michael Lok he had found a partner whose eagerness to see the project realized completely overshadowed the pain of any short-term discouragements. Accordingly, in the early months of 1576, they renewed their collaboration (if it had ever abated) and approached their prospective investors from the previous year. All pronounced themselves willing to proceed on the basis of their previously stated commitments, save for the outstanding matter of Frobisher's credit and credibility; but one of their number – Lord Burghley – attached certain strings to his participation. The £50 he had promised from his own pocket undoubtedly sharpened his attention, and he now personally intervened to improve the administrative arrangements:

> Now, in proceedinge to the preparacion of the voyage questions grewe amongst the venturars, according to the noate of condicion sett downe by my Lord Treasorer, who should take charge of the mony to be collected of the venturares, and who for the provicion and furniture of the shippes, and who in the conducte of the voyage with the shippes at sea . . .[3]

The last matter was certainly one that needed to be addressed, but otherwise Burghley's intervention seems surprising. That he should think a note of condition necessary hints at problems that must have been evident in the previous year; perhaps these had less to do with money or reputation than the gap between intention and ability that informed the efforts of the project's principal promoters. Though both Frobisher and Lok were enthusiastically committed to the project, neither seems to have had any appreciable experience of the mechanics of setting out a long-range voyage. Lok's role as London Agent of the Russia Company gave him the principal responsibility for supplying trade goods for the northern voyages, but not for outfitting the ships themselves. Frobisher, though a sea-captain of long experience, had largely relied upon other men to provide his vessels. The one occasion upon which we know him to have had a hand in the mundane detail of preparations for a voyage – that of the *Mary Flower* – had been an unmitigated disaster, logistically. More experienced hands were needed for this new venture, and were seen to be so by the shrewd Burghley.

According to Lok's testimony, the Lord Treasurer directed that responsibility for the various matters should be apportioned between the adventurers and certain others, mainly Muscovy men, who were long used to the business of setting out voyages across distant seas. Particularly busy in this respect was William Borough. A long-time Muscovy mariner (he had sailed in the *Edward Bonaventure* in the first, 1553, Muscovy voyage) and tutor of other mariners, drafter of the earliest known chart to provide for the depiction of magnetic variation and future author of a learned treatise on magnetic variation of the compass, Borough now took on the task of hiring ships' crews and advising upon the prospective course the expedition should follow.[4]

The purchase of equipment and liaison with its suppliers was principally Lok's task; his friend and fellow-adventurer Edmund Hogan initially took responsibility for attracting additional investors, until his signal lack of success inclined Lok to delve deeper into his own pocket. This ill-judged generosity seems gradually to have encouraged the convergence of responsibilities that Burghley had sought to prevent. In particular, the role of treasurer of the adventurers' monies seemed tailor-made for an accomplished accountant who had put up more than half the funds to set out the voyage. Even so, it seems that Lok had higher corporate ambitions than this. As late as 1577, in a petition he drafted to request the incorporation of a 'Company of Cathay' (allocating to himself its governorship), one of his articles provided 'Thatt Edmond hogan shalbe Tresourror for iij yeres'.[5] By that time, however, Hogan was about to move on to Morocco, to take up residence as the Queen's envoy there.[6] For better or worse – in Lok's case, much the worse – it was he who was to have the predominant stewardship of the finances of the enterprise throughout most of its brief and turbulent life.

Once the 1575 adventurers had re-pledged their money, active preparations for the voyage commenced. Meeting alternately at the houses of the two Williams, Burde and Bonde, the men charged with its organization made their plans. We have seen that other, ostensibly similar expeditions had been set out to open up new trades, but much of the detail of their character and composition has necessarily been a matter of speculation. However, for this new voyage and its two successors, it is possible for the first time to recall the smallest detail of their preparation – their financing and outfitting, the provision of every loaf of bread, plank, nail and scrap of canvas – due to the survival of the account books of the enterprise.[7] These were compiled principally by Lok himself, and remained in existence following the collapse of the enterprise only because their author required them as evidence during his long journey through the London courts and prisons to which their entries eventually consigned him. What was to be Lok's misfortune is our incalculable gain, however. In the pedantic detail of every purchase made by the busy treasurer and his agents, they provide an open window into the minds and motives of the men who set out the early English voyages of reconnaissance.

The first matter in the adventurers' order of business concerned old debts. In the previous year, armed with his new licence from the Muscovy Company, Lok had approached Matthew Baker, shipwright at the Queen's yards at Chatham and one of the foremost ship designers of the era, to commission from him a vessel of unknown size.[8] With the collapse of hopes for a voyage during 1575, the arrangement had been terminated. The adventurers had paid £5 for release of the bargain, and a further £5 to discharge one John Cockes, who had been hired as the prospective master of the unbuilt ship. Now, once more, Lok went to Baker to commission a new vessel, the *Gabriel*, a bark of 25 to 30 tons, with a pinnace of 7 tons (the latter to be used as a fishing boat to supplement the ships' victuals *en route* and as an inshore vessel). Another bark, the *Michael*, of approximately the same tonnage as the *Gabriel*, was purchased from two of the lesser adventurers, Christopher Andrews and Robert Martin.[9]

What sort of ships were these, that were intended to pass through an unknown, almost certainly inhospitable passage into the Pacific, sail on to Cathay and return home thereafter via the same strait? During the sixteenth century, the term 'bark' was applied more loosely than in later years; but usually it denoted a smaller vessel than the multi-decked galleons and carracks that shared an ostensibly similar rigging arrangement. Generally, barks were three-masted vessels, square-rigged on the fore and main masts, and fore-and-aft rigged on the mizzen mast. There was also, typically, a small, square sprit sail on a yard beneath the bowsprit. A bark could be anything from 20 to 120 tons (the bark *Denys*, which sailed with Frobisher's 1578 voyage, was listed at 100 tons), so it is clear that the *Gabriel* and *Michael* were particularly small examples of the type – smaller, probably, than many of the nondescript coastal craft that carried England's domestic port trade around her shores. Their precise dimensions are not known, but comparative analysis of contemporary vessels of equivalent tonnage suggests that their keels were no more than 42 ft in length, with beams of some 12 ft, and holds little more than 6 ft in depth.[10] Each had a single deck, with a low-charged midship that shipped water very easily in high seas, but which also allowed the use of oars in addition to sails, thus increasing their ability to manoeuvre in calm or sheltered waters.[11] The *Gabriel* also had a cabin constructed specifically for the coming voyage, probably for the use of Frobisher alone. To furnish the cabin, and ensure that their admiral did not go sleepless upon his epic navigation, the adventurers paid almost £4 to the aptly named Richard Ducke 'for beddinge'. The other mariners were to sleep, when circumstances allowed, in the low hold. In such conditions, their mode of living might politely be described as communal, but more accurately as appalling.

Inevitably, constraints of financing had determined the provision of such small ships. Not only were they cheaper to buy or build, but they required less men to work them; their loss, for the same reasons, would be markedly easier to bear than that of larger ships such as the *Lion*, whose abandonment in the Benin estuary twenty-two years earlier had so discommoded the backers of the first Guinea voyage. Nevertheless, there were obvious disadvantages to such economies of scale. The prospect of making an indeterminably protracted oceanic voyage with such modest living and storage space would have been daunting, even to highly experienced mariners; a disincentive that must have made recruitment of the best of their breed very difficult. To put the size of these vessels (and the relative comfort enjoyed by the men who would sail in them) into perspective, it may be recalled that Drake's flagship during his 1577–80 circumnavigation, the *Golden Hind* (formerly *Pelican*), whose reconstructed dimensions seem impossibly tiny to the modern eye, was of a relatively massive 160 tons.[12]

However, despite the tightness of the adventurers' corporate purse, it is evident that considerable care was devoted to outfitting the vessels. The *Gabriel, Michael* and pinnace cost £235 16sh. 8d. to build or acquire; but with their comprehensive refitting, including interior ceiling planks for the cabin, iron nails, bolts and spikes (rather than the more usual wooden varieties which were, ironically, less damaging to their mountings in the longer term), and brimstoning of their hulls, total monies spent on the fabric of the barks came to almost £450, or more than fifty per cent of the official stock in the voyage. Like Jason before him, Frobisher was expected to pass into the mythical East by economical means; but in his case it was intended that he should return safely.

In fact, the Argonauts of legend had been relatively numerous in comparison to these new voyagers. Frobisher's entire complement was intended to consist of just thirty-five men, including himself. The command structure was to comprise himself and two masters, Christopher Hall and Owen Griffin. A once and future Russia Company pilot, Hall was clearly the more experienced man; a native of Limehouse, that long-time reservoir of seafarers, he was hired – probably at the recommendation of William Borough – upon relatively high wages of £6 13sh. 4d. per month, 'as promised upon good successe of the discouerye' (an early example of the cash on delivery principle).[13] These three officers, with two gunners, a surgeon, a trumpeter, two cooks (one of them a cooper also), a purser (Nicholas Chancellor, son of the famous Muscovy navigator, Richard), a smith, three carpenters and twenty-one common mariners, were to pass to regions unseen by European eyes since the last of the Norse settlements had disappeared silently a century previously (at least two of these men were second choices; one of the original mariners, Simon Pearson, and, more seriously, the expedition's prospective tailor, Thomas More, had the wit to follow their better instincts;

Lok records an advance upon wages paid to them, but noted of each: 'he is rone away w(i)th the mony').[14] Again, like their predecessors at ancient Iolcus, this heroic but tiny complement was taken down to the water's edge – to Ratcliffe on the River Thames, east of London – and dined upon the occasion of the launching of the *Gabriel*. Their feast, of bread and small beer, lightened the adventurers' corporate purse by a further 19sh. There, perhaps, their new ship had her dragon's head mounted upon her prow; a mythical beast to guard her charges through the dangers of the near-mythical lands to which they were bound.[15]

Though the adventurers had no sound prior intelligence regarding their intended destination, they expected the coming voyage to be arduous. It was estimated that the round trip would be of some eighteen months' duration – much longer than any English voyage to date. Some hard-won practical experience was already available to the adventurers, however. The victualling lists for the *Gabriel* and *Michael* reveal that lessons had been drawn from the Muscovy voyages, particularly with regard to the debilitating effects of Arctic temperatures upon men's power of endurance.[16] Modern analysis of the lists for the second (1577) voyage has shown that each mariner's rations, ostensibly, provided him with between 5,500 and 7,000 calories daily.[17] There were to be four 'meat' days per week (of beef and, when this was consumed or spoiled, of bacon), and three of fish – principally salt cod, ling and haberdine (sun-dried cod); whilst further sources of protein (though of course it was not yet known as such) were provided by Suffolk cheeses. A large fishing net was also purchased to allow the men of the pinnace to supply their comrades with fresher produce *en route* to Cathay.

The standard, or rather, the only vegetable supplement to these staples was the humble pea, of which fully 40 bushels were laded, giving each man a weekly allowance of about 4½ lbs (other vegetable staples of the period, such as turnips and onions, rotted quickly in ships' holds). We know now that peas are a valuable source of vitamin C; but the recent discovery of large quantities thereof in trenches on Kodlunarn Island in Frobisher Bay, suggests that boiled cabbage syndrome may have overcome Frobisher's mariners several centuries before English public schoolboys gave the affliction a name. The mariners' other staple was ship's biscuit, of which 76 hundredweight was supplied, supplemented by 36 bushels of wheat to make fresh bread (a 'great basone of brasse' was purchased to allow it to be baked in the ships without need for proper ovens). Rice and oatmeal – usually only provided in small amounts for the sick, but in this case amounting to 13 hundredweight and 12 bushels respectively – were also provided for the common mariners' occasional consumption. Flavouring agents – the only common additives of the age – were vinegar, mustard seed and (a far less usual provision) a pipe of sweet oil.[18]

In an era prior to the distillation of rum, the bane and sustainer of the mariner was beer; 13 tons (of 240 gallons each) were purchased, including 5 tons from the Queen's stores, supplied by Frobisher's old acquaintance, the Earl of Lincoln, her Lord Admiral.[19] Three hogsheads (of 64 gallons' capacity) of aquavite – 'strong water' or spirits, distilled from one or more of a variety of ingredients – were acquired for consumption by Frobisher and his masters. Unusually, the adventurers also provided 5 tons of good wine-sack, purchased from William Bonde for the astonishingly high – and probably inflated – price of £100 (the shrewd Bonde thereby partially insuring his investment against loss even before the voyage sailed). Too great a quantity for the three 'officers' of the expedition – even for a voyage of eighteen months' duration – it was nevertheless almost unheard of that such an expensive product should be supplied for the use of common mariners. Yet clearly, not all of this was intended for trade, as almost a full ton had been consumed by the end of a voyage which, in the event, was to last less than four months. Perhaps the wine's provision was not intended as a mere luxury, nor even a way of keeping Bonde in the enterprise. Though as expensive as the *Gabriel* herself, its consumption would have much reduced the risk of acute enteritis: one of the most common ailments to afflict sixteenth-century mariners; contracted, usually, by drinking spoiled beer. Over twenty years earlier, in the Bight of Benin, Frobisher had seen the catastrophic effects of an unknown chronic illness upon English ships' crews, thousands of miles from home. With a complement of only thirty-five men in two ships, in seas potentially far further from England even than western Africa, he would have been happy to spend other men's money to avert such an experience.

What was missing from these victualling lists? With only air-drying, smoking and salting techniques to preserve food, fresh fruit and vegetables were an inconceivable luxury, even had their nutritional value been fully understood. Scurvy had been identified and named already, but its prevention and cure were not remotely in hand (though it has been suggested that the provision of 100 gallons of 'sallote oil' for the 1577 voyage indicates that the adventurers were seeking to ameliorate its worst effects). For this and most other deficiency related ailments, prayer and the doubtful science of the surgeon remained the mariners' only recourse. Nor was the total implied calorific value of their victuals necessarily over-generous. Much of what was taken was expected to spoil *en route*; and even had it not done so, the conditions which the mariners were to experience would drain their reserves of strength, notwithstanding the quantity of food available.[20] Even with such care and attention as the adventurers were qualified to give, the evidence of this and the later north-west voyages suggests that the ships' surgeons would more than earn their modest wages.

The surgeon of the *Gabriel* in 1576 was Philip Bocket (or Boquet), a Frenchman. The adventurers provided him with a surgeon's chest, purchased for £2 13sh. 4d. In addition, a grocer, Edward Elmore, supplied a variety of 'drugs', the nature and supposed efficacy of which indicate what was expected to afflict the mariners. Among habitual surgeon's aids such as camphor, turpentine, borax and castor oil were more doubtful palliatives: oppoponax, which '. . . purgeth thick flegm from the most remore parts of the body . . .'; rhubarb, 'it gently purgeth Choller from the stomach and liver, opens stoppings, withstands the Dropsie, Hypocondriack Melancholly . . .'; spica nardi, '. . . helps windiness of the Stomach and dries up Rhewms that molest the head; corralina, '. . . good for hot gouts, inflamations; also they say it kills worms . . .'; and calam aromatica, '. . . provokes the Urine, strengthens the lungues, helps bruises, resists poyson . . .'.[21] Other preparations included violent purgatives ('coloehuthis' or colocynthus, aloes and a milder laxative, myrobalani chebuli), diarrhoea relief (boli orientali), expectorants (ladderi) and – perhaps a lesson drawn from recent Spanish experiences – mercury ointment (araenti viva or argentum vivum); used, usually, to treat venereal diseases. Small quantities of prunes, raisins, currants, almonds, dates, liquorice, and sweet spices such as nutmeg, ginger and cinnamon were provided to assist the convalescence of anyone who survived the above afflictions, whilst the only relief from the often fatal malady of tooth decay – short of the dreadful promise of the surgeon's strong arm – lay in $\frac{1}{2}$ lb of cloves for which master Elmore charged 4sh. 4d. Finally, the more mundane but equally painful occupational hazards of shipboard life were anticipated. At least some of the eight dozen 'cruell gerdles' acquired for the voyage would have been withheld from trade to alleviate the pain of hernias, the most common muscular complaint of the seaman; whilst a different sort of relief – no doubt intended for Frobisher alone – was provided by the purchase of a single 'chamber pysse pote'.[22]

No voyage into unknown parts ever went entirely unarmed, but this was not an absolute priority of the 1576 adventurers. To defend against the incalculable dangers of the intended navigation, the expedition was provided with just five falconets – light, one-and-a-half-pound shot-firing ordnance, useful for clearing an enemy's deck but incapable of damaging a ship's fabric – and a selection of personal arms: calivers, a long fire-lock musket, pikes, bows and arrows, three rapiers and three daggers.[23] A final line of defence was provided by a large English Bible: possibly ineffectual against a concerted assault but at just £1 a relatively economical resource.

Clearly, given the type and level of armament, the expedition was neither expected nor intended to encounter Spanish or Portuguese ships that otherwise might have defended the perceived rights of their nations by sending the English barks to the sea-bed. The latitude in which the passage was expected to lie – at, or above, 60°N – was far from the known Atlantic possessions of the great sea-borne empires; however, once through that passage and into the Pacific Ocean (the *Mar de Sur*, as Lok referred to it), the situation was complicated by the absolute ignorance of the English voyagers and their backers.[24] They had no idea in which latitudes the countries lay that the expedition would visit, nor to which of these the Spanish or Portuguese empires might lay claim as their own spheres of economic interest. Should some hostile contact have been made in those waters, a timely and convincing display of disorientation would, it seems, have constituted the Englishmen's only realistic response. Unlike Drake, whose vessels' armament would be more than capable of supporting his private war against Spanish possessions, Frobisher was expected to proceed with the utmost circumspection.

That caution reflected the central aim of the 1576 expedition. Frobisher's biographers claimed that he had long dreamed of finding a north-west passage to Cathay. The voyage that was now to be set out might well realize this obsession, but not as an end in itself. He had been obliged to enlist the assistance and backing of merchants, and it was to be they and several of the Queen's Privy Councillors (most of whom were avid commercial speculators as well as the principal officers of state) who established the priorities of the expedition. Finding a north-west passage was a worthy aim in itself, but not of any intrinsic interest to canny investors if nothing was then 'done' with it: the age in which men set out to discover the unknown from purely scientific or cultural curiosity lay long in the future. Once through his passage and in the shadowy realm of Cathay, Frobisher was intended – whatever *he* intended – to initiate a commercial relationship with the competent authorities there, as the forefathers of the Russia Company had done some twenty years previously with the Tsar's agents at Archangel.

To do this, he needed tradeable commodities. In addition to the victuals, ordnance and other accoutrements of a long-range reconnaissance, the expedition carried what amounted to a miniature trade-fair of English manufactured goods. Hampshire kerseys, Devonshire friezes, bays, linens, ribbons, silk

ribbons, laces, cloths of gold, velvets, taffetas, satins, damasks, tufted mocad-
owes, lockeromes, hunscotts, fustians and sarsenets, children's straw hats, dog
collars, looking-glasses, silk purses, spectacles, 'London shears' for women's
hair, gold and silver rings, counterfeit pearls, diamonds, rubies and emeralds
(these latter items were intended either for the cozening of naive foreign customers or, possibly, to indicate the nature of what the Englishmen sought in
return): a cornucopia of the nation's commerceries, purchased from London
mercers, staplers and haberdashers, to a total value of £213 5sh. 8d. Even the
Russia Company, wounded by the loss of its former exclusive rights over the
north-west passage, somehow found the stomach to deal with the adventurers. Broadcloths to a value of almost £25 were supplied from the store-
rooms of Muscovy House – mainly manchesters and suffolks, 'redye dressed
and tilleted'.[25]

The most cursory examination of this manifest reveals that these goods
were not laden in quantities sufficient to realize a profit (unless those with
whom they hoped to trade proved so obliging as to buy up everything at more
than seven times the cost price). Even before the despatch of the expedition,
therefore, the adventurers must have been reconciled to foregoing the quick
returns that had blessed the early Guinea voyages. Again, these foreshortened
expectations had been determined in part by a simple lack of funds, but also
by the anticipation that trade with the East might not be a straightforward
prospect. With what little money was available, the merchandise seems to
have been acquired, not to trade *per se*, but as a selection of samples to establish what might be traded. In contrast to England's later reputation as the
workshop of the world, it was generally believed during the sixteenth century
that many – perhaps most – English manufactured goods were inferior to
those of foreign lands, particularly to those of the little known but awe-
inspiring Orient. It was probably the adventurers' principal intention to identify the optimum profitable cargo for a second voyage, should the barks reach
their goal in 1576 (surprisingly, quantities of one of the few, non-textile
English manufactured items that previously had sold well in Muscovy – the
humble copper kettle – were not purchased for the voyage, though Lok
himself, as London Agent, was almost concurrently involved in buying them
for the Russia Company).[26] Thus, a strategy had emerged from necessity; one
which, other than in its relative lack of sophistication, was not very different
from that of the modern trade mission.

And this enterprise, it is clear, was to be a purely mercantile venture. The
identity of the principal investors, the quality of the ships' outfitting and the
care taken in the mariners' provision all indicate that the expedition was

fundamentally different to the sort of surreptitious, *ad hoc* arrangements – occasional royal service apart – under which Frobisher had put to sea in previous years. How he felt about this is hard to say. He was not a merchant, nor informed by mercantile preoccupations; indeed, it is probable that by 1576 his dislike and distrust of men of business had become instinctive. Having robbed them for years, it was hardly to be hoped that he would show more regard for their priorities than their property rights. It was equally to be expected that they, in turn, should have expressed reservations concerning his fitness for this venture. Their efforts in 1575 to prevent Frobisher from having the sole command of the expedition must have rankled, no matter what the justice of their case; yet the roots of this incompatibility went far deeper than perceived slights and offences. Merchants existed by rules and precedents that were not only antipathetic to Frobisher's ambitions but directly obstructive. As a young man, he had tried, very briefly, to conform to their version of the world. It had not been a happy experiment. Since that time, his career had progressed along paths entirely distinct from the new, speculative ventures that had begun to expand English commercial activities beyond their traditional bounds. This had been largely a matter of circumstance, but of temperament also. He was probably fearless, over-endowed with energies that most men possessed in very small, discreet quantities, and he was almost certainly an inspirational leader to the common mariner; but he had also long been a parasite upon the industry of other men, serving his 'owne turne' and no other. He was not a particularly violent or reprehensible example of the species; merely a stereotypical, small-time sea-rover whose activities were spasmodically useful to the Crown but more often a niggling canker upon the lawful intercourse of nations. Now, with the north-west passage project, Frobisher had the opportunity to forge a new career; one that might well provide a corrective to the earlier disappointments. To achieve his new goals, however, he needed the backing of the very men whose company and priorities he had long spurned. In years to come, men such as they would better appreciate the qualities that Frobisher and his kind could offer against the spectre of an advancing Counter-Reformation. For the moment, however, they remained far from the sanguinary impulses that were eventually, under the shadow of war, to lead many of them to set out their own privateering voyages. In 1575, Frobisher – if he wanted their backing – was bound to *their* business: not one of picking a fortune from merchants' pockets, but of selling their kerseys, tuffed taffetas and children's straw hats to as yet unknown races.

This is not to infer that he had entirely surrendered to the bitter truth of the world and his place within it. The very lack of any definition to his ambitions meant that they might, given the opportunity, be realized in any number of ways. It was opportunity itself, above all, that he needed. The man who discovered a new passage to the East, who established a trade that would rival those of the Spanish and Portuguese empires, would have riches and glory enough – even if the means by which they were secured seemed inglorious. For the moment, therefore, this new liaison between instinctive enemies was an entirely constructive one. Sixteenth-century English merchants who required new markets to be opened in regions unvisited by Europeans did not have a large pool of talent from which to employ a sea-commander. One who possessed the will to attempt it had qualifications enough, even if his other qualities were best overlooked. With Michael Lok's generous under-writing of the official stock, the adventurers of 1576 held their strong reservations in check, and for a while this unnatural collaboration appeared to function well. It was only when success evaded the enterprise that the con-tradiction between Frobisher's priorities and those he had allowed himself to serve became insupportable. And by that time, the north-west adventurers had many other matters to distract them.

Experience gained in the Muscovy voyages of the previous twenty years had shown that the optimum time to set out a northern voyage from England fell during spring (Russia Company ships usually departed from Gravesend in the first two weeks of May).[27] There were a number of delays in the prepa-rations for the new voyage, however, and these were almost certainly caused by the adventurers' shortage of funds. With much greater moral courage than common sense, Michael Lok loaned half the monies required to set out the expedition, but he may not have been able to lay his hands on the cash imme-diately: almost £550 was no small sum to find, particularly from the purse of a man with eight children (none of whom was yet old enough to be other than a burden upon the family's finances).[28]

May, the preferred month of departure, came and went; it was only on 7 June that the tiny fleet raised anchor at Ratcliffe, where final supplies for the expedition had been laden. Portentously, the new pinnace – her handling perhaps unfamiliar to her crew of four – collided with another ship near Dept-ford, some two or three miles into her epic voyage, and had to be laid up at Greenwich that afternoon for repairs to her bowsprit and foremast. From a window of her palace of Placentia overlooking the river there, the Queen herself – perhaps reminded of their purpose by one of her courtiers – waved in the direction of the anchored barks, and sent an anonymous member of her guard to summon Frobisher to visit her the next morning and take his leave. Their interview was not recorded for posterity, though Christopher Hall reported that the gentleman told the ships' companies of her 'good liking of our doinges, and thanked vs for it'.[29] She also gave Frobisher letters of favour in Latin and Greek, recommending him and his expedition to princes of countries he would visit – presumably to reassure their prospective hosts that if they were dealing with interlopers, their efforts were at least officially sanctioned. Her gracious support was, of course, of a moral nature only. Having given her blessing, she had the adventurers charged for the expense of drafting, translating and carrying her letters to the *Gabriel*, and also for 'Lynininge the said ij letter(e)s of favour and to a paynter for culleringe the quenes M(aies)ties pictures therein'. The adventurers were even obliged to pay, it seems, for taking up the valuable time of her gentleman-messenger.[30]

By 12 June, the ships were anchored off Gravesend Castle. The Russia Company's fleet had marked its own point of departure from that mooring some three weeks earlier; Christopher Hall (who but for his present employment might have been sailing in that other voyage) now observed his latitude at the anchorage to be 51° and 33', and the variation of his compass at $11^{1}/_{2}$ degrees. All such prudent formalities being discharged, the *Gabriel*, *Michael* and their small pinnace departed from the mouth of the Thames that afternoon.

The strategy of the adventurers in setting out the voyage has been discussed, but in the absence of any known written instructions, the tactics, it seems, were to be Frobisher's. In the six weeks prior to leaving England, both he and Hall had received tuition in the theoretical techniques of oceanic navigation from the noted mathematician, astrologer and cosmographer, John Dee; who, apparently, had been introduced to the enterprise by Lok.[31] Dee's qualifications for this task were beyond doubt; he had provided much the same service for Richard Chancellor prior to the despatch of the 1553 north-eastern voyage, and subsequently he had tutored most of the Russia Company's apprentice masters. He was, probably, England's foremost theorist in the cosmographical arts, though the practical value of his tuition to the 1576 voyagers is difficult to assess precisely. To assist him in his new task, instruments and literature had been provided by the adventurers; yet there was only so much that his new pupils could have absorbed in such a short time (particularly Frobisher, whose former experience of oceanic navigation was negligible), and, as we shall see, the new voyagers were to experience conditions for which little data yet existed. On 26 June, Frobisher was to write to Dee from the Shetlands, expressing his and Hall's gratitude for

Dee's 'frendly Instructions: which when we use we do remember you'; but he would conclude with the unusually frank observation that they were his 'poor disciples, not able to be Scholars but in good will for want of lerning, and that we will furnish with good will and diligence to the uttermost of our powers'.[32]

This inferred ignorance of the mechanics of oceanic voyaging was not an uncharacteristic token of modesty on Frobisher's part; nor was the failing his alone. We have seen that there was a pronounced English backwardness with respect to the hydrographical sciences; but there were also more endemic problems facing sixteenth-century oceanic voyagers. Even with a good ship and fair winds, imperfections in contemporary techniques and practices of navigation made sailing into unknown waters a hazardous undertaking.[33] The principal task of the would-be navigator was to know precisely where he was, once out of sight of land. In fair weather, latitude could be observed readily enough with the mariner's ring and cross-staff (though high latitude sailing brought its own, peculiar problems, as we shall see); but the technique of establishing longitude was, and remained, a mystery. Theorists already suspected that what was needed to mark an east-west course was an accurate timepiece, sufficiently compact and robust to be taken to sea, yet they knew also that no such thing existed in their age. Even the measurement of a degree of longitude was not yet agreed upon, conceptually. Competent masters understood that it was a variable quantity – as early as 1527, Thorne had noted that 'the degrees of longitude neare either of the poles are nothing equal in bignes to them in the equinoctiall' – but the only English work to address this in a practical sense prior to 1576 was William Bourne's 1574 *Regiment for the Sea*.[34] This was rightly to become a hugely influential work for English navigators, but it is difficult to assess how widely used it was by 1576, just two years after the first edition reached the streets of London. We know for certain that the work was not purchased for use in any of Frobisher's north-west voyages, though it is possible that Hall already owned a personal copy.

Such technical and conceptual difficulties made the observation of longitude an intellectual conundrum for theorists and a practical impossibility for everyone else. Measurement of distance sailed – the only realistic method of establishing an approximate east-west position – was by the most primitive of a ship's instruments, the log and line: cast out for a finite time established by minute-glass or a carefully modulated chant. The inherent errors of this primitive technique were further exacerbated in practice by the English habit of assuming a standard 'mile' of just 5,000 feet (partially compensated for by using half-minute glasses of about 28 seconds' duration), which meant that a ship's way in the sea tended to be overestimated.

Direction was established by means of the sea-compass, but even here, conceptual errors prevailed. Designers understood that the proximity of metal affected a magnetic compass, but having gone so far as to replace iron pins in the compass binnacle with wooden pegs, they ignored the more profound effects of large quantities of ship's tackle and ordnance close by. Furthermore, the quality of individual compasses varied widely. Frobisher took with him a large brass meridional compass, probably supplied by England's foremost instrument maker, Humphrey Cole;[35] but he also took twenty further compasses, 'of divers sortes' (the 1578 inventories of the *Gabriel* and *Michael* reveal that each ship carried four deck-mounted compasses; the remainder would almost certainly have been of the smaller, unmounted variety). The provision of such numbers suggests that the adventurers were worried as much about the wrong sort of variation as about potential breakages. Realistically, given the intrinsic limitations of their constituent parts – and despite the compass card's division into quarter points, with a theoretical accuracy to within 0.3 of a degree – an observation within 5 degrees of true was probably the best they could achieve.[36]

The quality of information upon contemporary charts was a further problem, invariably making the best available example a blank one. That of the North Atlantic, drafted by William Borough for the coming voyage, was scored by rhumb (direction) lines; otherwise, it depicted only England, Scotland, northern Ireland and that part of Scandinavia known to Muscovy Company masters, and thus contained no pre-conceptual errors to confound a newly plotted course.[37] Such simplicity was important, as contemporary measures to make charts more accurate usually had the opposite effect. Until 1599, when the Englishman Edward Wright developed a means of depicting longitude on charts using Mercator's projection, the plane chart – one of the most basic tools of the navigator – depicted meridians of longitude in parallel. A course plotted in advance upon such a chart – for example, one lying due east to west – would inevitably draw a vessel increasingly south of its true course (or north, if the route lay below the Equator). A globe, properly etched, would prevent this; but ships' globes were few and expensive in the 1570s (Frobisher's adventurers purchased an etched globe – at £7 13sh. 4d. their most expensive instrument of navigation – but this was almost certainly intended for Dee's tuition of his new charges, rather than to be risked upon the voyage).[38]

Faced with these profound problems, the astute navigator would try to keep it simple, and that is precisely what Frobisher intended. Contemporary intelligence told him that the supposed Straits of Anian lay somewhere around, or north of, 60°N. Therefore, given that he had no accurate information on how far west the ships would need to pass before making a landfall (and given also the undoubted truth that the chance of meeting with Spanish ships increased the further south his own vessels made their passage), it was his intention to pass northwards to 60°N directly, and then to set a course as close to due west as possible. The latter technique, known as westering, had been used successfully seventy-nine years earlier by John Cabot, almost seventy years earlier by his son, Sebastian, and during almost every fishing season since that time by countless French, Basque and, sometimes, English fishermen visiting the Newfoundland banks. It made a virtue of Frobisher's limited skills and the poor data available to him; it did not – contrary to popular English prejudices following his return – make him a new Magellan, much less a Jason.

From Gravesend, where the assiduous master Hall had made his point of departure on 12 June, the two tiny barks and their now repaired pinnace passed out into the North Sea and set a northerly course. Passing Fair Island, Hall almost off-handedly noted in his ship's log that it 'did rise at the Southermost ende with a litle hommocke, and swampe in the middes'.[39] The observation was not a reflection of the island's importance to this or any other expedition, but of Hall's having commenced the plotting of the 1576 voyage in an entirely instinctive manner. The good pilot never ceased to add to his empirical knowledge of coastlines and their hazards, because to do so would be to render his craft a false and dangerous thing (as several of his colleagues were to discover during Frobisher's third, 1578, voyage). No doubt a similar observation was added that day to his personal rutter: the dog-eared, increasingly thick wedge of loosely bound paper that constituted his personal Bible.

Strong northerly winds off Harwich on 13 June drove the barks into the harbour there. For the next few days they struggled to put to sea, and it was only on 18 June that they came to Yarmouth Roads.[40] Once there, however, the winds turned favourable, and the expedition had an easy passage northwards to the Shetland Islands, which it reached on 26 June. Here, Frobisher briefly paused to stop up a small leak in the *Michael*'s hull, to send his and Hall's regards to Master Dee and to top up the ships' water casks (faulty casking – one of the banes of life at sea – could often be identified and repaired only after several days at sea). That same evening, Hall observed his latitude once more, at 59°–46′N, after which Frobisher and his thirty-four men set their vessels out into the Ocean Sea.

For three days they sailed west and by north, coming up to 60°N. The weather was fair but blustery until 30 June, when a severe storm arose that was to pound their small barks, almost without pause, until 8 July. Inevitably, they were driven off course, and for long periods obliged to 'spoon' (to run without sail before the wind); but using each brief break in the cloud cover to good effect, Hall periodically re-observed his latitude and corrected his course accordingly, and continued to note the variation of his compass upon the chart prepared by William Borough. None of these were easy tasks. Even discounting the effect of a rolling deck upon his observations, there was a further problem – one that must have been known to Hall already from his prior experience in voyages to Muscovy, but which nevertheless could not be corrected. In his narrative of the 1577 voyage, George Best commented upon this technical difficulty of high-latitude navigation: '. . . here the north starre is so muche elevated above the horizon, that with the stafe it is hardly to be wel observed, and the degrees in the Astrolobe are too small to be observed (in) minutes. Therefore, we alwaies used the stafe. . . .'[41] In other words, the only reasonably accurate method of observing their latitude was by the sun. Fortunately, the summer months at that latitude provide ample daylight, but the 'loss' of the Pole Star, particularly under the prevalent poor weather conditions, was yet a further complication to add to the manifest of guesswork that constituted the English pilot's method of making his way in the sea. Upon the yawing boards of the *Gabriel*, moving precipitously towards a place for which no rutter's lore yet existed, Christopher Hall applied what little science he had to hand, and struggled to keep his bow to the west. The *Michael*, her crew already dispirited, followed.

Hall's careful observations, however hampered, proved true. On 11 July, through high seas and low cloud, they had sight of land to their starboard – of mountains 'rising like pinacles of steeples', sharply profiled and topped with snow. No Englishmen had yet seen and reported upon this savage land, but lying at or about 61°N, the false geography of the Zeno brothers provided its spurious identity: '. . . by coniecture had owt of histories and cartes of cosmography yt should seeme to be the great Iland of Friseland . . .'.[42] This was to be Frobisher's first achievement as an explorer: to confirm in contemporary minds the existence of a non-existent island.

The landmass was in fact the southeastern tip of Greenland, the coastline between Prins Christian Sund and Kap Farvel, and though the mariners of the *Gabriel* and *Michael* were mistaken as to what they were seeing, the barks were precisely upon their predetermined course. Kap Farvel itself lies almost exactly at 60°N, and provides the logical point of departure from which to cross the Davis Strait north and westwards. For the moment, however, Frobisher did not press on. The barks, no longer in storms but buffeted by high seas still, lowered all but their top-sails. Whatever directions Frobisher had received from his backers prior to his departure are no longer extant, but given the likelihood that any landmass encountered on his passage would be unknown to Englishmen, he had probably been told to examine and assess all landfalls *en route*, to determine their potential as way-stations for future expeditions. True either to the adventurers' instructions or his own instinct to explore a new dominion, Frobisher took his ships in towards the strange shore before him.

Immediate impressions of this land suggested little prospect of a safe haven for subsequent voyagers: 'full of high ragged Roks all along by the coast . . . some of the Ilands of Ise were nere yt of such heigth as the clowds hanged about the Tops of them, & the Byrds that flew about them were owt of (sight) . . .'.[43] Hall took the *Gabriel* in as close to shore as he dared; even so, he could find no bottom when sounding with a 150-fathom dipsie. It was clearly impossible to anchor in such a depth of water, and so Frobisher ordered his ship's boat hoisted out to attempt to reach the land. As he and four others moved towards the new shore, their way was almost entirely clogged by ice, a hazard exacerbated by thick fog which made both advance and retreat equally fraught with danger. With considerable difficulty, they regained the *Gabriel*, and after the briefest discussion, Frobisher and Hall decided against a further attempt on their outward passage. In fact, two more years were to elapse before Englishmen stood upon 'Friesland'.

The *Gabriel*'s course was set westwards once more. At this point, she still had the company of the *Michael* and the pinnace; but at some time during the next two days, as they crossed Davis Strait, another violent storm arose, in which the small fleet was dispersed. Somewhere in that bleakness, over-whelmed by high seas, the pinnace sank with her four hands.[44] In the same storm, the *Michael* turned back to England. According to Lok's later account (written after he had the opportunity to interrogate Owen Griffin, master of the *Michael*),[45] the bark continued westwards for four days until her crew sighted what they took to be the coast of Labrador. At that point, with huge ice-fields before them and no obvious prospect of going further, her twelve mariners had taken their own counsel and decided to return to England. No blame was later placed upon them for this defection – at least, not publicly – but Griffin was not to be employed by the adventurers in subsequent voyages. Whether this was his choice or theirs is not known; £5 per month was good pay, even for an experienced master, but the *Michael* was to prove an unlucky ship, and a man excluded from the enterprise might well have blessed his own, better fortune as that of the adventurers foundered.[46]

Only Frobisher and the eighteen men of the *Gabriel* now pressed on towards the west. Almost immediately, however, they were threatened with the same fate that had sent the pinnace to the ocean floor. The storm that had pressed upon them for almost two weeks now increased massively in intensity; in mountainous seas, the low-waisted *Gabriel* began to ship water, until she lay almost over on her side. Most of the crew, according to Lok's account, regarded themselves as doomed men;[47] their captain, however, driven no doubt by the deadlier prospect of future unemployment, now robustly repaid his backers' pale faith in his commitment. As the *Gabriel* began to settle in the water, he clambered his way along her now-upturned chain wales, had his men cut away the mizzen-mast to lighten the drag upon her (they wanted to cut away the main-mast also, but sensibly he prevented this), and then adopted a technique familiar to latter day ocean-going yachtsmen: heaving upon the weather leech of the foresail to rock the *Gabriel* and empty her of water. His heroism, and his crew's supine despair, were doubtless overplayed by Lok for dramatic effect – even Frobisher could hardly have righted the *Gabriel* single-handedly – but the hyperbole did justice to his near-elemental lack of circumspection. Fear of the new and extreme is an ever-present theme in much of the contemporary literature of exploration (the tone of George Best's account of the voyages is a salutary example of this); but one searches in vain for any indication that Frobisher was discouraged, much less cowed, by the traumatic impact of unknown travails. It was a quality that did great service in a voyage of such incalculable dangers; but being in large part a symptom of monumental self-confidence, it had the capacity to bring disaster as readily as deliverance, as his nervous mariners may already have suspected.

Hall's journal, heavily censored at some time prior to publication by Hakluyt in the 1589 *Principall Navigations*, mentioned nothing of the episode; he merely continued to note the ship's course and the conditions they encountered, principally the ice bergs that grew more numerous as they moved westwards. For a while, making urgent repairs to the *Gabriel*'s beaten masts, they furled all sails and ran before the sea once more. Fortunately, the storm abated sufficiently to allow this; but even so, the same doubts that had afflicted the crew of the *Michael* seem to have gripped the *Gabriel*'s mariners also. Their captain, however, was less inclined to indulge the same degree of ship board democracy as had the hapless *Griffin*. Moved by his duty to his commission (as Lok claimed), or by the understanding that failed navigators enjoyed few further opportunities for glory, Frobisher allowed no prospect of turning about to lift his mariners' spirits. They pressed on 'by fay(re) and fowle', and, on 26 July, sighted an ice-bound land to the west, at 62°–2′N.[48] Again, however, large quantities of surface ice between the *Gabriel* and its strange shore proved a hazard, and Frobisher had her course adjusted to the south-westwards to circumvent it. Two days later, when a morning fog lifted, land proper lay before them, of 'marveilous great heith: which by the account of the course and way they iudged to be the Land of Labr(ador)'.

It was not a bad guess, given their existing data; but Labrador lay to the south by some 5 degrees of latitude, across the mouth of a vast strait that Fro-bisher was to enter in error two years later. What he and Hall caught sight of that morning was the present-day Resolution Island, off the southernmost tip of Baffin Island. Imagining this to be the extremity of a peninsula, Fro-bisher sensibly gave the first honours in this new land to his Queen, naming it Queen Elizabeth's Foreland (known more commonly thereafter as the Queen's Foreland).

The landscape before them was not significantly more inviting than that which they had left behind them across Davis Strait. An account of the fol-lowing year's voyage, written by Dionyse Settle, a gentleman-follower of the Earl of Warwick, provides as much evidence of the writer's fearful supposi-tion as of the visible nature of the land:

> The Countries . . . lye very highe with roughe stonie mountaines, and great quantitie of snowe thereon. There is very little plaine grounde, and no grasse, except a little, which is much like vnto mosse that groweth on soft ground, such as we get Turfes in. There is no wood at all. To be briefe, there is nothing fitte, or profitable for the vse of man . . . there is great like-lyhood of Earthquakes, or thunder: for that there are huge and mon-sterous mounteines, whose greatest substance are stones, and those stones so shaken with some extraordinarie meanes, that one is separated from another . . . there are no rivers, or running springes, but such, as through the heate of the Sunne, with such water as discendeth from the mountaines and hilles, whereon great drifts of snowe doe lie, are ingendred.[49]

Settle's habitual style was of the epic tradition, but in this instance his observations were astute. The topography of Baffin Island, even to more worldly, modern eyes, is almost uniformly grim. High, barren peaks puncture habitually grey skies; beneath their upper slopes, snow lies almost all year round upon unsheltered soil. Winds, strengthened by the rapid shifts in temperature as coastal thermals encounter cold fronts over land, scour and flatten the sparse, lichenous vegetation. There are no indigenous trees; only infrequent, low brush growth upon sheltered soil. The prospect was (and remains) extremely forbidding, but it was also entirely guileless, offering not the slightest promise of being a place in which Europeans could exist upon local resources alone. Across 400 years, we can only guess at the reaction of Frobisher's mariners to their first glimpse of this new and strange place, but the potential that warmer climes offered in abundance to most other contemporary voyages of reconnaissance was utterly lacking in the landscape before them.

On 28 July 1576, moving in towards that unknown shore, the Englishmen had a first taste of its novel dangers. The prevailing off-shore current sweeps south-west across the face of the land, making an attempt at landfall in poor visibility fraught with potential disaster. That same current, moreover, swiftly brings large numbers of ice bergs that threaten to shatter any vessel attempting to cross their path. Calved from the west Greenland coast and carried north around the head of Baffin Bay, these fragments are picked up each year by the Labrador current and driven southwards along Baffin Island's eastern coastline. By the time they reach the Grand Banks off Newfoundland they become relatively few and small (though even there, they represent a considerable risk to navigation, as the unfortunate crew and passengers of the *Titanic* were to discover over three centuries later); further north, off the entrance to Frobisher Bay, they retain sufficient bulk to present an unremitting danger. For wooden-hulled vessels, the hazard is an extreme one – particularly during the summer months, when the greatest incidence of calving occurs.

Even if a fair wind and current carried a ship safely through this near-suicidal passage, there was a further, unexpected hazard. Moving tentatively inshore, constantly tacking to avoid oncoming ice bergs, the men of the *Gabriel* expected to find a safe anchorage. This proved to be remarkably elusive. The continental shelf off southern Baffin Island is extremely narrow, and falls away steeply; much of the shoreline forms in effect the upper edge of a cliff-face which disappears down into darkness, several hundred feet below a ship's keel. During the days following their first sight of land, Hall was repeatedly to sound and find no bottom, even as close as a cable's length from the shore. As upon the shores of 'Friesland', the only means of landing upon much of this coastline was by utilizing the ship's boat, set out into the main current – a supremely hazardous business, even where the shore was a familiar one. And this was unlike any landfall that English mariners had ever seen.

Yet it was at least a firmament before them, the coast of which they took to be America – or, if they had passed too far to the north, of Asia, the supposed northern shore of the 'Strait of Anian'. Their present latitude was approximately 59°–30'N, and in light of the limited information they possessed, the prospect was more likely to be that of America; accordingly, Frobisher set the *Gabriel*'s course north-eastwards whilst attempting to keep the shore constantly in view. Prophetically, Hall noted that the current they fought against was such that 'a ship may driue a league and a halfe, in one houre . . .'.[50] By 31 July, having in the intervening days lost sight of land, they made out another headland to the north and west. The *Gabriel* had passed, as her crew would soon discover, across the mouth of a large, seemingly open body of water. This new sighting was its northern extremity, the mirror to Queen Elizabeth's Foreland. Again, attempts to land upon the shore here were frustrated by the prevalence of ice; so much so that after a brief reconnaissance they had to stand out to sea almost fifteen miles. It was not until 10 August that Hall, taking with him four men in the ship's boat, managed to land upon the most easterly of a group of islands around the northern 'headland' (in his honour, it was named Hall's Island – later Little Hall's Island, to distinguish it from its larger neighbour). Their stay on-shore was fleeting; Hall went to the island's highest point to reconnoitre but then re-embarked hurriedly when he noticed that the tide had risen more than a foot since their landing. It was the most cursory reconnaissance with which to honour a new land, but in another sense it had been disastrously protracted. Lok's later indictment against Frobisher provide the only detailed account of this brief but portentous visit:

In that first voyadge one a litle Ilande of Rocke of halfe a mile circuit w(hi)ch they namyd hawlls Iland, after the name of Christofer Hawlle, m(aste)r of Shippe, who was the first mane that landed thereon, Captaine Furbysher not beinge one land at all, but remayninge still in the Shippe at sea x. milles from yt, One this Rocke was fownde by chaunce by a maryner, namyd Robert Garrard, who was one of the v. men w(hi)ch afterwards weare taken w(i)th their boate, by the people of that Countrye, a blacke stoune, as great as a halfe pennye loafe, beinge one the grownd losse, w(hi)ch he thought to be a Seacoole w(hi)ch he brought

aboorde the Shippe to prove yf yt woold burne for fyre, whereof they had
lacke . . .'[51]

The significance of this 'halfe pennye loafe' sized stone will become apparent, but it is enough here to note that whilst Hall and his men had merely
been seeking a safe harbour for the *Gabriel*, they had laid the ground – thanks
to master Garrard's keen eyes and cold body – for the brief making and subsequent near-destruction of Frobisher's reputation, the impoverishment, disgrace and imprisonment of Michael Lok and the emptying of dozens of
adventurers' pockets. In its own, modest way, this half-mile meander was to
prove one of the most fateful excursions in the history of sixteenth-century
English exploration.

At the time, however, Hall's reconnaissance found little that might prove
of potential interest to this or future expeditions, and by now Frobisher's
attention was firmly fixed once more upon his primary goal. It was apparent
that the body of water to the westwards was more than a shallow bay. Given
that fact, he had a simple choice: to press on to the north and find an alternative location for the eastern entrance to the rumoured 'Strait of Anian', or
to examine the prospect that lay enticingly before him. Best later claimed that
Frobisher chose the former option initially, but that persistent and contrary
winds prevented him from passing further to the north. Only then, apparently, did he determine 'to make profe of this place, to see how farre that
gutte had continuance, and whether he mighte carrie himselfe thorough
the same, into some open Sea on the backe side.'[52] Once more, however,
Best seems to have been writing the story to build a suitable posterity.
Despite existing 'intelligence', it was generally understood – and evident in
the entirely featureless representation of north-eastern America in most contemporary charts and maps – that the nature of the region remained a matter
for speculation. The Strait of Anian had come to be accepted as a geographical reality; but its precise location and nature remained obscure. It might
well be only one of several routes into the Pacific, and no doubt Frobisher
was happy to test the present possibility. If the *Gabriel* did indeed pass further
north along the coast, it was for a matter of hours only, and against a current
that strongly urged her elsewhere. Whatever the truth of Best's claim for Frobisher's motives, both his and Hall's accounts show clearly that as early as the
morning after the examination of Little Hall's Island, Frobisher ordered the
prow of the *Gabriel* to be turned westwards into the mouth of this potential
passage to Cathay.

Skirting the body of land to the west of the North Foreland, which Frobisher had named Lok's Land in honour of his partner (and such it remains today), the *Gabriel* moved north-westwards, keeping the northern shore of the strait within sight. The early signs were hopeful; at the northern extremity of this passage, it would not have been possible to see its southern shore from the low deck of the bark. Though Frobisher and his mariners already knew the opening to be not nearly so wide as the known representations of the Strait of Anian, it nevertheless promised to carry them far to the west: perhaps as far as the *Mare del Sur* itself.

Once more, ice seems to have presented a persistent obstacle to their passage. A full day's careful sailing carried them only sixty miles into this body of water; there, in its middle passage, they sighted another island, which they named after the ship they stood upon. That choice that may have been made more as a fearful propitiation than to commemorate their vessel: the same day, Hall's log recorded that the *Gabriel* was by now 'weake from the wales vpward' and urgently in need of repair. Forty-eight hours later, they sighted a sound (possibly in the vicinity of the present-day Waddell Bay), where, anchoring in eight fathoms, the bark's crew re-caulked her hull.

The weather continued relatively calm, but very cold. On 16 August, Hall reported that they had acquired a quarter of an inch of ice upon the deck of the *Gabriel* within two hours, with neither wind nor rain to encourage it. The following day they sighted and named Thomas Williams Island (possibly the latter-day Culbertson Island), and on 18 August, thirty miles to the north-west, Burche's Island (almost immediately to be misrepresented on contemporary charts as Burcher's Island) in honour of John Burche, the carpenter-mariner who had first sighted it. Frobisher went on-shore here with Hall and eight other men – as Best claimed, to attempt to find and make contact with the local inhabitants.

The decision could hardly have been made upon a sudden whim, or in blind hope of stumbling across a previously discreet local aboriginal culture. Though no prior encounter was mentioned in any account of the voyage, some sight of human activity must have occurred already, as, almost immediately after the Englishmen reached the highest point of this island, seven or eight small boats were seen putting out from the eastern shore of the strait. Frobisher and Hall re-embarked hurriedly, but sent the *Gabriel*'s boat to entice them back towards the English ship. This first clear sight of white men seems to have left the local Inuit curious but unafraid; one of their boats followed that of the *Gabriel* until, seeing the ship, they cautiously put in to Burche's Island. Hall went ashore alone to parley (a strange risk for

Frobisher to take with his most valuable subordinate), and gave the Inuit presents of sewing needles – items which apparently impressed their new owners tremendously. One of them, making signs to Hall, agreed to go on board the *Gabriel*, where he was given a taste of the Englishmen's food and drink – 'but he made no countenance of liking any' – and thereafter set ashore once more, to report to his eighteen companions that the strangers were friendly.[53] At this, the Inuit overcame their reticence, and all agreed to board the strange ship.

> They bee like to Tartars, with long blacke haire, broad faces, and flatte noses, and tawnie in colour, wearing Seale skinnes, and so doe the women, not differing in the fashion, but the women are marked in the face with blewe streekes downe the cheekes, and round about the eyes.[54]

Crowded together on the deck of the *Gabriel*, the two races examined each other carefully. Hall attempted to question some of them and wrote down the words of their language phonetically, pointing at their bodies and rendering the corresponding sounds as closely as his own language allowed: prominent parts of the visible anatomy first – 'argoteyt' (hand); 'cangnawe' (nose); 'arered' (eye); 'comagaye' (leg); 'atoniagay' (foot); and then more detail – 'coblone' (thumb); 'teckerre' (forefinger); 'ketteckle' (middle finger); 'mekellacane' (fourth finger); 'yacketrone' (little finger); then their artefacts – 'callagay' (breeches); 'polleutagay' (knife); 'attegay' (coat); 'accaskay' (ship). At the same time, the Inuit exhibited an equal, if more practical, interest in the artefacts of the Englishmen, and were given many 'tryfles of haberdash'. It was a friendly, if cautious encounter, but to the modern eye it is obvious that the two races had a different understanding of what it signified. The exchange of gifts is a deeply symbolic gesture to European cultures: a clear and explicit denial of aggressive intent. The Englishmen considered that they were buying the friendship – or at least the acquiescence – of these people; hence their sense of betrayal when the Inuit later acted according to their own, unfamiliar mores. It has been written that sixteenth-century Europeans, confronted with the unbridgeable strangeness of alien cultures, saw what they wished to see and judged accordingly.[55] The events of the next few days were to provide a salutary example of this phenomenon, by establishing prejudices which, reinforced by the literature of the north-west voyages, would endure far beyond the life of the enterprise.

On 20 August, having waved off their guests, Frobisher took the *Gabriel* to the eastern shore of Burche's Island. Together with Hall and four men, he took to the ship's boat and put in towards some Inuit houses there. They were seen and withdrew, but the Inuit made friendly signs for them to return. Frobisher, Hall and four others went ashore to examine their homes and then brought one of the Inuit back to the *Gabriel*. He was given a bell and a knife, and Frobisher pressed him to act as their pilot through the passage. It is difficult to know how adequately the concept of 'passage' was conveyed, but the Inuk male agreed to assist his new friends, and indicated that they should reach its western extremity – whatever that might be – in no more than two days. When he made signs to go ashore to prepare his kayak, five men were detailed to carry him in the ship's boat to a point well away from his fellows, and then to retreat immediately. For some reason (which, inevitably, remains obscure), they disobeyed. Beyond a headland, screened from the *Gabriel*, three of them landed with the Inuk and were immediately seized by unseen hands. The two others signalled to the ship and then went to their assistance. They, and the *Gabriel*'s boat, were not seen again.[56]

If innocent of an overt act of abduction, the Inuit were certainly guilty of preventing the Englishmen from returning to their own kind. Their motives are unclear, but the episode marked the end of the brief period of fraternization. Though none of the narratives makes the point explicitly, the Englishmen seem to have been expecting trouble. The conquests of Cortes, Balbao and Pizzaro had given the white man a contempt for the martial qualities of many of these 'inferior' cultures, but even after fifty years of unbroken Spanish conquest and exploitation, a number of the Caribbean islands, the eastern Spanish Main and northern New Spain remained 'no-go' areas, from which stories of the bestial savagery of their inhabitants were brought back by the survivors of abortive expeditions and invariably circulated for the delicious edification of a fascinated European readership. Thus, Frobisher and his men had to deal not only with seemingly dangerous novelty, but prejudice also. The Tartar and the Carib were the dark nemeses of travel lore, and these new folk appeared to be the close relations of one of these races at least. When, two years later, George Best gave the English mariners' hostility the spurious legitimacy of necessary prudence – 'the capitayn did wisely forsee that these strange people are not to be trusted for any cause nor shew of freendship that they would make' – he was only acknowledging a generally held preconception that had, in the meantime, received much apparent support from his own experience.[57] By then, sluttishness, inordinate cruelty and cannibalism had also been put at the door of the Inuit by men who were incapable of seeing beyond the tainted evidence of their partialities.

On the morning following the abduction of the five Englishmen, their compatriots searched the immediate area thoroughly, firing off one of their falconets and repeatedly sounding trumpets as they marched, but found not the slightest trace of the missing men or their captors. For that day and the next, they passed around the shores of what was to be commemorated as Five Men's Sound, hoping to find some token that offered the prospect of their recovery. Meanwhile, fearing further aggression from the Inuit, Frobisher had canvas sheets nailed across the *Gabriel*'s midships (the deck was so low there that access from the water was easy) and ordered the chain wales to be blocked up. On the morning of 22 August, several Inuit kayaks came out from the shore towards the *Gabriel*. Most remained prudently distant, willing to talk but fearful of reprisals. Only one Inuk male, slowly enticed towards the bark, seemed to forget or discount the incident two days earlier. Frobisher himself leaned over the side of the *Gabriel* and performed a protracted mime: offering gifts to the man and throwing items of clothing into the water to have him retrieve them. The Inuk's reservations were gradually overwhelmed by his acquisitive instincts. Each time Frobisher threw something into the water, it fell closer to the ship's side. Eventually, the man was directly under the side of the *Gabriel*, and Frobisher leaned towards him with a bell gently ringing between his fingers. When the man cautiously reached out to take it, Frobisher dropped it, grasped his wrist and lifted him bodily, still attached to his kayak, into captivity.

The concept of prisoner exchange was either entirely alien to the Inuk or not explained with sufficient clarity. The captive remained unresponsive to threats and promises, despite the obvious evidence of Frobisher's capacity to do him harm, but 'for very choller & disdain he bit his tong in twayne within his mouth.'[58] The Englishmen seem to have offered him no greater hurt than he inflicted upon himself; nevertheless, George Best showed more foresight than he knew when, subsequently, he referred to the captive and his countrymen as 'this newe prey' – a first symptom, perhaps, of the understanding that Europeans could or would find no common ground upon which to meet a culture so strikingly dissimilar to their own.

With a prisoner in his hold, Frobisher finally had some token of his discoveries to place before his backers. It was a timely acquisition, as there was now an urgent decision to be made. On the evening of the day that the five Englishmen had been abducted, snow had fallen a foot deep upon the *Gabriel*'s deck. It was obvious that the weather was turning, the brief summer there having run its course, and the prospect of an approaching Arctic winter was yet another problem to face. The expedition's entire complement was now just thirteen men. Furthermore, they had lost their only ship's boat, and so could not put ashore except in one of the rare, shallow harbours where the *Gabriel* could be anchored within wading distance of the shore (perforce a very brief wading distance, given the water's ambient temperature). To go on, to force the passage and sail across the Pacific Ocean, was unthinkable, even had their assumptions concerning the 'strait' proved accurate. On 23 August, Frobisher assembled his men on the deck of the *Gabriel*. For once, he invited their opinions, and immediately discovered – as he must have suspected – a unanimous desire to be elsewhere:

> And they all agreed that, consydering their evell & weak state by the los of their Bote, & five of their best men & the weaknes & little hability of the rest of the men that were left in the Ship, being but xiij men & boyes, so tyred, & sik w(ith the) laboure of their hard voyage, passed as they were neither hable well to procede in any long voyage toward the Tyme of winter nor yet of (remaining more than that time) already passed than to procede (more) with great danger of the vtter (destruction of the enter)prise for ever after yf they should (not now pass) away.[59]

Even Frobisher himself, single-mindedly devoted to his own advancement, must have seen that Cathay was no longer a realistic goal. His crew could hardly go much further, even if their will remained strong (which, clearly, it did not), and the means were equally lacking. Once the inevitable decision had been made, it was implemented immediately. Commending their five comrades to God's mercy, or to that of their unfathomable captors, the mariners set the prow of the *Gabriel* eastwards towards the mouth of the 'strait' and the Ocean Sea beyond. At a point no more than twenty miles from the head of what was in fact a great bay, without yet understanding the significance of what he had done or had allowed to go unfinished, Frobisher's career as an explorer had reached its furthermost point.

The return voyage was swift and uneventful. By 27 August, the *Gabriel* was abreast of Queen Elizabeth's Foreland, and at the month's end off the coast of 'Friesland'. For five days thereafter, she ran along its shore, her crew searching for a suitable landing place.[60] Once again, as upon their outward passage, the Englishmen were kept from the land by ice, and storms followed them back across the Atlantic. In high seas, one man fell overboard but was heaved back into the ship by Frobisher himself (no doubt his gratitude was more fervently expressed than that of the previous beneficiary of his captain's great physical strength). Without further incident – or any that was considered worth reporting – the *Gabriel* came home to England. By 25 September she was off Orkney, and sailed into Harwich Road on 2 October 1576.

For four days, what remained of the expedition rested there, tending wounded and sick mariners, but on 6 October the *Gabriel* came south into the Thames. In London, Lok had received word of their coming, and his spirits, dampened by the dire predictions of the *Michael*'s crew (she had arrived at London on 1 September, proclaiming the *Gabriel* lost), lifted once more. Hurriedly, he visited an instrument-maker, laid out 8sh. for an ornamental globe and took it downriver to mount upon the bowsprit of the *Gabriel* as she sailed past the Queen's palace at Greenwich: no doubt to remind their sovereign of the magnitude of Frobisher's achievement.[61] In London, the welcome given to the mariners was one of almost unbounded enthusiasm. Despite their failure to realize any of the ostensible aims of the expedition, they 'were ioyfully received with the great admiration of the people, bringing with them their strange man and his bote, which was such a wonder onto the whole city and to the rest of the realm that heard of yt as seemed never to have happened the like great matter to any mans knowledge'.[62] In the *Gabriel*, Lok eagerly examined the Inuk man and agreed with much of Hall's description of the race,

> . . . strongly pight & made . . . very brode face, & very fat & fu(ll about) his Body. But his legs shorter & smaller (then the pro)portion of his Body requyred . . . His Culler of Skyn all ouer his Bo(dy & fa)ce, was of dark Sallow, much like to the tawny Mores; (or ra)ther to the Tartar Nation, whereof I think he was . . . (his) countenance sullen or churlish and sharp withall

as well it might have been under the circumstances, though Lok did not make the point.[63]

Marking the novelty both of his capture and his alien mien, two portraits of the man were made: one by Cornelius Ketel, the other by a Flemish Protestant refugee, Lucas de Heere.[64] At least one of these was a posthumous likeness; the unfortunate Inuk was to die within days of his arrival in England – according to Best, from a cold contracted upon the return voyage – having been fed, clothed and ineffectually nursed through his illness. A wax death-mask was made for Ketel's benefit so that he could complete the portrait carefully, after which the body was embalmed to be returned to its homeland. It was an honourable intention, but at some point became impractical (perhaps the embalming did not take successfully). Thereafter, surprisingly, his body was buried in consecrated ground, in St Olave's churchyard, Hart Street.[65] Thus, England's first experiment in the treatment of indigenous peoples had all the familiar hallmarks of later failures: callous abduction, patronizing if well-intentioned mistreatment, helpless tragedy and, finally, a pointless redeeming gesture.

However, the Inuk man had fulfilled his role to admiration. The strangeness of Frobisher's story, and the exotic evidence he had produced to support it, invoked a powerful and seductive sense of dislocation among a population that, with very few exceptions, was far more parochial than in England's subsequent days of empire. To the more fanciful – and there were many – it seemed now that England had her own Columbus, returned with stories of places perceived as stepping stones to something greater. His voyage was not the first English expedition to unfamiliar lands; but it was sufficiently novel, both in intention and execution, to seem a prodigious thing. It had not been a parasitical intrusion into the achievements of other nations, nor an aggressive act of brigandage upon their possessions; but a purely English voyage of reconnaissance to a place upon which no known white man had ever stood. Even without firm proof that Frobisher had found a passage, much less a new and lucrative trade with the East, his was popularly regarded as the first footstep in a virgin land – though one that was apparently pregnant with the promise of English increase.

To mark the feat, the adventurers agreed that portraits of Frobisher and Lok should also be commissioned from Ketel. No doubt these were intended to hang in the corporate headquarters of the great commercial entity to be established to exploit the new discoveries: to remind and inspire future generations of company men going about their exotic and profitable business. Lok, perhaps more sensitive than Frobisher to the posterity of his fellow merchants, appears to have insisted that his own portrait be of the same dimensions as that of the returned hero. The good master Christopher Hall was similarly honoured, though with a smaller portrait (as befitted a mere employee); but the largest, most expensive commission was for a great portrait of the *Gabriel*: the *Argo* of much bad poetry that soon began to circulate in commemoration of her late and glorious voyage.[66] Unfortunately, this likeness is no longer extant; it may well have been the earliest example of formal English ship portraiture.

All of this assiduous self-promotion undoubtedly had a propagandist purpose, but setting aside the obvious excitement his return had aroused, what precisely had Frobisher achieved? The immediate tally seemed to be that he had proved the accuracy of maps depicting 'Friesland', discovered the entrance (but not the exit) to a passage into the Pacific Ocean and established a provisional claim to a new land in the name of the Queen. None of these accomplishments could be exploited without further expense, and even then there was little chance of a swift profit for those who had laid out their money. Why, then, did the enthusiasm of the adventurers now seem almost to match that of the crowds that had welcomed Frobisher home?

In fact, it is clear that very few of the protagonists remained unconvinced of the great potential of his discoveries. Lok noted the observations that Frobisher had made in his supposed strait, and these reflected generally accepted beliefs regarding the nature and behaviour of water in an open passage:

> . . . the capitayn with (?) of his men went on (shore) on an iland mynding to have gone to the top of an high (moun)tayn to discover what he could of the Straicts of the Sea (&) Land about, & there he saw far the two hed Lands at (the) furdest end of the straicts and no likelyhood of Land to the Northwards of them & the great brode open betwene th(em) which by reason of the great Tydes of flood which they found coming owt of the same & for many other good reasons they iudged to be the West Sea whereby to pas to Cathay & to the East India.[67]

Furthermore, Richard Willes, composing his 'For M(aster) Cap(tain) Furbysher's Passage by the North-west', was told by Frobisher himself that the further the *Gabriel* passed into the 'strait', the deeper his mariners' soundings became.[68] By contemporary standards, all of this was strong and reasonable evidence that he had been on the right track. Nevertheless, it is strange that none of those who interrogated Frobisher upon his return asked him the question that in retrospect seems an obvious one. Given the evidence of his own observations, the movement of tides and the Inuk male's testimony, and even acknowledging the difficulties he faced at the western-most point of his navigation, why did he not devote just two days more to the business of reaching the far exit to the passage? To have stood upon the eastern shore of the 'Mare de Sur' – even had he done no more than to return immediately thereafter – would have confirmed his achievement to the world far more profoundly than any token of alien culture. That Frobisher had not apparently seen this seems inexplicable. If, for twenty years, the discovery of this passage had occupied such a prominent place in his dreams and ambitions, how could he have stopped at Five Men's Sound and turned homewards?

Perhaps the simplest answer is that he was making the most of what was,

in reality, a very poor hand. Despite the testimony of a single Inuk com-
mentator – of a race that Englishmen already believed untrustworthy – and
the evidence of tides that seemingly set from the west, Frobisher could not
be certain that he had entered the correct passage. With the loss of five men
and the ship's boat, and with most of the surviving mariners showing well-
advanced symptoms of exhaustion, he could have gone on only a little further
– to prove or, fatally, to disprove his passage. If the latter, what prospect would
he have had of convincing his backers to set out another voyage to seek the
route to Cathay in another place? He had returned without new commodities (or prospect thereof), the adventurers were already in debt to Lok's purse
and, most importantly, the lesson of other English voyages to new lands was
unequivocal: that to secure neither adequate return nor the promise of one
meant that profit should be sought elsewhere. The merchants and courtiers
who invested in 1576 were speculators, but they were not, with few exceptions, fools. Nor was Frobisher himself so optimistic as to imagine that their
enthusiasm would ride what he might present to them as a temporary setback.
This may seem an unnecessarily cynical interpretation of his motives, but we
should recall what he had been seeking: not a passage, or a new trade, but a
reputation and its commensurate rewards. With his present associates'
backing, Frobisher was presented with the first real chance of his career
to achieve these goals; yet this opportunity had not been granted upon
unlimited resources, and certainly not upon his boundless credibility. By not
allowing the matter to be settled either way in 1576, he had at least the occasion to argue that a further effort was needed; and this is precisely what he
set out to do:

And nowe he beinge thus retorned home againe of that first voyadge he
was examyned of his doinges therein; by Sir Will(ia)m Winter, M(aste)r
Th(oma)s Randolphe, Anthonye Jenkinson, Mychael Lok and others,
therevnto appointed by Commyssion of her M(aies)ties honorable pryvye
Councell concerninge the passage to Cathaj, at w(hi)ch tyme he vowched
to them absolutlye w(i)th vehement wordes, speches and Oathes; that he
had founde and discoverid the Straights, and open passadge by sea into the
South Sea called Mar de Sur w(hi)ch goethe to Cathaj / and by the waye
had founde divers good ports and harbors for passadge of all the navye of
her Ma(ies)ties Shipps, and affirmed the same by divers arguments of the
depthe and culler of the water, the sight of the heade landes one boathe
the sides of the Straightes at the west end thereof openinge into the broade
Sea, called Mar de Sur, and the setting of the tydes w(i)th a fludd frome

the west owt of the sayde sowthe sea / and by divers other arguments by demonstrac(i)on in the Cartes and Mappes, w(hi)ch things the Commissioners beleved to be trewe vppon his vehement speches, and oathes of affirmac(i)on . . .[69]

Ironically, the one piece of evidence that would have guaranteed the survival of the enterprise without the need for proof of the passage's existence was not produced by Frobisher, because he was as yet unaware of its significance. It was in the hands of Michael Lok, who had received it from Frobisher's hands on 13 October as a mere souvenir of the voyage. The sole token of Christopher Hall's seemingly innocuous examination of his eponymous island, it had laid since in the hold of the *Gabriel*, exhibiting little promise of either fortune or ruin. However, as two inert substances may combine to produce something reactive, the object's first contact with the person of Michael Lok triggered a process whose repercussions were still unfolding two years later. None of this was inevitable. Had Lok, prudent merchant and champion of corporate sanctity, acted in character and simply taken the gift in the spirit of its offering, he would have had something of considerable anecdotal value with which to divert visitors to his house and a useful paperweight into the bargain. But the sage lessons of husbandry that had brought him to a comfortable station within the second rank of London's mercantile community were unravelling. Already, his purse had been sorely depleted: opened prodigally in the service of long-held aims that had seamlessly evolved into obsessions as he grew into middle-age unfulfilled. Being an intelligent man, he probably had some inkling of the enormity of his commitment, but even that understanding would have brought with it an unpleasant corollary: that an investment beyond one's means required a commensurate return.

NINE

All That Glisters

Of the minor artefacts, baubles and other, assorted souvenirs that found their way into the pockets of the mariners of the 1576 expedition, few had the potential to do more than briefly astound the friends and relatives of their owners. Unfortunately, one particularly nondescript item, casually acquired by a mariner who thereafter became one of the first Englishmen to die upon North American soil, held a somewhat greater promise of disaster. Master Robert Garrard's halfpenny loaf-sized rock, taken from the barren ground of Little Hall's Island, had somehow survived the urgent scientific curiosity of men seeking to warm their bodies, to be brought, whole, to an English quayside. Here, it passed immediately into the possession of the man who, after Frobisher himself, most wanted the enterprise to succeed: 'This stone beinge thus brought home, Captaine Furbysher gave a pece thereof to Mychael Lok, sayenge that yt was the fyrst thinge that he fownd in the newe land, and therefore gave yt vnto him according too his promyse'.[1]

Lok took away his souvenir, regarding it as having thus become his property, and immediately set himself to the business of finding some value in it. Despite his later claims of an initial scepticism, the diligence with which he passed small pieces to a number of assayers until one of them presented him with the right result suggests that his critical faculties were already in abeyance.[2] Both William Williams, assay-master at the Tower of London, and George Needham of the Mines Royal, the first men to take small samples of the ore, declared it to be worthless. Others followed, with similar opinions, and also failed to quench Lok's hopes. At the beginning of January 1577, he gave a further piece of the ore to a Venetian goldsmith then resident in

London, Giovanni Baptista Agnello. It was a profoundly bad choice. At this time, Agnello was searching as assiduously for a reputation (and with as little discernment as to how it might be secured) as both Lok and Frobisher. Having sensed what his new client was seeking, Agnello had little difficulty in 'finding' gold in the ore, and on 18 January he presented a grain to Lok. When the provenance of the ore was revealed to him, Agnello immediately suggested a partnership to exploit this potentially huge find. From the first, he urged that theirs should be a discreet, even a secret partnership; that in a future voyage: 'sum devyse might be made to lade it as stones, for ballast of the shyp.'[3]

Lok later claimed that his duty to his Queen was paramount; that he only appeared to agree to Agnello's proposal to test further the potential value of the ore. In fact, he had little choice but to disclose the news. If more of this promising commodity were to be returned to England, he would need the assistance and pockets of other men and, crucially, royal permission in the form of some sort of licence. Yet there can be little doubt that, initially at least, he did not regard this as a matter for his fellow adventurers' attention – on the contrary, he appears to have treated the ore business and that of finding a passage to Cathay as entirely separate issues. Even Frobisher remained unaware of the progress of his partner's activities; when he went to dinner at Lok's house in January 1577 and asked of the ore, he heard only that all assays to date had proved unsuccessful.

By 28 January, Lok was in correspondence with Francis Walsingham informing him of the results of Agnello's assays. Prior to that, he had sent a brief memorial to the Queen herself, informing her of his activities (though not admitting to his motives). Despite his efforts to keep the matter between a few, select confederates, however, he was already losing control of the process. Walsingham demanded several pieces of the ore to have them assayed by others (Lok ignored his first 'request', which was made some time before 28 January; but on the latter date, Walsingham met Lok in person, demanded to see the ore, took hold of it and broke off three or four pieces). Agnello, meanwhile, began to push for an arrangement: either for he and Lok to despatch a ship to the newly discovered lands to mine more ore, or for himself, acting alone, to buy future shipments of ore at a rate of £20 per ton. Walsingham neither refused nor acceded to these requests. He had already given his samples of ore to Edward Dyer, poet and amateur dabbler in the physical sciences, and to a French apothecary, Geoffrey le Brumen. Both men carried out small assays, finding minute traces of silver and nothing else; but as long as the matter remained inconclusive (and neither Dyer nor le Brumen

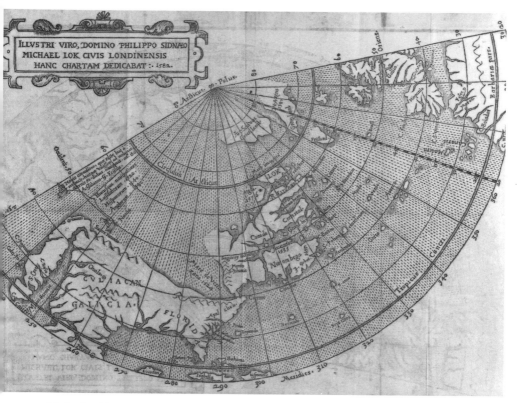

2. Michael Lok's 1582 chart of the North Atlantic from Hakluyt's *Divers Voyages* (1582).

were expert assayers), the Queen's secretary of state was too shrewd either to commit himself or leave Lok with the impression that a potentially vast new source of wealth was his to exploit alone. During February 1577, Lok passed between Agnello and Walsingham, transmitting the assayer's successive estimates and offers; Walsingham, perhaps hoping to tease out further information on the ore's true value, hinted that he might authorize a licence to allow Lok to set out a ship of 100 tons and secure more ore if Agnello could offer adequate sureties. This, and the Italian's increasingly urgent requests for a formal arrangement, seem to have quashed the last of Lok's prudence. On 6 March, he presented a written request to Walsingham, offering to pay Crown licence fees of £10 per ton of ore in return for a licence to transport and work the commodity. Once more, Walsingham remained non-committal; by this time, it seems that he was receiving information from other sources, and Lok's ability to influence events was dissipating.

Three weeks later, on 28 March, Lok and others met at the house of Sir William Winter, Surveyor of Marine Causes and Master of the Ordnance, to inaugurate the business of a commission, appointed by the Privy Council, to oversee preparations for a new voyage. There, Winter asked Lok to return the following day to discuss 'a matter of importaunce'. When they met once more, Winter revealed that he knew all about Agnello's trials upon the ore. Agnello himself had been anything but discreet; for several weeks, he had been communicating his 'findings' to Sir John Berkeley, who had spoken in turn to Sir William Morgan, who had informed Winter. Fascinated by the possibilities, Berkeley and Winter then introduced to the process one Jonas Schutz, a Saxon metallurgist who had worked previously for the Company of Mines Royal at Keswick.[4] Schutz subsequently assisted Agnello in several assays during January 1577, apparently unbeknown to Lok. Winter himself had arranged several further assays on a sample of ore (one, perhaps, that had been separated from the principal piece before its arrival in England), and now revealed to Lok that it was indeed valuable – with gold therein to the value of £240 per ton; far more than Agnello had admitted. According to Lok, Winter found this 'a matter to great for hym and me to deale withall, and belonged onely to the prynce'.

With this apparently expert confirmation of the ore's potential (Winter was a long-time investor in the Forest of Dean mines and, as Master of the Ordnance, must have had much understanding of refining techniques),[5] Walsingham's former reservations seem to have vanished. He had previously called the business 'but an alchamist matter'; yet he was now to increase his own stock in the new voyage four-fold over that for which he had provisionally subscribed prior to 28 March.[6] Within days, word of this prospectively vast new source of wealth was abroad in the City, for which Lok was blamed (he hotly denied it).[7] Guilty or not, his role in these subterfuges had been utterly inept. The temptation to keep the matter a near-secret had been overwhelming, but a practical impossibility nevertheless. Thinking himself to be the soul of discretion, he set into motion a chain of events that had swiftly escaped his capacity to influence them. Ironically, of all the participants in the 1576 venture, Lok had most fervently wished to see the exploitation of the north-west route to Cathay (and had emptied his purse to prove it); yet it was now he, with Winter, who bore the major responsibility for overturning the original objectives of the enterprise. With the prospect of fabulous wealth to be dug from a land as yet unexplored by England's rivals in Europe, the aim of finding a new sea-route to the Far East immediately became not so much an aside as almost completely incidental.

We need hardly wonder at the power of gold to deform men's power of judgement; but even so, the speed with which the enterprise reversed direction was remarkable. Why was it that Lok, Winter, Walsingham and others, whose shrewdness in their habitual businesses marks them out as men of considerable acumen, allowed their desires to so corrupt their sense of the possible? Did it really seem to them so likely that the first piece of rock picked up at random in this new land should be laden with precious metal? The answers, as to all matters of human motivation, are complex; but there was undoubtedly a powerful and persuasive lesson to be derived from the relatively recent Spanish conquest of central and southern America. Working against the healthy cynicism of the prospective investor was the apparent evidence of a continent that yielded up gold as easily as the known world yielded its soil. George Best, in the introductory narrative of his *True Discourse*, did no more than speak the mind of his generation when he asked:

For when was there euer heard of such abundance of gold and siluer . . . as in these days? No, Salomon himselfe, with all the pretious mettall of Ophir, which he (only one King) had in that only place, can not be comparable to the greate store of golde, and all other mettals, which dayly are digged out of the bowels of the earth, almost in all parts of the world.

Gold, it seemed, could be had almost everywhere. The largest conceptual obstacle facing the claims for Frobisher's ore was not that its discovery had been suspiciously easy but rather in the conflicting contemporary belief that gold was a 'hot' metal which did not form in the cold earth. Much later, on 15 November 1578, the Spanish Ambassador in London was to write a long relation to Philip II regarding Frobisher's third voyage, in which he observed 'it is incomprehensible that a land so cold as this can produce anything'.[8] This misapprehension was to have a wide currency until at least the mid-eighteenth century (long after it had been practically refuted); yet if Frobisher's discovery now seemed to deny the truth of this, it was only because he had an equally fallacious lore to support him; not least that the great prevalence of spiders observed in the soil of the new land 'as many affirme, are signes of great store of Golde. . . .'[9]

Clearly, contemporary metallurgy was no more exact a science than cosmography, as the tortured course of assays upon this New World ore during the life of the enterprise would prove. The element of doubt, both as to the general availability of gold and its particular presence in Frobisher's ore, was constantly present but did not necessarily breed circumspection. The only prior 'evidence' available to Michael Lok and his peers was that derived from Spanish voyages to mainland America; all of which seemed to return with an embarrassment of gold (a bounty that from the 1530s onwards had been supplemented by a torrent of silver). Logic, insofar as it had any part in the process, suggested that a commodity so easily secured had to be widespread. Lok continued to tout his piece of ore around London long after he should have become discouraged because he would not allow William Williams, George Needham and others to defy that logic. The observation that 'all that glittereth is not gold' already had a common currency in the late sixteenth century, and many London speculators continued to believe it even in the face of this new evidence; but to those who wished the enterprise to prosper it was a truth that recommended itself less and less as the body of 'evidence' regarding the ore grew.

With this supposed windfall suddenly before the adventurers, existing preliminary plans for a new expedition were immediately adapted, as were the assumptions that underpinned the enterprise itself. Elizabeth herself became an investor – the foremost of them, with stock of £1,000, partly met by the donation of one of her smaller naval vessels (the *Ayde*, built in 1560[10] and now valued at £750) to serve as Frobisher's flagship in the coming voyage. Her immediate motives are ambiguous. She had committed herself to the venture before knowledge of the ore became widespread, having instructed the Lord Admiral (Frobisher's old patron, the Earl of Lincoln) to provide the *Ayde* to the adventurers as early as 17 January.[11] Yet she was aware of Lok's progress with the ore – in writing – by 28 January at the latest, and it is prob-ably safe to assume that it was the prospect of gold, rather than trade, that caused her to increase her stock in the enterprise, and, not incidentally, give her the paramount say in any strategy to secure it.[12] If England was now set to emulate the stupendous experience of Spain and her New World treasure trove, she would not do so without the strictest royal supervision.

It may have been Lok's revelation to the Queen of this potentially stra-tegic resource that had brought into being the commission at which he and Winter incidentally touched upon the business of ore (though Lok himself had arrived at Winter's house that day still unaware that anyone except he, Agnello and Walsingham was involved). The consequences of its creation were profound, and reflected a new reality. The forthcoming voyage was not now to be organized by a few adventurers, nor would its aims reflect the aspirations of two men with a shared vision. Rather it would be subject to the absolute authority of the Privy Council, to whom the members of the commission – Sir William and George Winter, Anthony Jenkinson, Edmund Hogan, Thomas Randolphe and Michael Lok – would direct all matters for agreement or permission. From the moment of the commission's creation until the collapse of the adventurers' confidence some two years later, the north-west enterprise was to be conducted as a royal project in all but name.

Ironically, the only person who seems to have been entirely blameless for the usurpation of the north-west passage project was Martin Frobisher. At first, his silence on the matter was absolute; the only contemporary reference to his being exercised in the least degree by the ore he had brought home was the innocent question he asked during dinner at Lok's house. He seems, genuinely, to have regarded it as nothing more than that token he had promised to Lok prior to leaving England in 1576, and was probably surprised when, soon after 20 March, Lok told him of the full extent of his dealings with Agnello (having been ordered to do so by Francis Walsingham). However, once he understood the significance of the ore to his own prospects, he was not slow in adding to the momentum that effectively sidelined the original project:

> . . . And amongst other matters (the commissioners) enquired of them, what quantytye of this Ewre was to be had in that newe country, wherevnto Christofer hawl answered, that he coold not certanly tell what quantyty, for that he fownd no more but this stoune, nor sowght for no more, for that he regarded not this stoune, to be anye suche thinge, but he thought that where this was, there was more too be had / And therew(i)thall C. Furbysher vowched to the Com(m)issioners, w(i)th great speches & oathes, that there was Inoughe of yt to be had in that Countrye, too lade all the Queenes Shipps and sayd that as they sayled alongest in the straights he sawe the lyke thereof afarr of one that Iland, and one Loks lande alongest the shore, by the water lyenge lyke redd sande, glisteringe and one the rocks syddes of the shore, and at Gabriells Iland ynoughe of yt, w(i)th that Ewre of hawlls Ilande, w(hi)ch the com(m)yssioners did credyt and so certyfyed of their honors . . .[13]

So much for that apparently burning ambition, of some twenty years' standing, to discover a passage to Cathay. Undoubtedly, Lok had withheld information to which Frobisher had a right, and in doing so had provided a powerful incentive to shift the goals of the enterprise; but if the commissioners had heard the truth from their commander at sea as they had from Christopher Hall, the gold-mining project could hardly have been other than still-born. Once he had spoken out, that prospect evaporated. Though a second expedition to find the north-west passage remained a firm intention as late as 26 March 1577 (that is, before the news of 'gold' became generally known), its as yet unproven existence was hardly as promising a means of ensuring the continuity of his enterprise as the lure of English gold-mines. The future of the enterprise – with or without a passage to Cathay – was now secured by the strong underpinning that Frobisher provided to the wishful vision of Lok and Winter; he, in turn, ensured his own place within an expanded project. Later, when Lok and Frobisher were accusing each other of being the very cause and foundation of disaster, they might usefully have reflected upon their unwitting collaboration in creating the conditions for their own downfall.

For both men, there was to be an early and unwelcome implication of the redirection of the enterprise. Gold may have preserved their hopes, but it also imprisoned their ambitions. With imperishable optimism, Frobisher had addressed a petition to the Queen at some time prior to 30 March 1577, requesting that he be confirmed as High Admiral of the seas to the north-west and governor of all lands discovered by himself; with five per cent of profits accruing from the new trade and a one per cent levy upon commodities carried out of the new lands, for himself and his heirs in perpetuity.[14] We do not know if this request was even acknowledged, let alone considered (it was almost certainly drafted without the consent of Frobisher's fellow adventurers). Almost simultaneously, Lok was addressing a petition to the Queen to allow the incorporation of a 'Company of Cathay', with a charter based closely upon that of the Russia Company, giving it the same control over the potential new trade to the north-west as his former employers had retained to the north-east. This charter requested rather less for Frobisher's personal reward – a mere one per cent of the value of the Company's imports.[15] Again, however, the plea fell upon unheeding ears; the promise of gold, to a monarch beset by a perennial shortage of funds, had moved the agenda on somewhat. Many commentators have since spoken of the Company of Cathay as if it were a corporeal entity, but the appellation was an expression of a briefly shared identity, not of corporate reality. In March 1579, when the assets of the enterprise were being sold off to meet its debts, the Privy Council directed Burghley to pay monies for the Queen's re-purchase of the *Ayde* to Thomas Allen, Lok's successor as treasurer, rather than to the account of the adventurers, 'bi reason there is no soche corporacion or cumpany in lawe'.[16] This legal nonentity served the Queen admirably for two years. It provided a mechanism that allowed her to direct the enterprise without the substance through which its many participants might exercise their corporate privileges, or its creditors secure some form of redress in law. Eventually, however, this lack of legal form was to rebound with unpleasant consequences, not least for Elizabeth herself (and much more so for Michael Lok), but by then the contradictions of a corporate function without corporate responsibility had been fully worked through, with ominous implications for all participants. If the discovery and exploitation of a new trade were to have been the *raison d'être* of the Company of Cathay, the supposed discovery of gold, and the Queen's inevitable participation thereafter, ensured that it would remain a wraith.

It must have been a particularly bitter blow for Lok, therefore, when, in the following year, Elizabeth granted a charter to the admirably persistent Humphrey Gilbert, permitting him to discover, take possession of and govern any lands not already under the rule of a Christian prince. This also allowed for his heirs to assume the same rights in perpetuity, subject to a twenty per cent tax on profits arising from the enterprise to be paid to the Exchequer. Superficially, the terms and conditions of the charter were close to those requested by Lok (and even a little more generous), but there were fundamental differences. Most importantly, the Queen did not intend to invest in Gilbert's enterprise; therefore she had nothing to lose and a fifth of his profits to gain. Furthermore, it has been determined that Gilbert had almost certainly lost interest in the north-west passage by 1578, and was thinking instead of a colonizing project in the latitude of what would become the southern New England states; a scheme of the sort whose long-term financing and low initial yield offered very little temptation to a Queen who lived from one fiscal year to the next.[17] Colonization, *per se*, interested Elizabeth far less than it would subsequent generations of her countrymen.

Nevertheless, the most intriguing aspect of Gilbert's licence is not that it was granted, but what its terms might have meant to Frobisher's adventurers. It was couched in such broad terms that had their own enterprise survived for a year or two more, Elizabeth herself may well have become an unwitting interloper upon Gilbert's rights. Had Gilbert succeeded in his goals, efforts to enforce those rights would have provided a test of the limits of the Queen's patience with – and commitment to – the legalities she professed to support.

Meanwhile, Michael Lok, seduced by the promise of fabulous wealth, forsook his dreams of governorship and applied himself to the business of gold mines. Frobisher, never exercised in the least degree by trade, went swiftly wherever the prospect of advancement seemed most prominent. With the Queen herself as his principal backer, that prospect seemed, in the early part of 1577, to be filling his horizons. He had moved from the dark peripheries of society to bask in the glow of a modest but growing popular fame, sponsored by his sovereign and thus possessed of newly impeccable credentials. From the prisons of Guinea, Lisbon, Launceston, York and London to the patronage of Glorianna was a large step, even by the fluid standards of the sixteenth century. It was, of course, a smaller step to pass back again; but for the moment, such a fate seemed unthinkable. No intelligent opinion yet compared him to Columbus, but the less flattering analogies had begun to be set aside, or discreetly forgotten. Frobisher, energetically as always, prepared to add meat to the bones of this happy circumstance. With new lands to discover and exploit, gold to be had by the shipload there and a new reputation to gild with it, any misgivings he may have had that 'his' project had become the Queen's business paled before the prospect of an ambition gloriously realized.

TEN

The 1577 Voyage

Once firm decisions had been taken regarding the nature and aims of the coming voyage, the commissioners and their masters sought further financial backing with great energy but indifferent success. At the beginning of March, before the matter of ore became public knowledge, the Privy Council had addressed letters to the President of the North and the Mayor of Bristol, requiring them to invite the merchants of York, Newcastle, Hull and Bristol to share in the good fortune that had fallen upon the existing adventurers: '. . . their Lordships thincke good to desier that, seing by the successe of the last yere soche hope hath ben conceaved of the proffitt of that voiage as both her Majestie and their Lordships have entered into some charges and coulde wishe that others wold do the like . . .'.[1]

Whatever she and they could wish, it was hardly answered by the good merchants of these towns. The Earl of Huntingdon, who had been ordered to collect their replies, sent them on to the Council as early as 5 April; their form and content is not known, but none of those approached was to subscribe.[2] The first known provisional adventurers' list, dated 30 March, gave the names of forty-five men and women prepared to invest in the new voyage, with total subscriptions of £3,225.[3] Surprisingly, the subsequent public revelation of the ore and redirection of the aims of the enterprise away from prospective trading opportunities caused several of these – including a small group of Bristol merchants who may have been the only members of their profession to have responded favourably to the Council's invitation – to drop out. By the time the 1577 voyage was ready to sail at the end of May, fifty-eight adventurers were definitely committed, bringing new funds totalling £4,275.[4]

The response to the supposed discovery of gold seems, therefore, to have been relatively muted. This apparent lack of widespread interest in what promised to be a fabulously lucrative venture is puzzling, if the lure of gold was as powerful as contemporary literature suggests. Yet this was to be no sixteenth-century South-Sea Bubble or Grand Circular Canal project. Though participation in the venture was open (there is no evidence that efforts were made to restrict the number or type of investors), very few people succumbed to the temptation of its vast potential. The reason for this may have had as much to do with the structure as with the nature of the investment.

Though there is no extant statement of the terms of investment, it seems that new investors were offered only a limited participation in the scheme. The basic share-unit in the enterprise was £25. With a few exceptions – principally, of members of the Privy Council or Crown officers – those who became adventurers for the first time in 1577 took up the minimum investment of a single share (or of £50, which gave also a retrospective holding in the 1576 account – and, of course, in its debts). Either this was a measure of prudence on the investors' part, or, more probably, it represented their maximum permitted venture. It is improbable that the Queen wanted new subscribers to acquire a proportion of stock that would give them the right to massive returns of the order she was expecting for herself. Following the return of the 1577 expedition, a note of twenty-six prospective new adventurers – very few of whom were subsequently to subscribe – put each of them down for £25: a remarkable coincidence or, more likely, the reflection of a 'company' policy imposed by the Crown.[5] Lok's own, huge investment was an anomaly. He had made substantial loans to the enterprise in 1576, and would do so again in 1577; though a proportion of these were repaid (if slowly), the balance, for want of sufficient new subscriptions to redeem it, was converted into stock. In 1578, when even Lok was beginning to regret the implications of his enthusiasm for the enterprise, he managed to off-load £1,000 of his existing stock onto the Earl of Oxford; but no other investor, save for Lok and the Queen herself, came close to such a stake. Growing financial commitments were to result in the imposition of extraordinary assessments upon existing stock, but all subsequent attempts to raise 'new' money to finance the voyages or their collateral expenses concentrated upon widening the body of investors, not increasing the respective shares of current adventurers.

With this limited opportunity to make money, and with the Queen's heavy hand upon the enterprise, contemporary opinion – outside the immediate circle of adventurers and their kin – may have made a virtue of scepticism. Of the 'new' investors (that is, those who set down their names only after news of the ore had leaked out), fully eleven were Michael Lok's own children or step-children, with a nephew, Michael Lok junior; all of whom had taken up stock represented entirely by the elder Lok's loans that had yet – and were increasingly unlikely – to be repaid.[6] Whether the rest of London, meanwhile, was busily recalling precisely what does and does not glitter is hard to determine; what is certain is that the redirection of the enterprise from the search for a north-west passage to the exploitation of ore deposits in Meta Incognita brought a large shift only in the character of investment, with the mercantile proportion falling and that of the 'Court' rising from thirty-five per cent of the total in 1576 to some sixty-six per cent in 1577 – a small, if telling manifestation of the 'sure, certayne, and present gayne' principle so lamented by George Best.[7]

Whatever their social background, the identity of the new investors suggests that most had been brought in through their connections with existing adventurers, rather than by advertisement of the enterprise abroad. In addition to the Privy Councillors who had invested previously (all of whom continued as adventurers), the Lord Admiral Lincoln, the Earl and Countess of Pembroke, Sir Francis Knollis, Thomas Wilson (the Queen's principal secretary) and Lady Anne Talbot subscribed to the new voyage. Of lesser courtiers, the later Treasurer at Wars, Sir Henry Wallop, and Tower officials William Pelham, Richard Bowland and Geoffrey Turville (all officers of the Ordnance) also invested – as, inexplicably, did Edward Dyer, whose own, amateur assay of the ore had been so much more accomplished than those of Agnello and Schutz. Finally, Sir William Winter – the man (after Lok himself) most responsible for the subterfuges that had brought about the new ore project – was rewarded for his efforts by being allowed to subscribe for a full £200 of stock.[8]

Notwithstanding the City's doubts concerning the enterprise, the new voyage also included a further influx of Muscovy men. These were Thomas Allen and Richard Young (both assistants of the Russia Company in 1569), John Somers (a director in 1580), Anthony Marler (the longest serving London Agent of the Company in the sixteenth century) and Christopher Hoddesdon (former head of the English factory in Moscow and eventual Master of the Merchant Adventurers).[9] The motives of these men are harder to discern. Clearly, they were as moved by the failure of their Company to provide a consistent profit as those of their fellow Company men who had been persuaded by Lok in the previous year; but whether their participation in 1577 was merely a belated appreciation of this, or a response to the more immediate promise of gold, is difficult to establish. If the latter, they were being uncharacteristically loose with their money (though again, each of these men was sufficiently wealthy to risk £50 – in Marler's case, £25 – in an enterprise that just might provide a fabulous return).

The relatively underwhelming response to the new voyage had immediate repercussions. The finances of the enterprise were beginning to look strained, notwithstanding the fresh influx of capital. The budget for the 1576 voyage, under-provided by a half, had not run to its inevitable post-costs. Following Frobisher's happy return, therefore, no funds remained to pay off the crews of the *Gabriel* and *Michael*, who represented a continuing (and growing) expense to the adventurers. Some merchandise was re-sold to the original suppliers, raising almost £118; but the total cost of the 1576 voyage eventually reached £1,608, whilst its official stock had remained unchanged at £875. In the months prior to the setting out of the 1577 voyage, Lok's account books reflected (or, rather, deflected) the truth of this unsatisfactory position. In setting out the liabilities of the enterprise, he drew up separate accounts for the first and second voyages – in effect, treating them as distinct, terminable ventures – and 'sold' the equipment purchased in 1576 to the 1577 account without fully depreciating its value to reflect wear, tear and spoilage. In this manner, he managed to realize a paper profit of £75 on the 1576 account; though of course, the debts thereof had been merely carried over (a truth which not even Lok's fiscal gymnastics could disguise: he concluded his 1576 account with the pious exhortation 'And so by this first voyage is spent and lost of the stoke of li 875 the Sum of li 800 w(hi)ch god restore').[10] He then further blurred reality by running subscriptions for the 1576 and 1577 voyages together, implying – on the positive side of the balance sheet – a continuity that his massaging of the liabilities (and the allocation of £875 of 1577 subscriptions to pay off the existing debt) had belied. In effect, the present was bailing out the past and storing up problems for the future, for which the promise of vast returns would swiftly become less a matter of hope than of urgent necessity. Given the unhappy confluence of burgeoning costs, a disappointing level of new interest in the venture and the thin prospect of early income, Lok had little choice but to reflect the brightest possible position; but none of this augured well for an enterprise that had been intended to break away from the cycle of indebtedness that had plagued the early years of the Russia Company. Nor did the fine detail of the financial arrangements provide much comfort for Lok himself. Burghley, Leicester, Wilson, Gresham and others had set their names down for the second voyage, but they seem subsequently to have overlooked the small matter of handing over their money. Even after the return of the second voyage, Lok was issuing pointed reminders to these men that he had personally stood for their venture and would like the same repaid as soon as possible.[11]

Ironically, this relatively thin English interest in the forthcoming voyage was not to be reflected abroad. Soon, Philip II, the French Court and even the Tsar would seize upon its significance; and even before the despatch of the 1577 voyage, efforts were being made to discover precisely what it was that Frobisher had found. Several years later, the great Flemish cartographer, Abraham Ortelius, admitted to Richard Hakluyt that the principal reason for his visit to England in the early months of 1577 '. . . was to no other ende but to prye and looke into the secretes of Frobishers voyadge'.[12] Had Frobisher's countrymen been fired with even a fraction of Ortelius's curiosity, funds might have flowed much more freely; though in this case, their nation's much reputed natural reserve proved to be an entirely fortunate quality.

Nevertheless, optimism undoubtedly reigned within the company of adventurers prior to the despatch of the new voyage, even if it was founded upon shaky premises. With the impetus of New World gold mines to buoy them, the commissioners and Privy Councillors pressed on with their preparations. At the beginning of 1577, when Cathay had been their only goal, a proposal for the forthcoming expedition had been presented to Burghley. Then, a fleet of three ships and two barks had been envisaged, carrying merchandise to the value of £1,200. The total cost of this had been estimated at £6,280.[13] By 26 March 1577, expectations of potential investors were more modest. A new proposal of that date envisaged an expedition of 115 men in one ship and two barks, at a cost of £4,500.[14] Preparations went ahead on the basis of this latter plan, even after the public disclosure of the ore's existence, with a view to despatching the voyage no later than June. On 22 March, probably upon the basis of the draft proposals, Frobisher was given a commission to press the necessary mariners.[15]

Setting aside the scale of the expedition, its goals were hardly comparable to those of the previous year. The instructions that the Privy Council were eventually to issue for the new voyage reflected the fundamental shift away from the search for a route to Cathay.[16] Now, its principal task was to return to Frobisher's 'strait' and secure large amounts of ore of the type seized upon by the late master Garrard. Little Hall's Island was to be their first – perhaps their only – destination. If no suitable ore was to be had there, other sites in the strait were then to be surveyed. Once large-scale extraction had commenced, Frobisher was to take the barks *Gabriel* and *Michael* and explore the upper reaches of the strait, noting safe harbours and potential mining sites. He was to pass as far as the western exit to the strait in order to confirm its existence and nature, and then return to rendezvous with the now fully laden *Ayde*. Only if all samples of ore were definitely proved to be worthless on-site (a near impossibility, given the inherent technical failings of the small furnace that Jonas Schutz was to construct in the new land) was Frobisher to send home the *Ayde* and press on to Cathay with his two barks.

The outfitting of the new voyage reflected these developing aims. The quality and quantity of victualling matched that of the previous year (though providing for what was clearly expected to be a shorter voyage than the passage to Cathay); but the experiences of the 1576 expedition, when men who had been well fed nevertheless succumbed to exhaustion, persuaded the commissioners also to provide ample woollen clothing – gowns, cassocks, shirts, breeches, hoses, caps and shoes of 'winter lether' for all ranks.[17] Additionally, now that Best's 'new prey' had been identified as potentially dangerous, the coming expedition was to be substantially armed. From the Queen's ordnance at the Tower, Sir William Winter supplied the *Ayde* – at market value, naturally – with four minions (four-pounders), eight sacres (five-pounders), nine falcons (three pounders) and six double-chambered fowlers (the latters' weight of shot is not known, but at £5 a piece these were as expensive as the falcons).[18] The crews' personal armament included bows, 'black bill' pikes, darts and daggers.

Though eight professional miners from the Forest of Dean were hired to accompany the expedition, surprisingly little was spent on mining implements, which suggests that the commissioners expected the ore deposits to lie near or upon the surface, waiting to be harvested like a fallen crop of fruit.[19] Some £50 secured the necessary tools, but this sum included all materials for a small assaying furnace to allow ore samples to be tested on site.[20] Jonas Schutz, by now having supplanted Agnello as the Commissioners' favourite assayer (though Agnello continued to assist in conducting assays until at least the end of 1578), agreed to go on the voyage in return for a pension for life and £45 in advance.

Vestigial interest in exploring the north-west passage to its western extremity, and the even less likely eventuality that the barks *Gabriel* and *Michael* would pass on from there to reach Cathay, was reflected in the scant attention that these goals received in preparations for the voyage. Much of the miniature trade fair of commodities laden in the previous year had been sold off to meet the debts of the 1576 voyage. The remaining items were to be carried in the barks once more, though nothing further was purchased (monies intended for the provision of new merchandise in the 26 March plan had since been reallocated elsewhere). Any possibility of a profit arising, even upon a successful voyage to Cathay, was therefore unthinkable. To facilitate the momentous initiation of a new trade, just two merchants joined the crew and gentlemen of the *Ayde*; no doubt they were to transfer to the *Gabriel*, should the small likelihood of their intended employment become a reality. One of these men was Lok's servant and probable factor, Edward Selman;[21] the other was Thomas Marsh, possibly a relative of Anthony Marsh, servant of the Russia Company and Lok's successor as its London Agent in 1580.[22] Even this thin complement of businessmen was probably surplus to intentions; Selman's presence here and in the 1578 voyage (in the latter of which he would act as the expedition's semi-official chronicler) had less to do with the vestigial prospect of trade than the need to provide a pair of eyes for Lok and his fellow merchants, for reasons which will become apparent.

Frobisher's flagship in the coming voyage was, of course, the Queen's ship *Ayde*. Captain of the *Gabriel* was Edward Fenton, a gentleman follower of the Earl of Warwick who had seen service as a soldier in Ireland in the 1560s; and of the *Michael*, Gilbert Yorke, possibly one of Sir John Yorke's multitude of sons and, therefore, a cousin of Frobisher.[23] As we shall see, the number of 'other ranks' was eventually established at 120, though this total was comfortably exceeded, despite the Privy Council's persistent directions otherwise.

As in the previous year, Frobisher himself appears to have had little responsibility for the preparations to set out the new voyage. He was given money to hire mariners for the *Ayde*, and may have secured the participation of a number of the gentlemen who were to go in the voyage; but he was not a member of the commission that had the charge of setting the scale and character of the expedition. Lok later claimed that even without a defined role, Frobisher's efforts to intervene in these matters were wholly counterproductive. Before the definitive nature of the 1577 voyage had been established, he had allegedly argued for a substantially equipped expedition of three tall ships and two barks (perhaps this had been the genesis of the first, £6,000 plan for the expedition).[24] When its scale was subsequently revised for want of the necessary funds, Lok claimed that '. . . he made no smale raginge and owtragious speakinge amongest the Comyssioners . . .' in protest at their prudence.[25] The justice of the charge is difficult to establish (though clearly, it was vulnerable to challenge by the other commissioners, if false). Presumably, even Frobisher understood that the budget for the 1577 voyage was not likely to be generous, and that overstating his case might have the effect of pricing himself out of a voyage. Conversely, all the evidence of his dealings with and in the adventurers' money suggests that he was acutely prodigal of their resources. Lok, recalling the experience of opening his own purse in 1574–5 to support Frobisher's needs, may have warned his colleagues that their captain's input to the preparations for the voyage was best confined to dock-side recruitment: an activity for which his career as a privateer had given him much valuable experience.

More pertinent was the problem, manifest once more prior to the departure of the 1577 voyage, of Frobisher's autocratic temperament. In the previous year, it had been Lok who had struggled to convince his fellow adventurers that their commander at sea was fit to do just that. Twelve months later, it seems that Lok was as exercised by the problem as anyone. Though bound by the decisions of others on land, it is apparent that Frobisher was strongly opposed to sharing his command at sea. Exhortations to commanders to take 'good counsel' from their officers were habitually made in official instructions of the period, but rather in the spirit of those which urged monarchs to take the same from their privy advisers. The truth was that a sea captain, both then and later, exercised an authority wholly disproportionate to that of his land-bound equivalent (Francis Drake made particularly striking use of this latitude during his most memorable voyages). A good captain would seek advice, but whether he acted upon it was his decision alone; probably, Frobisher would not have minded the sentiment being expressed generally, though it seems that something more specific was envisaged:

When as the Commission(er)s had devised articles for his Com(m)ission, and Instructions for the direction and gov(er)ment of the voyadge, w(hi)ch weare confirmyd by her Ma(ies)ties honorable pryvie Councell, even by his owne advice, and for casualtye of deathe woold have joyned vnto him Capt. Fenton and some others of the gentillmen that went w(i)th him, he vtterly refused the same, and swore no smale oathes, that he woold be alone, or otherwise he woold not goe in the voyadge, for he had alredye a higher Com(m)ission vnder the broad seale then they coold gyve him anye, and badd them make what Com(m)ission they woold, for when he weare abroade he woold vse yt as he lyst, and afterwardes becawse he coold not be furnished w(i)th all thinges to his will, therew(i)thall he flonge owt of the doores, and swore by gods wounds that he woold hippe my m(aster)s the v(e)nturers for yt, at w(hi)ch words Captayne Fenton plucked him secretly, and willed him to be modest . . .[26]

An appeal to Frobisher's modesty was hardly likely to be successful, but Fenton had taken the point that his commander chose to ignore. Despite Frobisher's wrathful outbursts before the commissioners, the fact that he was to sail under the authority of the Broad Seal of England brought very serious disadvantages to a man who preferred to take his own counsel. The contrast between his own proclivities and those of Michael Lok emerges decisively in the respective manner in which they reacted to this 'higher commission'. For Lok, authority and regulation were components of that bedrock upon which his professional life had been raised. Despite his failure to become governor of a Company of Cathay, and the pronounced reduction in his capacity to influence events that the Queen's involvement had brought, he moved easily from the role of joint founder of the enterprise to that of merely one of several commissioners responsible to the Privy Council. But Lok's bedrock was Frobisher's millstone: a dragging, inertial weight to stay the pace of his ambitions. Upon land, he fretted at delays, the constant shortage of funds and the curbs placed upon the scale of his expeditions; above all, he reacted in a wholly negative way to the reality that these matters were now ordered without requiring his input. Once freed from the tyranny of other men's preoccupations, Frobisher would give full vent to his natural inclinations. Time and again during his latter two voyages to Baffin Island, he would follow the letter of his obligation to 'take good counsel' whilst simultaneously refusing to brook the slightest dissent to the decisions he wished to have made. It was a characteristic – perhaps the *only* characteristic – he was to share with Drake, his later colleague and, eventually, his bitter enemy.

Neither the commissioners nor their masters in the Privy Council could have been unaware of this problem. Thus, as we have seen, Edward Selman may have been appointed as the adventurers' – and particularly, the merchants' – representative on the voyage; a presence that may have been intended to incline their sea-commander to circumspection. However, stronger measures were also taken, should that intention prove excessively fond. For the first time, Frobisher sailed with instructions that set a precise order of priorities. What they did *not* provide for was any more freedom of action on his part than unforeseen conditions or events might demand. With the Queen's money committed to the enterprise, potentially expensive initiatives made in the cause of one man's personal advancement were not to be encouraged.

Unfortunately, if some of the priorities she demanded of Frobisher were not his own, neither were they those of her fellow adventurers. As Michael Lok and his fellow commissioners pressed ahead with their work, new instructions were incorporated by order of the Privy Council which had little relevance to the purely commercial enterprise envisaged originally. In addition to his stated complement of men, Frobisher was also directed to take with him a number of condemned prisoners, six of whom were to be set down on the coast of 'Friesland'. The remainder were to be left on-shore somewhere in the strait to winter there, observing climatic and other conditions to determine the best time of the year for subsequent expeditions to visit. To complement their worthy (if very unwilling) work, Frobisher himself was to chart the most defensible sites for 'possessynge of the countrie', and secure between three and ten of the local inhabitants, 'whereof some to be ould and the other yonge whome wee mynd shall not returne agayne thither; and therfore you shall have great care howe you doe take them for avoidyng of offence towards them and the contrie'.[27]

These new goals, peripheral to the main business of the voyage, must have given many of the adventurers a discreet spasm of foreboding. An enterprise devoted to generate the earliest possible profit was one thing – its motive could hardly fail to appeal equally to merchants, lords and poets – but proto-colonists and aboriginal hostages suggested something entirely more abiding, and expensive. The very last thing that the merchants in particular sought was an extended commitment to develop a presence in the new lands beyond that which was strictly needed to extract the ore. Their money, devoted to anything other than its immediate increase, was doing nothing more fertile than support a royal agenda. To the more prudent of their number, even the promise of gold may not have entirely quelled the first suspicions that Elizabeth, as was her habit, had secured a foreign policy on the cheap. When, therefore, the expedition departed from England at the end of May, the hopes of the adventurers were high; but for the first time they may have been tinged with a nervous appreciation that all that may be gold is not necessarily profitable.

Frobisher's small fleet set sail from Harwich on 31 May 1577.[28] From that moment, he was at odds with his detailed and onerous instructions. They had strictly provided for a maximum of 120 mariners, miners and gentlemen-soldiers in the *Ayde* and two barks. That number included the unfortunates who were intended to represent England's first experiment in judicial deportation, whose heinous offences included 'robbinge of a Tailors shoppe at Barnet', several robberies 'by the highway', 'stealing of a gelding & a mare price vi.li' and, in the case of the unfortunate John Roberts (a beggar), perjury: 'long repreved by her m(a)jesties comaundment'.[29]

It was known already, however, that Frobisher had exceeded this quota by at least twenty, and possibly as many as forty, men. On their first evening abroad from London, the ships had paused at Gravesend; they remained there until the following morning, so that the crews might receive communion from the hands of a minister of the town. Once out of the Thames that afternoon, Frobisher may have assumed that the matter of overmanning had been settled by default. At Harwich, however, letters were waiting which ordered him to set down his surplus. Even Frobisher could hardly continue to ignore his instructions in the face of remonstrations from the Privy Council; in obeying them, however, he decided unilaterally to adjust the Queen's priorities. The most expendable members of his complement seemed to be – and were – the condemned men. With a number of mariners also, he set them on-shore in Harwich harbour on the last day of May – not, it seems, under restraint, or even having taken their parole – and set his fleet towards the north thereafter.[30]

Its route towards the new lands mirrored that of the previous year, with minor deviations. On 7 June, they anchored in St Magnus Sound in Orkney to take on water, and spent some time thereafter trying to persuade the terrified local population that they were not pirates. In the previous year, the industrious but literal Hall had bothered himself only with his precise latitude off the Shetland Islands; now, however, the company included a number of would-be Mandevilles. The audiences for which George Best and Dionyse Settle were to set down their memoirs demanded far more substantial fare than a mere master's lore; and here, at Orkney, they aired their muses for the first time. Having the opportunity to devote almost an entire afternoon and evening to the study of the local culture and its mores, both men felt qualified to set down their conclusions with horrible condescension. Somewhat charitably, Best observed of the local inhabitants that 'their houses are but poore without, and sluttish enough within, and the people in nature therevnto agreeable';[31] whilst Settle, less inclined to circumspection, declared:

> The good man, wife, children, and other of their familie, eate and sleepe on the one side of the house, and their cattell on the other, very beastly and rudely, in respect of civilitie. . . . They dresse their meate very filthily, and eate it without salt. Their apparell is after the rudest sort of Scotland. Their money is all base.[32]

It is to be hoped (and was probably assumed by their literary persecutors) that the good people of St Magnus had no recourse to a bookseller.

From Orkney, the fleet's passage across the Atlantic could hardly have been more different than that of the previous year. The expected storms failed to materialize; the weather remained uncharacteristically temperate and the winds were almost always favourable. The ships' masters – Hall (*Ayde*), William Smith (*Gabriel*) and James Beare (*Michael*) – continued to mark their courses carefully, and their mariners set themselves to the myriad tasks that, even in fair weather, kept them from idleness; but the gentlemen's first experience of oceanic travel was not unakin to that of later generations of paying passengers. Settle remarked that they had so few impediments to their voyage that 'we had when we were so disposed, the fruition of our bookes, and other pleasures to passe awaye the time . . .'. Best reported their rendezvous with three English fishing boats returning from Iceland, to which they passed letters to take back to England, but was otherwise reduced to commenting upon the quantity of logs and brushwood that drifted past the *Ayde* (idly, Settle noticed them also, and then busied himself in speculation as to their ultimate source).

This pleasant cruise continued until 4 July, when a gunshot from the *Michael* signalled the first sighting of the coast of 'Friesland' in that year. The prospect of this alien place provided far more worthy grist for the imaginations of the literati. The sparse, 1576 description of the coastline provided by Hall was filled out handsomely, though unequally: Best's 'ragged and high lande, full of drift ise, and seemeth almost inaccessible . . .', was easily outshone by Settle's florid:

> Here, in a place of odoriferous and fragrant smels of sweete gums, & pleasant notes of musicall birds, which other Countries in more temperate Zone do yeeld, we tasted the most boisterous *Boreal* blasts, mixt with snow & haile, in the moneths of June and Julie . . . Al along this coast yce lieth, as a continual bulwarke, & so defendeth the Countrey, that those whiche would land there, incurr great danger.[33]

However colourfully couched, the latter observation was acute. The land before them seemed to hold out some small promise, with easy fishing and evidence of valuable white coral in the seas close to its shores; but both Settle and Best nervously noted the quantity of ice that floated before and on to the same shores: 'some 70. some 80. fadome vnder water, besides that which is aboue . . .'. Once more, the persistence of mists that half-hid such monstrous obstacles confounded attempts to effect a landing. First Hall and then Frobisher tried to reach the shore in their ship's boat (the latter upon at least

two occasions), but both were driven back by lack of visibility and the knowledge that large amounts of ice lay somewhere in the fog before them. For
four days thereafter, the small fleet passed westwards along the coastline,
searching without success for safe harbours and signs of habitation. Curiously,
having accepted once more the myth of the Zeno brothers' discovery of
'Friesland', Best noted that their chart compared very agreeably with his view
of the coastline before him. On the morning of 8 July, having neither a clear
opportunity to land, nor any convicts to set down as instructed, Frobisher
was obliged once more to modify his official instructions, and set the ships'
course to the west, towards his new land.

Almost immediately, the long-anticipated storms descended about the
fleet. The vessels were dispersed, each spooning before the wind for long
periods rather than chance their sails (the *Michael* did so from necessity,
having had her steerage smashed and her top-masts shattered). However,
despite losing the means of checking their positions for several days, the
masters' plots proved admirably proficient, and as the weather cleared on 17
July the three ships made contact once more. That morning, Frobisher sent
off the *Gabriel* and *Michael* on opposite north-south courses to attempt to
find some familiar landmark, but it was a mariner in the *Ayde* herself who
sighted Hall's Island, dead ahead, that evening.

The following day, when the *Gabriel* and *Michael* had rejoined the *Ayde*,
Frobisher took Jonas Schutz to Little Hall's Island in the *Ayde*'s pinnace, to
search for further samples of the black ore secured by master Garrard. During
several hours' scrupulous examination of the ground, they found nothing.
Best chose to regard this puzzling and irritating failure in a miraculous light:
'that being only one rich stone in all the Iland, the same should be found by
one of our Countreymen, whereby it shoulde appeare, Gods diuine will and
pleasure is, to haue oure common wealth increased . . .'.[34] However, their
initial disappointment – no matter how tortuously justified as a fortunate one
– was fleeting. A brief inspection of islands nearby apparently revealed traces
of a similar ore, and of recent human habitation. The mariners also found
some gulls' eggs, an unknown species of fowl and a young seal, all of which
they brought back to the *Ayde* and ate. On 19 July, Frobisher disembarked
upon Hall's Greater Island with forty of his best men (though with much difficulty once more, due to the quantity of ice lying off-shore), and thereafter
trekked some two miles inland to its highest point, which he named Mount
Warwick. There, the Englishmen raised a column of stones, the first mark of
possession in that new land, and prayed for their country's successful exploitation of its bounty.[35]

Before leaving the island, Frobisher and his men saw several Inuit climb Mount Warwick immediately after they themselves had evacuated it, apparently to examine the strange artefacts left there. They waved to the Englishmen, making signs that they wished to parley; with cries, according to Best, 'like the mowing of Bulles'. Both groups appointed two men as emissaries to approach the other. As in the previous year, this initial encounter was friendly, though both sides were extremely cautious. Each presented gifts – pins from the Englishmen and two bow-cases from the Inuit – and unsuccessfully offered the respective hospitality of their homes or ships to the other. Best – who may have been one of the two men appointed to speak with the Inuit ambassadors – noted their carefully off-hand manner with strangers:

> Their manner of trafficke is thus, they doe vse to lay downe of their marchandise vppon the ground, so much as they meane to parte withall, and so looking that the other partie, with whome they make trade, shoulde doe the like, they themselues doe departe, and then, if they doe like of their marte, they come againe, and take in exchange the others marchandise, otherwise, if they like it not, they take their owne and departe.[36]

The Inuit's excessive caution suggests either that they had some prior, hostile contact with other races (possibly from the south side of what is now Hudson Strait), or that word of the events of the previous year's expedition had travelled down the coast from the north-west. This quality of circumspection was to make it extremely difficult for Frobisher to obey his instructions – which, seamlessly, he now re-interpreted to apply to the folk of his new land, rather than those of 'Friesland' – to secure several of their number, and not a little hazardous. The following day, he and Hall went alone to parley with two men of the Inuit party. They appeared to be unarmed, and so Frobisher and Hall, after making 'certeine dumb signes and mute congratulations', fell upon them, probably upon a prearranged signal.[37] The prospective hostages refused to play their expected part, however. They broke free and leapt behind a nearby rock, from where they plucked their bows and arrows. Frobisher, though prone to fearlessness, was not entirely imprudent; hastily, he and Hall turned tail and sprinted for the safety of their men and boats, though Frobisher himself took a flesh wound in the buttock on the way (Best later put salve upon it by claiming that his admiral had 'rather speedily fled backe' only because he suspected a greater number lying in ambush). The prospect of the rest of the English landing party, advancing to protect their leader, did not deter the two fierce and aggrieved Inuit, who continued to fire their arrows and wounded several of Frobisher's men. It might have been the occasion of England's first military setback in her embryonic march to empire; fortunately, however, her mariners' spirits rose as Inuit quivers emptied. As their assailants, arrows and anger expended, began to retreat, a member of the landing party (an over-large Cornish wrestler named Nicholas Congar) pursued and brought down one of them with great violence. Frobisher, embarrassed but almost whole, had been provided with his first captive.

This encounter, however diverting, occurred as the fleet was enduring considerable dangers. Anchored in the small sound between Hall's two eponymous islands, it remained exposed to the endemic hazards of a wooden world. A fire on the *Ayde*, caused by an inattentive cook, had barely been contained (fortunately, a ship's boy had noticed the wrong sort of smoke issuing from a badly laid oven chimney and raised the alarm in time). Even more seriously, as the mariners were distracted by the fire, the weather turned once more. On the evening of 18 July, as Frobisher and his best men laid claim to the land, the remaining members of the expedition received a hard lesson in Arctic seamanship:

> . . . the ship and barkes . . . were forced to abide in a cruell tempest, chancing in the night, amongst and in the thickest of the yce, which was so monstrous, that euen the least of a thousand had bene of force sufficient, to haue shiuered our ship and barkes into smal portions, if God (who in all necessities, hath care vpon the infirmitie of man) had not prouided for this our extremetie a sufficient remedie, through the light of the night, whereby wee might well discerne to flee from such imminent dangers, which we avoided with 14 Bourdes [i.e., tacks] in one watch the space of 4 howres.[38]

With Hall on-shore also, it was left to the masters' mates of the *Ayde* and *Gabriel*, Andrew Diar and Charles Jackman, and the *Ayde*'s master gunner, Richard Cox 'being expert both in Navigation and other good qualities', to handle the ships deftly and preserve the expedition from disaster.[39]

Though the immediate crisis had been weathered, it was clear that the ships could not remain at their dangerous anchorage. Apparently, the crew of the *Ayde* found time to sink to their knees and give thanks to God for their deliverance (one senses here the presence of Best's artistic licence once more); but the wind and tides having cleared the mouth of the strait on 19 July, the ships were moved from their treacherous position. The northern extremity of the strait's mouth had proved too dangerous and, more importantly, bereft of that ore which Frobisher had promised in such vast quantities. According to Lok's later (and somewhat lurid) testimony, Schutz and his assistant goldfiners had not borne this disappointment lightly, falling 'intoo great greyfe, and into desperatt minde . . . and wisshed them selves rather dedd than alyve'.[40] Frobisher had sworn to the commissioners that another, red ore lay like red sand upon the northern coast further to the west; had this proved equally elusive, the fragile Schutz might well have suffered a relapse. Perhaps, then, it was merely tenderness – or, more likely, the need to prevent a reputed expert from challenging the verity of his former 'vehement oaths' – that now inclined Frobisher to direct his vessels towards the strait's southern shore. As yet unvisited, its promise – happy or otherwise – could hardly reflect upon his own judgement.

With only a few, infrequent exceptions, the south-western shore of Frobisher Bay is extremely forbidding to any vessel seeking a landfall. Cliffs rise almost sheer from the sea, and prevailing currents scour seasonal ice-floes along the lee shores, enticing and entrapping vessels which cross their path. The master's mate in the *Ayde*, Charles Jackman, was therefore fortunate to sight the entrance to a wide, shallow bay with adequate sheltering headlands, which was (and remains) named in his honour. The *Ayde* and the two barks anchored here on 21 July. A brief reconnaissance was enough to confirm that although many rocks thereabout shimmered with the promise of precious metals, it was, as Best pointed out, no more than 'blacke leade, and veryfyed the prouerbe All is not golde that shineth'. This speedy and accurate observation was as germane as it remains puzzling. If Best knew this – and Settle also, using an almost identical form of words – the mystery of how the rest of the ships' crews, the assayers, the merchants, courtiers, Privy Councillors and their usually thrifty monarch came to be deceived about other rocks elsewhere in this new land only deepens.[41]

Yet there was, it seems, evidence of more promising ore here. The reconnaissance parties found four sorts of ore broadly similar to that of Hall's Island, which promised to hold gold 'in good quantie'. Before any further exploration was attempted, however, there were important dues to be paid. On-shore in Jackman Sound, Frobisher had a trumpet sounded, his men gathered in a great circle, and they fell once more to their knees, giving

> . . . GOD humble thankes, for that it had pleased him of his greate goodnesse in preseruing vs from such imminent dangers, to bestow so great & hidden treasures vpon vs his poore and vnworthye seruants,

beseeching likewise the assistaunce of his holy spirite, so to deliuer vs in saftie . . .[42]

Their deliverance notwithstanding, the Englishmen's examination of the locality was fairly cursory thereafter, and the narratives reflected this. Best noted the discovery of a dead narwhal, spotted whilst Schutz was setting up his furnace to test ore samples found near Hall's Island, but otherwise had little to say for or against the country. Frobisher marched his men about five miles inland 'towardes the tops of the mountaines' and found nothing worth putting a claim to. It was probably the lack of means to sustain future expeditions here – even more pronounced than upon the northern shore of the bay – that inclined him to stay no longer. Having made that decision, he moved quickly, exercised by the harsh reality of what needed to be done before winter returned. On 26 July, he set out in the *Gabriel* and *Michael* for the northern shore once more, leaving the *Ayde* in the relatively safe waters of Jackman's Sound, to be sent for when he had established a base-camp.

Within twenty-four hours, the barks had crossed the bay, reconnoitred part of the northern shore and discovered a seemingly rich vein of minerals in a small sound, probably north of Lefferts Island, at the southern entrance to the present day Lupton Channel. By the following day, Frobisher's miners had extracted some ten tons of ore. Unfortunately, the site was dangerously exposed. On 28 July, ice drove with great force into the shore, making any lading operation fraught with danger; the *Gabriel* lost one of her remaining two cables and an anchor, and the *Michael*'s hull was almost rent during the break-up of a large ice berg against which she had been anchored. On the next ebb tide, the barks moved northwards up the coast, leaving their ore piled up in a cairn on the shore to be collected later. Frobisher named the bay Beare Sound, after James Beare, master of the *Michael* (its discoverer) and a small island therein Leicester's Island.[43]

The following day, the barks came into a much broader sound – almost a sub-bay system – dotted around with small islands and sheltered from the worst of the winds on three sides by low hills. More importantly, the screen of islands and favourable currents kept ice from drifting into the sheltered waters. Here there was room and safe anchorage for as many ships as they might ever wish to bring to the new land. Frobisher named it Countess of Warwick Sound to honour the wife of his chief patron, and a small island near its northern shore, somewhat unimaginatively, Countess of Warwick Island (the present day Kodlunarn Island). Upon initial investigation, this was found to hold such a quantity of seemingly valuable ore that Frobisher

immediately chose it as his base-camp, and sent the *Michael* to bring over the
Ayde from the southern shore. Immediately, he put his miners to work on the
island, and unnerved his gentlemen-companions by personally pitching in to
help dig ore from the hard ground; thus setting a precedent they could hardly
ignore. Best recalled 'euery man, both better and worse, with their best
endeuors, willingly laide to their helping handes';[44] but as he was over forty
miles distant across the strait when the episode occurred, it is probable that
his imagination, in this instance, was working with as much industry as the
reluctant gentlemen.

Meanwhile, those other gentlemen who had remained with the *Ayde* on
the southern shore were applying themselves equally industriously, though
much more intuitively, in their admiral's absence. Before he departed for the
northern shore, they had asked his permission to 'marche up thirtie or forty
leagues in the countrie, to the ende they mighte discover the inlande, and do
some acceptable service for their countrey.'[45] Frobisher, perhaps understanding the necessity of keeping 'gentlemen' upon short leashes (a lesson which
Drake was to learn within a few months in the South Atlantic), had refused
this; but in his absence, doing their country some service had recommended
itself once more, and irresistibly. To that end, and finding a little time on
their hands, the gentlemen of the *Ayde* started a small war.

Contrary to Frobisher's orders to return immediately with the *Ayde*, the
captain of the *Michael*, Gilbert Yorke, sent on the ships but remained on the
south shore with some thirty gentlemen-soldiers and two pinnaces. They had
caught sight of another group of Inuit, watching the Englishmen from a distance, and now Yorke acquiesced to the urgings of George Best and the ensign
bearer, Richard Philpot, to 'eyther allure them to familiaritie, or otherwise
take some of them, and so atteine to some knowledge of those men, whome
our Generall lost the yeare before'.[46]

A small landing party was set down upon the shore west of Jackman's
Sound, which then marched westwards, shadowed by the pinnaces. They soon
came upon a small Inuit encampment in a sheltered creek. It is not known
whether any attempt was made to parley with these people, but they proved
to be not nearly so trusting as their northern counterparts. Startled by the
novel apparition of well-armed Englishmen, they attempted to escape in their
boats, but were driven back from the sea by the approach of the two pinnaces. Thus trapped, the Inuit decided they were being given no choice but
to fight. They managed to injure one of the gentlemen for the loss of five or
six dead of their number, before the survivors fled in their kayaks, leaving an
old woman and a younger female with a baby, the latter wounded in the arm

by an English arrow. The victors of this short, vicious campaign (who later named the site of their triumph 'Bloody Point'), showed scant respect for age: the elder woman was stripped 'to see if she were clouen footed', but was then released by reason of her 'ougly hewe and deformitie'. The younger woman and child were secured and taken back to the pinnaces, to become the second and third of Frobisher's captives.[47]

Their recent and heartfelt recourse to the Deity had not brought the Englishmen to any more perfect example of the Christian ideal. Sorrowfully, Settle observed – perhaps initiated – the honourable tradition of placing the blame entirely upon the barbarous natives for their own, untimely deaths:

> Hauing this knowledge both of their fiercenesse and cruelty, and perceiuing that faire means, as yet, is not able to allure them to familiaritie, we disposed our selues, *contrary to our inclination*, something to be cruel, returned to their tents, and made a spoyle of the same . . .[48]

By a remarkable coincidence, their 'spoyle' included items of English clothing, taken from one or more of the five men abducted in the previous year. The desperate bravery and fierceness of their Inuit foe, and the discovery of English garments without the bodies that formerly had filled them – one doublet had many arrow holes piercing it – inclined the Englishmen to fear the worst of their enemy: that they were dealing with cannibals (though their captive, when questioned about this, 'earnestly denied (it), and made signes to the contrarie'). Without conscious irony, Best speculated that the wounded Inuit, some of whom had thrown themselves into the sea rather than be captured, did so because they suspected the Englishmen of precisely the same tastes.[49]

Following this sanguinary encounter, Yorke and his sated gentlemen took to their pinnaces and set sail for the Countess of Warwick Sound. By 3 August, all elements of the expedition were safely anchored there. As the Englishmen began to search its immediate environs, further traces of Inuit habitation were discovered, including several roundhouses, sunk into the earth and covered with skins. Best marvelled at (and was possibly disconcerted by) the drainage system of these houses, that managed to divert rainwater into under-trenches that kept the floor perfectly dry; fortunately, he was able to reconfirm his stout prejudices in observing other aspects of the Inuit's manner of habitation; particularly how: 'they defile these dennes most filthylie with their beastle feeding'.[50] Their male Inuk captive, taken into these houses, was apparently diverted by the tokens of his own folk. He described and demonstrated some of the artefacts, and admitted to his captors 'by signes' that he was entirely familiar with the story of the five Englishmen lost in the 1576 voyage. Again, the obvious question was put to him, and again, he was obliged to take pains to explain that neither he nor his countrymen were in the habit of eating human flesh.

This half-word of the five missing men was given further currency when the Inuit whose camp the Englishmen had attacked came to parley. They had followed the two pinnaces across the strait; now, with remarkable *sang-froid* (and, one suspects, not a little righteous outrage), they marched into the midst of their tormentors' encampment to complain of the late battle and demand the safe return of the abducted woman and child. Frobisher, perhaps startled by a display of courage more pronounced than even he might have considered sensible, used his male captive to bargain with them; offering to exchange their three for the safe return of his five men. Curiously, he was told that the latter were living still, to whom the Inuit offered to take Frobisher's letter: 'for they knewe very well the vse wee haue of writing'. If the latter observation was true, it confirms that the five men had lived for a time among the people following their capture, and supports similar claims made centuries later by the descendants of their Inuit abductors.[51]

Frobisher accepted this offer, and dictated his letter. He was by now addressing dead men, as he must have suspected: resurrected by the Inuit in the hope of recovering their own people. However, the morale of his men demanded the gesture. Cruel usage, poor pay and indifference to their worst suffering were expected by the common mariner of his betters, but outright abandonment in such a place was inconceivable. Frobisher's exhortation was therefore a call to arms and an urgent reassurance – but of his own men, not of the unfortunates who had been lost twelve months earlier:

In the name of God, in whome we al beleue, who I trust hath preserued your bodyes and soules amongst these Infidels, I com(m)end me vnto you, I will be glad to seeke by all meanes you can deuise, for your deliuerance, eyther with force, or with any commodities within my Shippes, whiche I will not spare for your sakes, or any thing else I can doe for you. I haue aboord, of theyrs, a Man, a Woman, and a Childe, whiche I am contented to delyuer for you, but the man which I carried away from hence the last yeare is dead in ENGLAND. Morouer, you may declare vnto them, that if they deliuer you not, I wyll not leaue a manne aliue in their Countrey. And thus, if one of you can come to speake with me, they shall haue eyther the Man, Woman or Childe in pawne for you. And thus vnto God, whome

I trust you do serue, in hast I leaue you, and to him we will dayly pray for you. This Tuesdaye morning the seauenth of August, Anno. 1577.

postcript. I haue sent you by these bearers Penne, Incke and Paper, to write backe vnto me agayne, if personally you can not come to certifye me of your estate.[52]

The Inuit returned for the letter on 8 August, and indicated they would be back within three days with a reply. That night, moved by their obvious courage, the entire expedition's complement huddled closely in their bivouacs and maintained constant watches against a surprise attack. The following morning, Frobisher decided to make their position more defensible. This was not merely in response to the danger posed by their immediate neighbours. His male captive had also given an uncomfortable indication that his people might not be entirely disorganized, making signs to warn them of the imminent arrival of an Inuk 'prince', whom he named Catchoe.

The Englishmen took the threat seriously. The revelation: 'gaue vs occasion to foresee what might ensue thereof, for he shewed by signes, that this Catchoe was a ma(n) of higher stature farre than any of our nation is, and he is accustomed to be carried vpon mens shoulders'. Prudently, Frobisher ordered that a small fortification be raised by enclosing a corner at the foot of a cliff-face and bulwarking it with casks filled with earth. He was obeyed promptly and enthusiastically; the mariners and soldiers thereafter naming their construction Best's Blessing in honour of its architect, and of their sincere affection for his art.

For the next few days, a group of armed Inuit paraded aggressively on raised ground overlooking the sound. Several times, they tried to ambush Frobisher and his men, luring them towards two or three of their comrades whilst a greater number lay hidden in defiles or behind rocks nearby. Almost certainly aware that the five missing Englishmen were already dead – and, probably, that their compatriots were not infinitely gullible – they may have been attempting to take further hostages to trade against their woman and child. The Englishmen were extremely cautious, however, and did not stray far from their camp except in large parties. When this strategy failed to entice any potential victims, the Inuit demonstrated in strength from a distance, hoping to intimidate where they could not persuade. However, this was a language with which their enemy was perfectly at ease; immediately, Fenton had his soldiers perform a mock skirmish to display their prowess, and Frobisher ordered a sacre to be fired from the *Ayde*. It was more than enough to deter the Inuit from making any more forceful demonstration, but the stand-off continued, and prevented Frobisher's men – brief sorties apart – from reconnoitring further sites around the sound for ore deposits.

There was a strong element of bluff in all of these demonstrations and counter-demonstrations. Notwithstanding the bloodshed on the southern shore and the mutual attempts at abduction, neither side wished to push the situation further. Clearly, the Inuit were pragmatic about their losses, but not in any hurry to incur more. Frobisher, for his part, had been cautioned not to give offence to the local population, and whilst the death of six of their number might well be considered offensive, it had not yet alienated them entirely. The mutual distrust exhibited by the two cultures had already hardened into dislike; but the Inuit, ignorant of the European inability to exhibit moral flexibility, seemed more willing to mend their differences. Unfortunately, the more developed culture, as ever, was the first to allow suspicion to descend into something more enduring. As we have seen, this was manifest most clearly in the readiness with which the Englishmen gave rein to their worst prejudices. The threat of cannibalism, the most feared of ancestral taboos, recurs constantly and vividly in the narratives. Best in particular seemed unable to comment upon any aspect of Inuit life without drawing evidence of it: '. . . but I doubt, our flesh is so sweet meate for them, that they will hardly part from so good morsels, if we come nere their ha(n)dling'. In light of this weight of preconception, and of any more fruitful experience to counter it, an armed and mistrustful truce was as much as could be hoped for.

Yet however strongly such xenophobia may have recommended itself, it could not entirely supplant the spirit of enthusiastic curiosity which continued to pervade the narratives of the voyage. Englishmen, whether experiencing first-hand the shock of the unknown, or reading of it from men such as Best and Settle, had a voracious appetite for novelty. To satisfy this hunger, Settle in particular made use of his time in Baffin Island to observe those apparently few customs and artefacts of the Inuit that did not hint at a taste for human flesh. Inevitably, his narrative is coloured by the certainty of his own culture's superior worth, but his eye was acute:

They are men of a large corporature, and good proportion: their colour is not much vnlike the Sunne burnt Countrie man, who laboureth daily in Sunne for his liuing. They weare their haire something long, and cut before, either with stone or knife, very disorderly. Their women weare their haire long, and knit vp with two loupes, shewing forth on either side of

their faces, and the rest soltred vpon a knot. Also, some of their women
race their faces proportionally, as chinne, cheekes, and forehead, and the
wristes of their hands, wherevpon they lay a colour, which continueth
darke azurine.[53]

This, and other descriptions provided by Hall and Lok, make it clear that
the Inuit's physical characteristics were not repulsive to English eyes. Their
domestic habits, however, tested the fastidious nature of men who themselves
were not far removed from brutishness:

They eate their meate all rawe, bothe fleshe, fishe, and soule, or something
perboyled with bloud and a little water . . . they neither vse table, stoole,
or table cloth for comelinesse: but when they are imbrued with bloud,
knuckle deepe, and their kniues in like sort, they vse their tongues as apt
instruments to licke them cleane . . . what knowledge they haue of God,
or what Idol they adore, wee haue no perfect intelligence. I thincke them
rather Anthropologi, or deuourers of mans fleshe, then otherwise: for that
there is no flesh or fishe, which they finde dead (smell it neuer so filthily)
but they will eate it, as they finde it, without any other dressing. A loathsome spectacle, either to the beholders, or hearers . . . as the Countrie is
barren and vnfertile, so they are rude and of no capacitie to culture the
same, to any perfection: but are contented by their hunting, fishing, and
fowling, with rawe flesh and warme bloud, to satisfie their greedie panches,
whiche is their onely glorie.[54]

These are untested prejudices, not observations; but if they appear unyielding to the modern eye we should recall the burden of ignorance that Best and
Settle unconsciously bore. Before the despatch of the 1576 voyage, the adventurers had purchased a copy of Mandeville's *Travels* as though it were capable
of providing useful information on what the voyages should expect. Such late-
medieval works, permeated with fantastical claims, were still, on the whole,
regarded as reliable. Only a century earlier, Caxton had published the *Mirrour
of the World*, in whose supposedly informative pages could be found sentient
fires, giants, mares made pregnant by the wind and an Ethiopian river that
froze by day and boiled at night.[55] The work was still popular in London
during the 1570s; immortalized in this and many similar pieces, the prejudices and fears of untravelled men were not yet dismissed as fiction, even
though no one could verify their assertions. Strangeness breeds fear, and fear
hatred; over half a century had passed since Columbus had found absolutely

no half-men, trolls or wood demons; but news did not travel well in the six-teenth century, particularly when those who possessed it did not wish it disseminated.

For Best and Settle, their camp surrounded by hostile aboriginals and a great and war-like prince of their people on his way, there was little incentive to search out the good in these folk. In a more practical sense, however, their commander showed greater – and uncharacteristic – circumspection. Faced with daily provocations and attempted ambushes, Frobisher refused to rise to the challenge: being, in Best's elegant phrase: 'more carefull by processe of time to winne them, than willfullie at the firste to spoyle them . . .'. Prudently, he curbed his soldiers' natural instinct to fight; the entire expedition was confined to the island mine-sites, unless individuals were given instructions to the contrary. This narrowed the span of their exploration and limited the types of ore that could be mined, but Schutz had found sufficiently promising samples of ore on their base island and upon another that lay two miles to the west (the present day Newland Island), which they had named Winter's Furnace. The Inuit could do nothing to interfere with traffic between these two sites, and without the distraction of war, mining could now begin in earnest. The Forest of Dean miners, assisted with varying degrees of enthusiasm by mariners and gentlemen, proceeded swiftly. In little more than a week, almost 200 tons of supposedly valuable mineral rock were extracted from ditches scoured into the islands' surface (excavations that scar the face of Kodlunarn Island to this day).

However, even with this industry well in hand, and the men 'determined lustily to worke afreshe for a bone voyage', Frobisher was not content. Perhaps the frustration of not being free to vent himself upon the Inuit made him look closer to home. If so, Christopher Hall was unlucky to be in the way. It will be apparent that his fastidious and painful temperament was not of a kind that recommended itself to a man of Frobisher's impulsive nature. It is probable, furthermore, that the latter's relative lack of skills as a navigator had been made uncomfortably apparent during their day-to-day working relationship. Later, there were to be several occasions upon which the two men clashed upon a point of judgement; but in 1577, the first symptom of their future antipathy grew from the most trivial of circumstances. Having been asked a question on some matter, Hall made the mistake of answering Frobisher without first doffing his cap, at which his admiral,

> beinge in a furyous humo(u)r of Temper, he openly revyled him w(i)th outrageous speaches and swore by gods bludd he wold hang him, and

offered to stryke him on the face with hys fyst which Captain Fenton did defend and Hawlle did quietly putt vpp, and all this w(i)thout anye cause but onely upon vayne suspicion of hawlles dewetyfull service . . .[56]

This was hardly the reaction of a man at peace with the progress of his mission. In the following year, Fenton himself and Lok's servant, Edward Selman, were to have a similar taste of Frobisher's infamous temper. It was a quality that lay too close to the surface throughout his career, temporarily stilled by happy circumstance but much more often inflamed by the frustrations, whether of inanimate or sentient cause, that he seemed unable to disregard or accept as being a part of the process of human intercourse. Whether manifestations of this quality exacerbated the habitual seethe of personal grudge and petty rank-pulling that permeated sixteenth-century shipboard life is hard to determine. We shall see evidence that Frobisher used discord – particularly, between his immediate officers and the other ranks – as a conscious tool to reinforce his own position (and, by inference, his intensely insecure sense of authority). He was not unique amongst his contemporaries in doing so, but he was certainly unfortunate in the high proportion of men he abused who left written testimony of it thereafter.

During the 1577 expedition, this self-indulgent discord was limited to its most senior officers, as the common mariners and miners were far too busy to exercise their more wilful inclinations. Freed from fear of the Inuit, the traffic of small boats passed busily between the Countess of Warwick Island and Winter's Furnace with their loads of ore. By 21 August, the *Ayde*, *Gabriel* and *Michael* were laden to capacity; 'bellies broken' or backs over-strained, the men were now exhausted, and, ominously, ice had begun to congeal around the ships. Best, a gentleman-soldier himself, found ample cause to applaud his peers, particularly those who had shared the hardships of the common mariner:

> It is not a little worth the memorie, to the commendation of the Gentlemen and Souldioures heerein, who leauing all reputation aparte, with so great willingnesse, and with couragious stomackes, haue themselues almost ouercome in so short a time, the difficultie of this so great a laboure.[57]

Courageous stomachs notwithstanding, there was little sound reason to remain longer in this unpleasant land once the ships' holds had been filled. On 22 August, the mariners and miners took down their tents; by way of farewell, Frobisher had bonfires lit and the company marched around their

small island with ensign flying, marking out their territory for the understanding and doubtful benefit of their troublesome neighbours. A volley of
shot rang out, both in farewell and in honour of their fair patron, the Countess of Warwick, 'and so departed aboorde'. The following morning, the ships
weighed anchor.

All that day, they lay becalmed in the Sound, low in the water but safe
from aboriginal vengeance. On the following morning, the ships' sails caught
a west wind, and the tiny fleet passed out of the mouth of Frobisher's supposed strait. They had explored its upper reaches no further than the island
upon which they had begun to extract the supposed wealth of empire – a distance, admitted Best, of no more than 30 leagues from its eastern entrance.
He later claimed that when Frobisher left the *Ayde* in Jackman Sound, it had
been merely to identify suitable mining sites before pressing on to 'discover'
the passage, but subsequent events belied this. Contrary to his statement, and
to Edward Selman's later assurance that Frobisher and others 'remaine prest
to explore the truth of that which is unexplored', not the slightest effort had
been made to further the cause to which the adventurers had first set their
money only eighteen months earlier. The instructions that had urged him to
send his barks on to the west had been inserted to cover all the perceived
options, but the perceptions themselves had been flawed. They had addressed
a failure-case: one that could hardly be established until the ships had returned
to England. For as long as gold occupied the minds of those who gave Frobisher his instructions, any further navigation of the region would require an
accidental, rather than an incremental, effort.

At the entrance to the strait, Frobisher directed his ships southwards,
hoping to find better weather before ice dragged the heavily laden vessels even
lower into the water. The prudence of their swift departure was immediately
apparent. Even at best speed towards more temperate regions, the ships were
not spared the perils of Arctic weather: a margin note in Best's *True Discourse*
incredulously reported 'Snow half a foote deepe in August'. When high winds
forced the barks to lower their sails, the ever-unlucky *Michael* became separated from her sister ships. Alone thereafter, the *Gabriel* and *Ayde* made good
time through storms, except during a brief, welcome lull, when repairs to the
battered *Ayde* were effected using rather drastic means:

The seconde daye of September in the morning, it pleased God of hys
goodnesse to sende vs a calme, whereby we perceiued the Rudder of oure
shippe torne in twaine, and almost ready to fal away. Wherfore taking the
benefite of the time, wee flunge half a dosen couple of our best men ouer-

boord, who taking great paines vnder water, driuing plancks, and binding wyth ropes, did wel strengthen and mend the matter, who returned the most parte more than halfe deade out of the water . . .[58]

Only slightly more comfortable than the *Ayde*'s 'best men', the captive Inuit were stowed securely in the *Ayde*'s hold. The man, apparently seasick and doubtless suffering from the afflictions that were soon to kill him, was nursed by the woman with great tenderness. For Best, this and their natural modesty – 'for the man would neuer shift himselfe, except he had firste caused the woman to depart out of his cabin, and they both were most shamefast, least anye of their priuie parts should bee discovered' – went someway to rehabilitate them in the face of their otherwise sluttish manner of living, particularly as they also had the discretion to 'never vse as man and wife'.

The *Ayde* and *Gabriel* became separated in mid-Atlantic during their castward passage. The *Gabriel* lost her master soon afterwards (the unfortunately clairvoyant William Smith, who fell overboard immediately after revealing a premonition of drowning),[59] but luckily met with a Bristol ship, probably returning from Iceland, that led her home. The *Ayde* came into Milford Haven on 23 September. Captain Yorke of the *Michael*, perhaps wisely in view of her reputation as an unlucky ship, had opted for the longer but more familiar passage via the Orkneys, and sailed into Yarmouth soon after the return of the other vessels.

The *Ayde* and *Gabriel* rested at Bristol. They may not have been sufficiently sea-worthy or adequately manned to make the further voyage to London (or the adventurers may have baulked at paying the further sea-wages of their crews), but the ore they carried needed to be put somewhere that might be secured against thieves. For almost a month, nothing was done. Eventually, it was left to Lok to address a memorial to the Privy Council, suggesting that the ore be placed in Bristol Castle under four locks, with keys to be held by the Mayor of Bristol, Frobisher, Sir Richard Berkeley (who seems to have gone down to Bristol on the Council's order to organize security there) and Lok himself.[60] Almost incidentally, Lok later revealed that it had been the original intention that the ore should be refined at Bristol, rather than London, possibly because of the proximity of the Forest of Dean lead mines and the refining expertise they provided.[61]

Meanwhile, Frobisher had gone on immediately to the Court, then at Richmond, to report the success of his voyage and be lionized thereafter by the Queen and her entourage. Possibly unintentionally, Best implied that her admiration for Frobisher's feat was not so much in regard to his skills as a navigator as the fact that among his men 'there was so good order of gouer-nement, so good agreement, euery man so readye in his calling, to doe whatsoeuer the General should commaunde': a telling reflection upon contemporary expectations of English discipline at sea.[62]

Nevertheless, Elizabeth must have allowed Frobisher some personal credit. The second voyage had returned safely, with much more than mere tokens of its visit. By the planting of the English standard in the new land, the Queen's right of possession had been established, as had that of naming it. With unerring perception, she chose *Meta Incognita* – the unknown limits. In recognition of Frobisher's success, she bestowed upon him an unspecified lease 'of a good lyvinge' and a gift of £100. Michael Lok later claimed that the money had been intended for the common mariners, but that their admiral kept it for himself. This is one of Lok's less likely charges, however; Elizabeth, sensitive to individual achievement and chivalric bravery alike, never seemed to concern herself with the condition of the faceless 'other ranks' who had borne the same dangers.[63]

ELEVEN

A Schisma Growen Amonge Us

Frobisher's triumphant return marked the zenith of his reputation as an explorer. Almost 200 tons of ore had been successfully mined and returned to England for the loss of only two men. The passage had not yet been proven, but it remained a possibility, and its course lay through a land to which England now had a strong claim by the standards of contemporary international law – or what, in its absence, was acceptable to princes. A godly nation had begun the 'purpose of manifestyng Gods mightie woorde and maiestie among those that feed like monsters and rather live like dogges than men' (Thomas Churchyard's charitable phrase),[1] and three examples of these unfortunates had been returned safely, though they lived no longer than the man abducted in the previous year. The captive Inuk male – his name, as closely rendered as Englishmen could make the Inuit tongue, was Cali-chough or Kalicho – entertained the mayor and people of Bristol, on one occasion rowing painfully up and down the River Avon in his kayak, demonstrating the Inuit technique of killing fowl (in this case, several unsuspecting local ducks) with his darts; but both he and the woman (referred to colloquially as 'Egnock', or, more accurately, Arnaq; the Englishmen mistaking a generic Inuit word for 'woman' as a personal name), died soon afterwards. They were buried, respectively, on 8 and 12 November, in St Stephen's churchyard, Bristol.[2] The ultimate cause of death in the man's case almost certainly arose from the severe handling he had received when brought down by Nicholas Congar (an autopsy upon his corpse, carried out by the surgeon Edward Dodding, revealed two broken ribs and a collapsed lung). The woman apparently succumbed to measles.[3] The adventurers paid for a wet-nurse to suckle the Inuk infant, named 'Nutaaq' (again, this was merely an Inuit word for 'child'), who survived a five-day journey to London and three days of lodging thereafter at the Three Swans Inn; but then he, too, died. In London, as in Bristol, a Christian cemetery – once more, that of St Olave, Hart Street – obligingly received a heathen upon hallowed ground.[4]

As in the previous year, the prospect – however fleeting – of members of an alien race encouraged much popular interest in the recent deeds of Frobisher and his valiant mariners. This was fed further by the swift publication in London of Settle's *A true reporte* and Richard Willes's *For M. Cap. Furbyshers Voyage by the north west* (the preface to his *History of Travayle*), which circulated news of the recent voyage throughout England. In the following year, a French edition of Settle's account was published in Geneva; two years later, German and Latin editions would follow, giving the story of the 1577 voyage a European currency.[5] Yet news of Frobisher's exploits had already passed much further than either Settle or Willes could have imagined. As early as the previous June, Philip II had been made aware of the expedition when his informants in England wrote to him, suggesting that although Frobisher claimed to be heading for Cathay, he might be intending to plunder the West Indies.[6] Between that date and 3 May 1579, the Spanish Ambassador Mendoza was to write upon at least eighteen further occasions to Philip, appraising him of developments in the enterprise. This was more than idle interest. The threat to the West Indies was soon understood to be illusory, but if Frobisher were to be successful in his northern quest, England would have a source of New World wealth to rival that of New Spain – and, technically, upon territory claimed by Spain under the Treaty of Tordesillas. On 7 October 1577, Mendoza revealed that he was sufficiently sensitive to his master's interest in Frobisher to have secured a spy to sail on the planned third voyage.[7]

There was also much immediate French interest in Frobisher, though hardly for the same reasons that had focussed Philip's attention. On 9 October, the French diplomat, Castelnau de la Mauvissière, wrote from London both to the French King and to Catherine de' Medici, informing them that

Someone called Forbichet is back from his voyage and new navigation with a certain quantity of gold ore, which they say will extract a great profit and that the English want to settle in the country that he had discovered on

*PICTVRA VEL DELINEATIO HOMINVM NVPER EX ANGLIA AD-
vectorum,una cum eorum armis,tentoriis,&naviculis.*

3. Woodcut of Inuit captives from the 1580 Latin edition of Settle's *True Reporte*. The Inuk male Kalicho is shown demonstrating his hunting prowess on the River Avon. By courtesy of the James Ford Bell Library, University of Minnesota.

the north side (of America) in the direction of Cathay, with the intention of establishing a New England . . .[8]

More ominously, La Mauvissière suggested that 'if your Majesties want to take part to this venture it will be very easy to do so without hindering the Spaniards and Portuguese conquests and the land given to them as a gift by the Pope'. He had worded it as an intended collaboration, but that was probably for the benefit of Walsingham's spies. What La Mauvissière seems to have envisaged was an opportunity for France to extend her own New World activities northwards before the English could back up a claim to title by planting sitting tenants there. Unfortunately, the French Ambassador's diplomatic bag had larger holes in it even than he imagined; Frobisher himself heard of this and other French interest in Meta Incognita, and used its implied threat for his own ends – with profound implications, as we shall see.

Further abroad, from Frankfurt, the Spanish Protestant exile Casiodoro de Reina wrote to the Landgrave of Hesse-Cassel, informing him of 'marvellous things' reported from England; of 'a noble man outstandingly gifted in nautical matters, which he took delight in all his life, whose name is Frobisher'. News of the supposed gold did not, however, impress Reina nearly as much as had Frobisher's prowess in finding it; of the whole business, he commented: 'as I'm writing, I can scarcely contain myself from laughing at this Lucianic lie'.[9]

Even western Europe could not fully contain the news of Frobisher's travels. From Moscow, the Tsar (exhibiting as much understanding of the discoveries as his western cousins) wrote to Elizabeth demanding the return of his three abducted subjects, members of the Paky Samwedy people taken by Frobisher, as he believed, from the 'Jugoria' (Yugorskii) region of Siberia.[10] At Plymouth, Drake was only now making ready to commence what would become his famous circumnavigation. Until his return three years later, and until the seismic ramifications of his achievement were well understood, no English seaman would so stir Europe's composure as Frobisher had by the very act of returning safely.

Yet if that attention was meat and drink to a man for whom reputation had been so hardily secured, it was also a fickle thing, to be preserved only by the swift extraction of significant amounts of gold from the ore. To date, however, a full year after samples of the ore had first been assayed, no verifiable extraction of any form of precious metal had been accomplished. For the moment, the perceived achievement of the voyages themselves remained strongly etched in the public mind; but the longer Frobisher's backers continued to lay out money without prospect of immediate return, the less reason he would have to regard his situation with the self-satisfaction that Lok later recalled:

> . . . noe smale joye was had of his arryvall, and noe smale increase of his reputacon, So that nowe xii or xx men weare to fewe to followe his horsse vppon this his retorne home . . . and nowe Captaine Furbysher havinge the thinge that he so mutch hunted for, grewe into such a monstrous minde, that a whole kingdome coold not conteyne yt, but as alredy by discoverye of a new worlde, he was become another *Columbus* so allso nowe by Conquest of a new world he woold become another *Cortes* . . .[11]

Even allowing for the ore's imagined potential, the comparison was hardly realistic. Cortés's booty, importantly, had been ready-refined and fashioned into convenient trinkets. What Frobisher had provided was a commodity whose value was as much a matter of speculation still as the passage he had attempted to find in 1576. Furthermore, the adventurers' commitments to date, though great, were still insufficient to see that speculation realized successfully. At the despatch of the expedition in May, less than £3,000 had been received from the total due subscriptions of £4,275.[12] Even with the further amounts that had trickled into Lok's corporate purse whilst the expedition was out of England, the clamour of creditors was becoming an embarrassing refrain. At the beginning of August, the Privy Council had attempted once more to widen the base of investment, writing to the Lord Mayor of London to remind him of the great benefit that the enterprise would bring to Englishmen, and asking that he secure further investors from among those 'substanciale merchauntes of the Citie' who were not yet venturers.[13] Not a single response is known to have been received, if indeed the mayor made any attempt to indulge the request. Ominously, that same letter had noted 'certen lewde speches raised concerning the gaines that shold rise' from the soil of Meta Incognita; an indication that the promises of assayers notwithstanding, much of London's mercantile community was coming to regard the gold mines of the Queen's new territories as a chimæra, and treating calls to participate therein accordingly.

The enterprise's growing financial problems did not make the outlook any more promising. The letter in which Lok outlined arrangements for storing the ore in Bristol Castle also contained a pertinent reminder that the mariners, soldiers and miners needed to be paid. As long as they remained as employees of the 'company', the meat and drink they consumed constituted a growing cost to the adventurers. Lok estimated that £800 would be enough to discharge them, 'but the w(hi)ch sayd money cannot be found in London uppon interest nor exchange nothw(i)thstandinge the dyllygens used by the Commyssyoners to take up the same . . .'.[14] In light of this embarrassing failure, he suggested a further two options: either the Queen's customs duties might be pressed for the purpose until receipts from gold extracted from the ore came in, or an assessment might be raised upon the existing stock of the adventurers. The latter option was, of course, more attractive to Elizabeth, notwithstanding Lok's warning that it 'would be very longe tyme and moche dyfficultye in collection'. An unsigned note dated 13 October again reported that money to discharge the men could not be found, even upon interest. Three days later the Privy Council, bowing to the inevitable, ordered an extraordinary assessment of twenty per cent upon stock, to be delivered directly to Lok 'beynge appointed to give bylles signed under his hand for suche sommes as he shall receave'.[15]

With hundreds of tons of ore at the forefront of their minds, the adventurers appear to have emptied their pockets willingly enough, if with less overt enthusiasm than before. By 24 December, Lok had received all but £22 of the £1,030 due, though by that time the cost of discharging the men had risen to £1,242.[16] This was the final charge upon the account of the 1577 voyage. To date, the enterprise had consumed a total of £7,400 – all spent wisely, if reports of the ore's worth were correct. The possibility they were *not* was one that few of the participants seemed willing as yet to contemplate.

In the weeks following his return, such trifles appear not to have troubled Frobisher. Money that was not bound for his own pocket was a matter, apparently, for accountants; from the moment he had stepped off the *Ayde* at Bristol, he had considered his duty to be so fully discharged that he seems not to have contributed in any way to the post-voyage arrangements. This had not been the intention of the commissioners. They had ordered him to take a full inventory of the *Ayde* and *Gabriel* at Bristol (no doubt to forestall the endemic pilferage that stripped ships laying at dock), but in his haste to be with the Queen at Richmond, he had given over even this responsibility to 'a false, Ruffyanly boye of his owne namyd John Commings'; who, according to Lok, had since 'gonne a rovinge . . . .'.[17]

Though a trivial incident in itself, it contributed to Lok's exasperation and growing disillusionment: not with the project itself, but with his former partner. His original faith in Frobisher's abilities and commitment, touching if somewhat fulsome, had begun to wilt as the gulf between their expectations grew and the problems of financing the enterprise deepened. The impoverished privateer who had come to Lok to seek his assistance just eighteen months earlier had acquired something of a popular status, and in the process may have allowed certain debts to slip his mind. Lok, who had risked so much to see the enterprise realized, was not a man to tear up such moral promissory notes unredeemed. In his accounts for wages, dated 31 November 1577, Frobisher is stated to be the only one of 143 men who had sailed on the voyage not to have received any part of his wages.[18] This may only have been a matter of Lok honourably providing for the little men first, but Frobisher's subsequent, violent outbursts against Lok's inability (or, more likely, refusal) to pay his wages suggests that the treasurer was happy to inflict a little understanding of the company's financial predicament upon its prodigal cause.

And finances remained the predominant issue. The 1577 expedition had been set out on the basis of the ore being worth approximately £240 per ton.[19] On its return, Jonas Schutz immediately oversaw the building of two furnaces

at William Winter's warehouse at Tower Hill; to test the new ore and, hopefully, confirm the results of earlier trials. By the end of October, he had completed a furnace that would allow a hundredweight of ore to be assayed. In
the presence of Frobisher, Lok, Winter and the English assayer Robert
Denham, Schutz assayed a sample and declared it to contain gold to a significantly more modest value of £40 per ton.[20] Yet even this disappointment
carried a further sting. Schutz claimed that much gold remained in the slag,
which he believed could only be extracted in a larger, much hotter furnace –
for which new monies would be required. An audit of the accounts of the
'Company of Cathay', conducted in 1581, claimed that two small ingots of
gold, weighing just under half an ounce, and two of silver (almost eight
ounces) had been produced from four hundredweight of ore smelted at this
and two succeeding assays at Tower Hill.[21] We now know that this was an
impossible outcome; almost certainly, Schutz had felt himself under pressure
to produce irrefutable evidence of his skills and had deliberately deceived his
employers. If so, he bore a large responsibility for the events that followed,
for this 'evidence' further delayed the day when an unequivocal assessment
of the ore's true value could be made. In drawing up an estimation of the
company's financial state a few weeks later, Lok unintentionally made clear
the vulnerability of its asset-base:

> all the minerall Ewar brought hom(e) by m(aste)r furbusher in the iij
> shippes in this voyage / to saye / cxl. tonnes Layed in the Castell at bris-
> towe xx. tonnes Laded in the tower at London and in the storehouse at
> tower hille Sum(m) clx. tonnes / the price and valew wherof cannott be
> knowne vntill yt be molten & refyned & tried.[22]

Yet if the apparent results of the October assay were hardly spectacular,
they held out at least a hope that costs already incurred during 1576 and 1577
could be recovered. The Privy Council, informed of the findings on 3
November, ordered a further large assay to be conducted. Not surprisingly,
the commissioners who witnessed the first assay were unsure of what they
had seen; Lok – who undoubtedly stood amongst their more gullible element
– wrote to Walsingham on 30 November, urging that Schutz's recommendations regarding larger furnaces be acted upon, and regretting the delay in
doing so: 'I know not wherto impute the fault, but to a *schisma* growen
amonge us commissioners, throughe unbelefe . . . .'.[23]

This schism was almost certainly fuelled by the gap between Schutz's perceived and actual talents. Saxon metallurgists enjoyed a high reputation in

Elizabethan England; much more so than their English counterparts – hence their disproportionate influence in the English copper-mining industry.[24] Robert Denham, who should have noticed the absence of any verifiable amounts of gold or silver in the October assay, probably allowed himself to be so blinded by the other man's putative abilities that any reservations he expressed were ambiguous. It is also undoubtedly the case that he *wanted* to be convinced. No assayer involved in the process – at least, none of those who were attempting to secure pensions in return for working the ore – had anything to gain by dismissing its potential outright.

So 1577 drew to a close without any likelihood of an early return upon the adventurers' stock or certainty of when one might be expected. Logic suggests that the failure to produce gold or silver from the ore definitively should have caused the adventurers to lose faith in the enterprise, but several events conspired to confound their scepticism. We have already noted the ambiguities of technology and reputation that clouded the results of successive assays. Furthermore, because of the extreme political sensitivity surrounding the supposed discovery of gold, it is almost certain that much of the information regarding the ore and its testing was being withheld from the majority of adventurers (that is, those who were not members of either the Privy Council or commission). Nor were the majority of adventurers simply being gullible, or even venal, in continuing to participate in the enterprise without any firm prospect of timely returns. There was a further issue: one that, for the mercantile investors in particular, made the abandonment of their investments a matter of final, rather than prudent, resort.

'If goods were lost much were lost, if tyme were lost more were lost, but if credit were lost, all were lost.'[25] For the man of business, John Isham's dictum would be apposite in any age; but it was particularly so during this period. Though promissory notes and letters of credit had largely replaced cash transactions as the medium of international commerce, there were as yet no satisfactory systems in place to remove the personal dimension in doing business, even for the great banking families. Credit – the personal credit of the merchant – was therefore an indispensable quality. To simply walk away from a venture in plain sight of one's peers and customers (particularly a venture of such high profile) invited the ruin of reputation, and thus of credit. Unless things began to look entirely hopeless, none of the adventurers wished to be seen to be the first to refuse to meet assessments on stock. That things did *not* yet look hopeless was a corollary of yet another development: the involvement, in November 1577, of a second German metallurgist.

Schutz had repaired his furnace following the first assay, and by 4 December he was ready to conduct a second large 'proof'.[26] Again, the results were disappointing: 'w(i)th danger of his lyffe, throughe the smoke', Schutz assayed another hundredweight of ore and apparently found it to be worth slightly more than £40 per ton. Once more, he claimed that much gold remained in the slag, and blamed his equipment for this poor showing. The Privy Council and Commission were becoming increasingly doubtful of his claims, 'butt chiefly they beleaved nothinge that was donne becavse the gold-esmithes and goldefyners of London and manye other namyd counynge menn had made many proofes of the ewer and coulde fynde noe whitt of goolde therein . . .'.

Had the Privy Council now believed the eyes and skills of their country-men, confidence in the enterprise surely must have been seriously compro-mised at this point; but Schutz had concluded his latest assay by undertaking to provide half an ounce of fine gold from every hundredweight of the ore. The offer seemed to deny the logic of any reasonable cynicism, particularly as it was made by a supposed expert. Walsingham in particular, whose com-ments upon 'alchamist matters' pretended doubts that his actions consistently belied, seems to have been very unwilling to disbelieve the reputation of a German metallurgist. His solution to the 'schisma' and its ill-effects therefore proved to be no solution at all: to assuage or otherwise confirm the misgiv-ings of the Council, he chose to engage further expert help – from precisely the same tradition.

Sometime during late November, a piece of the ore had come into the pos-session of Dr Burchard Kranich, a Saxon who had formerly been involved in the Cornish silver-mining industry. Kranich was a resident of the parish of St Clement Dane, who, upon occasion, had acted as a personal physician to the Queen (no doubt it was the exercise of this unlikely talent that now allowed him to intrude so prominently, via Walsingham's offices, upon the matter of New World ore).[27] On 9 December, a few days after Schutz's dis-appointing 'second great proof', Walsingham ordered Frobisher and Lok to deliver further samples to Kranich, who countered Schutz's offer with his own – again, promising to provide half an ounce of gold per hundredweight of ore.

The following day, Schutz and Kranich met for the first time. Each wished to be the sole assayer of the ore; thus, their mutual loathing and contempt was as immediate as it was contrived. Schutz 'dislyked the dealinge of Mr Burcott boethe for his evell manners and allso his ignoraunce in divers points of the works', whilst Kranich concluded tartly that 'yf Jonas had any couninge yt had longe since appered'.[28] Again, logic suggests that the rivalry of these two incompetents should have sounded the death-knell upon the enterprise; yet far from undermining further the hopes of the Privy Council and Commission, their struggle to obtain the sole patent to work the ore, and their apparent consensus on the value of the ore (if upon nothing else), rekindled the common conviction that gold and silver must be there to be had. Thus, in a striking example of collective self-delusion, it had become inconceivable to all concerned that the gulf between promise and result sug-gested that at least two of the three assayers were fools or liars (Robert Denham continued to assist in successive assays, though being only an Englishman his opinion was hardly heard). On 23 November, in a letter to Walsingham, Lok perfectly expressed this contradictory principle: '. . . the iij workmasters cannot yet agree together, eche is jelous of other to be put out of the work and therby lothe to shew their conynge or to vse effectuall con-ferens; but amongest them all we doo very playnlye see and fynd that the ure is very ryche . . .'.[29]

The Queen herself was no less confused by the assayers' epic struggle. To cover the odds, she granted patents to work the ore to all three men, and in doing so both perpetuated the cause of strife and encouraged the claimants to ever-greater dishonesty.[30] As their factiousness continued, Lok and Winter tended to support the claims of Schutz; particularly his contention that larger facilities were needed to smelt the ore properly. Frobisher, becoming impa-tient of Schutz's inability to produce the gold that would ensure his reputa-tion and fortune, transferred his loyalties to Kranich (it was he who personally carried the adventurers' £10 to Kranich to allow him to build a small furnace to make his proofs). According to Lok's later account, Frobisher was primed by Kranich to pester Schutz with unhelpful comments: saying firstly that he was laying his bellows too high during the smeltings, and, subsequently, that he should place them higher yet.[31] On 20 December, Frobisher demanded that Schutz allow Kranich to melt a hundredweight of the ore in his furnace. When Schutz refused, he made him dismantle it and show its manner of con-struction to his rival. Kranich, of course, criticized its method in minute detail, which only threw more fuel upon their rivalry.

Perhaps the only sensible suggestion made during these weeks came, aston-ishingly, from Frobisher himself, who had begun to take heed of the claim that larger and better furnaces were needed.[32] On 21 January, he suggested that 10 tons of the ore should be transported north to Keswick, to be smelted and tested in the copper-mine furnaces there. It was an excellent and timely suggestion, and Schutz did everything possible to have it rejected. The following day, he pointed out how expensive it would be to move and assay such a quantity of ore, and promised to conduct a further, large assay himself. In retrospect, his motives are perfectly clear: if the Keswick assay failed to show the value he had promised, his own technical inadequacies would be highlighted; if it succeeded, his patent would be swiftly removed and given to someone in the North. Schutz was undoubtedly less than competent as an assayer, but he was hardly a fool otherwise.

In fact, although he was not yet aware of it, Schutz was about to win the battle against his rival. Only days after his attempt to keep the ore away from Keswick, Robert Denham quietly approached Michael Lok and told him that he had found a strange kind of mineral ore at Kranich's house, containing substantial traces of silver, copper and lead.[33] When Kranich subsequently made a further assay upon the ore in the presence of Burghley and the commissioners, Lok and Denham were ready. The results of the assay, conducted using an additive identified as 'antimony', were promising; but Lok insisted that it was this additive that was responsible for the apparent success. When tested, the additive was found to contain silver in the proportion of 30 ounces to the ton, as well as copper and 'very muche' lead.

Attempting to bluff out this confrontation, Kranich stood by his findings and moreover threatened not take up his patent unless he was allowed to use the same antimony in future assays; but his credibility had been shattered. At best, he had been shown to be incompetent, unaware of the properties of the additives he employed; at worst, he was deliberately 'salting' his assays to produce false results. After 22 February, when this came to light, he was probably no longer in contention for the right to work the ore. Five days later, he was unmasked publicly. Somewhat obsequiously, Lok had repeated Denham's confidential observations to Walsingham and identified their source. On 26 February, the Queen's secretary confronted the hapless Denham and demanded the truth from him: 'therew(i)thall Robert Denham kneled downe and craved p(ar)don, alleaged his oathe made to Dr burcott not to reveale his secrets . . .' – and promptly revealed them in some detail.[34]

Kranich was disgraced, but the damage caused by his involvement was profound. The commissioners' flagging faith in the ore had not been further undermined by his deceptions: to the contrary, his efforts to secure the sole rights to work it, and Schutz's correspondingly strenuous defence of his own findings, had convinced them that their former anxieties were unjustified. An unfortunate corollary of this was that they now readily accepted the truth of the only point upon which both Schutz and Kranich had agreed: that much larger furnaces were needed to properly separate gold from the slag. Already, on 8 January 1578, the Privy Council had ordered the commissioners to take up 'at reasonable interest' £500 to allow work on these new facilities to commence. Unsurprisingly, as the merchants of London had largely resisted the temptation of investing in the enterprise, so the goldfiners and other financiers shied from laying out funds – at *any* interest, reasonable or otherwise – to build furnaces. Eleven days after making their hopeful direction, the Council succumbed to reality once more, and ordered Lok to collect £900 from the adventurers by means of a second extraordinary assessment, this time of twenty per cent upon stock: 'to the end that so good an enterprise and proffitable as this viage is hoped will prove after so great charges allreadie bestowed thereon; nowe not be hindered either for want of so small a som or not prosecutyng the triall of the sayd ore.'[35] It was a perfect refutation of the principle that good money should not be thrown after bad; but Lok obeyed, and no doubt lost a few more friends.

The original intention, as we have seen, was that any new furnaces required to process the ore would be built in or near Bristol. However, the difficulty experienced in supervising successive assays and then accurately reporting their results had shown this to be unfeasible. On 7 December, Frobisher returned to London from Bristol, having halted the preliminary works there. Nine days later, on the commissioners' order, Schutz rode into Kent with Frobisher and Lok to survey several sites; as the latter reported '. . . at Deartforde Jonas lyked the mills best of allothers for the comodious water and place.'[36] This was Bignoures Mill, a mile outside Dartford town, on a tributary of the River Darent. The existing buildings on site were devoted to wheat and malt milling and thus useless for this new purpose, but they had plentiful water courses, a primary requirement for smelting furnaces. On 12 January 1578, Schutz returned to the site with a German bellows-maker, Sebastian Copeland, and a furnace-maker, Henrick Williams, to measure out the ground there.[37] Two days later, he presented his structural plans to the Commission, and it was upon their recommendation of these that Lok was ordered to raise the new assessment upon 'company' stock.

Schutz's specifications envisaged an entire complex to be built from scratch, rather than attempt to adapt the existing buildings. The total cost, excluding maintenance and running charges (which were to be onerous, as the furnaces would require almost complete rebuilding after each assay) would rise to almost £1,900 – their sole purpose, to refine ore that was itself to prove entirely valueless. Yet the logic that built this monstrous facility was both profoundly warped and inescapable. Schultz's final assay at Tower Hill, conducted on 8 March 1578, was to reveal an apparent yield of just £23 15sh. per ton of ore.[38] This was accepted by the commissioners, probably because their capacity to distinguish between fact and their need for fact had been exhausted by months of worry and prevarication. But the revelation carried with it several unpleasant corollaries. To break even, let alone make a profit on monies already invested in the enterprise, more would need to be spent – much more. Preliminary plans for a new voyage, formulated on the basis of Schutz's estimate, were immediately drawn up by the commissioners and presented to the Privy Council with his report. They envisaged the mining and recovery of some 800 tons of the ore and its transportation in four or five ships (carrying a total complement of just 120 men). Its cost was estimated at £6,400, of which half would be needed to set out the voyage and half to pay off the crews upon its return. In light of the adventurers' existing commitments, these recommendations seemed to represent an exercise in wishful thinking. In the event, their costings were to be far exceeded. The latest estimates meant that vast amounts of ore (with a corresponding incremental commitment to the coming voyage) were required to provide any prospect of a worthwhile profit on monies expended so far, and only the new and expensive works at Dartford would have the capacity to realize that profit. For the unfortunate adventurers, each new occasion of heavy expenditure carried within it the perfect rationale for a further one.

TWELVE

The 1578 Voyage

From the moment at which the commissioners issued their report on Schutz's third 'great proof', probably on 10 or 11 March 1578, plans for the new voyage commenced in earnest.[1] For Frobisher, this was good news, though not entirely without certain intrinsic drawbacks. The profound growth of the enterprise, and the corresponding inflation of his place within it, would no doubt be to the benefit of his reputation; but an immutable law of physics was beginning to exert a less happy effect. As the cost of the enterprise also grew (and, in particular, the Queen's share of it), Frobisher's already much limited power to influence events was curtailed even further. Strictly drafted instructions required and allowed for little initiative, particularly of the sort that self-aggrandizing sea-captains of the period were all too inclined to exhibit. Though, ostensibly, he was the commander at sea of a large, independently financed project, Frobisher had become little more than the principal officer of the sort of Crown-controlled, semi-private enterprise that was to become the norm during the Spanish war.

The tardiness with which his due salary was paid was a depressing reminder of this. As pleasing as a reputation must have been to Frobisher, it required a certain style to complement it; yet even as late as the end of 1578, he would claim that he had received little recompense for more than two years' labours. For the first voyage, he stated that he had received £60.[2] Prior to the despatch of the 1577 expedition, he was allowed a further £250 for 'charges', of which he had received only £130; the balance of which he was 'fane to Lett rone for my aventure which doth Remane ther as he [i.e., Lok] is wyttnes . . .'.[3]

So for want of wages in hand, Frobisher had become an adventurer. The promises and claims with which he had secured his enterprise would now rebound to his own financial disadvantage, should the enterprise fail. Nowithstanding the skills and opinions of the assayers, it was probably he who could most clearly assess that possibility, because it was his testimony that had made his strait seem viable, that had first identified the abundance of ore to be had in Meta Incognita and would now, as we shall see, strive to increase the scale of the coming voyage beyond anything that the original adventurers had envisaged. To have received some small insight into those anxieties of his backers that he had, until now, entirely ignored should have been a salutary experience. There is no evidence to suggest that it was so; indeed, it seems that he did not in the least degree equate his own risk with that of his fellow adventurers. The one was a cause for personal disquiet; the other a necessity that Frobisher appears to have accepted with remarkable equanimity. Unfortunately for his ambitions, the enthusiasm of men who did not share his priorities – much less place them to the fore – waned as costs increased.

The truth of this was painfully apparent in the difficulty with which new investors were secured. To say the least, new interest – whether from the City or Court – was desultory. Soon after the return of the 1577 voyage, the least discerning speculator of the age, the Earl of Oxford (who may have been introduced to the enterprise by his father-in-law, Burghley), had put himself down for the smallest unit of stock, of £25.[4] In the intervening months, he had been approached, perhaps secretly, by Michael Lok, who was increasingly keen to liquidize at least part of his own, huge venture. Oxford carefully assessed the risks and potential rewards to be had from a venture that had cost much and provided nothing to date, and promptly took £1,000 of stock from Lok's hands. Welcome as this was to Lok personally, however, it was not new money (indeed, the transaction was not effected until after the 1578 subscriptions had been set down).[5] Another twenty-five potential investors had been named in the same preliminary list as Oxford. Only three of these were to invest (and one of them, John Dee, appears to have had his subscription paid by Michael Lok personally).[6] A grand total of just seven new investors actually subscribed (including two more of Lok's step-children), whilst four of the existing adventurers discovered the nerve or wisdom to withdraw from the enterprise. These included two of the original investors, William Burde and Christopher Andrews (the latter, one of the former owners of the *Michael*), who did not, upon mature reflection, answer the assessment to build the Dartford works, for which they now automatically forfeited their existing stock.[7] The two other defaulters, both 1577 adventurers, were Lady Anne Talbot and, significantly, Sir William Winter – who was, with Lok, the person most responsible for the genesis of the ore project.[8] Conversely (or, rather, perversely), after resisting its siren-lure for two years, William Borough finally discovered the funds on whim or plain bad judgement to risk his money in the enterprise. The only other significant new investors were Lord Hunsdon (the Queen's Lord Chamberlain) and the Countess of Sussex, both of whom participated for just £67 10sh. (that is, a minimum participation based upon combined 1576 and 1577 stock issues). The final new entrant in the list of investors was Ann Frances, widowed sister of two existing adventurers, the mercers Matthew and Robert Kindersley.[9] Additionally, though worthlessly, several men who had sailed in the first and second voyages, and others who were to command vessels in the coming expedition, were now admitted as adventurers *gratis*: 'in consideracion of their service'.[10] These included Edward Fenton, Gilbert Yorke, Christopher Hall and, a rare manifestation of corporate compassion, one of the common mariners, James Wallis: 'hurte and maymed by the countrey people'.

So it fell once more to the existing adventurers to provide the greater part of the necessary funds. This they did, but rather less readily now. Receipts from assessments raised to finance the Dartford works were still due from many of them, and a new charge was hardly likely to be welcomed. New initiatives to raise capital in the City proved as successful as previously – that is, not at all. The dislocation between the swift expansion of the scale of the venture and the waning enthusiasm of those who supported it (those that is, who had not been privy to, and could not be swayed by, the false enthusiasms of Schutz and Kranich) must have become increasingly apparent during these months. Only the heavy hand of the Queen and her Council upon the enterprise, with its remorseless power to cajole, provided the necessary momentum to allow the expedition to be set out on, or near, schedule. It is difficult to say whether Frobisher himself devoted much attention to this failing commitment and its implications for the future of 'his' enterprise; but as monies failed to come in at the expected rate, even he must have felt the weight of expectation – and the prospect of its unfulfilment – pressing much more acutely than before.

He was further distracted by his increasing involvement (despite Lok's misgivings) in preparations for the new voyage. In at least two documents he was named as a member of the Commission, though his presence thereon appears to have been occasional, and dependent upon the business at hand.[11] A section of accounts, amalgamated within Lok's books under the heading 'C. frobyshers boowk', shows that he received and allegedly disbursed almost £650 prior to the departure of the fleet at the end of May 1578.[12] This was mainly press money and funds for victuals, wages and armour, for which expenditure he was accountable to Lok's agent, Edward Selman. Almost immediately, there were rumours of his 'evill victualling' and misappropriation of funds; rumours which may have had a broader currency than among his fellow adventurers:

At the beginninge of this theird voyage C. Furbisher was sent by the Com(m)ission(er)s from London to Brystowe to Furnishe and dispatche from thence the Shipps Ayde and Gabriell for this voyadge, wherein he was mad(e) victuler of the Shippe Ayde, for the whiche victualls he had v^c pounds of mooney delyvered him before hande, but he did so evill victuall the same Shippe, that whereas the Companye allowed him mooney for to victuall her w(i)th fleshe iiij dayes in the weake, he served the men onely iij dayes and ij dayes in the weake therw(i)th and the rest of the weeke w(i)th fyshe and that so evill and so scarse, that thereby mutch sickenes grewe, and diu(er)s of them dyed, as the men do reporte /

He was sent into the west Countrye to provide cxx men myners, for this voyadge, for whose furniture he had mooney of the Companye before hande for their wages, ccxl. poundes, w(hi)ch is xl.^{s} for eche man, but thereof he payed theis men to some xx^s. to some xiij^s iiij^d. and to some nothinge the man, as his accoumpts declares, allsoo he had cxx^{li}. of mooney for their weapons & furniture, w(hi)ch is xx^s. for everye man to provide his weaponnes w(i)thall, but what weapons they had, or he for them is yet unknowen, for none doeth appeare anye wheare, but in the west Countrye is spread a Rumor that those myners beinge prest by Com(m)ission in her Ma(ies)ties name, manye of them afterwards wear chardged by favo(u)r, for showemakers, tailors musitians, gardeners, and other artyfycers no(t) woorkemen / And they weare furnished to Sea, at the chardges of the Townes and villadgs in manner of a subsidie, as yt is reported openly.[13]

It seems, therefore, that Frobisher may have attempted to recover his arrears of wages by means other than recourse to the pockets of his former benefactor Lok. The charge of bad victualling was later corroborated both by Fenton and Hall, but not until Frobisher had given further evidence of it.[14] For the moment, the accusation was not made public, but it seems likely that at some point immediately following his return from the 1578 voyage he was confronted by Lok and Selman; particularly as they, in turn, were accountable to the commissioners and Privy Council. Both men were to feel the sharp edge of his temper towards the end of the year; perhaps the genesis of his ire lay in a first, polite request for receipts, properly recorded and signed, and for the names of those men he had allegedly provided for. His dreams of fame and a fortune (the latter still far from being realized) were hardly to be furthered by tiresome reminders to improve his book-keeping practices.

With these worries, pressures and outright irritations, Frobisher may have seen arrangements for the voyage coming to fruition with some relief (indeed, Lok later alleged that he 'coolde take no rest, vntill he weare gonn one the waye to his newe Empier').[15] Officially, he was provided with a fleet of ten vessels. In addition to the four 'company' ships *Ayde, Gabriel, Michael* and now the *Judith* (of approximately 100 tons, purchased from William Borough), there were six officially chartered vessels that would transport the hundreds of tons of ore to be mined in Meta Incognita. These were the *Thomas Allen* (owned by the adventurer of that name), *Hopewell, Anne Frances, Thomas of Ipswich, Frances of Foye* and *Moon of Foye*. Little is known of these ships, but it seems likely that with the exception of the *Thomas Allen*, they were small but heavily built three masters of the sort that habitually carried England's commerceries across the Channel (one vessel which was to sail with the fleet unofficially was nicknamed the *busse*: the word traditionally denoted an inelegant, broad-beamed lighter used as the drudge-vehicle of sea-trade). If these ships were now intended to pass into dangerous seas and return with heavy loads of ore in their holds, they had to be both robust and – for their owners an important consideration – relatively cheap to replace.

With so many vessels, the scale of the voyage had passed far beyond that envisaged in the commissioners' preliminary report in March (though the amount of ore to be laded in the ships remained the same, at 800 tons). Yet the increased charges associated with the hire of further vessels were not the only additional burden upon the adventurers' pockets. Ominously, the Privy Council's instructions to Frobisher revealed that they were holding out the possibility of more than one further expedition. The Queen had a new land to govern; hopefully, its resources would provide a healthy profit to her Exchequer, but in the meantime the claim needed to be staked more forcibly than in the raising of a column of stones on 'Mount Warwick'. Furthermore, that claim, once made, needed to be protected. At some time before March 1578, an initial estimate for the coming voyage had been drafted. This document, in addition to providing for a much-expanded ore-mining operation, was the first to address requirements for a colony of 100 men to remain in Meta Incognita.[16] These were to earn their keep by mining a further 2,000 tons of ore before a fourth voyage returned for them, in addition to that mined and returned in the ships that would take them out to their new land in 1578. The cost of keeping these intrepid colonists (in victuals and wages) was estimated to be £4,800; but potentially the net return would be £40,000, if Schutz's latest (and least optimistic) estimate of the ore's value proved sound. Such a ratio of cost to return appealed enormously to the Queen and her Council, particularly as the colony would hardly be capable of generating any further costs in the intervening months. Accordingly, existing preparations for the voyage were adjusted to provide for this project: forty mariners, thirty soldiers and thirty miners ('pyoners') were now to be established – and supplied – in a suitably defensible site in Meta Incognita. As intended, it would have been the first English settlement in the New World, predating Ralegh's Roanoke colony by almost a decade. The colonists were to winter there under the command of Edward Fenton (now Lieutenant-General of the expedition and captain of the *Judith*); according to the instructions drafted for the voyage, he was to 'observe the nature of the ayre, and may discover and knowe the state of the countrie from tyme to tyme as moche as may be, and what tyme of the yeare the Straight is most free frome eysse'.[17] He and his men were also to explore the land and seas 'confynynge, borderinge, or lyinge' within 200 leagues of the colony, and to keep a weekly journal recording the detail of such matters: for the use of future colonists and, perhaps, their eventual administrators. The colony was initially to be provisioned for eighteen months, but this seems to have constituted a momentary lack of foresight on the commissioners' part; any relief expedition would have been attempting to retrieve the colonists – and, more importantly, the ore – in the depths of an Arctic winter.

The decision to establish a colony indicates how far the initiative had passed from the adventurers of the original joint-stock arrangement to the Queen and her Council. There was no conceivable rationale for a colony to men who simply wanted to realize a return upon their existing investments; no commercial logic in incurring heavy, incremental costs merely to keep men alive in a barren land to mine further quantities of ore that had yet to provide the merest profit. And even should that profit subsequently materialize, logic dictated that it would be far more prudent to set out a new voyage in 1579 with fresh miners, rather than attempt to employ men already weakened by a winter beyond the worst experience of Englishmen. The colony was there-fore a distraction from the immediate goals of the adventurers, but with the

Queen's priorities now so firmly identified with those of the enterprise itself, it was a project that they were obliged to underwrite.

It was also something that Frobisher had brought about, however unwittingly. When the commissioners had been discussing the scale and nature of the new voyage, he had intervened with an ingenious (and ingenuous) warning:

> . . . he enforced vnto the Comission(er)s manye arguments and reasons, howe requisite and needfull yt was to fortifie and to inhabit in that newe Countrye / And for to vrge the same to a greater furniture of Shippinge for his dominion, he vowched w(i)th oathes vnto the Comission(er)s, and w(i)thall shewe(d) a l(ettr)e (but redd yt not) w(hi)ch he sayd cam owtt of Fraunce, by a messenger of his owne, how that the French kinge did arme p(re)sently xij shipps, to passe to the same newe Countrye, to take possession of the straightes and to fortyfie at the mynes there . . .[18]

Later, Frobisher was to regret this shallow cleverness. Like the merchants, he came to consider the colony project a distraction, though his reasons were anything but commercial. If Edward Fenton were to be successful in his command of the first English colony in the New World, Frobisher's own achievement – whatever that was to be – would be significantly diluted: perhaps even recalled as no more than a footnote to a greater and more lasting deed. Precisely how and when he realized this is not known; but almost as soon as the colony project became a firm objective of the coming expedition, he was intervening to prevent its realization: '. . . with hevie Countenaunce he woolde cast owte speaches cullerably, sometymes sayenge that this great furniture of buildings for Capt. Fenton woold be to little purpose, Sometymes that they shoold hardely be able to plant them selues there, & dangerously to live there, and plainly sayd to Charles Jackeman at harwiche that they shoold not inhabit there . . .'.[19]

He was entirely prudent in his opinion of the colony's viability, though hardly to be credited for it. Such a plantation would have made that established at Roanoke seem a model of easy living by comparison. Fish apart (and even they had to be caught, in seas that were often treacherous for wooden-hulled vessels), there were few local resources that the Meta Incognita colonists might have secured had their own supplies spoiled or failed (an habitual risk), or if some natural calamity – fire or pestilence being the most feared and expected – afflicted their fledgling community.[20] Fresh water was available from a small spring on the Countess of Warwick Island itself; but if that dried up, further sources were at such a distance as to make the journey – particularly in the depths of winter – acutely difficult for men already weakened by extremes of toil and cold. Under such novel conditions, it is not difficult to imagine how tiring the mere effort of remaining alive would have proved. Add to these natural burdens the ever-present threat of Inuit aggression (in particular, their suspected taste for English flesh) and the psychological insecurity of not knowing when, or even if, a relief expedition might return, and the potential effect upon the colonists' morale can hardly be overstated.

Though circumstances would, fortunately, prevent its establishment, providing for this colonial experiment was an expensive business. The preliminary estimate proved to be quite accurate; the actual cost came to a few pennies less than £4,350, or roughly the cost of despatching an entire expedition in 1577.[21] The expense, in part, reflected the care with which this first English colony in the New World was planned. Despite the flawed and excessive optimism that had decreed it, there was considerable ingenuity evident in its outfitting. The colonists' equipment included a remarkable, prefabricated blockhouse: according to a provisional manifest set down by Edward Fenton, this was '. . . of timb(e)r heavie framed for o(u)r Lodging & storehowses conteyning 132 foote in Lengthe and 42 foote in breadthe with ij (bulwarks?) at either ende thereof conteyning in Lengthe (blank) foote and in bredthe (blank) foote with iij other bulwark(e)s of defence thereat adioyninge . . .'.[22]

With walls to be reinforced by bricks and mortar, the house was clearly intended to survive more than a single winter.[23] The *Gabriel, Judith* and *Michael* were allocated to remain with the colony, to allow further exploration of the straits and, presumably, to provide the means of emergency evacuation, should this prove necessary (though clearly, this would mean the abandonment of the ore they had mined). This might have proved difficult. Logic suggests that any abandonment of the colony would be both urgent and most likely to occur during the winter months, yet given the prevalence of pack ice in the straits, the commissioners had sensibly provided that the ships should be beached throughout the Arctic winter.[24]

Fenton's provisional list for the colony gives a good indication of its anticipated rationing – which does not appear to have been over-generous, given the expected conditions to be faced by the colonists. As in the second voyage, meat appears to have been provided for four days per week: this was, principally, beef (15,600 lbs, giving a daily allowance of 1 lb per man), supplemented by pork (three months' worth – 1,200 lbs) and bacon (six months at

$\frac{1}{2}$ lb per man per day).[25] The remaining three days' principal meal was to consist of fish – haberdine (dried cod) and stockfish – with cheese (1 lb per man per day), bread (two days out of three, with dried biscuit on the third), butter (3 lb per man per month) and, all-importantly, beer – 43 tons of 'small' or weak beer, and 90 tons of strong beer – giving an approximate daily allowance of 4 pints per man (this was by no means an excessive allowance, which suggests that locally drawn water, being untainted by proximity to prior human settlement, was considered an acceptable alternative). Vegetables were represented solely by the ubiquitous pea – four bushels per man, whether he wanted them or not. The usual flavourings – wine vinegar, mustard seed, sweet oil and, of course, salt – were provided to relieve the monotony of the diet, as were two surgeon's chests, to deal with the inevitable ailments arising from its deficiencies. A final item in the victualling lists shows that the colonists would not entirely lack company in their hostile new world: Lok's accounts also record the purchase of 2 quarters of 'pollarde meale for dog(e)s'.

There remains some doubt as to how the colonists were expected to spend their winter months. Clearly, they would be required to earn their generous keep by securing a further 2,000 tons of ore; however, the commissioners and Privy Council were by now well aware of how destructive to human tissue continuous, hard labour could be in such a climate. Unless, therefore, the colony was considered to be entirely expendable (and to the Queen, nothing that had taken large sums from her own purse was that), it seems that mining activity was to be confined to the brief summer, whilst the colonists' efforts at other times would be devoted to the more mundane task of not dying.

With the costs of other ships and men – those devoted to the extraction of some 800 tons of ore and its return to England during 1578 – the total cost, merely for the new voyage to set out from England, was £8,939.[26] To put this onerous commitment into perspective, Drake had set out six months earlier with three ships at a cost of some £5,000, ostensibly to discover and claim the supposed southern continent of Terra Australis. This, his famous circumnavigation, would provide a return upon the Queen's investment alone that was sufficient to pay off the national debt. Several adventurers in the Frobisher voyages – Leicester, Walsingham, Lincoln and William Winter – had also invested in Drake's project. Their concurrent, heavy involvement in Frobisher's enterprise, which to date had failed to provide income, let alone profit, strengthens the case of those who argue that Drake's plans for aggressive economic warfare were already known to his backers – or at least some of them – prior to his leaving England. If so, their prudence was admirable, as was the rationale that had dictated this new investment: gold that might – or might not – be scoured from the soil of an alien landscape could almost certainly be dragged from the pockets of His Most Catholic Majesty's subjects.[27]

To meet the costs of the huge new voyage to Meta Incognita, the charge upon adventurers still reeling from the assessment imposed to finance the works at Dartford was 135 per cent of their total investment in the first and second voyages (excluding all assessments). The Queen was rated at £1,350, Frobisher at £135, and Lok at a crippling £2,632 10sh. (this figure seems to have included his 1577 loans now converted to stock).[28] In total, £8,370 was raised to finance the voyage. More than £1,900 of this remained unpaid by 3 May 1578, and it is likely that this figure did not reduce considerably before the third voyage sailed at the end of that month.[29] What is surprising, however, is not the tardiness with which the existing adventurers met this new commitment, but rather that they bothered – the prudent Burde, Winter, Andrews and Talbot apart – to search their pockets at all. Again, their readiness to do so, in light of the existing burden of expenditure, is hardly to be explained as a manifestation of gold-fever. It was rather a combination of fear and ignorance: fear of the implications of personal default (and, of course, of the abandonment of existing stock), and ignorance of the true progress of assays carried out by Schutz and his assistants at Tower Hill. There was of course a degree of optimism still – new investors had been secured, if far fewer than had been anticipated – but the blithe assumptions that had brought in so many new adventurers in 1577 had faded to something far more hopeful, with all the uncertainties that hope, alone, entails.

Mindful of the weather patterns in the new lands, the Privy Council had directed that the expedition should be ready to sail by 1 May; but preparations, hampered by the tardiness with which money came in, fell behind schedule. The individual vessels of the fleet congregated at Harwich only on 31 May (Christopher Hall brought the *Ayde* and *Gabriel* directly from Bristol, where they had lain since the previous year). This was not, however, the fleet that had been planned and provided for in the official instructions. Separately, both Lok and Frobisher had arranged for further ships to sail with the expedition. Lok had gone into partnership with one Richard Fairweather, who provided a ship, the *Beare Leicester*, brought officially into the enterprise under charter-party shortly before the voyage commenced (her captain, Henry Philpot, was clearly well regarded; he was appointed subsequently to be a member of the expedition's 'land council' in Meta Incognita).[30] Frobisher, meanwhile, briefly in the West Country attending to the refitting and provisioning of the *Ayde* and *Gabriel*, had contacted some of his old confederates and arranged for several more, privately financed vessels to join his expedition as freight ships. At least two of these, and probably all, were former or active privateers; one, Hugh Randall's *Salomon*, of Weymouth, was the same ship that had joined the *Robert* and *Roe* in the capture of the *Mary* in 1569.[31] The other vessels were the *Emanuel of Bridgewater* (also identified in contemporary accounts as the *Manewall* or, more commonly, the *Busse of Bridgewater*), the *Emanuel of Exeter* (also known as *Armonell*) and a large bark, the *Denys*. Being included solely upon Frobisher's personal authority – it appears that he did not reveal their presence to the commissioners prior to the assembly of the fleet at Harwich – none of these vessels was admitted under charter-party, though in the aftermath of the voyage the freight charges of the *Salomon*, *Armonell* and the *Emanuel of Bridgewater* were accepted as the adventurers' responsibility: at an incremental cost, according to Lok's account books, of £1,000.[32]

The purpose of these additional, unauthorized vessels was not to ship ore clandestinely (even Frobisher could hardly have hoped to run a private operation within the enterprise); their inclusion was rather the final manifestation of that ill-founded optimism that had first brought Lok and Frobisher to their unlikely collaboration. Nevertheless, their somewhat disreputable owners may have believed that part of their intended cargoes had the potential to be misplaced upon their return passage. In the event, the Council's strict instructions regarding security prevented this, though it is not beyond the bounds of possibility that one of these vessels, the *Emanuel of Bridgewater*, later beached and wrecked at Smerwick Bay in western Ireland with some 110 tons of ore, had been heading for Baltimore or Kinsale with the intention of keeping her ballast from the reach of Admiralty Court officials.

Frobisher himself stood to gain little by associating these men with his enterprise, and much to lose in terms of reputation; it may be that he had allowed himself to be persuaded that their vessels' carrying capacity would provide an incremental profit for the adventurers, and that the latter would be sufficiently grateful not to baulk at the additional freight charges they would thus incur. If so, he was to be proven very wrong. The involvement of these unauthorized ships was to increase the carrying capacity of the fleet by almost forty per cent, and its potential for realizing a profit by not a single penny. Later, Frobisher was to rail at Lok and Jonas Schutz as the men most directly responsible for the failure of the north-west enterprise; but it was the cost of his unofficial freight ships – yet another onerous occasion of expense

– that tested to destruction the flawed logic that had sustained the adventurers throughout almost three years' false promise of gain. Lok was later to stress this in his accusations against Frobisher's conduct (claiming that the purpose of introducing the unauthorized vessels had been merely to inflate Frobisher's fleet, and therefore the prestige of its commander), whilst entirely passing over his similar, if lesser, culpability *vis-à-vis* the *Beare Leicester*.[33]

Though this particular proof of their fears was concealed from the Privy Council before the voyage sailed, suspicions regarding Frobisher's potential for disobedience were reflected in the precision with which the instructions for the voyage were drafted. Arrangements for the proposed colony apart, their major goals were almost identical to those of the previous year, except where hard-won experience dictated otherwise.[34] They ordered that the expedition should make directly for Countess of Warwick Sound, and re-establish their base camp there. Frobisher was to examine all likely sites in the immediate vicinity rather than conduct a broader reconnaissance as in the previous two years (though the promising deposits at Beare Sound were to be tested once more). Given the nature of the commodity the expedition was to obtain, security was a paramount consideration. All the extracted ore was to be carefully logged by location, type and condition; and samples of every type placed, with the results from assays thereon, into sealed boxes. Such assays were to be strictly observed, and conducted only by those specifically appointed to the task.

Security in the wider sense was also a matter of clear concern, but again, there were to be no pre-emptive measures which might in any way detract from the main business of ore-mining. In view of the difficulties with the local population in the previous year, Frobisher was to impress upon his men: 'rather to muche then any thinge to littell. . . . that in all yo(u)r doynges and theirs you so behave yo(u)r selves and theyme, towardes the said people as maye rather procure their frindships and good lykings towardes you by courtesyes then move them to any offence or myslikinge.' 'Offence' was presumably a reference to killing any more of their number, a belated recognition that the Englishmen's behaviour to date had not been best designed to foster amity with the Inuit; and one further item to be taken in the new voyage suggests that corrective measures were anticipated in this respect. Robert Wolfall, a preacher from the diocese of Bath and Wells, 'being of good reputation amonge the best, refused not to take in hand this painefull voyage, for the onely care he had to save soules, and to reforme those Infidels if it were possible to Christianitie.' If the infidels could not be conquered, they should at least be made decently pliable – after which, in the Spanish manner, they might be civilized to the point of extinction.[35]

The north-west passage, and the five men lost in 1576, had almost ceased to exercise the attention of the Privy Council. Almost as an afterthought, Frobisher's instructions directed that he was to proceed up the straits with the *Gabriel* and *Michael* to search for both only 'yf leasure and tyme wille permitt'; a broad hint that both matters were considered effectively dead in 1578. The instructions were careful to point out that even if Frobisher made this further attempt, he should also spend the time usefully, to search for further potential mining sites.

Because of the scale of the new expedition, the complexity of its aims and, not least, the investment it represented, Frobisher was explicitly ordered to involve his principal officers in decisions regarding all aspects of their task. On land, his 'council' would comprise Captains Fenton, Yorke (*Thomas Allen*, vice-admiral), Philpot (*Beare Leicester*), Best (*Anne Frances*) and Carew (*Hopewell*, rear-admiral); at sea, he was to consult the expedition's chief pilot, Christopher Hall, and ships' masters Jackman, Beare and Diar. Frobisher's reaction to these potential curbs to his authority will be discussed subsequently, but the specific naming of men with whom he should confer, rather than the more usual exhortation merely to take 'good councel', implies that the Privy Council were recalling once more and acting to curb his tendency to take his own counsel only. A prudent measure, it was also, ultimately, an optimistic one. As we shall see, Frobisher was to exercise almost untrammelled authority during the expedition (though his council would be called, and heeded, upon at least two occasions); yet this was not to be a uniformly unhappy experience. If sage counsel was a necessary curb upon sea-commanders' impulsive natures, there were, nevertheless, to be occasions in the coming voyage upon which a single, absolutist will would achieve what discourse could only confound. The events and implications of the 1578 voyage were to leave a stain upon Frobisher's reputation that would endure for years; it was a particular irony, therefore, that for all his readiness to alienate his officers, his abilities as a leader of men would never be displayed to greater, nor more fortunate, effect.

At Harwich on 31 May 1578, Frobisher issued his articles and orders to the captains of the assembled fleet. As with all such missives, they provide excellent evidence of which disorders were considered most likely to disrupt a contemporary expedition.[36] The important exhortations came first: swearing, dice, cards and 'filthy communication' were forbidden, and to assist the mariners in rising to these counter-intuitive challenges, divine service was to be held on each ship's deck twice daily, weather and other corporeal distractions permitting (such frequent recourse to God was common in naval ships during the period, though almost always in equally forlorn expectation of its efficacy).[37] On the conduct of the fleet itself, the ships were to remain within one mile of the *Ayde* at all times during their passage; she alone was to bear a stern light, and if this were to be put out, no other ship should attempt to go on before her in the sea. All captains were to repair to the *Ayde* each evening at seven o'clock for the daily report; or, if poor weather prevented this, to the *Thomas Allen*, where Christopher Hall would give them any new instructions on their course.[38] Two shots should be fired off and two lights showed, if any man were swept overboard (the orders refer only to a 'mischance', but no one would have misunderstood what was meant by that). The nightly password was to be a pious 'Before the world was God', to which the response would be 'After God came Christ his son'. Should any ship become separated from the fleet, she was to make for 'Friesland' and then for the straits (Best excised from his reproduction of these instructions the precise latitudes to which the ships were directed under such circumstances). Finally, if the fleet were attacked – it is not clear here whether the Privy Council was thinking of Spanish intervention or that of a rival, French fleet – it was to concentrate and fight in three divisions, centred upon the ships *Ayde, Judith* and *Thomas Allen*.

Instructions were the universal method of reminding sea-captains of their precise duties, but in this case their attention to the matter of discipline was unusually apposite. The expedition was not a naval affair (though the level of the Queen's commitment made that a moot point), and the constant references to the personal behaviour of the ships' crews, and to the wider matter of fleet discipline, strongly suggest an expectation of unruliness. The discipline that was to mark – some might say disfigure – English ship-board life in later generations was not, as yet, even remotely in sight. Contemporary penalties for slackness or insubordination were indeed harsh, but their implementation depended entirely upon the personal authority of the commander at sea: hence the considerable success of Francis Drake, whose ability to inspire his mariners and crush dissidence amongst his officers has been amply noted. Frobisher's own authority had proved to be considerable (even if his methods were often less than inspirational), but in this new voyage he had the company of eleven 'civilian' vessels. Owned by private individuals, they had been brought into the enterprise under purely commercial arrangements, with no vested loyalty beyond that which secured their freight charges.

Furthermore, they were to pass into a region that was almost certainly going to provide unpleasant surprises for the majority of their crews. There were many less arduous voyages during the course of the sixteenth century that suffered large-scale defections of ships when the attention or ambitions of their captains wandered, and the supposedly gold-bearing ore that Frobisher's 1578 fleet was to lade could hardly have made that prospect more remote. As we shall see, the singular achievement of this new expedition was not so much that it met most of its objectives, but that it did so in the face of many strong reasons to abandon the voyage entirely. If this untypical commitment and cohesion was an occasion for praise, a great part was due to Frobisher himself.

After receiving their instructions on the deck of the *Ayde*, the other captains returned to their ships and made ready to depart immediately, having been filled with a sense of urgency that had emanated from the Privy Council itself. The swift deterioration in weather conditions in Meta Incognita had hampered the 1576 and 1577 expeditions. In this new voyage, the planned departure date of 1 May had been intended to steal a march on the Arctic climate. This had proved impossible, but time could be recovered, even now. As the ships of Frobisher's fleet departed from Harwich that afternoon, they did not turn north, as in the previous two voyages, but south-east. The official instructions had stipulated only that 'you shall passe the landes of England, Scotlande or Irelande' – the precise course was not an issue to the Council, only the speed with which the passage was made; with this in mind, Frobisher (upon his own initiative, as far as we know) determined rather to sail westwards down the English Channel and launch himself into the Ocean Sea from western Ireland.[39]

It was to prove a sound strategy. On 3 June the fleet came to anchor at Plymouth to take on water, having briefly diverted its course off Folkstone to chase a French man-of-war that had attempted to shadow it; three days later they were off Cape Clear, where they encountered and gave succour to that most fortunate of ships, the little *Grechwinde*. From there, on a north-westerly course, the fleet took advantage of good winds, and even with a brief calm on 11 June and the contrary, north-east flow of the oceanic current off Ireland (which Best correctly surmised was the same current that 'runneth alongst into the greate Baye of Mexico'), it was safely off the coast of 'Friesland' by 20 June. The Atlantic passage had been made in just two weeks, and no ships had yet gone missing.

In the previous two years, icebergs off the coast of this inhospitable land had denied Frobisher a landfall, but the Queen and Privy Council remained determined to know its nature. His instructions, more explicit than in the previous year, required him to 'endevour to dyskover the new land . . . and to get best knowledge that you can of the state and nature therof'.[40] Despite his schedule, therefore, and the urgency that had permeated his instructions regarding the ore itself, Frobisher called over Hall from the *Thomas Allen*, and both men transferred into the smaller, handier *Gabriel*. They took the bark westwards along the coast, rounding 'Cape Frobisher' (Kap Farvel) on to the western coast of Greenland. There, through a break in the ice, they saw signs of life on-shore. In a pinnace, Frobisher, Hall and several unnamed gentlemen forced their way to the beach, where they immediately claimed the land on behalf of the Queen, naming it West England.[41] Within an hour, Edward Fenton and a party from the *Judith* joined him there, and they explored the tents of the local inhabitants, who, prudently, had fled at their coming.

This year, Frobisher took closer heed of his instructions regarding the 'new prey'. In the tents the Englishmen found seal skins, three boats similar to those they had observed in Meta Incognita and approximately forty white puppies; yet at Frobisher's order they purloined only a single whelp from this substantial brood (their trumpeter, Christopher Jackson, took another without permission), for which they left in exchange some looking-glasses, bells and other 'toyes'.[42] In another tent, they found iron nails and an iron trivet, which Best assumed to indicate that 'they haue trade with some civill people, or else are in deede themselues artificiall workemen' (i.e. artificers). When this brief examination was complete, Frobisher and his men withdrew to the shore, neither disturbing nor otherwise violating the possessions of the Queen's new subjects. Elizabeth had made it clear that she wished to enjoy her new territories in peace, a prerequisite of which was that the natives should be kept tractable.

The difficult feat of landing upon 'Friesland' having been accomplished, the expedition's overwhelming priorities reasserted themselves. The landing parties returned to their ships within two hours, though the high seas, fog and ice made their re-embarkation a hazardous business (Fenton spent most of the day in his pinnace, until the weather subsided sufficiently to allow him to come alongside the *Judith*).[43] For the next two days, the fleet passed west and northwards along the coastline of this new English possession. During that time, the ships remained in touch only with difficulty: according to Thomas Ellis, they fell into 'such a fogge and hidious mist, that we coulde not see one another: whervpon we stroke our drummes, and sounded our trumpets, to the ende we might keepe together'.[44] By 22 June, however, the mists had cleared; and having sighted and named a high cliff to their starboard *Charing Cross* ('for a certaine similitude' Best noted), Frobisher had his ships set their course west-north-west towards Meta Incognita.

Immediately, the entire fleet was thrown into severe danger. The weather, even by the harsh norms prevalent in Davis Strait, became uncharacteristically violent. In high seas, a fast-moving front of icebergs drove into the path of the fleet, and Frobisher was obliged to order the ships to turn southwards to run before this menace. Their new course was maintained for some three leagues only, but by the time this was corrected north-westwards once more, they had lost the *Michael* among the ice: gone, apparently, upon her now-traditional detour. No attempt was made to search or to wait for her; as Frobisher's orders had stipulated, any missing vessel was to make her own way, upon her own resources alone, to the pre-designated landfall. By 26 June, the *Judith* had also become detached from the fleet (the previous day, Hall – in the *Thomas Allen* – had recorded his latitude to be 61°–24′N, but Fenton's observation from the deck of the *Judith* less than twenty-four hours later was 62°–36′N, with the wind having fallen almost to calm in the meantime).[45] Though the separated vessels would have occasional sight of the other, far off amidst the ice-pack, almost seven weeks would elapse before the fleet fully re-assembled. Meanwhile its formation was to fragment yet further.

Fenton and Hall each recorded their first sight of land on 27 June, though in different locations. Fenton reported the *Judith* to be fifteen leagues off Hall's Island, but so beset with ice that she was forced to lay off to the seaward once more, to find some other way in. Four days later, he claimed to have sighted the Queen's Foreland (possibly he was right, though his observation of latitude on that day at 60°–15′N was wildly inaccurate, unless the *Judith* had somehow passed southward across the mouth of Hudson Strait and was off the coast of Newfoundland). Almost simultaneously, Hall was to the north, taking the *Thomas Allen* much closer in towards the mouth of the strait than the rest of the fleet. There, he definitely made out Lok's Land, Hall's Island and, later in the day, the Queen's Foreland. More importantly, he also noticed a great prevalence of ice in the strait itself.

The next forty-eight hours were to bring dangers beyond anything Frobisher and his men had yet faced in their new land. On the morning of 2 July, Hall brought the *Thomas Allen* out of the ice to rendezvous with the waiting ships and warn them of what lay before them. Unfortunately, his prudent reconnaissance was entirely unappreciated by his comrades in the fleet. Hall's own words best describe the tragi-comedy that followed:

I had byn hard aborde the yse, and cam of to tell my Amberall & the rest of the flete, that there was no way into the straightes, bycause the yse was so thick, so at my comming of, I met first with the M(aste)r of the Barke Dennis, whose name was Dabney, & told him, and he was partely perswaded, and so from him I spoke with Androw Diar, M(aste)r of the Hopewell, and perswaded him, so that the rest of the ships were to windeward, that I could not speake with them, so that Richard Cockes came sayling vp being to windewards, and I could not speake to him, he presently set vp his Mainetop sayle, and fortop sayle, and sayled in among the yse, and the bark Denis after him, the Salamon after him, the Fraunces of Foye after him, and one after another, to yt came to the 11. sayle and that was the Amrall, I next to him, and the Hopewell last of all. . . .[46]

The image of a hapless Hall, shouting forlornly to his incautious comrades as they disappeared into the ice and then following despairingly thereafter, is one of English maritime history's more endearing *vignettes*; but the consequences of their collective deafness were almost catastrophic. Initially, Hall's caution seemed excessive; the weather was particularly fine that day, and the ice seen clearly and brilliantly in sunshine did not frighten the mariners as it had in squalls and fogs. A favourable wind carried the fleet westwards into the strait, encouraging it towards its goal. But that same wind, and the equally favourable currents, also carried in huge amounts of gleaming, seemingly unthreatening ice behind them. A trap was forming, into which the fleet blithely ran with all sails set.

From deck of the *Ayde*, Ellis saw the *Michael* and *Judith*, far distant to the north, faithfully shadowing the fleet on a parallel course. At ten o'clock that evening it remained very light; Frobisher's ships had by then passed approximately thirty miles into the 'strait', being rather closer to its southern shore. At that point, the fleet came to a vast polynia within the ice, 'inclosed of every side, that we could neither get out nor in no way'. The experience was uncomfortable, yet still the weather remained fair, and Hall laconically called it 'a pretty plasser' for the ships of the fleet to ply up and down, waiting for an opportunity to break out.[47] But the thirteen vessels thus enclosed were about to experience more than mere confinement. Even whilst the weather remained fair, their good fortune began to evaporate. The bark *Denys*, attempting to manoeuvre with her sails raised, had her hull rent by an iceberg and sank within half an hour, though fortunately her entire crew was picked up by the boats of the *Ayde* and *Beare Leicester*. Ironically, the loss of the *Denys* was probably to preserve a further 100 lives, as will become apparent; but this early disaster seemed only to foreshadow a night of appalling loss. The ships' ordeal worsened dramatically around midnight, when the weather swiftly turned; a violent storm, coming in from the south-east and compacting the ice still further within the 'strait', tossed the ships and turned what had been a dangerous confinement into a deadly jousting contest with icebergs that now moved as precipitously as the vessels themselves. The four ships of the fleet that lay easternmost – *Anne Frances, Frances of Foy, Moon* and *Gabriel* – managed to force their way out into looser pack-ice, and spent the next few hours fending and pushing their prows towards the mouth of the strait and the relative safety of open water; the remaining eight ships, entombed in the vanishing polynia, prepared as best they could for the worst.

With cables, mattresses and tarpaulins stretched over the ships' sides as rudimentary fenders, the crews used every spare piece of wood (and many that could not be spared) to keep the ice from breaking against their hulls. Some captains anchored their vessels to the larger icebergs, hoping thus to coordinate their violent tossing; three-inch planks shattered like matchwood in men's hands as they plied desperately; the largest of the ships were lifted between clashing floes, well above their watermarks – 'mountaynes of ise tenne thousande tymes scaping them scarce one ynch, whiche to haue stricken had bin theyr presente destruction'[48] – these were conditions which no Englishmen (at least, none that had survived) had yet experienced. Their terror was magnified, furthermore, by the brutal understanding of their predicament: that there was no possible succour for any man who might, through God's mercy or blind good fortune, somehow survive the sinking of his ship in those waters; that even if, by some miracle, he might reach the shore, death would only be the slower and more painful for it. A single option only recommended itself to the desperate ships' crews – to somehow survive the night afloat and hope for the weather to turn once more.

Yet these eight ships had at least the thin comfort of an ordeal shared. To the north, closer in to the shore, the *Judith* was undergoing a more private agony.[49] The journals both of Edward Fenton and his master Charles Jackman related their torments in graphic detail (though of Jackman's journal only a fragment survives): torments which they still imagined to be the mere prelude to a year's painful sojourn in that land.

Earlier that afternoon, Fenton had been 'lykwyse alured by the beuty of (th)e day and fayrnes of the gole to enter the strat(e)s fyrther by 5. leages than the generall'. By three o'clock the following morning, the *Judith* was entirely enclosed by ice, with no free water in which to fend off the pressing floes.

The crew, demoralized by their seemingly deadly situation, almost gave up hope of salvation; but in that dark moment, Reverend Robert Wolfall called upon a higher authority even than Frobisher:

> . . . (he) moved vs to prayer layinge befor vs our p(re)sent danger and how we ought to behave (our)selues to godward in this distres to whom as it semed from this woorld we ware redy; (see)inge this his comfortable exhortation so quietned and revived o(u)r p(re)sent estate that the dangers wherin we ware was therby relented and made the more tollerable in yᵉ hope (we) had in god(e)s mersis. This his exortation fynished o(u)r captayn and m(aste)r by god apoynted our safegard incoraged yᵉ gentelmen and soldiers with pikes and owers to beare yᵉ Ise (from) the side of the shipp, the other with lyke diligenc chered his saylors with great currage and man- lynes to stand to ther labor and taklinge. Then every man imployed hymself to labore he cold best skyll of and as the spech goeth we laboringe for lyffe it (ples)ed god to send by 9 aclock to apeas the storme and open a glad in yᵉ Ise . . .[50]

If Jackman's words seem heartfelt, he did no more than give due recognition to the scale of their deliverance at the hands of (an obviously Protestant) God. Even Edward Fenton, usually a more taciturn journalist, waxed piously upon it:

> . . . after o(u)r hartie prayers made to god, he opened vnto us (as to the children of Israell in the brode sea) a litle cleare to the north-west wardes, wherinto we forced o(u)r shipp w(i)th vyolence And thus having given o(u)r selves to themercifull handes of god, he of his greate goodnes sente us p(re)s(en)tlie faire weather, wherby we gained some plaine to turne in all the forepart of the daie.[51]

That morning, the slowly clearing storm revealed a seascape of wreckage and near-destruction amidst the parting ice-floes. Across the ice-strewn strait, the broken and beaten ships of the fleet, singly or in pairs, limped eastwards towards the safety of open water. Astonishingly, no vessel other than the *Denys*, and not a single life, had been lost. It had been an occasion of unbe- lievable good fortune, but fortune favours those who rise to it. It had been an occasion also of inspired leadership: of making the best of very poor and fragile resources. If Frobisher may be condemned for his autocratic and inflex- ible nature, he deserves also the credit for confronting these dangers with a single-mindedness that might have evaded more balanced temperaments. He had allowed none of the ships confined within the polynia to face their peril unsupported: all the ships' boats had been set out so that their oarsmen might form a further defensive barrier, constantly shifting around the edges of the ice to congregate wherever the threat seemed – in every sense – most pressing. He had ordered the top-masts of the ships to be taken down and used as fenders against the ice, and at the most desperate moments of the night he had sent his men out on to the ice itself, to heave against the ships' sides with their shoulders. Several hundred men, fighting for their own lives only, could not have emerged unscathed from that ordeal; it required a single will, too stubborn to brook dissent or suggestion, to organize their deliverance. Upon a similarly desperate occasion almost exactly a decade later, beset by four of the deadliest ships of the Spanish Armada, he would exhibit the same striking resolve. Perhaps it required the purity of outright crisis to bring his often destructive energies to an effective locus; but that rare condition being achieved, we sense a near elemental quality of detachment in his reaction to adversity. Better men, understanding that accepting good counsel and weakness of leadership are not synonymous, may well have avoided such a consummate ordeal; it is by no means certain that they could have overcome it in so effective a manner.

Almost immediately, however, Frobisher was afforded an opportunity to exhibit the worst of his nature once more. For most of 3 July, urgent repairs were made to the ships to stop up breaches in their hulls and replace or repair broken masts; the following day, the fleet reassembled well out of the mouth of the strait and lay at hull, adrift. For several more days, less urgent repairs were undertaken, during which time little attention was paid to the fleet's position – clearly, no one was yet eager to make another attempt to gain their prearranged landfall. A persistent fog made observation difficult in any case, but on 9 July, the weather cleared slightly. There are two contrasting accounts of what then occurred. Even Best, Frobisher's faithful and uncritical biographer, was hard pressed to put it favourably:

> . . . the General with the Captaynes and Maysters of his Shippes, beganne doubtfully to question of the matter [i.e., of their precise position], and sent his Pinnesse aboorde to heare each mans opinion, and specially of Iames Beare, Master of the Anne Frances, who was knowen to be a sufficiente and skilful Mariner, and hauing bin there the yeare before, had well observed the place, and drawne out Cardes (charts) of the coast. But the rather this matter grew the more doubtful, for that Christopher Hall chiefe

Pylot of the voyage, deliuered a playne and publicke opinion in the hearing of the whole Fleete, that he had neuer seen the foresayde coast before, and that he could not make it for any place of Frobishers straytes . . .[52]

Hall, not writing for an audience, put it more bluntly:

. . . and I stode against them all, and said yt was not yt [i.e., the 'true' strait], And then I toke my Pinas, & rowed abord my generall, I told him that yt was not the streits, and told him all the marks of both the lands, that yt was not the Streicts, and he presently was in a great rage & sware by Gods wounds that yt was yt, or els take his life, so I see him in such a rage, I toke my pinas & came abord the Thomas Allin againe . . .[53]

Despite Best's claim for his admiral's willingness to take advice on the matter, Frobisher had already assumed the coastline before him to be the northern headland of his eponymous strait, and pronounced it so. Most of his captains and masters, whether from conviction or prudence, agreed. Only the estimable Hall, later supported by Robert Davis (master of the *Ayde*), refused to allow wishful thinking to constitute fact. Two years before, Hall had carefully noted the strength of the prevailing south-easterly current and had drawn his own conclusions on what its effect might be. Now, examining the coastline with greater care than his peers, he declared the fleet to have been driven to the south of the Queen's Foreland.

He was correct. His fellow masters, perhaps overawed by the strangeness of the land before them, had forgotten the primary requirement of their calling: to be adept pilots. Their rudimentary expertise in oceanic navigation – for many of them, this was their first experience of its peculiar rigours – needed to be supplemented by careful, even fastidious observation of coastlines, currents, types of stones on a sea-bed and anything else that might help to throw light onto a dark, unknown world. Such devotion to processes was necessary yet uncommon in an age of extremely variable standards. Frobisher's own method of making his way in strange seas, absent the dutiful Hall, was the antithesis of this, as its first independent testing proved.

Having tasted the sharp edge of his admiral's temper upon the deck of the *Ayde*, Hall went back to the *Thomas Allen*. He had better luck with her captain Gilbert Yorke, and with several others who were far more inclined to trust his opinion than that of Frobisher. The following morning, as the fleet prepared to move westwards into what most of them assumed to be the mouth of their 'strait', fog descended once more. Under its cover, the *Thomas Allen*,

Anne Frances, *Emanuel of Bridgewater* and *Frances of Foy* took the opportunity to turn about to the east, and slip away. It was not a mutiny, nor even desertion: they had simply put themselves in a position where, as their orders stipulated, they would be obliged to find their own way to the designated landfall, unencumbered by their admiral's idiosyncratic skills as a navigator.

Frobisher, leading those of his captains who were either too prudent or supine to stand against him, passed into a broad, open expanse of water. Fog continued to conceal its true nature or extent, though occasional breaks allowed them to see land to their starboard. On 16 July, Frobisher sent the *Gabriel* towards its shore, where members of her crew disembarked and spoke to several Inuit who had innocently wandered down to the water's edge to observe this unusual phenomenon (their friendliness, and willingness to exchange baubles with the English mariners, caused Thomas Ellis to conclude perceptively that 'they had small conversation with the other(s) of the Streightes').[54] The following day, Frobisher's ignorance of his position became unsustainable when the fog lifted entirely and allowed the ships' masters to observe their latitude. Immediately, Hall was proved to have been entirely correct: they lay at 62°–10′N, almost a full degree south of their expected position.[55] With feelings too deep to have been recorded for posterity, Frobisher turned his vessels about. They had penetrated what they were to name 'the Mistaken Strait' – actually, Hudson's Strait – to a depth of perhaps 200 miles, forty years before Henry Hudson himself entered it.

Yet this error, though embarrassing, had not been entirely unproductive. It has since been suggested that Frobisher pressed on beyond the moment at which he realized he was wrong because the passage in which he found himself seemed more promising than his own strait. Best claimed that he would have gone on to explore its headwaters – perhaps even forced his way into the South Sea, had his responsibilities to the adventurers not weighed upon him. Setting aside Best's cautious defence of his admiral's motives, there is probably some truth to the suggestion. Frobisher had sought a north-west passage to establish a reputation and its commensurate fortune, and he had served these same priorities by swiftly acquiescing to the gold-mining project that had supplanted his original goal. Two years on, with not a single ingot of gold to show for this shift in emphasis, why should he not have resurrected his hopes for the passage with equal promptness? Though he had not passed to the headwaters of his own supposed strait in 1576, he had gone as far as Five Men's Sound, at which point he must have seen both the north-east and south-west shores of Frobisher Bay simultaneously. That discouraging prospect, perhaps as much as that of a diminished and demoralized crew, had inclined him not to press further. Now, however, with a passage of seemingly oceanic dimensions before him (and a fleet of some eight vessels, all well-provisioned), the temptation to go on must have been powerful. Furthermore, such evidence as the men of the *Gabriel* had gathered before returning to the fleet was extremely encouraging: 'Oure menne that sayled furthest in the same mistaken straites (hauing the maine lande vppon their starboorde side) affyrme, that they had mette with the outlet or passage of water whiche commeth thorowe Frobyshers straites, and followeth as all one into this passage.'[56] If his own strait was but a tributary of this great passage of water (which, of course, it was not), then this mistaken strait was an opportune error indeed. Despite Best's implication that Frobisher made up his own mind to turn around, it is more likely that only the urging of his captains, and the palpable disregard of his orders that it would have constituted, prevented him from sailing on to the west to test this new and exciting possibility.

The fleet's return eastwards out of the Mistaken Strait was not without considerable peril, though again, this was due principally to the imperfections of observation that seemed to have dogged the expedition whenever Christopher Hall was absent from it. Not yet understanding that the Queen's Foreland was an island, Frobisher prematurely turned his ships northwards on 18 July, having cleared what they took to be that headland. In fact, they had entered the latter-day Annapolis Strait, to the west of Resolution Island. With good visibility and open water, the passage from there into Frobisher Bay would have been easy; but the fleet had neither. In fog once more, the ships unwittingly dispersed; the *Ayde*, according to Selman, losing contact with the other eight ships that remained with the fleet.[57] The sea-bed in that passage varies wildly between deep and extremely shallow waters; at one point, Best reported, the *Ayde* was 'faine to let an ancker fall with twoo bent of cable together, at a C. and odde fadome deapth, where otherwise they hadde bin by the force of the tides caried upon ye rocks again, & perished'. Those of the vessels that did not follow the *Ayde*'s example fell almost immediately into treacherous shallows, being driven upon their lee to a point where they ran over rocks which lay no more than 'halfe a foot' below the ships' keels.[58] Once more, ships' boats were put out ahead to sound for safe water; but several ships, pushed too closely in-shore by the strong current, were obliged to kedge (that is, to haul clear of the rocks) with their anchors: a technique that the crews increasingly assumed to be their last resort: 'wee were all without hope of helpe, euery man recommending himselfe to death, and crying out, Lorde nowe helpe or neuer: nowe Lorde looke downe from Heauen and saue vs sinners, or else oure safetie commeth too late . . .'[59]

Fortunately, the Lord once more rose to an English crisis. The following morning, visibility improved and the wind arose from the north; using it, the ships slowly edged away from their imminent graveyard and put out into open water once more. By 21 July, Frobisher's fleet was off the Queen's Foreland, bruised but intact still. At the foreland's western extremity, a wide, ice-filled channel was discerned (like the treacherous Annapolis Strait, it had been concealed during the fleet's westward passage by thick fog). Frobisher sent in the *Gabriel* to discover whether the channel passed north into his strait. She did so, proving the Queen's Foreland to be a large island, a feat commemorated (unfairly, given the *Judith*'s similar 'discovery' almost three weeks earlier) in the passage's present-day name, Gabriel Strait.

At her emergence into Frobisher Bay, the *Gabriel* encountered the *Thomas Allen*, which, since leaving the fleet eleven days earlier, had been plying across the entrance to the strait without making any discernible attempt to enter it. Upon finding that their admiral's arrival was imminent, however, Hall and Gilbert Yorke immediately turned the *Thomas Allen*'s prow north-westwards into the strait, towards Jackman's Sound. Ellis reported – from as far distant as the deck of the *Ayde* – that the *Thomas Allen* had been forced to make that manoeuvre by the great prevalence of ice that lay between her and the fleet, but Hall (the only eye-witness) offered no reason for their manoeuvre. The *Gabriel* followed the *Thomas Allen*, ostensibly under orders to head for the Countess of Warwick Sound independently of the fleet, though no doubt her crew was content to be in the company of a competent pilot once more.

Frobisher, meanwhile, attempting to bring the fleet into the strait's middle passage once more, pushed head-on into dense clusters of icebergs. At the first attempt on 26 July, the fleet almost suffered a reprise of the experience of 2 July, but hurriedly retired out of the strait before the trap closed. The following day, Frobisher ordered another attempt. By this time, however, more of his captains had had enough. Five of the ships – the *Anne Frances*, *Thomas of Ipswich*, *Moon*, *Salomon*, and *Frances of Foye* – simply ignored his orders and turned away to the seaward:

> . . . the remembraunce of the perilles paste, and those presente before their face, broughte no smalle feare and terror into the hartes of many con-siderate men. So that some beganne priuily to murmure against the Gen-erall for this wilfull manner of proceeding. Some desired to discouer some harborowe thereaboutes, to refreshe themselues, and reforme their broken

veselles for a while, vntill the North and North-west windes might disperse the Ise, and make the place more free to passe.[60]

George Best, the author of this accusation, was of course one of those to 'murmure'. This was his second defection, coming only three days after his ship *Anne Frances* had rejoined the fleet. Despite the brave tone of his *Discourse* – and the consistently good light that he cast upon his own role therein – there can be little doubt that Best fully shared the sense of hopelessness that infused many of the men, officers and mariners who had endured so much without yet having set foot upon the land they had been sent to exploit. By his own admission, the conditions in the ships, physically demanding beyond the imagination of modern seamen, were exacerbated by climatic extremes with which few contemporary Englishmen knew how to deal, particularly during the frequent storms they encountered:

> . . . there fell so much snow, with such bitter cold air, that we could scare see one another for the same, nor open our eyes to handle our ropes and sayles, the snow being above halfe a foote deepe uppon the hatches of oure shippe, which did so wette thorow oure poore marriners clothes, that he that hadde five or sixe shifte of apparell, had scarce one drie threede to his backe, whiche kinde of wette and coldnesse, togither with the over labouring of the poore menne ammidest the ise, breed no small sicknesse amongest the fleete . . .[61]

With one exception, these deserting ships were later to make their way independently into the strait, relying upon their own masters' opinions of when it was safe to do so. In the meantime, the fleet itself – or that small part which still trusted itself to Frobisher's judgement – pressed on into the ice. Again, he was warned that it was too thick ahead to proceed safely (this time by the master of the *Emanuel of Bridgewater*), and again, he ignored a voice of reason. Best's recollection of Frobisher's own rationale is perhaps the least critical passage in his *Discourse*; yet its flavour, even allowing for the gross misrepresentation of his Admiral's true priorities, illuminates something of an indomitability that rendered mere common sense almost superfluous:

> The Generall not opening his eares to the peeuishe passion of anye priuate person, but chiefly caryng for the publicke profite of his Countries cause, and nothyng at all regardyng hys owne ease, lyfe, or safetie, but especiallye respecting the accomplishement of the cause he hadde vndertaken

. . . determined with this resolution, to passe and recouer hys Porte, or else there to bury himselfe with hys attempte, and if suche extremitie so befell him, that he muste needes perish amongest the Ise, when all helpe shoulde be paste, and all hope of safetie set aside, hauing all the ordinaunce within boorde well charged, resolued wyth pouder to burne and bury himselfe and all togyther with hir Maiesties Shyppes.[62]

The prospective participants in this mass viking funeral appear to have been sufficiently moved (or terrified) to have dredged a further effort from their exhausted bodies. Slowly, the ships, 'with incredible payne & perill', edged north-westwards into dense ice, already more than three weeks overdue at their appointed landfall. Even now, Frobisher's poor skills as a navigator were displayed to the full. The *Ayde* overshot Countess of Warwick Sound and passed as far north as Gabriel's Island in the middle passage of the strait. Selman, with considerable exasperation, recorded Frobisher's successive misidentifications of Jackman's Sound, York Sound and Gabriel Island (the latter he confidently declared to be Pembroke Island, at the mouth of Countess of Warwick Sound). It was left to an expert navigator – Christopher Jackson, the *Ayde*'s trumpeter and purloiner of the illicit whelp in 'Friesland' – to discreetly point out his error.[63]

Finally, on the night of 30 July, the *Ayde* anchored off Countess of Warwick Sound. Taking his pinnace to the shore, Frobisher found Edward Fenton and his men already well established at the base-camp on Countess of Warwick Island. Their own story since losing contact with the fleet was, if anything, more desperate than that of their comrades.

Barely escaping the great storm of the night of 2 July, the *Judith* had emerged from the strait the following day. Only twenty-four hours later, she re-entered the treacherous passage, and since that time, neither the *Judith* nor the *Michael* had fled from it. Heroically (and imprudently), they had spent almost three weeks in constant mortal danger, struggling to make a landfall that at no time lay more than forty miles distant. On one occasion, the *Judith* was breached simultaneously on both her flanks by two clashing bergs.[64] Following hasty running repairs to her hull, she met with the truant *Michael* on 13 July, since when the two ships had remained together, fending off icebergs or grappling to them when there was no other recourse; drifting or towing their ships with the boats, constantly attempting to pass through the ice-pack towards Countess of Warwick Sound. At one point, both ships had been lashed to an iceberg 200 yards in diameter, 'w(i)th a hill in the middest of it', to allow their exhausted mariners some respite.[65] Such unremitting toil could not be maintained without a price, and by the evening of 20 July, Fenton's men had reached the limits of their physical endurance. Once more, however, at this uttermost point of danger, a minor miracle lifted them from despair. At six o'clock the following morning, they discovered that the current had brought about what main strength could not: the *Judith* had drifted during the night to within three miles of their goal. Once more, Fenton ordered his weary men into their boats. For the next few hours, they edged forward, taking soundings every few minutes; finally, at about midday on 22 July, they anchored off Winter's Furnace in the Sound. With fine (if consciously under-stated) style, Fenton drew a line under their ordeal in his log entry for the day: 'And being thus ancored (gave hartie thankes to god for his gracious and mightie deliveraunce from so manie greate and daungerfull perills) wente to dynner . . .'.[66]

Even now, however, so far overdue their schedule, they could not com-mence mining. Due to 'thindescrecon' of the purser of the voyage (either Nicholas Chancellor, purser to the intended colony, or Thomas Thornton, who had responsibility for the rest of the fleet), all their tools had been laden in the *Thomas Allen*. The members of the prospective colony were therefore confined to exploring the environs of the Sound, noting potential mining sites and observing the nature of what was to be their home for the next year. Encouragingly, in that bleak landscape Fenton saw a crane and some sign of deer; though 'not above ij or iij in a place', it seems to have convinced him that his colony had some chance of survival.

The arrival now of Frobisher's *Ayde* and several of the other vessels meant that the expedition's primary work could begin in earnest. The fleet as a whole was not yet entirely safe, however. Several ships remained out in the strait still, and on the night of 30 July, whilst Frobisher enjoyed supper with Fenton in the *Judith*, the *Ayde*'s anchor, slammed by an iceberg whilst being raised, smashed through the ship's hull. Emergency repairs to the breach were hur-riedly effected using a side of beef. According to Edward Selman, the acci-dent had occurred due to the incompetence or malice of the boatswain Walter Holmes and quartermaster John Hill, who had been told to watch for ice by Charles Jackman when he himself went below for his dinner (Jackman had been ordered to take charge of the *Ayde* by Frobisher). Selman, who was present, made the tactical error of rebuking the men; fortunately, they con-fined their retaliation to telling him to go to his cabin (that is, their words were delicately interpreted thus by Selman, who had been charged to write the expedition's official report), though he complained later that in doing so they 'abused me very much'. Trivial though the incident seems, his comments provide yet more evidence of Frobisher's poor method of maintaining discipline among the lower ranks:

> The m(aste)r (Jackman) can beare no rule amongst them, bycause he is not cowntenanced by the Generall, & therefore all things hath fallen owt the worse with vs, & that hathe caused me to speake more earnestly in this cause, for neyther the boatswayn, nor any officer yet hitherto hath byn obedient to the M(aste)r, & the disobedience of the officers doth cause the company allso to disobey and neglect their duties.[67]

With the bulk of the expedition now landed, however, and its schedule completely thrown out by the events of the previous weeks, there was little further opportunity for the exhausted mariners to be unruly. On 1 August they brought tents to Countess of Warwick Island and assembled them for use as miners' quarters, and the assayers began to conduct trials upon the first samples of ore. On the following day, the *Gabriel* came into the Sound with Christopher Hall on board (he had left the larger *Thomas Allen* anchored on the south side of the strait). The welcome she received was genuine but perfunctory; in view of the need for haste, her miners were greeted with shovels and immediately assigned to one of the mining sites. Fortunately, the size of the expedition deterred the Inuit from making any form of demonstration; without that threat, miners and mariners were soon swarming about the various mine-sites, bringing in samples from promising deposits to determine which of them should be worked. On 3 August, having all of his 'land council' present except Yorke and Best (the *Anne Frances* was still at sea), Frobisher issued the official orders to be observed on land.[68]

Security was the foremost consideration. No man was allowed to go anywhere except Countess of Warwick Island or Winter's Furnace without licence, and no independent assays of ore were to be undertaken or ships laded without express instructions. On discipline, anyone cursing, brawling or using 'discouered speeches' would be imprisoned; whilst the act of drawing a weapon in anger would cause the offender to have his right hand struck off. Due, perhaps, to the intervention of John Paradice, senior surgeon with the fleet, matters of hygiene received particular attention. No one was to wash in the spring of fresh water on Countess of Warwick Island, and anyone taking his 'easemente' except under the cliffs where the sea would wash away the ordure was to merit fourteen hours' imprisonment for the first offence (during which time, presumably, he would perforce be prevented from repeating his crime), and a shilling fine for the second. A final proscription anticipated wider environmental concerns by several centuries: any ship whose crew was caught in the act of throwing ordure or other rubbish overboard into the Sound was to suffer the loss of one ton's rate of freightage.

With the law thus forcefully stated, the disorders that might otherwise have pervaded the lower decks largely disappeared. Work proceeded swiftly, though not entirely effectively. Best later noted that many of the most adept miners were in the four vessels still abroad in the strait (his own included). Upon his own arrival in the Sound, the reliable Christopher Hall had been sent immediately in the *Gabriel* to fetch the *Thomas Allen* from the southern shore of the strait, but the other ships were to arrive at their own leisure. In the meantime, the pace of digging was hampered by heavy rain, though Frobisher did as much as he could, given his incomplete resources. Fenton and his men had begun the task of examining sites on the shores surrounding the Countess of Warwick Island; samples of the ore they had found there were immediately tested, and new mines were established at 'Fenton's Fortune' (possibly in Diar's Sound, the present day Victoria Bay), at the 'Countess of Sussex mine' (approximately six miles north-west of Countess of Warwick Sound) and at Sussex Island in Beare Sound, the site of the previous year's most promising finds. These outlying sites were usually assigned to one or two ships' companies; their miners were protected by soldiers and armed mariners, and their ships' ensigns flown above the mine as a beacon, to be lowered should the Inuit attempt to attack or otherwise disturb their work. To date, there had been no definite sightings of the 'newe prey' on the northern shore (though Fenton found traces of old indigenous habitation in what is now Napoleon's Bay); even so, given the lateness of the season, Frobisher took particular pains to ensure that the work should not be interrupted by even a single encounter of the sort that had dogged the previous year's work.

On 9 August, having deployed their existing resources as effectively as possible, the land council convened to discuss the establishment of the colony. It was now that the consequences of the purser's challenging method of lading the ships became apparent. Half of the frame for the colony's great house remained at sea (or, rather, under it: the *Denys* had gone down with a substantial portion), and many spars and other necessities for its construction had been expended in the struggle to fend off icebergs on the night of 2 July. This was unfortunate, but Fenton's more immediate concern was the ship *Moon of Foy*. She was carrying 84 tons of beer intended for the colony's consumption, and her continuing absence held out the frightening prospect of his men having to drink even more water than anticipated.[69] All of these shortages obviously impacted upon plans for the colony; yet even so, Fenton courageously offered to remain in Meta Incognita with just sixty men. The expedition's master-carpenters, summoned to the council's presence to give their estimate of the time needed to construct a smaller version of the great house – and without many of its expected component parts – observed the ancient tradition of claiming that the work could not be done in less than eight or nine weeks, even if the missing ships came in that very day (the expedition had at most only twenty-five days more before its departure, according to the timetable set out in its official instructions). It was therefore agreed – unanimously, according to Best – that the colony should not be established that year; 'and therefore they willed Master Selman the Register, to set downe this decree, and with all their consentes, for the better satisfying of hir Maiestie, the Lords of the Counsel, and the aduenturers.'

Lok later challenged this, claiming that when Fenton offered to remain with fewer men, Frobisher refused to consider the matter further, and used the carpenters' objections 'as with a sufficient cloke to cover his evill minde'.[70] Yet Fenton himself made no such claim; on this occasion – though perhaps motivated by jealousy of Fenton's future fame, should he succeed – Frobisher acted entirely properly, and in the best interests of the prospective colonists.

While the objectives of the expedition were being discussed in council, several of its ships remained somewhere out in the strait, struggling to make the agreed landfall. After choosing not to follow Frobisher on 27 July, the *Anne Frances*, *Moon of Foy* and *Thomas of Ipswich* had reassembled off the Queen's Foreland. A further attempt to enter the strait ended when ice enclosed them and breached several ships' hulls. Back in the safety of open water once more, a conference of captains and masters was called on the *Anne Frances*. The option of giving up and returning to England was beginning to seem attractive (particularly to the ships' masters, whose practical natures made more of pack-ice than putative gold-mines), but Best unctuously reminded them of their duty, and assiduously recorded it for posterity: '. . . that it would be so great and argume(n)t, eyther of wante of courage or discretion in them, as he resolued rather to fall into any danger, that so shamefully to consent to returne home . . . .'.[71] In the *Anne Frances*'s hold was a dismantled five-ton pinnace, intended for reconnoitring potential mining-sites; Best told the others that as soon as it could be assembled, he would personally attempt to cross the strait to find Frobisher. Meanwhile, the ships should keep company 'as true Englishmen, and faythfull friends, should supplye one anothers want in all fortunes and dangers'. Notwithstanding this sterling exhortation, the crew of the *Thomas of Ipswich*, led by Richard Cox, the estimable saviour of the *Ayde* in the previous year, took their own counsel on what constituted faithful friendship. That same evening, they silently turned their vessel's prow eastwards, out into the Atlantic and home.[72]

The next day, the two remaining ships found a good harbour in an inlet on one of the small islands off the Queen's Foreland. Whilst Best and his men explored the island and others around it, assiduously taking samples of ore according to their instructions, a carpenter-smith in his ship – clearly a man of great and undervalued skill – set to work on the pinnace. It was by no means a straightforward task, as the purser's curse had fallen upon Best's ship also. Most of the knees and nails that were to have held the pinnace together had been laded in Fenton's *Judith*; for want of the proper tools, the *Anne Frances*'s unsung hero was obliged to use the barrel of a ship's gun as an anvil and a pick-axe as a hammer, with which he somehow fashioned nails from smashed pieces of tongs, grid-iron from the ship's hatch-covers and their only fire-shovel. On 18 August, he presented the assembled craft to his captain, and promptly stated that he would not set foot in it himself 'for five hundreth poundes'.

'These wordes somewhat discouraged some of the company which should haue gone therin', recalled Best. Fortunately, the master's mate of the *Anne Frances*, John Gray, 'manfully and honestly' (and, possibly, a little weak-headedly) volunteered to accompany Best upon this potentially disastrous navigation, at which Captain Upcot of the *Moon* and seventeen other reckless braves similarly determined to test their luck to breaking point. The following morning, they departed in their fragile pinnace. Three days later, having been driven across the strait by a strong tidal flow that threatened to part them from their few nails, they sighted the *Beare Leicester*'s ensign, flying onshore just to the north of Countess of Warwick Sound.

Best and his companions knew nothing of this, the Countess of Sussex's mine, where miners from the *Beare Leicester* and *Thomas Allen* were busily gathering ore. They assumed that the Inuit had captured the ensign, and swore to recover it from 'those bad, cruell, and [yet again] man eating people', thus managing – in the same breath – to attribute both sophisticated motives and barbaric practices to the native culture. Fortunately, their mistake became obvious as they approached the shore and recognized their countrymen, 'wherevppon there was a sodaine and ioyfull outeshoote, with great flinging vp of cappes'. This was the morning of 22 August, and all elements of the fleet (those, that is, which had not deserted) were finally in contact once more, after an interregnum of almost seven weeks.

The prospect that met Best's eyes as he came into Countess of Warwick Sound later that day was akin to the tented boom-towns of later centuries, with scattered areas of activity centred upon the small island at the Sound's northern limit. To the west, 'Winter's Furnace' was largely quiet, its early promise of ore having proved illusory. Around the nearby shores of the Sound, the freight ships were anchored, awaiting orders to pick up their ladings of ore from pre-assigned sites. The *Gabriel* and *Michael* plied the strait between the Sound and Sussex Island in Beare Sound, the most distant outwork, bringing ore to lade in the flagship *Ayde*. On Countess of Warwick Island, two great trenches scoured out in this and the previous year were now idle (the ore being 'hardly had' from the ground there),[73] but the furnaces of Schutz and Denham worked almost continuously, grading ore by type and perceived value. To the north-east, 'Fenton's Fortune' had now proved to be a disappointment; the men working it had been carried either further south to join their colleagues at the more promising Sussex Island, or north to the Countess of Sussex's mine. On 18 August, a new mine-working was opened approximately six miles south and east of the main camp. Named Denham's Mount after the assayer, this appeared to provide the best samples of ore to date, and a platoon of long-suffering miners was hurriedly redirected once more.

In all of this frantic activity, with the weather expected momentarily to worsen, there could be no provision for rest-days. By the time that 'Denham's Mount' was opened, only 300 tons of ore had been mined (little more than a third of the intended quantity). As the pace of work increased yet further to compensate for this shortfall, some of the men, already weakened by their prolonged ordeal at sea, fell exhausted and died – the gentlemen-soldiers, belying their drone-ish reputation, among them.[74] Also, provisions were now running low: on 19 August, Fenton noted that the *Ayde* had only three firkins of butter remaining, and, three days later, that her supplies of fish were down to 250 'poor John' (haberdine) and the same number of stock-fish. Ominously, as stocks of food dwindled, surface ice began to form around the hulls of the ships at anchor in the sound, though as yet the weather remained calm.

Though all of these matters conspired to frustrate his schedule, Frobisher's temper almost held up. Since landing his fleet, he had acted with exemplary energy, spreading his resources cleverly and using them flexibly as assays upon samples from the various mine-sites proved or disproved their apparent value. Major decisions had been scrupulously referred to his land council, and all the extant sources (Lok's later blasts apart) suggest that they had been heeded by him. There were, however, further isolated incidents and general discontents that showed a more familiar side to his nature. He and Fenton argued hotly on 19 August over matters of discipline; the latter was particularly critical of the insolence of the boatswain of the *Ayde*, Frobisher's 'kinsman', Alexander Creake (their precise relationship is unknown) and one Edward Robinson, both of whom had refused to obey the Lieutenant-General's orders.[75] Once more, this insubordination appears to have been symptomatic of a wider discord between decks. Frobisher, as always more suspicious of men the closer their rank to his own, continued to encourage discord between the common mariners and the 'gentlemen' as a means of ruling by division. In this case, the argument soon grew to the broader matter of authority – specifically, Fenton's own – which Frobisher attempted to make him admit had been conferred by himself, rather than by the Privy Council: a claim that Fenton rightly dismissed with 'hoat woords'.[76] Lok – no doubt well informed by Edward Selman, whose own experience on 30 July had been ample witness to the indiscipline of the common mariners – later added his own observations. Of Alexander Creake, he claimed:

> . . . he is of great disordered lyef, who syns his retorne home is goone to Sea w(i)th others his like fellowes, one evill ventures. And also he [Frobisher] woold not punishe the disorders of hym and of Edward Robinson and others for anye complaynt mad too him, but rather maynetayned their disobedience booth against M(aste)rs Christofer Hawlle and Robert Davies and allso against Captaine Fenton beinge in that newe Countrye, whereby followed in that voyadge great spoyle and pilferye of the Shipps takle and furniture . . . and throughe there disordered and mutinus dealings amongest the men, great evill service followed in the Companies busynes, and great contenc(i)on and stryff grewe amonge the men in that newe Countrye betwene the marryn(er)s one thone p(ar)te and the gentillmen one thother parte, that they weare w(i)th their weapons to have joyned together . . .[77]

Being themselves 'gentlemen', the other members of Frobisher's land council appear to have taken Fenton's part, at least implicitly. Four days after the incident of 19 August, they forced a tribunal upon their admiral to consider the culpability of Creake and Robinson. Even Frobisher must have realized that there was little to be said in their defence, and had probably advised them so in the meantime. The two mariners made their submission, stating that they had not known Fenton had been appointed as vice-general of the expedition; a highly unlikely claim which, nevertheless, appears to have been accepted for the sake of preventing further factiousness. The two men were merely admonished and pardoned thereafter.[78]

Yet admitting the probable justice of these claims against Frobisher, and as deplorable as his jealousies appear to the modern eye, it would be wrong to overestimate their significance. There is much evidence that sixteenth-century discipline in general was harsh but not invariably effective; for all its brutality, it could neither entirely smother the contemporary Englishman's innate unruliness nor impose concord upon a seethe of petty feuds below decks. Any number of unhappier contemporary expeditions might be cited; indeed, by comparison to Drake's habitually lonely, paranoid and, sometimes, homicidal manner of government at sea, Frobisher's record was one of almost unbroken good-fellowship. Five years later, Edward Fenton, the man whose reputation Lok consistently defended in his blasts against Frobisher, was to command a farcical voyage in which the disorder of every group of mariners, gentlemen and merchants was to reach epic proportions.[79] By 1578, Frobisher, whatever his personal faults, had established a record of maintaining discipline in difficult circumstances, and his personal conduct during that year's expedition – brief furies apart – was untypically correct. During their stay in Meta Incognita, he managed not to threaten anyone with a dagger or a hanging, much less deliver one. Indeed, the care he showed for the common mariners' welfare was striking: on one occasion, he berated his old crony, Hugh Randall, captain of the *Salomon*, for being so assiduous in bringing ore from Beare Sound that he had not waited for a relief ship to provide protection for the miners there.[80]

His measures, pragmatic and – however unintentionally – humane, and the undoubtedly heroic response of the men, rapidly recovered the time that had been lost at sea. From 20 August, the freight ships began to depart singly from the Sound, to take up their allocations of ore mined elsewhere and thereafter return, fully laden, to the concentration area. No one yet paused in his labours as the time to depart approached, though from 26 August, Fenton and his men began to bury supplies and equipment that could not be stored in the ships for use by subsequent expeditions. Frobisher himself must have needed rest as much as any of his men, but the evidence of his movements suggests otherwise. On 24 August, he took a pinnace south to Beare Sound to oversee the lading there; he returned at night two days later, but on the following morning he set out north to 'discover mynes', coming back to Countess of Warwick Sound in foul weather the following night. Even then, the *Ayde* was found to have storage still for 10 or 12 more tons of ore, so, once more, Frobisher climbed into his pinnace to seek out and bring back the shortfall.

Meanwhile, Fenton, denied his colony, had one more task to discharge. On Countess of Warwick Island, he raised a small stone house, 14 feet long by 12 wide, and roofed it with wooden slats. Inside, he placed bells, pins, laces, combs, eye-glasses and other 'fancies', to bring back the Inuit and 'entice the people to some familiaritie against other yeares'.[81] His men also built an oven, and baked bread in it for the Inuit to taste. Beyond providing a home for these belated tokens of friendship, the house had a further, more scientific purpose: 'this I did to prove what the vehemencie of winde and weather would do therwith this winter, to thende, that if the nexte yere habitacion shoulde be performed there, that then by this litle begynninge, a iuste occasion and experiment should given how we shoulde deale in buildinge greater howses'.[82]

Once the house was completed, Fenton gave it a garden: peas, corn and other grain were sown around it to test the soil's fertility and the ability of European crops to survive the seasons there. The greater houses that Fenton envisaged were of course built upon the North American continent in time, but this tiny hovel was the first of them. Its foundations still remain, barely visible amidst the stark, sterile terrain in which they were set. No one ever dwelt within it, and, probably, no seed ever sprouted around its rude perimeter. Only the occasional curious Inuk came to bear witness to its long decay: at once a perfectly apt and forlorn testament to the brief, frenzied sojourn of Elizabethan Englishmen in that land, a land much too distant, in every sense, from those epitomes of wealth and increase they had sought to emulate.

On 30 August, all members of the expedition who were present in Countess of Warwick Sound assembled at Winter's Furnace for Divine service, led by Reverend Wolfall. For Best, the occasion was memorable in that 'the celebration of diuine mistery was (th)e first signe, seale, & confirmatio(n) of Christes name death & passion euer knowen in all these quarters' (either he regarded the Spanish presence in the New World to be too distant to qualify as those 'quarters', or the Catholic rite to be no such proper celebration). Following the service, Frobisher's land council convened for the final time. Even at this late stage, the matter of any further discovery of the strait had yet to be decided. Again, as with the colony, brutal reality was allowed to inform the captains' decisions. However slight the will to attempt a further reconnaissance, all of those present declared themselves in favour – in principle – of Frobisher completing his navigation. The means of doing so, however, were utterly lacking. The weather had proved almost deadly to the fleet already (that day, the *Anne Frances* had to be dragged aground, and eight great leaks in her hull mended). To attempt to push further into the strait seemed, even to the most daring, an act of suicide. Furthermore, as we have seen, the provisions for the expedition were severely depleted: in addition to normal wastage and the extraordinary damage done to the colony's supplies, the ships' own stores, thrown about in storms and impacts upon icebergs, or crushed by the poor stacking of coal and timber upon them, were almost consumed. The prospect of scraping together the resources to provision a further search for the western exit of the passage was therefore unthinkable. Starving, shut up in ice from which only a spring thaw would eventually provide deliverance, such an expedition could expect nothing more than its 'vtter destruction'. Again, the council of captains (apparently unprompted by Frobisher) exhibited impeccable good sense in dismissing the option out of hand.

As they wound up their deliberations, Frobisher took the occasion to issue orders for the conduct of the voyage homewards. Earlier orders governing the outward voyage remained in force, but given the imagined value of their cargoes, security was tightened even further. No samples of the ore were to disappear into pockets on the voyage to England, upon penalty of the offenders being named as 'fellons'. Nor were any of the ships to unload anywhere but at Dartford creek, where, hopefully, the great works now stood complete, awaiting the bounty of the New World. The crew of any vessel separated from the fleet and taken by an enemy should ensure that all maps and charts were destroyed before they were boarded, thus preserving England from the threat of interloping that her mariners had been all to eager to inflict upon other nations.

These matters being settled, and 'all other things being in forwardnesse and good order', Frobisher directed that the ships be made ready to sail, and then departed in a pinnace for Beare Sound, to supervise the final collection of ore there. The next day, with ice forming thickly in the Sound, the fleet weighed anchor and followed on to pick up the remaining miners and equipment *en route* to the mouth of the strait. Only the *Judith* and *Anne Frances* stayed behind – the crew of the former vessel to assist in re-launching the latter from the shore, where repairs to her hull had yet to be completed. Once these two ships put out into the strait the following day (and despite the plans for future years' colonies and accommodation with the strange 'countrey people'), almost three centuries were to elapse before a white man stood upon Baffin Island once more. Appropriately, Edward Fenton, the intended governor of

England's first overseas colony, was one of the last to depart the debris of proto-empire.

At Beare Sound on 1 September, Frobisher was lading the final consignments of ore into the *Gabriel* and *Michael* whilst the remaining ships of the fleet assembled at its mouth; only the *Emanuel of Bridgewater* came closer in to the island during the day, to take in her allocation of miners. The weather, meanwhile, had become ominously inconsistent. Periods of absolute calm alternated with brief, violent squalls that pushed the ships towards the rocks of the lee shore, the recurring nightmare of seafaring men. By the next morning, Frobisher still had not returned to his flagship. Christopher Hall (who had transferred into the *Ayde* for the return passage) hailed a number of other ships as they tacked laboriously away from the threat of running aground. None had any news of their admiral, but the master of the *Beare Leicester* told him he had sighted a pinnace in Beare Sound. Nervously, with only the *Ayde*'s foresails raised to manoeuvre, Hall edged her closer in to the land, to find Frobisher.

The previous day, the scene on-shore at Sussex Island had been chaotic. This was the most heavily worked mine during the latter stages of the expedition, and thus many miners – the complements of a number of ships – had been brought here from other sites.[83] Tossed by rising seas, several pinnaces lay at anchor, waiting for them to embark. As the light failed and high winds prevented the men from regaining their ships, Frobisher had his barks secured, their supplies distributed and tents raised to allow the company to remain the night upon the island. He probably hoped that the weather would turn during the night: and so it did, but much for the worse. The next morning, the mariners and miners of Sussex Island discovered that their means of returning to England had gone. As the tides and wind had strengthened, the ships of the fleet had moved off into the middle of the strait, their crews abandoning efforts to maintain their stations. One by one, the storm-beaten elements of the fleet, each imagining that other ships were closer in to Sussex Island (and dealing with the small matter of their stranded admiral and his miners), began to set their sails to escape the continuing danger of the lee shores. As strong north-westerly winds rose and drove them in the direction they were to take homewards, several gave up the struggle to remain in the strait. That night, even Christopher Hall, the most assiduous master in the fleet, listened too readily to men returning in the pinnace that he had sent out to recover Frobisher, who told him that the admiral 'came after' in the *Gabriel*. For several more hours, he lay at hull with the *Thomas Allen* and *Moon*, a double light lit at his stern to bring home any strays; but then at seven o'clock the following morning, having judged that his admiral had passed him in the night and was already ahead of the *Ayde*,[84] he set sail and laid a course out of the strait, for England.

In fact, Hall's assumption was correct. Frobisher was already at sea, looking for his fled fleet. He and the miners of Sussex Island were crammed aboard the *Gabriel*, *Michael* and a small pinnace (the latter alone, towed precariously behind the *Michael*, held twenty-six men, including George Best, who made the most of his ordeal in his *Discourse*). Fortunately, the *Judith* and *Anne Frances*, coming on after the fleet from Countess of Warwick Sound, met them off the Queen's Foreland and took in some of their excess. Even then, they remained in acute danger. In high seas, many ships in the fleet had lost their pinnaces during the previous forty-eight hours, the majority dashed against the hulls of their mother vessels by the high seas. The *Judith* herself had lost two pinnaces and a boat in the space of just a few hours on 2 September, and Best and his crew had only just boarded the *Anne Frances* when the pinnace that had carried them from Sussex Island shivered to pieces and sank.[85] None of the larger ships had remained to take in their full allocation of men; with twenty-two of the *Ayde*'s complement of miners, Fenton and Best were ordered to make for England. Frobisher dutifully remained in command of the crowded *Gabriel*, the vessel upon which he had begun his great enterprise two years earlier.

The homeward voyage was a confused, dispersed affair, the weather making a mockery of Frobisher's strict instructions that the ships should 'vigilently and carefully keepe company with the Admirall, and by no maner of meanes breake companye willingly now in our returne homewards'.[86] The fleet, partially separated even before it departed from the strait, was entirely scattered once into the Atlantic Ocean proper. Some vessels enjoyed relatively swift and uneventful passages thereafter: Hall's *Ayde* sailed south-eastwards through storms whilst her master – freed from the burden of Frobisher's oppressive rule – amused himself by experimenting with every conceivable combination of sails in various weather conditions and recording them for posterity in his log. The only notable excitement during this time was the near-death experience of one Francis Austen on 8 September: 'at that present 4. of clock, the sea let in at my Gen(er)alls cabban; & burst from the Cabban floors to the windows all the timber & bords into him who was at the helme . . .'.[87] Five other mariners of the *Ayde*, their bodies exhausted by the efforts of the previous weeks, failed to maintain the same grip upon life as the fortunate Austen had upon the cabin timbers, and were 'heaued ouerboord' thereafter with a minimum of ceremony (in all, Best later estimated that 'not aboue fortie' men died in the entire course of the 1578 expedition: a light tally for such a strikingly arduous venture).[88]

The *Ayde* had the company of the *Thomas Allen* until 10 September, when a broken mainyard obliged Hall to lay the flagship at hull briefly for repairs. Eleven days later, the *Ayde* met with the *Anne Frances*; her captain, George Best, hailed across and obligingly mentioned that Frobisher was 'in a great coller' against Hall for abandoning his admiral at Beare Sound (at which, no doubt, Hall experimented with even more sail).[89] By 25 September, the *Ayde* was in the Soundings, and came into Portsmouth three days later.

Fenton's *Judith*, overladen with men, lost the company of the *Anne Frances*, *Gabriel* and *Michael* in a storm on 8 September. Thereafter, she had a lonely passage homewards, not meeting any other vessel until 27 September, when she sighted the *Anne Frances* once more and the *Salomon* off the Scilly Isles. The *Judith* came to anchor at Weymouth three days later: 'the Shipp being p(er)soned w(i)th 67 men, the moste p(ar)te wherof infected w(i)th the skirvie and other gingerfull diseases'.[90] At that moment, ironically, the Privy Council was drafting an order forbidding Londoners to board Frobisher's ships because of an outbreak of plague that was currently sweeping the City.[91] It had not occurred to them that the crews they were seeking to protect were themselves a health risk.

A few days later, Fenton took the *Judith* to Portsmouth (a prearranged rendezvous); he heard that Frobisher had arrived there already, but had crossed the Solent to visit his old acquaintance Edward Horsey on the Isle of Wight; possibly to apprise him of the success of the voyage and promise him some part of the bounty returned in the *Salomon* of Weymouth.[92] Frobisher returned to Portsmouth on 6 October, gave command of the *Ayde* to Fenton, and hurried on to Court by horse the following day. Bringing the fleet's flagship past the Downs a few days later, Fenton overtook and dutifully captured a bark previously taken from its Breton owner by one Thomas Halfpenny, an English pirate. At Tilbury, however, Halfpenny escaped in one of the *Ayde*'s boats; according to Fenton himself, 'not without some suspicon that the watche was privie therunto, having good prooff that the Booteson sett on land ij of the p(ri)soners without my knowedg or the maisters.'[93] Alexander Creake, it seems, was still doing what came naturally: crossing Fenton and providing a small service to one of his kinsman's old colleagues.

Most of the other ships of Frobisher's fleet had arrived safely at one of a number of southern ports before the end of September. Only one vessel was lost – the *Emanuel*, or *Busse of Bridgewater*, whose homeward voyage was filled with remarkable incident. She had been last sighted almost upon a lee shore in Beare Sound (Selman had seen her danger, and commended her crew with a pious 'God be m(er)cifull vnto them'). Though feared lost, her crew managed to bring her safely out to sea through the Lupton Channel (the first Englishmen to make this navigation), apparently discover a new, fertile island in mid-Atlantic approximately fifty leagues south-east of the supposed Friesland (an imaginary island off another imaginary island, in fact), and, finally, suffer shipwreck whilst attempting to beach her at Smerwick Harbour on the west coast of Ireland on 26 September.[94] Much of her cargo of 110 tons of ore, dug from the Countess of Sussex mine, Diar's Passage and Beare Sound, was seized by the Earl of Desmond (who retained it, notwithstanding later directions from the Privy Council to return it to the *Emanuel*'s captain, Richard Newton).[95] Some of the ore may still be seen in and about the ruined walls of Smerwick fort, where it was used long ago to repair damage that English besiegers were to inflict barely two years following the *Emanuel*'s beaching, in a battle in which Frobisher himself was to figure. Sir John Norreys, one of the English commanders in that battle, would notice remnants of the ore scattered upon the beach and later write to Burghley, with unerring if heartless perception, observing them to be 'Captain Frobisher's new found riches, perished at Smerwick.'[96] As an epitaph upon three years' striving to emulate the fabulous example of Spain, an epic series of voyages into forbidding strange landscapes and, not least, the squandering of over £25,000, the comment was almost indecently economical.

THIRTEEN

The End of the Enterprise

Abraham Fleming's 'right heroicall heart of Britanne blood'[1] had brought home his large and heterogeneous fleet, virtually intact and carrying far more potential riches than expected. Whilst most of his captains had fled before storms and tides, he had stayed; risking his own life to recover every last miner and artificer from certain death. As he was a man who, palpably, had led by example rather than vain, flatulent exhortation, Martin Frobisher had much reason, he may have supposed, to think himself proven to his peers and backers.

Their gratitude fell somewhat short of fulsome, however. Since his departure upon the latest and largest expedition to Meta Incognita, nothing had happened to make their expenditure to date seem any more worthwhile. Indeed, their morale seems to have fallen steadily during these months as their commitments grew apace. No further assays had been conducted on the 1577 ore whilst the third voyage was abroad; even so, upon no greater evidence than the results of Schutz's final assay at Tower Hill during the previous March, the Privy Council and commissioners had been tirelessly spending the adventurers' money on the new works at Dartford. Begun at the end of April, these were completed a matter of days before Frobisher's ships arrived home. The complex consisted of 'two great workhousses, & two wattermylles, w(i)th fyve great meltinge furnaces in the same housses, & one great Cole-hous, & other necessarye workhouses . . .';[2] the river Darent had been dredged to allow the ore ships to dock near the Queen's House at Bignoures, where their precious cargoes would be unloaded and securely stored; and the mile of road between there and Bignoures Mill had been swept to prepare for carts to carry the ore to the furnaces that would – hopefully – tease out the wealth of the New World.[3] The largest refining facility in southern Britain now awaited only the arrival of the ore itself. 'God give it good success', Michael Lok had piously exclaimed a year earlier:[4] it was a sentiment that even the godless amongst them would have fervently acknowledged whilst counting what remained in their purses.

As the adventurers were praying for a fortunate end to their enterprise, Philip II had already ceased to fear the rise of a rival empire. On 31 March 1578, as preparations for the voyage commenced, the Spanish Ambassador, Bernardino de Mendoza, had written to his king to inform him of his pre-liminary investigations into the enterprise. It was his opinion then that ' the business must be a prosperous one to bear such heavy charges'.[5] By June, Mendoza's spies had secured samples of the ore clandestinely and had already determined that the 'gold' was marcasite (so worthless, in fact, that Philip II assumed that his agents had been discovered in their plot and samples of a false ore substituted by English counter-spies).[6] Within days of the expedi-tion coming home, Mendoza could report that 'they are not much pleased with his return, nor are the merchants interested in the business satisfied with the voyage . . .'.[7] On 15 November, having interviewed the spy he had planted in the 1578 expedition, he sent to Philip an extremely detailed and accurate narrative of the voyage. It has been suggested recently that in view of Mendoza's early and precise knowledge of assays carried out since the begin-ning of that year, that spy – possibly a double-agent – may have been the English assayer, Robert Denham.[8]

Mendoza had good cause to assume that the merchants were 'not much pleased'. Without the damning results of Spanish assays upon the ore, they may still have hoped for a good outcome to the business; but before the promised bounty could be transmuted from its raw state into the finished product for the purses of the faithful, long-suffering adventurers, there were yet more costs to meet. The return of the expedition with over fifty per cent more ore than had been planned (according to Selman, 1,250 tons – exclud-ing that lost at Smerwick in the wreck of the *Emanuel* – as against the expected 800 tons) meant that there were now significant additional freight charges to answer for. Before the end of October, the Privy Council ordered Michael Lok to collect a new assessment, this time of eighty-five per cent of existing subscriptions, to raise the £6,000 that was estimated as necessary to pay off the ships and men.[9] To forestall any hesitation among the adven-turers, the Lord Mayor of London, Sir William Cordell, was appointed to act as Lok's assistant, 'to calle before you suche parsons as shalbe found slak in payment, or shall refuse to pay their partes as aforesaid, and to perswade them eyther to pay the same presentlie, or els to comaunde them, as so dyrected by us, to appeare before us presently to shew cause why they doe not . . .'.[10]

If there was a single straw that broke the back of investment and finally crushed any lingering hopes for some good end to the enterprise, it was this final, huge call upon the adventurers' purses. For as long as the ore held out some promise of return, their prior commitments, though onerous, could be borne. But a demand for even more money, to pay off debts to which they had not given their agreement (and of which, probably, they had been unaware, until the bill was delivered), brought a decisive collapse in the adventurers' confidence. And it was confidence, rather than statute, that had been the fundament upon which the unincorporated 'Company of Cathay' was built. In keeping all matters of governance and direction in her own hands, Elizabeth had played a shrewd game; but now its implications rebounded unpleasantly. The only viable sanction that could be brought against those who simply chose not to pay was forfeiture – but of what? And who, moreover, would make that threat? Her Privy Council was full of men who were themselves reluctant to empty their pockets further – more reluctant, indeed, than their less well-informed partners from the City. In fact, the majority of the funds due upon this final, huge assessment that was eventually to be paid came from those supposedly canny merchants whom Best had memorably castigated; who 'never regarde vertue withoute sure, certayne, and present gaynes'. In stark contrast, the men of the Court ('from whence, as from the fountaine of oure common wealth, all good causes haue theyr chiefe encrease and mayntenance'), having seized control of the enterprise on the back of the hapless Lok's supposed evidence of gold and transformed it thereafter into a huge, quasi-public project, kept their purse strings tightly knotted. By the end of the year, with the first three great assays at the Dartford works (8 and 12–13 November, 29 December) having produced results that ranged from 'verye evill' to 'somewhat reasonable' and then 'but evill' once more, less than half the dues from the final assessment had been received.[11] In the following months, even that constipated flow of receipts would dwindle to nothing.

Meanwhile, the clamour of the enterprise's creditors had become deafening. Hurriedly abandoning any prospect of a future expedition – even whilst the ore remained unproven – the Council ordered the chattels of the company to be sold off or bartered to meet outstanding debts, of which the most substantial – and certainly the most pressing – were for wages.

The common mariners and miners of the 1578 expedition had braved fearsome hardships, and almost forty had died before the return to England.[12] A few of these casualties were entirely accidental, being lost overboard during the return passage; but the majority of mortalities were caused by ailments exacerbated by the effects of utter exhaustion, vitamin deficiency and frost-bite.[13] It is clear, moreover, that the true rate of mortality was understated: that a further, significant number died following the return of the ships to England (many payments of wages in arrears were made subsequently to the widows or relatives of men known to have survived the return passage). The rewards for these heroic endeavours were extremely paltry – and, furthermore, tardily paid.[14] Some were lucky and received their full dues within two months of their return – the miners appear to have been discharged first, with only a few outstanding sums due at the end of the year[15] – but many mariners received even less than the thin bounty for which they had signed up. For these unfortunates, their discharge was more in the manner of a rummage sale: a debasing scramble for oddments in lieu of cash. The account books provide the evidence of this in harrowing detail: to Edward Rigby, £1 18sh. 3d., of which he received 11sh. and 3d. in canvas remnants and a 'cappe'; to Philemon Wharton, paid £1 2sh. 8d., of which 8d. was for a cap and 2sh. for aquavite; most poignantly of all, to Edwarde Heale, due £5, of which his food and burial at Portsmouth stood for 10sh. 6d.[16] When ready money was found, it went as often as not to the 'ostis' who had allowed credit to a destitute mariner and fed him in wretched lodgings until the paymaster, Edward Selman, came visiting. For want of rich men's moral obligations being satis-fied, many of the common men who had so heroically served the enterprise enjoyed a bleak and hungry Christmas in 1578.

It is difficult to apportion the principal blame for this general evasion of responsibility; but indisputably, the centrifugal forces that had begun to pull apart the enterprise tugged most strongly at the two men who had first carried it to Court and City three years before. Frobisher had fulfilled the expecta-tions of his backers, almost to the letter. He had allowed himself to bend to their priorities, trusting to forces over which he had little control to advance his reputation and fortune. In doing so, he had exhibited fortitude, resolve, initiative and remarkably little natural aptitude for the navigator's art. But if his fame had been secured, his fortune most certainly had not. At a rate of £25 per month, his salary from the adventurers was now some seventeen months in arrears. In the scramble of creditors upon vanishing assets, the just rewards for his travails were unlikely to be forthcoming; blame, therefore, had to be laid at someone's door. The threshold upon which it came down most heavily was that of his former partner, Michael Lok.

In this, Lok unwisely colluded. After almost three years of serious personal commitment, of making substantial loans whilst simultaneously carrying the second largest investment in the enterprise, he had begun, belatedly, to look after his own interests. On several occasions he addressed letters to the Council asking for recompense for his service as treasurer (not an unreasonable request), and for interest on the loans he had made to the company of adventurers for want of subscriptions. The Council's continuing silence eventually forced his hand. In the midst of the pressing claims of creditors, he ensured that the outstanding freight charges of £450 for his own vessel, the *Beare Leicester*, were given priority.[17] He also submitted a claim for £1,200 for expenses (including the table diet of the commissioners who, it seems, had met habitually at Lok's house to discharge their business) and interest charges he had borne on his loans over three years.[18] There may have been some justice in these demands, and certainly, no one had devoted himself to the company's business so tirelessly as Lok; but his timing was exquisitely poor, nevertheless.

It was also his misfortune that his requests for recompense coincided with the first questions regarding his honesty. To save warehousing costs, a large amount of equipment used in the late voyage was stored in his house (probably a warehouse below his living rooms in Cheapside), pending its sale. Rumours began to circulate among the adventurers that he had purposely detained this against satisfaction of his claims. Lok denied this robustly, but the need for scapegoats had made the truth a dispensable commodity:

> . . . I have my howsse full paystered of the goodes of the companye dyscharged out of their ships come home, w(hi)ch is tackeling of ships, monytion, vyttells, and many od things, w(hi)ch is all by inventarye receved under the handes of the masters and offycers of the ships, w(hi)ch goodes I am ready at all tymes to delyver . . . And bycaus that sclanderous tonges wyll not be stopped by wordes, I make no answere to them, but abyde the time when God shall make my doinges knowen . . . .[19]

The busiest of these slanderous tongues was, unsurprisingly, Frobisher's. He had come to see in the treasurer's 'doble dealings' the prime cause and continuance of all his own frustrations. Since the return of the 1578 expedition, he had had the charge of paying off the mariners, miners and soldiers of the *Ayde*. For this, he had received some cash – principally the outstanding subscriptions of the Earl of Warwick, Thomas Gresham and Anne Frances – but had continued to press Lok for the balance. Lok provided only £61 more, though in the meantime he disbursed £944 for the Dartford works and detained a further £1,200 against the settlement of his own claims. He compounded this error of judgement by complaining (with very good reason) of the unreliability of Frobisher's own accounts, which were the principal evidence for the expenses the latter now claimed. In view of the pressures on both men, it is only surprising that some form of *dénouement* did not occur earlier; but matters finally came to a head on the evening of 20 November 1578, when Frobisher paid an unexpected visit to Lok's house, accompanied by a veritable mob of his 'sarving men' (all of whose wages, presumably, were also in arrears). The sight of tackling, munitions, victuals and other supplies from the late voyage, 'paystered' around the house, could hardly have calmed tempers. According to Lok himself:

> . . . there [Frobisher] openly in great radge and furye exclaimed one M. Lok, in this wise, sayenge thow hast cossyned my Lorde of Oxford of m^{li}, thow haste made false accompts and deceavyd the Companye of iij^m. pounds, thow hast not one groat venture in all theis voyages, thow art A bankeroot knaive, and swore by gods bludd he woold pull him owt of his howsse by the eares, All which villanus reproches M. Lok did beare quietly for that tyme, knowinge them to be false; and thinkinge C. Furbusher to be eyther dronke or made.[20]

With Frobisher repeating his claims in public ('in the Coorte, and in the Royal Exchange and everywhere in London', complained Lok),[21] they began to be heeded. In particular, the charge of making false accounts was taken up by others, principally those who had most to gain by doing so: the company's creditors. Lok's account books had been audited for the first time in August 1578 on the orders of the Privy Council (belatedly, they had come to doubt the wisdom of having so much control over the finances of the enterprise in one pair of hands). Thomas Neale, the Queen's auditor, had passed them, apparently without reservation. Now, with Frobisher leading the accusations against him, Lok was almost immediately suspended as treasurer (though initially this seems to have been presented more as a well-deserved 'rest'), and Neale was ordered by the Council to examine his accounts once more.[22] In Lok's place, another of the adventurers, Thomas Allen – a member of the Skinners' Company and the Queen's Merchant of the Baltic Stores – was appointed as the new treasurer, some time before 8 December. He was to prove precisely as successful as Lok in securing further funds to discharge the adventurers' obligations.

The specific charges that Frobisher had made against Lok were soon dismissed. The most cursory examination of the finances of the enterprise (as confirmed by Neale) showed that he had indeed invested over £2,000 of his own money; that his accounts, though 'lacking controllement', were basically sound (his detention of interests of money aside); and that the Earl of Oxford was perfectly capable of cozening himself without Lok's assistance. Yet despite being cleared of these accusations, the former treasurer was to go to prison on up to eight occasions in the next three years for non-payment of monies owed the creditors of the enterprise – a crime of which, ironically, he was palpably innocent.

Before the third voyage had sailed, the Council had directed Lok to enter into charter parties for the freight ships in his own name, though on behalf of the company as a whole.[23] It was an arrangement that had been intended to save time when a hundred other matters had pressed upon the schedule of preparations. Now that members of the Council itself were being pressed for the company's debts, they found it expedient to allow Lok's signature on these papers to speak for itself. As a means of escaping their own commitments, it was a sound strategy; as a cynical measure to divest themselves of a troublesome merchant whose own claims for wages and expenses significantly added to their potential liabilities, it was lamentably effective. By March 1579, the 'company' was involved in at least seven law suits against creditors – even against one of their own adventurers, William Borough, who was still owed £95 for the *Judith*.[24] But of course there was no company, only a hapless ex-treasurer. Borough, like Frobisher, decided that it was Lok's vindictive and self-serving nature, rather than a lack of funds, that kept him out of pocket. Within months, the accused was in prison as a result of this lawsuit; one of many such incarcerations.[25]

With Lok disgraced, the main cause of Frobisher's continuing financial embarrassment – as he considered him – had been removed. However, if he thought that Lok's successor Thomas Allen would prove to be more tractable, he was to be disappointed. Within days, he was accusing Allen of the same misdemeanours as Lok. On 13 January, Allen wrote to the Council, complaining that Frobisher 'doyth moche myseuse me' (Allen was also withholding funds in satisfaction of outstanding freight charges on his own ship).[26] Yet Frobisher himself was hardly untouched by rumours of financial malpractice. Lok's complaints regarding his accounts were palpably too just to be ignored. In January 1579, auditors found errors, or made disallowances, of £316 from a total of just £842 disbursed. Frobisher hotly – if unconvincingly – challenged their findings: 'if Evirye mans account be this narroly

Exsamyned you shall se moer must fall howtt then is fall howt as yett'.[27] The auditors chose not to be convinced or cowed; in particular, Frobisher's claim that much of the armour he had purchased for the expedition had been lost at sea by Hall's negligence was dismissed out of hand: 'for Armore he provided lyttell, and hath all styll himselfe with moche of the companys that is lackinge'.

These first, overt suggestions of impropriety, though not seized upon at the time, were to come back to stain Frobisher's reputation in subsequent years. Yet if he had taken money from the corporate purse, he was little worse than those who had detained monies towards their own 'expenses', and he had some high-profile debts of his own to discharge. Having become an heroic figure, he considered himself due a commensurate public image. This required resources, of which even now he had few. His pay for the three voyages, as stated, came to a total of £758, plus a further £175 for duties performed since the return of the final expedition.[28] This would have been a handsome reward for such poor returns as he had delivered, but those returns had now determined the likelihood of his recompense. Nevertheless, though now being far out of pocket, he had adopted a lifestyle which both reflected and complemented his fame: not least in having his retinue of 'sarving men' – useful for mobbing hapless treasurers, if little else – who were, according to Lok, costing the adventurers a further £400 merely in the act of following Frobisher's horse around.[29] Without any known source of income, what sustained their leader during this difficult time? Those precious instruments of navigation that Lok had charged be returned to the company were suspiciously unaccounted for, as was a quantity of the victuals and implements laded in the *Ayde* for the third voyage, which had remained on the ship following her return, rather than being inventoried and stored thereafter. As late as mid-1579, Lok claimed that these remained in Frobisher's hands still, with unaccounted goods or cash to the value of £564. The accusation was probably well founded; but amidst the mounting chaos of dislodged treasurers, unpaid bills and starving mariners to divert the attention of the Privy Council and commission, the minor frauds of their admiral at sea may not have been regarded by them as material. In an age wherein the provisioning of official projects was habitually marked by blatant graft, Frobisher merely acted his expected part and joined the scramble to take what he could.

Yet if he was short of money, he had at least acted to trim his more frivolous expenses. Whilst the 1578 expedition had been at sea, Walsingham had been discommoded by a petition from a woman in a poorhouse in Hampstead, on a matter of a debt of just £4:

In her most lamentable manner sheweth vnto yo(u)r honour yo(u)r humble oratrix Isabell Frobusher, the moste miserable woman in the world, that whereas your hono(u)rs said oratrix sometimes was the wife of one Thomas Riggatt of Snathe in the County of Yorke, a verie wealthy man, who left your oratrix well to live and in very good state and good portions unto all his childern. Afterwards she took to husband M(aste)r Captain Frobusher, (whom God forgive) who hathe not only spent that which her said husband left her, but the portions also of her poor children, and hath put them all to the wide worlde to shifte in a most lamentable case. And now to increase her misery she hauing not to reliefe herself her childerns childern of her said first husband are sent into her having a poor room within another at Hampstead near London for her to keep at whiche place she and they are for want of food ready to starve to your poor oratrix intolerable grief and sorrow. Your oratrix humble peticion is that wheras one M(aste)r Kempe gent. dwelling in the Wool Staple at Westminster gave his promise to pay her 4li for the said M(aste)r Frobusher (which he will not now pay) that without delay he may pay the same or that it would please your hono(u)r to help her with some reliefe vntil M(aste)r Frobusher's return to keep them from famishing – and she accordinge to her bounden duty will daylye pray God, etc.[30]

Despite the ostensible business of an unpaid debt, this is little more than a begging letter, from the wife of a man whose enterprise had the financial backing of half the Privy Council. If proof were needed of Frobisher's utter indifference to the state of his family, it is amply set out here. When he returned from the sea he had an opportunity to do something, however modest, to alleviate her plight; but the cost of keeping a retinue had proved too expensive to allow less urgent calls upon his purse. Existing evidence suggests that he made not the slightest provision for his wife and her children, either then or later. With this, her lonely plea from the poorhouse, the wretched Isobel disappears from history.

If this was the most poignant personal epitaph upon Frobisher's north-west enterprise, it was by no means the only one. The adventurers, whether of slighter or greater means, shared a common and growing sense of hopelessness in the early months of 1579. The only faint light in the gloom of their dying fortunes was the small, residual chance that some value might finally be teased from the New World ore. By now, however, even their touching faith in Saxon metallurgical expertise had been almost entirely extinguished. Schutz, to give him some small credit, appeared to have been doing his pale

best. Several times, he came near to suffocation in attempting to separate the
illusory precious metals from the slags he created in his furnaces; but time
and his credibility were running out. In successive assays carried out between
December 1578 and February 1579, he affected to detect the presence of gold
and silver, but this remained unseparated from the ore itself, even though
Schutz now had the 'addittaments' to the absence of which he had attributed
his former failures. An assay of 20 January was particularly dangerous, being
conducted in the presence of Frobisher alone. He had been ordered to attend
by the commissioners in his new role as surveyor of the works at Dartford,
an appointment made less in recognition of any intrinsic suitability for the
task than for the purgative effect of introducing a large, well-armed and
angry man into the assaying process.[31] Presumably this focussing of Schutz's
attention was at least partly responsible for the encouraging results of
this latest trial, which seemed to offer the promise of £10 per ton of ore
refined.

Promises, however, were no longer sufficient to contain Frobisher's impatience with those whom he now regarded, absent Michael Lok, to be the principal confounders of his ambitions. During successive visits to Dartford
during the early months of 1579, he appears to have acted as a salutary arm
to the Privy Council's more restrained exhortations, assaulting or threatening
virtually everyone involved in the process. Lok later claimed that upon various
occasions he 'would have mischeved' Edward Fenton (with his dagger),
'revyled' Michael Lok, his servant, Charles Sledd and Edward Castelyn
(bursar of funds at Dartford) 'w(i)th villanous speech and threatinings',[32]
struck Schutz, belaboured Richard Rawson (landlord of the Bull inn at Dartford) with a set of keys for the workhouses and 'bete Edward Selman abowt
the head, and w(i)th his dagger had almost cloven his head' (Selman had
made the mistake of confiscating another set of workhouse keys from Frobisher's kinsman and servant, William Hawke, presumably at the urgent
request of everyone involved in the smelting works).[33] At other times, seemingly oblivious to the damage and ill-will he had caused already, he attempted
half-heartedly to be conciliatory. Even as the last hopes for the enterprise were
fading, he had foiled offers by Schutz and Denham to buy part of the ore
and work it themselves; but almost immediately thereafter he had secretly
proposed to the same men an arrangement whereby they should all work the
ore on their own behalf. It need hardly be said that this magnanimous offer
to paper over past differences was summarily rejected by the disillusioned
assayers.[34]

Yet even Frobisher must have sensed the onset of an unwelcome reality by now. The north-west project was a singular episode in Elizabethan maritime enterprise. It was anomalous both in structure and intention: a protracted affair which provided no real evidence either that it would be profitable or not, until such sums had been invested that the option of cutting and running provided no escape worth having. For Frobisher in particular, this was not merely a matter of commercial regret, even with the loss of his own 'investment' in the enterprise. What he realized much too late – in part because the inflated scale of the project had inferred a spurious sense of permanence – was that the reputation it had brought him was bestowed upon a very short lease. His 'vehement oathes' had convinced the Queen, her Council and their commissioners; but when their promise was not realized, all that remained was the bare prospect of a new and very barren 'English' land across the ocean. That, we may assume with some confidence, was not regarded as a very attractive return upon squandered money.

For Frobisher, fame had come slowly. It had required a great deal of industry to achieve, and more to sustain; but, confronted by the bald imperatives of empty purses, it fell, swiftly. There were neither funds, nor the will, nor the hope to keep the enterprise that had created it from well deserved extinction. For as long as he practically could, he attempted to beat some life into his failing prospects (or rather, into those whom he considered capable of sustaining them); but if he had been the first to discern some potential in his project, he was the last – the obsessive Lok apart – to abandon it. The Queen – figurehead, overseer and driver of the enterprise – had ceased to believe that the hollowness of her Exchequer chests could be enriched in frozen wastes; her Privy Council members, whatever each of them believed privily, followed obediently and tried to prevent further reminders of outstanding dues from mentioning their own, large culpabilities; the other adventurers – courtiers, gentlemen, poets, and merchants – had already absorbed the bitter lesson of their own empty purses and had set themselves to other, more worthwhile businesses. Most of the ore, pristinely untested, was already mouldering in secure storehouses at Dartford, pending the final assays in May 1581 – ironically, performed by William Williams, the man to whom Lok had turned first of all in 1576 with his 'halfe-penny loafe' shaped piece of ore. Thereafter, as Camden later reported, the worthless bounty of the New World was cast out to repair the local roads.[35]

Lok himself was beginning his comprehensive tour of London's prison accommodation and a subsequent, forty-year odyssey to rebuild his reputation and fortune, crippled not only by his own debts but also by the burden of bonds to a total of £4,000 that he had given for the Queen's investment in his enterprise.[36] What he and his former colleagues left behind became a cautionary tale to London's commercial classes; ensuring that subsequent attempts to find a north-west passage would be modest, precisely planned affairs. The definitive epitaph upon the 'Company of Cathay' was the report issued by the Queen's auditors, Thomas Neale and William Baynham on 6 May 1583.[37] It revealed that almost £2,650 of adventurers' subscriptions remained outstanding (and there is no evidence that any of this was subsequently paid). The Queen herself owed nothing, but Privy Councillors, their wives and other courtiers accounted for almost £1,400 of the total, with the Earl of Oxford alone owing £540. Of the £400 that Frobisher himself had ventured – albeit unwillingly – £280 remained unpaid. He was also stated still to owe a further £294 from funds he was to have disbursed on the adventurers' behalf, which he was 'to paye presentlye to the said adventurars . . . except he can shew good cause to the contrarie'. Michael Lok, the 'bankerot knave' who had ventured a total of £2,180 and had given so much new business to London's gaolers thereafter, was found to owe just £27 10s.[38]

Fame Deferred: 1579–85

It is greatly to be feared that Furbisher has played us a trick . . .[1]

Notwithstanding the novelty of their collective experience, the discomfiture of sixty adventurers, their creditors and a putative English Columbus had hardly occupied the nation's attention during the three years of the north-west enterprise, though its demise may well have encouraged a general sense of *Schadenfreude* among those who had resisted the temptation to invest. The north-west venture was a curious episode in England's emerging maritime tradition, but its immediate implications were few, and entirely overshadowed by developments whose repercussions were to press upon the English nation as a whole. Whilst Frobisher and Lok had devoted their attention to their country's embryonic overseas trade empire and the incidental matter of their own enrichment, the real world – that bound by the ambitions of priests and princes – had moved to a point at which problems held in abeyance for almost a quarter of a century were closing upon some form of resolution. These wider issues were not of immediate – perhaps not of *any* – concern to Frobisher during this period; but their impact upon his future career, as upon those of many of his contemporaries, was to be profound.

When the *Gabriel* and *Michael* departed from Gravesend upon their first north-west voyage in May 1576, it seemed as though the governments of Elizabeth I and Philip II might yet preserve the peace that had served them well for decades, notwithstanding the pricks of English pirates, Spanish imperial designs and the incompatibility of the two nations' confessional preferences.

Since the conclusion of the 1574 Bristol treaty, official relations had improved slowly as commercial ties were re-established. In 1577, the venerable Anglo-Iberian trade was finally placed upon a more formal footing, when the Spanish Company was incorporated in London (Michael Lok, then still hopeful of profit from the soil of Meta Incognita, had been one of its charter members).[2] The founding of the company was an act of faith in the long-term ability of commerce to propound the benefits of self-interest above self-aggrandizement successfully, and reflected, at least for the moment, the desire to return to the state of pragmatic engagement that had hitherto proved of such inestimable value to English merchants.

Diplomatically, the replacement of the sanguinary Alva as Philip's regent in the Netherlands by the (slightly) more circumspect Don Luis de Requeséns, and the abolition of the notorious 'Council of Blood', were considered at first to be positive developments in England. For her part, Elizabeth continued to steer her policy towards the Low Countries with great circumspection, upholding Philip's absolute right to rule his subjects there whilst attempting to guarantee confessional freedom to the rebels. She wished, simply, for a fondly imagined but entirely illusory *status quo ante* of Charles V's time to be restored. Her failure to bring about that reversion was due not merely to the inherent contradictions of her policy, but also to the determination of too many of the lesser protagonists that any compromise should not succeed. Despite the desire for peace that informed the efforts of both Elizabeth and Philip, time and circumstance favoured those for whom any degree of relativism, no matter how conducive to good business, was unacceptable. Thus, by the time that Frobisher walked away from his enterprise in the first few months of 1579, the Queen had acquired much greater concerns than her squandered £4,000 and the prospective value of New World ore in Dartford cellars.

In the Low Countries, always the most volatile tinderbox to Anglo-Spanish affairs, the regime of the intelligent Requeséns was too brief to achieve anything lasting (though at least one of his proposed solutions to the crisis – the breaking of the dykes and subsequent inundation of the rebellious provinces – had hardly been intended to win the hearts and minds of his subjects).[3] On his sudden death in March 1576, Philip appointed his own half-brother, Don John of Austria, the hero of the battle of Lepanto, to succeed as Regent. By the time Don John arrived in the Low Countries late in November that year, it was already much too late for a peaceful resolution of the confessional crisis, even had the goodwill existed to attempt it. Late in October 1576, the occupying 'Spanish' troops – a heterogeneous body of

Iberians, Germans and Italian mercenaries – mutinied for want of wages far in arrears. Overnight, the entire edifice of Philip's authority in the Low Countries crumbled. In this vacuum, the States-General was convened by almost all the provinces to consider measures to counter the threat of the marauding troops. A treaty, the Pacification of Ghent, was proposed both in haste and hope of securing some local advantage from Philip's temporary weakness. It recognized William of Orange as Stadtholder of Holland and Zeeland, and called upon him to expel the mutinous army and restore the apocryphal 'ancient liberties' enjoyed during the reign of Philip's father. The laws against heresy were also suspended, and although the States-General acknowledged Philip as their sovereign lord, they refused to allow Don John to assume his regency unless he accepted the terms of the Pacification. Meanwhile, on 4 November, what was to become known as the Spanish Fury fell upon Antwerp; starving Spanish troops sacked the city, destroying or pillaging a civic wealth derived from centuries of commercial dealing; a despoliation from which the former entrepôt never recovered. The episode shook Europe – particularly its Protestant portion – and was uniformly counter-productive: rather than appear as a local Spanish triumph, it confirmed the helplessness of official Hapsburg policy in the Netherlands and invited only further resistance to what now seemed to many to be both an immoral and inchoate power. With no effective army to hand, and even the chronically cautious Elizabeth threatening to finance the Prince of Orange's campaign to crush the mutinous Spanish army, Don John had no choice but to acquiesce to his new subjects' demands. In February 1577, he issued the Perpetual Edict, which accepted all the terms of the Pacification of Ghent.

The moment has been called the high-water mark of Elizabeth's Netherlands policy,[4] but in reality it held out a promise of nothing but renewed conflict. The suspension of the laws on heresy had benefited the rebels, but in the manner of all moral absolutists, the extremists amongst them were no less intent upon total victory than was their Spanish master. The removal of Philip's troops from the Low Countries, one of the principal terms of the recent treaty, took away the most immediate source of strife; but it also removed the means by which civil order could be maintained or restored. These were fundamental problems that, unsolved, could hardly assist in the process of finding a lasting settlement; but they were not the only obstacles. The very person of Don John, in his new office, represented a new and harsher policy towards the rebels, notwithstanding the concessions with which he had commenced his regency. His own experience, reinforced no doubt by recent humiliations, had taught him that problems were best and

most decisively dealt with at the tip of a sword. Rumours circulating soon
after his appointment had it that he wished finally to pacify the Netherlands
only as a preliminary to the invasion of England, following which he would
marry Mary Stuart and assume the English throne himself. Such ambitions
seemed distant in the early part of 1577 as the Spanish army marched southwards out of the Low Countries; yet the history of the revolt of the Netherlands was one of extreme reversals of fortune. Having made one perfunctory
(and spurned) attempt to make peace with William of Orange, and receiving a number of death threats from extremists – probably Calvinists – who
hardly understood the limits of what they had achieved to date, Don John
brought his painful career as a conciliator to a premature end. In July he
slipped out of Brussels unnoticed, raised a number of loyal Walloon troops
and seized the citadel of Namur. From there, he sent word to the Spanish
army to turn about and return to the Netherlands.[5]

Elizabeth, urged by Walsingham and others finally to take up the role as
champion of Protestant liberties, reluctantly allocated £100,000 for the
succour of the rebels should Don John revoke the Perpetual Edict. She also
urged the States-General to appoint William of Orange as their military commander. Their reaction was infuriatingly ambiguous. Most of the provinces
remained predominantly Catholic, and fundamentally loyal to their prince;
though they asked for English troops to come to their assistance, the States-
General announced that they wanted a compromise that would be acceptable to Philip also. Yet they also demanded of him the impossible: that Don
John be replaced as their regent by Archduke Matthias of Austria, the
Emperor's brother.

Exasperated at this exercise in un-*realpolitik*, Elizabeth turned once more
to her familiar role as mediator, though making strong representations to
Philip to maintain the Pacification of Ghent. His reply was swift and uncharacteristically decisive. Alexander Farnese – Prince of Parma, satrap of Spain
and the foremost general of his day – was ordered to take command of the
Spanish army and lead it back into the Netherlands. On 31 January 1578, the
combined forces of Don John and Parma virtually annihilated the States-
General's army at Gembloux. In the aftermath of the battle, Elizabeth no
longer had room to manoeuvre; despite her deep fears of semi-permanent
continental entanglements, she was obliged to provide further loans to the
rebels merely to keep the Protestant cause from extinction. Even direct military intervention was considered, not least when the States-General, made
desperate by their defeats, offered sovereignty over the Netherlands to the
French King's brother, the Duc d'Anjou. Fortunately, Elizabeth soon per-

ceived he was not the threat he seemed; and the intransigence of the States-General in failing to seek a peaceful settlement with Philip post-Gembloux further cooled her enthusiasm for their cause. Despite the urgent pleas of Walsingham and Leicester, she was not yet ready to edge into that vacancy they held open for a Protestant champion. Yet there could have been few who did not regard the relationship between Spain and England as having been further defined by the events of 1578, and almost entirely for the worse. Neither Elizabeth nor Philip had sought to intrude overtly upon the other's rightful sphere of princely authority, but the fundamental relationship between England and Spain was tipping once more, with conditions for their enmity being set out by proxy.

Martin Frobisher, having almost entirely abjured his responsibility for the fate of the north-west enterprise by the early part of 1579, might have expected to find a role in the unofficial response to Parma and Don John. His personal credit at the time, however, was such that he would have been hard pressed to put to sea – legitimately – in a coracle. The greater part of his wages for three years of admiralship upon the Ocean Sea remained outstanding, and some of the balance had disappeared into the bottomless pit of the enterprise itself. As we have seen, he may have detained in his hands certain goods and chattels belonging to the enterprise, and possibly also the monies he had diverted by means of his 'evil' victualling of the *Ayde*, but most of this was surely spent in covering the wages of his so-called serving men, before they, too, abandoned him for a brighter prospect. In March 1579, when Thomas Allen was attempting to sell off the assets of the defunct 'Company of Cathay', he asked £80 for the *Gabriel*. Frobisher, perhaps in an uncharacteristic burst of sentimentality (or possibly searching for the means by which to put to sea upon his old business), had bid for her. Allen had not taken this offer seriously: he had merely observed 'I thinke redye monye is owte of the way w(i)th him.'[6] There was no longer even a Michael Lok to stand for food and lodgings whilst something profitable sailed into view. Prospects, for Frobisher, could have been little better in 1579 than in the dark days of 1574.

However, his recent failure had not been complete. Men who did not found new empires for their sovereign, or fill her coffers with unimaginable bounty, did not necessarily qualify as unemployable. Even as he was busily destroying his old partner's reputation and hindering the progress of assays at Dartford, Frobisher's skills as a sea-captain had been commandeered by the Privy Council, though in a modest way. In February 1579, with the north-west enterprise flagging beneath the weight of its debts, he was briefly diverted from his preferred business to be employed as captain of the Queen's ship, the *Foresight*, to transport Duke John Casimir, prince-regent of the Palatinate and veteran Protestant mercenary, to Flushing. It was a task that even his recently disappointed Queen felt he might discharge without further undue attrition upon her purse (and may well have been intended as a deliberate device to neutralize his unremittingly obstructive efforts at Dartford). Her pale faith was justified: Frobisher ensured the safe transportation of the Duke and his troops for the princely reward of ten guineas;[7] though even upon this official business, he made one last attempt to resurrect his almost vanished prospects. On their short passage across the Channel, he broached the matter of the ore that languished at Dartford to his distinguished passenger. Duke Casimir, possibly unaware of the almost uniformly pessimistic results from the Dartford works, subsequently wrote to Frobisher from the Low Countries, promising to secure six good assayers in Germany and send them back to England.[8] He did not do so, however; and this seems to have been the final occasion upon which Frobisher exercised himself on behalf of his dead enterprise.

For the next few months, he effectively disappears from the records; possibly, he was busily canvassing for work amongst those who had recently been his paymasters, though without any discernible success, as we shall see. Fortunately, the Queen's problems, as ever, provided limited but useful opportunities for a man with an empty stomach and the will to fill it. In the latter part of the year, despite recent Spanish successes in the Low Countries and the danger to the Protestant cause there, the most immediate 'foreign' issue for Elizabeth lay closer to home – in Ireland, a place in which Frobisher himself had previously done some useful, if limited, business.

The endearingly persistent James Fitzmaurice had fled from Ireland following the collapse of his rebellion in the early 1570s, and had since remained in Europe. He had not allowed his lack of success to dampen his ardour for making war against the English, however. In recent years he had passed constantly between the Courts at Rome and Madrid, pleading for assistance for a further uprising. Philip, anxious to keep the threat of English interference in the Netherlands to a minimum, was not inclined to give Elizabeth a spurious counter-justification for her aid to his rebellious Dutch subjects, and offered only verbal encouragement to the desperate Irishman. The Pope, however, was less constrained by the earthly preoccupations of princes. He gave his blessing and a little money to Fitzmaurice, and promised pardons and indulgences for any and all Italian bandits currently despoiling the trade routes of the Cisalpines, who might choose to join this holy cause – an offer that even Fitzmaurice must have dreaded proving popular. Back in Spain once more, and deserted by Frobisher's sometime acquaintance Thomas Stukeley (who was to have joined in an Irish campaign with him), Fitzmaurice managed only to raise a small band of disaffected Spaniards, Portuguese and Catholic Englishmen.[9] With these, and little more than moral support from the Spanish King, he landed on Irish soil at Dingle Bay, on 17 July 1579.

His arrival caused a brief panic in England, until the size of his 'army' became apparent. Fitzmaurice's cousin Desmond initially hinted at his continuing loyalty to the Queen's cause; but subsequent murders by his brother, John FitzGerald, of Sir Henry Davells (agent of Sir William Drury, Lord Justice of Ireland) and the Provost Marshall of Munster, and Desmond's continuing failure to declare outright for the Queen, resulted in his being proclaimed a traitor on 2 November 1579. Undoubtedly this was a premature opprobrium, but thirteen days later, Desmond gathered his followers, rose to his own bad press and sacked the town of Youghal, with the slaughter of all who resisted. A new rebellion, manufactured by the stupidity of the Queen's servants in Ireland, had commenced; though James Fitzmaurice, its original cause and promoter, was by now dead, cut down in a skirmish in Connaught.

Martin Frobisher's previous Irish service may have recommended him for new employment there, but its catalyst lay in more recent connections. Several men who had backed his voyages to Meta Incognita were to play key roles in this new stage of the pacification. Sir William Pelham (who had come to Ireland to oversee the construction of fortifications) took charge of English forces when Sir William Drury died following the English defeat at Springfield; Sir William Winter was appointed admiral of the squadron sent to support the land forces and interdict any foreign attempts to assist the rebels; and Sir Henry Wallop, the Treasurer at Wars, crossed to Ireland with the Queen's money to finance their exertions. It seems that Frobisher was involved in the fleet preparations from August at the latest; early in September, the Privy Council ordered him and others to hold themselves in readiness to take command of the Queen's ships.[10] It is most likely to have been Winter (no doubt petitioned by Frobisher) who had put him forward for employment, though the role he was given – to captain the ship *Foresight* once more as a transport for troops and supplies – was very similar to that which he had discharged in Irish waters almost eight years earlier. In light of the brief but significant profile he had enjoyed during the north-west enterprise, this was a strikingly modest appointment; perhaps the most telling indication of how far his stock had fallen amongst those best placed to advance his career. Nevertheless, as poor a prospect as a small naval campaign promised to be, there was a curious symmetry here to the opportunities afforded by the cause of the Earl of Desmond. Almost certainly, Frobisher was one of the few men to have had the promise of money both from its promotion and extinction.

The land campaign of Ormond and Pelham was unattractive but effective; they confined Desmond's forces and allies to Kerry (where there were few existing resources to sustain them), and then systematically despoiled the countryside to prevent the enemy from foraging. From the sea, meanwhile, Sir William Winter used his fleet with as much economy and success as when, almost twenty years earlier, he had confounded the French naval campaign to support Mary Stuart's cause in Scottish waters.[11] His four vessels – *Revenge* (commanded by the young Walter Ralegh), *Swallow*, *Foresight* and *Merlin* – moved steadily up the Shannon river, landing ordnance occasionally to reduce and take the castles that stood for Desmond, and at Dingle Bay they caught and destroyed Fitzmaurice's small fleet. Gradually, Desmond's position became desperate; but further risings elsewhere in Munster, Connaught and Leinster, and the recall, through ill-health, of the excellent Pelham (superseded by the diligent but pedantic Lord Grey), put fresh heart into his rebellion. To fan the flames further, a mixed force of Spanish volunteers and Italian mercenaries, the latter raised by the Pope, was carried into Smerwick harbour by a Spanish fleet in September 1580, and immediately occupied the fort there.

Grey's appalling massacre of this force (ably abetted by the supposedly cultured Ralegh) has been well documented, and needs little further discussion here. Winter's absence – he had returned to England to refit his squadron – had allowed the enemy force to land unchallenged, but he swiftly redeemed this innocent error. His small fleet returning immediately to Ireland, invested the fort from the sea and played an active part in the very brief siege. It seems that Frobisher's *Foresight* was not present at this stage in the campaign, having been driven back by storms; she is not portrayed upon the Smerwick map of 1580, and there is some evidence that she was docked at Gillingham harbour during November 1580 as the final, bloody stages of the siege of Smerwick fort occurred.[12] However, Frobisher was not entirely unemployed in the meantime. On 28 September, he addressed a memorial to the Privy Council – possibly at Winter's request – concerning the provisioning of the fleet that had done such sterling service in Irish waters. Entitled 'M(aste)r Furbisshers Informac(i)on touching (th)e defect of Victels',[13] it noted the standard naval allowance for victuals of 1 lb of bread, 2 lbs of beef and a gallon of beer per man per day; but claimed that the pursers had provided little more than half that amount, and poorly at that: 'And for the godnesse of the victualls whyle I was their let all the Capte(i)ns and compan(i)es saye what it was, for I saye it was ill' – a forthright and courageous statement from a man who, having been the source of so much recent Privy Council business, might well have felt it wiser to keep his head below the parapet.

He concluded his memorial with a statement that was intended to reflect only upon the 1580 expedition, but which might have stood as the epitaph upon almost every failed official venture for the following twenty years: 'These thinges beinge consyderyd yf the former allowance be not full and the victuall good, it is not possible to prolonge the tyme of servyce beyonde the proportion of victuall: But yf her Ma(ies)ties allowance be full, and the victuall good, it maye be drawne to som longer tyme vppon an extremyty.'

'To some longer tyme' . . . many of the newer English naval vessels, designed to be weatherly and fleet, had poor storage space in comparison to their enemies' ships;[14] but that necessarily limiting factor should not disguise the perennial difficulty that English sea-commanders experienced in attempting to loosen the purse-strings of their thrifty monarch. Shortage of supplies had been the principal cause of Winter withdrawing prematurely from the coast of western Ireland, thus allowing the Spanish fleet to disembark an army there. Mercifully, this was a small and, very soon, a dead army; but that its showing had been so poor was for Elizabeth a matter of good fortune, not prudent anticipation. Nor were the implications of her frugal policy confined to operations in British coastal waters. It will become all too clear that several plate fleets, upon whose safe arrival the entire edifice of Spanish power had come to depend, were to cross the Atlantic and reach their home harbours unmolested because would-be English predators were elsewhere, replenishing their ships' empty holds. Frobisher may have been repeating a common complaint, but it is to his credit that he made the attempt at all. Importantly, it is an indication also that his opinion continued to carry greater weight than his wider reputation, even in the immediate aftermath of the north-west debacle.

With the recapture of Smerwick, the major naval activity of the Munster campaign came to a close. By the end of 1580, Frobisher was ashore in England once more with neither gainful employment nor any prospect of it. The Irish service and Flushing voyage had been useful short-term businesses for a man with a large hole in his pocket, but they offered no promise of resurrected fortune. During these winter months, in a burst of desperate optimism, he petitioned the Queen to intercede to allow him to take possession of an unspecified lease, granted some five years earlier (perhaps one of the few tangible rewards of his brief career as an *agent-provocateur*).[15] He had been attempting to secure it from the former lessee through the courts – without success, it seems: 'I was dismyssed to the Com(m)on lawe, w(i)thout my charges, to my farder trouble, & longer detracting of tyme, thinking therby to wearye me . . .'. This suit had been a further drain upon his slender resources; the tenor of his request for some other favour: '. . . eyther to imploye me in yo(u)r p(re)sent s(er)vice, or ells to bestowe yo(u)r gracious relief vpon me, that I maye but lyve to be redye when you shall have occasion', hints far less at idle unemployment than encroaching destitution; though even now, he joined his plea with a veiled threat to return to something of his former habits, should such favour not be forthcoming: 'I desier but to lyve w(i)th credit as yo(u) s(er)vant, w(i)th a peny the daye, rather then vnder forayne princes, w(i)th greter revenue'. That the loss of Frobisher to a foreign prince might have been considered a serious blow in the aftermath of the north-west enterprise is doubtful; nevertheless, the Queen, perhaps wishing to reward him for his recent diligence whilst reminding him of its cost to her, offered him the post of Clerk of the Ships: one of the offices of her rudimentary naval administration. The idea may have occurred to her in recalling his recent forthright comments on the 'defect of Victels'; if so, and she was now a making a point, it was a humorous one. That she should consider a man of Frobisher's near-pathological aversion to administrative detail appropriate for the post, or its duties comprehensible to him, is almost beyond belief. Nevertheless, he obtained letters patent which provided for an annuity of £33 6sh. 8d., plus 3sh. 4d for each day occupied entirely in the duties of the clerkship, and £6 per year for boat hire.[16] It was hardly lucrative, though the income would have been useful enough in such thin times; however, even this modest sinecure was offered with strings attached. Frobisher was to succeed to the post only after the present incumbent, George Winter, had vacated it 'by decease, departure, surrender, forfeyture or other determinacyon'. In fact, William Borough directly succeeded Winter as clerk on 24 March 1581, which indicates that Frobisher had immediately sold on his patent to a man who was more prepared to dirty his hands in the business of naval administration.

This is the last known reference to Frobisher's activities during 1580, and indeed, for some time to come. For the next twelve months, he almost disappears from recorded history. His employment in official service so soon after the demise of the Meta Incognita enterprise indicates that he retained some reputation as a sea-commander, but his aspirations to glory and renown had been brutally pegged, as the level of his new responsibilities indicated. Unlike Drake – or, later, Ralegh and Essex – he had not been such a debtor upon the Queen's trust to merit personal disgrace as he fell; nor, realistically, were her expectations of his talents as high as of theirs. His was rather the fate of the underperforming but periodically useful servant, to be shifted to where his skills could best be utilized or, if necessary, contained. As long as there was an urgent need for a competent sea-commander, Frobisher could expect some small profferment; but peace, or even an end to crisis, brought only bad news. This was entirely the consequence of the inherent flaws in his character. In a commercial environment, he had proved himself a disastrous associate; not only because he had chosen too often to go his own way, but also for the contempt in which he held the aspirations of those whose money had sustained him. The hand, having been bitten, was now withdrawn; and Frobisher was confronted with all the consequences of the gulf between his imperishable self-regard and his achievements to date. It could not have been a happy prospect.

A full year, and no word of his activities. To pass from prominence to utter oblivion was not an uncommon fate in an age that had few reliable media of record. For the years between 1590 and 1595, the known activities of such a renowned figure as Francis Drake, disgraced in the aftermath of the disastrous 1589 expedition, can be comprehensively summarized upon a single page: men who were not capturing the public imagination or fighting some lesser, domestic matter through the courts tended not to leave marks of their passing. Yet the seeming totality of Frobisher's disappearance remains puzzling. He had become associated with enough prominent members of the government to leave traces of his movements, if only in the wake of their attempts to avoid him. Sir William Winter had moved the Queen to provide a brief employment in Ireland, and possibly Warwick or Leicester had put him forward for the small service to Flushing; it would be reasonable to suppose that other former adventurers of the 'Company of Cathay' were also sounded out by an increasingly penurious ex-explorer, yet none of them has left evidence to suggest that he was. Between December 1580 and the following November, the only known reference to Frobisher places him at an official reception in Bermondsey, where, as we shall see, he was by no means the guest of honour. To fill in the remaining months of anonymity, we are reduced to speculation.

One possibility, drawn from what we know of Frobisher's temperament and experience, recommends itself strongly. Having reached for glory and stumbled badly, he had several choices before him. The first (and most easily accomplished) was to go hungry. Another was to seek out a new project: a new opportunity to secure the rewards, both tangible and honorific, that had eluded him in Meta Incognita. That prospect, relying as it did upon other men's judgement of his abilities, was, to say the least, a remote one in 1581. However, there was a further option open to Frobisher: one in which he might utilize those peculiar skills that had provided his only palpable rewards to date. At the end of 1580, he disappeared, with no obvious means of support-ing himself (much less the family he had already chosen to abandon). Yet when he next emerged into the light of posterity, it was with a little money in his pocket and a partially rehabilitated reputation. Perhaps it was neither outright war nor trade, but the exercise of war *upon* trade, that sustained him now as it had done a decade before.

There is no documentary evidence to prove that Frobisher returned to pri-vateering in the early 1580s, but circumstances could hardly have been more favourable. Ostensibly, there was little official need for the efforts of private expeditions, and the Admiralty Court issued few letters of reprisal during this period. The Queen's relationship with French Catholics – the Guise faction apart – was reasonably good once more; this reflected in her financial support for the Duc d'Anjou against the Spanish Regency in the Netherlands. As far as it was in her power to determine, her involvement in that tortured con-flict ended there. Despite recent Spanish successes, she did not yet openly allow Englishmen to attack Spanish shipping in European waters, for fear of anticipating something that several of her Councillors were already regarding as an inevitability. As always, however, what the Queen meant, said and did had only a vague correspondence. Without the means to police her home waters effectively, she hardly attempted it. English privateering had become truly endemic, and tended to follow the course of royal diplomacy in one direction only – that is, towards further depredation. Proscriptions against piracy continued to be imposed, and continued to be ineffectual. Admiralty Court records for the period between the end of Elizabeth's 'official' involve-ment in France in 1573, and the near unrestricted issue of letters of reprisal against Spanish ships in 1585, show a continuing stream of petitions against known and anonymous malefactors.[17] As in previous decades, such claims from foreign plaintiffs tended to be dealt with tardily and unsatisfactorily, so it is probable that only a relatively small proportion of depredations against non-English ships was reported officially. Furthermore, the penalties enforced against captured malefeasants were – occasional sanguinary examples apart – incredibly light. This was an era in which any act of felony upon land, no matter how trivial, would invariably bring the most condign punishment; yet privateers who had despoiled vessels carrying hundreds of pounds' worth of goods often languished in gaol for no more than a matter of days before their backers secured their release.[18] One pertinent example of this phenomenon was provided by Hugh Randall – Frobisher's erstwhile colleague in the privateering and ore extraction trades – who was committed to Weymouth gaol in 1581 for abetting piracy, yet almost immediately obtained his release on bail, despite the order for his arrest having come from the Privy Council itself.[19]

The situation was not so much the result of a lenient sentencing policy *per se*, but of the perennial clash between national policy and the interests of local officials, many of whom were active associates of those they imprisoned; and, equally, of pressures created by the increasingly overlapping jurisdictions of the Admiralty Court and Privy Council. Where aspects of international law – as yet a virgin area of jurisprudence – were developing under the impetus of numerous pleas for redress, the Admiralty Court often found itself sidelined or hamstrung by its masters, many of whom were too close to the matters they adjudged. It also contended with changing attitudes to the offence itself. Half the coastal population of England had long conspired to thwart the Admiralty Court's authority, but by the early 1580s long-time malfeasants had acquired more distinguished company. As time passed, what had once been lamentable had become merely habitual; increasingly, members of the highest strata of English society who had formerly supported privateers in clandestine ways did so more openly. Again, we may cite an instance that was by no means untypical of this trend. In 1580, three Hamburg merchants petitioned the Queen regarding the seizure of three of their vessels by English ships, one of which was owned by Henry Seckford, Groom of the Chamber and Keeper of the Privy Purse. Seckford had not even attempted to disguise his involvement: his name – that of the ship also – was painted gaudily upon her bow. Yet even such a distinguished occasion of piracy provided little opportunity for retribution (and Seckford's position at Court undoubtedly ameliorated the offence). The suit, scrupulously presented in the Admiralty Court by its plaintiffs, was still awaiting settlement in the reign of James I.[20]

Only very occasionally, when outright pirates made the mistake of hindering Crown policy too overtly (without having first secured the right connections), was justice as swift and as brutal as the offence merited. Between 1582 and 1585, the Admiralty Court's ineffectuality in policing the coastal towns caused the Queen to suspend its judicial authority.[21] In the interregnum, her policies were implemented directly, if no more consistently than before. At Wapping, on 30 August 1583, nine men went to the scaffold on the Privy Council's order, having been found guilty of acts of piracy. Indeed, even before their trials commenced, the Council had announced that 'We intend to have a convenient number for example to be executed . . .' – and, furthermore (to ensure the magistrates concerned were not unduly swayed by such minor distractions as the need for evidence), they listed ten names of those to be so condemned, from a pool of some forty-three men originally arraigned.[22] The crimes of the condemned men had been exacerbated by repeated acts of cruelty to the crews of captured vessels (principally to encourage them to disclose their full manifests),[23] but also, and far more significantly, by the organized nature of their trade, which had made one town in Dorset – Studland – a freebooters' entrepôt to rival Baltimore. Then, as now, wrong-doing underpinned by persistence and, worse, by proficiency required sterner gestures in response; but what is most significant about this episode is not the severity of the sentences passed but their arbitrariness. The tenth man on the condemned list, William Arnewood, identified as a 'gentleman', was released almost immediately and had returned to his chosen employment several months before an official pardon was issued (he was not, according to surviving records, an informer). His less fortunate colleagues, it seems, had disqualified themselves from such leniency by being both pirates *and* expendably low-born; perfect material from which large but inexpensive points might be made. Then, as always, station had counted much more than mere culpability.

Elizabeth herself offered august proof of this. Guardian, arbiter and upholder of the commonwealth, she was a willing accomplice to acts of piracy when the deed was to her own advantage. At the very moment when Frobisher, having called in such small favours as he could secure from his former backers, was looking around for gainful employment, she was accepting her dues from the most spectacular act of piracy in English maritime history – Drake's seizure of the Spanish carrack *Nuestra Señora de la Concepción* (or *Cacafuego*). With such an example looming before him, is it likely that Frobisher would have jibed at returning to the one profession at which he was adept? The evidence of his past and future career suggests not. If he disappears from our view in 1581 – and indeed, for long periods during this decade – it was, very possibly, because he was at sea upon business that thrived more profitably in the dark.

However, he was no longer the petty offender whom Dr Lewes had chased through the ports of southern England. Having made something of a reputation – even in a manner which had caused many men to rue the day they had first heard his name – it seems that Frobisher was not now entirely cast out of the company he had acquired during the previous seven years. The north-west passage scheme has occupied our attention for obvious reasons, but England was a place stirred by projects throughout these years – half-plans, fluid, shifting proposals and dimly perceived opportunities that sought to exploit any and every chance to pluck a profit from someone else's purse. The overwhelming example of Drake's circumnavigation swiftly eclipsed the salutary lesson of Frobisher's failure; indeed, it so completely wiped clean the slate that the prudent Burghley was obliged to act as a braking influence upon several schemes intended merely to set ships into the Pacific to prey outright upon Spanish possessions. Yet Burghley himself, and other members of the Privy Council such as Leicester, Warwick, Pembroke and Walsingham, were as much speculators as they were their sovereign's principal officers of state. If some were more fastidious than others about the company they were prepared to keep, or less inclined to see in their own efforts a deliberate, Protestant response to a looming Catholic threat, they were all aware nevertheless of how few men could be relied upon as a safe pair of hands to carry their projects forward. Whatever Frobisher's culpability in one particularly ill-founded investment, he was almost certainly regarded as adept at the business of taking ships across oceans and returning them safely. This, even in the late sixteenth century, was by no means a common talent.

Circumstances were bringing the need for such talents to greater prominence at the turn of the decade. One event in particular, though not in itself a *casus belli*, dramatically altered the perceived balance of power in Europe and fostered an urgent anxiety amongst many Englishmen. This was the union of the Crowns of Portugal and Spain in 1580: the result of a short, decisive campaign which, seemingly overnight, almost doubled the extent of territories under Spanish control and – ominously for England – provided Spain with offensive naval resources in the Atlantic for the first time.[24]

Though this enlargement of Spanish power had repercussions for almost every state in Europe, it had taken few people unawares. The death of the Portuguese King Henry had been anticipated since the moment he ascended the throne, two years earlier. When the expected event was announced on 31 January 1580, Philip II – by marriage, the leading claimant to the throne – moved swiftly.[25] Alva crossed the Portuguese frontier with a Spanish army whilst Philip's foremost admiral, the marquis of Santa Cruz, blocked the Tagus estuary with his fleet, thereby sundering the seat of Portuguese government from its overseas possessions. By summer, the strategy anticipated

as long ago as 1524 by the marriage of Charles V to the Portuguese Infanta
had been realized: Philip was acknowledged as the new king of Portugal by
the nation and all its possessions save the Azores, where Terceira and several
other islands offered their fealty to the only realistic Portuguese claimant, the
Prior of Crato, Don António. His was a pitifully small dominion to set against
the fruits of Philip's aggressive and successful campaign, but the fact that he
was proclaimed at all provided Elizabeth with a fig-leaf of legitimacy in refusing to accept the union of Crowns as an accomplished fact.

To men like Walsingham and Leicester, the union of Crowns was further
fuel for their contention that the earth had not room enough for Philip II
and the forces of the Counter-Reformation. Elizabeth herself was sufficiently
moved to treat Francis Drake as a hero, rather than a pirate, when he returned
to England following his circumnavigation on 29 September that year
(though the £160,000 that fell as her share of his booty made his impeach-
ment effectively impossible in any event). Brazenly, she wore jewels taken
from the *Cacafuego* at a reception on New Year's Day 1581 at which
Ambassador Mendoza was present.[26] He saw what he was intended to see:
that Philip was not the only monarch who could take what he wished with
impunity.

The two events – Drake's phenomenally successful return and the absorp-
tion of the resources of the Portuguese empire by Spain – provided the
impetus for a rash of new English projects: the one for its fabulous example,
the other because it offered the opportunity for England to encroach upon
Portuguese possessions 'legitimately'. Walsingham, as always urging a more
active policy against Spanish interests, drew up (or possibly redrafted in his
own hand) a charter for a company to establish a permanent trade in the Far
East; anticipating the creation of the East India Company by a generation.[27]
The document may have been intended as no more than a discussion paper.
Certainly, it was not considered seriously – firstly, because it envisaged Drake
as the incorporated company's governor, an appointment that would have
been extremely provocative to Philip II; and, more practically, because the
scope of the company's authority – 'soche domynions and contreys sytuate
bayonde the Equynoctyall line' – would have made half the globe a theatre
of operations for an aggressive, Spaniard-hating sea-rover. If, however, the
Queen and her Council were not prepared to see Drake's intentions given
corporate respectability, the potential of one or several further voyages to
exploit his new spice islands contacts was irresistible. Trade with the East
remained a powerful motive for English expansionists, whether amongst the
more 'respectable' sort, such as Lord Burghley and leading members of the

1. Martin Frobisher, by Cornelius Ketel, 1577.

2. Queen Elizabeth, I by an unknown artist.

facing page:

3. (*top*) Philip II, King of Spain, by an unknown artist.

4. William Cecil, 1st Baron Burghley, by Arnold van Brounckhurst, 1570.

5. Sir Francis Drake by an unknown artist, commissioned soon after his return from the 1577–1580 circumnavigation.

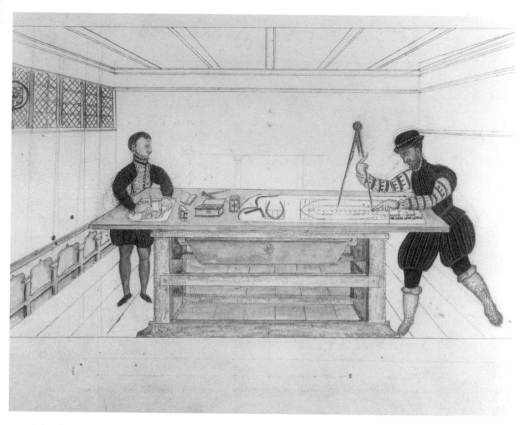

6. The shipwright Matthew Baker, architect of the bark *Gabriel* and the ship *Judith*, in his draughting office: possibly a self-portrait, from *Fragments of Ancient English Shipwrightry*.

9. Skirmish at 'Bloody Point', by John White, 1577.

facing page:

7. (*top*) 'Kalicho', Inuk captive: portrait by John White, 1577.
8. 'Arnaq' and 'Nutaaq', Inuit woman and child captured at Bloody Point: portrait by John White, 1577.

10. Armada campaign. The fleets re-engage of Gravelines, 29 July 1588, by Henrik Cornelizoom Vroom.

Muscovy Company; or amongst those whose speculative activities complemented a more robust political agenda against Spain. The dimly perceived opportunities presented by recent events now brought these disparate elements together to find a scheme that might take best advantage of Drake's achievements. As it transpired, the nature of the project was to evolve constantly as the respective motives – lawful trade, outright plunder or a creative synthesis of both – were argued and counter-argued by their proponents.

On 20 December 1580, Mendoza reported to Philip II that the Queen had sent word to the Azores to stand fast for Don António, and that English ships were being readied by Leicester to follow up Drake's late successes.[28] On 9 January 1581, he wrote again with more specific information which suggested a broad strategy for England to secure the entire Portuguese East Indies trade and simultaneously attack Spanish possessions in the Caribbean. Drake, he had heard, was to take ten ships around the Cape of Good Hope to the Moluccas; Francis Knollis (Leicester's brother-in-law and son of the Queen's Treasurer of the Household), would sail into the South Seas with an as yet undetermined force, whilst Humphrey Gilbert was to take six ships to Cuba, where he would establish and fortify a position. Interestingly, Mendoza mentioned also that Martin Frobisher was being encouraged to revive his northwest passage scheme, a suggestion that further illustrates the flaws of the Spanish intelligence network in London.[29]

Tentative preparations for some form of English response commenced, but by April no definite strategy had been decided upon. Mendoza again reported on the matter to his king, noting that a meeting had taken place between Walsingham, Leicester, Drake, John Hawkins, William Winter, Richard Bingham and Martin Frobisher, 'all the latter being experienced mariners'.[30] A preliminary scheme, endorsed by Burghley and dated that month, envisaged a fleet of eight ships and six pinnaces 'to be furnyshed to the sees in warlyke manner', with 1,000 men victualled for four months, the cost of which was estimated at £10,320.[31] Seven captains were named as potential commanders, including Drake himself, Richard Bingham, John Brewer, one Gregory, and three of Frobisher's 1578 captains, Luke Ward, Gilbert Yorke and Edward Fenton.[32] Frobisher himself was not mentioned in this document.

This note was the first indication that the ephemeral plots anticipated and reported by Mendoza at the turn of the year had hardened into a specific scheme: one that was to become known as the 'First Enterprise'. This proposed that an English fleet should fortify the island of Terceira as a future base of English activity in support of Don António, after which it would cruise in the vicinity of the Azores, awaiting the Spanish treasure fleet. If this was missed, the English fleet was to proceed to the West Indies, where it would 'range all the co(a)st . . . and sacke all the townes and spoyle whersoever they fynd them by sea or land'.[33]

The scheme was a gamble that, whatever the intentions of its promoters, might easily have brought England to outright war with Spain in 1581. It was only the fact that the fleet would sail under the flag and authority of Don António, rather than of Elizabeth, that might have prevented Philip from regarding the expedition as an outright declaration of war by England (a very shaky *might* indeed, given the evidently English origin of its component parts). The Queen herself, as ever, was not entirely committed to the scheme. She sought French support, financial as much as political: the Duc d'Anjou was currently pressing his claim for her hand in marriage, and this was a palpable way of testing his commitment. Anjou, not entirely blinded by her charms, offered nothing; and though Burghley reported that Elizabeth had become 'very cold' on the idea, desultory preparations for the voyage continued into the summer of 1581. On 29 August, Walsingham ordered the expedition's provisions to be sold off. The expedition, still at anchor, had cost £13,000 to date.[34]

In truth, the First Enterprise had been an unconscionably risky proposal. Burghley had refused outright to accept its alternative strategy of sacking the Spanish Caribbean, and had scored through that section of the proposal with his own pen. In 1581, so soon after his spectacular circumnavigation, any enterprise that set Drake loose against Spanish possessions – even if beneath a Portuguese flag – would have been an unequivocal declaration of hostilities.

Briefly, a further option – the 'Second Enterprise' – was considered: a slightly less controversial scheme wherein a fleet of up to fifty ships would sail to Calicut during 1582 to trade with Portuguese possessions; a voyage to be undertaken in partnership with Don António (again, Terceira was to be fortified on the outward passage to provide a base for future operations).[35] It is difficult to say how seriously this project was promoted, but it foundered when the Portuguese Pretender, tired of Elizabeth's prevarications, abandoned hope of effective English assistance and took himself off to France to raise more steadfast support there.

Though the Second Enterprise had swiftly followed the First into oblivion, Leicester, the principal promoter of the original scheme remained keen to put his money to some profitable use. Another, more modest project – in effect, a creative resurrection of the first Moluccas scheme – was touted among his friends and associates. This envisaged an intentionally ambiguous voyage, in which two or three ships would sail on an ostensibly peaceful expedition to trade in Moluccan spices. Such a scheme had several advantages. Being essentially a private venture, it had the potential to escape the close scrutiny and restrictions that would inhibit a Crown project. This gave it a certain flexibility – that is, lawful trade might easily be supplemented by less orthodox means of acquisition, should a suitably laden carrack hove into view *en route*. To facilitate such an agenda, however, it was vital that Leicester and his fellow investors be allowed to put their choice of man in command.

Or rather, their second choice. Drake, himself an enthusiastic supporter of the new project, was to be its third most substantial investor after Leicester and the merchant Henry Oughtred, with a personal venture of £667;[36] but Elizabeth would not allow him to take command of even this supposedly less controversial expedition. Someone else was needed: less provocative to Philip II but with the authority to carry the expedition to its far destination. Of those names appended to the April estimate for the 'First Enterprise', none was considered suitable – at least, not by the latter part of 1581. On 7 September, Mendoza had another name, let slip from the mouth of Leicester himself. The same day, he reported to Philip II: 'Leicester says that the Queen will fit out 3 ships to sail about Christmas under Frobisher, and if the adherents of Don Antonio are found numerous in the East Indies they will effect a landing, otherwise they would carry merchandise for trade, and go to the Moluccas.'[37] By 1 October, Mendoza was reporting that the scheme had been slimmed down to a single vessel of some 300 tons, but on 4 December, he claimed that the voyage would after all be undertaken by three ships, including, probably, the *Galleon Leicester* (formerly *Galleon Oughtred*), currently the subject of negotiations between Leicester and Henry Oughtred.

The circumstances that led to Frobisher's appointment are not known. Burghley had apparently not considered him suitable as recently as April, but that had been an entirely different venture – at least, in the Lord Treasurer's mind. It is not clear, furthermore, that Burghley had personally chosen the names he had set down. Certainly, the first of these – Drake's – would not have been his preference.[38] The others were fairly uncontroversial, but hardly capable of inspiring the loyalty of men required to pass around half the globe. Someone else had been needed; someone other than those considered acceptable by Burghley.

Leicester and Drake did not share the Lord Treasurer's concern to have a commander who would stick to the letter of his official instructions; but from their perspective, what were Frobisher's qualifications to lead this expedition? He had experience of commanding a large number of ships upon an ocean voyage, and a good record of preserving his men from unnecessary casualties. These were laudable qualities, and extremely apposite for the new project; but they were probably not, in themselves, decisive. The principal attraction for Leicester and Drake may have been a further talent; one that Frobisher had perfected *prior* to 1576, in voyages that had much less to do with lawful trade. Though his experience since then had brought him a certain reputation as an effective commander, it certainly did not push him forward as the first choice of men devoted only to extending England's commercial interests; but neither Leicester nor Drake could be accused of having such a narrow preoccupation.

Frobisher's connection with the project may, possibly, be dated from his attendance at a formal reception, held in Bermondsey in April 1581, to celebrate the successful return of Drake's epic voyage. The Queen was there, and so too, therefore, were several foreign diplomats. One of these was the French Ambassador Castelnau de la Mauvissière, who spotted Frobisher in the crowd. The Frenchman engaged him in conversation, asking of his late north-west venture. Frobisher was reported to have spoken of '. . . the profit that the Queen would find if by the same means he shortens by two-thirds the way needed to reach . . . all Asia, but he never has the time to begin his voyage as he wants to do another time because he lost time searching for gold mines in which profit is small and the expenses high.'[39]

The words of a frustrated, disappointed man in his cups, possibly; made more bitter by the contrast between his own fortunes and those of the guest of honour at that reception. Yet Francis Drake was also interested in the north-west passage. He had sought its western exit whilst in the Pacific (though not with any great assiduity), and apparently he now expressed the opinion to Frobisher that he should make a further attempt to find it – perhaps this was the 'encouragement' picked up and later reported by Mendoza to his king. Superficially, it was hardly more than polite conversation, yet it seems to have been made with a firm, though unrelated purpose. From their first acquaintance, Drake does not seem to have regarded Frobisher merely – or even principally – as a navigator. They had probably not met prior to that occasion, but already they shared enough mutual contacts, particularly among the large pool of privateers that infested West Country ports, for Drake to know precisely where Frobisher's best talents lay. Given the true, secret aims of the forthcoming venture, it is not unlikely that almost immediately he came to see in this aggressive Yorkshireman a surrogate for his own, denied presence in the voyage.

Several men who had accompanied Drake in 1577 – John Drake and William Hawkins the younger among the most prominent of them – were also to sail with the new expedition, and their priorities had little to do with peaceful trade. Once before, the Pacific Ocean had been their almost unguarded hunting ground; it was certainly Drake's – and very probably Leicester's – intention that it should be so once more. In light of this priority, what sort of man would they have sought to lead their expedition, if not one to whom the vessels of other nations were a natural prey?

Whatever was privily discussed that day at Bermondsey, the speed with which Frobisher was involved in the preparations for the voyage was striking (notwithstanding the relatively recent lessons of the north-west enterprise), and confirms the early ascendancy of the Drake party within the project.[40] He was apparently enthusiastic about the intentions of its backers (or rather, certain intentions of some of its backers), and invested £300 of his own money – funds from unknown but probably disreputable activities – to prove it. We may be sure that the return he was seeking had very little to do with the trading goods, some £2,000 in value, that were to be carried in the voyage;[41] nevertheless, having made a palpable commitment to the project, he worked hard to see it succeed. It was he who, on behalf of Leicester, negotiated and signed the final sale agreement for the *Galleon Oughtred*,[42] and also initiated an offer on the adventurers' behalf for a second ship, the *Edward Bonaventure* (the Earl of Oxford, one of the principal adventurers, was involved with him in these negotiations; it seems, therefore, that he bore little malice in respect of his recent, heavy losses in a matter of New World ore).[43] Letters to Frobisher from Simon Fernando (the Portuguese pilot of the *Galleon*) and his old lieutenant Edward Fenton, touching upon a lack of money for supplies and Fenton's dislike of William Hawkins, indicate that he assumed a good deal of responsibility for the smooth progress of the project – and, surprisingly, a conciliatory role between the factions that very quickly established their positions on opposite sides of the enterprise.[44] In September, Drake wrote to Leicester, offering a ship of 180 tons for the voyage as part of his own venture, 'but if yo(u)r L. w(i)th m(aste)r Furbusher thinke best to have the little new barke and the 2. pinaces I will bestowe the like'. Drake concluded, with uncharacteristic deference: 'I am willinge to follow the directio(n) of yo(u)r L(ordship) and m(aste)r Frobusher in ev(er)y respect.'[45] Frobisher may also have personally selected and arranged for the hiring of many of the mariners for the voyage: a margin note to the preparatory arrangements drawn up by Leicester's secretary, Arthur Atye, makes a brief reference to 'the speciall men M(aste)r Frobisher desireth'.[46] It is clear, therefore, that his input into this voyage was much greater than in the 1576 north-west expedition, and in light of this, it seems all the more perplexing that on 27 February 1582 he was removed – seemingly without warning – as the expedition's prospective commander, to be replaced by Edward Fenton.[47]

There were in fact several, possibly related reasons for this abrupt reversal. Upon Burghley's initiative, many aspects of the organization of the expedition had been put in the hands of alderman Sir George Barne, William Towerson and John Castelyn, all senior members of the Russia Company (the first two had attempted to resist Frobisher's north-west project on his initial approach to the company in 1574, whilst the brother of the latter gentleman, it will be recalled, had previously tasted the sharp edge of his temper at the Dartford works).[48] Their involvement had been secured not least because their expertise in setting out long-range trading voyages was apposite – *if* this was to be a trading voyage. In giving them these responsibilities, Burghley may have spoken of the secret agendas of some of the adventurers; certainly, the appointees' efforts, as the preparations progressed, were increasingly devoted to hampering the more aggressive aims of Leicester and Drake. They put their own men into the ships, including some who were almost certainly not those whom Frobisher regarded as 'speciall men'. Nicholas Chancellor, purser in the three north-west voyages, was so appointed for the *Edward Bonaventure*; Richard Fairweather the younger, son of Michael Lok's partner in setting out the *Beare Leicester* in 1578, became master's mate on the *Galleon Leicester*; and most provocatively, the chief pilot appointed to carry the expedition to its goal on what was to have been Frobisher's flagship was one Christopher Hall of Limehouse. When Mendoza reported to Philip that Frobisher had refused to lead the expedition because the Muscovy Company had forced a 'lieutenant' upon him, it was possibly Hall to whom he referred, rather than Fenton, with whom Frobisher seems to have worked amicably throughout the winter of 1581–2, and who had been expected to join the expedition for a number of months beforehand.[49]

Barne, Towerson and Castelin seem to have gone further than merely recommending suitable officers for the expedition; in a document which Taylor ascribes to the Russia Company, draft instructions for the expedition appear to anticipate and deflect the potential for trouble: 'That noe other gentlemen be appointed to goe on the voiage but the three captaines specified, the rest to be Factors and meere Seamen: for avoydance of superfluous

Charge and hindrance of ye voiage, and those to be appointed by soche as are committes for the voiage.'[50]

In other words, the less influence over the arrangements for and aims of the voyage that Drake and his friends enjoyed, the better. On 20 March, following Frobisher's removal, a meeting was held at Muscovy House to finalize the respective number of mariners, merchants and gentlemen who were to go on the voyage. As Taylor has observed, it seems to have been convened almost solely with the intention of keeping the number of 'idle men' – that is, those who would go for reasons that had nothing to do with honest trade – to a minimum.[51] Three days earlier, Henry Oughtred had written to Leicester, complaining of the company's malign influence on the preparations: ' . . . we might have bene on the vyage long synce (at less) charges and a muche speadyer retorne had (there not been) lyngeryng convocations of the Moskovia Howse (who) have over greate speech as many of judgement . . .'.[52]

The priorities and manpower imposed by the Muscovy men probably made Frobisher's continuing involvement impossible, even had they been willing to see him command the expedition. Though the ostensible purpose of the voyage had been to trade, he had in reality been offered the opportunity to be set loose in the Pacific with two well-armed ships, to revisit Drake's towering achievement there but with far greater resources. It is difficult to envisage a purpose or opportunity that accorded more perfectly with every fibre of Frobisher's being; yet as the Russia company's hold on the priorities of the coming expedition tightened, that prospect not only diminished – it was replaced by an implicit obligation to submit himself to merchants' priorities once more.

On the Russia Company's part, they were aware of Frobisher's antipathy to the dragging process of lawful trade, and had good cause to fear it. They had an ally in Burghley, whose eagerness to antagonize Spain was less than that of Leicester, and certainly much less than Drake's. Whether this distrust of Frobisher's motives was sufficient in itself to have him removed against the wishes of the Drake party is questionable, but there seems also to have been a more immediate issue – that of his alleged dishonesty.

Michael Lok's previous tirades against Frobisher had been fuelled by their mutual hostility; but his accusations regarding the misappropriation of mariners' funds, theft of company equipment and 'evill victualling' seem to have received considerable circumstantial support from Christopher Hall and Edward Fenton during preparations for this new enterprise. Richard Madox, appointed as chaplain on the voyage, later reported in his personal diary that

Hall accused Frobisher of having been given £1,600 for victualling the *Galleon Leicester* and *Edward Bonaventure*, but that he had spent only £500 of this and pocketed the rest; that Fenton believed the expedition light of 20 tons of beer 'by Furbushers meanes' (on 18 October, Madox would express a similar fear in his diary: ' . . . would God all that beer that we look forward to and bought with silver could be found in the hold of our ship. But it is to be feared that Furbusher has played us a trick . . .'); and Madox himself surmised that a minor epidemic of colic on the *Galleon Leicester* was caused by Frobisher's 'man', Anthony Fisher (perhaps the mariner of that name who sailed in the 1578 expedition to Meta Incognita), whom he suspected of having tainted their wheat supply with cheaper rye.[53]

The ultimate source of these accusations may have been the purser of the *Galleon Leicester*, Nicholas Chancellor, the man with principal responsibility for supplies and disbursements. Chancellor had much previous experience of Frobisher's methods of handling funds in the three north-west voyages, and was a known associate of Michael Lok. He was also, most pertinently, a Muscovy man; and may have thought it proper to inform his employers of what they should expect. If the warning was given, it was apparently heeded and the necessary evidence quickly found. The swiftness of Frobisher's departure from the enterprise, and lack of documentary information as to its cause, suggests a matter of some embarrassment, dealt with decisively.

It would have been of small comfort to Frobisher at the time, but the merchants' worst fears for his leadership were comfortably exceeded by the performance of his replacement. The voyage, under Fenton's command, was an unmitigated disaster. Frobisher's substitute had not been a popular choice, even before the ships departed from England. Henry Oughtred regarded him as much inferior to William Hawkins: that 'his experience is verye small his mynd highe, his (temper) of the manne(r) colerick, thrall to the collycke and st(ubborn) . . .'.[54] Oughtred was almost certainly partial (friends of Hawkins were most definitely not partisans of Fenton also), yet Fenton had moved on considerably in the world since acting as vice-general in the 1578 north-west voyage, and this may have contributed in no small way to the 'highe' attitude he now displayed. He had married Thomasina, daughter of Benjamin Gonson, former Treasurer of the Navy, and thus had become John Hawkins's brother-in-law (his stark antipathy towards William Hawkins seems to have been with regard to the young man's personal loyalty to Drake and his priorities, rather than directed against the family as a whole, with whom he enjoyed an amicable relationship). Prior to 1582, his record of command at sea – particularly during the 1578 voyage – was an honourable one. Certainly, the jealousies he seemed to have aroused in Frobisher during their former association hints at qualities that an impartial observer might regard as laudable. Yet the consistency of recorded opinion expressed against him in this new enterprise suggests that he had learned too much of Frobisher's methods of government at sea without acquiring the strength of character to sustain them.[55]

Fenton's small fleet passed as far as Plymouth before internecine warfare commenced. The two parties on board – merchants and 'Drake's men' – clearly had irreconcilable expectations of their voyage; their admiral, fearing mutiny from all quarters, began to exhibit tokens of paranoia and indecisiveness to almost clinical proportions. An over-long, feverish visit to the west coast of Africa, Fenton's apparent plan to make himself king of the Atlantic island of St Helena, their complete ignorance of the waters through which they sailed (even Christopher Hall's skills failed him utterly),[56] the constant bickering and subsequent threats of court martial (at one point Fenton considered turning his guns on the *Edward Bonaventure*), the defection of the *Edward* after an indecisive battle with Spanish ships off St Vincent and the loss of the small bark *Francis* – the catalogue of mishaps, disasters and inadequacies made Frobisher's leadership during the north-west voyages seem like a model of sage government. Whatever Frobisher's own expectations for the 1582 voyage might have been, it is almost certain that he would have provided a better return for all parties. Being at one with the priorities of the Drake party, he would have needed to placate only the merchants (a less boisterous element, particularly at sea), whose reservations would in any case have dissipated upon a successful conclusion to the enterprise. With that measure of harmony imposed, to have reached the Moluccas should not have been too onerous a task. Once there, it would have required a poor effort indeed not to make some form of profit, and any ship sighted upon their passage – of whatever nation, one suspects – would only have added to the dividend paid out upon their return. Though provocative, the original choice of Frobisher had not been entirely unwise; like Drake, he provided a happy blend of strong leadership and weak scruples.

This felicitous voyage had not taken place, however. Cast out of the 1582 enterprise by merchants, his £300 venture lost in the subsequent debacle (though possibly partially covered by his idiosyncratic victualling practices), Frobisher was once more unemployed. This time, however, he lay under no cloud; indeed, almost immediately after his removal, he received a small but surprising consolation prize, when, on 17 March 1582, the burgesses of Southampton made him a freeman of the town, probably in recognition of the significant new business he had put their way in the preceding months whilst the 1582 expedition was being outfitted there.[57] Furthermore, having been the personal choice of Drake and Leicester, and playing no part in the disasters of the voyage itself, his reputation was undamaged. To the contrary, the total eclipse of Fenton's reputation, and of everyone who sailed with him, may have helped stifle accusations regarding Frobisher's alleged embezzlements; perhaps, even, it placed his record during the north-west voyages in a rounder perspective. The corruption of captains was regrettable but endemic, and accepted as a fact in sixteenth-century England: it was rather their conduct and effectiveness at sea that made, or destroyed, reputations.

On 26 April 1582, Ambassador Mendoza, who had been watching preparations for the voyage carefully, informed Philip II that Frobisher, though removed from command of the enterprise, was preparing three further vessels with the intention of reaching the Moluccas before Fenton's expedition.[58] This supplementary expedition never sailed, though the project must have been active when Fenton's ships departed from England. From the South Atlantic, Madox later reported that Fenton gave two captured Spanish friars letters of safe conduct, addressed to Frobisher, requiring him not to molest them but rather to hasten to follow Fenton's ships around the Cape of Good Hope.[59] The intended voyage was probably stayed for the same reasons that Drake's proposed 1581 expedition had been aborted, but the fact that it was advanced so far reflects the continuing interest of Leicester and Walsingham in breaking into the Pacific. In reporting it, Mendoza had put together two and two because he was aware that the Leicester–Drake–Frobisher connection remained unsevered. It was one that was to be in existence still when Frobisher next emerged fully into the light of posterity.

Again, however, the end of his involvement in a prominent enterprise marked the beginning of a period of anonymity and – ostensibly at least – of unemployment. Between 1582 and 1585, there are few extant references to Frobisher, and most relate to the same scheme. In 1583, Sir George Peckham published *A true reporte, of the late discoveries, and possession, taken in the right of the Crowne of England, of the New-founde Landes* to promote wider interest in Humphrey Gilbert's scheme for the English colonization of North America (Peckham himself had obtained assignments under Gilbert's 1578 patent to occupy and exploit up to four million acres of virgin American soil). In this work, Peckham reproduced a poem purportedly written by Martin Frobisher, in which the discoverer of the supposed north-west passage lauds his own achievement and dares other to follow:

A pleasant ayre, a sweete and firtell soile,
A certain gaine, a never dying praise:
An easie passage, voide of loathsome toile,
Found out by some, and knowen to me the waie.
All this is there, then who will refraine to trie:
That loves to live abroad, or dreades to die.[60]

Literate members of Frobisher's expeditions to Meta Incognita might well have discovered their former travails to have been 'voide of loathsome toile' with a degree of bitter amusement – as much, perhaps, as at the prospect of their former commander putting pen to paper to run off a few lines of doggerel. This was almost certainly Peckham's romantic deception, but it had been made in the service of a good cause, and may not have seemed so implausible then as now. In an age in which headless men were still believed to rule fantastical lands, even an erudite Frobisher remained a possibility.

Yet there was a more practical strand to his involvement with Peckham. In June 1582, articles of intent were signed by a small syndicate of adventurers intending to offer shares in a scheme to exploit Peckham's licence.[61] Its principals were named as Sir George Peckham himself, Sir Thomas Gerrard, Sir Edmund Brudenell, Sir William Catesby, William Shelley, Philip Basset, Sir William Stanley, Richard Bingham and Martin Frobisher. Several of these men were prominent Catholics, their intention being to found a colony of like-minded souls far from the malevolent influence of the Recusancy Act; but the latter three were to have a more immediate role in the scheme.

The first article of the agreement provided the statement of intent: '. . . the next intended voyage for possession or conquest of parts of America, and set them to sea before the last day of March next (that is, March 1583) by the conduct of Standley, Bingam or Forbusher or one of them authorised as General by Sea.' Article 32 refined this: 'Standley, Bingham and Forbusher agree to be ready for the seas before 31 March, and undertake to discover four islands and 4,000,000 acres on the adjoining mainland, without any action unjustifiable in England.'

The scheme did not proceed on its stated schedule. Spanish diplomatic efforts to block it, with their disheartening implication that preserving Spanish rights over the New World took precedence over the welfare of fellow Catholics, seem to have been successful. Stanley, furthermore, was assigned to Irish duties in January 1583 and was effectively removed from the project. Nevertheless, Peckham continued to plan for an American colony; he received further assignments of land from Gilbert, and joined his rights to those of

Sir Philip Sydney, who himself had received assignments totalling some 3,000,000 acres of territory. Gilbert, meanwhile, prepared his own fleet to take possession of his patented lands across the ocean.

His death at sea on 9 September 1583 was a fatal blow to existing projects for western planting, though preliminary arrangements for Peckham's voyage continued after a fashion. By this time, it seems that Frobisher had become the most likely man to lead it. On 1 April 1584, Hakluyt wrote to Francis Walsingham from Paris, making a reference to 'those westerne voyages', partly on behalf of Sir Horatio Palavacini, the Queen's indefatigable debt-collector in the Low Countries. Hakluyt wrote that Palavacini, 'yf he were moved therunto by the least word from yo(u)r honor', would venture £100 either in a scheme of Christopher Carleill's (according to Quinn, this was possibly a plan conceived by Carleill and Walsingham to double-cross Gilbert);[62] or, 'if master Carlile bee gon, yet yt might come in good time to serve M(aste)r Frobishers turne, yf yo(u)r wisdome shold like wel of yt, seeing he setteth not forth as I vnderstand vntill beginning of May . . . '.[63]

Notwithstanding the apparent firmness of Hakluyt's assumption (or Palavacini's implied interest), the scheme appears to have died soon after. Peckham found it impossible to raise sufficient interest in a colonizing scheme amongst the merchants of Southampton, Bristol and Exeter, and in London there was little sympathy for its strong Catholic agenda. Peckham himself was in prison before the end of the year, having been discovered harbouring Catholic priests; without him, only Sir Philip Sydney continued to press for a new voyage, but Elizabeth personally forbade him to pursue his project. For Frobisher, who doubtless cared nothing for the confessional complications inherent in his prospective employment, the comfort of a reputation partly restored continued to be but a poor return for yet another aborted venture.

There is a further, curious reference to his activities, dating from the year 1582, which places him as a member of an embassy to the Court of the Danish King Frederik II.[64] If this was indeed an 'embassy' in the diplomatic sense, it seems highly unlikely that Frobisher was a part of it. Even setting aside his involvement with the Leicester–Drake project in the early months of that year, and his subsequent association with Peckham (which, together, required him to be in England until at least the end of June), he had no previous – and indeed was to have no future – experience as a diplomat. In fact, it would be difficult to conceive of someone less versed in the subtleties that diplomacy demanded of its practitioners. Nevertheless, developing English interests in the Baltic that year allow us to speculate that Frobisher might indeed have travelled to the region, if only in a supplementary capacity. Thomas

Allen, former north-west adventurer and merchant of the Queen's Baltic stores (the 'Queen's Merchant for Danske'), was a frequent voyager to Poland and 'Eastland', and may have found some limited employment for his former associate in one of the voyages that served to replenish England's precious stocks of tar, hemp and masts. However, what evidence we possess implies that theirs had been an uneasy relationship – particularly after Allen succeeded Michael Lok as treasurer of the enterprise – and this makes their continuing association seem unlikely. A more realistic possibility dates from the latter part of 1582, when the Eastland Company presented a proposal to the city council of the Hanse port of Ebling and their titular lord, the Polish King Stephen Bathory, requesting permission to establish their entrepôt there.[65] This, conceivably, was backed up by simultaneous English representations to the Danish King, who was extremely sensitive to any extension of English economic power in the region (vitally, he controlled the Øresund through which the Eastland Company ships had to pass to enter the Baltic). If this mission did indeed take place, it is not unlikely that Frobisher was employed to transport it. The only firm extant evidence for the episode is in the letter Frederik II wrote to Elizabeth in August of that year, saying that he had recently 'approached' Frobisher and asked him to command a Danish expedition to Greenland to re-emphasize the Danish-Norwegian claim to that land (it is equally possible that they were no more than correspondents, though the wording implies personal contact).[66] Frobisher, apparently, expressed a willingness to take up the appointment, subject to obtaining his Queen's permission. Nothing more came of the offer (there is no extant reply to the king's letter); Frederik's claims were probably considered a potential threat to, or infringement upon, England's own claim to 'West England' as established by Frobisher himself in 1578; though English confusion regarding the geographical realities of Greenland was probably more germane in ensuring Elizabeth's silence on the matter. Frederik seems to have made a further approach to Frobisher in 1586, and received a short letter, dated 21 March 1587, which promised a more detailed response.[67] None seems to have been drafted subsequently.

Neither this episode nor any other of Frobisher's half-tastes of employment during these years suggest that his career was about to recover in any significant manner from the disaster of the north-west enterprise. However, one other document, drafted sometime during 1583, offers firm evidence that his reputation remained more robust than his prospects. Resentment of John Hawkins's stewardship of the navy by his fellow officers (Sir William Winter in particular was a long-term brake upon his intentions) had risen to such a pitch by the latter half of 1583 that the Privy Council appointed a commission, drawn from its own numbers, to investigate the claims and counter-claims of the protagonists.[68] The commissioners were Burghley, the Lord Admiral Lincoln, Lord Chamberlain Howard, Francis Walsingham, and the Chancellor of the Exchequer, Sir Walter Mildmay. With two exceptions, these gentlemen had very personal (that is, financial) reasons to think ill of Frobisher; yet his was among the names appointed as a sub-commission from which the commissioners could obtain additional assistance and advice, should this prove necessary. Other sub-commissioners included Drake, the Ralegh brothers and Henry Palmer, so this was by no means a list of unemployed or journeymen sea-captains. There is no evidence that Frobisher was ever called upon by the commission, but that is hardly relevant. That he should have been named at all is the clearest indication of the entirely sensible distinction made between achievement and ability, by a Queen and Council who had extremely finite resources upon which to call.

Nevertheless, reputation without employment was at best a thin gruel. A non-existent literary career, a peripheral involvement in western planting, a highly doubtful interest in the arts of diplomacy and a probable return to privateering apart, Frobisher's activities during these years are at best half-glimpsed in a very sparse paper-trail. Once more, lack of evidence may indicate only that he was not caught despoiling the wrong ships; what is certain, however, is that his involvement in the 1582 Moluccas scheme was the last in which he was to commit himself to the priorities of those whom he preferred to rob. For the final twelve years of his life, he was to set himself to occupations in which his skills and objectives would be aligned far more precisely than had been allowed by the suffocating restrictions of trade and commerce – though in the process, paradoxically, he would find many merchants becoming much more sympathetic to his own preoccupations. Whether, for Frobisher, this was the beginning of self-awareness or merely a matter of necessity cannot be determined; but he was to find a much happier place in the service of those for whom war with Spain was not only an inevitability, but a vast opportunity also.

PART THREE

The End of Peace: 1585–88

The earth was made for the children of men, and neither the Spaniard, nor the Frenche, hath a prerogative too dwell alone, as though God appointed them a greater portion then other nations.[1]

FOURTEEN

Broken Amity

The slide towards outright Anglo-Spanish conflict was, as we have seen, a complex process. It has been the subject of many exhaustive studies, to which the present author will add little of substance. Again, however, a brief recapitulation is necessary to illustrate how Frobisher's later career was both a product of, and fertilizer upon, the roots of that conflict.

One of the most profound developments during these years was the conceptual shift away from old certainties as to where the greatest threat to England lay. France, for as long as she had existed as a recognizable polity, had represented the principal potential danger to English interests – even to English independence. The occasional period of amity between the two countries had almost always resulted from mutual exhaustion or fear of a third power whose interests, briefly, seemed inimical to both; all had been less in the nature of true peace than temporary deferrals of the inevitable. The French Wars of Religion changed this historic relationship. They removed, for many decades, the possibility of substantial French interference in English affairs, and in so doing rendered old fears and hatreds largely redundant. Once Elizabeth had in turn expunged the memory of Calais and her own, increasingly unconvincing claim to the throne of France, Anglo-French relations slowly stabilized. Guise and the Catholic League continued, periodically, to present a threat to English interests, and the danger of an Angevin champion of Dutch interests in the 1580s offered a brief, fraught glimpse of a new and unwelcome concentration of power; but France herself could no longer threaten England effectively without Spanish assistance.

As we have seen, English antagonism towards Spain was, in contrast, neither deeply rooted nor, for many years at least, perceived to be natural. As a nurturer of heresy, Elizabeth's rule was of course anathema to Catholic princes throughout Europe; but that this did not necessarily mean that her removal was universally considered obligatory, or even desirable. The political interests of Philip II, so often teased by the activities of English privateers, would nevertheless have been ill-served by an outright Guise victory that united the Crowns of England and Scotland in the person of the Catholic Mary Stuart (in this context, it should be recalled that successive popes had been unsuccessfully urging Philip to restore the Catholic faith in England since July 1568).[2] Elizabeth's religion, though distasteful to the Spanish king, remained very much a subordinate matter for as long as circumstances dictated it should. It was only when the imperatives of sovereign power and spiritual conscience began to converge that the slide towards open conflict began to seem less of a matter of regret than of approaching resolution. Yet that conflict was by no means unavoidable, even as late as 1580. Elizabeth did not wish for war with Spain, and Philip, for a time at least, was happy to oblige. Princes, however, do not always determine the fate of nations.

Elizabeth was not – and could not be – a populist ruler in any sense, but her subjects' priorities and their consequences were to exercise a huge influence upon her policies. Unfortunately, the common man did not possess her acute sense of where England's strategic interests lay, nor care to look beyond his own, narrow partialities. Popular antipathy towards Spain, growing throughout the 1570s, had largely dated from 1567, when the Duke of Alva's polyglot army had marched into the Netherlands to expunge the canker of resistance to Hapsburg rule. English sympathies with the rebels had since grown stronger, but were, to say the least, disingenuous: they pretended an affection towards a race that had long been their closest trading associates but with whom, by 1567, many no longer chose to trade. In 1566, popular riots in Antwerp and elsewhere had not brought English merchants flooding into the country in a display of confessional solidarity – it had sent them elsewhere, looking for an alternative, less troublesome venue. They had found it in Hamburg. The charter of the Merchant Adventurers was adjusted to allow them to maintain the regulation of their trade outside Antwerp, for so long the seat of their government, and the venerable economic ties between England and the Netherlands began to unravel thereafter.[3] As this sundering of old certainties assisted the physical process of disengagement from their old Burgundian relationship, it also allowed the ever sentimental English to condemn Spanish excesses in the Low Countries without suffering the once inevitable economic penalties of doing so. We must assume that the adjectives 'plucky little' did not have common currency in sixteenth-century England; but it is fair to say that growing English sympathy with the cause of the rebel provinces was fuelled more by the apparent size of the odds against them – and by implications of their defeat – than by any substantial sense of brotherhood.

Meanwhile, isolated events elsewhere further encouraged anti-Spanish feeling in England, no matter where the justice of a particular cause lay. Deprived of the traditional object of his contempt by the temporary neutralization of France, the Englishman found a satisfying substitute in the Spaniard, whom he came to regard – with very little evidence – as a cruel, objectionable creature, both cowardly and overbearing. Hawkins's defeat at San Juan de Ulua in 1568 generated a popular, if brief, fury in England, and the establishment of the Council of Troubles – the so-called 'Council of Blood' – in the Netherlands, which formalized the persecution of those with whom many Englishmen shared a creed (if only in opposition to Rome), created antipathies that fed a growing perception of Spanish power as morally wrong, if not actually evil. Though England and Spain mended their relations at a political level in the early 1570s, English popular opinion – outside commercial circles – hardly acknowledged this. Gradually, the economic jealousies and spiritual antipathies that had previously driven English interlopers to circumvent or encroach upon Spanish interests developed into something more: a sense of direct rivalry. Nations need the currency of hatred for very few years before mistrust becomes instinctive enmity, particularly where there is little desire to have it otherwise. Long before the Queen or the majority of her councillors came to regard war with Spain as inevitable, the mass of her subjects had unthinkingly accepted their own truth: that enduring friendship between England and Spain was impossible, no matter how it had seemed formerly.[4]

Popular xenophobic sentiment aside, a growing degree of self-interest was generated by economic activities which replaced the older commercial ties. The English market at Antwerp had collapsed, submerged beneath long-term economic problems and confessional strife; what followed was not simply the resurrection of the same activities in a different location, but the rise of an alternative economic sub-culture. Whilst the exportation of English cloths remained a paramount activity, it was supplemented by the growing volume of trade from more distant markets – many of which lay within the bounds of Spanish-Portuguese interests – and also by another, increasingly important source of foreign earnings: prize goods seized upon the seas.

At the beginning of her reign, the Queen's use of the privateer as an instrument of policy had been sporadic, though of necessity it became more prevalent as her relations with Catholic Europe degenerated. Occasionally, as we have seen, she sought to curb or even end the activities of English privateers; yet the *djinn*, once released, could not be forced back into the bottle. Throughout the 1570s, even in the face of those half-hearted efforts to reestablish the rule of law at sea that we have noted previously, more and more of the foreign produce entering English homes came from stolen, rather than traded, cargoes.[5] Gradually, the concept of privateering as a legitimate activity had become acceptable to the English people, because its fruits were derived from a source that they were coming to accept as their natural enemy. When, in June 1585, an entire generation of English merchants – many of whom had formerly lamented the activities of privateers – abandoned their struggle to preserve legitimate commercial links with Spain, they crossed only a personal Rubicon. Upon its far bank they found most of the rest of English society, waiting for them. What was soon to become a national obsession – the interception of the Spanish treasure fleets – may easily be mistaken for an appropriate strategy of war; in fact, it may be more accurately described as the culminating ambition of a profession that had already staked out its partialities in a thousand lesser encounters.

English and Spanish diplomatic activity did not so much reflect these certainties as stagger on behind, tied to the imperatives they generated. Naturally, where Anglo-Spanish spheres of interest clashed head-on, the potential for further discord was greatest. The most intractable issue remained the Low Countries, where Elizabeth had tried to maintain a policy of honest broker between Philip II and his rebellious subjects since 1572. She sincerely believed that Philip had a legitimate right to uphold his rule in his own possessions, even to use of force to achieve it; had she believed otherwise, how might her own claims to, and actions in, Ireland, have been justified? Thus, her attempts to preserve the rebels from extinction were not based upon any sense of natural justice – it is probably fair to say that she loved their Calvinist element no more than Catholics, though the latter represented a far greater threat to English interests – but rather upon the political consequences of that extinction. An overwhelming Catholic victory in the Netherlands, even if that of an ostensible friend to England, was an unthinkable prospect. Outright Spanish victory remained preferable to an alternative, French domination of the Low Countries, but even that fundament of English policy was subject to the vagaries of time and chance. If, subsequent to the victory of the Counter-Reformation in the Netherlands, France also reverted entirely to Catholicism and ended its long enmity with Spain, how long might England survive the peace? The rebel provinces were therefore a vital resource; by simply continuing to exist, they provided England with a foreign policy by default, though it was one that required an extremely deft touch. How to ensure their continuance without causing an irreparable breach with Spain was the central problem of Elizabeth's Netherlands policy. Yet even had she been allowed to pursue its solution unhampered by her subjects' narrower agendas, it is hardly possible that she might have succeeded.

For Philip II in turn, peace with England had always seemed preferable to war. What made this impossible, eventually, was the widening chasm that lay between his understanding of his imperial dignity and the extent to which Englishmen were prepared to acknowledge it. He was, in the strictest sense, more sinned against than sinning. The seeds of his antipathy towards England lay not so much in the organic hatreds of clashing religious dogmas (regarding which he had long exhibited remarkable circumspection), but in their physical corollaries: Elizabeth's interference in the Low Countries and the increasing pin-pricks of English encroachment upon his more distant possessions. As time passed, he came to see these irritations as being far less the fruits of political necessity or individual enterprise than as the reflection of a concerted policy: as though Englishmen had come to regard Spain herself as unworthy of their respect or friendship. Though by temperament a cautious man, he was also the ruler of a large swathe of the known world. His personal pride was admirably flexible when circumstance and God required, but that of his station could not allow itself to be tested indefinitely if his subjects were not to draw all the wrong lessons. Whether the necessary physic for this ailment was war could not yet be determined at the beginning of the 1580s; but the more that Englishmen considered it so, the more their assumption gained a natural momentum that Philip had little reason to resist.

FIFTEEN

The West Indies Raid

Francis Drake's personal declaration of war with Spain, it has been said, pre-dated that of his Queen by a decade; a claim that rather underestimates his enthusiasm. The mauling of Hawkins's third slaving expedition had been a cathartic experience for Drake (though he himself had managed to escape the debacle), and the various projects he had undertaken since that time had been underpinned by the same obsessive strategy – to attack the economic and mili-tary power of Spain at every opportunity. Like Frobisher, he had sought fame and fortune for their own sake, but in the process he had not allowed himself to be distracted from the one infallible means by which those goals might be realized – stealing the assets of the Spanish empire. His involvement in the 1582 Moluccas project was merely a continuation of the work of his circum-navigation, though it is almost certain that the Spice Islands' trade would have been only a secondary priority had he commanded the later expedition. He had been prevented from doing so because the Queen, knowing perfectly well his capacity for generating events that possessed their own momentum, did not wish to anticipate a conflict – a very expensive conflict – that might yet be avoided.

Time, however, was on Drake's side. Philip II's dominions were so widely dispersed that nexes of conflict were created by the very refusal of other nations – particularly those with ocean-going vessels – to accept a world-order decreed by papal bull. For many years, the antagonisms created by the Refor-mation had been subordinated to the needs of men's purses; but the further the strands of English interests expanded into the oceans, the more likely a reckoning between the largest Protestant power and the Spanish Hapsburg

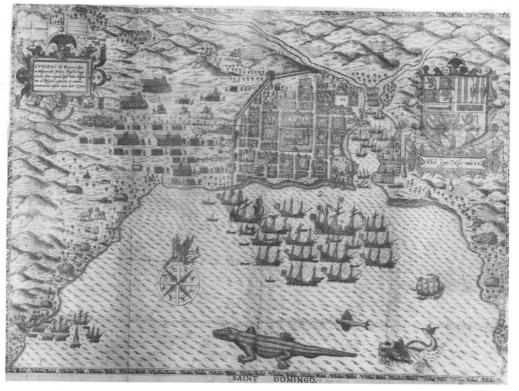

4. View of Santo Domingo by Baptista Boazio. By courtesy of the John Carter Brown
Library at Brown University.

dominions became. In Drake's mind, that likelihood had long been a certainty. The apparently decisive success of Parma in the Low Countries, the
occasional threat of Spanish intervention in 'English' affairs (that is, Ireland),
and, above all, Philip's seizure of Portugal's vast overseas empire in 1580: these
ominous developments did not exacerbate his near feral hatred of Spain –
they merely confirmed its prudence.

We have seen that other, powerful men shared Drake's opinions. In particular, Walsingham and Leicester had long pressed Elizabeth to undertake a
more active, Protestant policy against the political tide of the Counter-
Reformation. Their own practical efforts did not stop at organizing sea-
voyages to interlope upon Spanish interests; by the early 1580s, Walsingham
in particular had begun to assemble – or to create – evidence to support his
claim of a Catholic world-conspiracy against England. In 1583 he uncovered
the Throckmorton plot (having tracked it minutely almost from the moment
of its conception), which exposed Spanish complicity in a plan for a Guise
invasion of England: a stratagem to be priorily assisted by the assassination
of the Queen. Mendoza, who had been in direct contact with its leading

English agent, Francis Throckmorton, was promptly expelled from the Court, despite a virtuoso display of diplomatic bluster.[1] He was the last Spanish ambassador to reside in England during Elizabeth's reign.

In that same year, the resurgent forces of Catholicism seemed poised for final success in the Low Countries. Parma's expulsion of the Duc d'Anjou's troops removed the final French barrier to Spain's re-conquest of her rebellious provinces; in 1584, he swept through the southern Netherlands, plucking out the cities that stood against Spanish rule, until Flanders and most of Brabant had been pacified. Only Brussels and Antwerp, isolated and unsupported by external allies, remained as outposts of resistance. With the death of William of Orange, struck down by a Calvinist fanatic in July 1584, it seemed that the Protestant cause in the Netherlands approached extinction.

Apocalypses, however, tend to be supra-denominational. A month before William's assassination, even as the rebels felt the ring of Spanish iron closing about them, the Duc d'Anjou, heir to the French throne, died. In life, he had been Philip's enemy; in the act of dying, he became his nemesis. The man who now stood next in line to succeed Henry III was a Protestant, Henry of Navarre. For Philip, this was an horrific prospect. It offered to him the mirror-image of Elizabeth's worst fears – in this case, that the Spanish Low Countries might be crushed between two irredeemably hostile, Protestant powers; that in the longer term, the Catholic faith in France might be entirely extinguished. Direct Spanish interference in French affairs, something Philip had always prudently sought to avoid, now became a matter of dire necessity. Within seven months of Anjou's death, he had secretly committed himself to an armed alliance with Guise and the Catholic League. He had also taken a further, profound step, though one determined by inescapable logic rather than conscious intent. Now that his worst fears for France had come to pass and overt action was unavoidable, why should he continue to compromise his most fundamental principles in seeking an English friendship that could no longer be of benefit to Spain? Slowly, circumstance pushed the English and Spanish monarchs towards a conflagration that both had feared for decades.

Yet at this seemingly final hour, faced with the apparent total failure of her policy in the Netherlands, the threat of active Spanish support for the Catholic League and Philip's desire to see her dead a matter of public knowledge, Elizabeth sought to influence the course of events by all means short of war. Though even the prudent Burghley was by now convinced of the inevitability (if not the desirability) of war, and even as John Hawkins was urging naval operations against Spain's Atlantic islands, her East Indian stations, the annual Basque fleets to the Newfoundland Banks and other economic targets upon the coast of Spain itself, the Queen was prepared only to support a new expedition to the Moluccas: to strike at Portuguese economic interests there as a means of hurting Spain indirectly. Plans for this expedition were formulated as early as November 1584 and provided for a fleet of eleven ships, four barks and twenty pinnaces. She ventured £17,000 towards the anticipated costs of £40,000, but, as before, the prospect of Drake leading the enterprise was too frightening for her to contemplate. In April 1585, with preparations well advanced, and the aims of the project generally known throughout Europe, he was detained in London.[2]

Arrangements for some sort of undertaking continued, however. From Paris, Mendoza – now Spanish Ambassador to the French Court – continued his sterling work. In May, he informed Philip that Leicester was reported to be outfitting several ships for an unspecified project (though to Philip, his plate fleets remained the obvious target).[3] It was this continuing perceived threat to his *flotas*, coupled with news of the despatch of the first Virginia expedition under Richard Grenville in April, that caused Philip to see the beginnings of an officially sanctioned, coordinated English strategy against Spanish overseas possessions. To confront it he moved swiftly and – by his own standards – drastically. In 1585, as in the previous few years, Spanish harvests had proved inadequate to meet the needs of the home population. To make up the shortfall, Philip had issued limited immunities from religious proscription to allow English grain ships to trade directly with Spain. On 29 May, with almost all of these vessels still moored in Spanish ports, he ordered their detention. One of these, the *Primrose* of London, staged a spectacular escape from Vigo and returned home with the man who had attempted to seize her, the *corregidor* of Biscay. He was found to be carrying orders from Philip which appeared to indicate that the seizure of English vessels had been an initial step in a scheme to send a sea-borne expedition to the Netherlands, possibly as a preliminary to an invasion of England.[4]

That same month, a delegation from the States-General, reeling from the successes of Parma and of the Catholic League in northern France, took the equally drastic step of offering sovereignty over the Low Countries to Elizabeth. It was inconceivable that she would have taken on such an open-ended commitment to the rebels' cause (which is precisely what they had hoped for in making the offer); nevertheless, she promised an English expeditionary force that might, given further successes by Parma, be set directly against Spanish troops. By 1 July, Drake's commission to command the planned expedition had been reinstated, and general letters of reprisal were issued by the Admiralty against all Spanish shipping: 'as if it were in the time of open war between her Majesty and the said King of Spain'.[5] It has since been established that the Court of Admiralty did not refuse a single application for these new letters, nor, it seems, ask any of the usual questions that the proofs of claim required.[6] Drake's younger brother Bernard took immediate and industrious advantage of the new policy. He had been preparing ships to follow Grenville to Virginia; instead, he sailed directly for the Newfoundland Banks, seized an entire Spanish-Portuguese fishing fleet there, and, for good measure, several Portuguese sugar ships on the return passage.[7] Elsewhere, a swarm of privateers, sensing something of a return to the former golden age, urgently fitted out their ships for voyages to the Spanish coast. For England, the safeguard of the seas was no longer diplomacy, but ships – the more the better – set out upon them.

Francis Drake's schedule for the coming expedition (mis-dated 25 April 1585) provided striking modifications to the original aims of his voyage.[8] He was now to secure the release of English ships in Spanish ports before moving into the Atlantic to intercept the West Indies fleet. From there, he was given the further options – possibly to be exercised at his own discretion – to despoil Spanish settlements on the Main and establish an English base from which future attacks upon Spanish New World possessions might be mounted.

It is clear that no matter how hard Elizabeth had tried – and subsequently would try further – to avoid war with Spain, these 'instructions' (or, more probably, priorily agreed objectives) represented a personal Rubicon. What had been entirely unacceptable aims in the still-born 'First Enterprise' of 1582 now received her tacit, if not official, sanction. It is difficult to overstate the provocation they represented. The produce of the Spanish Main and New Spain was the life-blood of Philip's empire; the new project was not merely intended to slow its flow, but to slash the very arteries that carried it. It has been memorably said that when Drake fired his first shot upon Santo Domingo, the seat of the *Audiencia* of the Islands, he 'tore away the dissimulation which for 59 years had veiled the activities of the English in the Caribbean'.[9] If this was not yet to be a war of armies in the field, Drake was about to correct any misconception that the treaty of Tordesillas had settled the world in favour of Spanish and Portuguese interests.

The scale of the coming expedition was a message in itself. Drake was now to sail with a total of twenty-five ships – including the Queen's ships *Ayde* (recently reconstructed and enlarged from 200 to 250 tons) and *Elizabeth*

Bonaventure – and some eight pinnaces. His lieutenant-general was Walsing-ham's son-in-law, Christopher Carleill, recalled from Irish service specifically to serve as commander of troops in this expedition. Carleill was a land-soldier; he was intended to lead the forces that might be required to face Spanish colonial troops. Drake therefore required another lieutenant; a vice-admiral to take charge of the fleet should he himself fall. This time, there were no lists and no merchants to raise objections to the logical choice. Drake's appointed vice-admiral was Martin Frobisher.

Frobisher's flagship was the *Primrose*, apparently the same ship that had gained so much glory in the Biscayan adventure.[10] She was at least partly owned by the Hawkins family (probably by John himself), but financed principally in this voyage by a consortium of London merchants. In stark contrast to their colleagues' attitude of a very few years earlier, Frobisher's appointment did not scare these law-abiding citizens into making the sort of representations that had removed him from the 1582 Moluccas enterprise. In fact, it is likely that they were now quite enthusiastic about the choice. The seizure of English ships upon the Spanish coast had, irrevocably, cost Philip the support of his most steadfast allies in England – her merchants. Their reputed horror at the event eclipsed any former, discreet misgivings they may have entertained regarding the treatment of English Protestant prisoners and the idiosyncratic practices of Spanish customs officials. So pro-found was its effect upon the City – where most of the more substantial Anglo-Spanish traders resided – that her merchants were rumoured to be outfitting a war-fleet of their own, though this proved to be mere bravado. Nevertheless, several of the same men who had formerly worked to have Frobisher removed from command of the 1582 expedition may have been among those now eager to have such a proven fighter as their captain.[11] The fact that Frobisher was commanding a converted merchantman inclined Corbett to suggest that he was the merchants' first choice of commander, but this seems to test their newly sanguinary impulses beyond the bounds of prob-ability. It is clear, rather, that he was posted as vice-admiral by the Queen herself.[12]

Frobisher's appointment, after years of anonymity and unemployment, seems an overly confident token of faith in his abilities – until one considers the qualities required of Drake's second-in-command at sea. He would need to be relatively strong-willed, adept at holding together a fleet at sea and, above all, obedient to a higher – *the* higher – authority. Elizabeth had long feared the implications of Drake's inability to avoid trouble and his refusal to take any counsel that contradicted his own. In contrast, Frobisher had a record of (largely) following official instructions, and would not hesitate or fear to remind Drake of them, should the need arise. By appointing both he and Carleill personally, the Queen had sent a message that even Drake could not ignore: it was to be his expedition, but the authority was hers.

That hint seems to have been taken, at least initially. On 17 September, just three days out of England, Drake dined Frobisher and Carleill aboard the *Elizabeth Bonaventure*, an occasion that Carleill later reported with great warmth:

> he proceded with longe discorce of many things conserninge the voyadge and with earnest protestation amonge the rest of the trust which he ded and dayly had to repose in vs two: above all men elce, and withall requiringe in frindly sorte to be advartysed by us of any thinge which we coulde wyshe to have altered or amended/ on so much that for my owne parte I can not say that evar I had to deale with a man of greatar reason or more carefull circomspection.[13]

The image of a circumspect Drake, much less one that invited dissension – no matter how constructive – is an unlikely one; and Carleill, it must be said, was not to be one of the most critical of Drake's subordinates (he would stand almost alone against the other land-captains when, at Cartagena, they petitioned Drake to curtail the expedition).[14] Nevertheless, events show that Drake was careful to seek his immediate lieutenants' advice throughout the voyage, even if he promptly ignored it thereafter.

Acknowledging Frobisher's peculiar talents, we sense a measure of discomfort in his role as Drake's vice-admiral. The two men had not sailed together previously, and, despite the superficial similarities of temperament that they shared, it would have been an optimistic opinion indeed that regarded them as *sympatico*. Though also of an habitually violent and martial disposition, Frobisher appears not to have shared Drake's instinctive hatred of Spain or Spaniards *per se*; nor that urgency born of a sense of some international Catholic plot being brought to maturity. One imagines Drake's frequent and loud blasts against Spanish perfidy being received with some puzzlement, even irritation, by a man who regarded Spaniards – if he regarded them at all – as his unwilling professional associates. Perhaps it was only the promise of an employment offered by the Queen herself – and, of course, the chance to get at one of the Spanish Indies fleets – that persuaded Frobisher to accept a subordinate position with *el Draco*. By 1585, he had been a beggar – perhaps a sea-beggar also – for far too long to be discriminating about his commissions. A man seeking to regain a reputation needed to be seen; and to sail with Drake was, undoubtedly, to be seen.

The fleet departed from Portsmouth on 14 September 1585. It did so hurriedly, before all preparations had been completed; probably to forestall the habitual last-minute intervention by the Queen to modify and dilute the fleet's instructions.[15] The victualling of the ships was unfinished, and orders of conduct had not yet been issued by Drake; the consequences of both oversights were to undermine the fleet's effectiveness and its chances of success. Nevertheless, the expedition was a truly impressive force, the largest English naval force to pass into the Atlantic to date, and the calibre of its other leading officers reflected its importance. Rear-admiral on the *Galleon Leicester* was Francis Knollis, son of the Queen's Treasurer of the Household and Leicester's brother-in-law; whilst several other vessels sailed under men absolutely loyal to Drake personally – his youngest brother, Thomas, William Hawkins the younger, Thomas Moone, John Martin and George Fortescue – men who had accompanied him on his circumnavigation and who still, even in 1585, unconditionally shared his priorities.

Once clear of Portsmouth, the fleet sailed south-westwards, towards the Spanish Atlantic coast. Off Finisterre, Frobisher's *Primrose* took a Biscayan fishing vessel and, the following day, five French merchantmen returning from Spain with cargoes of salt. Four of these he released unharmed, but the fifth, the *Madaleine*, was co-opted into the fleet 'becawse wee fownde no bodie in her, ther (men) weare runne ashore for feare'.[16] She was renamed the *Drake* – not, we may be certain, at the insistence of Frobisher.

On 27 September, the fleet came to Bayona in the Bay of Vigo; there, it anchored and Drake took 700 men into the town harbour to negotiate with the local governor for the impounded English ships. An envoy was sent to demand of the Englishmen their intentions; with no further reason to keep these opaque, or to pretend an amity that had finally died, their reply was admirably concise: 'answer was made we were men of warr & sought nothyng but what we could winn by force'.[17]

Yet Philip had already relented of his hasty strategy and ordered the release of all detained ships; the Governor of Bayona was therefore able to point out to his unwelcome guests that any English vessels wishing to visit his ports could come and go at will. Nevertheless, Drake sent a contingent under Carleill up-river, to search for any ships that might still be held. Whilst upon this task, his men piously burned a cargo of 'trashe belonginge to the hyghe chur(ch)' and sacked a small religious house before returning to Bayona. They lost only one straggler, whom the locals somewhat peevishly decapitated.

Carleill had observed the proprieties of war, and provided the governor of Bayona with an excellent excuse not to resist. Under an exchange of hostages which the latter arranged with Frobisher and Drake ('they concluded between themselves that peace should be wholly entertained in all parts'), mariners from the English fleet went on shore to purchase food and lade water.[18] From 28 September, severe weather kept the English ships in the bay; in the meantime, their further provisioning from the neighbourhood's slender resources proved a slow business. It was only on 11 October, after returning their respective hostages with every token of mutual regard, that the Englishmen and their obliging Spanish suppliers parted company.

In Madrid, meanwhile, Philip sought to anticipate the expedition's goals. He understood Drake's motives perfectly, but not his precise aims. To the Spanish King, the most trying aspect of this and subsequent English long-range raids against his possessions was not the material damage they inflicted, but the diversion of resources required to cover all their potential targets adequately. Looking at the options before him, Philip was aware that his resources were spread too thinly. The Tierra Firme *galeones* and New Spain *flota* were the obvious primary targets, but once at sea, these fleets were more or less thrown upon their own resources (standing instructions to make themselves elusive made their interception by friendly or enemy vessels equally difficult).[19] Drake might also be planning to sack towns in the Canaries or Verde Islands, or to strike at the rich Caribbean ports of Santo Domingo, Cartagena, Havanna or Nombre de Dios. All these cities and towns needed to be warned and, if possible, reinforced; yet the continuing threat to Spain's possessions and interests closer to home – most notably from the still-active Portuguese pretender Don António – prevented any large-scale response to Drake. As John Hawkins had obliquely inferred to Burghley in his 'second memorial' of July 1584, England's only truly effective strategy in a conflict with Spain would be one of deliberate attrition; her only substantive advantage lying in the ability to tie down or demolish resources that might otherwise be utilized against her.[20] Hawkins's considered opinion proved to be well founded: in logistical terms, the despatch of Drake's fleet – whatever its eventual achievement – did more to ease the pressure that might otherwise have been applied to the Netherlander rebels than anything undertaken by the ineffectual Leicester and his 6,000 men.

In fact, Drake's intended first target was that which Philip had most suspected – the plate fleets. Leaving the Bay of Vigo, he separated his fleet (which, however, remained in contact), with Frobisher's *Primrose* leading a squadron of thirteen ships.[21] The manoeuvre was sensible; to catch a prize at sea was a matter of chance, and the further the net could be spread, the more that chance was favoured. Unfortunately, the English fleet was chasing a wraith. The ships of the New Spain *flota* had reached their home ports whilst the English fleet was still at Plymouth (Drake was to learn that he had missed the prize of prizes when he encountered and spoke with the captain of a French man-of-war, off Palma in the Canaries, who told him that seventeen Spanish ships, laden with the wealth of New Spain, had passed by him some twenty days earlier).[22]

The late despatch of the expedition had therefore undermined one of its principal (if unstated) goals; and its subsequent diversion to Vigo for supplies removed any chance of catching any strays from the *flota*. Yet even following this lengthy and expensive detour, Drake was obliged to seek further victuals in the Canaries rather than proceed directly, as he had intended, to the Cape Verde Islands. In a gale, somewhere between the coast of Spain and the Canaries, the *Primrose* and the *Drake* lost contact with the other English ships, but rejoined the fleet on 17 October. On 3 November, the English force attempted to put in at Palma to take on water, but was discouraged by a lack of safe anchorage and, more immediately, by cannon fire from the local garrison – a shot from which was said to have passed between Drake's legs as he stood in the flagship's gallery in discussion with Frobisher and Carleill.[23] Prudently, the three principal commanders decided to sail on and seek out more welcoming harbours, but these proved elusive. At Ferro, southernmost of the Canary Islands, they found the locals impoverished by recent French attacks and unable to supply provisions 'suffycyent to serve the fleet 2 dayes', a claim that Drake accepted, probably on the evidence of their thin faces.[24] From there, the fleet doubled back eastward to the Barbary coast (where a large catch of sea-bream, porgy and dogfish relieved their pressing food shortage) and then to Santiago in the Verde Islands, which, according to the expedition's provisional schedule, Drake had already determined to sack, possibly in reprisal for 'the great wrongs' done to William Hawkins the elder four years earlier, when several of his men had been attacked and murdered during a visit there.[25]

Santiago was deserted when the English fleet arrived there on 16 November. Shots were fired at the ships during their first night at anchor in the harbour, but the lack of any prospect of a relieving force from Spain seems to have drained local morale. Carleill disembarked between Porto Prayo and Santiago with 1,000 men, and had advanced to the latter by dawn. Looking down into the town, the small English army saw fifty cannon drawn up to block their advance, primed but now abandoned. Carleill had them fired off to signal that the town was taken and also, gallantly, to mark the anniversary of the Queen's coronation, twenty-seven years earlier to the day.[26]

Drake remained at Santiago for twelve days, resting his men and plundering what remained of the town's wealth. The mariners and soldiers took whatever they could find – oil, meal and fresh fruit – and even stole the local hospital's brass bells; but the town had been stripped entirely of its gold, silver and church plate by the retreating population. Bravely, if unwisely, the Governor of the town (an Italian) came to negotiate terms. He was mistaken for a spy and searched, yielding up fifty pieces of gold from his trousers. The author of the *Primrose* journal revealed the Englishmen's scant respect for the conventions of diplomacy: 'Wee kepte him in prison & vsed a certaine kinde of torment to make him confesse'.

A short expedition inland to the settlement of Santo Domingo yielded no better rewards; the English force took the town for the loss of just one man,[27] but finding nothing worth having more than burning, they withdrew back to the coast. The only useful discovery thereafter was a small fleet of seven abandoned caravels containing bread, wine, oil and sugar, which the Englishmen emptied and set adrift. They withdrew from the island on 29 November (having first attended to such minor administrative matters as hanging a ship's steward who had confessed to buggering two cabin boys), leaving both Santiago and Porto Praya in flames.[28] Frobisher remained with his pinnaces to evacuate the 100-strong rearguard, but no further resistance was encountered from the island's defenders as they embarked.

The evacuation apart, Frobisher's role in the raid was largely passed over by contemporary sources; but during his time on the island he had an opportunity to practise the unfamiliar role of conciliator. Having taken Santiago, Drake – who was still ordering matters that should have been settled before the fleet left England – required his men to take an oath of obedience to the Queen and to his own person as general of the expedition. Of all the captains, Francis Knollis alone refused to take any oath other than that due to the Queen; possibly because his religious convictions – or his social standing – made the form of a common soldier's oath unacceptable. His attitude hardened in the face of (probably intentional) disrespect shown to him by Drake's chaplain, Philip Nichols. Nichols, the author of the contentious oaths, stood far too much upon his own authority in declaring during a sermon that 'if there were any man so foolish or so proud or so fleshly harted as to refuse these o(a)thes beforesaide, he thought him an ill member in the action, and not worthy of the socyety.'[29] Several gentlemen, led by one Thoroughgood, complained of Nichols to Drake, who was, typically, enraged at this perceived disloyalty to his own person (he may also have dwelt upon the example of Knollis's brother Henry, whose defection with three ships from Humphrey Gilbert's 1578 expedition had ruined any happy prospect for that enterprise).[30] Drake's 'acustomed furies' needed careful handling, particularly as Thoroughgood spoke on behalf of up to fifty men, loyal to Knollis personally, who threatened to leave the fleet and return home.[31] Frobisher, with other captains gathered in council for the purpose, seems to have provided that care. As was his habit when warring with his subordinates, Drake took pains to draw up documentary evidence of his reasonable attempts to secure the dissidents' abject surrender. He framed a memorial, demanding to know under what terms Knollis could be reconciled, or, failing that, whether the men faithful to him would be content to go on with their service.[32] Frobisher and four of the principal captains took this to Knollis, and attempted to persuade him to reconsider his stand. They were unsuccessful. Knollis was obdurate, but he had powerful friends, and could hardly be dealt with in the same manner as was the unfortunate Thomas Doughty, seven years earlier. Drake was therefore obliged to exercise an unfamiliar degree of self-control, but the episode is yet another example of the posturing that marked contemporary hierarchies at sea (and a further yardstick against which to set Frobisher's own record as commander). When the English ships departed from Santiago on 29 November, the rift had not yet been mended. Knollis was deprived of his rear-admiralship pending a more formal arraignment; but the fleet sailed on without defections from his men.

Retribution for the Englishmen's depredations in Santiago descended swiftly thereafter. Within two days of their departure, sickness swept through the fleet; in Drake's ship alone, over 100 men were stricken, and sixty or more in Frobisher's *Primrose*. November in the Verde Islands had been extremely hot, and the English seamen's diet had remained as inappropriate as upon Wyndham's voyage to Guinea thirty-two years earlier, thereby exacerbating the effects of this new affliction. Many of the Englishmen mistook it for the disease which the Spaniards called *Calentura*, the burning ague: reputed to be caused by the infected evening air, *La serena*, and so deadly that any who were caught abroad in it would invariably die. The affliction that struck Drake's fleet may have brought symptoms that were superficially similar to this mythical distemper; but there was a far more likely source of infection in the Englishmen's enforced proximity to several contagious patients held in Santiago hospital; and, indeed, in the probable trans-island passage of the pneumonic plague that was currently ravaging Spain itself.[33] Whatever its precise provenance, between 200–300 men – fully ten per cent of the English fleet's complement – were to die in an Atlantic passage of only eighteen days' duration.

By 21 December, the survivors had reached the West Indies, and were anchored off Dominica (the expedition was now almost a month overdue, according to the schedule set out in Drake's instructions).[34] From there, the ships passed to St Christopher's Island on Christmas Eve, where they remained for several days; resting the sick and burying more of their dead. Here, Drake, Frobisher and Carleill discussed their first Caribbean objective, and settled upon Santo Domingo in Hispaniola: 'being the auncientest and chiefe inhabited place in all that tract of country thereabouts'.[35] Again, the counsel of senior officers seems merely to have confirmed Drake's earlier decision, as expressed in his provisional schedule, which stated that he intended to sack Rio de la Hacha on the Main: 'unless he t(urn aside to Hispaniola) and the city of Domingo . . .'.[36]

On the short passage north-westwards from St Christopher's Island, two Spanish barks were taken (one of them by Frobisher's *Primrose*) with cargoes of food, tobacco and hides. Most usefully, they acquired a Greek pilot, who agreed (possibly having been encouraged by the same 'certaine kinde of torment' as had the Governor of Santiago) to take the English ships into the harbour of Santo Domingo. By the evening of 31 December 1585, the fleet lay off the town, making ready to seize its first major prize.

The town's preparations to receive Drake's assault were woefully inadequate. Its Governor, Cristóbal de Ovalle, had received prior warning of an anticipated attack from Spain. He later claimed that news of the English fleet and its appearance occurred almost simultaneously;[37] yet even if this were true, he should have fortified Santo Domingo months earlier in response to the lessons of Grenville's visit to Puerto Rico and Hispaniola during the previous May, which had highlighted the vulnerability of Spanish Caribbean settlements before well-armed English ships.[38] Such feeble measures as Ovalle had taken anticipated an assault from the direction of his harbour. However, whilst Drake presented his fleet in conformity with the Governor's assumptions, Carleill led a nine-mile overland march from the west during the night of 31 December/1 January and fell upon the virtually unprotected west wall of the town. A brief sortie was made from the town by 100–150 Spanish troops, a single cannonade thundered from three guns placed over the town gate (killing two or three English soldiers), and then the garrison and what remained of the town's population promptly fled into the fort above Santo Domingo. Drake and his men entered the town virtually unmolested, and established themselves whilst the Spanish garrison quietly dispersed into the countryside.

'Thus the Spaniardes gave vs the towne for a Newyeers gifte', recalled the anonymous author of the *Primrose* journal.[39] It was not as well favoured as expected, however. The English soldiers and mariners found plentiful stocks of food, spices and clothing, but, again, virtually all the gold and silver plate had been removed by the fleeing townsfolk. The discovery of a further commodity in a galley in the harbour – almost 400 enslaved Turks, Moors, Negroes, Greeks and Frenchmen – added little to the value of the haul but provided many extra mouths to feed.

The day after the city's capture, Drake sent a Negro boy under flag of truce to ask for a parley. Unfortunately, he met first with officers from the captured galley, who courageously set upon him with their swords and killed him. Drake responded by hanging two friars he had captured in the town;[40] but these formalities being discharged, the Englishmen set themselves to persuading the enemy to negotiate. In the absence of gold and silver to be had by force (or, indeed, of anyone to whom that force might be applied), Drake was obliged to employ his only real bargaining counter – the town itself. Organizing his soldiers into squads, he began systematically to destroy it, neighbourhood by neighbourhood. After ten days of such despoliation, the *Audiencia* sent an emissary to discuss terms. Drake demanded 200,000 ducats (about £48,000). The following day, three more Spanish officials came to the town, and offered 20,000 ducats if Drake would go away without causing further damage. Drake's response, inevitably, was to cause that further damage. Each day for almost three weeks thereafter, the negotiators returned to the town, failed to agree terms, and watched another neighbourhood burn. In the meantime, house-to-house searches ahead of the firing parties revealed small caches of personal jewellery and gold – not enough to satisfy English expectations, but sufficient to dull the disappointment of the growing understanding that the town's ransom was not going to be spectacular. Drake himself was beginning to weary of negotiating with men who, though clearly distraught at seeing the seat of their government put to the torch, had neither the means nor the will to stop it. He was also sensitive to his own, worsening problems.

Already, the capacity of the English expedition to achieve its optimistic objectives had been sorely reduced. The ague that had caused such heavy fatalities during the Atlantic crossing continued to torment the Englishmen; by the end of their occupation of Santo Domingo, almost 500 would have died: perhaps twenty per cent of their entire complement. Also, considerable dissension continued amongst Drake's captains with regard to the treatment of Francis Knollis – indeed, now that they were at leisure to consider the matter, the problem worsened. Several fights broke out between the respective partisans of Drake and Knollis following a makeshift court martial on 10 January, and up to forty soldiers had to be imprisoned for disobedience and 'contempt' in monks' cells in the cathedral (laconically christened 'the Marshalsea' by the English mariners).[41] With such distractions, Drake was eager to put to sea once more and restore his men's discipline. Accordingly, on 30 January, it was his nerve that broke before that of the enemy. Arriving for their daily meeting, the Spanish negotiators offered a ransom of 25,000 ducats (approximately £6,000) which Drake reluctantly accepted, promising in return to evacuate the town.[42]

The English soldiers withdrew to their ships the following day, taking every moveable piece of booty that the town had yielded, save for a number of hides and sacks of sugar that Drake presented to the leading Spanish negotiator, García Fernández de Torrequemada (who very properly accepted them on behalf of all the citizens of the town). The Englishmen also took away with them about twenty Frenchmen released from the galley, and sixty Turkish and Negro slaves who presumably thought to try their luck with Drake. The other slaves were sold back to their owners, though only when the chattels in question agreed to it. By modern standards, the transaction was ghastly; but by his own and other contemporary lights, Drake had treated the slaves with a consideration that bordered on tenderness.

Although the plunder from Santo Domingo had been extremely disappointing – Drake's provisional schedule had estimated the haul would be in the region of 500,000 ducats – news of the town's seizure and sack reverberated throughout Europe. Having traded with impunity upon the very coast of Spain, Drake had now despoiled one of the principal centres of Spanish government in the West Indies – the most venerable city of the Spanish New World. Reports of his deeds remorselessly exaggerated their physical achievement, but in the effect they had upon Spanish prestige, rumour was as useful a tool of war as palpable damage.[43] The message had been sent out, not least to Philip's many creditors, that English ships could pass at will into the heart of Spain's overseas empire and threaten the sources of their loan repayments.

Drake's next target was Cartagena, the entrepôt of the Spanish Main, where shipments of pearls, silver, gold, cochineal and hides were habitually amassed before their transportation to Spain on the Tierra Firme *galeones*. Expectations of this city were even higher than of Santo Domingo, with the provisional schedule estimating plunder worth 1,000,000 ducats. Haste was therefore essential: it was assumed that word of the sack of Santo Domingo would have crossed the Caribbean within days, and any delay could only assist

Cartagena's defenders in further fortifying their city. From Santo Domingo, therefore, the English fleet sailed directly south for the Main, pausing only at Cape de Vela to allow Frobisher to take a pinnace to seek out a house that was rumoured to be a storehouse for pearls.[44] The search was swiftly abandoned when nothing was found, and, by 9 February, Drake's fleet was off Cartagena.

In fact, the *Audiencia* of Santo Domingo had been inexcusably tardy in warning their compatriots at Cartagena. It appears that word was sent across the Caribbean only after Drake's departure from Santo Domingo; even so, little prompt action was taken by those upon whom this curse now threatened to descend.[45] The hazardous navigation into Cartagena's outer harbour (a narrow, twisting channel surrounded by shallows) had disinclined the Governor to devote much energy to fortifying it – or, indeed, any of the alternative approaches. Only when refugees from Santo Domingo arrived with exaggerated stories of Drake's strength did a resulting last-minute panic bring about some worthwhile improvements to the town's defences. Women and children were evacuated, valuables removed from the town, and trenches dug along the spit of land – *La Caleta* – that screened the outer and inner harbours from the sea. A chain was also hung between the two shores of the entrance to the inner harbour; a measure that was to give Frobisher in particular an unpleasant, if wholly anticipated, experience.

To reach Cartagena's outer harbour, the English fleet was obliged to sail westwards past the city. Drake paraded his ships in warlike array to make a useful psychological point and then, without pause, the leading vessels turned hard to port and passed through the horns of the harbour. Shoals, contrary tides and other impediments notwithstanding, the entire English fleet entered without incident into a sound that the author of the *Leicester*'s journal estimated to be capacious enough 'to contayne all the shippes of England'.[46] That night, as at Santo Domingo, Carleill was despatched with a strong force (Spanish accounts put the English force at between 500 and 1,100 men, though the lower figure is more feasible), to march across *La Caleta* and frontally assault the city's principal line of defence. In a divertive attempt, meanwhile, Frobisher prepared a small fleet of pinnaces to attack the forces screening the inner harbour.

It was here where the chain prevented further ingress that the most effective Spanish defences had been organized. Sixteen pieces of ordnance, mounted in a stone blockhouse to which one end of the chain was secured, covered an entrance barely the width of two ships. Frobisher, with captains Fenner, White and Crosse, brought their small boats against the chain, but were so swept by shot that the rudder of Frobisher's skiff was blown away, and: 'mens hattes from there headdes & the topp of our meane maste beaten in peeces, the Oares striken owte of our menes handes as they rowed & our Captaine [Frobisher] like to have him slaine'.[47]

Behind the chain, anchored in the inner harbour, two galleys formed a further line of defence. These were in the charge of Don Pedro Vique y Manrique, ostensibly the commander of all Spanish troops on the Main. He had 650 Spanish soldiers with him, in addition to a number of armed Negroes and 400 Indian auxiliaries; but his intended role in the coming battle is not entirely clear. He had the ability to sweep *La Caleta* with his guns, thus seriously harrying Carleill's advancing troops. He did not do so, however; nor did he land more than a small proportion of his men to support either *La Caleta*'s barricades or the blockhouse party. It may be that some of his Turkish galley slaves were not chained at their oars, and that he was wary therefore of dispersing his men or otherwise committing them at the cost of leaving his ships unguarded. It is also clear from the later deposition sent to the *Audiencia* of New Granada that Vique was an extremely cautious man (it was he who had ordered the chain over the inner harbour, which protected his vessels but also removed their ability to assail the English ships directly).[48] In the event, the galleys' only contribution to the fighting was a brief engagement in which they fired their ordnance at Frobisher's pinnaces when they reached the blockhouse chain, which added much to Frobisher's discomfort but nothing to the effective defence of the city.[49] During this desultory bombardment, the accidental firing of a powder cask in one of the galleys created panic among the Spanish mariners; Vique unsuccessfully exhorted his men to stand firm, and then – with their desertion *en masse* – he reluctantly scuttled his small fleet into the inner harbour. It was possibly one of the most inglorious feats of sixteenth-century Spanish arms; the wretched Don Pedro was later court-martialled and sentenced to death for his part in it, though perhaps in view of the fact that even his craven showing had far surpassed that of his men, the sentence was subsequently commuted to life imprisonment.

Meanwhile, Carleill's force, confronted by thousands of poison-tipped staves thrust into the ground to hamper any landward advance, waded along the shoreline of *La Caleta* and reached the barricade that barred access to the town. About 500 Spanish troops from the city lay behind the obstacle, waiting to repulse the Englishmen. However, the defences closest to the shoreline were weak, and Carleill's men had no difficulty forcing their way through. In the dark, the already demoralized Spanish troops panicked and fled 'vpon the first

5. View of Cartagena by Baptista Boazio. The English fleet is shown entering the harbour and, later, at anchor. By courtesy of the John Carter Brown Library at Brown University.

volley of our shot'.[50] Only their old but valorous commander, Don Alonso Bravo Hidaldo de Montemayor, and his ensign bearer, Cosme de Blas, resisted the English advance; though in doing so the first was wounded and the second slain. Pushing past the last of this brief resistance, Carleill's men charged into the town and clambered over further barricades that had been erected at the end of each street. Here, they found only local Indian levies willing to put up a fight, whose poison-tipped arrows caused several English casualties. Given this breathing space, their Spanish employers gratefully fled from the town, 'with theyre horses or theyre heeles'.[51]

About the time that the English soldiers entered Cartagena, Frobisher withdrew his pinnaces from the blockhouse assault, perhaps having received a pre-arranged signal from Drake or Carleill. The harbour fortifications no longer served any defensive purpose for the beaten Spanish forces, and their occupants surrendered the following day when it became clear that no other resistance remained. One of the Spanish officers defending the blockhouse, Captain Mexia Mirabal, later claimed that Drake had been angered by Frobisher's withdrawal and had taken command of the pinnaces to make a second, equally unsuccessful assault upon the inner harbour chain.[52] None of the more definitive English accounts mentions such an episode, however, and the episode seems highly improbable; Frobisher's fellow officers in the attack – particularly Fenner – had, like their vice-admiral, proven records of bravery under fire. Drake, furthermore, would hardly have risked his own life to make a point in a battle that had already been won. Frobisher's assault had been a stratagem to keep a significant proportion of Spanish ordnance from the direction of the main English effort for the commitment of a relatively small part of the attacking force (one, moreover, which had not carried sufficiently heavy ordnance to penetrate the defences it assaulted).[53] There is no suggestion that the genesis of the two men's future feud lay here before the enemy's blockhouse; it was rather in the city itself that their understanding of the respective rights and obligations of admiral and vice-admiral may have provided a first niggling discontent.

By dawn, the town of Cartagena and its immediate environs were entirely in English hands, and Drake requisitioned the house of the courageous Don Alonso as his headquarters. As his men busily set themselves to finding hidden treasures among and beneath public buildings and private houses, the city's Governor, Pedro Fernañdez de Busto (an unheroic but extremely shrewd politician) and the bishop, Don Juan de Montalvo, returned to ask the conqueror's terms. As at Santo Domingo, a small gulf in their respective negotiating positions quickly became apparent. Drake demanded 400,000 ducats to evacuate the town, and the governor and bishop offered 5,000: at which 'our generall assured them that he wolde consume theyre towne with fyer yf they did not speedely agree for the ransome of it'.[54]

Fortunately for Don Alonso, his wife was less anxious about preserving her worldly wealth. She sent to Drake a suit with buttons of gold and pearl and some unspecified emerald jewellery, to Carleill an emerald brooch and ring and to Frobisher an emerald ring. Don Alonso's ransom was officially set at 6,000 ducats, though Drake decently remitted 1,000 of this to stand as the 'rent' due for his occupation of the Spaniard's house. He also took his wife's gifts into account. Don Alonso was an honourable and courageous foe, and Drake, always self-consciously chivalric, treated him as such. When, finally, the balance of his ransom was received, Drake provided a written receipt for it; and when Don Alonso's wife fell ill, the old man was given leave to go into the country to bring her home. She died soon after, but Drake allowed her body to be brought into the town and buried in the priory, following a solemn requiem mass which he – fervent Protestant though he was – attended.

The Governor of Cartagena was not nearly so burdened by courtly sentimentality. The removal of most of the town's wealth prior to its capture had
provided another threadbare prize for the hopeful English invaders; a disappointment he was not inclined to soften by making premature concessions.
The pace of negotiations on the precise figure to ransom the town was further
hampered by the expectation by both sides of a relieving Spanish fleet. Drake
began to apply his patented urban-clearance plan to areas of central Cartagena as he had done at Santo Domingo (according to the Governor's official
despatch to Philip II, the Englishmen commenced with the city's churches
'to which they showed themselves to be most inimical'),[55] but these outrages,
visited upon buildings already cleared of their valuables, did not rush the
Governor into paying for what he might secure for free, given time. In the
meantime, the heat of the season had brought the supposed *Calentura* upon
Drake's men once more. More than 100 were to die during their stay in the
town; the rate of mortality became so high at one point that the corpses (even
that of Captain Fortescue of the bark *Bonner*) were thrown overboard from
the ships 'without any other solemnety'. This wasting strength of the English
forces, added to the disappointment of plunder, the growing factiousness of
the common soldiers and niggling attrition of combat (the Captains of the
Francis and the *George*, Thomas Moone and John Varney, were killed on the
same day by a single Spanish sniper), began to tell upon English morale. Eventually, even Drake's infamous resistance to taking counsel was worn down: in
a formal resolution presented to him on 27 February 1586, Drake's land captains urged him to evacuate the town on best terms, rather than try to hold
out for £100,000, 'which seems a matter impossible to bee performed for the
present'; and to give order for the expedition to sail directly for England (the
sea-captains – Frobisher included – were not involved in this rare display of
popular resistance; they were keeping their own company in the less pesti-
lential environment of the outer harbour and sea beyond, watching out for
the expected Spanish relief force).

Though he had initially invited their input, Drake seems briefly to have
resisted his captains' forthright petition, and tried to bribe them out of their
resolve with a distribution of gold and silver; but only Carleill considered
the offer.[56] Meanwhile, negotiations with the Spanish Governor had slowly
brought the price of the town's ransom up to 110,000 ducats (£27,500). With
his growing problems of illness and indiscipline, this was just acceptable to
Drake; the Englishmen withdrew from the town to new quarters at the inner
harbour blockhouse and at a fortified abbey a quarter of a mile distant. For
ten more days, they remained, re-victualling and watering their ships and

allowing their surviving wounded and sick to convalesce. Eventually, the Spanish paid a further 1,000 ducats to remove them from the abbey but baulked at paying for the return of their blockhouse, which was subsequently blown up. The English fleet sailed from Cartagena on 31 March, further burdened with a growing collection of freed Negro and Turkish slaves.

Two days later, the citizens of the city, wearily examining the damage to their homes, were horrified to see the English ships once more off *La Caleta*. The *New Year's Gift*, a ship taken at Santo Domingo and drafted into the fleet, had begun to leak heavily (she had been over-laden with brass cannons taken from the two galleys sunk in Cartagena's inner harbour). Drake had therefore brought the fleet back to what he knew to be a safe haven still, to strip her of her cargo before scuttling her. He assured the Governor that his men would not attempt to despoil the town once more, but asked to be allowed to remain long enough to bake bread for the homeward voyage. It was not a request that could be sensibly refused; so keen were the Spanish not to give Drake an excuse to have another go at them that they posted wardens to ensure than none of the townsfolk bothered the Englishmen at their business except to assist them by bringing wood and water.[57] It was a striking display of enlightened self-interest; one whose logic the Governor was later hard-pressed to explain to his furious king.

On 14 April, to the inexpressible relief of its reluctant hosts, the English fleet finally departed from Cartagena, and set a course northwards. To date, it had secured booty in goods and ransoms of approximately 150,000–200,000 ducats (about £41,000–£55,000). Allowing for the costs of outfitting the expedition (and, of course, discounting the human cost of more than 600 lives to date), this hardly constituted a profit. Something more was needed if the English descent upon the Caribbean was to be regarded as an outright success. Both English and Spanish sources suggest that it had been Drake's original intention to sail eastwards to take and hold both Nombre de Dios and Panama (this was stated explicitly in Bigges's *Summarie*, though only hinted at in Drake's provisional schedule).[58] It is not known whether Elizabeth either knew or approved of any design more long-term than merely to pillage and sack these cities – certainly, any act of conquest that, if successful, would have sundered the Spanish empire and placed a strategic English presence in its midst could not have been tolerated by Philip II. However, the conditions that might have brought about this fatal confrontation were already lacking. It was possible for the English force, even in its weakened state, to take the cities – if their defences were as poorly arranged as those of Santo Domingo and Cartagena they could have offered little effective resistance – but the effort was hardly worth its attendant risks. Though the potential booty of these places had previously been assumed to be enormous (particularly that of Panama, which, according to Drake's schedule: 'doth [receive] all the treasure that cometh by water from the new kingdom of Peru, which may be taken without resistance; this town may be a prey of a million of ducats'),[59] the general and considered opinion among Drake's men had come to be that the riches of the Spanish Caribbean had been vastly exaggerated. In any case, the loss of about one quarter of his entire complement made Drake's holding of the isthmus against any substantial relieving Spanish force a near impossibility. Pushed by his captains, or sensible of the problems he faced, Drake abandoned any prior intention of attacking the isthmus.

The fleet did not yet turn homewards, however. After touching briefly at the Cayman Islands and replenishing their stocks with crocodile and turtle-meat, the English ships made the easternmost point of Cuba, Cape San Antonio. From there, they passed to the island's northern shore, and spent almost two weeks thereafter cruising in the area – either lost, confounded by contrary currents or hoping to intercept the Tierra Firme *galeones* out of Nombre de Dios whose customary first port of call was Havanna (if the latter, their wait was hopeless; the fleet had been indefinitely detained by Philip, pending word of Drake's departure to England). By 14 May, they were back at Cape San Antonio once more, where wells were dug to gather sufficient springwater to fill the fleet's casks.

Yet even now, the English ships did not turn eastwards. On 23 May, their course was directed to the north, towards Florida. Drake's intention, a goal he had probably determined upon even before the expedition set sail from England, was to visit Ralegh's colony at Roanoke in the Carolina Banks. None of the accounts mentions any council convened to discuss the matter before the expedition made for the Florida coast; indeed, Bigges's *Summarie* claims that it was only at an assembly of captains called by Drake off the Spanish settlement of St Helena that it was decided to seek out the English colony. Yet this chronology is hardly feasible. There would have been neither reason nor advantage in passing to the Florida coast at all, if not to press on northwards thereafter to find the colony. Nor is it likely that the same captains who had so bravely discouraged Drake from pressing north-eastwards in the name of profit would now agree to press northwards in the name of good fellowship. The evidence strongly suggests that it was Drake alone, of all the expedition's officers, who wanted to go to 'Virginia'; and probably for a priorily determined reason.

It has been suggested that there was a significant degree of coordination between the plans of Walter Ralegh and Drake for their respective ventures in 1585, and such evidence that we possess supports this.[60] Ralegh, the chief promoter of the Roanoke colony (he had secured his half-brother Humphrey Gilbert's colonizing patent upon the latter's death), was also a backer of Drake's expedition, and so must have had the opportunity to discuss the matter with him. To Drake himself, it was a distraction at best (though one he was willing enough to oblige) but for the colonists of Roanoke, the benefits of collaboration would prove invaluable. The first most lasting service that Drake could provide to them was that which he undertook from the moment he discerned Spanish activity upon the Florida coast: to remove the greatest potential threat to any English colonial presence on the North American coast.

On 27 May, the ships' watchers made out a beacon on the Florida shore.[61] Behind it, they found a fortified Spanish settlement: that of St Augustine. Ostensibly, there seems little reason for Drake to investigate this place further (whose existence, until that moment, had not been suspected). His men's prior experience at Santo Domingo and Cartagena, the probability that the settlement (far more modest in scale than the cities) would not be worth the plunder, his land-captains' growing urgency to return to England – all suggest that the English fleet would have been inclined to ignore the new challenge. Yet not only did it pause here, but after attacking and dispersing the Spanish garrison (in an assault in which Frobisher and Drake led twenty men into the fort and repulsed a subsequent attempt by local Indians to recapture it for their Spanish masters), the English force razed the town and fort so thoroughly as to render it uninhabitable.

Only Bigges's *Summarie* provided the reason for such brutal treatment:

In this place called S. Augustine, we vnderstood the King [i.e. Philip II] did keepe as is before said, one hundred and fiftie souldiers, and at an other place some dozen leagues beyond to the Northwardes, called S. Helena, he did there likewise kepe an hundred and fiftie more, seruing for no other purpose, then to keepe all other nations from inhabiting any part of that coast. . . .[62]

The destruction at St Augustine was therefore punitive. For any English colonizing experiment on the eastern coast of North America to survive, it needed to be far from the hand of Spanish intervention. Twenty years earlier, de Laudonnière's French Florida colony had been brutally expunged by Spanish iron, and to a man of Drake's partialities this was lesson enough. The English expedition subsequently came upon the more northerly Spanish settlement of St Helena and spared it, but only because they had no pilot to guide their ships through the shoals that guarded the entrance to its harbour.[63] Despite Bigges's later claim to the contrary, the English visitation upon Florida had been far too deliberate to have resulted from a last-minute whim.

Yet having decided to call in at the Roanoke settlement (where Drake also intended to set down the many freed slaves he had accumulated from Santo Domingo and Cartagena to serve as labour for the colony), there remained the small matter of finding it. Though the 1584 voyage of Amadas and Barlow had reconnoitred the Carolina Banks, there is no evidence that the precise latitude had been made available to Drake prior to his sailing. Also, he did not know if or precisely where the colony had been subsequently established, as Grenville's 1585 Roanoke expedition had returned to England more than a month after his own fleet had departed. It was a matter, then, of tracking the North American coastline until contact was made.

St Helena was the northernmost extent of the Spanish presence on the eastern American continent. The Englishmen saw no other trace of 'civilized' habitation until 9 June, when a large bonfire on the shoreline of Hatarask Bank signalled the presence of their countrymen. Leaving the ships outside the so-called Port Ferdinando (the colony's landing place, a small island in a shallow inlet just north of Cape Hatarask), Drake and his captains took their pinnaces into Roanoke Sound, and were greeted by the colony's commander, Ralph Lane.

Drake's discussions with Lane again suggest a premeditated plan to assist the colony. Even before they met, Drake had sent a letter with Captain Edward Stafford (one of the men they had first sighted from the sea), in which he offered any provisions necessary to the colony.[64]

The offer was timely. The promised supply ship from England and the relief expedition under Grenville were overdue by several months; in the meantime, some of the local Indian tribes had become resentful of the English presence. Lane had recently attacked his principal adversaries and prevented a threatened confederation of tribes, but only one group of native Indians – those of Croatoan – were friendly to the Englishmen. As the colony's supplies could only be gathered locally through their good offices, Drake's munificent offer provided an urgent lifeline for the colonists.

However, the goods that Drake provided, though generous enough in view of his own shortages, were insufficient to sustain the colony for more than a few months. Furthermore, the bark he allocated to remain with the colony – the *Francis* – having been almost fully laded with the promised tools, victuals and other equipment, was caught in a hurricane on 12 June. She disappeared out to sea and did not return thereafter (she was commanded by one Abraham Kendall; possibly the same Captain Kendall who had commanded the ill-fated bark *Denys* in Frobisher's 1578 north-western voyage).[65] Drake then offered a replacement vessel, the 170 ton *Bonner*, but she was far too big to navigate the shoals within the banks and was therefore useless for Lane's needs. At a council of colonists on 16 June, the decision that most of them had probably hoped for was made, and Lane asked Drake to transport them all back to England. He readily agreed, having little faith in the colony's future without its promised relief from England. The colonists were embarked in the fleet with such haste that much of their equipment was simply thrown into the boats haphazardly, and three colonists who were at that moment somewhere in the hinterland with the Indians were simply abandoned. The fleet sailed on 18 June, closing the book upon England's first overseas colony.

Unlike Frobisher's prospective colonial experiment eight years before, the Roanoke project had been viable. It failed, perhaps not so much upon a point of supplies, or even the poor choice of site; but because the necessary mindset that allowed Europeans to exist far from their native lands for years at a time had yet to be acquired by Englishmen.[66] With the burden of dislocation and disillusionment upon the settlers, even relatively small setbacks had assumed the proportion of insurmountable problems. Two years later, another colony was to be established at Roanoke, but the intervening Spanish war prevented its re-supply or relief. Without a Drake to save them, the unfortunate colonists were to suffer the full implications of their neglect. For many years thereafter, Indians of the region claimed that a measure of white men's blood ran in their own veins; perhaps the most optimistic claim for the fate of the second Roanoke colony.[67]

Drake's fleet reached Portsmouth on 28 July 1586, having encountered *en route* no plate fleet or other distraction worthy of recollection in any of the journals or accounts of the expedition. It had taken bullion, jewels, ordnance and other commodities to a value of some £60,000; after disbursements for wages, approximately £40,000 remained, giving the adventurers therein a return of approximately £6 for every share subscribed. Even this modest return was not paid promptly, however; the report of a royal commission into the voyage, dated June 1587, ordered that they were to be paid 15sh. per £1 invested, with the possibility of a further 12d. to follow when receipts from the sale of all prizes and equipment were received.[68] Though not the financial disaster that Frobisher's 1575–8 enterprise undoubtedly had been, the expedition had hardly realized its vast promise.

Yet the blow to Spanish morale had been profound. A Breton ship, coming from Seville to Plymouth in April 1586, had reported (false) word from Spain that Drake had taken Nombre de Dios, Panama and Cartagena, and 'runneth through the country like a conqueror'.[69] Philip II's inability to provide adequate protection or even relief to his vulnerable colonies had highlighted the devastating ability of sea-power to carry a campaign to the weakest strategic links in his empire. It was a lesson he was to learn well but expensively; and in doing so he was to justify fully Hawkins's theory that the threat of an English fleet worked to far better effect than its actuality.

And what of Frobisher? The narratives give very few glimpses of the second ranking sea-officer of the expedition. Such fragmentary evidence as we possess suggests that he discharged his duties with diligence, restraint and, when required, courage. Lack of detail to fill out that judgement is frustrating, but it probably indicates no more than that Frobisher had displayed a competence which discouraged comment from those who wrote only of incident. His attack upon the Cartagena chain was notably courageous, and though only a diversion to Carleill's flanking attack, it was undoubtedly expected to be bloody. The fact that Drake gave it over entirely to his vice-admiral says much of his reliability under fire, as does his subsequent joint-leadership of the attack upon the fort at St Augustine.

Perhaps, given Drake's notoriously autocratic nature and unwillingness to brook dissent, Frobisher had merely surrendered himself to the pleasures of being at sea upon lawful employment once more, with its added fillips of an occasional battle and chance of spoils. If this is the case, he was as one with the majority of his fellow captains. The orders that Drake issued for the conduct of his fleet, though tardy, were typically constrictive. Initiative, on the whole, was discouraged; there are frequent references in the various sources to captains' councils at which 'decisions' were taken, but it is probable that these were rubber-stamping affairs to ratify what Drake and a small circle of personal favourites had decided upon already (as, two years later, William Borough claimed of similar councils convened during the Cadiz raid).[70] The project – and its absolute direction, once out of reach of Elizabeth's heavy hand – were his; other men tended to be mentioned in the accounts of the voyage only when they crossed him or died unpleasantly. The most significant appearances of Frobisher – as a conciliator between Drake and Knollis, or commanding the fleet of pinnaces at Cartagena – reflected either another man's troubles or a brief, rare moment of independent action.

Yet this paucity of evidence may also reflect a coolness between the men: the first manifestation of their later, well-documented antipathy. Frobisher was not a member of the West County circle that produced the famously incestuous mix of sea-faring adventurers; his name is often appended to those of Hawkins, Drake, Gilbert, Ralegh and Grenville as though he were a part of their world, rather than simply of their profession, but this was not the case. Until 1585, he had at best a glancing acquaintance with Drake. They had been associated briefly during the Moluccas scheme of 1582, but under the Earl of Leicester's absolute direction this had been no more than a distant and impersonal relationship (and beneath such an overweening authority, the matter of their own respective dignities had not been in point). Their collaboration in the West Indies raid was not one of equals, but it was as close as they ever came to forming a professional bond. Thereafter, the relationship was wholly antagonistic. Having tasted Drake's leadership once, Frobisher seems to have developed an aversion for it – and for the man's undoubted record of success in exercising it – that grew, eventually, into violent dislike. When next offered the chance to serve with Drake, he would refuse outright (even though he was in effect disobeying his Queen), and, moreover, he would not care to disguise his reasons for doing so.[71] Long before Frobisher made his famous attacks upon Drake's character during the Armada campaign, the grounds for their mutual repugnance appear to have been fully laid out.

That later clash reflected far more closely the fundaments of their respective natures than did the apparent show of harmonious government that blessed the 1585/6 campaign. Both men had a sense of their own infallibility, even when all the evidence had it otherwise. Frobisher's absolute and unquestioning support of his appointed commander in the West Indies raid was not a token of loyalty, but of the consistency of his belief in strong leadership – a belief that had brooked not the slightest dissent to his own rule during the three voyages to Meta Incognita. True democracy at sea was an impossibility, and Frobisher, no less than Drake, considered the only 'good counsel' worth having was his own. But there are limits even to sage principles. Having been appointed to the voyage by the Queen herself, Frobisher had enjoyed a measure of her reflected authority. It is not unreasonable to suppose that on occasion he had considered himself qualified to offer his opinions to Drake, even where they had not been sought. It is equally likely that he had been ignored, notwithstanding Drake's earlier promise to take his counsel. Uncharacteristically, Frobisher had kept his own counsel thereafter, but later he made it clear that he would never again serve with, or under, Drake. It was a wise decision: one which illustrious men subsequently sought to honour by keeping the two as far apart as was practicable.

Ironically, given his own reputation for financial improbity, Frobisher's principal role in the aftermath of the voyage was, with Carleill and Sir William Winter, to certify Drake's account of expenses on the voyage to the commission appointed by the Privy Council to discharge the enterprise. The accounts were passed without contention; in fact, the auditors – or at least two of them – went out of their way to praise Drake's 'worthiness' and excused any gaps in the accounts, by reason that his personal secretary had died during the voyage and, therefore, that any errors would rebound to his disadvantage.[72]

The latter claim seems doubtful; Drake does not appear to have handed over the personal gifts he received from Don Alonso's dutiful wife, and may even have confiscated those presented to Carleill and Frobisher as, according to the letter of his own orders to his fleet, he had the right to do. A further bone of contention was that whilst his own wages were paid very soon after his accounts were certified, funds were thereafter exhausted in paying off the surviving mariners and soldiers, and both Frobisher and Carleill apparently had the greatest difficulty in securing their own dues. As late as 8 May 1587, Carleill was still owed £400 (the Privy Council wrote to William Winter on that day, asking him to pay £280 on account),[73] whilst Frobisher's wages were even more tardily paid. Another order to Winter, dated 12 May 1588 (a day upon which Frobisher readied one of the Queen's capital ships to engage the Armada), allocated a mere £150 in respect of his 'expences outwardes' in 1585.[74]

It would seem, therefore, that the famous West Indies raid proved no more profitable for Frobisher than for the adventurers who had backed the scheme in the hope that Spanish possessions in the New World were as rich as was rumoured. The voyage had consumed a full year of his life, achieving great political and little financial success. In its aftermath, Frobisher had good reason to think himself rehabilitated in the Queen's eyes, yet her good opinion alone was hardly recompense for the experience. Superficially at least, he was no better placed to advance his ambitions in late 1586 than had been the unfulfilled Moluccas raider of 1582. Despite any obvious sources of enrichment, however, it was at this time that he went back to Yorkshire and began to acquire the beginnings of the large estate that was to be so minutely described in his will only eight years later. In the latter part of 1586 he obtained the farm of Altofts; where, instead of occupying his childhood home, he built a new house 'neare the Parke' – possibly a mile to the south of the old manor (in that same year he was being sued by a neighbouring landlord, John Freston, in a dispute over pasture land in the area).[75] He also acquired – either at this time or subsequently – leases on manors at Glass Houghton and Brockholes (the latter with at least 100 acres), mills at Castleford and a messuage at Heath.[76] On 29 September that year, one Henry Middlemore wrote to Burghley, asking for a grant of certain unidentified lands and livings formerly owned by one Abington, noting that he understood them to be recently bestowed to Frobisher.[77] We can only speculate upon where, when and how Frobisher found the money for these acquisitions, but again, the possibilities are limited. It may be that he had disregarded, or otherwise freely interpreted, article 6 of Drake's orders to his fleet: that 'no man of what condition soever retayne or kepe to himselfe any gould, siluer, Iewellry, or any thinge of speciall price, for that there shalbe order taken where the same shalbe delivered . . .',[78] but this would have been risky, given Drake's dogmatic nature. There is the possibility that he received some form of *ex gratia* award from the Queen herself, by right as her appointee on the voyage; but this seems even less likely (if she did not have his wages promptly paid, a bonus could hardly have been more readily forthcoming). A far more probable source of enrichment, as we have seen, was that which he may have nurtured in the years between 1580 and 1585, in preying upon the lawful commerce that plied the ports of north-western Europe.

Even before the unrestricted issue of English letters of reprisal in May 1585 declared open season upon the vessels of Spain and her possessions, the Queen and the Admiralty had virtually abandoned large-scale attempts to regulate the pace of their countrymen's depredations. When Drake's fleet approached the Bay of Vigo at the commencement of his West Indies raid, armed English merchantmen were discovered there in force already, patrolling Spanish coastal waters in the hope of freeing the grain ships or taking compensation from Spanish prizes. These ships and their crews had not sprung into existence overnight to redress that recent wrong: there was a large body of relevant expertise upon the seas already, to which any number of outraged merchants could repair. In that long-standing broil of individual (and individualistic) enterprise, there would have been many opportunities for a man with robust sensitivities to make or add to a fortune. It will remain a matter of speculation whether Frobisher followed this business during the years prior to Drake's West Indies raid, but privateering is still the most feasible – and available – occupation to have provided for his energies and needs. Following his return to England in 1586, speculation is no longer necessary. From that moment almost until the hour of his death, eight years later, the privateering profession welcomed the return of an old craftsman, his appetite for the chase not only whetted by years of semi-respectability but under-pinned by a new and entirely welcome writ – that of the monarch who for-merly had sought so industriously to curb his tastes. As war approached, Frobisher discovered that his acquisitive instincts and the needs of his Queen had become almost entirely complementary.

SIXTEEN

The Slide: 1587–88

The hundreds of seizures and despoliations that had supported a generation of English privateers since the late 1560s were, by any measure, small acts of war against Spanish interests. Considered individually, however, none provided the provocation that might have triggered an open conflict. What had been missing was a palpable element of strategy, though the collaboration of the Queen and her ministers with many supposedly renegade freebooters had often been evident to Philip and his ambassadors in England. The events of 1585/6 were a new departure. As we have seen, it was in this year that the Spanish king first discerned in the activities of Drake, Ralegh and Grenville a general strategy of English arms against his interests. In the Low Countries too, it seemed that Elizabeth had chosen to confront Spanish ambitions head-on. In December 1585, Leicester disembarked at Flushing with his army of 6,000 troops, marking the first official English invasion of European soil since 1563. Even had the Earl's martial talents been one-tenth of those of his adversary, his brief – to reorganize the States-General's demoralized forces and reverse Parma's recent gains – was impossibly ambitious; nevertheless, a formal English presence upon 'Spanish' territory was an outright act of aggression that Philip could neither absolve nor overlook. Leicester himself poured oil upon the flames in February 1586, when, upon his own initiative, he accepted the title of Governor-General of the Netherlands from a States-General that was eager to offer any device to keep the English alliance intact.[1] Ostensibly, the act appeared to confirm that Elizabeth had at last decided to accept sovereignty over the Low Countries. In fact, she was furious at Leicester's presumption, but Philip had ceased to believe that her tantrums meant anything.

He was by now convinced that the conditions for war – both in Europe and his far-flung Spanish American possessions – were being set aggressively by her Protestant ministers of state. As a consequence, he listened more readily to the urgings of his own counsellors – in particular, to the arguments of his secretary, Juan de Idiáquez, and of the marquis of Santa Cruz that a conflict with England, 'simply as a defensive measure devoid of aggressive or ambitious intent'[2] though inevitably expensive, was unavoidable.

The logic employed by Idiáquez was as formidable as Santa Cruz's intended solution. Spain's continuing failure to crush the revolt in the Low Countries, the damage to her ocean-going trade, the resistance of France to the Hapsburg hegemony in Europe – all these problems would be expunged by the defeat of Elizabeth and the installation of a compliant, Catholic monarch upon the English throne: a monarch who would be far too busy reversing the English Reformation to exhibit independence of thought or action for years to come. At Philip's request, Santa Cruz resurrected a scheme he had first proposed in 1583, soon after his overwhelming defeat of Don Antonio's French fleet off Terceira (the occasion of which, incidentally, first made plain the potential of joint Spanish-Portuguese sea-power wielded aggressively). Then, over-confident of success – and falsely reassured by the cravenness with which certain vessels he had assumed to be English had fled the battle – Santa Cruz had argued for an immediate invasion of England to cauterize the wound of rebellion in the Low Countries. Philip had refused to accept his urgings, believing that the moment was not right for such schemes: 'since they depend on propitious timing and on chance occurrences which may create an opportunity in the future'.[3] The dryness of this observation had then disguised a deep reluctance which, three years later, had been freed from almost all of its underpinning logic. On 12 March 1586, Santa Cruz presented his plan once more, but this time as a proposal to counter a threat to Spain that was no longer provisional but clearly identifiable. It provided for a fleet that would have required the entire commercial and naval tonnage of the empire to meet – a total of 556 vessels, to transport a conquest army of 55,000 men directly from Spain to England.[4] The scale of the plan was therefore wholly unrealistic, but the fact that it had been resurrected at all carried two profound implications: that Philip was finally set upon some form of resolution to the English problem, and that the debate upon its nature had begun. Even as the Spanish King once more cooled his admiral's martial ardour, he ordered him to commence a concentration of warships at Lisbon. The enterprise was as yet an indistinct beast, but it had been given a name.

Rumours of Santa Cruz's plans were circulating in Spain as early as 15 May

1586, when letters from Biscay, published in England as Spanish advertise-
ments, repeated a general belief there that he was preparing a 'great army for
England of 800 sail of ships'.[5] Shrewdly, the reporter called it only a 'Spanish
brag', but that was hardly the point; when an autocrat allowed the tongues
of his people to wag in such a precocious manner, it meant that they were
being prepared psychologically for war, and that their King wanted the same
to be known abroad. Philip's other preoccupations, moreover, were beginning
to order themselves – with a good deal of assistance from Elizabeth – in such
a way as to make an English adventure more attractive. In that same month,
Mary Stuart 'secretly' communicated with Mendoza in Paris (Walsingham
was perfectly aware of her letter and its contents), offering to relinquish the
rights of her son James to succeed to the English throne in Philip's favour.
Philip himself was extremely interested in the proposal; so much so that he
encouraged, at least tacitly, another attempt on Elizabeth's life – the so-called
Babington plot. It failed dramatically; two weeks after the return of the West
Indies expedition, the ring-leaders were arrested and Mary Stuart's complicity in the scheme became apparent (her means of communicating with
the hapless Babington – via messages concealed in her beer-barrels – had been
devised and supervised by Walsingham himself).[6] The hapless Queen of Scots
was arrested and put on trial for treason: an event which both provided Philip
with his first legitimate reason to intervene in English affairs and – should
the court that tried Mary incline to harshness – removed any prospect of a
'French' succession to Elizabeth.

Slowly, all the good reasons for not dealing with the English problem were
dissipating. The next step – a catalyst for direct intervention – was provided
by Mary's execution in February 1587. Despite Elizabeth's almost convincing
expressions of revulsion at the deed, it had removed the most important inter-
nal threat against her; but the occasion had also presented the Spanish King
with an opportunity to move as the avenging hand of Christendom as a
whole. What might have been regarded merely as an act of unwarranted
aggression against another kingdom would now be seen – by all right-minded
princes – as a pious undertaking. Furthermore, with the dead Mary's obliging offer still in his hand, the King of Spain was now, in some eyes at least,
the legitimate successor to the English throne. For Philip, after decades of
attempting to reconcile conflicting spiritual, economic and political necessities, the requisites of Kingship and Godliness had finally, and precisely,
aligned themselves.

The extent to which England was ready to meet this challenge has been
the subject of much speculation. English public finances were in a parlous

state during these months, but then they almost always were. Burghley, increasingly resigned to the coming conflict, had managed to scrape together a war-chest of approximately £300,000, but much of this was subsequently squandered in support of the profligate Leicester's ineffectual campaign in the Low Countries. Additionally, the English acquisition of Flushing and Brill that had brought Leicester's fruitless intervention opened a further seeping wound in the Exchequer's resources that Drake's disappointing haul from the West Indies raid could hardly begin to patch. If war were coming, England was in no fit state to pay for it.

For her part, Elizabeth had long been aware that an enterprise against England was contemplated; perhaps even before Philip himself was firmly set upon it. From the moment in June 1585 when the *Primrose* had brought the captive *corregidor* of Biscay and his incriminating instructions to England, she was justified in believing that the Spanish King had committed himself. He had not; but Elizabeth lacked the spies at his Court that might have told her otherwise. She was therefore obliged to respond, but in some manner that did not further deplete her vanishing funds. There was no question that England might take the offensive at sea, much less in a land campaign. Thus, requests for further funds during these months from James VI, Henry of Navarre and the States-General were ignored as the Queen and Burghley devoted themselves to devising a realistic – that is, a cheap – strategy.[7] We do not know what alternatives were considered, but the only truly feasible option swiftly emerged as a clear favourite. If Philip could not be turned from his plans for England, he might be delayed. The best way to ensure that was to cut off the principal source of his armies' wages; and the only means by which this could be achieved was the interruption of his economic life-line. In 1585, for the first time, an English attempt to seize one of the West Indies plate fleets had received both official backing and naval vessels to help achieve it. It had failed, as every similar attempt during the sixteenth century was to fail; but that did not make each subsequent attempt any less worth-while. At the cost of a few ships' victualling and crews' wages, contributed towards a larger, privately funded expedition, Elizabeth had the opportunity simultaneously to enrich her own, depleted Exchequer and impoverish Philip's. As a strategy, therefore, it possessed the two overwhelming qualifi-cations to engage her support, and made a further attempt in 1586 almost obligatory.

Once more, however, prevarication and the spreading of commitments undermined any chances for success. By June 1586, John Hawkins had assem-bled five of the Queen's ships and thirteen armed merchantmen: their purpose to intercept the West Indies (or Portuguese East Indies) fleets. He was not then allowed to depart. As part of the Queen's over-nervous response to one of several, periodic rumours of a Guise invasion, he was ordered instead to 'ply up and down' the Channel, ready to thwart the expected French Catholic fleet. It was not until 6 August, when it became clear that the French ships had moved southwards against the Huguenot fleet at La Rochelle, that the Queen was sufficiently reassured to allow Hawkins his attempt upon the Indies fleets.[8] By the end of the month he was off the Portuguese coast, but it seems that most of the expected ships were already safely at Lisbon. Hawkins managed to take a small straggler from the *flota* and three other vessels, but these did not even cover the cost of his expedition.[9] He was back in Plymouth before the end of October, due, no doubt, to inadequate vict-ualling. As thin as its prospects had proved, this cruise was to be the last sub-stantial English naval effort of 1586.

Yet as the following year commenced, it was no longer possible to ignore the consistency of intelligence emanating from Spain and Portugal. Santa Cruz was assembling the royal galleons at Lisbon; further concentrations – including, possibly, the Tierra Firme *galeones* – lay at Cadiz, and unusually heavy sea-traffic from Spain's Mediterranean ports was observed passing west-wards through the straits of Gibraltar.[10] Furthermore, the shocking commit-ment evinced by her execution of Mary Stuart appears to have galvanized Elizabeth. Having provided Philip with the moral right to avenge that act, she fully appreciated how swift his response might be and moved accordingly to stall it. On 15 March 1587, Francis Drake was ordered to prepare a puni-tive expedition of four royal ships and such armed merchantmen as might be secured. Its purpose, for once unqualified by a chronically cautious monarch, was to interrupt Philip's war preparations by whatever means Drake saw fit: a commission for which he had waited most of his adult life. He himself pro-vided two ships, the *Drake* (formerly the *Madaleine*, to whose French owners he had quite correctly given compensation) and the *Elizabeth Bonaventure*; the Levant Company, whose vessels were habitually required to fight their way home through screens of Moslem privateers, provided four powerfully armed ships; and ten other merchant vessels joined the fleet at the promise of a share of Spanish booty.[11] On 2 April, having composed his famously florid farewell to Walsingham ('the wind commands me away', etc.), Drake slipped anchor at Plymouth. Several days later, a royal messenger hurried into the town, bearing Elizabeth's exhortation that Drake should not 'offer vio-lence to any of [Philip's] towns or shipping within harbouring, or to do any act of hostility upon the land'.[12] It was too late for such caution in every sense, but she probably understood that. No doubt the letter was intended for publication at home and abroad: as upon almost every other occasion that Drake put to sea, the Queen needed her alibi.

The 1587 expedition, in contrast to so many others of the age, must be reckoned an almost total success. Named after its first and most spectacularly achieved objective, this was the famous Cadiz raid: a synthesis of purpose, opportunism and fantastic good fortune which, albeit indirectly, was both to hamper Philip's capacity to wage war that year and increase Elizabeth's ability to resist him. At Cadiz, Drake caught and incapacitated about thirty Spanish ships (though few of these were intended for the assembling Armada); at Cape St Vincent, he stormed and captured Sagres Castle, destroying Henry the Navigator's famous library there; finally, having swept out to the Azores to make a belated attempt upon a plate fleet, he captured the Portuguese carrack *San Felipe*, returning almost fully laden from the East Indies. Her cargo brought booty worth some £140,000, of which the Queen's share came to £40,000.

Yet as lucrative as it had proved, the most profound effects of the raid were entirely psychological. Philip had no idea that the expedition was the final English raid of that year, and was thus obliged to protect the incoming Indies fleets that carried the means of financing his forthcoming English adventure. Accordingly, Santa Cruz was ordered to employ his existing concentration of Spanish warships from Lisbon to provide cover and escort duty in the Atlantic. The task was not discharged safely until the end of September, after which Philip's foremost sea-commander, physically and emotionally exhausted, returned to Lisbon and promptly took himself to bed, from which he did not stir for weeks. The strains also told upon Philip himself, who seems to have suffered an almost total nervous collapse in November.[13] The enterprise of England, intended to have been set forth in the autumn of 1587, was definitely off for that year.

For once, the English had had an indisputable victory. Yet the very success of the raid blinded Drake, and, to a certain degree, even the prudent Hawkins, into misunderstanding its significance: they had come to the conclusion that such operations might be sufficient in themselves to maintain England against Spain; that war could be kept far from English shores by the assiduous application of sea-power alone. For Hawkins, this meant semi-permanent patrols off the Azores to take successive treasure fleets and thus strangle Philip's capacity to make war; for Drake, it was an unremitting campaign against the Spanish and Portuguese ports that sheltered the gathering war fleet (with, of course, every opportunity to seize further plunder taken in the meantime). Unfortunately, their ambitions anticipated English abilities by some two centuries. Sixteenth-century England had neither the administrative structures nor the resources to maintain ships 'on-station', nor even the proper understanding of what was required to allow it. The ships themselves were probably not sufficiently weatherly to withstand the attrition of more than one voyage each year – much less so their crews, whose victualling was almost always inadequate for more than a few weeks at sea. No matter what daring her sea-commanders had shown in carrying their flags to the furthest corner of the Spanish empire, Elizabeth's navy was a force designed to protect home waters; it was not, in any sense, a strategic instrument of global warfare. Reality imposed itself at the very first attempt to further this apparently strategic design when, as a corollary of his sterling work to reorganize the manning of the Queen's ships, Hawkins attempted to push his scheme of outfitting a squadron of ships to patrol the Atlantic for up to six months. It does not seem to have been seriously considered, much less attempted. Had it been so, it would have struck upon the rock of victualling agents, their paymasters, the Privy Council and the Queen herself – who continued, quite sensibly, to be obsessed by the implications of Philip managing to send just half of his fleet northwards whilst Drake, Hawkins and the other leading captains were at sea, attempting to emulate the success of the Cadiz raid.

For all of its material success, therefore, the 1587 expedition did not alter the balance of power or, to any palpable degree, resources. Strategically, Spanish losses to Drake were more than balanced by Parma's seizure of Sluys on 26 July in that year and the abject failure of Leicester's land campaign. In the aftermath of England's striking naval success, Spanish and Portuguese ports were not blockaded, supply convoys maintained their duties unmolested, and, most ominously, the Tierra Firme *galeones* arrived safely at Lisbon, carrying 16,000,000 ducats' value of bullion as ballast in their holds. The Great Enterprise – interrupted but hardly weakened – proceeded.

In fact, the scales tilted further in favour of Spain as the months passed. By spring of the following year, Philip's other strategic problems in Europe – all of which might otherwise have created potential distractions from the Great Enterprise – had eased considerably. Chastened by its utter failure, Leicester's army withdrew from the Netherlands in December 1587. Days earlier, Guise achieved a brilliant victory over Henry of Navarre's German mercenaries at Auneau. The political ascendancy he derived from this – particularly in the further sidelining of the ineffectual Henry III – was wholly advantageous to Spain. In Paris, Mendoza collaborated closely with Guise throughout the winter of 1587/8, and received strong assurances of support for the proposed invasion of England: most usefully, a promise to secure the French Channel ports to provide logistical assistance to the Armada, should this prove necessary. On 12 May 1588, this strengthening alliance was further buttressed by the 'day of the barricades', when Henry III's already feeble ability to influence events in his own kingdom was finally extinguished. Almost all of Paris rose in revolt, and the King was forced to beg Guise to placate the mob – a mob that in any case stood firmly for the Guiseoise cause. Royal authority in France had effectively collapsed, and north of La Rochelle itself, there was no longer a port in France that would send out ships to interfere with a Spanish fleet moving against England. Only the Netherlander rebels, deprived of their English army and representing no incremental threat (being at war with Spain already), now stood against Spanish arms. For Philip II, the residual reasons for not turning against England had dissolved in such a manner as to hint at the hand of God urging him forward: a welcome reassurance to complement the powerful urges of logic and necessity.

SEVENTEEN

The Winter Guard

Drake had been given his ships and the freedom to use them aggressively upon the coast of Spain, and Hawkins, deep into the stewardship of his 'Second Bargain', was busily upgrading the Queen's ships and the infrastructures that supported them in dock and upon the seas. Lacking the reputation and influence of these men, what role did Frobisher have in the preparations for the coming war? In June 1587, Mendoza reported to Philip that Richard Grenville had been ordered to take out four ships to re-supply and reinforce Drake's expedition off the Spanish coast. Grenville had refused, apparently because he would not serve under his upstart Devonshire neighbour. Frobisher had then been considered in his place, 'who they thought would agree with Drake better than the other'.[1] A few days later, Mendoza expanded upon what he took to be the Privy Council's reasoning: that they considered it necessary to send some person who would not challenge Drake's authority, but defer to him unreservedly. If this was indeed what was required, Frobisher was not the man for the job. Before the end of June, Mendoza again wrote from Paris, saying that the Earl of Cumberland intended to go out to reinforce Drake, 'although Captain Frobisher is appointed to the command, which he refused.' Grenville had perhaps put it more explicitly, but Frobisher too had found a single taste of Drake's autocratic leadership a rich and sating experience, and had little desire for more of that which the hapless William Borough was currently sampling off the coast of Spain.[2]

For the months following the return of the West Indies expedition, we have no information on Frobisher's movements. The rigours of such an arduous expedition may have inclined him to take a rare leave of absence from the sea – possibly, the business of searching out suitable properties in Yorkshire provided the excuse to indulge himself in this manner. However, by the turn of the year there was little doubt in English minds that war with Spain loomed, and a man of Frobisher's talents was not likely to be underemployed. Few others available for service in the Queen's ships had his experience of keeping a diffuse command together upon the seas: a talent which, in an age of composite fleets, could hardly be over-esteemed. His employment in Drake's West Indies raid had, undoubtedly, been more than a probationary post; the Queen herself had regarded his presence therein as a necessary corrective to Drake's independence of mind, and he had acquitted himself dutifully. Now, however, he received his definitive reinstatement in her good offices, when, during the summer of 1587, he was appointed to the command of a small Channel fleet of seven naval vessels – ostensibly with the sort of opaque, unspecific remit that Elizabeth was always happiest to provide.[3] His flagship was a familiar vessel, the *Foresight*; he took command of her on 18 August, as 'Capten and Admyrall', upon wages of 16sh. per day. The squadron was at sea for eighty days until 31 October; after a month's refit, it returned to its station until the turn of the year.[4]

Though Hawkins's accounts for the navy tell only the bare detail of these movements, it is clear that Frobisher's role was a modest mirror to Drake's: the sentinel facing the other extremity of Philip's English strategy. As the Cadiz expedition had interrupted preparations for the great fleet gathering in Iberian ports, Frobisher's was set out to intercept any and all Spanish sea-traffic with the Low Countries, to strangle the Spanish King's means of supplying and communicating with his government there. For the first time, therefore, he received a royal appointment that recognized precisely his principal talent. If any man could smell out a Spanish merchantman, scurrying northwards below the horizon with packets of letters and pay for hungry mercenaries, it was one who had devoted the greater part of his adult life to doing just that – preferably in darkness or foul weather, when the chances of being disturbed at his trade were minimal. However, he was now committed to broader, more august duties. As the principal naval commander in the Narrow Seas, he was to provide cover and support for Leicester's ultimately unsuccessful attempt to save Sluys for the Dutch rebels; a task that may have given the Earl some sleepless nights, after an unnamed but trusting hand – possibly that of Burghley or Howard – directed that Frobisher be given charge of carrying his treasure-chest to the Low Countries.[5] There was also, not least, the duty of preventing Parma's invasion army from making its short but fateful passage across the Narrow Seas (an attempt which, it was still believed in England, might be made without naval support from the Armada).

After months of anonymity, there is suddenly a flurry of references to Frobisher as he went about these several businesses. In July, intelligences to Philip II from Spanish spies in England reported that he was about to sail to take up station off Dunkirk to thwart attempts by Catholic privateers to seize the English ships that supplied the rebels.[6] In October, Mendoza wrote to his master from Paris, noting that Frobisher's squadron was still on station there, though prevented from chasing the privateers in-shore by the uncharted shoals that flanked the Dunkirk Roads.[7] From Frobisher's own correspondence to the new Lord Admiral Howard and others, it is clear that he was working with considerable industry to justify the Queen's rediscovered faith in his abilities. Throughout the autumn months of 1587, he busily chased both Spanish ships and the rumours of an approaching campaign that they carried. In a letter to Leicester on 17 September, he reported upon his recent reconnaissance of Antwerp and 'the Dunkrykes', and of the varying success of his efforts to blockade the coast. For once, he seems to have made an attempt to discern which of his potential victims were friendly to England, though this was not always easy. He complained that the Netherlander rebels (perhaps loath to allow their commercial traffic to be interrupted by such minor distractions as war) were issuing ships with blank passports in Leicester's name, and asked for 'some synamente or by some selle of yo(u)r owne with these we maye knowe whom to staye and whoo to lett past'.[8] During the winter months (that is, following 2 January 1588, when his squadron returned to port to refit once more) his correspondence ceased, though this had more to do with high seas than inaction. When better weather allowed him to resume his station and send out his pinnaces once more, his industry was immediately apparent. On 9 March 1588, Howard wrote to Walsingham, to inform him that Frobisher had spoken to the crews of two ships coming from Lisbon; they had told him – perhaps under persuasion – that the great Armada was to sail on 15 March. The following day, Howard reported that Frobisher had put into Margate roads with first news of the death of the Prince of Condé, and that Henry of Navarre was also thought to be in great danger. On 13 April, Howard received another letter from Frobisher, concerning word of the Spanish fleet being at sea (it was not), of large-scale movements of Parma's troops in the Low Countries, and of the interception of a fly-boat off Calais, which was found to be carrying a hundred pilots (including two Englishmen) bound for service in the Armada.

It is evident, moreover, that Frobisher was becoming something more than the Lord Admiral's eyes and ears at sea. Howard instituted an unofficial war-council during the early months of 1588 (its composition was later confirmed to Walsingham in a letter of 19 June).[9] Initially, this appears to have comprised Howard's nephews Lord Thomas Howard (second son of the executed Duke of Norfolk, now restored to his dignity) and Lord Sheffield, Francis Drake and John Hawkins; but very soon Frobisher and Thomas Fenner were admitted for their counsels. Very diverse temperaments had thus been assembled at the Lord Admiral's order, yet a consensus swiftly emerged upon how to prosecute the coming war. Howard seems at first to have favoured (or at least acquiesced to) a defensive concentration in the Channel and North Sea to deny Parma a crossing into England – a proposal that recommended itself all the more strongly for being precisely the one Elizabeth herself favoured. In the face of his new council's urging, however, he become an enthusiastic proponent of an aggressive pre-emptive strategy: to take the battle to the coast of Spain. Later, on 14 June 1588, as his fleet fought contrary winds at Plymouth, he was to write to the Queen as their mouthpiece: 'The opinion of Sir Francis Drake, Master Hawkins, Master Frobisher and others that be men of greatest judgement (and) experience, as also my own concurring with them in the same, is that (the) surest way to meet with the Spanish fleet is upon their coast, or in any harbour of their own, and there to defeat them'.[10] In defending this strategy the following day, the Lord Admiral referred to his advisors as 'men of greatest experience that this realm hath.' Undoubtedly, Drake and Hawkins were still seduced by the imagined strategic lessons of Cadiz, and Frobisher was always ready to carry a battle to the enemy; but their urging of an offensive tactical policy at this late hour reflected an inescapable truth: that the only other realistic alternative – to challenge and seek to defeat a Spanish fleet off the English coast – allowed no possibility of failure, if England were to be saved by other than a bloody campaign upon English soil. Though Drake's desperate exhortation of 13 April – that 'the advantage of time and place in all martial actions is half a victory; which being lost is irrecoverable' – may have been regarded as a truism even then, it was absolutely timely nevertheless, even if the means by which such an advantage might be secured did not yet lie in English hands.[11]

Inevitably, the entreaties of Howard, Drake, Hawkins and Frobisher broke against the twin rocks of thrift and caution. Ships at sea were more expensive to maintain than ships in dock – particularly during spring and early summer 1588, when unseasonable storms were battering anything that put to sea – and the floor of Elizabeth's war-chest was now clearly visible. Hawkins had done great work in bringing her naval vessels up to fighting standard, but the cost had been enormous. Total naval expenditure (including the new ships programme) had risen from £17,903 in 1585 to £29,391 in 1586, £44,000 in 1587 and a near insupportable £90,813 in the Armada year.[12] With such attrition upon the public purse, pennies had to be counted carefully. Once under sail, men began to earn their sea-pay and victuals (the latter costing the Queen 7½d. per man per day at sea),[13] and food brought to a quay-side to provision a departing fleet had a habit of going bad before lading. Until Elizabeth could be sure that Philip was irrevocably set upon his enterprise, she was loath to loosen the reins upon her prodigal sea-commanders. She was also still exercised by the all-too-likely inability of an English battle-fleet on a southerly course to sight or engage a Spanish fleet moving north upon its great business.

Yet Philip, too, was burdened by the march of time and its commensurate costs. The marquis of Santa Cruz, worn out by his cares and duties, died at the beginning of February (he was sixty-two years old, though he looked at least ten years older).[14] His fleet, battered by its unwonted convoy duties, lay rotting and typhus-ridden at Lisbon: at least as much in need of urgent repairs as its English counterpart had been in the previous year. Even less so than Elizabeth, Philip had few 'professional' alternatives who might have filled Santa Cruz's role effectively. Aware also that the growing problems of his ships required something more than an admiral's touch, he now chose Don Alonso Pérez de Guzmán el Bueno, Duke of Medina Sidonia and Captain General of Andalusia: the premier grandee of Spain and one of the few Spaniards to emerge from the Cadiz episode with his reputation enhanced. Then, ignoring the somewhat inflated rumour of *el Draco*'s invincibility, he had led a relief force of militia into the port to prevent its sacking by the victorious Englishmen. In recognition of his feat – which made him the only Spanish officer to have distinguished himself in a campaign against Drake – he was appointed as Spain's supreme naval commander: to work an administrative miracle at Lisbon and then to put to sea to achieve its martial equivalent.

Medina Sidonia was a courtly, affable man, in whose veins ran the blood of a true civil servant. Indeed, his attention to detail was one of his most apposite talents, honed over several years' experience of outfitting the *flotas* for their annual trans-Atlantic voyages.[15] Nevertheless, he accepted his appointment very reluctantly, having first begged to be excused and, recommending in his place, the *Adelantado Mayor* of Castile. This heartfelt (and undoubtedly sincere) suggestion was refused, and the new admiral reluctantly took up the poison chalice, his reward for having priorily exhibited a degree of competence. Haunted by the possibilities of failure – and tormented already by a premonition of his own death – he set himself to the great business in hand, with its potential for disaster firmly in mind.

The new admiral's most pressing problem was the timetable he had inherited. For years, Philip had reacted to the depredations of English privateers and the policies of their Queen with remarkable self-control; but having determined to rid himself of that twin canker, and being thwarted in his original schedule, he now pushed for a resolution with indecent haste. From the end of 1587, the resources of southern Portugal and Andalusia were consumed to supply the gathering Armada.[16] Any measure to achieve the overwhelming concentration of force that the needs of an overstretched empire had long prevented was now attempted, as if the entity existed to serve the purpose, rather than the reverse. Santa Cruz's 1587 fleet, a mongrel aggregation of sixty ships (few of them Spanish), stiffened by a core of thirteen royal galleons, was joined at Lisbon by the eight Cadiz galleons that regularly guarded the Indies fleet – all of them sound, relatively new ships – and the twelve remaining galleons of the once powerful Portuguese navy (one of which, the *San Martin*, was to be Medina Sidonia's flagship). From Naples, four galleases – large, hybrid warships carrying both lateen sails and banks of oars – were summoned to join the Spanish fleet, and two large carracks were hired from Venice and Genoa, which arrived at Lisbon by the end of April. To support the principal warships, merchantmen were hired or commandeered in ports from Bilbao to Barcelona – some even from the Low Countries – and armed from the steady stream of ordnance issuing from the foundries of Madrid and Lisbon. By April 1588, a fleet of some 130 sail was in being, if not yet battle-ready: supplied with 2,431 pieces of ordnance and a stupendous – though ultimately superfluous – stockpile of 123,790 rounds of shot.[17]

Yet it was not so much the quantity of materiel assembling at Lisbon that concerned Medina Sidonia as its quality and disposition. The administrative paralysis encouraged by Santa Cruz's decline and death had fostered a malaise that permeated the core of the fleet. In principle, ships were constantly maintained in a sea-worthy condition (a corollary of the pressures placed upon Philip's resources by English raids); but this meant that shore-leave for the mariners of the fleet was grudgingly and infrequently granted – and, furthermore, that frequent ship-board epidemics struck down the maximum number of seamen. Without a firm purpose – nor even, latterly, a commander – to keep them distracted from their unhappy lot, morale amongst the lower ranks had become extremely poor. Consequently, desertions and sickness took a heavy toll; the total complement of Santa Cruz's fleet had fallen from approximately 12,000 men to little more than 8,000 by the time that

Medina Sidonia took command.[18] Yet if he was no match for his predecessor as a leader of men, the Duke – whose own, vast estates required a semi-regal administration – was a born logistician. Immediately upon arriving in Lisbon he issued a stream of orders: ill-sorted ships' supplies, thrust haphazardly into gun-decks, were cleared, sorted and re-stacked; rotting food barrels were removed and replaced or repaired; medical facilities for the large number of sick seamen laid up in the ships were improved from non-existent to merely lamentable; repairs to the ships themselves began to be undertaken in a systematic manner, with each ship's officers responsible – for once – for the correct application of administrative orders in their own vessel.

To provision a fleet of this size was a titanic undertaking. The harvests of Andalucia were requisitioned by the King's officials, who had entered the provinces armed with the powers to persuade, to cajole and, ultimately, to make off with their reluctant suppliers' produce.[19] A large proportion of the provisions thus secured was spoiled *en route* to Lisbon, but the ships' vict-ualling lists showed that the Armada would eventually depart from Lisbon with 110,000 quintals of biscuit, 4,000 quintals of rice, 6,000 bushels of beans, 3,000 quintals of cheese, 6,000 quintals of bacon and the same of salt fish, and 11,000 pipes (of 126 gallons) each of wine and water.[20] To bring this vast bounty into Lisbon, absolute priority was given to the vessels that carried it. No ship that was not employed to service some aspect of the coming campaign was allowed to sail from or into the Tagus estuary, where beached vessels, their hulls being repaired and re-caulked, littered the shores and inlets for miles. To enable this frenzied programme to be maintained, the timber supplies of central Portugal were exhausted; but by the latter part of April, the work was done. Insofar as any contemporary fleet could achieve the task that Philip had set in the appointed time, the great Armada stood ready, awaiting its orders to sail.

As Medina Sidonia laboured on a Herculean scale, the concentration of the English fleet had commenced. In December, Elizabeth ordered Drake to gather a squadron to operate from Plymouth to seize any Spanish and Nether-lander vessels braving the western Channel.[21] He was given five of the Queen's ships – *Revenge, Hope, Nonpareil, Swiftsure* and *Ayde* – and a further twenty-three vessels by 5 February (most of the latter were armed by merchantmen, dazzled by the prospect of service with the age's paramount purloiner of Spanish wealth).[22] Still more ships were to come to Plymouth in the follow-ing weeks, until Drake had over sixty vessels under his command. It was not, in its component parts, a fleet that might have borne close enquiry of its antecedents. At the moment of supreme national crisis, that perennial sustainer and curse of Elizabeth's foreign policy, the privateering industry, had gathered to repay their Queen for decades of intermittent royal patronage. When England's ships set out to face the Armada, many of them – particularly those set out by the ports of Dorset and Cornwall – would be known to the Admiralty principally through the legal cases they had generated in former years.[23]

At Queenborough, meanwhile, Howard assembled eight of the Queen's galleons, soon to be joined by the now-deceased Earl of Lincoln's ship, *White Lion*, and seven smaller vessels; in the Channel, Sir Henry Palmer commanded a flotilla of nine ships – mainly armed coasters – whose role was to screen the Low Countries (Sir Henry Seymour succeeded Palmer in this post in April); and at Chatham, the most powerful ships in the English fleet – the four 'great ships of the navy', *Triumph*, *Elizabeth Jonas*, *Bear* and *Victory* – prepared to enter the Channel.[24] There, on 21 April 1588, Martin Frobisher transferred out of the *Antelope* (his flagship since 1 January) to take command of the largest of these – probably the largest vessel in either the English or Spanish fleet – the *Triumph*.[25]

The four great ships, the nucleus of Elizabeth's navy, had been Hawkins's particular concern during the winter months. As recently as 12 October 1587, the report of the chief shipwrights at Chatham had been extremely critical of their condition; of the *Triumph*, they observed: 'The same ship we find much decayed in the timbers, but most in the quarters . . . she cannot be of any long continuance except these imperfections be remedied. Nevertheless, in considering her strong building, with a little addition to the same, it bringeth us in good hope that she may answer any sudden service that may be required, specially for the summer season.'[26] Their optimism was well founded. Medina Sidonia's frantic efforts at Lisbon had the effect of enthusing Hawkins's workmen also; by the time of his final pre-campaign report to Burghley on 17 July 1588, he was able to claim that '. . . the four great ships, the Triumph, the Elizabeth Jonas, the Bear and the Victory, are in royal and most perfect estate; and it is not seen by them, neither do they feel that they have been at sea, more than if they had ridden at Chatham.'[27]

By contemporary standards the *Triumph* was a monstrous vessel, of more than 1,000 tons. With a keel fully 100 feet long and a beam of 40 feet, she was – and was intended to be – a sea-going fortress. Built in 1561, probably one of the very last of the older, high-charged designs, her full-strength complement was 350 mariners, 50 gunners and up to 330 soldiers (though the declared accounts of the navy show that Frobisher carried only 498 men in total during the campaign).[28] Her armament, according to Sir William Winter's report of

30 December 1585, consisted of nine demi-cannons, four cannon-periers, four-teen culverins, seven demi-culverins, six sacres, two minions, four port-pieces, ten fowlers and twelve bases – a total weight of ordnance of 68 tons.[29] Given the rapid development of English shipbuilding technology during these years, it is likely that she was already obsolete by 1588; but like one of the mammoth battleships of the twentieth-century's wars, whose demise was foreseen long before the last of them went to the breakers' yards, she needed only to close and engage to render her limitations academic.

This, the largest of the Queen's ships, was also one of the most expensive to maintain, provision and – unthinkably – to replace, should she go to the sea-bed during the coming campaign. Frobisher's stewardship of the *Triumph* was therefore a singular act of faith in his abilities. Probably, it was a recognition of his limitations also. When we consider the role that the Queen and Howard must have envisaged for a ship of such imposing dimensions, the qualities required of her captain become evident. Her size was undoubtedly intended to intimidate the enemy, but bulk comes with its own, intrinsic disadvantages. In any complicated manoeuvre, her relative unwieldiness would be likely to put her at a disadvantage against more modern and agile vessels (though Frobisher would disprove this assumption in spectacular fashion during the approaching campaign). In a head-to-head maul, however, her weight of ordnance and ability to absorb punishment might prove decisive. This latter possibility had become something of a preoccupation to Howard. English tactics in the coming sea-battle reflected a generally held perception of Spanish abilities: particularly, that the Spanish *tercios* were superior to their English counterparts. At Terceira, six years earlier, Santa Cruz had manoeuvred his Spanish-Portuguese fleet to within boarding range of the French enemy, and his troops had annihilated Strozzi's mercenaries thereafter; with that lesson of Spanish martial superiority all too plain still, the ships of the Armada were expected to repeat a well-proven – and well-known – tactic. To counter it, the English intention was to stand off and attempt to pound the Spanish fleet into dissolution – a new and untested strategy for men whose principal preoccupation to date had been to close with and board an enemy, using minimum force in order to preserve the cargoes and ships they wished to steal.

It was understood, nevertheless, that reality does not always conform to intentions. Should such tactics fail, and the enemy manage to lay their grappling irons across some of the English ships, the massive *Triumph* would be a particularly tempting target. Her soldiers would be hard pressed against a determined assault by picked Spanish troops, and so the man who commanded her needed to be as much a fighter as a sailor – someone, moreover, who could not be cowed by reputations. If Howard chose Frobisher for this task deliberately, he had made a shrewd decision. During the campaign, elements of the Spanish Armada repeatedly mistook the giant *Triumph* for the English flagship and directed their attentions accordingly. Howard, in the *Ark Ralegh* (now renamed the *Ark Royal*), a smaller vessel but the most modern ship in the navy, was able to direct his forces without attracting the constant pounding that Medina Sidonia in the *San Martin* was obliged to endure.

The strategy implied something of a slur upon Frobisher's abilities – a recognition of steadfastness rather than tactical brilliance. Yet there could have been no more appropriate role for him in the coming maul. He was utterly reliable in combat, a pounder who could be assigned a position and forgotten thereafter; and with the *Triumph*, he had been given the instrument to realize this potential. She was an imperfect yet intimidating giant, one that, if English tactics failed to prevent the Spaniards closing, was almost certainly expected to be in the thick of the coming conflict. Rarely can the manifest of a vessel's qualities and failings have reflected so closely those of her commander.

The clash of fleets, hurriedly provided for and expected by even the most optimistic peace-mongers, was nevertheless slow in coming. During April, Howard's ships – troubled by unfavourable weather and lack of victuals – lay first at Queensborough and then Margate. Since his appointment as commander of the combined English fleet in the previous December, Howard had been kept firmly in the Thames estuary and eastern Channel, covering the Low Countries against an attempt by Parma to bring his army across the Narrow Seas in its fleet of barges. This strategy was elucidated in detail in a Privy Council document of 15 February 1588, which shows clearly the depth of self-delusion under which the Queen and her principal ministers officers made their assumptions, both of the threat before them and of England's capacity to meet it. In addition to preventing the Armada and Parma's forces from concentrating, a diversion to Portugal was also considered (to stir the Portuguese people into attempting some unspecified – and no doubt suicidal – disruption of the Spanish war effort), as was an expedition to the Azores, 'to intercept some Indian fleets'.[30] Quite how these aims were to be achieved concurrently was not touched upon, but as long as each was considered to be a viable goal, the division of English forces was unavoidable. In having several strategies to meet several threats, the Queen thus fell by default upon the very worst option. In the early months of 1588, Drake's force alone stood ready to engage the entire strength of the Armada in the western Channel.

Had it done so, it would then have been almost impossible for the squadrons of Howard and Seymour, fighting prevailing south-westerlies, to join him from Dover and Margate in time to prevent his destruction. On 30 March, Drake, giving his 'poor opinion' of this strategy to the Privy Council, once more urged a more forward, aggressive policy:

> If her Majesty and your Lordships think that the King of Spain meaneth any invasion in England, then doubtless his force is and will be great in Spain; and thereon he will make his groundwork or foundation, whereby the Prince of Parma may have the better entrance, which, in mine own judgement, is most to be feared. But if there may be such a stay or stop made by any means of this fleet in Spain, that they may not come through the seas as conquerors – which, I assure myself, they think to do – then shall the Prince of Parma have such a check thereby as were meet.[31]

Howard, prompted by Frobisher, Thomas Howard and Sheffield (who remained under his direct command; Fenner's *Nonpareil* was already at Plymouth with Drake), strongly agreed. As early as 17 April, pushing this strategy, he set down a hopeful memorandum, noting which of the ships should 'go with the Lord Admiral towards the West Country'.[32] Walsingham supported him from within the Council, but it was not until 21 May that the Queen finally relented, and allowed Howard to move his ships westwards. Once in receipt of his new orders he did not dawdle; two days later, at eight o'clock in the morning, his fleet – thirty-eight ships and pinnaces – was off Plymouth, where Drake's sixty sail came out to meet it. There, Drake was appointed vice-admiral of the combined fleet and Hawkins its rear-admiral. For two days thereafter, their ships took on water in Plymouth, after which, the fleet's dispositions agreed, they prepared to sail south-west with the first favourable tide, to meet and defeat the Armada at sea.

Three weeks later, they remained at Plymouth still. The appalling weather that had laid upon the Channel during the spring and early summer months kept the ships firmly in harbour. As usual, the fleet had been provided with victuals for a month only, commencing from 19 May. Ships' companies were therefore obliged to make inroads into their sea-stores; on 28 May, Howard reported to Burghley that the supply vessels, allocated to follow the fleet from Chatham, were not nearly ready to sail, and that in consequence the fleet had only eighteen days' supplies remaining. Nevertheless, he remained committed to an early battle, if for entirely practical reasons: 'God send us a wind to put us out, for go we will, though we starve.' Unfortunately, God did not oblige, and starvation began to seem the more likely outcome. Marmaduke Darell, the assistant Surveyor of the Victuals, frantically scoured the countryside around Plymouth to provide a further six days' supplies (and ran up debts of £900 in the process); but it was only on 22 June that victualling barges from London brought a further month's victuals for the fleet.[33] These administrative distractions, and rumours that the Spanish fleet's departure from Lisbon was imminent (or that it had already sailed), gradually reduced Howard to alternating moods of despondency and self-justification. At the end of May, he wrote plaintively to Burghley:

'there is here the gallantest company of captains, soldiers and mariners that I think ever was seen in England. It were pity they should lack meat when they are so desirous to spend their lives in her Majesty's service. I would to God I did know how the world went with our Commissioners; for if I know nothing I must do thereafter, and think of the worst.'[34]

By 23 June, having tried and failed three times to put to sea, Howard's nerves had frayed quite through. The tenor of his correspondence, even to the Queen herself, had become almost hysterical: 'For the love of Jesus Christ, Madam, awake thoroughly, and see the villainous treasons round about you, against your Majesty and your realm, and draw your forces round about you, like a mighty prince, to defend you.'[35]

It was no longer clear whether those 'villainous treasons' emanated from agents of the Spanish Crown in England, the victuallers of the fleet or the very weather that kept his fleet in Plymouth Sound; but Howard needed a battle, and very soon. His intention, bolstered by the urgent pleas of his council, had been to catch the Spaniards off their own coast, but it was not merely poor weather that made this unlikely. On 9 June, Walsingham had acknowledged that Howard was 'minded' to go to Bayona, but warned him that the Queen would prefer him, as always, 'to ply up and down in somme indifferent place between the coast of Spain and this realm, so as you may be able to answer any attempt that the said fleet shall make either against this realm, Ireland or Scotland'.[36] In other words, though Howard had now come to the west to force a resolution with the Armada, he was still being required to cover the same perceived threats that had formerly been his charge at Margate. With such blithely unrealistic instructions, it is hardly surprising that he could not be calm.

Conflicting reports of Spanish movements did not make his task easier. On 23 June, he mentioned a report 'from a sure fellow', suggesting that the

Armada would first put into a French port to take on a Guise army. The following day, Drake wrote to Walsingham that the 'Spanish forces are decried to be near at hand in several companies on our coast . . .'; and Thomas Fenner, in a memorial dated 14 July, reported the sighting of thirty sail off the Lizard on 19 June.[37] None of these reports could be ignored; yet equally, none could be regarded as definitive. The Armada might already be off Sluys, or it might lie under the waters of Biscay; the English Admiral's eyes at sea had been effectively blinded by the fog of a war whose precise form remained as yet obscure.

At the beginning of July, however, Howard received the reliable word that at least part of the Armada was approaching the Channel (a detachment of some fourteen sail had been sighted about fifty miles southwest of the Lizard). In fact, the entire Spanish fleet had been at sea since 30 May, though its progress northwards had been hampered by unweatherly stragglers and contrary winds. By 12 June, the main body of its ships had passed only so far north as Cape Finisterre. There, worried by the attrition upon his stores, Medina Sidonia held his fleet for several days, waiting for the last of his victualling boats to bring their bounty. Supplies of fresh water in particular were very low, principally due to poor casking. On 19 June, Medina Sidonia's council of war heard the details of these problems, and thereafter voted to put in at Corunna to re-supply the Armada.[38]

It was a fortuitous decision. About fifty ships of the fleet had come to anchor within Corunna harbour when a great storm swept north-eastwards from the Atlantic. The vessels still at sea scattered precipitously to avoid destruction upon lee shores; two days later, most limped into the Vivero and Gijon harbours, but more than thirty ships remained unaccounted for as late as 24 June. From his quarters in the *San Martin*, Medina Sidonia gratefully accepted what he wished to believe was the hand of God, and dictated a letter to his King, suggesting the enterprise be postponed for another year, or even that a further effort to secure peace with England be made. The reply came swiftly, and as he must have expected.

On 5 July, Howard's ships finally managed to warp out of Plymouth to take up a screening station in the western Channel. The English fleet was divided into three squadrons (though remaining in contact), with Howard's vessels in the centre, Hawkins's to the north off Scilly and Drake's off the French coast near Ushant: 'thus we are fain to do' the latter complained, 'else with this wind they might pass by and never the wiser.'[39] It was the soundest strategy under the circumstances, but futile nonetheless. The same north wind that had allowed the English fleet to put out of Plymouth Sound had also driven the scattered remnants of the Armada back into Corunna, to rejoin the main body of their fleet. Some of these stragglers had been sighted by the southernmost ships of the English fleet; Drake and Hawkins tried to follow, hoping to surprise the Armada whilst in harbour, but after three days of struggling against a wind that had perversely veered southerly once more, they brought their ships back into the Channel. By 12 July, the entire English fleet was at Plymouth once more, its victuallers scouring the already emptied town to replenish its exhausted supplies.

Howard's ships had barely sighted an enemy ship to date, yet the cost of keeping this fleet in being – a fleet far larger than any that England's rudimentary naval establishment had yet attempted to supply – was already prohibitive. For the four 'great ships' alone, the monthly victualling bill was £1,551 (to meet it Hawkins asked Burghley for charges of £10,191 to 13 July); the twenty ships set out by the City of London required in victuals and hire charges some £2,300 per month (in a letter of 10 July, the London mercer Thomas Cordell pointedly advised the Privy Council that the Lord Mayor and Common Council of London would victual these vessels at their own charge 'for one month longer'); whilst Drake's squadron required almost £9,400 for its service to 28 July.[40] Howard concluded an account of this grim tally with the good news that he had fully £500 remaining in his own hands, but that Her Majesty should find a further £19,070 as soon as might be convenient.

Not surprisingly, as the man most responsible for finding the necessary funds (and with no real idea of how he might continue to do so), Burghley was losing a little of his customary generosity of spirit. In a letter to Walsingham, he somewhat callously observed: 'I marvel that where so many are dead on the seas the pay is not dead with them . . . A man would wish, if peace cannot be had, that the enemy would not longer delay, but prove, as I trust, his evil fortune'.[41]

Fortunately for the Lord Treasurer's peace of mind, the enemy was about to relieve the pressure on his nation's ledger. Even as Howard dropped his anchor in Plymouth Sound on 12 July, the great Armada was plying out of Corunna. Nine days later, the Lord Admiral of England managed to scrawl a short note to Walsingham: 'Sir – I will not trouble you with any long letter; we are at present otherwise occupied than with writing.'[42] On the rare balmy afternoon of 19 July, Captain Fleming's bark *Golden Hind* had rushed into Plymouth harbour under all sail, having sighted the main body of the Armada off the Lizard. Immediately, Howard ordered all of his ships that were not still revictualling to warp out of harbour and assemble off Rame Head. The tide was against them that afternoon, and even allowing for delays to finish the odd,

apocryphal game of bowls it was a slow business; but by the end of the following morning, the English Admiral had a fleet of fifty-five sail, including all
the Queen's principal galleons, anchored outside Plymouth Sound (Frobisher's
Triumph had emerged from Plymouth harbour with the ten rear-most vessels
of the fleet, her tardiness almost certainly the fault of a design which made her
unhandy when embayed). This haste, though entirely driven by a prudent
wish not to be caught by the enemy in harbour, was to create problems for the
English fleet. Many of its ships remained at the dockside still, their hatches
splayed to accept the provisions that the busy Darell had wheedled from his
parsimonious masters; as battle was joined (and particularly, once the size of
the Spanish fleet was understood), Howard's pleas for these vessels to join the
English fleet were to become progressively more urgent.

Notwithstanding the attrition upon his nerves, the Lord Admiral's first
manoeuvre at sea was one that required considerable steadiness. On 20 July, as
he issued his final instructions for the ordering of the fleet, he discovered that
the enemy was now as close as Fowey, some fifty miles to the west. Rather than
throw himself directly between the Armada and its goal, the English admiral
stood his fleet well out to the south-west that afternoon. In the early evening,
the Armada was still to the westwards, her mast-heads glinting in the glare of
a setting sun; but by midnight or soon after, Howard had achieved the important and skilful feat of passing across the face of the approaching Spanish formation to steal the weather gauge. As dawn arose on 21 July, the English ships
were to the west, following the Armada as it moved grandly up the Channel.

Medina Sidonia had expected an early attack, and the first sight of his
enemy did not disabuse him. As the main body of the English fleet formed
to his south-west, he noticed more English ships on his port flank, coming
late out of Plymouth and moving westwards along the coast, to double behind
the Armada and join their compatriots. For the first time, he realized that the
fleet against him was to be in little part inferior to his own. Accordingly, he
had the entire Spanish fleet brought into its crescent or 'bull's horns' formation: a battle order of a deep centre (in which the vulnerable transport and
supply ships were herded) supported by thinner, more manoeuvrable wings.
At about nine o'clock, after the respective fleets' admirals had exchanged
absurdly chivalric challenges ('the Lord Admiral sent his pinnace, the *Disdain*,
to give the Duke of Medina defiance'),[43] Howard led his ships against the
shoreward wing of the Armada – the Levant squadron of Don Alonso de
Leiva – and the clash that two monarchs had spent three decades avoiding
commenced.

EIGHTEEN

'The Warre of 21 Julie': The Armada Campaign

After years of acquiescence, gradually unveiling threats and fearful anticipation, the war fleet of Spain – *la Gran Armada* – had finally come about its great business. The precise bounds of that business, however, remained slightly obscure still, even to those who would discharge it. Philip's instructions to Medina Sidonia were at once explicit and imprecise. They directed the Spanish Admiral by laying down broad objectives and, to a lesser extent, setting out the goals for which the great Armada was being so expensively set forth.[1] What they did not – could not – do was address the operational dispositions of the fleet, nor anticipate the precise circumstances under which the ships of the Armada and Parma's army would effect their concentration. These instructions, moreover, were not new. They had first been outlined by Philip in letters to Santa Cruz and Parma in September 1587, and had not been developed further in the intervening months.[2] They directed that as Medina Sidonia entered the Channel, he was to send word ahead to Parma in one of the fleet's *pataches*, to allow him to prepare his land forces for their imminent rendezvous. Medina Sidonia had been cautioned that he should not seek a battle at sea before that rendezvous was effected, though he should of course protect himself in the meantime. Only if he caught elements of the English fleet separately – particularly Drake's western squadron – should he engage them aggressively. Interestingly, this qualification to the instructions indicates that Philip had anticipated Elizabeth's strategy of dividing her fleet and keeping the Lord Admiral off the Downs: one that, if not successfully argued down by Howard (ably supported by Drake, Hawkins and Frobisher), would have given the Spanish fleet a decisive local superiority at each stage of its passage up the English Channel. Ideally, Philip wished for Medina Sidonia to avoid a sea-battle altogether, in which case he was to land 6,000 of his fleet's soldiers in England with Parma's army. If, in the meantime, Parma had managed already to cross the Channel in his fleet of barges (how he might have achieved this considerable feat unsupported by a Spanish fleet was not touched upon), the Armada was to secure the Thames estuary and Downs, thereby dominating and protecting the passage to Flanders. Thereafter, the principal task of the Spanish fleet would have been fully discharged. It was to be Parma's task alone to reduce Elizabeth to submission, re-establish the unregulated practice of Catholicism in England, ensure the repatriation of all English troops in the Low Countries, and secure recompense for English depredations at sea.

In view of his own claim to the English throne, Philip's demands of a conquered English Queen appeared to be remarkably lenient; in fact, they reflected his understanding of the art of the possible. If the Low Countries could not be retaken and Protestantism expunged there, what chance would there be for taking England herself? For all its imposing scale, the Great Enterprise was not to be a conquest but a punitive expedition only; even the demand for recompense was, on Philip's specific instructions, to be a negotiable matter pending satisfactory resolution of the principal terms. As for any sea-battle that could not, despite Medina Sidonia's best efforts, be avoided, Philip left everything to his admiral; his only tactical direction was the obvious one – that Spanish ships should close with the enemy's vessels and board them, using the superior number and quality of Spanish soldiers to offset the suspected advantage of better guns and gunnery skills amongst the English fleet.

Given Philip's reputation as a man who could not delegate responsibility, these instructions were remarkably open-ended. The aim of concentration was stated, but that was all. No further thought was given to how the great ships of the Spanish fleet could enter one of the small, shallow ports of Sluys, Nieuport or Dunkirk; how Parma might otherwise bring his army out to the Armada under the guns of the rebel squadrons that pestered the coast of Flanders; or, most pertinently of all, how the English fleet might be neutralized to allow the joint Spanish forces to descend upon England unhindered. The only hint that Philip anticipated difficulty in this respect was in his order that Medina Sidonia should seize the Isle of Wight as a base for operations if he received definite word that Parma was unable to cross the Narrow Seas. Any subsequent action would be a matter, the instructions directed, for Medina Sidonia and Parma to work out between themselves.

Thus, the Armada entered the English Channel on 20 July 1588 with no precise plan with which to achieve its first goal – the rendezvous with Parma's army. Moreover, Medina Sidonia had known since 1 May that previous estimates regarding the number of troops that Parma had available for his descent upon England had been wildly optimistic. Rather than the 30,000–40,000 expected, Parma sent word that he had a total of 17,000 foot-soldiers and only 1,000 cavalry (though even this modest number must surely have been sufficient to have overcome Leicester's levy-bands who were currently – and far too belatedly – practising their drilling techniques at Tilbury).[3] Even more ominously, Parma's promised 300-strong fleet of ships, plates and hoys in which to carry them had somehow reduced to a collection of mere barges, many of which had oars alone to propel them. It seems astonishing, therefore, that even before he entered the Channel, Medina Sidonia did not appreciate that, absent a miraculous degree of English negligence, the goal of transporting the army of the Netherlands safely across the Narrow Seas required him to comprehensively defeat the English fleet beforehand. This fundamental misapprehension – one which did not dissipate during the campaign – only emphasizes the gulf between intention and possibility that fatally undermined the Spanish strategy.

The first action, on 21 July, set a pattern for much of the following campaign: one that was determined far more by circumstance than conscious intent. There has been much written on the relative attributes of the two fleets, and of their potential. It was assumed for many years that the Spanish fleet was superior in weight of 'broadside' but lacking in manoeuvrability. Other, revisionist theories have since attributed to the English ships a technological edge, particularly in weight and range of guns and in the skills of the gunners themselves (this, as we have seen, was a contemporary belief also). One recent, comprehensive survey of the respective fleets' abilities concludes with the unambiguous statement: 'What seems certain is that the Spanish Armada was at such a decisive disadvantage in firepower in both weight of shot and range, that it was probably incapable of winning the sea battle on whatever terms it fought'.[4] The claim is almost certainly accurate (only some thirty of Medina Sidonia's vessels were fully armed, purpose-built warships),[5] but it does not acknowledge a wider probability – that neither fleet was capable, alone, of securing an outright victory.

The inherent limitations that each faced were profound, and probably insuperable. To wield such a huge concentration of ships in a coherent, unified manner in battle was a task beyond the ability of any sixteenth-century naval commander (a fact of which most, if not all, of those involved were well aware). The progress of the Armada in the following days – and English attempts to splinter its formations – was marked by innumerable small actions, rather than the grand clash of fleets of a Cape St Vincent or Trafalgar. After each of these indecisive encounters, the Spanish fleet reassumed its stately (if increasingly ragged) progress eastwards up the English Channel, rather in the manner of a dignified grande dame whose *décolletage* had been rudely disturbed; her assailant, meanwhile, followed on, ready to pounce once more when opportunity permitted.

The deployment of an effective strategy by either side – had one been conceived – would in any case have been hampered by the shortcomings of contemporary science and naval tactics. The thunderous volleys of shot fired by each of the protagonists, so prodigal (at least on the English fleet's part) of their painstakingly accumulated stocks, had remarkably little effect upon the fabric of their targets. The technologies that would allow naval forces of future centuries to annihilate their enemies at sea had yet to be conceived; in their absence, the only realistic means of sinking an enemy ship were by scuppering her, firing her to the water line or driving her on to a reef. And even if contemporary gun-design had been up to the task of ship-killing, the means of applying it effectively were equally lacking. The art of the broadside (that is, as a coordinated discharge of shot) had not yet been developed, requiring as it did a degree of training and discipline that was beyond the contemporary mariner.[6] A similar failing in his commanders made fighting in line of battle, the means by which that greatly superior weight of shot might be brought to bear locally, another distant prospect. Though ships sometimes passed an enemy line-ahead to deliver their volleys (indeed, the English use of such a formation during the first day of the Armada campaign has been regarded by some authors as innovatory),[7] it was not yet conceived as a manoeuvre to break the enemy's formation. A 'line' of warships during this period was more in the nature of a disorderly queue, each taking her turn to engage in a succession of single vessel-to-vessel jousts, after which she would either turn to present the guns on her other flank or withdraw, so that her crew might – very slowly – reload her ordnance.[8] Sea-battles, unless they took the form of land-battles translated to water (such as those fought at Lepanto and Terceira), were simultaneously extravagant of effort and thrifty of result.[9] The developing character of the Armada campaign provides a striking example of this, and was afterwards so confirmed by the most pertinent – and expert – contemporary opinion of English skills: that of the master-gunner, William Thomas, who asked of the battle he had just endured: 'What can be said but our sins was the cause that so much powder and shot spent, and so long time in fight, and, in comparison thereof, so little harm?'[10]

In view of these limitations, it is probably reasonable to assume that as the respective fleets departed from their home ports, each had a broadly equivalent potential to do the task for which it had been assigned. That is not to say that their prospects were equally well favoured, however. The flawed strategy that had set out the Armada without providing for the means by which Medina Sidonia and Parma could effect their concentration was to turn a difficult objective into a near-impossible goal. Conversely, the English fleet was undoubtedly to enjoy local advantages throughout the campaign due to its relatively modest aims, greater proportion of weatherly vessels and generally better armament: all of which would further hamper Spanish hopes for success. Nevertheless, there were to be few occasions when either fleet possessed the initiative outright. In the action off Gravelines (on the hottest day of combat), the English rate of fire rose briefly to more than ten times that of the Spanish ships;[11] yet even at this moment of apparently overwhelming superiority, the tally of enemy vessels sunk directly by English gunfire was precisely one – the *Maria Juan*; though two others – the *San Felipe* and *San Mateo* – were so damaged that they had to be abandoned, and later sank. Even these ships had sustained serious structural damage only after English vessels – which greatly outnumbered them locally – had closed to musket range and pounded them over the course of several hours. It may well be that under this prolonged and profoundly ineffectual assault, the Spanish ships' knee-pins had simply shivered loose, fallen out and that the hull timbers parted thereafter – a case of being shaken to death, rather than broken under the weight of shot.

Nor does the once prevalent image of plucky little English ships dancing around huge, cumbersome Spanish galleons stand much scrutiny. The English fleet undoubtedly contained a higher proportion of modern ships (and of seamen to soldiers in their complements); but the principal English vessels were on average as large, if not larger, than those of their opponents.[12] If Englishmen seemed to handle their ships more deftly, it was mainly because they were manoeuvring about formations – largely consisting of many slow-moving transports, hulks or *urcas* – that their opponents were attempting to preserve. The Spanish record of seamanship during the battle was certainly equal to that of the opposing fleet, as may be witnessed during the battle of Gravelines, when the Armada was able to reconstitute its battle formation from the initial chaos of its flight from Dunkirk, and do so, moreover, in the face of unremitting English attacks.[13]

At the end of the battle, the Spanish fleet was decisively beaten; but it was beaten by unspectacular attrition, by the profound demoralization of its mariners (who suffered terrible casualties between decks from the same shot that did so little mortal damage to the fabric of their ships) and, finally, by the weather. The military defeat – that is, one inflicted by conscious English policy – was by no means overwhelming. The truth of this is evident in the nature of the battle itself, for had the supposed inadequacies of the Spanish force (and the corresponding superiority of its English enemy) been as profound as is sometimes claimed, the fact that the Armada was not annihilated during its passage eastwards up the Channel would be inexplicable.

Given these unremarkable truths, the whole debate upon the relative performance of the fleets becomes peripheral. The insurmountable problem for both forces was not so much their respective skills and technological abilities as the nature of the encounter itself, which was entirely beyond the experience of any man of either fleet. The perception of the enemy's strength and abilities was undoubtedly important in determining the developing strategy of the battle; but even so, neither Howard nor Medina Sidonia were to truly understand what damage they had inflicted upon the other, nor even what they themselves had sustained. In such a fog of war, human will and morale counted for far more than technology. At the beginning of the battle, it is probably fair to say that both admirals were more concerned with avoiding defeat than actively seeking an all-out victory. At its conclusion, nothing had happened to make either of them believe that they had been capable of more.

At the close of the first day's fighting on 21 July, however, the psychological advantage remained firmly with the Spanish fleet. That morning, the sight of the Armada manoeuvring into its defensive formation had dispelled any lingering English misconceptions regarding the calibre of their enemy. As Howard moved against the landward wing of the great crescent, Drake, Hawkins and Frobisher attacked the opposite flank as it moved eastwards past Eddystone. For more than an hour, some of the most powerful English ships – Drake's *Revenge*, Hawkins's *Victory* and Frobisher's *Triumph* at their head – paid particular attention to the large galleon *San Juan de Portugal*, flagship of the vice-admiral, Juan Martínez de Recalde. It has since been suggested that Recalde – a sailor of immense experience and courage – wanted to draw the English ships into a close mêlée in which the superior numbers of Spanish troops and mariners could play a decisive role, and that to do this he deliberately turned his ship into the path of the pursuing enemy.[14] If so, his tactic was not successful. Even Frobisher, the most impulsive of men, was content to remain out of range of the *San Juan*'s grappling irons and pound her with his culverins. Eventually, after more than an hour of standing alone against some of the principal ships of the English fleet, Recalde was 'rescued' by elements of his Biscayan squadron (they had sailed on initially, apparently oblivious to his predicament).[15] By the time the English ships were forced to withdraw, they had inflicted so little damage that Recalde was able to make running repairs without slackening his speed. The total tally of attrition comprized two hits upon his mainmast, a little disarrayed rigging and a handful of casualties. Rarely can so much ammunition have been spent so harmlessly.

The only substantial damage done to the Armada that day was self-inflicted. The flagship of the Andalucian squadron, Pedro de Valdés's *Nuestra Señora del Rosario*, collided with a neighbouring vessel and lost part of her bow; upon the Armada's other wing, the flag of the Guipúzcoan squadron, the *San Salvador*, was severely damaged when her magazine blew up. The *Rosario* was taken in tow but fell away from the other ships when her ropes parted. The *San Salvador*, still burning, was nursed into the safety of the fleet and most of her crew taken off. The Armada, virtually intact, sailed on to the east.

This failure to draw first blood decisively, and the awesome spectacle of the Spanish fleet's disciplined formation sweeping onwards as if untroubled by the best of the English forces, undoubtedly unnerved Howard. In his day's despatches to Walsingham, he praised the valour of his captains but concluded: 'Sir, for the love of God and our country, let us have with some speed some great shot sent us of all bigness: for this service will continue long . . . .'. He also had Drake write 'haste, post haste', to Seymour, waiting with his squadron at Dover, to warn him to have his ships ready for what bore down upon them; and he begged the Earl of Sussex to send out any ships still lying at Portsmouth to join the English fleet.[16] To the observer, the sense of a harsh awakening is almost palpable. For years, Englishmen had despoiled the cities and ships of the Spanish empire by concentrating superior forces at the location and time of their choosing, defeating second-string or demoralized colonial troops with relative impunity. Among the less perceptive, these successes had bred contempt and, dangerously, a degree of complacency. Faced now with the concentration of Spain's finest seamen and soldiers, it had become unpleasantly clear during the span of a single day that the enemy was a worthy one – one, moreover, for whose defeat no tactics had yet been conceived.

The only bright news for the English mariners – though certainly not for all of them – was the news of Drake's capture of the *Rosario* during the night of 21/22 July. Valdés's ship (abandoned, as he later claimed, by the rest of the Spanish fleet) was sighted off Start Point by the *Margaret and John,* an English privateer commissioned into the English fleet. After exchanging fire with the larger Spanish vessel, she withdrew into the English formations and reported the *Rosario*'s presence. Howard explicitly ordered that the enemy vessel be ignored. Drake's *Revenge* was on watch that night, leading Howard's *Ark Royal* by a single lantern light at her stern. Sometime in the late evening, when full darkness had fallen, Drake seems deliberately to have doused his light. Howard, imagining his own ship to be falling behind, put on sail and almost blundered into the rearguard of the Spanish fleet ahead of him. Drake later claimed that he had gone off to investigate some vessels to the seaward and then, returning, had happened upon the *Rosario* by pure chance. Once upon her, his luck had held true. Valdes, hearing that it was the infamous *el Draco* himself who demanded his surrender, meekly obeyed; though his own ship carried at least the fire-power of the *Revenge*. It was England's first – and by far the easiest – success of the campaign.

Even so, in the immediate aftermath of the incident, Howard might have wished the *Rosario* adrift still. Absent rules of consortship, Drake and the Queen had the principal claim to prize money. To a lesser extent, the crews of the ships *Roebuck* (which had accompanied the *Revenge*) and *Margaret and John* might have expected a share of the takings; but both seem to have been disappointed. Most of the other English captains, whilst ambivalent about Drake's behaviour, must have rued their own poor fortune and yet another example of his fabulous luck. One, however, had much stronger feelings. Two years earlier, Frobisher had served under Drake; an experience he had chosen not to repeat. Some worm of dislike or resentment had embedded itself at the time, nurtured almost certainly by the prospect of Drake's successes and self-righteous arrogance. In a man of Frobisher's often unstable temperament, the creature found ready and warm incubation; now, fed by Drake's cavalier – and, more importantly, profitable – disregard of his orders, it re-awakened in monstrous disproportion. This new transgression, furthermore, struck upon a rare matter of principle. Though Frobisher himself had long enjoyed a career in seizing ships despite explicit instructions to the contrary, his ire at Drake's success – gained in the very act of betraying his station in the fleet – was overwhelming. Nothing could be done or said amidst the trials of battle, but once on-shore, he was to make it his business to slander Drake's character beyond reason or prudence. Thus, Medina Sidonia had accomplished two objectives on 21 July, though only one of these had been intentional. He had kept his fleet's formations intact, and he had rekindled a deadly animosity between two of the English fleet's senior commanders.

For Howard, it had been a day of historic significance, though in the event signifying very little. The first clash of fleets had resolved nothing; nor had it illuminated Spanish intentions. For the next few days, he would continue to agonize over the Armada's precise goal; both he and Seymour, waiting with a small fleet of coasters off the Downs, tended to discount the theory that Medina Sidonia must attempt to rendezvous with Parma and his fleet of invasion barges *before* landing upon English soil. Seymour had openly offered his opinion that the Spanish fleet's destination was the Isle of Wight, or possibly Sandwich in Kent, either of which could be seized and held with little difficulty.[17]

Not understanding the limitations of the Spanish strategy (Elizabeth herself had only received the full picture on 17 July, thanks to Walsingham's efforts),[18] Howard's intention during the next few days – beyond the increasingly hopeful aim of destroying the enemy outright – was to consist almost exclusively of keeping the Spanish fleet from moving too closely in-shore as it passed along the English Channel. To some extent, his stealing of the weather-gauge from the Armada had made this more, rather than less, difficult. As long as the prevailing wind came from the south-west, it was easier for the Spanish ships to make the English shore than it was for their enemy to prevent it. This often conflicting ambition to hold both the weather station and the initiative was reflected in the contradictory nature of developing English tactics. Howard wished above all to draw the Armada away from the English coast, but his attempts to throw a screen of ships between land and the Spanish fleet – attempts in which Frobisher was to figure prominently – were to bring more and more Spanish ships to precisely where he did not want them to be. It was hardly what Drake would have done, but unlike his fiery subordinate, Howard had to think as much of the land battle he had to prevent as the sea-fight he was expected to win.

Details of Martin Frobisher's role in the first day's fighting are sparse. His attack upon Recalde's *San Juan de Portugal* had been as ineffective as that of Drake and Hawkins; a sobering result for the commander of the most powerful ship in the English fleet. The following day saw no serious action, providing a pause in which Frobisher had ample time to brood upon Drake's latest windfall. The rest of the English fleet, waiting for reinforcements and further supplies from Plymouth and Portsmouth, did little more than to shadow the Armada eastwards; in the afternoon, the crippled *San Salvador* (whose crew had failed to scupper her prior to abandoning ship) was taken in tow by English ships, and Lord Thomas Howard found leisure enough to set foot upon a Spanish vessel for the first and last time in his life.

To the east, meanwhile, Medina Sidonia – exercised by the growing understanding that his 'bull's horns' formation slowed his rate of manoeuvre in dealing with threats to its extremities – divided his forces. A powerful rearguard was organized, containing perhaps two-thirds of his ships, whilst he himself led a smaller vanguard that would challenge any oncoming, eastern wing of the English fleet. This done, however, he made no further effort to engage the English ships, and the day ended as quietly as it had begun.

The events of Tuesday, 23 July, in striking contrast, removed any doubts that a war was now being waged. At dawn, the wind veered easterly, giving the Armada the weather gauge. To the north and east, Portland Bill was visible; behind it lay the broad, inviting expanse of Portland harbour and the town of Weymouth. To Howard's preoccupied mind, this was a dangerously ideal anchorage at which to land invading troops, and the Armada had the lee position to do it. It is clear that he remained uncertain of his ability to defeat the Spanish force (which surely would not have disembarked its troops under the guns of an enemy fleet); hurriedly, therefore, he took his ships north-eastwards to attempt to turn the Armada's landward flank and herd it out to sea once more. His timing was impossibly optimistic; Medina Sidonia set a course to deny the English manoeuvre, and with the wind in his favour it became clear that his ships would reach Portland Bill first. Realizing this, Howard then adopted the drastic expedient of turning his fleet entirely about, coming south and east; either to draw the Spanish fleet after him, or, even more optimistically, to outflank its opposite, seaward wing.

Not all of his ships followed, however. Anchored under the lee of Portland Bill, Frobisher's *Triumph* and five armed merchantmen (including the busy *Margaret and John*) remained.[19] They may have been there since before dawn, or, possibly, they dropped anchor only when the English fleet turned about; but as most of the Armada followed Howard's ships and tried to engage them at close quarters, Don Hugo de Moncada's four Neapolitan galleases – *San Lorenzo, Napolitana, La Girona* and *Zuniga* – again imagining the *Triumph* to be the English flagship, came up to attack her before her 'admiral' could find a favourable wind and escape back to the safety of the fleet. These were, probably, the most heavily armed vessels in the Spanish fleet, and certainly the most manoeuvrable in a calm. Each carried up to fifty guns and between 170–265 soldiers: their purpose, above all, to realize that strategy of close, maul and conquer that Santa Cruz had demonstrated to such devastating effect at Terceira.[20]

With this powerful force bearing down upon him, Frobisher did not attempt to flee. Conventional wisdom had it that galleys and galleases were galleon-killers to be avoided at all costs. Fourteen years later, Sir William

Monson and Sir Richard Leveson would engage a Spanish fleet of eleven galleys off Cezimbra, in the fight to take the carrack *San Valentine*. Their feat (seven English galleons and three pinnaces scattered the galleys, sinking two of them) was then considered to be a singular one. In his *Tracts*, Monson himself observed that it 'has been seldom seen or heard of, for ships to be the destroyers of galleys'.[21] In this case, however, Monson was talking up his own record. He must have been aware of a previous occasion, on the morning of 23 July 1588, when Martin Frobisher initiated a tradition that paid scant respect to existing lore. Engaging Moncada's galleases, he devoted himself to giving them a hard lesson in close-in fighting, their supposed *forte*. As they approached his squadron, he concentrated the fire of the *Triumph's* lower-tier guns into the rowing decks of the enemy vessels (each gallease had 300 rowers, sited beneath their gun decks),[22] thus reducing their manoeuvrability in the in-shore waters by smashing their oars and – a bloody corollary – butchering their means of propulsion. The only vessel of the *Triumph's* escort known to possess a significant armament was the *Merchant Royal*, a Levanter (commanded by the estimable merchant-privateer Robert Flicke); but all the English merchantmen fought well – even the little *Mary Rose*, a victualling boat that had been drummed into the English fleet as it beat out of Plymouth harbour, three days earlier.[23] As upon the night of the great storm in Meta Incognita ten years earlier, Frobisher had organized his forces superbly at a moment of extreme crisis, with a flair that hints strongly at outright enthusiasm for the task. Intending conquest and glory, Hugo de Moncada found himself fighting instead for his own survival. It had been his misfortune to present a man of limited talents with the conditions to fully realize them; a man who, having neither experience nor fearful preconception of Spanish naval tactics, chose to instill a harsh, corrective lesson in the maul.[24]

This hot action continued for some ninety minutes. Frobisher may well have been perfectly content to prolong it until his opponents had struck their colours or burned to the waterline; but a change in the wind to south-south-west pushed the landward wing of the Armada to the east, at which Howard – still attempting to turn its seaward flank – was able to see the *Triumph's* predicament, as such he believed it to be. He turned the *Ark* about once more, and led seven other ships to Frobisher's rescue. Medina Sidonia followed, with sixteen large galleons of his vanguard. As the opposing forces moved northwards once more, the two admirals fought a close running battle, until the wind turned to the English advantage and the damaged Spanish ships broke off to rejoin their fleet. The day ended with the Armada still in touch with the shore, though the English seemed to have recovered the weather gauge.

Frobisher's presence under Portland Bill has since been the subject of much discussion. It has been implied by most commentators (whatever they make of his subsequent actions) that he had been negligent in allowing himself to become separated from the fleet – and, moreover, to become stranded upon a lee shore. Mattingly alone suggests that it was rather a cunning ploy to lure Spanish ships on to the treacherous shallows of the Shambles reef, where they could be despatched easily or – perhaps of more immediate interest to Frobisher – taken as prizes.[25] If such prizes could not be had, glory would indeed have provided an adequate compensation: to have destroyed such vessels would, undoubtedly, have added glister to his reputation. Yet to have anchored off Portland Bill (and thus deliberately to have become separated from the remainder of the English fleet) seems a strange tactic to have chosen if either of these aims was foremost in Frobisher's mind. Indeed, his luring of the four galleases (whose hulls displaced much less water than his own vessels and were capable of manoeuvring in a dead calm) had offered a potentially deadly return in shallow, lee waters. This appears to leave only the charge of negligence: of Frobisher failing to notice that he had drifted too far inshore. However, with the wind having blown from the east that morning, it is difficult to see how he could have unintentionally drifted north-eastwards away from the main body of the English fleet. If we look no further, the episode remains a puzzling one.

However, one theory that does not seem to have been considered actively is, to the present author, the obvious one: that Frobisher was off Portland Bill to deny, or at least to make hazardous, a potential landfall to any elements of the Armada that might attempt it. His admiral was burdened above all by the threat of a Spanish landing, and the extremely capacious Portland Harbour appeared to be a magnificent base for the invasion of southern England. The danger had been specifically identified in Howard's strategic summary of 27 November 1587: 'Portland (a likely place). The reason why Portland is also an apt place to land in, is for that there is a great harbour for all his ships to ride in, and good landing for men. The isle being won is a strong place for retreat, the country adjoining (for) champaign, where, with great commodity, he may march with his whole army'.[26] With such a threat all too clearly in mind, it is hardly too fanciful to suppose that either Howard or Frobisher himself – intuitively or otherwise – would have done something to forestall this danger. There is much that hints at necessity and very little of design in the English fleet's tactics that day, but there can be little doubt that Frobisher's small force did more good – and damage to the enemy – at its supposedly negligent anchorage than it might have done elsewhere. When Medina Sidonia committed more ships to that small segment of the conflict, it was to rescue his own vessels rather than administer the *coup de grâce* to the enemy. Thus, he surrendered the initiative he had enjoyed since sunrise – and, furthermore, found himself suffering the greater damage in exchanges with the opposing English ships for the first time since the conflict began, as Howard's squadron, forming another rudimentary line-ahead formation, swept his flagship with repeated volleys of shot. For almost an hour, it seemed that the *San Martin* herself might fall into English hands, until she was rescued by a number of her galleons. If, in being substantially responsible for the nature of the day's actions, Frobisher had been at fault, it was an error that had proved entirely beneficial to the English cause.

After a day of such desperate manoeuvres, both fleets seem to have drawn back once more. The only English action on 24 July was against the damaged ship *Gran Grifon* (flagship of the *urcas* squadron) and the vessels that came to her aid. Periods of almost dead calm, the need to repair the previous day's damage, and, in Howard's case, to urgently replenish his ships' almost vanished stocks of shot and powder, otherwise kept the two fleets from engaging. That evening, drawing lessons from the enemy's redeployment, he organized his fleet into four squadrons, and appointed the supposedly remiss Frobisher to command one of them.

The appointment was not a matter of paying dues to seniority – at least half a dozen other men in the fleet had as much (or more) right to command as Frobisher – but rather a shrewd recognition of his qualities, particularly, his coolness under fire and his will to fight. So far, any damage done to the Armada had been minimal. The English ships had manoeuvred well, but their longer-range guns seemed to have proven almost ineffective. Time might provide better fortune; but time was not on Howard's side. The further that the Armada passed, intact, eastwards up the English Channel, the more likely – he believed – that it would eventually force a landing upon English soil: perhaps, even, with Parma's army in the midst of its great formation. If the Spanish fleet was to be decisively defeated before that happened, the Lord Admiral needed commanders who would not shirk a closer maul than had occurred to date. In recognizing Frobisher's talents to this end, he did not flatter him – certainly not in the expendability he implied – but his trust was hardly an act of faith. Within musket shot of four of the most dangerous ships in the Spanish fleet, Frobisher had kept the most unwieldy English vessel out of their grasp whilst inflicting something of a drubbing. It was a demonstration of an art that other English captains were increasingly to emulate in the coming days. The men of the Armada were beaten psychologically before their fleet met disaster because the growing persistence of English attacks allowed no time for repairs, wounds or shattered nerves to be adequately tended. Frobisher's own efforts in the next few days were strongly to reflect – perhaps exemplify – this strategy of attrition.

Howard's dispositions following the fleet's reorganization indicate much of his faith in his subordinate's terrier-like persistence. The Lord Admiral himself, with the squadrons of Drake and Hawkins, stood out to sea, hoping to take the weather gauge on the following morning and out-manoeuvre their enemy; the fourth squadron – Frobisher's – was placed well to the landward, ready to deny the prize that even Philip II had identified as a fine anchorage for his fleet – the Isle of Wight.

At dawn on 25 July, Frobisher was as close in-shore as he had been two days earlier, but this time there can be no doubt as to his intentions. He was off Dunnose Head, in harm's way, blocking the eastern entrance to the Solent. During the night, in a dead calm, he had taken his squadron ahead of the Spanish vanguard – perhaps using his ships' boats, or the slightly brisker in-shore current – and had overlapped its leeward flank.[27] For the first time since battle had been joined, the English fleet had seized a potentially decisive tactical advantage. At that moment, Frobisher was as close to immortal fame as to the sea-bed beneath him: if the wind arose from the east as it had in the previous two days, the Armada's formation would have been breached: half of its vanguard pushed back upon the rearguard, crowding in the Spanish ships and drastically reducing the number of guns that could be brought to bear against an English fleet whose own target would have been gratifyingly grouped. Had it fallen out thus, the *Cacafuego*, the *San Felipe*, the *Rosario*, the good fortune that seemed to fall upon Drake's head like rain – all these bitter accumulations of grudgery would have dissolved in the sweetness of a victory (and, incidentally, its commensurate prizes) to which Frobisher would surely have laid a principal claim.

Again, however, and almost disastrously, his luck deserted him. In a dead calm at first light, the *San Martin* lay close enough for the *Triumph* to do further damage with her culverins. Frobisher began to fire upon the Spanish flagship as soon as his guns could be brought to bear, an occupation that filled his time pleasantly whilst he waited for the wind that would allow him to close for the kill. When that wind came however – at about seven o'clock – it did so from the south-west, and brought with it a dozen of the principal

Spanish galleons, set upon rescuing their flagship. Facing such a threat, there was no question but that the *Triumph* must withdraw. She could not do so, however: Frobisher, obsessed with the decisive moment, had placed himself far too closely upon the lee shore. What followed was in some ways a reprise of his action off Portland Bill, but this time fully a quarter of the Armada's most effective ships bore down upon him; and what, two days earlier, had been a shrewd tactical manoeuvre was now a suicidal gamble in the process of failing spectacularly.

The other ships of Frobisher's squadron were slightly to the west and seaward of their flagship. Most of them managed to withdraw before the looming threat; only the little *Mary Rose* and Fenner's *Nonpareil* remained, selflessly committing themselves to share the fate of the *Triumph*. The crisis developed in the slow motion of a two-knot breeze; any thoughts of strategy refined to a matter of whether the Spanish galleons could close with the *Triumph* before her boats pulled her out of the lee-calm. Several other English vessels slowly bore up, risking their own safety to send in further ships' boats, until fully eleven had the *Triumph* in tow. The *Bear* and *Elizabeth Jonas*, two of the three other 'great ships' of the English navy (commanded by Lord Sheffield and Sir Robert Southwell respectively), gallantly attempted to stand between the *Triumph* and the Spanish galleons, but had only partly succeeded when a freshening breeze suddenly veered eastwards, and the *Triumph* set her sails to catch it. Several accounts – both Spanish and English – comment upon the excellent seamanship that carried her swiftly to safety: skills that were no doubt sharpened by a looming prospect of butchery.[28] Within minutes, undamaged, the *Triumph* and her flock of small boats were joined by the approaching English fleet. It had been, to quote a later tempter of the fates, a close-run thing: from being within a hair's-breadth of becoming England's hero, Frobisher had only just saved himself from the ultimate disgrace of being the only English commander to be taken by the Armada.

Yet even this local crisis had proved beneficial to the English cause. The Spanish vanguard's pursuit of Frobisher (and his earlier pounding of the *San Martin*) had distracted Medina Sidonia's attention from what was happening elsewhere. When he finally turned to assess the wider situation, it was to witness almost his entire fleet bearing north-eastwards towards his position – driven on by the pursuing squadrons of Drake and Hawkins. Slowly, the greater part of the Armada was being herded towards the treacherous rocks of the Owers shoals, off Dunnose. Once he realized this, the Spanish Admiral's reaction was swift and decisive; he led his fleet about to the south-eastwards, and by evening had lost any chance of regaining the English coast.

Howard had successfully discharged his most immediate and burdensome task: a Spanish landing on English soil had been prevented. It was the first day of fighting that he chose to regard as a definite English victory, and he was not unmindful of the men who had helped to bring it about. The following morning, he called to the *Ark Royal* Lord Thomas Howard, John Hawkins and Frobisher, the supposedly wilful officer who had stood almost alone between the Isle of Wight and the Armada. According to Stow, the Lord Admiral used the occasion to make a point:

> (he) was desirous to advance certaine personages to the degree of knight-hood, for that, behaving themselves manfully, as well with their ships as their good advice, they were worthie that degree of honor, and so much the more worthie in that, being farre separated from all courtly favour, which manie times imparteth the chiefest honours unto the least deserving men, they declared their valour in the eyes of the fleet.[29]

With hindsight, it seems almost a slur upon Hawkins's noble efforts that they should have been recognized at the same moment as the rather less notable feats of an unregenerate freebooter; but the previous three days' fighting had brought Frobisher's peculiar abilities to the fore no less than those of the deliverer of the English navy. Their respective careers, though sharing superficial points of similarity, had progressed in vastly different ways. What, for Frobisher, had been the only secure employment of his life had provided merely the foundation upon which Hawkins had built an august reputation and a formidable talent. Yet battle – this battle – was a great leavener of prior achievement. The habitual constraints imposed by a society that required conformity to accepted mores were, however briefly, suspended; in that pause lay opportunity, and Frobisher had seized it by applying talents which, in less violent times, had brought him close to ruin. Other men, throughout the English fleet, had done the same but not, perhaps, with the single-mindedness that had characterized his actions off Portland and Dunnose. If, as Stow suggested, courtly favour bestowed the 'chiefest honours' unfairly, the horrors of war – for Frobisher – had provided an opportune corrective.

The next day, the English fleet resumed the chase. Howard had determined not to waste further shot until he could rendezvous with the English squadron in the eastern Channel. His ships therefore shadowed but did not close with the Armada as it moved towards Calais Roads. At Whitsand Bay, the English fleet was replenished and reinforced by the thirty-five ships of Seymour's command; whilst Medina Sidonia, anchored off Calais, forlornly waited for

Parma and his army of the Netherlands to emerge in their fleet of barges. They did not come. Parma, closely marked by Justin of Nassau's cromsters and now convinced that to attempt to cross the Channel in the face of the English fleet would be suicidal, wrote ingenuously to Medina Sidonia that he would be ready in six days' time, and not earlier.[30] Two days later, English fire-ships drove the Armada from its moorings, and battle was rejoined with a vengeance off Gravelines.

Frobisher's role during these days has not been recorded, but on 29 July his squadron was immediately behind Drake's in the line that savaged Medina Sidonia's flagship off Dunkirk. Drake gave the *San Martin* a single broadside before moving off to the north-east, where a powerful force of Spanish galleons was re-assembling. Frobisher, ignoring the turn of Hawkins's ships directly behind him, chose to remain with the *San Martin*, pouring cannon shot into her flanks from within musket range and attempting to finish what he had begun off Dunnose.

If there was a single instance that distinguished the respective talents of Drake and Frobisher, it was here amidst the clamour of a battle which both men had sought so eagerly. In breaking off to attack more dangerous formations, Drake never lost sight of his role within the day's tactical dispositions (though it is hardly likely that the day 'would have been marked with one of the most brilliant battles of all times', as Corbett believed, had the other English ships followed his example).[31] Frobisher, desperate still to have his prize – either in his hands or upon the sea-bed – and knowing no other way of gaining a victory than in the maul, simply chose to pretend there were no broader goals than those directly before him. His failure to take the *San Martin*, not least because of a fine shielding action by some of the principal commanders of the Armada (a mirror of the English ships' rescue of the *Triumph* off Dunnose Head), merely added to the sum of his frustrations. It did not, even for a second, incline him to draw any lessons regarding his tactical error.

The Armada campaign, as a clash of opposing forces, effectively ended at Dunkirk. The Spanish fleet, denied its rendezvous with Parma but seemingly almost intact still, passed on northwards. Yet it had lost seven of its precious first-line ships, twenty per cent of its effective fighting complement and almost all of its morale, in addition to the indeterminable structural damage caused by English guns. Medina Sidonia did not seek to make a landing upon the coast – even when the English ships had called off their pursuit – but had his fleet sail on, to meet its scattered destiny in unseasonably stormy seas off Scotland and western Ireland. The English ships followed as far as the Firth of Forth, and then, their supplies exhausted, they turned about. On 8 August, at Harwich and a dozen ports in the Thames Estuary and Medway, the battered ships and their equally battered companies were greeted with nervous relief. The Queen herself came to Tilbury to express her heartfelt thanks to Leicester's levies who had done nothing. Her heroic mariners, in contrast, were left to die decently of their wounds, untended and unpaid, upon the docksides.

For the principal commanders, the aftermath of the campaign was a little more rewarding. Their failure to destroy the Spanish fleet dampened any inclination to celebrate, and until word of its titanic losses began to trickle back to England, fear of a Spanish landing – possibly in Ireland – persisted. Yet insofar as the invincible Armada had proved to be an ineffective weapon against the English fleet, it was a victory – the first major setback to the seemingly unstoppable rise of Spanish power. Unsure still of the campaign's outcome, Elizabeth nevertheless confirmed the shares of spoils taken by her sea-commanders.

It was upon this matter that Frobisher's own satisfaction was further soured. It seems that in the course of just a few days he had moved on from merely resenting Drake. His envy at the seizure of the *Rosario* was undoubtedly intense, but envy alone cannot explain the purity of his emotions. There were after all richer and, ostensibly, more talented men with whom he enjoyed an entirely fruitful working relationship. Drake's career, however, was the epitome of what Frobisher's had failed to be and stood as an affront to his personal and professional failures. Confronted by this prodigy, the discrepancy between his talents as he understood them and his achievements did not merely rankle: it seems to have subsumed any possibility of self-criticism and redirected its energies towards something entirely malevolent and, ultimately, self-destructive.

With leisure now to feed his worm of envy, Frobisher's ranting against the duplicitous Drake was at first scurrilous, and then openly slanderous. At Harwich, in the presence of his ennobled companions Lord Thomas Howard and John Hawkins, he claimed of Drake that he

> . . . tooke Don Pedro [of the *Rosario*], for after he had seen her in the evening, that she had spent her masts, then lyke a coward, he kept by her all nyght, because he wold have the spoyle. He thinketh to cozen us of our shares of xv. thousande duckatts, but we will have our shares, or I will make hym spend the best blood in his belly. . . .

On the matter of courage, he was even more scathing:

> Sir Fra. Drake reporteth that no man hath done anye good service but he, but he shall well understand that others hath done as good service as he, and better too. He came braginge up at the firste, indede, and gave them hys prowe and hys broade syde, and then kepte his lowfe and was gladde that he was gone agayn, like a cowardly knave or traitor – (the other) I rest doubtful, but the one I will sweare.

Frobisher, whose 'strategy' throughout the battle had been to find the thickest brawl and plunge into it, even now remained incapable of understanding what Drake had attempted to do off Gravelines and elsewhere. In the midst of his diatribe, however, there was a small but valid point. Doubts still remain as to whether Drake had deliberately doused his light on the night he captured the *Rosario*, and indeed, whether he had been specifically appointed to keep the fleet's way in the dark. Frobisher himself believed so, as did others: 'Then saide he [i.e., Frobisher], Sir Francis was apointed to beare a lyght all that nyght, which lyght we looked for, but there was no lyght to be seen, and in the mornyng when we shuld have dealt with them, there was not above fyve or syx (ships) next unto the Admyrall, by reasone we sawe not hys lyght.'[32]

In keeping the matter alive, Frobisher was undoubtedly talking a fight – and also, if unwittingly, putting a case on behalf of many of the fleet's mariners who would earn little more than grief for their efforts – yet their officers were no doubt embarrassed by the persistence of his vendetta. As negligent of his orders as Drake may have been on the night of 21 July, there can be little doubt that, generally, he was envied his success. This was not an age of professional navies; men such as Drake, Hawkins and Frobisher took their short-term commissions dutifully but with an eye on life beyond the next discharge. To serve the Queen did not mean that an enterprising commander could not serve his own ends also, and prizes were the generally accepted perk in a service that often ended in unpensionable mutilation or death, and much less often in the timely receipt of one's remuneration from a grateful sovereign. Wages, for Frobisher, meant 20sh. per day whilst at sea;[33] which, even if speedily paid (and there is no evidence to suggest they were), seems insignificant in light of approximately £4,000 that Drake took as his share of the *Rosario*'s bounty. It has since been claimed that Frobisher's share of prize money from the Armada campaign was a massive £4,979,[34] but this assumption has arisen from a misreading of the declared accounts of the navy. These show that Frobisher received this precise amount – but in 1590 – for the victualling of 620 men during that year's Atlantic campaign (typically, he was never to provide proper accounts for the money's disbursement, as the executors of his estate were being pointedly reminded as late as 1595).[35] In February 1590, Hawkins set out a warrant for £1,531, 'What ys received vppon the warr of the 21 of Julye. And what ys to be p(ai)d to S(i)r Martin Frobisher knight out of that Warr',[36] but from this he abated £230 18sh. 4d. for sea stores and rigging paid for by other hands, which indicates that the payment was substantially a reimbursement, not an award. There is no evidence that any significant sum fell to Frobisher as prize money. At the end of the 1588 campaign, there were only two major Spanish ships in English hands, and having provided Drake with his due share of the *Rosario*'s worth, the Queen was hardly minded to scatter further largesse except upon repairs to her fleet. If Frobisher's hatred of Drake seemed excessive even whilst the battle raged, it was teased further by the respective padding of their purses in its aftermath.

That animosity, at least on Frobisher's part, proved to be enduring. As late as November that year, Mendoza gleefully reported to Philip that 'the differences between Drake and Frobisher still continue'.[37] Indeed, in the immediate aftermath of the Armada campaign, it seems that Frobisher may not have directed his ire upon Drake's reputation alone. During August, immediately after the campaign, the Privy Council gave order to Lord Buckhurst: '. . . that his Lordship doe committ Gill of Brighthempson (hauing uttred slaunderous (words) against the Lord Admirall) to the gaole, there to remayne in irons untill uppon his Lordship's retorne it maye be better examyned whether Capten Furbusher used anie such speaches or no . . .'.[38] The nature of these 'speaches' is not known. It may be that the Privy Council had misheard rumours of Frobisher's outbursts against Drake and mistakenly assumed their target to have been Howard; but it is also possible that Frobisher was less than impressed by what he considered to be Howard's timidity in not bearding Drake for the *Rosario* episode. The matter was serious enough for him to be summoned before the Council two weeks later (undoubtedly the reason for his absence from Howard's war council at Dover on 21 August), where he appears to have been absolved of any indiscretion.[39] There is no indication that after this date he and Howard were in any way estranged, and certainly, the official *Relation* of the campaign which was drafted under Howard's direction contained no criticism of Frobisher's own conduct, implicit or otherwise.

As rash as Frobisher's tantrums against Drake had been, they were not entirely unsupported. Others would also express their distaste – albeit in more measured terms – at the vice-admiral's role during the campaign. On 12 August, Seymour wrote to Walsingham: 'But if my Lord himself [i.e. Howard] should come into the Narrow Seas, and that Sir Francis Drake should attend as Vice Admiral, I pray you let me be called home; for by that I find by experience, by good observation, some seers of antiquity are not the same persons they are deemed.'[40] Lord Sheffield appears to have shared this poor opinion, and even Howard himself, who had been careful not to criticize Drake too strongly in his report to Walsingham, could not have been happy in recalling the *Rosario* incident.[41] Drake's dousing of his lantern almost led to the Admiral himself being taken by the Spanish fleet, a disaster that would have resounded to his own immortal infamy. Drake was certainly aware of the tension that the episode generated. He considered it necessary to pass on a written note of Howard's 'honourable using' of him thereafter to Walsingham, requesting that he show it to the Queen, which implies that he was trying to cover his reputation.[42] He also very sensibly had Frobisher's outbursts at Harwich put in writing and witnessed, possibly as insurance against the hour when the latter attempted to make good the threat to rearrange his tripes. Scourge of the Spanish empire he may have become, but the diminutive *el Draque* could have given himself few odds in such an encounter.

The Armada campaign, that great enterprise anticipated by all its protagonists to be a decisive event, marked only the beginning of a long and bitter struggle that tested the sanguinary tastes of an entire generation. After a spectacular opening campaign, Drake was to have a bad war; Frobisher's, in contrast, was to be one of improving fortunes and creeping respectability. Despite his obsession with Drake's successes, his own reputation had been entirely rehabilitated during the 'warre of 21 July'. No one had fought more valiantly; and valour, even more than strategic ability, was prized by a race for whom war yet remained a chivalric occupation. Amidst the welcome noise of congratulation from new and rediscovered acquaintances, the only small occasion for personal regret during these days might have arisen from a brief intelligence received from a London poorhouse, where Isobel Frobisher, after years of neglect and abandonment, had finally obliged her husband by dying. The tragedy appears not to have diverted Frobisher from his new preoccupations for even a moment, nor the smallest funds from his wages to provide for her children (if, indeed, they survived their mother). In previous years, he had not allowed sacramental obligations to encumber his search for honour;

now, with that happy prospect before him, a potential embarrassment had obliged him by expunging itself in a timely manner. The nation, briefly enamoured of its new hero, did not choose to weigh this dark consequence of his indurate nature in the slightest degree. Unlike the Earl of Leicester, indelibly cast as the pitiless nemesis of Anne Robsart in contemporary lore, Frobisher had long managed to put a sufficient cloak between reputation and responsibility, and now he reaped the benefit of that prudence. Whom the gods first make mad are not, it seems, invariably destroyed thereafter.

PART FOUR

The Queen's Admiral: 1588–94

You have woone yorselfe reputation . . .[1]

NINETEEN

Narrow Seas and Treasure Fleets

In the aftermath of the Armada campaign, there was no coordinated English strategy to follow up the dimly perceived victory. News of the Spanish fleet was still scrappy and unreliable; the Privy Council seems to have believed that one of its options after leaving English waters was to descend upon Protestant Denmark. Sir Horatio Palavacini wrote to Walsingham on 12 August, implying or suggesting that the Earl of Cumberland should hold himself in readiness to take a fleet to assist the Danish King or, possibly, to browbeat him into putting up a fight. Frobisher was mentioned as Cumberland's lieutenant, though this brief intelligence apart, there is no evidence that any such project was seriously envisaged.[2]

Elizabeth, meanwhile, beset by clamours for money to discharge her mariners, had a vague longing for Drake to go to the west to seize a Spanish plate fleet (or two, if he could manage it), and went so far as to issue tentative orders to that effect. Howard, in a tactful letter to Walsingham on 27 August, pointed out that none of his ships would be fit to be set out into the Atlantic until they were first laid up and repaired. In another note, written twenty-four hours earlier, he appointed Sir Henry Palmer to command a squadron of eight ships to patrol the Narrow Seas for two months, and named Frobisher to succeed him at the end of that time. The document is damaged; only the identity of one of Frobisher's ships – the *Antelope* – is given, though we know from other sources that his flagship – a small 'revenge', perhaps – was to be Drake's recent command. The following day, Howard left Dover for London, and Frobisher was appointed, with Sir William Winter and Sir John Hawkins, to command the fleet in his absence.[3]

Frobisher remained in command of the *Triumph* until 15 September, after which he transferred into the *Revenge*.[4] His role in the succeeding months seems to have been similar to that in the previous year – to intercept the traffic of war materiel being carried from the Iberian Peninsula to Philip's armies in the Low Countries. By the end of November, his fleet – now the *Revenge, Golden Lion, Elizabeth Bonaventure, Repentance, Isaac, John, Unity* and *Bark Waye* – had begun to seize Spanish and Netherlander vessels in the Channel.[5] On 1 January 1589, as Seymour stood down from his spell in command of the fleet that guarded the Downs, Frobisher succeeded him; transferring his flag from the *Revenge* to the *Vanguard*.[6] In Paris, Mendoza – lacking access to the Lord Admiral's correspondence – misunderstood the purpose of the change in command. On 12 January, he wrote to Philip, reporting rumours that Frobisher was to transport 6,000 Dutch and English soldiers from Zeeland into England in preparation for Don Antonio's attempt on Terceira (thus revealing that at least one of the prospective aims of Drake's 1589 expedition was anticipated already). As late as April, Spanish sources in London still believed Frobisher to be the man appointed to lead this expedition.[7]

If Philip was being led to expect great things of Frobisher, however, the reality was a little more mundane and predictable. The enthusiasm – and lack of discrimination – with which his new squadron performed its interdictory role during these months suggests that he and his subordinates were attempting to recompense themselves for the financial disappointments of the Armada campaign by more habitual methods. Before the year was well advanced, a steady stream of Dutch, German and French pleas to the Privy Council and Admiralty Court indicates that many vessels which were, may have been and certainly were *not* assisting the cause of Spain or the Catholic League had been taken by the Channel fleet: paperwork that must have brought back unpleasant memories of Dr Lewes's burdensome pursuit of Frobisher some two decades earlier.[8]

However, having consistently portrayed Frobisher as a ruthless pursuer of innocent vessels, we should recall also the ambiguities of his new role. The known facts behind some of these incidents illustrate how blurred the distinction between 'good' and 'bad' prize could be, and how profitably a man might exploit the grey areas in between. Henry IV's envoy in London, Jean de la Fin, Seigneur de Beauvoir la Nocle, complained of a seizure by Frobisher's fleet in a string of letters to the Privy Council. In October 1589, the *Golden Lion* (the ship that had carried William Borough and his mutinous crew away from Drake's fleet at Cadiz two years earlier), stopped and seized a Breton vessel, the *Gerosme* of Paimpol. She had been carrying approx-

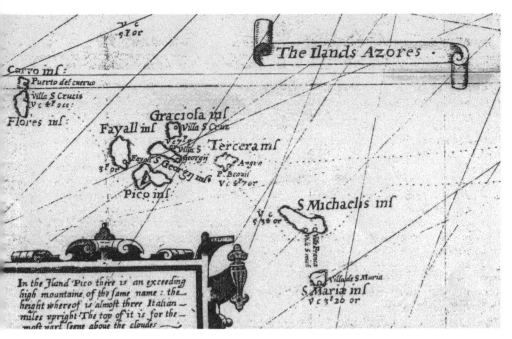

In the Jland Pico there is an exceeding
high mountaine of the same name: the
height whereof is almost three Italian
miles vpright. The top of it is for the
most part seene aboue the cloudes

6. The Azores, in whose waters Englishmen habitually awaited sight of the returning plate fleets. Author's collection.

imately 9,000 crowns' value in wheat and cloth, owned jointly by two syndicates of merchants: one based in Paimpol, the other in the neighbouring town of Morlaix. The merchants of Paimpol claimed that they were loyal to their King and had letters to prove it; those of Morlaix were 'Leaguers', and thus their share of the cargo was good prize for Frobisher.[9] Beauvoir admitted the latter claim, but demanded restitution of the remainder. The Admiralty concurred, and ordered Frobisher to comply. His response was to return the *Gerosme*, but retain all of her cargo, claiming (without offering any evidence) that the French King had granted him the right to seize all French cargoes of food bound for Spain. Several more protests to the Privy Council ensued, and several more reminders to Frobisher to comply were duly issued. The masterly prevarications and evasions that he employed to avoid these orders were clearly garnered from venerable experience. At first, he claimed that the loyal proportion of the *Gerosme*'s cargo had been surrendered to the Queen's officers. When that failed to quell Beauvoir's complaints, he agreed upon at least two occasions to meet with the French envoy to settle matters, and simply did not turn up for these appointments. In the meantime, Beauvoir had written to the Privy Council regarding another of Frobisher's prizes, a ship of le Havre worth more than 18,000 crowns, which he had sent on to Wales – probably to Milford Haven, another notorious entrepôt of the

privateering trade – without paying the French King's due of fifth of the prize
money or, indeed, notifying the French envoy of the seizure (as he was obliged
to do). Frobisher, blithely indifferent to these complaints, merely proceeded
about his business with even greater industry. By May 1590, Beauvoir was
writing to the Council that he was heartily sick of receiving complaints from
wronged French merchants, and in October, offered the hopeless – but
undoubtedly astute – opinion that Frobisher would never pay the King's dues
on all the Leaguer ships he had taken.[10]

It would be unfair, however, to conclude from the above that Frobisher
had been victimizing France only. Other seizures, of Dutch and German
vessels, generated even more correspondence. His taking of one vessel in
particular – the *Yongfrau* of Pomerania – created a volume of legal correspondence that the Privy Council did not even begin to address, but wearily
handed to Sir Julius Caesar: Judge of the Admiralty Court, step-son of
Michael Lok and himself a former investor in the north-west enterprise.
This comprised, variously, petitions of one Hendrick Voets for restitution
of monies and goods belonging to Hendricks de Haese of Amsterdam; of
Francis de Fort, claiming that Frobisher took ten bags of coin from the
Yongfrau; and of Michael Leman and others, merchants of Holland and
Flanders, demanding the release of the ship and its cargoes.[11] On other occasions during 1589, petitions against Frobisher were made by the alderman and
company of the steelyard for the release of Hanseatic vessels and goods
detained at Dover; by Joachim Skeale, a Swede resident in Lubeck, for the
restoration of his ship (the *Rose*) and her cargo of winesack; and by George
Johnson of Rotterdam, on a matter of £70 recompense for goods taken out
of his (unnamed) ship.[12]

Though Frobisher was not brought to task officially for any of these seizures
(which indicates that all were at least partly 'good' prize), their diplomatic
repercussions, and those of other, more discreet activities, were not inconsequential. In July 1590, Thomas Wilkes and Thomas Bodley, Elizabeth's diplomatic agents in the Netherlands, wrote to the States-General, asking them
to take steps to quell the wave of popular anti-English sentiment generated by
the activities of men such as Frobisher (they mentioned him by name in their
petition).[13] The fact that he was known personally to the States-General as
the exemplar of their problem is perhaps the single most striking testimonial
to his business; certainly, he was, with Hawkins, the most senior English naval
commander to be named with such persistence in the correspondence of the
Admiralty Court. However, as irritating as these seizures were to those who
were required to soothe the outraged friends of England, there can be little

doubt either that they were personally profitable to Frobisher, or that his actions were at least tacitly condoned by the Privy Council, notwithstanding the stream of half-hearted warnings they despatched to his small fleet. It is not hard to see why this should be. In any war, collateral casualties were expected and unless these depredations impacted severely upon England's relations with a friendly power, few resources could be devoted to repairing the damage. Even fewer actually *were* devoted to the problem when its fruits were profitable to the Crown also, as Frobisher's undoubtedly were. By 15 March 1590, he owned or leased a property on Tower Hill specifically to deal – on his own account and on behalf of the Queen – in the goods he had taken at sea. A note of that date from Henry Billingsley and Thomas Allen, endorsed 'At ye house of S(i)r Martin Frobisher knight in his counting house', reveals that the two skinners were purchasing hides there 'belonging to her Ma(ies)tie, w(hi)ch weare broughte by Sir Martyn frobisher . . .'.[14] If Frobisher was acting directly as Elizabeth's official agent for the disposal of his ill-gotten cargoes (rather than have her take a profit through the more normal but cumbersome Admiralty arrangements), it would seem that the Seigneur de Beauvoir la Nocle and the owners of the *Yongfrau* and other seized vessels were devoting a lot of time to very little purpose.

In the midst of these partially illicit activities, however, Frobisher did not neglect the letter of his employment. One group of prisoners, taken from a Spanish 'Frygott' captured by his fleet in the Narrow Seas, was sufficiently important to be taken directly to Court, then at Nonesuch, for interrogation.[15] On 6 May 1589, Frobisher reported to Howard that he had captured a hoy carrying another suspected Spanish spy, who upon being taken, 'caste ouareborde tou paketes of Letares'. The same ship carried 'three pore men, their wifes & childern', whom Frobisher somewhat dismissively set ashore at Dover and directed 'to goe where thay will'.[16] Three days later, he sent another note to Burghley, the longest missive he is known ever to have written. At the end of April, the Privy Council had asked for his opinion on the strategic value of Ostend to the Protestant cause (almost certainly with the intention of reducing or withdrawing the English garrison there).[17] It may have been a subject which raised particularly strong feelings in Frobisher, or perhaps the request had flattered his vanity; whichever is the case, he set himself to providing more than even the Council had expected. Unfortunately, this was one of his few surviving pieces not to have been taken down by a secretary; his own, extremely neat hand sets out the arguments, but so also does his own spelling and grammar. A brief taste here will suffice to emphasize the advantages of employing trained clerks:

Consethrenge the charge the enemy is at w(i)th sondri garesones to kepe
the frontares of those wayste contres tou presarve those contres w(i)thin if
he shall haue theme at lebarte beyeseydes the wellthe & trade thate wolle
growe tou the enemye beye it / for if we shoulde geue it ovare thes somare
we cannote so muche ruianate or drounde it bute thate wolle recouare it
before wintare & make it w(i)thin one yere a betare harbrou then donkerke
for it hathe hade five times as mane peaers belongenge tou it as evar don-
cerke hade . . .[18]

Discounting the headache that deciphering them must have given to
Burghley, Frobisher's comments were perceptive, and their underpinning
logic far-reaching. Years of standing close in to the Dutch and Flemish coasts,
harrying Parma's supply lines and strangling the commerce of Philip's once-
wealthy provinces, had given him insights that may have escaped greater
but more detached intellects. What the Queen and Burghley might wish to
be free of would, he had seen, rebound vastly to their disadvantage, should
it be lost:

'it wolbe a fare wores nebare [neighbour] then dunkerke for it dothe stande
so derecteleye in the waye that all shepes moste parforese falle w(i)th in
seyghte of it to go in tou floshene [Flushing] if it be lete go tou the enemy
there can nothenge pase frome floshene nor tou floshene w(i)thoute grete
conning & then haue tha all thate coste [coast] clere for all there mene of
ware . . .'.

The hapless privateer, rescued from oblivion in the Marshalsea at the whim
of Master Secretary Cecil, now lectured the great Lord Burghley upon
strategic realities and the true costs of cost-paring. In this, and in events of
which he could as yet have no inkling, Frobisher had begun to exact a modest
recompense for the galling prospect of Drake's glittering career. Indeed, the
process mirrored a very satisfying dip in the latter's fortunes. At the very
moment that Frobisher sat at his table in a cramped cabin, straining to use
what small learning he possessed to the best effect, Drake and Norreys were
abandoning the seige of Corunna, the prelude to their larger failure before
Lisbon and the pointless demonstration at Vigo. If Frobisher's suggestion that
Ostend was worth keeping at any price was likely to displease the Queen, it
was as nothing compared to the £49,000 she had invested (and was in the
process of losing) in this, Drake's supposed riposte to the Armada campaign.
And, in July, as Howard was writing to Walsingham regarding which ships

were to go 'to the west' with Frobisher and which should remain under Palmer in the Narrow Seas, Norreys and Drake received the summons they must have been dreading: to come up to London, bringing their accounts for the late voyage with them.[19] Their fears were not misplaced; within months, as Frobisher searched for Spanish treasure ships off Portugal – Drake's former hunting ground – his old nemesis languished at Buckland in disgrace, charged with such weighty tasks as chairing a committee to investigate Plymouth's water supply.[20]

Frobisher's newly enhanced reputation, deriving particularly from his role as one of the five principal sea-commanders during the Armada campaign, had brought commensurate responsibilities; but this new commission, first hinted at in Howard's July correspondence to Walsingham, reflected something more. Commanding a Narrow Seas squadron was a natural extension of the necessary, mundane war duties that complemented the more dramatic yet fleeting moments of battle. The rotation of competent men in this role – Seymour, Palmer and Frobisher – ensured that the Spanish army's tenure in the southern Netherlands remained fraught with supply difficulties and the more immediate threat of further mutinies for want of pay. However, these passive aims, though important, could not be decisive in themselves, nor relieve the pressing problem of England's war expenses. What was needed was the means of delivering a mortal blow to Spain's ability to prosecute the war. Invasions of Spain and Portugal, as had recently been made amply apparent, were not the answer; nor was an expensive over-reliance upon Dutch martial abilities. The only feasible proactive policy, as always, was to seek the ruin of Spain in the Atlantic Ocean, across which her vulnerable plate fleets alone provided the means for Philip II to prosecute so many, simultaneous conflicts. For the next few years, Frobisher was to be more closely identified with this strategy than any other man, John Hawkins excepted. He was not chosen for this role by default (the Queen did not trust her expensive fleets to whomsoever was to hand), but because his performance during the Armada campaign had shown him to be a remorseless pursuer of an ordained goal, and, perhaps even more importantly, because he remained desperately hungry for those tokens of success whose surfeit seems to have blunted Drake's appetite.

The principal naval effort of 1589 after the Drake-Norreys fiasco was intended to follow up and complement the semi-private expedition of the Earl of Cumberland, who in June had sailed with the evergreen intention of intercepting one of the Indies fleets. As usual, the voyage had been ill-equipped, and Cumberland had spent too much time in the Azores, attempting to water his ships (the lessons of Drake's 1585 raid, requiring additional funds to put right, had been ignored). Thus, he had missed any chance of taking a plate fleet at sea, a feat that was becoming ever more difficult. Following the appalling attrition upon Spanish sea-forces during the Armada campaign, the Caribbean had swiftly become infested with English privateers, operating in the knowledge that Spain could no longer send more than a handful of ships to guard her treasure. This should have made the task of chasing the plate fleets much easier; yet with Philip's silver rendered so vulnerable, Spanish sea-commanders had become extremely wary, and their tactics developed accordingly. When, therefore, several ships of the 1589 *flota* managed to reach Angra in the Azores unscathed, they chose to remain, safe in the harbour there, until Cumberland had expended his supplies and returned to England. In the face of such a perceptive strategy, he was able only to take a single, stray ship of the *flota* (it was subsequently wrecked in a storm), and a few smaller prizes, before hunger did what Spanish martial might was no longer capable of achieving.[21]

Frobisher's new expedition was intended to cruise off Portugal and take any part of the treasure fleet that might (and so easily did) evade Cumberland: the first manifestation of a 'twin-net' strategy that was to be repeated in the following year by Frobisher and Hawkins. On 30 August 1589, he was given a commission authorizing him to press men in the south-western ports, though this referred only to 'certain special service in the south and west seas'.[22] A few days later, a list of ships reserved to his command named the *Golden Lion, Elizabeth Bonaventure, Advice* and *Repentance*.[23] Since 18 June, he had reassumed station in the eastern Narrow Seas, having rotated once more with Seymour; but on 9 September, he transferred out of his flagship *Rainbow* to take command of the *Elizabeth Bonaventure*.[24] He was at sea by the following day, though once more carrying a clutch of orders designed to extract the maximum use of his forces at a minimum outlay from the Queen's purse. Thus, instead of passing directly to the Portuguese coast, Frobisher went first to Dieppe, which the Catholic League had been attempting to invest. Sir Edward Stafford wrote to Walsingham on 15 September to inform him that the Leaguers had retired, and that Frobisher (who had put into the harbour that day) had determined that he was no longer needed and immediately set sail once more.[25] From Dieppe, the squadron passed directly to Cape Sagres; there, under bombardment by the guns of the fort, Frobisher cut out a large Biscayan vessel at a cost of some damage to the *Repentance*.[26] He then stood out to sea, probably in or near the 'Burlings' (the Boerlingas islands, off Cape Carvoeiro), and patrolled the known approaches of the Indies fleets.

The same fourteen ships of the *flota* that had out-waited Cumberland's small fleet left Angra on 27 October, on the final, dangerous leg of their voyage to Lisbon.[27] For once the English net held, and Frobisher himself sighted the Spanish ships two days later. However, the extremely extended formation of his squadron meant that he was entirely unsupported; further- more, some of the treasure ships were of the new *gallizabra* type – lighter, low-decked vessels with only vestigial fore and aft castles, heavily armed but designed above all to move quickly through the water. The testimony of four friars, taken in the Biscayan prize and later released, claimed that Frobisher had not dared to attack the Spanish ships' close formation unaided.[28] Before he was able to concentrate his own resources, the plate ships had reached the safety of the Tagus estuary, though it was reported that the English squadron subsequently took the tardy flagship and vice-admiral of the *flota* (though these had already discharged their cargoes of silver bullion at Angra).[29] However, as Frobisher returned to England with these and two lesser West Indiamen taken subsequently, a severe storm descended about his fleet. The two principal Spanish ships sank with their cargoes off Eddystone, though to his credit, the English Admiral managed to overcome his bitter disappoint- ment sufficiently to have their stricken crews pulled out of the water. The remaining prizes, if relatively modest in light of the expectations that had set out the expedition, provided enough booty to ensure that a further attempt to seize the plate fleets would be made in the following year.[30]

There was one other seizure made by Frobisher during his 1589 voyage. The vessel, unidentified in any document, was detained briefly and then allowed to depart unmolested. One of her passengers, a Genoese merchant named Paolo Porta, was given a letter by Frobisher to be presented to Philip II. The Spanish King accepted this from Porta's hands on 22 December, and promised to read it; in the meantime, he referred the merchant to Secretary Idiaquez, who sent him on to England with a promise of a passport for Frobisher and one other gentleman to come to speak with Philip.[31] The letter appears to have been an offer by Frobisher to assist with the Spanish capture of Flushing; as with his approach sixteen years earlier, a token of personal treachery that would not have been in the least objectionable to the Privy Council. Any prospect of cozening the Spanish King was worth the attempt; indeed, such offers seem almost to have become an English national sport. Ralegh, too, was known to have touted his services to Philip, as, possibly, had many other, lesser men whose stratagems were conducted beyond the scope of official record.[32] It is hardly surprising that such tokens of faithlessness had become part of the currency of a war waged upon the pretences of faith, and most if not all of these schemes seem to have been blithely used or ignored by Burghley and Walsingham as circumstances required. In Frobisher's case, Porta made a deposition in England on 13 April 1590 (possibly to Burghley himself), which makes it very likely that the mysterious initiative had been sanctioned or even authorized by the Council itself. Nothing could, or did, come of the matter. Frobisher's obvious indifference to the finer points of his own religion undoubtedly made him an attractive figure to those who could convince themselves of his capacity to turn; but he was now beyond such treacheries. If, in 1573, a half-hearted approach to an unemployed (and near unemployable) privateer had not secured an English traitor, no weightier promises to an admiral were now likely to succeed.

Following his fleet's return to England, Frobisher resumed his winter guard in the Channel (Palmer had commanded the squadron in his absence: officially, from 10 September until 31 December).[33] It appears that his first major task in the new year was to assist in the evacuation from Cherbourg of Lord Willoughby's disease-ridden expeditionary force. The commission had been given first to Luke Warde, one of Frobisher's former lieutenants in the north-west voyages, whose original instructions offer a further example of Elizabeth's regard for her men: 'And because divers of the souldiers are diseased and troubled with infirmities, it is thought meete you shall have care to receave only into her Majesties shippes the Lord Willougheby and suche of the better sorte as maie be conveniently placed in them, to avoyd the pestering and infecting of her Majesties shippes . . .'.[34] With a number of armed merchantmen (presumably to disembark those not considered of the 'better sorte'), Frobisher was in the mouth of the Seine before 20 January, and appears to have disembarked the army with as much despatch (and certainly with more legitimate authority) as Willoughby had demonstrated in coming to France.[35] Chateuneuf, the French Ambassador, wrote to Walsingham from Dover on 6 February, mentioning that Frobisher had already arrived in the port, disembarked the stricken army and had departed once more for the coast of Zeeland.[36]

In early March, word reached the Spanish Court from its agents in London that Frobisher had put into the Thames a few days earlier with five or six prizes, the fruits of this brief cruise.[37] In the meantime, preparations for a major new Atlantic expedition had commenced. As early as December 1589, preliminary plans to set out Hawkins with six ships were being discused; but by the turn of the year, the size of the proposed force had increased to thirteen vessels.[38] This enlarged fleet was to be split into two elements, and Frobisher – whose new-found reputation as one of the few English commanders actually to have sighted a plate fleet at sea must have counted for much – was appointed as joint-commander. The English fleet was ready to sail by mid-February, but as with Hawkins's 1586 expedition, the Queen then ordered it to be detained in port.[39] Once more, her Council had received news of a threat from the sea: this time, of a Spanish design to reinforce the Catholic League forces in Brittany. All available shipping was detained in English harbours until the size and nature of the threat could be gauged; as their own fleet was the most obvious means of challenging any major Spanish action, Frobisher and Hawkins kicked their heels in port for almost four months, whilst other English ships – among them the little *Hawk* and *Fancy* – were hurriedly despatched to the French coast to find the rumoured Spanish force.[40] On 11 June, the joint admirals received further instructions from the Council, ordering them to remain at Plymouth until the end of the month, after which, if they had heard nothing more, they were to depart upon their intended voyage.[41] Unfortunately, the long delay in setting out the expedition meant that yet another opportunity had been lost. Though it was the 1590 New Spain *flota* that the English ships were intending to intercept, the long-delayed 1589 Tierra Firme *galeones* had arrived at Lisbon only during March 1590, bringing five million much-needed ducats for Philip's depleted treasury. Had Hawkins and Frobisher been allowed to sail on schedule, they may well have placed themselves between the Azores and Lisbon in time to intercept them, with a force powerful enough to take on and defeat the *gallizabras* in detail. Success would have been by no means inevitable (absorbing the lessons of earlier voyages, Spanish ships seem now to have made for the Azores in a slightly higher latitude than previously), but the delay meant that perhaps the best English chance ever to intercept Philip's plate ships had dissipated even before the fleet sailed at the end of June.[42]

When the expedition was finally allowed to leave Plymouth, its two elements separated; Frobisher had command of the larger squadron of seven ships: the *Revenge* (his flagship once more), *Golden Lion*, *Elizabeth Bonaventure*, *Dreadnought*, *Crane*, *Quittance* and *Advice*.[43] This year, it was he who was to lie well out into the Atlantic, patrolling the approaches to Flores and Terceira whilst Hawkins provided the line of secondary interdiction off the coast of Portugal with six ships.

By 25 July, Frobisher's ships were off Mont-St-Michel (as we shall see, both he and Hawkins had been further delayed in indulging their habitual practices on the southward passage), where he met with a small fleet of vessels out of Lyme Regis. Some of its mariners later claimed that he had told them of his intention to land upon the coast there, but this was almost certainly misinformation designed to percolate back to Philip's spies in London.[44] A few days later, his squadron was in the Azores, near Terceira. By now, he had a fleet of twenty vessels, having brought several English privateers into consortship on the passage south. Already, they had missed several ships of the 1590 New Spain *flota*, which had put into Viana at the beginning of August;[45] nevertheless, Frobisher remained on station for a further month, taking a number of small prizes off Corvo, the most north-westerly of the island group. In light of his late departure, this strategy was sound, providing the last opportunity to take stragglers. At the end of a month's cruise, however, provisions for his fleet had been almost entirely consumed. As usual, the Queen's policy had been formulated without the resources to support it, probably in the hope that some divine good fortune would place the Spanish ships directly in Frobisher's path as he arrived in his patrol area. To his credit, he sought desperately to extend his fleet's capacity to remain at sea. Perhaps recalling the civilized arrangement he and Drake had negotiated with the Governor of Bayona at the outset of the West Indies raid five years earlier, he decided to rely upon the perennial need of Spain's provinces for hard currency. The fleet made for the island of Fayal, where the 'Portuguese' fortress, the *Castello Branco* – manned by Spanish troops – had been demolished in the previous year by Cumberland's expedition. Frobisher may have hoped not to find any serious opposition on the island; as it transpired, the fortifications had been hastily rebuilt and re-garrisoned. Even faced with this potential threat, he decided to send an envoy to the fortress, offering 'good friendship' and English cash for victuals and water. The courtesies of war had long since been exhausted, however, and the commander of *Castello Branco* replied to this optimistic proposition forthrightly – by shooting the envoy. Frobisher, outraged at a flagrant violation of a flag of truce, was powerless nevertheless to do more than promise to return later and visit his wrath upon the island; a threat that, without the means of sustaining his Azores station, lacked its customary credibility. By 9 September, his fleet was back in Plymouth, with scant results to show for his efforts.[46]

Hawkins, patrolling the seas around the Burlings, was barely more successful. He had used his own resources at Plymouth to supplement the Crown's provisioning, but even so, his ships had victuals enough to remain on station for just six weeks. In the event, it was not nearly enough. One of his own vessels, cruising independently, captured a carrack and brought it into Dartmouth, but Hawkins himself returned to Plymouth in October with only a few small prizes. The entire expedition had cost more than £17,000 to set out;[47] it is highly unlikely that it came even close to covering that with prize monies.

Yet despite their modest returns, the expeditions of 1589 and 1590 were extremely effective, if a strategy is to be judged by the damage it inflicts upon an enemy. English interest in the Spanish treasure fleets was a venerable pre-occupation, but these latest manifestations were subtly different than those of previous years. Whilst Frobisher and others sailed, as always, with the primary intention of enriching themselves and their Queen, it is clear that the policy of denying Philip his principal source of income was beginning to assume a parity with the seizing of it. Surprisingly, Frobisher himself had become a leading proponent of this potentially selfless strategy, though in so ambitious a manner that his proposals could hardly have been sanctioned by his parsimonious Queen. In an undated note to Burghley – the wording of which makes it clear that Howard had urged him to convey his opinions – Frobisher had argued, not necessarily for the benefits of putting Spanish gold in English hands, but of keeping it out of Spanish ones:

> For no doubt if they came home this year [i.e. the plate ships] they will have [perforce?] wast them sent to meet them, so as there must be (sufficient sent) to overthrow them, for although eight good ships of the (Queen's) Majesty's will be able to beat them they shall be able to (take too) few of them; for when they come to fly it is the number that take them, for when every ship makes shift for her(self, the) multitude must perform the chase. So that my opinion is that there may be no less than eight g(alleons) of the Queen's Majesty's and twelve good merchants, and all th(e) men of war that may be gotten to accompany them. The Queen's majesty were better bestow a hundred th(ousand) pounds to overthrow them if she gain not one penny by (it, than to) let them pass . . .[48]

For Frobisher, such a policy 'in being well considered is to the Spaniards of as great danger as anything that may happen to them'. Interestingly, he also made the case for catching the plate fleets in the narrow end of the 'funnel' – that is, in the Florida Channel at the beginning of their home voyage – rather than allowing them to use the width of the Atlantic to escape their pursuers. In making this proposal, of whose boldness he asked Burghley's forgiveness, he had come to understand – not least from his own, frustrating experiences – the fundamental flaws of a policy half-forged in expectation of fabulous gains; though in making his plea he was as optimistic of the Queen's largesse in setting right that policy as Hawkins had been.

There was nothing original about this concept of commerce destruction

(Walsingham had been arguing the case for several years), but for a man of Frobisher's sterling venality to have become so convinced of its truth indicates something of the currency it had come to enjoy. The value of the theory was self-evident, in that the enemy feared its adoption above all others. The 1589 and 1590 expeditions – and several, smaller-scale private English raids upon the Caribbean itself – unnerved the Spanish authorities: not because of the possibility that they might encounter his fleets by chance (which long experience had shown to be most unlikely), but because English ships were patrolling systematically with the intention of severing Spain's economic lifeline. Neither expedition was to seize a significant prize, but in 1590, the timetable of the *audiencia* of Santo Domingo was so disrupted by the threat (real and perceived) of English interdiction that it was obliged to detain that year's combined fleet at Havana, despite Philip's urgent instructions that it should depart from thence no later than 25 July.[49] Frustrating though this decision proved for Frobisher and Hawkins personally, it was to have widespread consequences. For want of the expected annual transfusion of capital, Philip was obliged to default upon his debts to Italian bankers (several were ruined); his standing army in the Netherlands, that perniciously voracious consumer of New World silver, was rendered incapable of offensive action during 1590; and – a direct corollary – Henry IV was able to defeat the armies of the Catholic League in the Low Countries that year. To Linschoten (an impartial observer), reporting the utter disruption of Spanish commercial traffic in the Azores in 1589/90, the English 'are become lords and masters of the sea, and need care for no man'.[50] Poor comfort that it may have been to Frobisher, who no doubt had entertained dreams of taking another *Cacafuego* or *San Felipe*, his career had come to enjoy a European significance.

As always, however, such momentous tides were muddied by the less estimable – if inevitable – consequences of setting out privateers upon the nation's business. On their voyage south, both Frobisher and Hawkins had been at their old occupation of seizing vessels owned by England's allies, even to the detriment of a strategy that might, if successful, have secured the wealth of the Indies. Perhaps, anticipating the frustration of yet another failure to intercept a plate fleet, they had indulged their habit with even greater enthusiasm than usual, thus ensuring that greater disappointment. The industrious Beauvoir la Nocle wrote to Burghley as early as 2 July (possibly within forty-eight hours of the incident), asking for assistance to check upon eleven French vessels taken by the two squadrons; as ever, he wanted 'loyal' cargoes and vessels returned and the King's fifth paid on the remainder. On 11 and 17 July, respectively, the States of Zeeland and the States-General wrote to complain of the seizure of Dutch ships carrying cargoes of cochineal, ginger and silver worth some 100,000 florins – all of which both Frobisher and Hawkins subsequently claimed had belonged to Spanish merchants.[51] It was also alleged that the crews of these vessels had been maltreated by the English mariners. For once, the Privy Council moved swiftly; on 25 July, they ordered goods belonging to merchants of Holland, Zeeland, Danzig and Hamburg to be released. Neither Frobisher nor Hawkins seems to have obeyed. The matter generated at least eight further missives from the Council, who, as late as November, were expressing their considerable ire at this blatant disregard of its authority (Hawkins seems to have received the brunt of these complaints; perhaps the Council, recalling the counting-house at Tower Hill and its illustrious share-holder, had by now given up on Frobisher).[52] As appears to have been their habitual practice, municipal officials at Plymouth colluded to muddy the Admiralty Court's investigation; the Council wrote to the Mayor in October regarding his continuing failure to deliver up goods belonging to one George Siguine of Calais, taken in one of Frobisher's prizes:

> . . . you have refused to deliver the whole quantitie and porcions mencioned in the same because they where not marked accordingly. Forasmuch as it is alleged that the markes have been washed out of sondry hodgsheads of wines and mallasses, and certeine cases of gilt leather belongeinge to the said merchantes which are perfectly and apparently knowne to be the proper goods of the said Siguine . . .[53]

On 14 November, Burghley drew up a note estimating that Frobisher had taken 'bad' prize belonging to merchants of Holland and Zeeland to the value of £1,154.[54] M. Noel de Caron, representative of the States-General, confirmed this with his own manifest of stolen monies and goods, presented to the Admiralty Court, showing that cargoes of cochineal, figs and other goods worth almost £1,200 were missing.[55]

As provocative as these seizures had been, there is evidence that both Frobisher and Hawkins had good reason to regard certain Netherlander ships as fair game. Their claims regarding the ultimate ownership of these vessels' cargoes were in some cases based upon the best evidence – that of their own eyes. An unsigned note to Burghley, dated 14 May 1591, claimed that the *Catherine* of Amsterdam, bound for Spain but taken *en route* by Frobisher, had been carrying some two tons of iron nails; other evidence from Admiralty Court records indicates that such practices remained widespread.[56] If the enterprising shipowners of Holland, Zeeland and England were not prepared to sacrifice their trade in the cause of their liberties – particularly, if they remained willing to sell vital war materials to Spain – then clearly some further discouragement had been both necessary and proper.

There were other complaints of Frobisher's performance during the 1590 expedition, though these were largely circumstantial in nature. One Thomas Davies, whose precise identity is unclear, addressed a detailed critique to Ralph Lane (Lane had become a member of Howard's council of war following the end of the Armada campaign).[57] Davies had sailed with Frobisher on the Azores raid, probably in the *Revenge*. Most of the complaints he made in his letter were couched in general terms – of the poor provisioning of the fleet, the misrule and dishonesty of its captains – who 'fall at variance, then in malice, they discourse such abuses as are done and committed by them' – and the undermanning of the ships with inferior sailors (the last was an abiding problem in contemporary naval expeditions, particularly during wartime, when calls upon their limited numbers were heavy).[58] But he also alleged that Frobisher deliberately failed to engage a heavily laden Spanish fleet one night – this seems unlikely unless, as in 1589, these were fast, well-armed *gallizabras* – and that he had taken several friendly French fishing boats: giving one, with its catch, to 'a kinsman'. Furthermore, he provided a paper-trail for the £1,154 value of seized cargoes that Burghley had noted elsewhere (indicating, perhaps, that he was the Lord Treasurer's man, placed in the fleet to provide such intelligence). In the latter case, however, his arrows were misdirected; the fate of the proceeds from these goods indicates little more than that Frobisher was looking after his men. Every penny raised was distributed between the commanders of the Queen's ships – *Golden Lion*, *Elizabeth Bonaventure*, *Dreadnought* and *Crane* – as Davies was forced to admit – to be disbursed subsequently 'for the vse of her Ma(ies)ties shipps'. In other words, Frobisher had done no more than oblige the merchants of Holland and Zeeland to assist in financing the war against their common enemy: one which some of them may have been seeking to abet. In doing so, he was acting within his Queen's laws, and, incidentally, providing much needed funding for her cash-starved navy.[59] Though we have little evidence to determine the scale of the practice, it may be that a significant proportion of prizes taken at other times by Frobisher and his naval colleagues was similarly put to correcting the deficiencies of the Queen's naval administration.

Even admitting the justice of some of Davies's charges, it is difficult to condemn outright the acquisitive habits of Elizabeth's captains. This and other episodes illustrate the anomalous role that they discharged during these officially organized expeditions. Their commissions bound them to duties that served their sovereign, yet the skills such duties demanded had been honed, in many cases, in entirely selfish pursuits. These skills could be requisitioned, but not independently of the peculiar moralities they had generated. For many such men, taken from their habitat of choice to lead England's sea-borne response to the threat of Spanish hegemony, brazen self-interest was to remain an imperative – particularly as the expected rewards for legitimate naval service were both extremely modest and hardly secured. The fierce sense of duty that we discern also was something else: often involuntary, but almost always unstinting, even to the detriment of personal safety. The manner in which these supremely uncomplementary qualities were manifest – in men like Drake, Hawkins and Frobisher – has since determined our perception of their worth; yet as we have seen from one man's career, it is not always easy to discern where self-interest ended and duty began. Some were able to make a virtue of their cupidity – Hawkins, for example, had long thrived in, and contributed to, an economic sub-culture that made Plymouth such a haven for illicitly seized goods; yet the effectiveness of his tenure as Treasurer of the navy (for which he is principally recalled) was hugely informed by the same experiences. If, for Frobisher, the chance to make even this limited withdrawal from temptation did not arise, there can be little doubt that the dutifulness he displayed in naval office was more than a convenient adjunct to his venal instincts.

Having partially exonerated him and his kind, however, we must also note evidence of the Frobisher tradition being followed by a new generation at this time. On 15 August 1589, the English merchant and sometime spy Otwell Smith wrote to Walsingham from Dieppe, informing him that ships from the town had recaptured a Breton bark, laden with Newfoundland fish, that previously had been taken by a Scottish privateer named Turner. The bark's prize crew – including one 'Martin Frobisher junior', had been incarcerated in Dieppe jail upon suspicion of throwing its original crew overboard.[60] The young felon was probably the son of John Frobisher.[61] His life and career prior to the occasion of his employment with Captain Turner are entirely anonymous, though his pedigree was impeccably appropriate for his chosen profession. The charge of throwing the Breton bark's crew overboard seems not to have been validated. Had it been, the French authorities would almost certainly have considered it a hanging offence, yet Martin junior was at large once more by the early part of 1590, and sailed with his uncle in that year's Azores voyage as captain of the *Dreadnought* (he was that kinsman whom Davies, almost certainly with justice, had identified as the recipient of the elder Frobisher's largesse).[62] In the same manifest of stolen goods that had signally failed to shame Hawkins and the elder Frobisher into making restitution thereof, M. de Caron had specifically identified Martin junior by name, alleging that he had purloined fifty-eight bags of money and cochineal worth over £2,400 from the *Damoiselle* of Purmerend; though he noted also that the crime was 'without any hope of satisfaction, by reason young martin is in prison for other piraces & not able to satisfy for anything' (a margin note states 'They haue warrant(e)s to arrest young Frobisher, w(hi)ch they may execute at their pleasur(e) . . .').[63] The younger Martin had also become known to that other indefatigable chronicler of his uncle's depredations, Beauvoir la Nocle, who claimed that part of the prize from the *Damoiselle* was money belonging to some loyal merchants of Vitre.[64] To have garnered such attention in so short a career speaks well of the boy's industry, and had he lived longer he might have surpassed even the elder Martin's record as a source of employment for the Admiralty Court. Like his uncle, however, the younger Martin Frobisher was soon to find dry land a far more dangerous environment than the yawing deck of a privateer.

For the elder Frobisher, the end of the 1590 expedition brought, for some weeks at least, the resumption of his habitual station in the Channel. On New Year's Day 1591, one M. Moucheron wrote to Burghley regarding the compensation he had received in respect of the previous year's voyage, which suggests that Frobisher had been persuaded to prise open his money chest, if only slightly (he had parted with just £70; perhaps to satisfy that restitution sought some nineteen months earlier by George Johnson of Rotterdam).[65] An unsigned, undated intelligence letter, written by a Spanish spy, probably in February or March, almost certainly overstated the facts in claiming that both Frobisher and Hawkins were out of favour since their last voyage, though – a silver lining – Drake's credit was also stated to be 'worth nothinge', and had been so for some time.[66] Nevertheless, the two commanders of the 1590 expedition appear to have been censured for their supplementary activities and, for a while thereafter, Frobisher at least seems to have followed his commission a little more closely. During 1591 there were no known approaches to the Admiralty Court in respect of his seizures (other than on-going correspondence regarding those made during 1590), which suggests that it was the legitimate prey of Spanish vessels that received the brunt of his attention. Here again, however, there are very few references, and these unenlightening; in May, for example, Howard wrote of two Spanish ships taken by Frobisher which were to be sold off (being too unweatherly to be pressed into Crown service); the receipts to be used to build two 'nimble' ships for the navy.[67]

Lack of further evidence of Frobisher's sea-activities during the latter part of 1590 and for much of 1591 may indicate also that he was spending one of his brief periods as a landsman. Though the manner and means of his living would hardly indicate it, he was adding significantly to his properties at this time. In November 1591, he obtained from the Queen the leasehold of the manor of Whitewood, near Featherstone in Yorkshire, for an unspecified amount; and of Finningley Grange in Nottinghamshire, for a fee of £949.[68] It may also have been during this year that he acquired the manor of Wasenfield (near his existing properties at Heath), a house in Walthamstow (Essex) and unspecified holdings at Blackstone (Yorkshire) and Rockeley (Nottinghamshire) – all properties that feature in his will. A cursory glance at a map reveals that Walthamstow apart, Frobisher was building a portfolio of lands and properties lying within thirty-five miles, principally to the south, of his ancestral home at Altofts. The concentration is both significant and poignant. However rootless a life his career had demanded of him, age and wealth (and the prospect of one day enjoying it) had at last brought out a parochial side to his restless nature. Ties of kinship and ancestry – so long held in abeyance or disregarded entirely – had begun to re-exert their pull upon him as the prospect of comfortable retirement loomed.

These imperatives were to be manifested most strongly in what, for Frobisher, had long been unfamiliar, perhaps even painful considerations. With his acquisitions in the area, he had come to have the status of a landed gentleman; yet even now he did not enjoy its commensurate lifestyle. Even more than Drake or Hawkins, Frobisher had been wedded to the sea. His first marriage – a tragic association for the unfortunate Isobel and her children – seems to have been no more than a distraction; an episode that he chose to forget long before it ended with her pauper's death. Since then, he had accumulated a substantial estate without building the social structure to fill it. Though probably a fond uncle to his nephew Martin – whose brief, feckless career mirrored much of the worst of his own – he was at best a cold and distant icon to the remainder of his family. One imagines his visits to Altofts to have been fleeting, forbidding affairs for his servants and kin; his brief appearances as local magistrate a superficial imprint upon the social life of the district.[69] Without an immediate family to stand proxy for his absent authority, Frobisher was a name, but not a presence, in West Yorkshire.

He moved to fill this vacuum at some time before October 1590, when he married for the second time.[70] Dorothy, daughter of Lord Wentworth and widow of Paul Withypool of Ipswich, was a mature woman with a grown daughter, and presumably there was little expectation of her providing a male heir. Details of the provenance of her relationship with Frobisher, his approach, courtship and any other evidence of his tender feelings for her are entirely absent. One is left with an overwhelming sense of affairs briskly put in order: a mutually satisfactory arrangement that would provide Dorothy with a measure of security and Martin with an off-the-shelf family. The final, missing piece to an elusive conventionality, acquired, it seems, with little more ceremony than the wealth that supported it.

Yet as Frobisher built the estate that would be the physical monument to his achievements, his capacity to enjoy their fruits was diminishing. The reward of diligence, from a monarch who had too few reliable lieutenants, was yet further duty; and in discharging it there were to be new frustrations.

TWENTY

The Madre de Dios

Despite three years' failure to engage or take significant elements of the plate fleets of New Spain and Tierra Firme, English attention – one might say obsession – remained firmly fixed upon the goal; the more so because it offered the only realistic hope of alleviating the costs of an increasingly expensive conflict. The war was not progressing favourably for England, despite the total failure of the Armada campaign. Defeat being the best of tutors, technical improvements to Spanish shipping and administration since 1588 had created new threats for England's navy and her myriad private voyagers, who, in the manner of all victors, had derived fewer lessons from their relative successes. Philip, absorbing the bitter truths of the 'warre of 21 Julie' and the enduring attempts upon his plate fleets, had gradually upgraded both his ships and the administrative arrangements that protected his New World lifelines. English operations against Spanish vessels had, subsequently, become bloodier and less profitable. In 1591, as Frobisher remained on-shore to tend to his growing estate, Lord Thomas Howard's attempt to intercept the *flota* had brought out a Spanish fleet of fifty-five ships under Alonzo de Bazán, brother of the late Marquis of Santa Cruz. Wisely, and precipitously, Howard had fled; leaving Grenville to die gloriously (and pointlessly) in the last fight of the *Revenge*. The *flota* was badly mauled, but by weather rather than English ships, and though the loss to Spain was substantial, it did little to ease England's financial problems.

Now tiring of the unprofitable attrition upon her own ships, Elizabeth refused to surrender to Hawkins's promptings to set out a predominantly naval force in 1592 as she had done between 1589 and 1591.[1] If a new,

large-scale attempt to make a golden rendezvous with the silver galleons were
to be organized that year, the principal cost of its failure was not to be borne
by the Crown. Even the strategically important task of blockading the Spanish
coast was given over to a form of 'private' enterprise – to the ever-reliable
Cumberland, whose perennial need of a profit was a far sounder safeguard
than any more explicit token of loyalty.[2]

Thus, the principal English effort in 1592 was financed from a variety of
sources. Preliminary discussions regarding an expedition that year may have
originated amongst the London merchants who had so profitably set out
Robert Flicke, the grocer turned privateer, to reinforce Howard in the Azores
the previous year;[3] but their influence in formulating the aims of the venture
was minimal. Though not wishing to bear the brunt of costs, the Queen was
careful to maintain a firm official direction of any concentrated force. She
put up ten per cent of the necessary funds, principally in the form of two
royal ships, the *Garland* and *Foresight* (no doubt over-valued for the purpose
of establishing her share of prizes, as was her habit).[4] The Ralegh brothers,
Carew and Walter, were also major investors, and Walter in particular soon
took upon himself the leading role in organizing the expedition.[5] Cumberland, though stretched by his current commitments, provided five of his own
ships, and John Hawkins also invested heavily. The London merchants,
perhaps discouraged by the Queen's implicit control of the scheme – and her
refusal to allow them a more equitable division of the 1591 prizes taken by
Flicke – eventually ventured only a minor share, of some £6,000 (the coincidence of this and their share of the 1591 prize monies suggests that the
same merchants were allowing their money to 'roll' in the new venture).

On 28 February, Walter Ralegh was given a commission to command the
expedition.[6] It seems that his was the name most acceptable to the disparate
elements that had backed the project (probably this was more to do with his
intimacy with Elizabeth than any real faith in his abilities as an admiral),
though the Queen remained loath to allow her current favourite to go to sea.
Ralegh himself, whilst keen to see the expedition set out, was almost equally
reluctant to leave. He had no experience of commanding fleets, and loved the
sea no more than had his half-brother, Humphrey Gilbert. Elizabeth's own
misgivings provided him with the excuse to find an adequate substitute for
his own presence on the expedition; on 10 March 1592, he wrote to Robert
Cecil: 'I have promised her Majesty that if I can persuade the companies to
follow Sir Martin Frobiser, I will without fail return, and but bring them into
the sea some fifty or three score leagues, for which purpose my Lord Admiral
hath lent me the Disdain.'[7] Given the experience he had gained during the

1589/90 Atlantic compaigns, Frobisher's appointment as Ralegh's substitute was hardly remarkable, yet it is interesting nevertheless. Drake, of course, still lay under a cloud; but Hawkins, though busy still upon his renovation of the royal ships, was as available for service at sea as he had been in 1590 (his first request to resign from the Navy Office would not be made until July that year, and even then he was to express himself ready to take up other, more active service).[8] Alternatively, it would have created no great difficulty for Cumberland himself to have assumed overall command at Finisterre; he was at that moment already off the Portuguese coast and therefore aware of the latest intelligence of Spanish movements. Neither man seems to have been considered, however. Despite his failures in 1589 and 1590, his regrettably enduring habits *vis-à-vis* his treatment of friendly ships, and the lingering rumours regarding his honesty, it seems that Frobisher was acquiring something of a reputation for reliability.

As it transpired, Ralegh's intentions fell out precisely. On 4 May, he led his fleet out of Plymouth Harbour. The following morning, Frobisher came up in the *Disdain* and transferred into the *Garland*. For several days thereafter, Ralegh supervised the handing over of the fleet, possibly persuading many of his reluctant gentlemen friends and officers to accept the much harsher authority of his replacement. On 13 May, the fleet was forty leagues off Finisterre; there it met with thirteen Flemish and French ships, on board one of which was an Englishman who recently had been in Cadiz.[9] He informed Ralegh and Frobisher that Philip had ordered that the plate fleets should not sail from the Main or New Spain that year. Ralegh took this information back to England in the *Disdain*, whilst Frobisher pressed on, searching for a different prey.

It has been suggested that Frobisher merely implemented Ralegh's strategy during the coming campaign, but this seems unlikely.[10] Burghley and Howard wrote to Ralegh on 23 May, hinting that the Queen had authorized Frobisher to choose his station to intercept the enemy, and subsequent events confirm this.[11] Even before the fleet sailed, news reached England of the expected return of five Portuguese carracks from the East Indies; ships that almost certainly would not have the protection now afforded to Philip's plate fleets. From the moment at which Frobisher assumed command of the expedition, his dispositions were clearly directed towards their capture. Though the expedition had sailed southwards as a single unit (taking *en route* a Biscayan ship with cargo valued at £7,000),[12] it was soon deployed in two divisions to increase the chances of intercepting the carracks. The largest squadron remained under Frobisher himself, whilst a second comprising Sir John

Burgh's *Roebuck* and Robert Crosse's *Foresight*, with a number of barks, operated independently (a third squadron, Cumberland's five ships under John Norton, joined Burgh in the Azores).[13] Again, a two-tier strategy was employed; Frobisher took up the station of secondary interdiction, using his ships to screen the seas around the Burlings, whilst Burgh moved west to the Azores, where the carracks were expected to put in before attempting the final leg of their long voyage to Lisbon. At Flores, Burgh met with and was joined by two London ships, the *Green Dragon* and *Prudence*. As was the practice of English vessels sailing together with the same purpose, they and Cumberland's vessels entered into a consortship arrangement with Burgh's force (their contract was only a verbal one, however; an oversight that was to cost them dearly when prize monies were eventually allocated).

At the end of July, ships of Burgh's fleet intercepted the Portuguese carrack *Santa Cruz* as she approached the port of Angra, and chased her westwards towards Flores. In two separate encounters over two days, the *Santa Cruz* had managed to fight off the English vessels, but to escape such relatively swift and determined carrion proved impossible. Her captain, despairing of rescue, beached and burned her, together with her precious cargo, rather than allow the English mariners their prize. He and his crew were captured by their pursuers; under interrogation, he admitted that three other vessels were expected (in fact, two of these – the *Bom Jesus* and *Santa Bartolomeo* – had been lost with all hands in the Indian Ocean some months earlier, at the very start of their voyage). With this information, Burgh stood off to the west of Flores, where the carracks had been ordered to rendezvous with the Indies fleet's escorts. His ships patrolled the waters for several days, each vessel two leagues from its neighbour to increase the area of search.[14] On 3 August, the *Dainty* – the smallest ship in Burgh's squadron – sighted a huge vessel on the horizon. She was the Portuguese carrack *Madre de Dios*, fully seven decks high and of 1,600 tons. As imposing as her dimensions were, however, her cargo was even more impressive. Her purser's manifest subsequently revealed that she was carrying Moluccas pepper, cloves, cinnamon, camphor, cochineal, musk, amber, calicoes, silks, Chinese porcelain, ivory, ebony bedsteads – and a small matter of precious stones, to the value of 400,000 crusados.[15]

Having suffered a disappointment with regard to the *Santa Cruz*, the Englishmen did not stint in their efforts to secure this vast new prize. A vicious, close battle ensued, with the tiny *Dainty* taking on the carrack alone, 'with the slaughter and hurt of divers of her men', until the *Green Dragon* could come up in support.[16] Meanwhile, the *Foresight* and *Roebuck*, both attempting to close with the *Madre de Dios*, became entangled in each other's cables and were for a time unable to contribute anything to the increasingly hard-fought battle. The captain of the Portuguese ship, like his countryman in the *Santa Cruz*, tried desperately to beach his vessel upon a nearby island, but the *Foresight* managed to move to deny her access to the shore until the *Tiger* and *Samson* also came up. Finally, after three further hours of pounding, surrounded by English ships that gradually had closed and lashed themselves like parasites to her hull, the *Madre de Dios* fell to half a dozen boarding parties. In the aftermath of the fight, the carrack resembled a charnel house between decks. According to a contemporary account, 'no man could almost step by (but) upon a dead carkase or a bloody floore';[17] but in the frantic search for the cargoes that had nearly eluded them, the English mariners cared little for whom or what they trod upon. Crosse's crew from the *Foresight*, and possibly those of the *Dainty*, *Samson* and *Tiger* also, spent the night of 3 August plundering the carrack's holds whilst Burgh was distracted elsewhere, struggling to keep the badly damaged *Roebuck* afloat.[18] When he managed to board the *Madre de Dios* the following day, proper care was, for once, provided to the fallen enemy. English surgeons treated the wounded, and Burgh gallantly allowed the survivors and few passengers to leave on a freshly provisioned bark, the *Grace of Dover* (unfortunately, she was subsequently intercepted by the bark *Bond of Weymouth*, and her passengers despoiled of a further 50,000 ducats' worth of diamonds, which possibly had been concealed in the seams of corsets or yet more intimate places). About 400 Negro slaves had been chained in the holds of the *Madre de Dios*; these were put ashore at Flores and Corvo. The carrack herself, still sea-worthy despite her mauling, was carried as a prize to England.

While this epic capture was taking place, Frobisher was still in the Burlings, assiduously searching for prizes that had now been accounted for in full. Commanding a fleet that represented an even more diverse conglomeration of interests than was usual, he seems to have had a great deal of difficulty keeping his ships with him.[19] In consortship, and not therefore subject to the harsh discipline of outright naval service, several of the merchantmen's crews proved unable to resist the temptation to go off and do a little private business among the Spanish coastal traffic. Some time before the capture of the *Madre de Dios*, Captain Thompson's *Dainty* had taken a drubbing from an intended prize during one such unauthorized leave of absence. When he returned to the fleet and complained of his plight, Frobisher sourly expressed the hope that more of his fleet would experience the same and thus become better disposed to staying with their flagship.[20] His pointed comment was ignored, however, even by the man to whom it was most forcibly directed.

Within days, Thompson had carried off the *Dainty* to the west, without leave once more, to take his courageous place in Burgh's memorable encounter.

Always sensitive to his own bad luck, Frobisher must already have harboured dark premonitions regarding that year's expedition. In mid-August, the *Green Dragon*, returning to her station after briefly re-provisioning in England (and, more importantly, off-loading her illicit share of the *Madre de Dios*'s spoils), brought a letter for him from William Monson, dated 12 July, that bore the exhortation 'give these with speed, speed, haste, post haste'.[21] Monson had only recently escaped from captivity in Lisbon following his capture during Cumberland's 1591 expedition, and was able to provide much useful intelligence both upon what ships were arriving at Lisbon and what might be expected in the following weeks.[22] Unfortunately, his letter, written a month before it was placed into Frobisher's hands, was in effect an historical document. It mentioned that one of the carracks was already safely in Lisbon, but that the others were expected: 'the height [i.e., latitude] they held in was 43°; therefore in any wise keep to the northward of the Burlings . . .'. Monson also warned him of eighteen Spanish warships at Caescaes in the Tagus estuary that were being readied to meet the carracks and would hopefully hand out the same punishment to their English pursuers that Grenville had received in the previous year. In fact, there was no longer any reason for them to put to sea; Frobisher did not yet know that, though he could account for the *Madre de Dios* and *Santa Cruz* at least. In a letter to Burghley, he claimed that there had been another carrack, 'the third, it was my hard hape to misse at the Burlinges in a darke night, havinge sight of her light, the seventh of Julie'.[23] The possible existence of this, a third surviving ship of the Portuguese fleet, was corroborated only by Portuguese prisoners from the *Santa Cruz*, who claimed that a carrack named the *San Bernardo* had made the swiftest passage of any of the vessels that had departed together from Goa.[24]

Ghost ship or not, her elusiveness left Frobisher almost frantic for success. It may have been a lingering hope of taking her that kept him off the Portuguese coast even after receiving word of the capture of the *Madre de Dios*. However, his indecision ended on 31 August, when he met with the *Foresight* at about 47° N. Captain Crosse must have boasted at some length of his activities on the night of the carrack's capture; Frobisher, doubtless moved more by envy than outrage, wrote to Burghley on 4 September, to remind him that Crosse had not only disobeyed his instructions to keep the *Foresight* with the fleet, but had taken her away with 'such welth as he hath aboard him, w(hi)ch is given me to understand to the valew of tenn thousand pound(e)s'.[25] Plunder of the magnitude that Crosse had hinted at was not something to be left to other men; even as he dictated his letter, Frobisher was taking his ships swiftly northwards (the letter was begun just north of the Burlings and was endorsed 'from the Lizard'), almost certainly with the intention of intercepting the *Madre de Dios* and her remaining escort at sea, to put in his claim to an admiral's share of her booty. Under rules of consortship, he was entitled to a proportion of the prize money even though he had not been present at her capture, but the point could hardly be made too strongly under such remarkable circumstances – particularly by a man who was all too well aware of the Queen's habit of renegotiating consortship terms without priorily informing her 'partners'. His rather transparent excuse for leaving his station, relayed to Burghley in the same hastily drafted letter, was that Crosse had told him the carrack needed cables, anchors and sails, all of which he could supply: so, 'for the better saftie of her (I shall) keepe betwixt the Lizard and Hushinge' (Ushant) and escort her to the Isle of Wight.' Plaintively, he also put in a near oblique reference to his share of the spoils: 'I hope your honours will consider the authoritie I have by her Ma(ies)ties comission and my owne poore reputation so longe as I comandeth not in any thinge, but for her ma(ies)ties service.'[26]

Frobisher failed to make that rendezvous (the *Madre de Dios* was brought into Dartmouth on 7 September) or any other profitable one. On the way north, he took only a lone Spanish caravel, with, as he despairingly put it, 'not one real of plate of piece of gold as God help me, but sixteen reals that was found about one man' (his 'hard hape' was holding fast, if by now he was reduced to stripping bare his captives in the search for pennies).[27] In retrospect, it is clear that this failure was expensive for everyone who expected a legitimate return upon the expedition. Frobisher knew already of the depredations of the English prize crew – and, possibly, that some of the mariners had mutinied – even before the carrack reached England; hence his dark promise to Burghley, scrawled as he hurried northwards, that 'I do not doubte yf I meete w(i)th them but to pacifie all thinges'. That promised pacification had not occurred, and the plundering of the *Madre de Dios* that had begun at the moment of her capture continued throughout her voyage northwards, making her lighter in the water by almost two feet by the time she reached England.[28] Only the *Roebuck* remained to escort her into Dartmouth, the other ships having slipped away to sell their wares in Portsmouth (Sir John Burgh, it was rumoured, had plundered from his captains in turn).[29] When the carrack reached the dockside at Dartmouth, Burgh was unable or unwilling to prevent further pillaging. Forewarned of her arrival there, London jewellers had swiftly despatched their agents down to the West Country with orders to buy up all the precious stones they could secure from men who neither knew nor cared to know their true value. One particularly enterprising mariner parted with

> 320 sparks of diamond, a collar of a threefold roll of pearl with six tags of crystal garnished with gold, a small string of pearl with a pelican of gold, a small round pearl garnished with gold, two chains of two-fold pearl with buttons of gold and two small jewels hanging unto the ends thereof, also three silver hafts for knives and a silver fork.[30]

The total loss was enormous: of the estimated half a million pounds of booty, all but £141,000 disappeared into the pockets, caps and other orifices of men whose custom was to enrich the taverns and bawdy houses of southwest England for months to come. Walter Ralegh, recently imprisoned by the Queen for having seduced and married one of her ladies-in-waiting, was hurriedly released on parole and sent down to Dartmouth (accompanied by his gaoler) to try to slow the haemorrhage of lawful prize into unlawful pockets. He took charge of the operation from Robert Cecil, who had been sent ahead by his father to investigate the losses and punish the pillagers (and had already written to Burghley on his scant success, claiming that he could almost smell the amber and musk on the sailors as they strode past him).[31]

The task was largely hopeless. In their own report to Burghley, George Barne, Hugh Offley and Thomas Cordell, appointed as commissioners to recover the carrack's stolen cargoes, commented laconically of the men they examined: 'we holde it loste labor and offence to God, to minister Oathes vnto the generallitie of them.'[32] To make matters worse (if that were possible), some of the other officials charged with recovering the loot were happily set upon their own enrichment. On 2 October, one of these worthies, William Broadbent, wrote to Hawkins to report on his lack of progress even as he was busily buying up 1,800 diamonds and 200 rubies from a mariner for just £130 of his own money.[33] At the end of that month, Drake and other commissioners were ordered to place the ships carrying prize goods under Frobisher's command for their passage from Dartmouth to Chatham.[34] Upon that brief, frustrating, business, the unsuccessful commander of a fabulously successful expedition would have heard the jangle of illicit prosperity reverberating about Dartmouth – for a few weeks at least, the boom-town of the West Country – and seen the wealth of the Indies transmogrified into other men's prize monies.

Or rather, the Queen's prize monies. Elizabeth decided that the burden of losses from the plunder should be borne equitably – that is, by everyone except herself. Because the consortship arrangement that Burgh had entered into with Cumberland's vessels had not been set down in writing, she had the excuse to take almost £80,000 as her share, on a ten per cent investment in the project. Cumberland received only £36,000 when a division in consortship should have yielded £66,360 (though even this was a fine profit upon an outlay of £19,000, and far happier than his usual, unlucky efforts); whilst Ralegh, whose bed-chamber conduct the Queen refused to forgive, shared a paltry £24,000 with Hawkins upon their joint outlay of £34,000 (they had been allocated £36,000, but from this was abated £12,000 for the syndicate of London merchants who, strictly, were due £15,900 under consortship division).[35]

What was to be Frobisher's eventual share of the disappointing pot of prize monies we cannot say; but the frantic tenor of his reminder to Burghley suggests he was perfectly aware of what even an admiral might expect from the Queen's share of the spoils. He was upon wages, of course (of 30sh. per day), yet wages do not compensate for the loss of plunder such as that of the *Madre de Dios*.[36] It seems that he made a further, small profit upon the sale of goods from several small prizes taken around the Azores (including a cargo of Brazil sugar he had seized on 15 July);[37] though here again there was much private pilfering of booty at the quayside at Plymouth, where his prizes were landed. In view of his larger disappointment and long experience of the Queen's idiosyncratic division of spoils, it is likely that not a little of this pilferage was Frobisher's own doing.[38]

Yet if his personal gain from the expedition was insignificant, the repercussions of this and the earlier Atlantic voyages were beginning to determine Spain's strategy both at home and with regard to her allies. The capture of the *Madre de Dios* heaped further misery upon the failing fortunes of the Fugger family, the financiers of Augsburg to whom Philip had hypothecated her cargoes against his debts to them (the ship was probably not insured, as English, Dutch and Protestant French plunderings had made merchant ships a very poor risk to lay money against).[39] The other carracks of the East Indies fleet had been lost also, and it is clear that the dash for home these ships were increasingly obliged to make during unseasonable months – thus running the twin risks of enemy ships and natural hazards – compromised their safety and threw even more doubt upon the reliability of the resources that underpinned Spain's lines of credit.

This was not the only illogicality forced upon Philip by English actions at sea. His need to prosecute his several wars, and the maintenance of pressure upon his western approaches, resulted in a vicious circle of expenditure and commitment that both encouraged and demanded further, heavy commitment of resources – resources which even the Spanish Crown could not afford to maintain indefinitely. To replenish the losses of 1588, a new fleet of Spanish naval vessels had been built between 1589 and 1592 – the *gallizabras* that had caused much frustration to English efforts (not least Frobisher's own). Yet to pay for this programme, it was more vital than ever that the bullion ships came home safely – for which purpose many of the new vessels were then committed. English depredations undoubtedly became less effective after c.1590, but the resources required from the Spanish treasury to bring about this process of modernization were enormous. If England could not win a military conflict against Spain, it was very possible for Spain to lose the economic struggle against the demands of her own, swollen commitments.

The loss of the *Madre de Dios*, therefore, was both of strategic significance to Spain and infinitesimal comfort to Frobisher. Without a significant portion of her bounty, his continuing employment may have been a necessity (even had he wished it otherwise), though a distraction from the business of ordering his new estates on land. His activities immediately following the return of the 1592 expedition are obscure. It is possible that he returned to his former Channel duties for a number of weeks, though the stream of complaints to the Admiralty regarding his liberal understanding of the concept of enemy shipping had by now almost dried up, and the declared accounts of the navy are not helpful in identifying any futher naval employment. A Fugger newsletter, written in Venice on 12 February 1593, suggested galleons were being fitted out at Lisbon because Drake, Frobisher and 'other great corsairs' had sailed to intercept the plate fleets; but this was merely an anticipation of a reprise of the previous year's expedition (and the suggestion that Frobisher and Drake were collaborating says much about the quality of Fugger intelligence).[40] In fact, Frobisher appears to have been involved in more immediate and personal business. On 25 February, little more than a week after the newsletter was issued, the Council summoned him to appear before them. Mysteriously, they gave no reason for this, stating only that he would be enlightened when he arrived at Court.[41] Their obliquity reflected the delicate and embarrassing nature of the matter. A fortnight later, Frobisher stood before the Judge of Admiralty once more, though this time it was not his own reputation on trial. He was there to represent the Queen herself, in a suit brought by the Earl of Southampton and Ralph Bowes regarding the title on a prize taken at sea by Frobisher but claimed by Elizabeth.[42] The irony could hardly have been lost even upon the unimaginative Yorkshireman. If he had neither the grace nor learning to become one of Elizabeth's intimates, nor the authority to keep his venal captains with him at sea, nor even the plain luck to secure for himself a portion of the riches that fell to his subordinates, he had at least come to be publicly acknowledged as her Majesty's legitimate accomplice in defending shaky claims to illicit prize cargoes.

Only a few days after visiting the familiar rooms of the Admiralty Court (for the final time in his career, it seems), Frobisher became involved in a new project financed by Walter Ralegh and the Anglo-Welsh merchant Thomas Myddelton. Myddelton was a member of the Grocers' Company, a part-owner of sugar-refineries in London and a long-time investor in privateering voyages, both passively and in his own right as a ship-owner. He had also handled much of the financial administration of the joint-stock 1591 and 1592 treasure fleet projects (then, he had been perhaps the most assiduous pursuer of the pilfered treasures of the *Madre de Dios*, faithfully documenting his progress in a series of letters to an anxious Burghley during the latter months of 1592).[43] As with many other English merchants who had enthusiastically accepted the necessities of war, such projects were by no means peripheral to his habitual mercantile activities. Much of the sugar refined in his London factories came from unwitting Spanish suppliers, either directly or from his purchases of the Admiral's 'tenth'.[44] It was he who had acquired, for £200, the prize cargo of Brazilian sugar that had represented Frobisher's only palpable gain from the 1592 voyage. This new venture, one of several in which he collaborated with Ralegh, was probably another small-scale expedition set out to hamper the flow of Spanish sea-traffic into the Low Countries (while enriching the pockets of the hamperers, of course). Frobisher was hired to command Lord Thomas Howard's *Disdain*, the same ship that had carried Ralegh home from the 1592 expedition.[45] His wages were set at 30sh. per day (but at a generous £3 per day whilst at sea);[46] as it transpired, he was employed from 6 March 1593 for a total of 199 days, of which seventy-two were spent at sea. It was a modest venture, though bringing comfortable recompense for a man between major projects (indeed, the fact that Frobisher accepted such a role so soon after the prestigious Atlantic appointments may indicate that he had placed a little too much of his existing capital into property in the expectation of future profits from prizes). No details of the voyage are known, but that it has not otherwise been noted in any contemporary document is hardly unusual. It was almost certainly identical in intent to the many, small-scale privateering raids that increasingly supplemented England's official, cash-starved prosecution of the sea-war during the 1590s. From the evidence of Myddelton's accounts, it achieved little in the way of profit. It was yet another voyage, moreover, in which Frobisher clashed with the mercantile element – in this case Myddelton himself, who, in a summary account dated 5 January 1594, was plaintively claiming personal expenses of £34 which he wished to deduct from Frobisher's dues, 'w(hi)ch he ought in all reason to allowe vnto me, as others have donn in the lyke case w(i)thowt any grudging'.[47] Even now, as a successful naval commander and a relatively wealthy man, it seems that Frobisher could not resist the opportunity of picking a merchant's pocket.

In one respect, however, the voyage was notable. Unobtrusively, it drew a line beneath a tarnished record that had commenced over thirty years earlier with the sea-fight against the *Katherine*. When he stepped off the *Disdain* at Dartmouth in September 1593, Martin Frobisher at once walked away from a small, insignificant employment and his life's one enduring career. He probably had no inkling of the moment, and certainly, he would have had no reason to turn and look back at the *Disdain* with more than his usual longing, or regret for the thinness of his prizes, or whatever emotion best described the leaving of his chosen habitat: but it was here, upon this dockside, that his history as a privateer came to an end.[48]

It had been a long and mainly inglorious occupation. He had sent warning shots across the decks of dozens of lawfully despatched vessels; boarded them with weapons drawn; no doubt politely ignored the official documentation waved in his face by frantic masters; briefly checked their cargoes to ensure that they were worth the trouble of seizing, and then taken them into whichever port he was using at that moment to evade the sharp eyes of Admiralty clerks. It was not a record to set down upon a memorial, but it had enriched him as no official service had come close to doing. Glory and honour had largely escaped him; but wealth, eventually, had not. If there was a lesson to be had from the pursuit of his several employments, Frobisher had taken it: that a reputation might or might not be earned – but undoubtedly, it could be bought. Yet ironically, having grown wealthy in avoiding it, he was at last to achieve a degree of honour entirely unsullied by venality.

For some months following the return of the *Disdain*, Frobisher was at Altofts, attending to the unfamiliar *minutiae* of the country gentleman's life and obligations. Nothing is known of the course of his relationship with Dorothy and how, following several years of marriage by correspondence, she and he adjusted to this unfamiliar proximity; but the two families' connection was further cemented at about this time by Dorothy's daughter's marriage to Martin Frobisher junior, who – having fathered a daughter, also named Dorothy – promptly died. Typically, the last known detail of his short life was gleaned from a Privy Council order to the Judges of the Admiralty, on a suit brought against him by merchants of Drogheda regarding his illegal seizure of a ship off the coast of Brittany.[49] The precise date and cause of his death are unknown, but it is almost certain that his uncle had regarded him as the intended heir of the Frobisher estate. In the early days of August 1594, probably soon after this bereavement, Martin senior was obliged to re-cast his will to reflect the altered circumstances of his own marriage and the loss of Martin junior.

This document, still extant, must have generated considerable legal fees.[50] It attempted to anticipate every possible permutation of premature death and wilful act of sterility among the surviving Frobisher clan. And this was, it is made palpably clear, a blood clan. If Dorothy had expected to acquire her husband's estate, she was to be disappointed. Frobisher's bequests to her were not ungenerous, but their terms were constrictive. She was to keep her own jewellery and the clothes she already owned, though only a third of the household draperies and linen. She was also to have the furniture and bedding of her chamber (and that of the chamber in which her daughter, waiting-women and chamber maids lay), £200 worth of plate, all the furniture in the Walthamstow house (though 'none other'), his two coaches with their white horses and the pick of six of his other horses (once certain individual bequests of colts had been made), ten cows and half his flock of sheep. In addition, she was to have an annuity of 200 marks (£67) and the right to reside at Frobisher Hall for forty years or until her death. Her daughter Mary was to receive a substantial portion of £200, probably by right of her marriage to Martin junior; and the fruits of that brief union, the infant Dorothy, would inherit the same sum when she reached fifteen years of age. If, however, the elder Dorothy attempted to challenge any part of his will, all these bequests were to be invalidated, and she was to receive only what recourse to the law would allow her.

The bulk of Frobisher's estate – the manors, messuages and lands he had accumulated – were now to go to Peter Frobisher, eldest surviving son of John Frobisher (referred to in at least one document as 'Captain', though his career and qualifications are entirely obscure).[51] If, however, Peter should die having produced no male heir, the estate would pass in turn – under the same conditions – to Darbie Frobisher, eldest son of the deceased Davy, or to Francis Brackenbury, son of Frobisher's elder sister Jane, or to Richard Jackson, son of his younger sister, Margaret.[52] For each of these potential beneficiaries in turn, the production of a male heir was the necessary *quid pro quo* to prevent the inheritance from passing to another branch of the family.

This painful quest to preserve an unbroken male inheritance was a common feature of contemporary wills, reflecting social norms in which female inheritance effectively meant either life-long spinsterhood for the recipient or the outright surrender of one family's assets to another. In another sense, however, it was also a poignant declaration of Frobisher's fidelity to his lineage; the more so for the seeming exile from natural kinship and domesticity that his career had determined. For all of his undoubted cupidity and self-serving disregard of matrimonial commitments, the fruits of that elusive goal he had so tirelessly sought in icy straits, fever-laden Caribbean cities and the holds of other men's ships were not now re-cast in forms to serve the memory of a new Columbus, as Michael Lok had once implied. His acquisitions, modest and scattered, were rather those of the rural, parochial gentleman who provided for his kin, and, at most, their local reputation. Filial obligation had played little visible part in Frobisher's career; it was to show itself, at the last, as a life-long preoccupation.

A few other remembrances commemorated the tiny circle of near anonymous individuals who had been to him more than mere acquaintances. His long-faithful servant (and, probably, his secretary) William Hawke, who had been at his side upon the three voyages to Baffin Island and dozens of other, less reputable voyages, received an annuity of £6 13sh. 4d.[53] Frobisher's 'lovinge Friende' Thomas Colwell (of whom we know nothing) was to receive a gelding worth £10 'for his paynes he hathe taken at the deliverye of this my will', as well as £20 in money if, subsequently, he was required to act as a referee in any contested action (if – as seems likely – Colwell was a lawyer, their loving friendship may have been nurtured in the great volume of Admiralty Court business that Frobisher had put his way over the years). Other than these few implied tokens of friendship, Frobisher's other bequests were as modest as they were predictable. To his sister Jane, he bequeathed a small annuity from the income from his properties, and to her daughter the same; though to Katherine, her granddaughter, he provided a lump sum of £40, possibly as a dowry for a girl coming to marriagable age. To Edith Frobisher, the unmarried daughter of Davy, he bequeathed the same; though in her case it may have been intended to tempt a likely suitor into considering an ageing spinster. To Edith's sister Anne, who was married and in no need of a dowry, he gave only £10. The most curious bequest to a female was that made to one Mary Masterson, who was to receive the yearly rents from the lease of his estate at Brockholes, or, when this expired, an annual gift of £20 'duringe her naturall liffe'. The award was substantial, and curious; Masterson may have been an old and valued family servant, or perhaps the widow of another, equally anonymous friend; it is perhaps too much to hope of Frobisher's sense of duty that he might now, after years of indifference, have provided for one of the children of the wretched Isobel.

When, on 7 August 1594, he scrawled his name upon every one of the sixteen leaves of this document and had it witnessed by Thomas Colwell and his otherwise anonymous acquaintances Anthony Lewes, Timothy Perrot and Richard Farrer, Frobisher ordered his affairs for the last time. He was fifty-nine years old or thereabouts – not a great age, even in those harsh times, for someone hardy enough to have survived the rigours of the crib. He was in robust health still, and his great natural strength not significantly diminished. On land at least, he was a respectable country gentleman of means and reputation, who had raised the name of his family to a prominence last enjoyed during the reign of Edward I. He was a major landowner in the county of his birth, with a further country seat at a fashionable distance from London for those occasions when official business called him to the south. The dispositions he made in his will suggest that his liquid capital, though not abundant, would have allowed him a life of considerable ease during his remaining years. All of this was cause for satisfaction, for a man who could allow himself that leisure; but there is nothing in what we know of Martin Frobisher's character that suggests he was capable of this small degree of self-equilibrium. Financial security and the social status of the respectable landowner had undoubtedly been his long-term goals; but the means by which he had pursued them had generated their own, contrary pressures. He had gone to sea by the age of eighteen, since when the pull of the landsman's life had diminished progressively even as the siren-call of ambition drew him on. In this, he was not so different from his enduring enemy, Francis Drake. Drake had set down his own land roots at Buckland Abbey, near his beloved Plymouth; yet he, also, had become a stranger to the firmament that had nurtured him (his disgrace in 1589 undoubtedly made his tenure upon it more protracted than he might otherwise have wished). Both men seem to have made their acquisitions more with an eye to posterity than upon a comfortable retirement. Each was to make a brief attempt to enjoy the spoils of their efforts in the practice of domestic harmony and the intercourse of local life. However, like men released into normal society after long-term confinement, its mundane dislocations ultimately proved too hard for either of them to bear lightly.

Even as he was arranging his estate, making the acquisitions and dispositions that reflected the successes of his later career, Frobisher was writing letters to the Queen herself: asking – perhaps begging – for a central role in England's major effort against Spain that year. Her answer, for once, was timely. Less than three weeks after signing his will, Frobisher left Altofts for the final time – to go back to the sea, his chosen place of abode. Over the course of four decades he had made the journey many times, though not always from the same point of departure. More often than not, he had joined a ship secretly, or at least unheeded by Admiralty officials; employing the discretion of a man with neither lawful licence nor good intentions. A brief campaign, a few prizes taken; quiet thanks and payment from a supposedly respectable shipowner, and then on to the next commission: this had been the occupation of his life. It had been interrupted by the lure of the northwest passage and the promise of gold to be had cheaply from the rocks of Meta Incognita, by the furies of the War of 21 July and by the growing need that the Queen had of his talents; but the fame of these brief asides should not disguise the truth of a career whose despoliations had defined Martin Frobisher. He was an habitual privateer who happened also to have made three voyages of discovery; an unabashed redistributor of other people's wealth who had come to be one of the Queen's most reliable sea-commanders. Now, however, at this uttermost point of his life, Frobisher became something more. On 27 August 1594, he set sail from the Thames for the last time under the authority of the Broad Seal of England, as Elizabeth's 'trustie and welbeloved' admiral: the guardian, moreover, of one of her precious armies. When he returned to England barely twelve weeks later, it would be as a dying man, and – finally – as a hero.

TWENTY-ONE

The Crozon Peninsula: El Leon, 1594

For all that war had encouraged striking dislocations to England's social order, certain fundamentals remained intact. As privateers became senior naval commanders, and merchants and noblemen in turn became privateers, the underlying priorities of Elizabeth's foreign policy remained unchanged, constant as the tides that bore her ships to sea. That policy, which had set out fleets, armies and the very occasional subsidy, had essentially defensive goals: to prevent the domination of the Narrow Seas by either France or Spain, and – a possible element of such a strategy – their support of hostile parties at the Celtic fringes who might effect the 'pacification' of England by proxy. The Queen's own support of the Netherlander rebels had been against instinct and nature, particularly so given their troublesome Calvinist element (she would have considered the adjective tautologous); but it had been necessary to prevent the triumph of the Counter-Reformation in the Low Countries, the most imminent and dangerous shore to England's own. Her use of privateers, and her tacit approval of outright piracy, were similarly recourses of need rather than of choice; but as tactical policies they had proved both mildly profitable and a means by which the Guiseoise and their Spanish paymasters had been prevented from concentrating overwhelming force against England.

In contrast, the English trans-oceanic expeditions of Hawkins, Drake, Frobisher and others, that have captured the imagination of every subsequent generation, were, even at their most effective, mere adjuncts to the main business of preserving the Act of Uniformity and the Tudor succession. These edifices were fragile, despite the overwhelming support they derived from the vast majority of Elizabeth's subjects. Sixteenth-century Englishmen considered themselves to be a relatively poor and weak nation; their often-expressed bravado and apparent self-confidence the symptoms, rather than the disproof, of a fundamental fear of submersion or extinction. The voices of propagandists for the expansion of England's trade and power – Dee, Gilbert, Peckham, Hakluyt, even Michael Lok – are heard so clearly across the centuries because their every proposition was amplified by the sense of urgency they felt: a sense that time was marching against, rather than in the cause of, England's interests.

Six years after the destruction of the great Armada, there were still few indications that those interests might weather the war, much less triumph. The fright occasioned by the 'warre of 21 Julie' had not dissipated in the aftermath of England's tactical successes, and with good reason. There was never to be a decisive English victory, at sea or upon land, that would end the long conflict with Spain, because sixteenth-century England was incapable both of gathering the necessary resources and providing the mechanisms by which they might be applied. Though Spain was subject to the same intrinsic limitations, and in turn played up the destruction of Grenville's *Revenge* principally because it was the only English capital ship she was ever to take, Englishmen remained deeply aware that the war, which they could not afford to lose, was not being won. The conflict continued, seemingly without possibility of a resolution favourable to England. The inherent weaknesses that ate at the economic foundations of the Spanish state were not yet generally understood; to the contrary, the prospect of her great, elusive fleets plying the Atlantic, bringing to Philip II's coffers an apparently illimitable bounty of silver, seemed to contemporary eyes to represent an awful permanence. Though all logic said otherwise, it was believed by her enemies that Spain could afford to lose the odd Armada.

Furthermore, there was little evidence that Philip II's enduring failure to realize his objectives in the Low Countries and elsewhere had in any way disheartened him. He has since been portrayed – usually by Protestant propagandists – as variously power-crazed, dull, chronically indecisive, manipulative and inhumanly cold. There may have been trace elements of all these qualities in his nature, but his overriding characteristic was dutifulness. More than any other monarch of the age – more so even than Elizabeth – he understood his responsibility to the office he occupied, and he suffered commensurately in discharging it. To a less driven soul, the loss of the invincible Armada might have been decisive; a peace of sorts – perhaps that so fervently urged by Medina Sidonia – might have been sought; patched together to please no one yet allow his king's sovereign dignity to be preserved. Yet to a

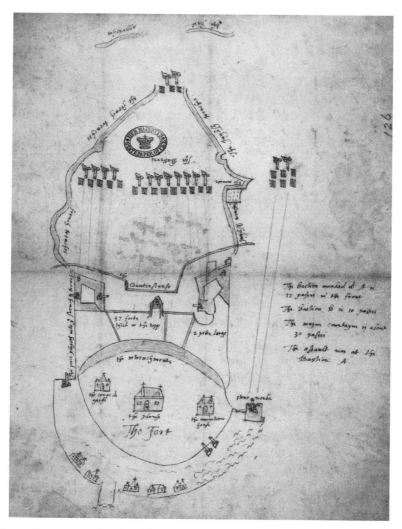

7. Crozon Fort, a campaign sketch by Sir John Norreys. By courtesy of the Public Record Office, London.

man who struggled so forcefully to administer God's will, something that could only be construed as the wages of divine displeasure required penitence, not the buttressing of a transient earthly pride. Philip, accordingly, blamed himself and his commanders for that defeat and devoted a great deal of repentant effort to its lessons. Most ominously for England, he swiftly came to realize the significance of the failure of Parma and Medina Sidonia to effect a liaison, and absorbed its most palpable corollary: that only with the seizure of a secure, deep-water port, in or near the English Channel, could he safely concentrate the resources needed to launch a full-scale invasion of England, should a further opportunity present itself.

From 1590, Brittany became the focus of this preoccupation; and in particular, the fine, capacious harbour of Brest. Though the French king Henry IV was a long-time ally of England, he had neither the resources nor inclination to prevent Brittany – far from Paris and traditionally turbulent – from falling under the control of the Catholic League. If a Spanish army could be landed there, the first and most important precondition for any future scheme to fall upon England would have been discharged. The greatest potential danger to this operation would arise if English and Dutch ships intercepted the force whilst at sea, or, worse, whilst disembarking. In the event, Hawkins, sailing late from Plymouth in 1590 towards a longed-for rendezvous with the plate fleets, saw the ships of the Spanish expeditionary force moving north along the French coast but made not the slightest attempt to engage it – though, with six of the Queen's vessels, an interception would hardly have failed.[1] Elizabeth's detention of Frobisher and Hawkins in port that year had therefore helped to preserve Philip's *galeones* and yet done nothing to prevent that which she had most feared: the establishing of a small but threatening Spanish force upon French soil: at Blavet, on the southern coast of the Brittany peninsula.

To a degree, this failure had reversed the logistical situation. For years, Philip had stretched his resources too thinly to cover all the perceived threats that small English forces could bring to bear upon his widespread possessions. Now, it was Elizabeth who was obliged to send an army to Brittany to counter the Spanish threat; to fortify and reinforce her vulnerable southern ports and keep her own galleons battle-ready; to spend thousands of pounds she could not spare to counter a threat which Philip could maintain or increase quite economically.

The English response to the threat – the small army that landed in Brittany in 1592 – was commanded by Sir John Norreys, veteran of the Irish wars and land-commander of the disastrous 1589 English raid upon Spain and Portugal. If this new commission was intended to punish him for his performance in the latter campaign, it succeeded admirably. Based in the almost indefensible town of Paimpol (Elizabeth had refused to meet the cost of fortifying it), permanently short of supplies, his troops riven by disease and ignored by their specious French allies, it was to Norreys's considerable credit that he managed to keep his army merely in being. Even so, by the end of 1593, morale among his 1,000 remaining effectives was so low that it seemed improbable they could continue to constitute a military threat.

In the early part of the following year, rumours of a prospective Spanish reinforcement of Blavet began to filter back to England. Ships returning from the northern Spanish coast – almost certainly privateers – reported that ports there were filling up with troops.[2] Obviously, these were intended for a purpose; the most likely, and dangerous, would be an advance upon Brest, which still remained loyal to the French King (though having made his memorable decision regarding what Paris was worth, Henry's was by now a Most Catholic Majesty). Alarmed by this threat, and moved by Norreys's repeated pleas for reinforcements, Elizabeth sent an envoy, Oliver St John, to investigate the situation in Brittany. The over-sanguine St John arrived at Brest, strolled around the town walls, and, upon seeing no Spanish troops, returned home thereafter to reassure his Queen that the panic had been just that.

Yet even as St John perambulated, the threatened Spanish reinforcements had already reached Blavet. The commander there, Don Juan de Aguila, assembled about 5,000 troops and a flotilla of a dozen ships, some of them modified galleys intended specifically for in-shore operations. At the end of March 1594 he moved swiftly, carrying his force by sea out of Blavet to the south side of the headlands that dominated Brest roads. Here, upon the Crozon peninsula, Aguila quickly raised a substantial fortification; by 25 April, it was virtually complete, and the Spanish commander re-embarked the bulk of his forces. In the new fortress which he named *El Leon*, he placed a garrison of 400 troops, supported by six field guns within the fortifications and six ships stationed directly below the headland. The estuary, and the walls of Brest itself, were now completely dominated by a well dug-in Spanish force.

In England, insouciance turned to panic once more. It was assumed that the erection of *El Leon* was the immediate prelude to an all-out assault upon Brest (the assumption was correct; Aguila had returned to Blavet only to await the remaining tranche of his promised reinforcements). A small English fleet was hastily assembled in the Thames, intended to bring Norreys's army down the coast from Paimpol to Brest, or, if necessary, to evacuate it altogether. By 13 July, 1,000 English troops under the command of Sir Thomas Baskerville had been brought hastily (though efficiently) out of Holland and transported by sea to the coast of Brittany. In London, plans were laid (or, more accurately, bandied) by the Privy Council, to organize a further relief army of up to 6,000 men and a fleet necessary to support it.[3]

In the meantime, Norreys had been doing surprisingly well. As yet lacking any reinforcements, he had moved quickly down the coast, hoping to prevent the Spanish forces from linking up with their Catholic League allies. His approach unnerved the ineffectual French rebels, who immediately withdrew to fortified positions around Morlaix. More surprisingly, Aguila himself, who had returned to *El Leon* with several thousand more men, retired hastily after re-provisioning the fortress. Without a shot being fired, the dispirited and under-provisioned English army had dispersed two larger forces and placed them both upon the defensive.

Having made hasty arrangements for the siege of the Leaguers at Morlaix, Norreys briefly returned to England to report upon his progress and needs. Formerly the commander of a forgotten army, he now discovered himself to be something of a popular hero. Large-scale recruitment drives were hastily initiated across southern England, and many prominent gentlemen adventurers, Ralegh amongst them, petitioned Lord Howard for a ship in the fleet he was known to be preparing. Initially, Howard intended to command the fleet himself, whilst a rumour had it that Norreys – despite his excellent record – would be replaced at the head of the enlarged army by the Queen's current favourite, the Earl of Essex.[4] By the end of July, however, the scale of the expedition, and its command, had been modified. The implausible Essex had been discounted (if indeed he had been seriously considered), Norreys was confirmed as commander of the assembling army and Howard had stepped down to make way for someone from whom both less and more was required. To the chagrin of others who had petitioned the Queen for the job, Martin Frobisher was appointed as admiral of a fleet of five royal ships (*Vanguard*, *Rainbow*, *Crane*, *Quittance* and *Moone*) and six armed London merchantmen.[5] It was almost certainly upon the occasion of this happy news reaching Altofts that the presence of masters Colwell, Lewes, Perrot and Farrer had been urgently requested to arrange the matter of final bequests and dispositions of his estate.

Frobisher had petitioned for the post, but so too had others. Why then had he been appointed to replace Howard, the kingdom's premier sea-commander? Obviously, the size of the fleet as eventually constituted was not such as to require a Lord Admiral to direct it, but neither was the transportation of a such a significant force (comprising a large number of Elizabeth's best troops) a matter of routine. Eight years earlier, Leicester had been given a similarly precious English army to take to the continent; so too had Norreys himself, with Drake, in 1589. The prodigal and ineffectual use they had made of these expensive resources thereafter had been salutary experience, and the Queen had no intention of suffering a reprise. Almost certainly, lessons had been learned, and the claims of station were now obliged to defer to those of ability. The task intended for the mariners of the new fleet was a flexible one. Their first duty was to carry the English army safely to Brittany, but Norreys was also to call upon them as reinforcements when required: a role in which their leader would necessarily have been subordinate to the land-commander. Several of the men who may have been considered for the role, their self-esteem enriched by proximity to the Queen, may have jibed at Norreys's direction; in which case England would have had yet another campaign by committee. In contrast, Frobisher's talents were supremely apposite. He had landed troops and fought with them upon several occasions during the 1585 West Indies raid, and his appointment to command the *Triumph* during the Armada campaign seems to have been made above all with his qualities as a tactical fighter in mind. As a soldier, he was undoubtedly a proven quality, and he was also capable of deferring to a higher authority when necessary. Most importantly, unlike men such as Ralegh and Essex he did not enjoy the Queen's favour for any reason other than his practical abilities, and was therefore to be trusted to regard the terms of his commission literally, rather than as a manifest of the possibilities before him.

When the campaign was over, the Queen wrote to him by her own hand. The tenor of her letter indicates something of the subtle changes in his standing and reputation that had brought him from lawless adventurer to admiral. Though it contains nothing of the intimacies she reserved for her more personable correspondents, there is a certain familiarity apparent, perhaps even a warmth, reflecting something of the slight yet undeniable convergence of two profoundly contrasting lives that war had brought about:

Elizabeth R.

Trustie and wellbeloved, wee greet you well: Wee have seen yo(u)r (letters) to our Threasurer, and our Admyrall, and thereby perceave yo(u) (love) of o(u)r service, as also by others, yo(u)r owne good carriage, wherby (you) haue woone yo(u)r selfe reputation, wherof for that wee imagine it wilbe comfort vnto yo(u) to vnderstand; wee haue thought good to voutsafe to take knowledge of it, by o(u)r owne hand writing – Wee knowe yo(u) are sufficientlie instructed from o(u)r Admyrall besides yo(u)r owne circumspection howe to prevent any soddaine mischiefe by fire or otherwise vppon o(u)r Fleet vnder yo(u)r charge, and yet doe wee thincke, it will worke in yo(u) the more Impression to be by o(u)r selfe againe remembered, who have obserued by former experience, that the Spaniard(e)s for all their boast(e)s, will trust more to their devises, then that they dare in deede, w(hi)ch force, looke vppon yo(u). For the rest of my direction, wee leave them to suche l(ett)res as you shall receave from o(u)r Consaile. Geuen vnder o(u)r Privie Signet at o(u)r Mann(o)r of Richmond the xiiij^{th} of November in the xxxvj^{th} yere of o(u)r Reigne.[6]

As her cautionary words make clear, Frobisher had not been chosen as the expendable option. Elizabeth's armies, even more than her ships, were precious things to be husbanded carefully and returned, preferably undamaged. The speed with which Norreys's forces were assembled and outfitted is a testament to the urgency with which the situation was viewed; it was most certainly not an indication that they were easily come by. The orders issued by the Privy Council before the expeditionary force sailed emphasised that its objectives were extremely limited and not to be exceeded in the field, no matter what success it enjoyed.[7] *El Leon* was to be reduced and Brest roads cleared, but Norreys was not to risk Elizabeth's precious ordnance and men by committing them to any further task. In particular, however successful the outcome of the planned operation, he was forbidden to move on to Blavet to attempt to expunge the Spanish presence entirely from French soil. The instructions may have reflected a very little confidence in the raw recruits that constituted almost half the assembling army, but more probably it was a matter of money. Even in the days when France had represented the only threat against England, the great and expansive land across the Channel – Burghley's 'bottomless pit' – had provided too many expensive lessons regarding grandiose schemes of conquest. If the coming expedition was to have many superficial similarities to more modern, combined-arms raids, it was principally because it was intended to be in and out as quickly (that is, as cheaply) as possible.

Norreys's army had assembled by the Thames on 12 August, ready to embark upon Frobisher's ships. However, contrary winds held them in port for two weeks thereafter. During this time they suffered almost 300 desertions, but gradually the untrained levies amongst their charges were drilled into a state of bare competence. Finally, on 27 August, the fleet sailed for Brittany. The commanders' initial intention was to put in at Morlaix, where Baskerville's force had joined with Marshal Aumont's loyalist French army to attempt to take the town. They had been partially successful, but lack of ordnance prevented them from storming the small fort there, which continued to hold out. The English fleet was now to reinforce this effort; however, the coastline proved treacherous, and local pilots could not be found to lead the troop transports to shore. Norreys now asked Frobisher to land them further to the east, at Paimpol.

The army disembarked there without incident or interference from the Catholic League's troops, after which Frobisher, temporarily set loose upon his own initiative, embarked upon a minor campaign that was as swift as it was effective. His fleet returned to Morlaix and landed the siege train in the face of the enemy defenders; a feat accomplished without loss of men or, far more importantly, field pieces. In a flash of inspiration – one, possibly, that recalled Drake's demonstration before Cartagena, almost nine years earlier – he ordered his ships to sail past the besieged garrison with all their guns run out. The prospect provided a strong hint that the rebels promptly took. They surrendered immediately to Baskerville and Aumont, and the fort was occupied without need of Norreys's army to march westwards to supplement a time-consuming and distracting siege.

By 6 September, Frobisher had brought his fleet around to Brest roads. The Spanish ships had already withdrawn, probably at word of the size of his force. He was able to invest *El Leon* from the seaward without interference, and to put several hundred of his mariners on-shore to cover the landward approaches. He also landed a number of ships' guns, but their suitability for siege work proved to be marginal (the siege-train remained at Morlaix). A month subsequently spent in assiduous bombardment was to have very little effect upon the fort's thick walls, and the many guns remaining in the ships themselves could not be elevated sufficiently to bring to bear on the fort's seaward side. Supplies of powder began to fail, but in late September, timely reprovisioning by a squadron of Dutch vessels allowed Frobisher to continue his leisurely pounding whilst waiting for Norreys to bring his army from Paimpol. However, his examination of the fort's defences had provided a salutary experience; on 6 October he wrote to Burghley, urging that the Anglo-French forces should take *El Leon* and hold rather than raze it, as the Spaniards would only return and rebuild it otherwise.[8]

Unfortunately for the brisk timetable the English commanders had set themselves, Aumont refused to allow Norreys and Baskerville to use the docks at Morlaix (the over-cautious Frenchman would allow only French Catholics to enter the town). They were obliged, therefore, to march their army overland across the west Brittany peninsula. Further bickering, and Aumont's insistence that the combined Anglo-French army seize the town of Quimper on the way, meant that Norreys and Baskerville were not before *El Leon* until 1 October. By this time the combined force had only 1,000 effectives remaining, and the siege train, which they had been obliged to leave behind at Morlaix, had not yet arrived by sea.

Frobisher, ever impatient, began to chafe at these unnecessary delays. Clearly, it had been his own efforts that had comprised the main thrust of the English offensive to date; but their rewards had been minimal, and threatening to fail altogether. On 11 October, he complained to Burghley that his supplies were low, that the country thereabouts could not provide twenty days' supplies for their men, and that he could not keep the privately armed merchantmen in his fleet with him much longer.[9] In the meantime, the weather had turned, bringing torrential rain that somehow managed to generate large quantities of mud where previously there had been little soil, making the local roads impassable by cart. The English army could not therefore be supplied by land, though the reluctance of the population thereabouts to assist in any practical way made this something of a moot point.

To add to the allies' woes, the first serious assault upon the fort, carried out by Aumont's newly arrived royal troops on the 9 October, had been repulsed by the Spanish garrison with depressing ease, after which the besiegers settled into virtual inactivity for want of the English siege-train. Only on 23 October was the battery, supplemented by further guns from the English and Dutch ships, in place before the fort. Even then the bombardment could not commence; most of the ordnance had first to be mounted on gun carriages assembled from ships' spars and other inappropriate sources (the west of Brittany, then as now, had few suitable trees). Even the gunners' trenches had to be built up, rather than dug down, with soil scraped together and turfed over bedrock; they were raised so far from their target, moreover (due to the accuracy of the Spanish defenders' own cannon), that their efficacy was further reduced. Nevertheless, on the day that these onerous preparations were completed, Norreys gave the order for a preliminary English assault on the fort's curtain wall, to neutralize the Spanish guns bearing on the English battery.

This assault, like the earlier French effort of 9 October, was a disastrous failure. Some of Norreys's soldiers, led by gentlemen-volunteers, managed to scale the two bastions that flanked the main, landward wall of the fort; but their efforts were immediately repulsed. At the battery, meanwhile, a barrel of gunpowder was ignited by a stray spark, taking with it six others. Fifty of the English force's precious gunners were injured, several very seriously, and two were killed outright. A final, unauthorized charge by the English rearguard resulted only in some forty further casualties, including two dozen dead. Despondently, the French commander, watching this disaster from his own trenches, decided that the fort could only be taken by under-mining: a process that would require months of quarrying down through the hard granite that composed the headland.

Disease, foul weather and a successful Spanish sortie against French positions on the 30 October reduced morale still further. By now, Aumont himself had fallen sick, and, having received word that Aguila had finally moved out of Blavet to make a demonstration against the allies, he wished to raise the siege entirely. Frobisher was furious. On 5 November, he wrote to Burghley and Howard: 'I am ashamed to write to your honours of these delays of the french. For this present day we should have battered and assaulted it by an agreement made betwixt ourselves'.[10] The following day, Norreys and he followed the weary Aumont around the siege trenches, pestering him to agree once more to an all-out assault. By evening, the Marshal had given way, and committed himself to a supreme effort on the following day.

The fortifications of *El Leon* remained almost intact. The wall which faced the shore battery was 37 ft thick, and merely scuffed by the attention it had received to date;[11] the only useful purpose served by the English guns had been to clear the ramparts of enemy soldiers temporarily. However, French pioneers had managed to mine a small section of the wall under cover of darkness; its detonation, at noon on 7 November, was the pre-arranged signal for a general assault to commence. Aumont and Frobisher personally led their men across an approach causeway barely 250 yards wide, into the face of the fort's main battery of five guns.

The breach created by the mine was narrow and defensible (though many Spanish soldiers fell as English and French ordnance was brought to bear upon it), but someone – a traitor or a fool – opened the fort's main gate. Frobisher's mariners were closest to it; he personally led them into the opening, forcing back the Spaniards who had rushed frantically to fill it. A bloody mêlée ensued; *El Leon* was taken step by step, each foot of ground resolutely defended by men who did their utmost to redeem their compatriot's error. Their English and French enemies, who had endured weeks of foul provisioning, disease and constant sniping from the fort's walls, fought equally fiercely, and largely dispensed with the courtesies of war.

The battle – or, more accurately, the slaughter – lasted for some five hours. As darkness fell, the allies crushed the last of the defenders' resistance; dozens of Spanish soldiers leaped over the walls of the fort into the sea, but as they reached the safety of the English and Dutch ships their heads were held under water by the mariners. Of a garrison of some 350–400 troops, only some five to nine men, hiding in the rocks below the fort, survived to surrender (in a rare, and far too belated, gesture of compassion, the allies sent these supposedly fortunate men back to their commander at Blavet, who promptly hanged them for cowardice).[12] Several hundred Frenchmen also died, as did approximately sixty Englishmen. Frobisher, Norreys and Baskerville were among the wounded.[13]

Suffused with renewed enthusiasm for his task, Aumont now begged Norreys to bring his forces against Blavet, to assist in expelling Aguila and his troops entirely from French soil. The Queen's instructions had been explicit, however; in any case, the English mariners refused to go on without their injured admiral, a canny excuse for inaction that was portrayed as a touching testament to his leadership. The following morning, English pioneers blew up the walls of *El Leon* with the remainder of their powder, whilst their commander-at-sea had himself propped up in bed to dictate his report to Howard:

My humble dutie my honorable good L(ord) the vij[th] november by a battrie, vndermininge, and a verie dan(gerous) assault wee haue taken this fort, w(i)th the losse of ( ) of our people but non of any accoumpt, They (defended) it verie resolutlie, And never asked mercie, So were put all to the swoord savinge five or six th(at hid) themselues in the Rock(e)s, many of them were slaine (by) our canonn and greatt ordenaunce in defendinge of (the) breatch w(i)th there Captaine one Perithos: It was tyme for vs to goa through w(i)th it for D(on John) is Aduanst w(i)thin six leagg(e)s of our armie w(i)th an intente to haue succoured them. Sir John Norr(is) doth rise this daie and doth martch toward(e)s th(em) to a place called old Croydon: —[14]

Wee are about to gett in our ordenaunce as fast as (wee) can and so to make our repaire homeward(e)s, Sir (John) Norris would willinglie have some five hundred of sayllers for his better streingth, against the day of meetinge w(i)th Don John, w(hi)ch I would verie willinglie have don yf we had vittles to contin(ue) our fleett heare for the tyme: —

I was shoott in w(i)th a bullett alongst the huckell bonne So as I was driven to have an ins(ision) made to take out the bullett. So as I am neither to goa nor ride, And the mariners are verie vnw(illinge) to goa except I goa w(i)th them my selfe: yett (yf) I finde yt to come to an extremitie we will (do) what we are able, yf we had vittles it were easilie done, but heare is non to be had. I ha(ve) according to y(ou)r honours derections tow shippc to Plymouth and Dartmouth, we most p(re)sentlie (goa) away yf they come not to us w(i)th vittles: —

This bearer is able to certiffie y(ou)r honours all thing(e)s at large. So w(i)th my humble p(rayers) to the almyghtie for y(ou)r increasse in ho(nour). Croydon this viij[th] of November 1594.

Yo(u)r honours most (humble) to comande. M(aste)r Mondaie arived the xxviij[th] October at Brest, and brought w(i)th him a thousand crownes for our vittlinge the w(hi)ch was distributed amongst the shipp(e)s.

Martin Frobisher.[15]

'. . . yf we had vittles to contin(ue) our fleett heare for the tyme'. This is the last extant correspondence to which Frobisher ever set his name, and still he was being tormented by the perennial complaint of Elizabethan seamen – lack of adequate supplies. Even from the evidence of his career alone, there is a strong case to be made that the single most profound brake upon English ambitions in the later sixteenth century was not gun technology, or poor strategy, or lack of resources *per se*; but the abiding failure of the Queen and Privy Council to provision their sea expeditions adequately for the jobs to which they were assigned. Had they done so, perhaps blind luck might have played a lesser part in English strategic plans – perhaps, even, the storming of *El Leon* might have been unnecessary, and its fatal consequences avoided.

Victorious but hungry and diseased also, Frobisher's mariners re-embarked into their ships. On 12 November, they sailed out of Brest roads and set their course directly for Plymouth – where, as usual, very little provision had been made for their return. In many cases, men were discharged with worthless papers promising some future recompense, and the force that had been so quickly organized fell apart with similar despatch. Somewhere in one of the buildings that crowded the old town, that dissolution was emphasized by another, more private ending. Characteristically, Frobisher had considered his injury as an irritation to be borne with indifference. On the brief crossing back to Plymouth, his ship's surgeon may have attempted to dress the wound and noticed the first hint of a sourness in the air above it. He may have had the courage to bring this to the attention of his (doubtlessly peevish) patient, or perhaps there was no longer need for an expert opinion. By the time that the ships docked, Martin Frobisher would have been in great and increasing pain, and perfectly aware of the smell emanating from his corrupting thigh: 'He was shot in the side, the wound being not mortall in it selfe: But swords or guns have not made more mortall wounds then proves in the careless or skillesse surgeon, as here it came to passe.'[16]

If carelessness, it had been encouraged by too much custom for too few hands in the aftermath of that bloody affray. Though the ball had been removed swiftly by the field-surgeon, its wadding, or 'bumbasto', remained unnoticed within Frobisher's wound. Too high upon his thigh to be treated by recourse to amputation, the infection, once active, could not be halted. Frobisher probably understood this even before the fleet docked in Plymouth harbour. In the brief time remaining, he may have sent word to his wife, his heir and his few friends; but none of them – other, perhaps, than the silent, long-serving William Hawke – could have been with him in Plymouth before he died. His only company, that of the rude mariners with whom had spent the greater part of his life, left no memorial of his passing. Whoever closed his eyes, called in the surgeon to disembowel the body and found the linen to enshroud what remained did so anonymously; perhaps because they had first stripped the cadaver of its few baubles in the time-honoured tradition. Absent the sentiment that marks the passing of beloved men, the process could have been marked only by a brutal efficiency.

No naval gazette then existed to carry the news to his professional colleagues. Word of mouth, a few discreet intelligences sent by the occasional literate mariner to his family – these were the only immediate memorials for a man who died much as he lived: violently and precipitously. There is no evidence that any guard of honour was provided to mark the body's passage from Plymouth to London, and almost certainly, there was no occasion of overt pomp to mark the ceremony that laid it to rest in the south aisle of St Giles-Without-Cripplegate on 14 December 1594. There is no mention of his death in any of the correspondence of the Queen or her Privy Councillors; no record of the reactions of any of his peers or former subordinates. If a monument was commissioned at the time, it was almost certainly placed in St Giles's graveyard and subsequently obliterated, either in 1603 or 1665, by church wardens desperate to find room for the great number of plague-dead of their parish.[17] Almost three hundred years later, in December 1940, elements of the *Luftwaffe* completed their honest work during a series of fire-bomb raids which gutted the church. Today, the sympathetically restored building has entirely lost its graveyard. It stands now upon a vast square, surrounded – and dislocated – by the stained, brutalist façades of the Barbican Centre, as though a particular effort has been made to expunge not only the physical evidence, but also the memory, of its charges in eternity.

For one of those charges, there remain now only two surviving contemporary memorials: the register of St Andrew's, Plymouth: 'Nov. 22nd. Sir Martin Frobisher, knight, being at the fort built at Brest by the Spaniards, deceased at Plymouth this day, whose entrails were here interred, but his corpse was carried hence to be buried in London'; and, even more succinctly, an entry in the parish register of St Giles: 'S(i)r Martyn Furbusher, Knyght; 14th day.'

Their principal sustainer dead, Frobisher's family passed swiftly from recorded history as if hastening to be gone. Peter Frobisher, the beneficiary of his cousin Martin junior's untimely death, assumed the Frobisher inheritance. We do not know whether Dorothy Frobisher attempted to challenge the terms of her husband's will, but those expectations she had been given were hardly realized. Nor were any ambitions Frobisher himself might have had for his estate's posterity honoured. Peter handily side-stepped the requirement that he should breed by promptly selling off the entire inheritance in parcels – even Frobisher Hall, which Dorothy must have entertained hopes of dying in one day – and, probably, drank or gambled away the proceeds thereafter. He remained childless; having managed to rise to the dizzy rank of Justice of the Peace in the West Riding by 1608 (an inevitable corollary of his acquisition of the Frobisher estate, rather than of any innate ability), he fled to the sinks of London once his uncle's inheritance was spent, and, according to Fuller, died soon thereafter, 'necessitous & obscurely'.[18] Dorothy Frobisher seems to have relinquished her right to occupy Frobisher Hall almost immediately. This may have followed the occasion of her third marriage, to Sir John Saville, Baron of the Exchequer;[19] though equally, she may have allowed Peter Frobisher to buy out her portion prior to making this fortunate – and, one suspects, very necessary – alliance. Thus relieved of its collateral obligations, the Frobisher clan abandoned its brief fame and descended once more into comfortable, rural obscurity.

Even as Frobisher, hastening to be gone to sea once more, had set down his will, he probably knew what would come of it. Fuller later recalled an anecdote which, for all its lack of provenance, gives a curiously resonant impression of a man wearied in the pursuit of a goal which, at the last, he may have regarded as unworthy of the chase:

'And upon the publishing of the said will, an old officer under him desired him to consider well thereof, for his kinsman was a weake man & not fit to manage it: To the w(hi)ch he replyd; my will shall stand, Itt – meaning his Estate – was gott at sea, it will never thrive long at land; w(hi)ch proved too true.'[20]

It had been a career that, upon occasion, had plumbed the depths of banditry; yet it deserved more than this sad epitaph. Countless foreign merchantmen, going about their lawful business upon the high seas, had been plundered; the treasure fleets of Spain had raced in and out of safe harbours, chased by a feral yet unsatiated hunger for the bounty in their holds; a life had been lived far too sparsely upon the pitching deck of a ship, unfulfilled by any of the unremarkable pleasures that less driven souls take as their right – all this had transpired, ultimately, to allow a young, possibly dissolute simpleton to expire prematurely in the gutters of a city that had once, however briefly, welcomed his benefactor as its new Jason.

Two thousand miles from England, in Ottoman Aleppo, Michael Lok would have heard the news of his former partner's death as he went about his business as the consul of the English Levant Company. His reaction is unrecorded, but it was not likely to have been one of satisfaction. Lok had proved himself a fool in his own affairs, and bore a grudge as easily – and, certainly, as vocally – as any man who had seen his reputation stolen from him; but few other Englishmen were as shrewd in understanding the nature and necessity of the sinews with which their country flexed her latent power. There can be little doubt that the outrage he had so minutely expressed in reams of self-justifying appeals to the Privy Council had survived the years since the collapse of the north-west enterprise. Every day, he had the evidence of his miserable estate before him to sustain that pain; why else would a man of some sixty-two years have braved the hardships of a long sea-voyage to take up an employment that paid him precisely half that which he had earned twenty years earlier, when Frobisher had first come knocking upon his Cheapside door? Yet even with this rich vein of injustice to feed his bitterness, he could not have been insensitive to his own guilt. Lok and Frobisher may have come together by chance, but no unconscious agency had then forged their alliance – it had been one of opposites, driven by the same goals of profit and peer-recognition. Their failure was as likely as it was costly, yet as an intelligent man, Lok could not have blamed Frobisher alone for his fall, and he admitted as much, though obliquely: '. . . but God who is the director of all mens well doynge, hathe styll drawen my mynd, and as it were forced me (notwithstandynge my often repugnance, throughe feare of Lak of Mayntaynance for my great famylye to the study of this matter) for summ good purpose, vnknown to me . . .'.[21] A man of Lok's acute piety could not have allowed the consequences of personal folly to be absolved so easily.

Remarkably, Michael Lok had over two decades of active life before him. He would hear also of the deaths of Drake and Hawkins; of Burghley and Ralegh; of Elizabeth herself. He would see the union of the English and Scottish Crowns in the person of a Stuart; the event that English foreign policy had striven for decades to confound. He would celebrate the end of the war against Spain and the first, faint beginning of her decline. He would see – most comforting of all to his partialities – the establishment of the first permanent English colonies in America. By his own account, he would dream more of the north-west passage, and, notwithstanding the successive failures of Davis, Waymouth, Hudson, Button, Gibbons and Baffin to find it in his own lifetime, he would never cease to believe that it existed, somewhere, waiting for men to make a reputation upon its navigation.[22] As late as the year 1615, he would be dragged into an English courthouse to be sued for debts still outstanding for pitch 'and other things' supplied to the north-west enterprise, and thus still find cause to regret he had ever come to hear of Martin Frobisher.[23] He would never, even briefly, recover a fraction of the honestly earned wealth he had squandered so prodigally to the hurt of his name and great family. One by one, his sons were to die before him; having made their modest place in the world, they would leave tokens in their wills to 'my poore father', forgive his long-standing debts to them and dutifully beg God to relieve his poverty;[24] yet even to the hour of his own death, Michael Lok would fail to free himself of the implications of that urgent, flawed preoccupation he had shared with his nemesis. Their lesson was universal, and all too plain – that a man in search of a reputation crosses hard ground on the way, and gathers wounds.

TWENTY-TWO

Encomium: Thy Brute and Name

Contemporary memorials of Frobisher's life and career are few, and unsatis-factory. Even before his body had been placed in its tomb, an unattributed ballad entitled 'Sorrowfull songe made vppon ye valiant Souldier Sir Martin Frobisher who was slayne neere Brest in Fraunce' was in circulation (a copy was entered into the Stationers' Company register on 4 December 1594).[1] Earlier in the same year, Thomas Blundeville had published his *Exercises*, in which he praised Frobisher's north-west voyages and desired that 'he might be made much of', without commenting further upon the character of the man he lauded.[2] Philemon Holland penned Latin verses on Frobisher's feats in 1620;[3] whilst two years earlier, a brief commemorative verse, composed by the rightly anonymous 'A.H.', was commissioned to accompany Frobisher's portrait in *Baziliogia, a book of Kings*:

> *The noble flames that glow'd in his stout brest*
> *Could ne're be quencht, nor by that Ice opprest*
> *Of Northern Seas; His praise let him not want*
> *Whose worth deserves a print of Adamant*
> *That he may still guide ships whose fame let grow*
> *So long as sea shall have an Ebbe and flow.*

In a less wanton vein, several monographs on the voyages were published in Europe to satisfy remaining interest in the north-west voyages, but these were based largely upon the published accounts of Settle and Ellis, and did not add to what was already known. In the second edition of his *Principal*

Navigations, Hakluyt reproduced most of the English accounts and journals of the voyages, and allowed them to speak for an achievement that had already been pored over and dismissed as a vainglorious episode of the recent past. Camden's is the only near contemporary appraisal: 'a most valorous man, and one that is to be reckoned amongst the famousest men of our age for Counsell and Conduct, and Glory gotten by Naval Exploits . . .'.[4] A later tribute by Fuller, based upon Stow, was more measured but brief; it recalled Frobisher as 'verie valiant, but withal harsh and violent (faults which may be dispensed with in one of his Profession), his service at eighty eight is loudly resounded in our chronicles . . .'; though it provided also a percipient appraisal of the north-west enterprise: '. . . yet no wise man will laugh at his mistake, because in such experiments they shall never hit the mark who are not content to miss it'.[5]

Few of the relevant portions of those chronicles mentioned by Fuller have survived, if indeed he was being more than merely charitable to the memory of a man who since has stood in the shadow of his more successful contemporaries. Ironically, Frobisher's most enduring legacy was the flawed data that his three north-west voyages provided to successive generations of cartographers, though he can hardly be blamed for the interpretations they placed upon it. Inexpert maps of Frobisher's 'strait', produced by Lok and James Beare, had a brief currency;[6] but subsequent reconnaissances of the area, most immediately by John Davis in 1585–7, resulted in the 'Greenland Transfer' – the wholesale mislocation of the known geographical features of Meta Incognita on to the southern landmass of Greenland, in an attempt to reconcile the enduring belief in the Zeno data with reality. This error, first promulgated upon Emeric Molyneux's 1592 terrestrial globe, remained in currency, with increasing refinements to its imagined topographical detail, until well into the eighteenth century. 'Friesland' – the principal cause of the error – enjoyed almost as venerable a life, until its persistent failure to materialize finally brought its removal from charts of the northern Atlantic. Similarly, the mysterious 'Busse Island', that product of the over-ripe imaginations of the crew of the *Emmanuel of Bridgewater*, engaged the imagination of successive Atlantic voyagers (Henry Hudson was the first to seek it actively, on the outward passage of his 1609 voyage); but then it, too, faded from the preoccupations of cartographers.[7] As these errors were understood and corrected, the tally of Frobisher's imagined achievements was duly, and unfairly, adjusted downwards.

What may be added to these thin commemorations? We may begin by dispensing with that which Frobisher was not. His name is often grouped with those of Grenville, Hawkins, Drake and Ralegh; yet the implied association is misleading. Though these men may have shared a physical proximity with Frobisher at certain times during their careers, their society was not his. Grenville was old gentry – as Frobisher might also claim with some justice – but with none of the rudeness of carriage and temperament that character-ized the Yorkshireman. Hawkins was, ostensibly, a more realistic peer; though his abilities brought him as close to setting the terms of his achievements as commoners might in that unequal age. Drake, probably, was the man whose career Frobisher most directly compared to his own, without ever under-standing the disparity between their respective talents that made one man's glory the other's enduring frustration. Even less likely comparisons may be made with the half-brothers Humphrey Gilbert and Walter Ralegh, whose intellect and courtly *mien* were as alien to Frobisher as fine wines to a cowherd, and probably as palatable. All these men's lives have become part of the currency of event-history, and thus they have been given a community of identity that is entirely spurious. They shared with Frobisher a number of mutual connections, and, in some cases, a life passed upon the deck of a wooden ship; and that is all.

That life, bereft of much of what we might consider to be 'normal' human intercourse, had few domestic entanglements. Both in the media of record and the obscuring glare of their kinsman's career, Frobisher's blood-relatives were at most bit-players whose glancing impact upon certain episodes in his life served principally to emphasize their absence at other times. Only one of his siblings is known to us as more than a name: John Frobisher, in a literal sense, the silent partner in their privateering relationship, gives an abiding impression of having had as many scruples as his more famous brother – though also, perhaps, a greater ability to avoid the reach of Admiralty offi-cers. The only other blood-relation to achieve any palpable form in extant records was the roguish Martin Frobisher junior, but this active and endear-ing young man died too soon to provide posterity with more than passing entertainment. George Gascoigne referred to the elder Martin as 'cousin' in his preface to Gilbert's *Discourse*; but this was a distant relationship indeed (their respective great-grandfathers had been father- and son-in-law).[8] The silent William Hawke, Frobisher's faithful servant – again, a 'cozen' – seems to have been closest to him in a physical sense, though he was almost cer-tainly not an intimate. The 'mvtinus and disordered' Alexander Creake,[9] another kinsman – the only man besides Frobisher himself, Christopher Hall and Luke Warde to have sailed in all three north-west voyages – comes to life only in the furious accusations of Michael Lok and Edward Selman.

Another kinsman, Frances Brackenberry – husband of Frobisher's sister, Jane – sailed in the 1576 and 1577 voyages; but other than receiving untypically generous recompense, he seems to have enjoyed no greater role than that of personal servant to his brother-in-law.[10] Similarly, one Thomas Frobisher sailed in the 1578 voyage (again, as a common mariner), but we cannot establish with certainty that he was a kinsman also.[11]

If Frobisher's family remains elusive, his close acquaintances are even more remarkable for their anonymity. His 'lovinge frinde', Thomas Colwell – the only person ever to be so distinguished – makes his first appearance in Frobisher's will, as though he had sprung into being during the final year of his friend's life as a mourner-to-be, hired to make up numbers in an ill-attended funeral cortège. As for women – whether wives, lovers or friends – they play so little part that one might be tempted to assume that Frobisher enjoyed less conventional tastes, had he shown even the remotest interest in, or evidence of, close male companionship. Only the Queen herself – his backer, employer and, eventually, his partner in prize monies – is a persistent presence, and it is likely that she met him upon no more than half a dozen occasions during the entire course of her reign. This is a life almost without personal memorial: a manifest of exile from the commonplaces of human society. Even the place in which Frobisher's body was laid to rest carries no more meaningful association with his life than its proximity to lodgings he was renting at the time of his death – as if it, too, were chosen principally to emphasize the transitory nature of his corporeal estate.[12]

With such threadbare material, it is inevitable that Martin Frobisher has been the most discreet of historical characters, notwithstanding the brazen intemperance that marked his career. Needing better evidence of his nature, commentators have defaulted, on the whole, to the safer adjectives; 'valorous', 'bluff' and 'harsh' being amongst the most commonly appended.[13] Occasionally, wild divergences surface; certain observers, regarding Frobisher from a distance, have severally dismissed him as having a character of 'simplicity and integrity', of being 'a stiff-necked martinet' – or, most surreally, of being endowed with 'superior mental qualifications'.[14] Untempered, these vignettes do more to conceal than illuminate. Frobisher has always been a tempting target for over-simplifications, but his character, despite its raw and prominent edges, was complex: a weave of uncomplementary qualities that formed early and evolved only slowly in the face of repeated frustrations.

Nevertheless, to discern his positive qualities or identify their symptoms remains a daunting task. Too often, the darker side of his nature did not so much obscure his virtues as obliterate them. Michael Lok's summary of his performance during the north-west enterprise was supremely partial, but almost certainly identified key flaws in his character:

> . . . he is soo arrogaunt and obstinat in his gouernment at Sea, as the Shippem(aste)rs Hawlle, Jackeman, Davis, Gibbes, and others will no more be vnder his gouernment / And so insolent in his dooings amonge the Com(m)issioners, as they are werye of his Companye / And soo prodigall and disordered in the Companyes busines, as manye of the venturers are minded to meddle no more w(i)th hym / And so full of lyenge talke as no man maye credytt hym in anye thinge that he doethe speake / And so impudent of his townge as his best frynds are most of all sclandered of hym when he cannott have his waie . . .[15]

Too many contemporary witnesses corroborate the justice of these charges for them to be the product of malice alone. Frobisher's weaknesses of temperament were palpable, and became spurious strengths only in the force with which he exhibited them. During the life of the 'Company of Cathay' (and probably for many years before that), whatever capacity for self-criticism he possessed was subsumed into an arrogant and unyielding refusal to take good counsel or acknowledge his own bad judgement, even when the evidence of it was undeniably before him. In those brief, elusive moments when his fame and reputation seemed assured, this unwavering self-delusion was not tempered: if anything, it solidified further in the warm glow of an almost impervious self-regard.

None of this will be revelatory, even to the most charitable observer. It is obvious that Frobisher's struggle to break free of the worst of his nature consumed very few calories indeed, and what remained reflected few of the conventional virtues. Yet such mitigations as one may discern, whilst unquestionably discreet, are not entirely negligible. His reputation as a harsh and violent commander is well deserved; but his hugely uncertain temper, perhaps the most pronounced aspect of his character, does not seem to have reflected an underlying cruelty. The one known occasion upon which he participated in butchery – the taking of *El Leon* – was a battle in which neither side sought or gave quarter. At other times, his rages were extreme but inchoate, and almost certainly fuelled by frustration rather than vindictiveness. During his long years as a privateer, there is no evidence that having robbed his victims, he ever felt inclined to torture them or cast them overboard thereafter – an all too-common practice among his professional colleagues. In this respect (if in no other), he is a more attractive figure than the supposedly cultured

Humphrey Gilbert, who built a reputation upon Irish corpses long before he cast his eyes further west; or than the polished yet cynical Walter Ralegh, who readily subsumed his humanity to direct the cold, protracted and entirely gratuitous massacre at Smerwick fort; or even than Francis Drake, whose often outspoken piety and chivalry were tainted by an acutely petty and unforgiving nature. Conversely, what has often been considered one of Frobisher's few indisputable virtues – his bravery – was rather fearlessness, with all of its concomitant indiscretions (of which his mortal wounding, at the head of men whom any prudent commander would have directed from the rear, was the last and best example).

When we recall this career in detail, the implications of the inconsistencies and dislocations that informed Frobisher's character are sharply evident. During the north-west enterprise, he displayed an enduring inability to engage the affections of his officers; yet at other times – in the West Indies in 1585, and during the Armada and Brest campaigns, when his unequivocal subordination to a higher authority removed any opportunity for self-aggrandizement – he discharged his duties ably and, upon occasion, with great élan. His skills as an explorer have been consistently overestimated: throughout the north-west voyages, he was served by men whose skills in the art of navigation were in almost every way superior to his own; yet upon the morning of 23 July 1588, when he denied Portland Bill to the four galleases of the Armada, he conducted a masterclass in ship-handling and close-in fighting that few of his contemporaries were capable of emulating. He was an incorrigible thief of other men's goods, their ships and even their victuals; yet during the course of his 1578 voyage he led by peerless example, risking his own life in violent seas when most of his fleet had fled, to recover every one of the miners who would otherwise have perished in that unforgiving land. He had a reputation as a harsh disciplinarian – almost certainly, this was the principal reason why his appointment to command the 1592 expedition in Ralegh's place was so unpopular – yet as the record of that voyage shows, he had little of the natural authority that allows better commanders of men to maintain discipline at more than an arm's length distance. He was, at several points in his career, a treacherous consort of pirates – in some ways an archetype of that unattractive breed – but his capacity for faithlessness did not, apparently, outlast his association with his equally faithless colleagues; perhaps this had been merely a necessary quality in a profession that drew strength from the darker side of human nature. And the one, enduring trait for which there can be no mitigation – his utter coldness to his first wife and her children – is strangely at odds with the unstinting efforts he made to provide for the posterity of his blood-kin, rather than for his own, immediate comfort.

The sum of what these qualities represent is very difficult to determine, but from their insoluble parts, a kernel of something indisputably more considerable emerges. Frobisher's achievements were entirely outshone by those of Francis Drake, his nemesis; yet if he possessed only a small fraction of Drake's abilities, he enjoyed an even slighter share of the fabulous good fortune that underpinned the latter's glittering career. And as Drake languished in disgrace for a failure that far eclipsed even Frobisher's worst moments – the 1589 English riposte to the Armada campaign – the Queen's 'trustie and welbeloved' admiral slowly, and steadily, achieved something of the recognition he had so desperately sought. 'You haue woone your selfe reputation': by her own hand, Elizabeth – the parsimonious monarch whose money he had so profligately disbursed – acknowledged this, even as the poison spread through his body. It was a fame to which he had come belatedly, but it bore a far more truthful aspect than that which his dreams of Cathay and gold mines had briefly promised. His self-promotion had been by no means exceptional in an age in which many Englishmen – particularly those who caught the Queen's eye in a more personal sense – decked out their stalls with pretty words and prettier manners. The pretensions of such handsome favourites as Leicester and Essex, for example, whose sovereign's partialities blinded her to their true qualities, rose far above their talents and fell spectacularly thereafter. Frobisher, a stranger to their chivalric culture and mores alike, was able to rely only upon his record: one that grew more impressive as his ego (almost certainly unwillingly) absorbed the bruising lessons of earlier failures. At *El Leon*, the moment of his greatest personal misfortune, it reached its apogée. Though his ships had brought an English army to that place, he was not its leader; nevertheless, Norreys gave to him the honour – and danger – of leading the English assault, because he recognized that to do otherwise would have been a tactical error. 'It was tyme for vs to goa through with it': the man who committed himself to his final battle upon such sublimely economical logic at once made plain his credentials and wrote the definitive epitaph upon them.

Can this then be regarded as a 'successful' career? To the extent that it progressed to a degree of distinction, the impartial observer might reasonably conclude that it was. To Frobisher, however, who seems never to have resolved precisely what, in a personal sense, constituted success, it almost certainly fell short. We began with Kettel's portrait, and even at the last there is nothing more revealing of the storms and humours of this supremely restless man.

The likeness is captured at a moment of imagined triumph, yet still there is not the slightest trace of satisfaction or ease in its unremitting glare. Frobisher's demons surmounted the mere dips and peaks that briefly disturb more placid temperaments, waging a war that consumed whatever thin prospect of equilibrium lay within. His life and career were defined by this conflict; its collateral effects in turn impressed and alienated those whose own lives crossed its troubled path, and massively buttressed the poor luck that he seemed to regard as the principal impediment to his advancement. What might have constituted success to such a inclement psyche – had its flaws permitted such a resolution – is beyond our capacity to determine.

Martin Frobisher is one of English maritime history's more uncomfortable icons. He was a popular hero in the purest sense: anti-intellectual, impatient of subtleties and, fatally for his prospects, entirely innocent of the byzantine arts that greased a man's progress in an age of double-dealing and back-stabbing. Yet his boundless, shameless ambition, unhampered by a genius that might have realized more than a part of it, was of a quality that defined the age itself. Old certainties and hierarchies had broken down and were being reconstructed in a form whose ultimate nature was as yet indistinct. Even the supreme symbol of the continuity of the English polity – the Crown – was possessed by a dynasty that had come from nowhere and would soon, as everyone knew well, pass into oblivion once more. Half or more of the aristocratic families that surrounded it had risen from common stock almost within living memory, their new wealth and estates built uneasily upon the ruins of another, bygone continuity. In the fifty-nine years that had passed since Frobisher's birth, the fundaments of English society had shifted more, perhaps, than at any other time prior to the Industrial Revolution; in that flux, fractures formed which seemed to offer fair passage through the barriers that men erect for their mutual reassurance. Many were successful in negotiating these treacherous paths, many more were not – above all, the effort was all. Frobisher's career was both an exemplar and a product of this often self-destructive urge. Ultimately, he aimed higher than his reach allowed; but in falling short he expended a prodigious, inchoate energy that renders any rational assessment of his career almost superfluous. The failures and successes that marked it were not so much pegs upon which we may hang a definitive epigraph as mile-stones upon a life lived transiently and restlessly, uncomforted by any sense of belonging or association. For Frobisher himself, its enduring disconsolation was that he was unable to pause upon his head-long flight and recognize its urgency as a symptom of self-doubt rather than conviction: to understand that what he chased was not a fulfilment of obscure and shifting ambition, but the wraith in the universal mirror of his turbulent age.

> *O blissefull Brute, farre better be thy lucke,*
> *The powers supernall prosper still thy saile;*
> *Of sowre assaulte the sweetnesse who should sucke,*
> *But he, whose paines in perill did preuaile?*
> *Long last thy lucke, thy fortune neuer faile,*
> *Not as Vlysses aged and vnknowne,*
> *But Gallant like arriue among thine owne.*[16]

TWENTY-THREE

Postscript

As the white men abandoned the island, the Inuit returned; no doubt hesitantly at first, then with greater daring as the weeks and months passed and the great ships did not return. Over the following years and decades, it became their habit to take some remnant of their visits – a tile, a piece of ironstone ballast, a shard of a smashed earthenware vessel – useful commodities to a culture upon whom nature had bestowed particularly thin resources, but tokens also of their repossession of the land. Their old, former name for the island is not known, but it became to them, and remains, 'Kodlunarn' – white man's island.

In 1862, almost 300 years after Martin Frobisher had departed from the land where his hopes for fabulous fortune died, Captain Charles Francis Hall – an American descendant of Frobisher's principal and much-reviled master – revisited the Countess of Warwick Island; the first white man known to have done so in the intervening centuries. When he approached them, the local Inuit were friendly, and keen to speak of an episode that remained an important part of their oral tradition. An old woman told him how, long ago, her ancestors had captured five white men; how, subsequently, these strangers had wintered with the Inuit and built a large boat with a mast and sails. Desperate to return to their home, they had tried to depart too early in the new season, before the ice had cleared, and had been driven back on to the harsh shores of Meta Incognita. They had tried once more thereafter, and found clear water, and went away to meet their fate in the icy waters of Davis Strait.[1]

Other Inuit spoke of the stone house other white men had built upon Kodlunarn; how first they had come in a single ship, then three, and then many.

They recalled how five of their own people had been killed by the white man, and four more kidnapped. These statements were precise, but carried within them no implied judgement or censure; they were merely the exercise of an obligation – to preserve the memory of past events by the process of reiteration.

Captain Hall was curious, but interested more in the memory of the white men than the means by which they were remembered. Nevertheless, an elderly Inuk described to him the process of how the people laid up their immortalities:

> When our baby boy gets old enough, we tell him all about you, and about all those kodlunas who brought brick, iron and coal to where you have been, and of the kodlunas who built a ship on Kodlunarn Island. When the boy gets to be an old Inuit he tell it to other Inuit, and so all Inuit will know what we now know.[2]

Recent excavations have confirmed Kodlunarn and its environs to be an archaeological site of major importance in Canadian prehistory; but even in acknowledging this the power of the European mode of recollection is implicitly diminished. The process of archaeology is one of re-accessing a dead place; of opening a time-hole into lives that have, in distance, become alien. For the Inuit who have recently taken possession of their ancestral lands once more, the past has long lived with the present, unsundered by the limitations imposed by linear time. When Europeans first came to Meta Incognita, two divergent cultures touched glancingly, their reactions a brief encapsulation of the fears, uncertainties and misplaced trusts that have dogged human history. In that time and place they recoiled, and remained distinct. Of the two, it was the more sophisticated, European culture that disappeared thereafter: extinguished by its own imperative to advance into new forms. The "primitive" culture has survived, if barely. Beset by the pollutions of proximity and the lure of superficially more rewarding lifestyles, the younger Inuit neither seek nor hope to retain an oral tradition that recalls their first contact with the *kodlunas*. Their elders, however, still hold a fading recollection of the place in which white men built a boat, even of the method by which its mast had been stepped in, and of how these strangers lived amongst the people for a time before dying.[3] A generation more, and this will be gone; and so too, finally, will Martin Frobisher. For the moment, he is recalled still; if not in name, then in the marks he left upon another culture; not in archives nor artful reconstructions, but through the exercise of human memory.

Such a fame even he might have regarded as an achievement.

Note on Known Portraits of Martin Frobisher

The 1577 portrait by Cornelius Ketel (Bodleian Library: Poole Portrait 50) it almost certainly the only accurate likeness of Frobisher. In 1589, Lord Howard of Effingham commissioned a series of tapestries from Henrik Corneliszoom Vroom to commemorate the English victory in the Armada campaign. These were destroyed in the fire that consumed the Palace of Westminster in 1834, but engravings of the tapestries, made by John Pine in 1739, have survived. In the margins of a number of these, a series of vignettes portrays the principal commanders of the English fleet, amongst whom, in tapestries 4, 7 and 10, are apparent likenesses of Martin Frobisher. Given the practical difficulties of assembling England's premier seamen to sit for these portraits during wartime, the limitations of accurate portraiture in the medium and, not least, that the images of Frobisher therein are dissimilar to Ketel's posed portrait, it is probable that Vroom's tapestries were intended to be representative, rather than idiosyncratic, likenesses. The only other two known portraits of Frobisher, by Robert Boissard (c. 1595, reproduced in *Baziliogia, a book of Kings*, f. 124) and Willem van de Passe (c. 1592/3, first reproduced in Philemon Holland's *Herwologia*), are rudimentary engravings, and almost certainly unreliable.

Notes

ACMC	Acts of Court of the Mercers' Company	*CSPS*	Calendar of State Papers . . . Spain
APC	Acts of the Privy Council	*CSPV*	Calendar of State Papers . . .
BL	British Library		Venice
CLP	Calendar of Letters & Papers (Foreign and Domestic) Henry VIII	*DNB*	*Dictionary of National Biography*
		EKR	Exchequer King's
CSPD	Calendar of State Papers, Domestic series		Remembrancer
		HCA	High Court of Admiralty
CSPF	Calendar of State Papers, Foreign series	HL	Henry E. Huntington Library
		PCC	Prerogative Court of
CSPI	Calendar of State Papers . . . Ireland		Canterbury
		PRO	Public Record Office, London

ONE: EARLY LIFE

1. Autobiographical note of Michael Lok; BL Cotton MSS Otho E VIII, f. 48r (fire-damaged).
2. In old Scandinavian, 'Altofts' means 'old house', or possibly, 'deserted site' (*Concise Dictionary of English Place Names* (1959 edn), pp. 8, 476); both interpretations indicate that this was already a venerable foundation when given its surviving name.
3. Summoned before the Privy Council in 1566 on a charge of piracy, Frobisher gave his age as twenty-seven 'or there abowte' (PRO SP/12/39, 86); an error almost certainly deriving from ignorance or indifference, rather than vanity. Most of the genealogical information reproduced here has been communicated to the author by a collateral descendant, George Frobisher, whose work has entirely supplanted the earlier efforts of John Hopkinson (1610), Thomas Fuller (1662) and William Wheater (1868).
4. The quotation is taken from *Troilus and Cressida*; act 4, scene 5. l. 165. The author is grateful to Susan Amber, vicar of All Saints, Normanton, who researched and confirmed the matter of the surviving physical evidence of Altofts Manor. Local rumour places it

at the junction of Normanton and Stanley Ferry roads, near the western extremity of the modern village, though this cannot be substantiated at present.

5.   Steffanson and McCaskill, *Frobisher*, i, lxxxix.

6.   Wheater, 'Ancestry', p. 854.

7.   The *DNB* entry for Sir John Yorke of London notes that Flower's *Visitation of Yorkshire* (1563/4) infers the two Sir John Yorkes to be father and son, whilst the 1568 *Visitation of London* regards Sir Richard Yorke (brother of Sir John the elder) as the father of the London Yorke. It is George Frobisher's opinion that Sir John Yorke of Yorkshire was his namesake's father.

8.   The Parish register of All Saints, Normanton gives Bernard Frobisher's date of burial as 1 September 1542.

9.   BL Harleian MS 4630: 'A collection of the Pedigrees and descants of Seuerall of the Gentry of the West Riding of the County of Yorke'; the document is certified (possibly retrospectively), Oxford, 1733. Today, the Frobisher arms may be seen in the west window of St Giles Cripplegate, with those of Oliver Cromwell (who was married in the church), John Milton and the earls of Bridgewater.

10.   Francis Frobisher is identified as a member of the Council on 31 December 1558, 10 November and 17 December 1560, 20 January and 20 June 1561 and 14 May 1562 (*CSPF*, *passim*). He was also a Justice of the Peace in the West Riding from November 1551 at the latest (PRO SP/11/5, 6).

11.   It is possible that David, Martin's elder brother, was also despatched to the house of Sir John Yorke but, unlike Martin, thrived there. Many years later, one of the few extant documents to refer to him identified him as 'citizen and merchant-taylor of London' (Patent Rolls Elizabeth I, c66/1016, no. 1658). The coincidence of his stated profession and that of his uncle seems significant.

12.   Michael Lok: BL Cotton MSS Otho E VIII, f. 48r.

13.   Dickens (*English Reformation*, pp. 292–3) summarizes research on Yorkshire schools during the Dissolution period.

14.   All extant references to Yorke's home speak only of its situation in 'Walbrook'. In the absence of a precise address, it is not known whether they refer specifically to the thoroughfare of that name, or to Walbrook ward generally.

15.   BL Cotton MSS Caligula E IX, f. 206: Frobisher's report to Lord Howard on the destruction of *El Leon*; 8 November 1594.

TWO: LONDON AND YORKE

1.   Preface to Clement Adams's account of Sir Hugh Willoughby's 1553 voyage; Hakluyt, *Principal Navigations, etc* (1598–1600), ii, p. 239. The present author's references to the *Principall Navigations* of 1589 are to the Hakluyt Society facsimile edition (1965). For the *Principal Navigations* of 1598–1600, the MacLehose edition (Glasgow, 1903–5) has been utilized. The first and second editions are hereafter cited as *PN* 1589 and *PN* 1598–1600.

2.   England's historic links with Antwerp have received much valuable attention. For the antecedents of the cloth trade, see Carus-Wilson, *Medieval Merchant Venturers*; on its mechanics, chapters 2 and 3 of Willan, *Studies* are valuable. The most comprehensive survey of the state of the trade in the mid-sixteenth century is contained in Ramsay's two-volume work on the end of the Antwerp mart (*City of London* and *Queen's Merchants*). Ramsay is also unsurpassed on the mercery trade in the Low Countries; the introduction to his *John Isham* is particularly enlightening.

3. Ramsay, *City of London*, p. 2. The fairs themselves increasingly became occasions for the settlement of outstanding bills.
4. For William Lok's activities, see McDermott, 'Michael Lok', pp. 119–24.
5. Wood, *Levant Company*, pp. 2–5.
6. Shillington and Wallis-Chapman, *England and Portugal*, pp. 133–5, 141–2.
7. Marcus, 'First English Voyages to Iceland', p. 314.
8. Hakluyt (*PN* 1598–1600, xi, p. 25) first reproduced anecdotal evidence, provided by the London merchant Anthony Garrard and Southampton merchant Edward Cotton respectively, of two English voyages to Brazil, by Robert Reniger and Thomas Borey (merchants of Southampton) in 1540, and by one Pudsey (also of Southampton) in 1542. (Reniger also has the doubtful distinction of being the first known Englishman to take a Spanish plate ship when, in 1545, he intercepted and despoiled the *San Salvador*). See also, R.G. Marsden, 'The Voyage of the Barbara' *Naval Miscellany*, ii, (1912), pp. 3–66.
9. Clay, *Economic Expansion and Social Change*; ii, p. 107.
10. Ramsay, *English Overseas Trade*, p. 20.
11. Willan, *Russia Company*, p. 2.
12. Several leading London merchants obtained a measure of royal patronage in recognition of their outspoken stand against the papal opposition to Henry VIII's divorce from Katherine of Aragon. For example, the mercer William Lok received a pension of £100 and the post of Gentleman of the Privy Chamber following an incident in Dunkirk in 1533, when he tore down from a church door a copy of the papal bull excommunicating Henry VIII for his marriage to Anne Boleyn (BL Add. MS 43827, f. 2v).
13. On contemporary English backwardness in the techniques of oceanic navigation, see McDermott and Waters, 'Cathay', pp. 353–9.
14. Sebastian Brant, *This present boke name the shyp of folys of the worlde . . .*, quoted in Parker, *Books to Build an Empire*, p. 18.
15. Statistics gathered for a single year – 1519–20 – clearly indicate this imbalance. Goods subject to duties carried out of England in English ships had a total value of just £1,187; those in foreign ships, £37,780 (Burwash, *English Merchant Shipping*, p. 206).
16. John Day's letter to 'the Almirante Mayor' remains the only evidence for this English voyage (see Ruddock, 'John Day', pp. 225–33).
17. Accounts of these voyages were produced by Hakluyt, *PN* 1598–1600, xi, pp. 23–5, 91–2.
18. Waters, *Art of Navigation*, pp. 83–4. Cabot's royal pension was set at some £300 per annum – a substantial figure by contemporary standards.
19. The author uses the term 'scholar' here in its widest sense; very few of the new 'scientists' were academicians.
20. Waters was the first to make this point (*Art of Navigation*, p. 91). See also McDermott and Waters, 'Cathay', p. 358. The 'rutter' (Fr. *routier*) was a printed or, more often, a hand-written pilot's manual containing sketches of coastlines, soundings, latitudes of well-known points of departure, distances between major ports, data on reefs and any other information gained empirically by the pilot himself and appended thereto.
21. The opinion is that of Waters, *Art of Navigation*, p. 104.
22. McDermott and Waters, 'Cathay', pp. 357–8.
23. Hakluyt, *PN* 1598–1600, v, p. 76.
24. *CLP*, ix 263; other English merchants who routinely supplemented Cromwell's diplomatic efforts in the Low Countries included Stephen Vaughan, John Gresham and William Lok.
25. Challis (*Tudor Coinage*, p. 87) infers that several men appointed personally by Cromwell to the Tower and Southwark Mints during the 1540s obtained their offices as sinecures, rather than by reason of any relevant prior experience.

26. *DNB*; Yorke, Sir John.
27. Beer, 'London', p. 34.
28. When Somerset was arraigned, it was rumoured that 'before the apprehension of the Lords he would have Sir John Yorke because he would tell many pretty things concerning the Mint' (PRO SP/10/13, 65; quoted in Brigden, *London and the Reformation*, p. 513).
29. *CSPS*, xi, 62.
30. Beer, *Northumberland*, p. 96.
31. White, *Ward of Walbrook*, p. 68.
32. *DNB*; Yorke, Sir John; Challis, *Tudor Coinage*, pp. 178–9. In 1551 alone, Yorke supplied 10,000 oz of silver, earning personal commissions of between £3,525 and £5,000.
33. PRO Customs Accounts 87/4, 167/1; SP/12/6, 52; EKR Port books, 4/2; summarized in Willan, *Muscovy Merchants*, p. 131. See also page 38 note 28 below.
34. Yorke's plot, like that of many other major merchants, may have been sited further east, below London Bridge; the drawbridge that allowed vessels larger than a waterman's boat to pass through the bridge had ceased to function around the year 1500 – perhaps another reason for the relative decline in the volume of trade landed at Queenshithe and Vintry, which stood up-river from the bridge.
35. Beryn has been identified by Hair and Alsop, *English Seamen*, p. 14.
36. Quotation from Michael Lok; BL Cotton MSS Otho E VIII, f. 42v.
37. Challis, *Tudor Coinage*, p. 107. Ludicrously, this debasement was intended to provide the funds whereby the same coinage could be revalued later in the same year. Yorke played an important role in formulating this plan, and may have been its conceiver.
38. Willan, *Russia Company*, p. 1; *Muscovy Merchants*, p. 121. Yorke was one of the first assistants (or directors) of the company, responsible for the administration of its corporate laws.

THREE: THE GUINEA COAST, 1553–55

1. Croft, *Spanish Company*, vii.
2. Englishmen had also traded directly, individually or collectively, with Portugal for many years, but this was principally an importation business; direct English exports – that is, not through Antwerp – were statistically insignificant, and remained so throughout this period. For example, duties paid on all English commodities exported directly to Portugal in 1567/8 came to just £263 10sh. 6d. (Shillington and Wallis-Chapman, *England and Portugal*, p. 134).
3. One known Englishman, Thomas Tison, was the resident Hispaniola factor of the Thorne brothers, Robert and Nicolas, during the 1520s (Andrews, *Trade, Plunder and Settlement*, p. 61).
4. Willan, *Russia Company*, p. 5.
5. It has been pointed out that the treaty of Medina del Campo specifically granted English merchants in Spain the same rights of trade with the 'older' Spanish Atlantic colonies as their Spanish counterparts (Connell-Smith, *Forerunners of Drake*, p. xiii). Certainly, they were subjected to the same onerous regulations and taxes as Spanish traders; however, there is no evidence (and nor does Connell-Smith infer) that any Englishmen were ever permitted to operate outside the specified Spanish ports appointed by the *Casa de la Contratación* in Seville; much less that they were permitted to trade directly, in their own ships, to the New World.
6. Hakluyt, *PN* 1598–1600, v, p. 76.

7. Hakluyt, *PN* 1589, p. 81: translation from Garcia de Resende, *Lyuro das obras* (Lisbon, 1545): an account of the embassy from King John II to Edward IV, requesting him to stay the ships. The plea was made in 1481. For early English interest in Portuguese over-seas possessions, see also Scammell, 'The English in the Atlantic Islands', pp. 292–4.

8. Blake, *Europeans in West Africa*, ii, p. 269. There is strong evidence in the Plymouth Customs Accounts that Hawkins sent the *Paul* on a fourth voyage to Guinea and Brazil in 1540, though he did not sail in her.

9. The only first-hand evidence for the voyage was a letter from James Alday (who had sailed with Wyndham) to Michael Lok, later provided by Lok to Hakluyt for inclusion in *PN* 1598–1600 (vi, pp. 136–7). Alday, himself of very dubious reputation (he is known to have despoiled Spanish ships in the 1540s), used the occasion of this letter to volunteer for service in Frobisher's 1576 voyage, declaring himself ready to risk his life therein 'to the uttermost point'. Superficially, it would seem that he gave even more than this, as his is one of the names missing from the list of surviving mariners paid off following the return of the voyage (PRO Exchequer King's Remembrancer E164/35, p. 27). However, this rep-resents a rare gap in Lok's accounts; Alday subsequently commanded an unsuccessful Danish expedition to Greenland in 1579 (Gad, *Greenland*, I, pp. 194–5). No doubt his experience in the 1576 voyage was considered qualification enough for this appointment.

10. Willan, *Studies*, p. 98.

11. Hakluyt, *PN* 1598–1600, vi, p. 138.

12. Willan, *Studies*, p. 99.

13. The account of James Thomas, in Hakluyt, *PN* 1598–1600, vi, p. 140.

14. *CSPF*, 27 May 1562.

15. Eden, *Decades*; reproduced in Hakluyt, *PN* 1589, p. 83.

16. *APC*, v, p. 304; 7 July 1556.

17. A regulated trade, in which merchants or their factors traded individually, and on their own behalf, required – at the very least – that an existing and identifiable political author-ity controlled the trading area, to allow activities to proceed unmolested. In the absence of such authority, joint-stock arrangements provided more effective means both of spreading the risk of investment and, eventually, of negotiating new trading privileges locally on behalf of its subscribers. Most importantly, it removed the element of physi-cal danger to the persons of those subscribers, exposing only the hired representatives of the 'company'.

18. Braz D'Alvide to John III of Portugal, 25 August 1552; reproduced in Blake, *Europeans in West Africa*, ii, p. 308.

19. Hakluyt, *PN* 1589, p. 85; the *Primrose* was a new ship, built in 1551.

20. As Master of the Ordnance, Wyndham may also have arranged for the furnishing of the *Primrose* and *Moon*.

21. PRO SP/70/32, 72.

22. Michael Lok; BL Cotton MSS Otho E VIII, f. 48r.

23. Report of the Spanish Ambassador; *CSPS* 1547–53, 92.

24. Nichols, *Diary of Henry Machyn*, p. 38.

25. Hakluyt, *PN* 1598–1600, vi, p. 148.

26. Hair and Alsop, *English Seamen*, p. 11.

27. Hakluyt, *PN* 1589, p. 97.

28. PRO E351/2195: though only three years old, the *Primrose* was sold off by the Crown fol-lowing her return, being riddled with a particularly voracious variety of tropical wood-worm. For the subsequent legal moves to secure the mariners' due wages, Blake (*Europeans in West Africa*, p. 288, n. 1) summarizes the High Court of Admiralty records. There is other, corroborating evidence of Yorke's rapacious nature: whilst he was briefly

in prison during 1553, his tenants at Whitby brought an action against him in the Court of Requests, complaining of rent increases of 122 per cent imposed in the two years since Yorke had acquired the abbey and its tied properties (*DNB*; Yorke, Sir John).

29. Willan, *Muscovy Merchants*, pp. 85, 103.

30. BL Add. MS 43827; Heath, 'William Loke', p. 10; Madden, *Privy Purse Expenses of the Princess Mary*, pp. 152, 161; McDermott, 'Michael Lok', p. 121.

31. *CLP*, viii, p. 404; Hakluyt, *PN 1598–1600*, v, p. 63.

32. On 19 November 1553, less than three weeks after his release, Yorke was attending Mass at St Stephen Walbrook (his parish church) where the Queen's own chaplain, John Feckenham, preached (Nichols, *Diary of Henry Machyn*, p. 48).

33. It has been determined that during the entire course of the sixteenth century, only four men (other than Lok himself), knighted whilst in the office of alderman or sheriff, did not succeed to the mayoralty (Beaven, *Aldermen*, I, p. 87).

34. BL Add. MS 43827, f. 13. The manuscript is a small, bound volume of the recollections of Rose Hickman, half-sister of Thomas Lok and wife of Anthony Hickman. Hickman and Lok also jointly built (or purchased) a ship, the *Mary Rose*, named after their respective wives. Hickman was more fortunate than his partner; having escaped to the Low Countries following his release from prison, he remained outside England until the accession of Elizabeth. Following his return, he resumed his career with admirable despatch: in 1560, he was named as one of the wardens of the Mercers' Company (McDermott, 'Michael Lok', p. 122; Herbert, *Livery Companies of London*, I, p. 296).

35. Supra, pp. 29–30.

36. Hakluyt, *PN 1589*, p. 96.

37. Ibid., p. 92.

38. PRO SP/70/37, 72: '. . . they were gladd sondry tymes to use hym to make dyvers jornayes to those that dwelt a myle or two of from the said castell, to gett victualls, as goates, pultry, and other, for to supplye their necessitie; for that thay themselves durst not, for perill of their lyves, doo it.'

39. Blake, *Europeans in West Africa*, ii, p. 360, n.1.

40. Richard Willes, 'For M. Cap. Furbyshers Passage by the North-west', printed in Richard Eden's *History of Travayle*.

41. These future associations may have reflected in part a narrowing of the respective fortunes of Frobisher and the Yorke clan. The succession of Mary Tudor – an event that Sir John Yorke had sought energetically to prevent – appears to have carried implications beyond his immediate imprisonment. Though he had retired fom the Mint in 1552 as a wealthy man (and subsequently realized a significant profit on his Guinea investments), he was unsuccessfully petitioning Cecil in 1560 for the post of master at the new extension to the Tower Mint (Challis, *Tudor Coinage*, p. 125): an indication that the intervening years had been less than uniformly fortunate.

42. PRO HCA/14/37, 250.

43. Blake, *Europeans in West Africa*, ii, p. 279.

44. The date was researched in parish records by George Frobisher, who kindly supplied it to the author.

FOUR: DIVERS AND SUNDRYE PYRACIES: 1560–71

1. PRO SP/12/132, 19: 'Anno Domini 1552, Roger Hunt, clerk of the Admiralty, went into Cornewall, with commission from the Lord Admirall, to apprehend Strangwaies, Kelligrew, and their company, did in that his service forth, and send out ships to

intrap them . . .'; reproduced in Marsden, *Law and Custom*, I, p. 225 (modernized spelling).

2. Much of the remaining information reproduced here is derived from Levy, 'Henry Stranguishe', pp. 133–7.

3. PRO HCA/13/13, 65, 35. The relevant Admiralty records were first identified in Marsden, 'Early Career . . . Frobisher.' Many sixteenth-century Admiralty Court records held in the PRO – the examinations and exemplars being the most substantial among them – remain unindexed to this day. The unbound bundles in particular are extremely fragile and hardly able to survive random trawling; the present author is therefore deeply appreciative of the signposts left by Marsden's work and, no less, of the invaluable overview of the records provided by K.R. Andrews in his introduction to *English Privateering Voyages*.

4. Lok's personal piety (manifested in his 1553 pilgrimage to Jerusalem), and the devoutly mercantilist sentiments he shared with his brothers, make it unlikely he would have condoned – much less participated in – piratical ventures during this period. Furthermore, he appears to have been of a conscientious and cautious nature; in 1561 he refused to command a voyage to Guinea because of the state of the ship proposed and the tardiness of its backers in despatching it in time to catch the cool season: '. . . the sequell whereof must by reason turne to a great misery to the men: the which for my part (though it might turne me to as much gaine as the whole commeth to) yet would I not be so tormented, as the sight thereof would be a corsive to my heart . . .' (Hakluyt, *PN* 1598–1600, vi, pp. 255–7).

5. The term 'privateer' will loom largely in this study. Applied to sixteenth-century practitioners of the art, it is, strictly speaking, anachronistic. Unfortunately, there is no satisfactory alternative. A contemporary term – 'likedealer' – had fallen out of use well before the end of the century (Marsden, 'High Court of Admiralty', p. 85), whilst 'voluntary' – sometimes used to distinguish ships set out under legal commissions from pirate vessels – also had a relatively short currency and is now too evocative of other, unrelated activities to be useful. The author is therefore inclined to favour seventeeth-century ubiquity at the expense of accuracy. The present work's general discussion on privateering owes much to K.R. Andrews's pioneering work on the subject. He and others may also regard as careless the present use of the term 'privateer' to refer to men who acted, indisputably, as outright pirates; however, the author regards it as necessary to distinguish those who often committed acts of banditry under the protection of recognized letters of reprisal from men who regarded any form of legal authority as entirely superfluous.

6. The royal proclamation that granted letters of reprisal against French vessels also stipulated that 'no man which shall go to the sea by virtue hereof presume to take any thing from any of their majesties' subjects or from any of their majesties' friends . . .' (HL, *Proclamations*, II, no. 435). However, Ramsay (*City of London*, p. 125) points out that the Admiralty Court was soon pestered by a deluge of complaints of Spanish and Netherlander vessels being despoiled.

7. During the first few years of Elizabeth's reign, Philip made repeated references in private correspondence to the bitterness of acquiescing, however tacitly, to her heretical rule. However, setting aside the economic benefits of friendship with the English people, the inevitable prospect of French power being enhanced by the neutralization of Protestant England was far too great a price to pay for religious conformity. It is no coincidence that his willingness to consider active measures against English interests, whatever their immediate provocation, commenced only *after* the collapse of French power during the wars of religion.

8. Parker, *Philip II*, pp. 152–3. Parker's work is the latest and, in the present author's opinion, the most lucid examination of the mind and motives of Philip II.

9. Read, *Cecil*, p. 240.

10. HL, *Proclamations*, II, no. 508.

11. The estimate was that of Sir Thomas Chaloner, English Ambassador to the Spanish court (Read, *Cecil*, p. 289). It was almost certainly a significant exaggeration, but the perception was clearly driven by the striking level of English activity against foreign vessels.

12. HL, *Proclamations*, II, no. 513.

13. Ramsay, *Queen's Merchants*, p. 13.

14. HL, *Proclamations*, II, no. 523.

15. Ramsay, *Queen's Merchants*, p. 13.

16. PRO SP/12/39, 86. In December 1584 the Earl was committed to the Tower for his alleged part in the Throckmorton plot. Six months later, he was discovered dead in his bed with a bullet in his heart, a wound that a hastily convened jury concluded was self-inflicted.

17. PRO HCA/13/15, 98; Levy, 'Henry Stranguishe', p. 134; Rowse, *Tudor Cornwall*, pp. 307, 317–18; Andrews, *Elizabethan Privateering*, p. 16. Killigrew appears to have been a particularly shameless specimen of the breed. Captured in 1556 by a royal squadron set out to curb privateering, he subsequently admitted that his ship, the *Sacrett*, had been gifted to him by the French King in recognition of his talents as a privateer (Glasgow, 'The Navy in Philip and Mary's War', p. 324).

18. PRO HCA/25/1, 6 March 1552(3); reproduced in Marsden, *Law and Custom*, I, p. 173: '. . . by all the tyme of ther beinge at the seas, honestly behave and demean themselves, and doo not robbe, spoyle, infest, trouble, evill intreate, apprehende, ne take any Portingales, Spaniardes, or any other persouns whiche be in league and amitie with her majestie . . .'. One of the principal reasons for taking bonds – other than to incline those paying them to a degree of circumspection – was to ensure that the Lord Admiral secured his 'tenth' on any prize goods taken at sea that might otherwise disappear before his officials could check cargoes at a voyage's end.

19. PRO HCA/13/15, 45.

20. PRO HCA/14/6, 5.

21. For Bowes's subsequent relationship with Frobisher, see pp. 68, 71.

22. C.f. the later evidence of Walter Darbie (PRO SP/12/39, 86), who claimed that he had known Frobisher 'evir sence his brother and he wer in trowble at the sute of Master Apleyard, beinge abowte towe yeres last past.'

23. PRO HCA/25/6; 15 July 1564; *APC*, vii, 28 September 1564.

24. HL, *Proclamations*, II, no. 525.

25. *CSPS*, 1558–67; 16 July 1565.

26. Ibid., 23 July 1565.

27. PRO HCA/13/15, 45.

28. The Spanish Ambassador to Philip II; *CSPS*, 1558–67; 27 May 1565.

29. The Spanish Ambassador reported a rumour that Appleyard intended to go to sea on an officially sanctioned mission to curb the excesses of English privateers (ibid.; 18 September 1564).

30. Both depositions are contained in PRO SP/12/39, 86.

31. This was probably one of Cooke's elder two sons, Anthony or Richard; the younger Edward and William had only recently come down from Cambridge after receiving their Master's degrees. Their father, Sir Anthony, was a former tutor of Edward VI, father-in-law of William Cecil and the man who had carried the Act of Uniformity to the House of Commons (*DNB*; Cooke, Sir Anthony).

32. PRO HCA/13/14, 45. On Killigrew, see also Mathew, 'Cornish and Welsh Pirates in the Reign of Elizabeth', pp. 337–48. As a scion of the family that virtually ran the privateering infrastucture in Devon during the 1560s, Killigrew was well placed to act as Frobisher's 'agent' in distributing his illicit prizes.
33. PRO SP/12/39, 86.
34. PRO SP/12/40, 2.
35. Elliot, *Europe Divided*, pp. 122–3.
36. Frobisher's own admission: PRO SP/12/39, 86.
37. *APC*, vii, 28 November 1566.
38. BL Lansdowne MS 107, f. 89. The document is undated, and may not have been extant when Frobisher gave his testimony to Dr Lewes.
39. BL Lansdowne MS 149, ff. 27–8.
40. PRO SP/12/39, 86.
41. Ibid.: '. . . a trill blacke shipp muche like to theires beinge a Scottishman did borde one Fleminge in the mowth of (th)e Thames before Margat and departid him selfe to the seas, Levinge his boate and his men on bord the same whoe came fower times to and froe withe the boates ladinge of wares, and afterwarde the said scott departid to the Sea . . .'.
42. *APC*, vii, 31 October 1566.
43. BL Lansdowne MS 139, f. 317.
44. Ramsay (*Queen's Merchants*) provides the most comprehensive summary of these negotiations and their importance both to England and the Netherlands.
45. *CSPS*, 1558–67, as dated.
46. PRO HCA/13/17; 9 June 1569: Frobisher '. . . did furnishe, p(re)pare & sett furthe vnto the seas ij severall shipps in warlyke fashion, to s(er)ve the prince of Navarr & Conde agaynst the Frenche which were ther enemies by ther com(m)ission grantid. And this shipp as he seith was callid the Robert.' The precise identity of the *Robert*, and how Frobisher came to command her, is not known, though Thomas Bowes later claimed that he himself had purchased the vessel from one Captain Pulverton (PRO HCA/3/14, 123). A vessel of that name was sponsored by the Earl of Cumberland twenty years later (Andrews, *Elizabethan Privateering*, p. 248), but it is hardly likely to have been the same ship.
47. Andrews, *Elizabethan Privateering*, p. 255.
48. Ibid., pp. 16–17.
49. Ramsay, *Queen's Merchants*, p. 144.
50. PRO HCA/13/17; 9 June 1569.
51. PRO HCA/24/43, 229.
52. This was the beginning of a long association. The *Salomon* and her owner, Hugh Randall, joined Frobisher's fleet in 1578 for the third voyage to Baffin Island.
53. Friar was an unlucky choice of victim. He appears to have suffered much at the hands of privateers, and in consequence, had become strikingly litigious, as many court examinations during this period attest (PRO HCA/13/16 & 17).
54. In fact, Frobisher was obliged to admit that Vaughan had caught the *Mary* only because the *Roe* was faster than his own vessel.
55. PRO HCA/13/17; 9 and 15 June, 7 July 1569.
56. PRO HCA/14/9, 57.
57. Ibid., 216.
58. Ibid., 257, 346.
59. Ibid., 256.
60. PRO SP/70/107, 236. As so often in Frobisher's career, he appears not to have regarded

the agreement as constituting an obligation on his part. As late as 1591, following the death of Bromley, he was being sued in the Court of Requests for repayment of the loan (PRO REQ/2/207/64).

61. PRO HCA/13/17; 10 February 1570.
62. PRO HCA/38/7: warrant originally issued on 25 April 1569.
63. PRO HCA/14/9, 197. Overton proved reluctant to relinquish 'his' wines. On 3 February 1570, Friar sued him for their return (HCA/13/7, as dated).
64. PRO HCA/14/10, 231.
65. PRO SP/70/110, 562.
66. PRO HCA/14/9, 89.
67. HL, *Proclamations*, II, no. 585; 1 March, 1572. Historians have since been divided upon the precise degree of premeditation that resulted in the sea-beggars' expulsion, and in particular, whether their subsequent capture of Brill and Flushing was part of a pre-agreed strategy between Burghley and de la Marck. It is the present author's opinion that the plot, if indeed such it was, represented by far the most sophisticated – and successful – occasion of geopolitical subterfuge undertaken by Elizabeth's government, and the likelihood of its prior intention should be judged accordingly.
68. On 1 March 1565, the Privy Council appointed Chichester to examine the coastlines of Devon and Cornwall to identify likely landing sites for stolen goods (*APC*, vii, as dated). Killigrew, famously ambushed in July 1556 by a squadron of the Queen's ships as he returned to Plymouth, was imprisoned but subsequently released to serve in the 1558 Brest campaign as commander of the naval vessel *Jerfalcon* under Admiral Woodhouse (Glasgow, 'The Navy in Philip and Mary's War', p. 341).
69. Cooper (*Ambassadeurs de France*, I, p. 214), reproduces correspondence of Archbishop La Mothe Fénelon, dated 25 February 1569(70), which suggests that Frobisher had recently been set out with three ships by the vice-admiral of Devon, Sir Arthur Champernowne. Unless the piece was mis-dated, this must have been a rumour only (or possibly word of a projected voyage), as Frobisher remained in the Marshalsea until at least mid-March of that year.
70. PRO SP/12/80, 31. The vessel was identified by Sir Henry Radcliffe as the *Carrack Sydney*, though as the *Carrack Lane* in bonds given by her owners, Thomas Lane and Richard West, to Frobisher for good behaviour (PRO HCA/3/15; 17 November 1571). There is no evidence that Frobisher transferred to another ship during this period; it seems probable, therefore, that the *Sydney* was renamed following her refitting.
71. PRO SP/12/80, 54 (iii).
72. PRO SP/12/78, 15; Radcliffe to Cecil: 'The farmers and honest inhabitants with some of the constables of the sea-coast adjoining came to me making their moan that they could not be sure certain of any servant they had for they would openly say that why should they serve for five nobles or forty shillings a year and might make their share at sea within one week four or five pounds.' Quoted in Andrews, *Elizabethan Privateering*, pp. 44–5 (modernized spelling).
73. *CSPS*, 1568–79, p. 341; the Ambassador claimed that Frobisher was set out with four 'well-found' vessels.
74. Oppenheim, *Royal Navy*, p. 177.
75. Pulman (*Privy Council*, p. 191, n. 14) cites a number of such commissions given during 1572–3.
76. In contemporary usage, the term 'hulk' had no negative connotation; it usually denoted a carvel-built vessel, typically a merchantman, that was robust enough to be requisitioned into naval service. Such vessels usually required extensive refitting, however, and were probably unhandy as fighting ships. The name of Frobisher's 'flagship' suggests that she

was a large and particularly high-charged design, which would not have helped in this respect.

FIVE: THE AMBIGUOUS PAPIST: 1572–74

1. Collins, *Sir Henry Sidney*, I, p. 24.
2. Simancas Archives L.8336, f. 27, 4 May, 1570; quoted in Falls, *Irish Wars*, p. 139.
3. *CSPS*, 1568–79, p. 210.
4. As late as 21 April 1576, the Privy Council wrote to Thomas Beale in the Netherlands, requiring him to ask the Prince of Orange to adjust (or, possibly, to rescind) Frobisher's 'passport' (PRO SP/70/138, 642). It is not known when he first took up this commission.
5. PRO HCA/14/11, 17, 41; 13/19, 29.
6. Supra, pp. 57, 85.
7. *CSPI*, II, p. 32; Falls, *Irish Wars*, p. 101.
8. Frobisher's testimony, given on 4 December 1572, is contained in PRO SP/63/38, 48.
9. Rowse, *Grenville*, pp. 121, 149.
10. Bodleian Library, Carte MS 56, f. 83.
11. Kervyn De Lettenhove and Gilliodts Van Severen, *Relations politiques des Pays-Bas*, vi; document 2591, p. 750.
12. *CSPS* 1568–79, 385; the calendar attributes the document to an unspecified date in May 1573, but this appears to be erroneous.
13. Kervyn De Lettenhove and Gilliodts Van Severen, *Relations politiques des Pays-Bas*, vi; document 2605, 2607; pp. 786, 789.
14. Ibid., documents 2620, 2641–2; pp. 803, 846, 850.
15. In fact, Montgomery's next action was his abortive 'invasion' of the coast of Normandy in the following March (MacCaffrey, *Queen Elizabeth and the Making of Policy*, p. 180).
16. Williamson, *Sir John Hawkins*, pp. 242–53.
17. Supra, n. 4.
18. *CSPS*, 1568–79, 420; 3 September 1575.
19. Wheater, 'Ancestry', p. 857.
20. Williamson, *Hawkins of Plymouth*, p. 62.
21. *APC*, v, as dated; Izon, *Stucley*, p. 28. The latter work is a volume in the 'Rogues Gallery' series, and should thus be treated with caution; it is, however, the only published source for much information on Stukeley's career.
22. Levy, 'Henry Stranguishe', p. 135.
23. Though citing no evidence, Izon (*Stucley*, pp. 45, 47, 51–3, 59–60) infers several occasions upon which Stukeley, Frobisher and Thomas Cobham may have collaborated in privateering ventures during the 1560s.
24. Wheater, 'Ancestry', p. 857.
25. *APC*, viii; 23 November 1573.
26. Falls, *Irish Wars*, pp. 107, 109.

SIX: THE NORTH-WEST PASSAGE

1. The phrase is taken from Thomas Ellis's 'In praise of Maister Martine Frobisher', in his (1578) *A true report of the third and last voyage into Meta Incognita, etc*; reproduced in Stefansson and McCaskill, *Frobisher*, II, p. 46.

2. *The discourse of syr Humfrie Gilbert knight, to prooue a passage by the North-west to Cathaya, and the East Indies*; reproduced in Hakluyt, *PN* 1598–1600, vii, p. 163.

3. Gilbert's *Discourse* was not published until 1576: ironically, to promote Frobisher's own forthcoming attempt.

4. *A new interlude, etc*; lines 859–64. The work was published in London by Rastell himself. He had outfitted an expedition of two ships and put to sea, but was abandoned by his crew off the Irish coast when he refused to commit acts of piracy (Williamson, *Cabots*, p. 246; Parker, *Books to Build an Empire*, p. 24).

5. Reproduced by Hakluyt, *Divers Voyages*, p. 38.

6. Andrews, *Trade, Plunder and Settlement*, pp. 53–4.

7. The most recent and comprehensive discussion of this little-known voyage is that of Quinn, *Cabot*, pp. 13–16.

8. Hakluyt, *Divers Voyages*, pp. 18–19. Quinn points out that having turned south and followed the coast of North America possibly as far south as 36°, Cabot's may have been the first English voyage to have returned using the Gulf Stream drift (Quinn, *Cabot*). It was a manoeuvre to be repeated, possibly unwittingly, by Rut in 1527.

9. Quinn, *Cabot*, pp. 13, 14 n.1.

10. All known documents referring to Rut's voyage are reproduced in Williamson, *Cabots*, pp. 104–11. Curiously, Richard Hakluyt (who was the first to mention the voyage, if obliquely), claimed that he had received his information from Martin Frobisher and one Richard Allen – possibly the London mercer of that name (*PN* 1598–1600, viii, p. 2). How Frobisher came by this information, and how reliable it was, cannot be established. It is possible that John Dee was the ultimate source, as Christopher Hall – with Frobisher a pupil of Dee's prior to the despatch of the 1576 north-west voyage – was another source quoted by Hakluyt on early north-west voyages.

11. An account of this voyage was printed by Hakluyt (*PN* 1598–1600, viii, pp. 3–7), which reported the alleged admission of a (prudently anonymous) member of Hore's crew: 'If thou wouldest needes know, the broyled meate that I had was a piece of such a mans buttocke'.

12. Andrews, *Trade, Plunder and Settlement*, p. 54.

13. McDermott, 'Company of Cathay', p. 150–1.

14. For the chronology of maps portraying the Zeno brothers' claims, see reproductions in Shirley, *The Mapping of the World*, pp. 122–39.

15. Quinn, 'Context of English North-west Exploration', p. 11.

16. It seems that Gastaldi (1561) must be given credit either for coining the term 'Strait of Anian' or for being the first to utilize it.

17. BL Lansdowne MSS 100/4: 'A Discourse concerninge a Straighte to be discovered towarde the North-weste, passinge to Cathaia and the Orientall indians, with a confutacion of their errour that thinke the Discoverye therof to be moste convenientlye attempted to the Northe of Baccalaos.' The endpaper to the manuscript is annotated in Burghley's hand 'M(aste)r Grynfold(e)s voyadg/Discovery of a Streight in ye N.W. Passage to Cathay & ye E.Indies.'

18. Cammocio, for example, showed the western exit of the strait descending almost to the tropic of Capricorn, a characteristic repeated by Gerard de Jode (1571), Tommaso Porcacchi (1572) and, most pertinently, by Humphrey Gilbert in 1576 (for these maps, see Shirley, *The Mapping of the World*, pp. 138, 146, 160).

19. BL Cotton MSS Otho E VIII, f. 239. The brief refutation is in a collection of papers thought to have been gathered originally by Michael Lok, though it is not set down in his hand.

SEVEN: MICHAEL LOK

1. The suggestion is that of McFee, *Sir Martin Frobisher*, p. 26. Mc Fee's is a 'Golden Hind' series volume which makes for stirring reading, but, citing no references, cannot be considered reliable.

2. The company's objections had been entirely protective; yet their comments, appended to Gilbert's petition to the Queen (PRO SP/12/42, 5 (ii)), were worded as though they strained to accommodate this potential interloper. Thus, to his request for rights of exploitation, they merely reiterated their own prior claims, but added that they: 'desyer the good advise, helpe and conference of M(aste)r Gilbarte yf yt please hyme, with reasonable condytions to enterpryse yt or to assyste theme therein'. Only to his specific request for the right of himself and heirs to take the custom of goods and merchandises derived from this exploitation did the company (quite legitimately) make an overt objection, on the grounds that his request was 'derogatorye to pryveledges' enjoyed by them.

3. BL Cotton MSS Otho E VIII, f. 41v.

4. Michael Lok: BL Cotton MSS Otho E VIII, f. 43r.

5. Michael Lok: PRO SP/12/129, 44 (i).

6. PRO EKR/164/35, p. 24.

7. Willan, *Russia Company*, p. 131.

8. Willan ('England and Russia', pp. 310–12) summarizes the statistics drawn from state papers and Port Books. The number of vessels despatched by the Russia Company in any one year appears to have fluctuated significantly. In 1566, it was claimed that fourteen ships sailed to St Nicholas, but just five in the following year. Until Russia acquired the port of Narva in 1581, Russia Company ships carried on a trade there which was maintained distinct from their Russian activities. The volume (if not the value) of this trade appears to have peaked in 1570, when thirteen ships sailed to Narva; though returning, according to the Spanish Ambassador Geurau de Spes, with little more than 10,000 crowns' worth of spices.

9. Technically, the mercers were a guild; the entity existed to regulate the trade itself, rather than to act as a 'company' with corporate activities *per se*. However, by the mid-sixteenth century, members of the mercers' and other guilds almost always referred to their respective associations as companies, and it is this form that the author will subsequently employ.

10. Best, *A True Discourse, etc*, reproduced in Collinson, *Martin Frobisher*, p. 70 (hereafter Best: Collinson). Best, a gentleman-soldier who would sail in the 1577 and 1578 northwest voyages, had by his own account travelled privately through Muscovy prior to 1577.

11. Warwick and Leicester were of course brothers; their nephew, Philip Sydney, was at Leicester's house at Kenilworth for much of 1575, rather than upon more distant service with his father in Wales (Boas, *Sir Philip Sidney*, p. 28), and may have been introduced to the project there. The Earls of Sussex and Leicester, though not related, were reconciled during the mid-1570s after years of outright rivalry at Court. Sussex also left much evidence of his high regard and personal affection for Burghley, whilst the latter's long patronage of Walsingham (excepting a brief period of tension during the early 1580s) is a matter of indisputable record (for the complexities of these relationships, see Pulman, *Privy Council*, pp. 47–9).

12. McDermott, 'Company of Cathay', p. 150.

13. Again, the suggestion is that of McFee (*Sir Martin Frobisher*).

14. Lok's extremely partial references to this period are variously contained in PRO SP/12/129, 44 (i); SP/12/119, 67 and BL Cotton MSS Otho E VIII, ff. 43r–44v.

15. In support of this, Lok himself referred to a 'former acquaintance' with Frobisher (PRO SP/12/129, 44 (i)), without providing further details.

16. The quote is from Lok's half sister, Rose Hickman; BL Add. MS 43827, f. 14v (see McDermott, 'Michael Lok', p. 125). Thomas appears to have died a few days before 30 October 1556; his burial in St Thomas Acre on that day, in a grave next to his father, Sir William, was noted by Machyn (Nichols, *Diary of Henry Machyn*, p. 117). However much against his will or inclination, Thomas's trouble to fashion himself to 'the popish religion' was apparently all too successful: his burial service was conducted by Henry Pendleton, personal chaplain to Bishop Edmund Bonner, stalwart of the Marian Counter-Reformation.

17. Michael Lok's own testimony (BL Cotton MSS Otho E VII, f. 42r) implies that he moved directly from the Low Countries to France, Spain and Portugal, and from thence eastwards into the Mediterranean. There is also the evidence of the first Pardon Roll of Elizabeth's reign, upon which Lok's name appears (Cal. Patent Rolls, Eliz. I, 229): 'Michael Lock, citizen and mercer of London, alias merchaunt venterer'; this was almost certainly in respect of a former proscription regarding his Protestantism.

18. PRO SP/12/129, 44 (i).

19. Halliwell, *Diary of John Dee*, p. 8: entry for 10 December 1595: 'M(aste)r Lok his Arabik bokes and letter to me by M(aste)r Berran his sonne'.

20. BL Cotton MSS Otho E VIII, f. 42r. The claim is hard to accept uncritically, as there were no English ships of this size known to have sailed to the Levant in this period; indeed, there was probably no English merchant ship of that tonnage in existence. It is far more likely that Lok sailed in a hired vessel – most probably Venetian in origin – carrying his own goods and those of his brothers, for whom he acted as factor.

21. PRO SP/12/8, 32. An affectation derived from his time in Spain, Lok often signed himself 'Mighell' or 'Miguell'.

22. BL Harleian MS 541, ff. 165–75; PRO SP/12/108, 16.

23. BL Cotton MSS Otho E VIII, ff. 47v–48r.

24. Prior, 'Reviled and Crucified Marriages', p. 128.

25. PCC prob. 1/42b; ff. 233r–235r: quoted, with modernized spelling, in Brigden, *London and the Reformation*, p. 562.

26. BL Cotton MSS Otho E VII, f. 42r.

27. Of Lok's brothers, the two eldest, Matthew and Thomas, were dead by 1557. John Lok's date of death is not known, though the inquisition post mortem upon Sir William Lok's estate, dated 24 October 1561, was almost certainly inaccurate in merely noting that 'the said Henry Locke and Michael Locke still survive' (Fry, *Inq. Post Mortem*, i, p. 228), as John Lok was refusing to make a Guinea voyage in the same year (supra, p. 49, n. 4). Henry died in 1571; partly worn out, no doubt, by the sheer effort of being married to the remarkable and extremely unconventional Anne Lok, whose pious (and, possibly, sexual) devotion to John Knox had caused her to abandon her husband and flee to Geneva with Henry's children, one of whom died there (Collinson, 'Role of Women in the English Reformation', p. 281). They were briefly reconciled before Henry's death.

28. The phrase is that of Willan, *Russia Company*, p. 26.

29. Ibid., p. 27. As late as 1576, possibly even following the return of Frobisher's first voyage to Baffin Island, Lok was defending the company's remaining privileges in respect of the Narva trade against interlopers in a piece entitled 'Certayne notes of Summ practises of evell dysposed Englishe men in England and in Denmark' (PRO SP/12/108, 16; though undated, this must have been written in the latter part of 1576, as it refers to the first Dutch voyage to St Nicholas which took place during that year).

30. It seems that the London Agent was not necessarily appointed for a finite term. Lok's

predecessor, John Broke, had served from 1565, and may only have been removed in 1570 upon suspicion of financial mismanagement. Subsequently, Anthony Marler was to occupy the position (with brief interruptions) for the greater part of the period 1580–1600 (Willan, *Russia Company*, pp. 26–7).

31. BL Add. MSS 43827, ff. 2–3.
32. Machyn, *Diary*, 28 August 1550: a public feast was given after the burial, and a dole of money distributed to the poor.
33. Beaven, *Aldermen*, I, p. 207; ACMC, I, p. 49.
34. BL Cotton MSS Otho E VIII, f. 42r.
35. PRO SP/12/129, 44 (i).
36. Ibid.
37. Best: Collinson, p. 70: '. . . hee repayred to the courte (from whence, as from the fountaine of oure commonwealth, all good causes have theyr chiefe encrease and mayntanance) . . .'. The reader will notice occasional references to 'court' and 'city' investors in the subsequent discussion of the north-west enterprise. Contemporary Englishmen often made that distinction unequivocally; however, as any student of Tudor history will know, it is in fact extremely arbitrary, and implicitly ignores interactions created both by the speculative nature of the Elizabethan aristocracy and their often intimate association with men of business. The terms are employed here by the author only to identify the provenance of connections through which adventurers of the 'Company of Cathay' were introduced to the north-west enterprise.
38. Ibid.
39. Bonde was to die a matter of days before the 1576 voyage departed from England; his investment was assumed by his son, also named William. As one would assume of the then freeholder of Crosby Hall, Bonde died a very rich man. The owner of five ships, he bequeathed gifts of gold to each of their masters, £100 to a maidservant as a dowry, and £2,000 to each of his four children (Fry, *Inq. Post Mortem*, ii, p. 98; PCC 26 Carew).
40. In the case of several of the adventurers, it is difficult (and probably pointless) to attempt to determine the provenance of their association with Lok. Lionel Duckett, for example, was a leading member of both the Russia and Mercers' Companies, and had close links with the Lok family that had stood for years, if not decades. Similarly, Thomas Gresham's charter-membership of the Russia Company cannot be said to have been more or less relevant than his own family's long association with William Lok and his children.
41. See Ramsay, *John Isham*, p. 87. In 1564, Lok and Hogan were associated in the purchase of silks recovered from the wreck of the ship *Philip and Mary*. Matthew Field was also a sugar importer in partnership with another of Michael Lok's brothers-in-law, Richard Hill or Hilles, who had married Sir William Lok's twentieth child, Elizabeth (Willan, *Studies*, p. 132; Bramston, *Sir John Bramston*, p. 10.)
42. PRO EKR E164/35, p. 3.
43. On the search for further investors, see infra, pp. 163–4, 205–6.
44. Patent Rolls 17 Eliz. 66/1126.
45. PRO SP/12/129, 44 (i).

EIGHT: THE 1576 VOYAGE

1. Willan, *Russia Company*, pp. 27, 132.
2. See p. 88.
3. PRO SP/12/129, 44 (i).

4. Borough's *Discours of the Variation* was published in London by John Kingston. It was bound together with Robert Norman's *The newe Attractive* . . . : 'one of the first truly scientific books ever published in England' (Waters, *Art of Navigation*, p. 153). Norman dedicated his own work to Borough.

5. PRO SP/12/110, 22.

6. Hogan had long-term contacts there through his former trading activities, possibly as an arms-dealer. As ambassador, he was involved in purchases of saltpetre for the production of gunpowder (most extant information on Hogan's career is summarized in Willan, *Studies*, pp. 147–51; and Bovill, 'Queen Elizabeth's Gunpowder', pp. 181–7).

7. Lok's accounts are contained principally in PRO EKR E164/35, 36. His accounts for the outfitting of the third (1578) voyage were separated from the rest at some time before 1830, and are currently held in the Henry E. Huntington Library, San Marino, California, MS: HM 715. All references to the HM material cite the original folio markings. The PRO material is incompletely foliated; however, in c. 1821, Craven Ord, Secondary of the King's Remembrancer Office, paginated the manuscripts, and it is to this enumeration that all subsequent references are made. To date, the only complete transcription of these accounts (PRO and HL) is that of the present author, in his unpublished thesis 'Account Books of Michael Lok, etc'.

8. Baker was responsible for the first theoretical method of calculating a ship's burden (Oppenheim, *Monson*, iv, pp. 50–1). Rodger (*Safeguard of the Sea*, p. 219) suggests that the ship *Galleon Leicester* (originally *Galleon Oughtred*), built in 1578 to Baker's design, was the first large vessel to be built from a paper draft. Baker's famous schematics, preserved by Samuel Pepys as *Fragments of Ancient English Shipwrightry* (now in the Pepys Library, Magdalene College, Cambridge) are the earliest extant technical drawings of English ships.

9. PRO EKR E164/35, pp. 9–10. Baker's associate in building the *Gabriel* was another leading English shipwright, John Addye, later the 'framer' of the *Galleon Oughtred* (Donno, *Madox*, p. 114; infra, p. 275). The *Michael* was stated by Lok to be of 30 tons, though the designation of the *Gabriel* as Frobisher's 'flagship' suggests that the latter was the more substantial – or more weatherly – vessel.

10. Friel, 'Frobisher's ships', pp. 303–5.

11. Some four dozen oars were purchased for the 1576 voyage: PRO EKR E164/35; p. 11.

12. PRO SP/12/136, 35. However, with a crew of eighty, the *Pelican* was not appreciably less crowded than either the *Gabriel* or *Michael*.

13. PRO EKR E164/35, p. 27. As late as 1600, a more usual master's rate of pay was £4 per month (Davis, *English Shipping Industry*, p. 138).

14. PRO EKR E164/35, p. 19.

15. Ibid., pp. 14, 11: 'for carvinge of the dragon(e)s hed, li 0. 10. 0.'

16. In his *Discourse*, George Best (who did not sail in the 1576 voyage) incorrectly claimed that the expedition was provisioned for twelve months (Best: Collinson, p. 71).

17. The author's thesis discussion on victualling for the voyages has been comprehensively superseded by Watt ('Medical Record', pp. 613–19).

18. A standard 'pipe' measure was of 126 gallons.

19. Ale was of course a popular beverage also, but being brewed without hops it would not keep for the duration of a long sea voyage.

20. It has been shown that members of a modern (1957) trans-Arctic expedition, provided with ample cold-weather clothing and a daily calorific intake of 5,000–7,000 calories, nevertheless lost significant body weight (ibid., pp. 612, 617).

21. All quotations from Culpepper, *Physicall Directory*, pp. 4, 7, 9, 16, 53.

22. Watt, 'Medical Record', p. 611; PRO EKR E164/35, pp. 44, 48.

23. PRO EKR E164/35, pp. 12–13.
24. BL Lansdowne MS 100/1, f. 1r: Lok here mis-states the Spanish form *Mar del Sur*.
25. PRO EKR E164/35, pp. 22, 43, 46–52.
26. Collingwood, *Elizabethan Keswick*, p. 187 (accounts for 1576; London, 31 August): '. . . to Mr Look for the Muscovite Company, 27 kettles and 2 sheets, £4. 10. 0.'.
27. Willan, *Russia Company*, p. 49.
28. This was the amount he advanced prior to the ships' departure (PRO EKR E164/35, p. 3). With the post-costs of the voyage still to be met, his loans in 1576 were to rise to some £800.
29. Hall: *PN* 1589, p. 615. Hall's account was heavily censored by Hakluyt, who removed all references to latitude.
30. PRO EKR E164/35, pp. 24, 28. The total cost of being provided with these letters was £8 19sh. 4d. A further entry in the accounts notes: 'paid for reward to the Queens man of the garde that came a bord the ships at Blackwalle, li 0. 10. 0.' (ibid., p. 19).
31. BL Cotton MSS Otho E VIII, f. 44r. For the most recent and detailed examination of Dee's involvement in the enterprise, see Sherman, 'John Dee's Role', pp. 283–98.
32. Quotation from Taylor, *Tudor Geography*, p. 262 (modernized spelling). The letter was probably set down at Frobisher's order, perhaps by Christopher Hall; known examples of Frobisher's own correspondence are not nearly so articulate. The texts and instruments of navigation purchased by the adventurers are listed in PRO EKR E164/35, pp. 16–17. Given their limited practicality in everyday use at sea, the author has previously offered the opinion that the texts were purchased for tuition purposes only, and not to be risked in the voyage itself. However, his attention has recently been drawn to the suggestion that Sir Philip Sydney, paying a visit to the *Gabriel* immediately prior to her departure, saw in her cabin 'the only six books in English on geography and navigation, one of them dedicated to his father ' (Boas, *Sir Philip Sidney*, p. 33: the work dedicated to Sir Henry Sydney was Thomas Hacket's 1568 translation of André Thevet's *Les singularitéz de la France Antarctique*). These books may of course have been removed before the *Gabriel* departed from England; Lok was not subsequently to complain of their 'disappearance', as he did of the instruments of navigation taken to sea by Frobisher.
33. The discussion on instruments and techniques of navigation is drawn largely from McDermott and Waters, 'Cathay'.
34. Quotation from Hakluyt, *Divers Voyages*, p. 41. The most recent reproduction of Bourne's *Regiment* is that of Taylor (Hakluyt Society, Second Series, 1963). Bourne provided a diagram of a half dial which, by drawing a piece of string or thread between its circumference (latitude) and diameter (length of a degree of longitude in miles), would give the approximate true length of a degree of longitude at every five-degree division of latitude (p. 241).
35. PRO EKR E164/35, pp. 16–17: 'for divers Instrumentes for Navigation . . . paid to Humfrye Cole and others.' For Cole's role in the enterprise, see McDermott, 'Humphrey Cole', pp. 15–19.
36. PRO SP12/129, 37; reproduced in Friel, 'Frobisher's ships', pp. 332–43. Waters (*Art of Navigation*, pp. 28–9) provides a damning list of the known failings of contemporary English compasses.
37. Borough's chart is extant, and held in the Marquess of Salisbury's collection at Hatfield House. For a technical discussion of this important English artefact, see Waters, *Art of Navigation*, appendix 10a.

38. The fact that Lok hurriedly purchased another globe for decorative purposes following Frobisher's return (see p. 148) suggests that the expensive version was safely under lock and key elsewhere.

39. Hall: *PN* 1589, p. 616.

40. Michael Lok's account of the first voyage (probably compiled with the help of Christopher Hall): BL Cotton MSS Otho E VIII, ff. 47v–54r (hereafter Lok: 1576).

41. Best: Collinson, p. 155. Although the cross-staff was graduated up to 90 degrees, its graduations above 60 degrees became so small that the slightest error of observation resulted in a divergence of several degrees from the true reading (Waters, *Art of Navigation*, p. 54).

42. Lok: 1576, f. 48v.

43. Ibid., ff. 48v–49r.

44. Only one of these unfortunates – John Hammond – can be identified by name (PRO EKR E164/35, p. 18).

45. Also known as Griffith.

46. Griffin's rate of pay is taken from PRO EKR E164/35, p. 18. Alexander Creake, boatswain of the *Michael* and 'kinsman' of Frobisher, may, on evidence of his behaviour at other times (infra, pp. 237, 243), have been a focus for their discontent.

47. The phrase is Lok's.

48. Lok: 1576, f. 49r.

49. Settle: *PN* 1589, p. 629.

50. Hall: *PN* 1589, p. 620.

51. BL Lansdowne MS 100/1, f. 2r.

52. Best: Collinson, p. 72.

53. Lok: 1576, f. 50r.

54. Hall: *PN* 1589, p. 621.

55. Elliot, *The Old World and the New*, p. 21.

56. The most likely explanation for this seemingly suicidal act is that the burden of several weeks spent in a world circumscribed by the rails of the *Gabriel* made the siren-prospect of *terra firma* – even that particularly bleak version – irresistible.

57. Best: Collinson, p. 73.

58. Ibid., p. 71.

59. Lok: 1576, f. 53r–v (fire damaged: author's reconstruction supplied in parenthesis).

60. The time devoted to this now minor aim suggests that Frobisher had set too northerly a course after leaving Baffin Island, made some point on the western coast of Greenland, and then followed its coastline south-eastwards.

61. PRO EKR E164/35, p. 28.

62. Lok: 1576, f. 53v.

63. Ibid., f. 54r.

64. PRO EKR E164/35, p. 30: 'for makinge a great picture of the whole bodye of the strainge man in his garment(e)s . . . li 5.' On De Heere's portrait, see Sturtevant and Quinn, 'This New Prey', p. 75. This was not commissioned by the adventurers.

65. PRO EKR E164/35, pp. 28, 30, 127. Later, this was the official church of the Navy Board, in whose pew Samuel Pepys habitually slept through Sunday afternoon sermons.

66. Ibid., p. 128. In 1578, even as calls upon the adventurers' purses were becoming intolerable, further portraits (of Edward Fenton and George Best) were commissioned from Ketel, at a cost of £6 (ibid., p. 184).

67. Lok: 1576, f. 50v.

68. Willes's piece is reproduced in Stefansson and McCaskill, *Frobisher*, I, pp. 135–45.
69. BL Lansdowne MS 100/1, f. 6r.

NINE: ALL THAT GLISTERS

1. Lok: 1576, f 46v.
2. 'Mr Lockes Discoors touching the Ewre, 1577'; PRO SP/12/112, 25. This document provides much of the evidence for Lok's 'secret' dealings prior to the general revelation of the ore's supposed value after 29 March 1577.
3. Ibid.
4. For a detailed examination of the role of Schutz and other assayers in the enterprise, see Baldwin, 'Frobisher's metallurgists' pp. 401–76.
5. Ibid., p. 416.
6. PRO SP/12/111, 48 (ii); EKR E164/35, p. 85.
7. PRO SP/12/112, 25: 'And thus by this means of the doynges of S(i)r John Barkley and S(i)r William Morgan dealynge therin w(i)th others their parteners, and w(i)th the Douchemen their workmen vtterly w(i)thout my knowledge, or ells by the meanes of others, who have pece of the vre for prooffes of others, and not of me, the secreatnes of this great matter is discoursed so as it is abroade / And bycause that I doo vnderstand . . . that the blame is layed all on me, as author of the spech(e)s that now is abroade of this great treasour, I doo by this wrytynge purge my sellfe of that vntrew surmyse.'
8. Allaire, 'Martin Frobisher', p. 580 & n. 41.
9. Settle: Hakluyt, *PN* 1589, p. 629.
10. But commissioned only in 1562 (Oppenheim, *Royal Navy*, p. 120, n. 9).
11. Murdin, *Papers . . . Burghley*, i, pp. 303–4.
12. PRO SP/12/112, 25.
13. BL Lansdowne MS 100/1, f. 1v.
14. PRO SP/12/119, 31.
15. PRO SP/12/110, 48.
16. *APC*, xi, 6 March 1578(9).
17. Quinn, *Gilbert*, I, p. 188.

TEN: THE 1577 VOYAGE

1. *APC*, ix, 6 March 1577.
2. PRO SP/12/25, 9.
3. PRO SP/12/111, 48 (ii); Collinson, *Frobisher*, p. 109.
4. PRO EKR E164/35, p. 87. New subscriptions came to a total of £5,150, but £875 of this was allocated to covering the debt of the first voyage.
5. PRO SP/12/119, 44; Collinson, *Frobisher*, pp. 163–4.
6. The precise patrimony of the younger Michael has not been established, though the terms of the will of Lok's first wife, Jane (PCC 14 Holney) indicates that they had no son of that name.
7. See McDermott, 'Company of Cathay', p. 160.
8. Subscribers list from PRO EKR E164/35, pp. 85–8.
9. Willan, *Muscovy Merchants*, p. 75; *Russia Company*, p. 287; Rabb, *Enterprise and Empire*, p. 379; Zins, *England and the Baltic*, p. 103.

10. PRO EKR E164/35, p. 4.

11. PRO SP/12/119, 30.

12. Hakluyt, *Discourse of Western Planting*, lines 1838–40.

13. PRO SP/12/111, 49; Collinson, *Frobisher*, pp. 104–5; appended to which was the first of several requests that the Queen grant articles of incorporation to the 'Company of Cathay'. Lok later claimed that it had been Frobisher himself who had pressed for an expedition of this size, and that his failure to secure it brought further tantrums against the commissioners for the voyage (BL Lansdowne MS 100/1, f. 2r). In this case, however, he was clearly shifting at least part of the responsibility from his own shoulders.

14. PRO SP/12/111, 48 (i); Collinson, *Frobisher*, pp. 105–7.

15. Patent Rolls, 19 Eliz.12/2604.

16. There are three extant versions of the instructions, held in PRO SP/12/113, 12; BL Add. MS 35831 and BL Sloane MS 2442. There are minor differences of detail and emphasis between them, and it is not known which represents the definitive version.

17. PRO EKR E164/35, p. 124.

18. Information on the weight of shot for contemporary ordnance is drawn from Corbett, *Spanish War*, appendix A.

19. PRO EKR E164/35, p. 111. The miners' wages, at 20sh. per month, were equivalent to those of the common mariners.

20. Ibid., pp. 104, 120.

21. Selman was to refer to Lok as 'my master' in his account of the third, 1578, voyage (BL Harleian MS 167/40, f. 166v).

22. PRO EKR E164/35, p. 111; Willan, *Russia Company*, p. 196.

23. In 1596, Yorke was to have the doubtful honour of being appointed as vice-admiral of the fateful Drake/Hawkins expedition upon the death of Sir John Hawkins, almost immediately after which he himself expired (Andrews, *Drake and Hawkins*, pp. 40, 95).

24. The wording of parts of the proposal – in particular, the seemingly premature request that '. . . it would please Her Ma(ies)tie also to graunt aucthoritie to M(aste)r Frobysher, for the governement of the men in obediens' – appears to reflect Frobisher's own priorities rather than those of the adventurers as a whole. However, its concluding request for the incorporation of a company of Cathay was almost certainly not Frobisher's. Lok, therefore, may have colloborated in drafting this note.

25. BL Lansdowne MS 100/1, f. 3r.

26. Ibid.

27. PRO SP/12/113, 12; the version in BL Sloane MS 2442 directed Frobisher to secure three or four Inuit 'at the most'.

28. There are two contemporary sources for the 1577 voyage: that of Best – an eye-witness account this time, as he sailed as Frobisher's lieutenant on the *Ayde* – and of Dionyse Settle: Hakluyt, *PN* 1589, a gentleman-soldier who enjoyed the patronage of that other great privateer, George Clifford, third Earl of Cumberland (Settle's *True Report* was dedicated to Clifford). Hakluyt reproduced a version of Settle's original account, without dedications, in *PN* 1589, pp. 622–30 from which the present author's references are cited. Though Christopher Hall sailed once more with Frobisher, now as master of the *Ayde*, his ship's log or journal for this year is no longer extant.

29. The names and offences of these unfortunates are contained in PRO SP/12/112, 46. Lok claimed that Frobisher set them ashore for 'frinshippe and mooney, sayenge that they weare vnrewly knaves w(hi)ch would make mutynyes in the Shippe . . .'. (BL Lansdowne MS 100/1, f. 2v).

30. Lok's wage lists makes it clear that even after setting down these men, Frobisher retained a complement of 143 men (PRO EKR E164/35, pp. 65, 118, 146).

31. Best: Collinson, p. 123.

32. Settle: *PN* 1589, p. 623.

33. Best: Collinson, p. 125; Settle: *PN* 1589, p. 623.

34. Best: Collinson, p. 128.

35. It has been suggested informally to the author that the column was raised as a marker from which Frobisher attempted to observe his longitude. This represents a striking over-estimation of his interest in – and ability to solve – one of the fundamental problems of navigation. The theory may have been given anachronistic encouragement in recalling Captain C.F. Hall's experience upon Mount Warwick almost three centuries later, when he lamented the turn in the weather because: 'I had fixed a capital point by sun to take my angles of various mountains, bays, headlands, etc.' (Hall, *Arctic Researches*, I, p. 14).

36. Best: Collinson; p. 130.

37. Settle: *PN* 1589, p. 624.

38. Ibid.

39. Cox later blotted his record when, as pilot of the ship *Thomas of Ispwich* in the 1578 expedition, he led the crew in mutiny against her captain and prematurely returned to England (Best: Collinson, pp. 264–5; BL Lansdowne MS 100/1, f. 8v).

40. BL Lansdowne MS 100/1, f. 1v.

41. Settle's wording, '. . . yet they verifie the olde Proverbe: All is not golde that glistereth', is so close to Best's that the probability of their active collusion is strong.

42. Best: Collinson, p. 135.

43. Though the channel between the Blunt Peninsula and Leffert's Island is called Beare Sound today, the precise location of that feature so named by Frobisher has not been definitively established.

44. Best: Collinson, p. 137.

45. Ibid., p. 135.

46. Settle: *PN* 1577, p. 625. Settle mistakenly identifies the ensign bearer as 'Walter' Philpot, but Lok's wage lists (PRO EKR E164/35, p. 112) show only the name of Richard Philpot.

47. This brief but bloody encounter is portrayed in a watercolour now held in the British Museum. The style of the piece makes it almost certain that John White was the artist. White made further drawings of the Inuit captives returned from the 1577 voyage, which indicates that he may have been personally present in the 1577 expedition (Sturtevant and Quinn, 'This New Prey', pp. 96–7). However, if he did indeed sail in the voyage, it was as a volunteer; there is no indication in Lok's wage lists that he was paid by the adven-turers for his troubles.

48. Settle: *PN* 1589, p. 626 (present author's emphasis).

49. Best: Collinson, pp. 142–3.

50. Ibid., p. 138.

51. Infra, p. 433.

52. Best: Collinson, p. 147.

53. Settle: *PN* 1589, p. 627.

54. Ibid., p. 23.

55. Beckingham, 'Near East, North and North-east Africa'; Quinn, *Hakluyt Handbook*, i, p. 186.

56. BL Lansdowne MS 100/1, f. 2v–3r.

57. Best: Collinson, p. 152.

58. Ibid., p. 154.

59. Ibid., pp. 153–4: 'This Mayster was called William Smyth, beeyng but a yong man, and a very sufficient Maryner, who beeyng all the mornyng before exceeding pleasaunte, tolde hys Captayne hee dreamed that he was cast ouer boorde, and that the Boateson hadde hym by the hande, and coulde not saue hym, and so immediately vppon the ende of hys tale, hys dreame came right euelly to passe, and in deede the Boateson in like sort helde him by one hande, hauyng hold on a rope with the other, vntill hys force fayled, and the Master drowned.'

60. PRO SP/12/115, 35.

61. PRO SP/12/122, 62; Collinson, *Frobisher*, p. 175: 'And thearevppon hee [Jonas Schutz] should have gonne to Brystowe too have builded the furnaces theire for the greate woorkes'.

62. Best: Collinson, p. 225.

63. BL Lansdowne MS 100/1, f. 6v.

ELEVEN: A SCHISMA GROWEN AMONGE US

1. Churchyard, *A prayse, and reporte of Maister Martyne Forboisher's Voyage* (London, 1578); quoted in Stefansson and McCaskill, *Frobisher*, II, p. 230.

2. The dates and location of their burial were researched by Alison Quinn, and reported in Cheshire, Waldron and Quinn, 'Frobisher's Eskimos in England'.

3. PRO SP/12/118, 40 (i); ibid., p. 29.

4. PRO EKR E164/35, pp. 150–2: 'paid for charges of the nurse w(i)th the strainge childe at the 3. Swanes, 8sh. . . . for charges of the same nurse at london to retorne to bristowe . . . li 1. 11. 0.' The location of the 'Three Swans' cannot be traced definitively; possibly it is to be identified with one of the establishments of that name in Old Fish Street or Dowgate (both of which were destroyed in the 1666 fire). Neither the child's burial, nor that of the Inuk male in the previous year, was recorded in St Olave's parish register (Sturtevant and Quinn, 'This New Prey', p. 84).

5. An Italian edition followed in 1582. For the known editions of Settle's work, see Stefansson and McCaskill, *Frobisher*, II, pp. 226–7 and Parker, *Books to Build an Empire*, p. 72.

6. Archivo General de Indias, Seville, Indiferente 739, no. 28; quoted in Allaire, 'Martin Frobisher', p. 576.

7. Allaire, 'Martin Frobisher', pp. 577–81.

8. Read, 'Castelnau de la Mauvissière', p. 286.

9. Hessiches Hauptstaatsarchiv, Marburg, Gef. 628: reproduced and translated by Kinder, 'Casiodoro de Reina', p. 108.

10. PRO SP/91/1, 1a; 26 January 1578.

11. BL Lansdowne MS 100/1, ff. 3v, 6v.

12. This is Michael Lok's claim; PRO SP/12/119, 30.

13. *APC*, ix, 4 August 1577.

14. PRO SP/12/115, 35.

15. PRO SP/12/116, 24.

16. PRO SP/12/126, 32; ibid., 12/130, 35.

17. BL Lansdowne MS 100/1, f. 5v.

18. PRO EKR E164/35, pp. 142–6.

19. PRO SP/12/112, 25; Collinson, *Frobisher*, p. 98.

20. PRO SP/12/122, 62; Collinson, *Frobisher*, p. 175.

21. PRO EKR E164/36, p. 331.
22. Ibid., 35, p. 159.
23. PRO SP/12/118, 54; Collinson, *Frobisher*, p. 195.
24. Collingwood, *Elizabethan Keswick*, pp. 1–29.
25. Ramsay, *John Isham*, p. 172.
26. PRO SP/12/122, 62; Collinson, *Frobisher*, p. 176.
27. Donaldson, 'Burchard Kranich', pp. 309–10.
28. PRO SP/12/122, 62: 'A little bundle of the tryeing of (th)e North-west ewre. By D. burcot, Jonas Schutz, Baptista Agnillo, etc'; PRO SP/12/122, 61: 'From D. Burcott Touchynge his Cunynge and offer about Triynge the Ewre'; both accounts written by Michael Lok: reproduced in Collinson, *Frobisher*, pp. 178, 181.
29. PRO SP/12/118, 36.
30. PRO EKR E164/35, pp. 151–2: 'paid for fees of pattent of Jonas sutz paid to m(aste)r Balyfe Clarke of my lord kepare, li 5. 5. 0 . . . to m(aster) Balyfe, secretarye to my Lorde kepare for fees of the Q(uenes) pattent geven to burcote, li 3. 5. 0. . . . for fee of the Q(uenes) pattent geven to dename, li 3. 5. 0 . . .'.
31. Ibid., p. 152; PRO SP/12/122, 62; Collinson, *Frobisher*, p. 178.
32. Collinson, *Frobisher*, p. 177.
33. Ibid., p. 178.
34. BL Lansdowne MS 100/1, ff. 4v–5r.
35. PRO SP/12/122, 10; Collinson, *Frobisher*, p. 173.
36. PRO SP/12/122, 62; Collinson, *Frobisher*, p. 178.
37. Frobisher's servant and kinsman, William Hawke, had been sent to Lincolnshire to bring Sebastian from the Grimethorpe mine works where he plied his habitual trade (PRO EKR E164/35, p. 151).
38. PRO SP/12/123, 5.

TWELVE: THE 1578 VOYAGE

1. Frobisher's commission to press mariners for the voyage was issued on 23 March (Patent Rolls, 20 Eliz. 12/2886).
2. Lok's accounts (PRO EKR E164/35, p. 20) show that Frobisher was paid a total of £80 in respect of the first voyage, though part of this may have been a reimbursement of expenses.
3. Ibid., p. 288. Lok disagreed; he claimed that Frobisher had been paid a further £253 for the period 20 September 1577 to the end of May 1578 at a rate of £1 per day (HM 715, f. 19).
4. PRO SP/12/119, 44.
5. Lok's initial subscribers' list (HM 715, ff. 1–3) does not give Oxford's name; it appears that their negotiations took place subsequently, perhaps whilst the ships were at sea.
6. PRO EKR E164/36, p. 228.
7. Andrews's ship-owning partner, Robert Martin, appears to have died in the period between the despatch of the 1577 and 1578 expeditions; an amount equivalent to his pro-rated investment in 1577 was taken up the following year by one Elizabeth Martin – probably his widow (HM 715, f. 3).
8. The precise extent of Winter's participation, and the point at which he withdrew, is not easy to determine. The final auditors' report on the enterprise (PRO EKR E164/36, p. 319) suggests that he invested a total of £300 in the enterprise, of which £60 remained

outstanding in 1581. However, in the assessment raised for wages due at the return of the second voyage (E164/35, pp. 129–30), his name is already missing from the list of adventurers. He is shown, however, as owing £40 in the later assessment to meet the building costs of the Dartford works (E164/36, p. 173).

9. She does not appear to have been associated with the ship of the same name that was to be hired by the adventurers as a freight vessel and captained by George Best in the coming voyage; the owner of the *Ann Frances* is named in Lok's accounts as one Francis Lee, who was also to purchase the *Judith* from the adventurers following the return of the 1578 voyage (HM 715, f. 23; PRO EKR E164/36, p. 18).

10. PRO SP/12/123, 50, reproduced in Collinson, *Frobisher*, pp. 210–11.

11. PRO SP/12/122, 9; BL Lansdowne MS 100/1, f. 6r.

12. PRO EKR E164/35, p. 296.

13. Lok's allegations: BL Lansdowne MS 100/1, ff. 6r–6v.

14. Infra, pp. 279–80.

15. BL Lansdowne MS 100/1, f. 6r.

16. PRO SP/12/124, 1; Collinson, *Frobisher*, pp. 209–10.

17. PRO SP/15/25, 146.

18. BL Lansdowne MS 100/1, f. 6r.

19. Ibid., f. 7v.

20. In his *Discourse*, Best noted the presence of bears, deer, foxes, rabbits (probably hares) and an abundance of wild fowl; but the latter apart, such commodities might only be realistically secured in the face of interference – or worse – from the now-aggrieved Inuit.

21. HM 715, f. 26.

22. Magdalene College Library, Pepys MSS 2133, f. 12.

23. Lok's accounts record the purchase of 10,000 bricks 'for the building(e)s at newe Lande' (HM 715, f. 12).

24. 'Paid to thomas bodnam Carpinter . . . for Crabes for the Landing of the Shipp(e)s that shall remayne in the new Land' (ibid., f. 8).

25. Watt ('Medical Record', pp. 615–16) points out that pork and bacon, being more durable commodities, were probably intended to be consumed only after stocks of beef had been exhausted. The quantities given by Fenton's provisional list are close enough to the eventual victualling for us to regard it as the definitive plan for the colony.

26. HM 715, f. 26.

27. On what Drake's backers may or may not have suspected, see Andrews, *Drake's Voyages: a reassessment etc.*, p. 57.

28. HM 715, f. 3.

29. PRO SP/12/124, 2.

30. HM 715, f. 25. An advanced freight payment of £100 to Richard Fairweather prior to the departure of the voyage was passed by the auditor; however, the charges of victualling the *Beare Leicester* were later disallowed.

31. Supra, p. 68. Randall may have had another reason for wishing to be associated with an enterprise that kept him out of England for a few months; in the previous October, he had been brought before the Privy Council in the latest of a number of actions against him for abetting acts of piracy (*APC*, x, 1 October 1577).

32. PRO EKR E164/36, p. 92. The *Denys* was lost at sea before she could take on any ore. The freight charges of the *Beare Leicester*, the ship that Lok himself brought into the voyage against instructions to the contrary, came to £450. Lok of course ensured that this debt was paid as a priority. The freight charges for the other 'unofficial' vessels were paid tardily, if at all. Those of the *Salomon* were eventually met, not by the adventurers,

but by the Exchequer: her owner Hugh Randall petitioned the Privy Council in 1580 for the outstanding debt (*APC*, xii; 1 June 1580). They granted him the right to levy £630 from money and goods forfeited by persons engaged in the unlawful exportation of corn from Devon (Patent Rolls, 23 Eliz. C66/2162: 22 October 1580).

33. BL Landowne MS 100/1, f. 6v.

34. PRO SP/15/25, 81; Collinson, *Frobisher*, pp. 212–18.

35. In 1584, Richard Hakluyt perceptively commented upon the utility of taking evangelical ministers in this and other English voyages: 'yet in very deede I was not able to name any one Infidell by them conuerted' (*Discourse of Western Planting*, p. 11).

36. Best: Collinson, pp. 228–31.

37. Andrews, 'The Elizabethan Seaman', p. 248.

38. The presence of the expedition's chief pilot on the *Thomas Allen*, and Gilbert Yorke's command thereof, indicates that she was intended to act as the *de facto* 'flag' of the noncompany vessels.

39. In contrast to those for the 1577 voyage, sources for 1578 are plentiful. There is Best's *Discourse* once more; Christopher Hall's ship's log for the *Thomas Allen* and, on the return passage, the *Ayde*, is comprehensive and uncensored (BL Harleian MS 167/42, ff. 184–200; hereafter Hall: 1578); the *True Report* of Thomas Ellis, one of the gentlemen who sailed in the *Ayde* (reproduced in Stefansson and McCaskill, *Frobisher*, II, pp. 33–45; hereafter Ellis: 1578); the account of Edward Selman, also in the *Ayde* (BL Harleian MS 167/40; hereafter Selman: this has been previously published – imperfectly – in Collinson (1867) and reprinted without correction in Stefansson and McCaskill; all references in the current work are to the original manuscript); the ship's log of Edward Fenton, captain of the *Judith* (Magdalene College Library, Cambridge; Pepys MS 2133, ff. 17–75; hereafter Fenton: 1578); and a fragmentary journal, unsigned but usually attributed to Charles Jackman, master of the *Judith* (BL Harleian MS 167/41; hereafter Jackman: 1578).

40. PRO SP/15/25, 146.

41. There is some disagreement as to the date upon which Frobisher's landfall in 'Friesland' occurred. Hall, Willes, Best, Jackman and Selman claim it was 20 June, Fenton the previous day. The present author has gone with the recollection of the majority.

42. Best: Collinson, p. 233; Hall: 1578, f. 188r.

43. Fenton: 1578, p. 21 (Fenton's journal is paginated, rather than foliated).

44. Ellis: 1578, p. 36.

45. Hall: 1578, f. 189r; Fenton: 1578, p. 24.

46. Hall: 1578, f. 189v–190r.

47. I.e., a pleasure.

48. Best: Collinson, p. 238.

49. As, undoubtedly, was the *Michael*, but her master's log has not survived.

50. Jackman: 1578, f. 182.

51. Fenton: 1578, pp. 25–6.

52. Best: Collinson, pp. 240–1.

53. Hall: 1578, f. 190v.

54. Best: Collinson, p. 246.

55. Lok claimed that even then, it was left to two mariners named Stuborn and Lunt to point out his error (BL Lansdowne MS 100/1, f. 8r). Thomas Stuborn and John Lunt had sailed in the 1577 voyage also, in the *Gabriel*.

56. Best: Collinson, p. 245.

57. Selman, f. 170r.

58. Best: Collinson, p. 246.

59. Ibid., pp. 246–7.
60. Ibid., p. 248.
61. Ibid., p. 250.
62. Ibid.
63. This was Lok's claim; BL Lansdowne MS 100/1, f. 8r.
64. Fenton: 1578, p. 32.
65. Ibid., p. 34.
66. Ibid., p. 38.
67. Selman, f. 172v.
68. The instructions are reproduced in Best: Collinson, pp. 256–8.
69. Or, possibly, the *Thomas of Ipswich*, if Ellis's version is more accurate.
70. BL Lansdowne MS 100/1, f. 7r.
71. Best: Collinson, p. 262.
72. With considerable (but ineffectual) foresight, Captain Tanfield of the *Thomas* of Ipswich had privily spoken to Best regarding Cox during their conference of that day: that he 'did not a little suspect the sayde Pylot Coxe, saying, that he had neyther opinion in the man of honest duetie, manhoode, or constancie' (Best: Collinson, pp. 264–5).
73. Respectively, the Ship's and Reservoir trenches.
74. Fenton: 1578, p. 50. His mortality list for the day included one Philip Ellard, 'a gent'.
75. Robinson was a persistently disruptive influence, and an enduring enemy to Fenton. Sailing in the 1582–3 Moluccas voyage, he responded to a general order forbidding the crew to go on-shore without leave: 'he woulde ask me [Fenton] leave butt go and comme as he listeth and cared not a farte for the best in the Shipp . . .' (Fenton's log, 16 June 1583; Taylor, *Fenton*, p. 147.
76. Selman, ff. 174v–175r. Lok later claimed (BL Lansdowne MS 100/1, f. 7r) that Frobisher had indeed set his seal to Fenton's commission; but only at the very hour of his departure from London, and upon the insistence of the commissioners for the voyage who had heard his tirades against the proposed colony and wished for some overt sign of his commitment to its foundation.
77. BL Lansdowne MS 100/1, f. 7v.
78. Selman, f. 175v.
79. See p. 281.
80. Fenton: 1578, p. 54; 23 August.
81. Ellis: 1578, p. 44.
82. Fenton: 1578, p. 69.
83. According to Lok (BL Lansdowne MS 100/1, f. 8r), Beare Sound was 'wheare most of their ladinge was had'.
84. Selman, f. 178v.
85. If this was the same, nailless pinnace that on 19–22 August had made the short but fraught voyage across Frobisher Bay to find the fleet, it seems that she had been substantially reinforced in the intervening days.
86. PRO SP/15/25, 146.
87. Hall: 1578, f. 197v.
88. Best: Collinson, p. 280.
89. Hall: 1578, f. 198v.
90. Fenton: 1578, p. 69.
91. *APC*, x, 29 September 1578.
92. Horsey was also a long-time acquaintance of Hugh Randall, her owner, and may have partly financed her outfitting for the voyage. In 1577, following the return of that year's

expedition, he put down his name as a prospective investor in the enterprise (PRO/SP/12/129, 44), but subsequently withdrew at some point prior to the despatch of the expedition that year. That withdrawal, and Randall's subsequent participation in the voyage, may not have been unrelated events.

93. Fenton: 1578, p. 73.

94. Thomas Wiars, boatswain of the *Emanuel of Bridgewater*, wrote a short report on this interesting Atlantic passage, which was later published by Hakluyt (*PN* 1589, p. 635). Wiars was described in the title thereof as a 'passenger' in the ship; possibly because he had shipped in her following his failed application to be a mariner in one of the official vessels of Frobisher's fleet, 'being found vnfytt for service' (HM 715, f. 181): an assessment which, in light of his observations during the return passage, appears to have been extremely percipient.

95. *APC*, xi, 25 March 1579. The locations from which the *Emanuel*'s cargo was mined are provided by Selman's account of the voyage, f. 177v.

96. *CSPI*, 74/56: 22 November 1580.

THIRTEEN: THE END OF THE ENTERPRISE

1. Abraham Fleming, *Rythme Decasyllabicall, upon this laste luckie voyage of worthie Capteine Frobisher 1577*; the first of two poems commissioned from him in the preface to Settle's *True Reporte*.

2. PRO EKR E164/36, p. 327.

3. For the building campaign at Dartford, see McDermott, 'Dartford furnaces', pp. 505–21.

4. PRO SP/12/125, 35.

5. *CSPS* 1568–79, 484.

6. Philip II to Mendoza, *CSPS*, 1568–79. 13 June 1578.

7. Ibid., 7 October 1578.

8. For the transcription of this report and possible identification of the 'spy', see Allaire, 'Martin Frobisher', pp. 581–5.

9. PRO SP/12/126, 20; Collinson, *Frobisher*, pp. 319–20.

10. PRO SP/12/126, 21; Collinson, *Frobisher*. p. 320.

11. PRO SP/12/127, 8; assay results reported by Lok, BL Lansdowne MS 100/1, ff. 9r, 11v.

12. This was Best's estimate. The difficulty of assessing post-voyage mortalities during the period is always a problem; morbidity was usually significant (c.f. Fenton's comment upon scurvy and 'other gingerfull diseases' in the *Judith*), and could only have been exacerbated by acute physical exhaustion.

13. Watt ('Medical Record', pp. 619–28) provides the most recent and comprehensive discussion of the mariners' ordeal.

14. Lok's accounts show that rates of pay for the common mariners and miners varied between 20–30 shillings per month, depending upon experience and/or seniority.

15. PRO EKR E164/36, pp. 159–64.

16. Ibid., pp. 105–8; another pitiable story was that of Nicholas Jones, a senior mariner who had sailed in the *Judith*. At the end of November 1578, Lok's account books showed his wages of £10 10sh. remained outstanding. Eleven days later, Jones, lying sick at the house of one John Evans in Limehouse, made out his will, leaving this sum to his host 'sayinge that he was the beste worthie thereof for he had been more like a father unto him than a friende . . .' (PRO EKR E164/36, p. 57; Probate 11/9171/16, f. 437).

17. Thomas Allen to the Council, 8 December 1578; PRO SP/12/127, 12.

18. PRO SP/12/129, 44 (i).

19. PRO SP/12/127, 20.

20. BL Lansdowne MS 100/1, f. 10r.

21. Ibid.

22. Neale's second audit, of January 1579, was later inserted in Lok's account books (PRO EKR E164/35, pp. 61–79), probably by Lok himself. It implied that Lok detained some £2,115 of the adventurers' funds in his hands at that date, though much of this was probably in the form of those goods and equipment 'paystered' around his house for want of alternative storage space.

23. PRO SP/12/149, 42 (xi): '. . . to require you to vse the best diligens ye may be able, for the furderyng of the departure of the said shippes as sone as may be . . . that forasmooche as by the generall assent of the venturars Michael Lok is appoynted to be Tresorer of the Companye, we thynk it most convenyent that the Charter-partyes of the freightment of the sayd shippes shold be made in hys name in the behalfe of the whole Companye.'

24. PRO EKR E164/36, 29.

25. Lok's imprisonments were almost certainly not consecutive. In his diary entry for 13 September 1580, John Dee recorded: 'Lock browght Benjamyn his sonne to me: his eldest sonne also, called Zacharie . . .' (Halliwell, *Diary of John Dee*, p. 8); yet by Lok's own testimony, between the years 1579 and 1581 he was to be imprisoned in every London gaol save Newgate, and wrote to the Privy Council from the Fleet in June 1581 to request a *quietus est* upon the bonds he had stood for the Queen's venture (BL Lansdowne MS 31, f. 42v).

26. PRO EKR E164/36, 332. As late as May 1581, the auditors Neale and Baynham noted that Allen still detained some £475 towards the unpaid freight charges of his ship. Borough, who briefly succeeded Allen as treasurer, was also cited in the report as detaining £17 10sh. 4d. 'for his owne paynes taken in the forsaid busynes'.

27. PRO EKR E164/35, 294.

28. PRO EKR E164/36, 336.

29. BL Lansdowne MS 100/1, f. 10v.

30. PRO SP/12/151, 17.

31. BL Lansdowne MS 100/1, f. 11v.

32. Frobisher's rough treatment of Edward Castelyn may in part have reflected a longstanding grudge; Castelyn was one of the small group of merchants who had profited hugely from the second Guinea voyage of 1554, in which Frobisher himself had proved so expendable.

33. BL Lansdowne MS 100/1, ff. 9r–9v, 11v–12r. Lok refers to Hawke as Frobisher's kinsman, and Frobisher himself refers to him as 'cozen' in his will. Allowing the broad latitude of the term 'cousin' in contemporary usage, their precise relationship remains unknown.

34. Ibid., ff. 12v–13r.

35. Camden, *History*, p. 216.

36. It has been suggested that Lok was never to be released from these bonds (Shammas, 'Invisible Merchant', p. 103). This seems highly unlikely. His personal loss of some £2,250 in the north-west enterprise effectively, if not legally, bankrupted him; and there is no evidence that he managed to recoup more than a fraction of that sum in the following decade (see McDermott, 'Michael Lok', pp. 132–5). It seems probable, therefore, that unless the Queen had determined to enjoy a particularly protracted, vicious and, ultimately, pointless revenge, these bonds were withdrawn or allowed to expire during one of Lok's several confinements.

37. PRO EKR E164/36, pp. 317–41.

38. Willan, *Russia Company*, p. 27, n. 2: 'Locke has the doubtful distinction of being considered the role model for Shylock by that curious group which regards the 17th Earl of Oxford as the author of Shakespeare's plays'.

INTERLUDE: FAME DEFERRED: 1579–85

1. Donno, *Madox*, p. 212.
2. *Cal. Patent Rolls*, viii, 19 Eliz.. Lok's name also appears in the 1604 charter of the resurrected Spanish Company (Croft, *Spanish Company*, document 641); see also McDermott, 'Michael Lok', p. 134 on Lok's continuing Spanish connections.
3. Parker, *Philip II*, p. 136.
4. Wernham, *Before the Armada*, pp. 329–30.
5. Geyl, *Revolt of the Netherlands*, pp. 152–60; MacCaffrey, *Queen Elizabeth and the Making of Policy*, pp. 218–31.
6. PRO SP/12/130, 10; Allen to Walsingham, 20 March 1579. The *Gabriel* was subsequently sold to James Beare and his brother Samuel for £60; the *Michael*, perhaps reflecting her reputation as an unlucky ship, raised a mere £48 16sh. 8d. (PRO EKR E164/35, 233; E164/36, 26).
7. PRO E351/2215: 'Martyn Furbusher Capitaine on her Ma(ies)ties Shipp named the Foresighte, transportinge of Duke Casamere ou(er) to Flushinge by the space of xxj dayes begin the xj[th] of Februar(ie) and endinge the iij[de] of Marche 1578(9) for his diet at xs p(er) diem . . .'.
8. BL Lansdowne MS 100/1, f. 12v. Lok is the only source for this alleged correspondence.
9. Stukeley found a more worthy crusade: he went off to serve with the army of King Sebastian, to perish gloriously at the battle of El Ksar el-Kebir with the flower of the Portuguese nobility.
10. *APC*, xi, 29 September 1580.
11. Winter's impressive 1560 Scottish campaign is summarized in Loades, *Tudor Navy*, pp. 210–12.
12. List of ships at Gillingham and Rochester, October–December 1580; derived from the declared accounts of the navy (PRO E351/2377) and noted in Glasgow, 'Elizabethan ships', pp. 157–65.
13. PRO SP/63/76, 71.
14. Rodger, *The Safeguard of the Sea*, I, p. 218.
15. PRO SP/12/151, 16.
16. PRO SP/40/1, 119.
17. PRO HCA 13/21–25, 14/14–23, *ad finem*. There is a contemporary (though entirely anecdotal) statement which gives a flavour of the problem (BL Add. MS 30222: quoted, with modernized spelling, in Senior, 'Judges of the High Court of Admiralty', p. 336): 'Note that in the time of Dr Lewes, there were so many piracies and spoils committed, that the Queen joined several Drs in commission with Dr Lewis, for his assistants in those cases of spoils'. Lewes was Judge of the Admiralty Court from 6 October 1558 until his death on 27 April 1584.
18. PRO SP/12/118, 26 (Proceedings of the piracy commissioners, October–November 1577) provides a pageant of known felons bailed upon fines of no more than £100.
19. Lloyd, *Dorset Elizabethans*, pp. 38–9.
20. PRO SP/12/234, 54; *APC*, xi, 19 March 1580. For attempts by judges of the Admiralty Court – particularly Dr Lewes's successor, Sir Julius Caesar – to have their authority upheld, see Andrews, *Elizabethan Privateering*, pp. 20–5.
21. Marsden, *Select Pleas*, I, xiv–xvi.

22. PRO HCA 14/22, 165, 181; discussed in L'Estrange-Ewen, 'Organized piracy', pp. 41–2.

23. One of the condemned men, William Valentine (alias Vaughan, alias Baugh), habitually extracted information by applying burning brands to the persons of his victims; another, Stephen Heynes (alias Carless) had on one occasion been begged by his own crew not to torture their captives further (ibid., pp. 37–8).

24. It has been pointed out that until 1580, Philip's was predominantly a Mediterranean galley fleet, built to counter the Ottoman threat (Quinn and Ryan, *England's Sea Empire*, pp. 91–3); with the Union of Crowns, he obtained the means to pursue more than a strictly defensive policy in the Atlantic.

25. His wife was the legitimate daughter of John III of Portugal, grandfather of Sebastian, the previous occupant of the throne.

26. *CSPS*, 1580–6; Mendoza to Philip II, 9 January 1581.

27. PRO SP/12/140, 44. Walsingham's petition closely resembles the 1573 proposal of Richard Grenville, from which it was probably derived (though there is no evidence that Grenville was personally involved with this new initiative).

28. *CSPS*, 1580–6, as dated.

29. Ibid.

30. Ibid., doc. no. 82. Bingham had commanded the *Swiftsure* in Winter's squadron at Smerwick (PRO E351/2216).

31. PRO SP/12/148, 46; reproduced in Taylor, *Fenton*, pp. 6–7.

32. Gregory may have been the 'master Gregory' who had charge of the ship *Christopher* during Drake's circumnavigation (Corbett, *Drake*, i, p. 228).

33. PRO SP/12/148, 47; Taylor, *Fenton*, pp. 7–8.

34. Donno, *Madox*, p. 19.

35. The First and Second Enterprises were probably considered concurrently, as they are outlined in the same document.

36. PRO SP/12/150, 96; Taylor, *Fenton*, p. 10.

37. *CSPS*, 1580–6, as dated.

38. In August, Burghley had set out a memorandum (BL Lansdowne MS 102, f. 104) which, though broadly favourable towards the proposed venture, had specifically identified Drake's presence thereon as a threat – in terms of the reprisals it might generate – to any and all English shipping falling within Philip II's grasp.

39. De la Mauvissière to Henry III, 9 April 1581; Bibliothèque Nationale, Les Cinq Cents de Colbert, no. 337; reproduced by Allaire, 'French reactions', p. 592.

40. Several commentators – exercised, perhaps, by the coincidence of certain names in both of these projects – have been tempted to assume a degree of continuity between the north-west enterprise of 1576–8 and the 1582 Moluccas scheme: even, perhaps, to consider one as the natural successor of the other. Rundall (*Narrative of Voyages*, p. 32) regarded the 1582 scheme as the fourth 'north-west' voyage; Rabb (*Enterprise and Empire*, p. 151) recognized the dissimilarities but ran the two ventures together in his computer-generated overview of Elizabethan investment; and even Manhart ('The English search', pp. 92–8), whose analysis of the north-west enterprise is otherwise perceptive, implies a continuity between the motives of the two enterprises. All appear to rely heavily upon the belief that Drake's interest in discovering the north-west passage not only survived his circumnavigation but formed a central aim of the 1582 expedition. However, as the original instructions for the voyage show, Frobisher was specifically ordered not to seek out the passage (BL Cotton MS Otho E VIII, f. 88). Only when he was safely removed from the enterprise was Fenton permitted, in the final version of the instructions, to 'bee inquisitive' regarding the passage – but again, only providing he did not attempt to sail

further north in the Pacific Ocean than 40°N (Hakluyt, *PN* 1589, p. 645); a qualification that effectively rendered the objective superfluous.

41. PRO SP/12/150, 96; BL Cotton MSS Otho E VIII, f. 105; Taylor, *Fenton*, pp. 10, 12.

42. PRO CO/1, 156; 1 October 1581: The purchase price was £2,800, of which £800 was to stand as Oughtred's venture in the enterprise.

43. BL Cotton MSS Otho E VIII, f. 86; Taylor, *Fenton*, pp. 18–19.

44. BL Cotton MSS Otho E VIII, ff. 82, 103; Taylor, *Fenton*, pp. 22, 27–8.

45. BL Cotton MSS Otho E VIII, f. 98 (not reproduced by Taylor).

46. BL Cotton MSS Otho E VIII, f. 87; Taylor, *Fenton*, p. 14.

47. The diary of Richard Madox (Donno, *Madox*, p. 89) is terse and uninformative: 'M. Furbusher was discharged of the viage and M. Fenton put in his place'.

48. Supra, p. 254.

49. Once at sea, however, Fenton took the opportunity of settling an old score. In his diary, Madox recorded: 'He [Fenton] told me how Furbusher delt with hym, very headly sure, and how that Furbusher was not the mariner he was taken to be as I easyly (be)leave' (Donno, *Madox*, p. 129: 6 May 1582).

50. BL Cotton MSS Otho E VIII, f. 251; quoted in Taylor, *Fenton*, p. 18.

51. BL Cotton MSS Otho E VIII, f. 151; Taylor, *Fenton*, pp. 35–6.

52. BL Cotton MSS Otho E VIII, f. 127 (fire-damaged); Taylor, *Fenton*, p. 34.

53. Donno, *Madox*, pp. 185, 187, 211–12; PRO EKR E164/35, p. 301.

54. BL Cotton MSS Otho E VIII, f. 127; Oughtred to Leicester, 12 March 1582; Taylor, *Fenton*, p. 34.

55. George Barne also formed an early and unfortunately accurate opinion of Fenton, if Madox's diary (29 May 1582) is to be trusted: 'The master [Christopher Hall] towld me Alderman Barne thowght our generaul but a folish flattering fretting creeper and so I fear he wil prov' (Donno, *Madox*, p. 139).

56. Madox's opinion of Hall, initially quite favourable, worsened as the voyage progressed. On 22 December 1582 (a few days before his own death at sea), he referred to the master as ' a vain and arrogant man who has learned to indulge his inclinations at the expense of others . . . and enhanced the strength of another while catering to himself and his own belly' (Donno, *Madox*, p. 267; modernized spelling).

57. Book of Oaths 1496–1704, Southampton Municipal Records; cited in Quinn, *Gilbert*, I, p. 58.

58. *CSPS*, 1580–6, as dated.

59. Richard Madox, 9 December 1582; Donno, *Madox*, p. 257.

60. Peckham's *True Reporte* is reproduced in Quinn, *Gilbert*, II, pp. 435–80.

61. Brudenell MS O.i. II; reproduced in Quinn, *Gilbert*, I, pp. 257–60.

62. Quinn, *Gilbert*, I, p. 79.

63. PRO SP/12/170, f. 2v–3r; quoted (with modernized spelling), in Taylor, *Writings and Correspondence*, p. 209.

64. Gad, *Greenland*, p. 196.

65. Zins, *England and the Baltic*, p. 70.

66. Diplomatarium Groenlandicum no. 13, p. 11; discussed in Gad, *Greenland*, p. 197.

67. Diplomatarium Groenlandicum no. 17, p. 12f; Gad, Greenland, p. 197.

68. PRO SP/12/186, 47.

FOURTEEN: BROKEN AMITY

1. Thomas Churchyard, *A prayse, and reporte of Maister Martyne Forboisher's Voyage* (London, 1578); quoted by Stefansson and McCaskill, *Frobisher*, II, p. 231.

2. Parker, *Philip II*, p. 157.

3. Ramsay, *Queen's Merchants*, p. 165. English cloths soon returned to the Netherlands via Hamburg and Emden, in defiance of Alva's prohibitions.

4. It is not within the scope of the present work to examine the growth of the 'Black Legend' of Spanish perfidy. Maltby's *Black Legend* remains the best analysis of this.

5. It has been estimated that during the years 1569–72, immediately following the English merchants' final abandonment of Antwerp for their new Hamburg mart, the shortfall in supplies of spices, sugar and other luxury goods formerly purchased in the Low Countries was probably made good by the activities of English privateers (Ramsay, *Queen's Merchants*, p. 145).

FIFTEEN: THE WEST INDIES RAID

1. Wernham, *Before the Armada*, p. 364: Mendoza had denied any involvement in the plot, claiming, magnificently, that he 'was not born to disturb kingdoms but to conquer them'.

2. Williamson, *Hawkins of Plymouth*, pp. 226–7; BL Lansdowne MS 41, f. 9; Keeler, *Drake's West Indian Voyage*, p. 10.

3. *CSPS*, 1580–6, 4 May 1580.

4. Corbett, *Spanish War*, p. xi.

5. PRO SP/12/180, 15; Corbett, *Spanish War*, p. 36 (modernized spelling).

6. Oppenheim, *Monson*, I, p. 126, n.8. Oppenheim credits Marsden's research on the point, which was confirmed subsequently by Andrews (Youings, *Raleigh in Exeter*, p. 13).

7. Andrews, *Elizabethan Privateering*, p. 92.

8. BL Lansdowne MS 100/1, f. 98; reproduced (with modernized spelling) in Corbett, *Spanish War*, pp. 69–74. The schedule (or a copy thereof) was taken on the voyage and – apparently – updated by Drake to include events occurring up to and including the sack of Santiago, after which it was probably sent back to England to apprise the Queen of his progress to date. Though the document is not signed or otherwise acknowledged either by the Queen or Burghley, its probable use as a means of communicating Drake's progress indicates that its provisions – in their entirety or as individual options – were almost certainly agreed prior to his departure from England. That approval, however tacit, carried implications that were far too sensitive to be certified overtly (however, see also Adams, 'Embargo', pp. 61–2, who casts doubt upon the significance of its contents).

9. The phrase is that of Wright, *Further English Voyages*, p. xxx.

10. The name *Primrose* was commonly bestowed upon English ships (both naval and privately owned) during the period, and there is no definitive proof that Frobisher's command was in fact the vessel that had brought back to England the *corregidor* of Biscay in May 1585. Mendoza's intelligences to Philip implied that she was Leicester's ship; Keeler (*Drake's West Indian Voyage*, p. 283) summarizes known references to a ship of that name, and confirms that a *Primrose* was partly owned by Hawkins but also by London merchants. Adams ('Embargo', p. 45) identifies the Biscayan *Primrose* unequivocally as belonging to William Bonde junior, though he cites no authority for this. In the absence of firm evidence otherwise, the present author agrees with the consensus that the vessel in Drake's 1585 fleet was *probably* that which had sailed from Biscay in May.

11. Keeler, *Drake's West Indian Voyage*, pp. 13 n.5, 283.

12. Corbett, *Drake*, II, p. 13; *APC*, xiv, p. 63.

13. Carleill's *Tiger* journal; Keeler, *Drake's West Indian Voyage*, pp. 72–3.

14. See p. 313 and n. 56.

15. In his despatch to Walsingham from Vigo, Carleill delicately observed that he had not been 'the most assured of her Ma(ies)ties p(er)serverance to let vs go forwarde' (PRO SP/12/183, 10; 11 October 1585).

16. Journal of the *Primrose*; Keeler, *Drake's West Indian Voyage*, p. 180.

17. BL Cotton MSS Otho E VIII, f. 235; Keeler, *Drake's West Indian Voyage*, p. 108.

18. PRO SP/12/183, 10.

19. It is strictly appropriate to refer to both the New Spain and Tierra Firme fleets as 'flotas'; however, the author will additionally refer throughout to the unofficial term – *galeones* – with which contemporaries often distinguished the ships bringing home the bounty of Tierra Firme from those of New Spain.

20. BL Lansdowne MS 43, ff. 20–1; discussed in Williamson, *Sir John Hawkins*, pp. 408–10.

21. *CSPV* 1581–91, p. 133; Keeler, *Drake's West Indian Voyage*, p. 89 n.2.

22. Master's journal of the *Galleon Leicester*, 28 October, 1586; Keeler, *Drake's West Indian Voyage*, p. 127.

23. Ibid., p. 128.

24. BL Cotton MSS Otho E VIII, f. 235; anonymous newsletter reproduced in Keeler, *Drake's West Indian Voyage*, p. 110; the *Tiger* journal (ibid., p. 95) corroborates this.

25. Walter Bigges, *A Summarie and True Discourse of Sir Frances Drake's West Indian Voyage* (London, Richard Field, 1589); Keeler, *Drake's West Indian Voyage*, p. 234. Bigges, a soldier, was one of the land-captains in the West Indies raid.

26. Ibid., p. 227.

27. 'Whom the Spaniardes meetinge cut of hys head & ryppnge hys bellie tooke owt his hart & carried them awaie but let his boddie lie' (Journal of the *Primrose*; Keeler, *Drake's West Indian Voyage*, p. 189).

28. Journal of the *Leicester*; Keeler, *Drake's West Indian Voyage*, p. 148. The steward, Thomas Ogle, apparently confessed his crime 'and died penitently'. Bigges's *Summarie* does not discuss the episode in detail; it merely refers to 'an odious matter'. The severity of Ogle's sentence – for a crime that was, to say the least, an habitual one in long sea voyages – may have reflected the fact that the offence had been perpetrated in the *Bark Talbot*'s steward's room.

29. Journal of the *Leicester*; Keeler, *Drake*, p. 142.

30. Quinn, *Gilbert*, I, p. 40.

31. The phrase is that of the author of the *Leicester* journal; Keeler, *Drake's West Indian Voyage*, p. 143.

32. Ibid., pp. 145–6.

33. Journal of the *Primrose*; Keeler, *Drake's West Indian Voyage*, p. 187 ('Wee fownde abowt 20 sicke persons all Nigros, lyinge of verie fowle & fylthie Diseases'); PRO SP/12/186, 20; intelligence from Spain, 16 January 1586; Corbett, *Spanish War*, p. 59. Williamson (*Hawkins of Plymouth*, p. 292) has also pointed out that the high proportion of soldiers carried in the ships meant that the expedition was over-manned, at a ratio of c. one man per one and a half tons of shipping; doubtless a contributory factor to the high mortality rate.

34. Corbett, *Spanish War*, p. 70; the schedule had anticipated the fleet's arrival at Dominica on 29 November.

35. Bigges, *Summarie*; Keeler, *Drake's West Indian Voyage*, p. 238.

36. Corbett, *Spanish War*, p. 70.

37. *Audiencia* of Santo Domingo to Philip II, 14 February 1586; in Wright, *Further English Voyages*, p. 32.

38. Grenville's expedition of five ships and two pinnaces had sailed from England on 9 April 1585, carrying the first Roanoke colony.

39. Journal of the *Primrose*; Keeler, *Drake's West Indian Voyage*, p. 194.

40. A Fugger news letter, written by an unnamed correspondent from Santo Domingo in February 1586 (following the English withdrawal), offered a different reason for their deaths: 'The enemy brought with them a parson of the Lutheran Faith in order that he should proselytize. When two preaching monks opposed this, they were imprisoned, hanged and died martyrs' (Klarwill, *The Fugger Newsletters*, p. 93).

41. Journal of the *Leicester*; Keeler, *Drake's West Indian Voyage*, p. 151.

42. Bigges, *Summarie*; Keeler, *Drake's West Indian Voyage*, p. 259.

43. A Fugger news letter from Madrid dated 5 April 1586 suggested that Drake's haul had been approximately two million ducats (Klarwill, *The Fugger Newsletters*, p. 103).

44. Ibid., p. 159.

45. See Wright, *Further English Voyages*, p. 24, n.2; it seems that word of the sack of Santo Domingo did not reach Cartagena until 24/25 January.

46. Keeler, *Drake's West Indian Voyage*, p. 161.

47. Journal of the *Primrose*; Keeler, *Drake's West Indian Voyage*, pp. 198–9.

48. Archivo General de Indias, 72/5/18, Santa Fé 89/5; Wright, *Further English Voyages*, pp. 74–5. This was the claim of several of his subordinates, who stated that they had wished to attack the English fleet in the outer harbour. However, the contradictory (and self-serving) claims of the various deponents who gave their testimony in this document make any single version of events unreliable.

49. Keeler, *Drake*, p. 200; the anonymous author of the *Primrose Journal*, perhaps overplaying the drama, claimed that the gunfire from the galleys was 'woonderful'. It seems to have been anything but that in reality.

50. Bigges's *Summarie*; Keeler, *Drake's West Indian Voyage*, p. 249.

51. Journal of the *Leicester*; Keeler, *Drake's West Indian Voyage*, p. 164.

52. Archivo General de Indias, 72/5/18, Santa Fé 89/3; Wright, *Further English Voyages*, p. 82. The claim is given particular attention in Kelsey, p. 267, but Mirabal's source of information is obscure; in referring to the incident, Mirabal himself stated only 'it was said that . . .'.

53. Kelsey (op. cit.) believes that the wording in Bigges's *Summarie* implies that the attack upon the harbour blockhouse was a main attempt, and not a diversion. The present author cannot find the same implication therein: 'At this instant we might heare some peeces of artillerie discharged, with diuers small shot towards the harbour, which gaue us to vnderstand, according to the order set downe in the euening before by our Generall, that the Vizeadmirall accompanied with Captaine Venner, Captaine White, and Captaine Crosse, with other sea Captaines, and with diuers Pinnaces and boates *should giue some attempt* vnto the litle fort standing on the entrie of the inner hauen, neare adioyning to the towne, though to small purpose, for that place was strong . . .' (Keeler, *Drake's West Indian Voyage*, p. 249; present author's emphasis). Note also Bigges's only other reference to the incident, in his commentary appended to the Boazio map of Cartagena in the *Summarie's West Indian Voyage*, where the action is described thus: 'Certaine Pinnaces of ours which intertained a little skirmishe with the Fort of the Hauen . . .'. There is little here to suggest that Frobisher's force was expected to carry the harbour chain and take the blockhouse.

54. Journal of the *Leicester*; Keeler, *Drake's West Indian Voyage*, p. 166

55. Archivo General de Indias, 72/4/6. Santa Fé 37/1; Wright, *Further English Voyages*, p. 161.

56. Journal of the *Leicester*; Keeler, *Drake's West Indian Voyage*, pp. 171–3.

57. Journal of the *Primrose*; Keeler, *Drake's West Indian Voyage*, p. 203.

58. Keeler, *Drake's West Indian Voyage*, pp. 210–77.

59. Again, the shining optimism is that of the provisional timetable in Drake's schedule; Corbett, *Spanish War*, p. 72.

60. Quinn, *Roanoke*, I, p. 32.
61. The sources disagree upon the date here; the *Primrose* Journal has it as 27 May, the Boazio map text the following day, and Bigges's *Summarie*, 30 May. The present author has arbitrarily fallen with the only account that was written on the day itself, or very soon thereafter.
62. Bigges, *Summarie*; Keeler, *Drake's West Indian Voyage*, p. 269.
63. Ibid., p. 270.
64. Quinn, *Roanoke*, I, p. 289.
65. This is Quinn's suggestion: ibid., p. 291, n.1.
66. Quinn's comment regarding English settlement in the New England area *(New American World*, III, p. xviii) is apposite in this respect: 'The English explorations were extensive, and we still do not understand fully why they did not master before 1612 the art of establishing English communities there.'
67. The fate of the Roanoke colonists is comprehensively discussed in Quinn, *The Lost Colonists*.
68. BL Lansdowne MS 52/36; reproduced in Corbett, *Spanish War*, p. 92.
69. PRO SP/12/188, 1; ibid., p. 66.
70. PRO SP/12/200, 57.
71. See p. 332.
72. PRO SP/12/195, 79: 'his man Cottell died in the journey who had the chief charge of his accounts, whereby he could not but forget much and receive great loss' (Corbett, *Spanish War*, pp. 92–4: modernized spelling).
73. *APC*, xv, pp. 75–6.
74. Ibid., xvi, p. 63.
75. BL Harleian MS 4630, f. 192.
76. Prerogative Court of Canterbury (PCC) Wills; 46 Scott.
77. PRO SP/12/193, 69.
78. Journal of the *Leicester*; Keeler, *Drake's West Indian Voyage*, p. 130.

SIXTEEN: THE SLIDE: 1587–88

1. Wernham, *Before the Armada*, p. 376.
2. Quotation from Elliot, *Europe Divided*, p. 316.
3. *CSPS*, 1580–86, 237.
4. Pierson, *Armada*, pp. 63–4.
5. PRO SP/12/184, 24; Corbett, *Spanish War*, p. 77. See also Parker (*Philip II*, p. 217) on the laxity of Spanish security measures.
6. For the Babington plot, (and Walsingham's direction thereof), see Pollen, *Mary Queen of Scots, passim.*
7. Wernham, *Before the Armada*, p. 383.
8. *CSPV*, 24 October 1586.
9. Oppenheim, *Monson*, I, p. 134.
10. Corbett, *Spanish War*, pp. 192–3; Pierson, *Armada*, pp. 65–6.
11. PRO SP/12/200, 1; Corbett, *Spanish War*, pp. 99–100; the Levanters included the *Merchant Royal*, which was to do sterling service alongside Frobisher's *Triumph* at Portland Bill in the following year.
12. PRO SP/12/200, 17; Corbett, *Spanish War*, p. 100.
13. Kamen, *Philip of Spain*, p. 273.

SEVENTEEN: THE WINTER GUARD

1. *CSPS*, 1587–1603; 27 May, 6 June, 20 June 1587.
2. Corbett, *Drake*, II, pp. 104–5.
3. PRO SP/12/209, 15.
4. PRO E351/2224.
5. Frobisher to Leicester, 17 September 1587; BL Cotton MSS Galba D II, f. 59: '. . . and presintelye my Lorde seinte me order to tayke in the tresure / and so Refared vnto yo(u)r Excelinces derecksione for thatt sarves . . .'.
6. *CSPS*, 1587–1603; 28 July 1587: despatch entitled 'The new confidant's advices from England'.
7. Ibid., 2 October 1587.
8. PRO SP/12/209, 12, 15; BL Harleian MS 6994, f. 120; in Laughton, *State Papers*, I, pp. 103, 106, 150. All quotations taken from Laughton are presented with modernized spelling and grammar.
9. PRO SP/12/211, 37; Laughton, *State Papers*, I, p. 210.
10. PRO SP/12/211, 18, 26; Laughton, *State Papers*, I, pp. 200, 202.
11. PRO SP/12/209, 89; Laughton, *State Papers*, I, p. 146.
12. Oppenheim, *Royal Navy*, p. 161; Parker, 'Dreadnought Revolution', p. 289.
13. PRO SP/12/208, 35;4 Laughton, *State Papers*, I, pp. 53–4.
14. The portrait in the Museo Naval, Madrid depicts a distinguished yet snow-bearded old man.
15. Pierson, *Armada*, p. 43.
16. For the Armada's outfitting, Pierson (*Armada*) and Fernandez-Armesto (*Spanish Armada*) are comprehensive.
17. Fernandez-Armesto, *Spanish Armada*, p. 10.
18. Pierson, *Armada*, p. 100.
19. Fernandez-Armesto, *Spanish Armada*, pp. 4–7.
20. Ibid., p. 10. A quintal varied between 101.5 lbs and 155 lbs; though usually equating to the former (Oppenheim, *Royal Navy*, p. 398, n.2).
21. Drake later told Petruccio Ubaldino, his uncritical and trusting Italian biographer, that this commission (not extant) ordered him to go to the Spanish coast and disrupt any concentration of the Armada whilst it lay in port (Corbett, *Drake*, II, p. 125). This seems to be a case of wishful thinking, or of history re-written. As we have seen, the Queen took great care during these months to fight off the urgings of Drake, Hawkins and Frobisher that the war should be carried to the Spanish coast.
22. PRO SP/12/208, 53; Laughton, *State Papers*, I, p. 64.
23. On some of the West Country ports' contributions to the English fleet, see Lloyd, *Dorset Elizabethans*, pp. 162–200.
24. PRO SP/12/208, 52; Laughton, *State Papers*, I, pp. 62–3.
25. The movements of Howard's captains between their various commands, summarized from the declared accounts of the navy (PRO E351/2225), is presented with admirable thoroughness in Oppenheim, *Monson*, I, pp. 159–61.
26. PRO SP/12/204, 20; Corbett, *Spanish War*, p. 225. It should be noted, however, that the report – by the shipwrights Matthew Baker and Peter Pett – may have been more critical than necessary, as it provided a rare opportunity for them to criticize their old enemy Hawkins (Williamson, *Sir John Hawkins*, pp. 374–6).
27. PRO SP/12/212, 61; Laughton, *State Papers*, I, pp. 274–5.
28. PRO E351/2225.

29. PRO SP/12/185, 34; Corbett, *Spanish War*, p. 301; Oppenheim, *Royal Navy*, p. 124.
30. BL Cotton MSS Vespasian C VIII, f. 12.
31. PRO SP/12/209, 40; Laughton, *State Papers*, I, p. 124.
32. PRO SP/12/209, 99; Laughton, *State Papers*, I, p. 159.
33. PRO SP/12/210, 35; 211, 70; 212, 16; Laughton, *State Papers*, I, pp. 186–7, 235, 243–4.
34. PRO SP/12/210, 36; Laughton, *State Papers*, I, p. 190.
35. PRO SP/12/211, 50; Laughton, *State Papers*, I, pp. 225–6.
36. PRO SP/12/211, 8; Laughton, *State Papers*, I, p. 193.
37. PRO/SP/12/211, 51; 12/211, 53; 12/212, 10; Laughton, *State Papers*, I, pp. 227, 228, 238–9.
38. Pierson, *Armada*, pp. 116–17.
39. PRO SP/12/212, 17; Laughton, *State Papers*, I, p. 247.
40. PRO SP/12/209, 82; 212, 30, 61(i); Laughton, *State Papers*, I, pp. 141, 251, 276–9.
41. PRO SP/12/212, 66; Laughton, *State Papers*, I, p. 284.
42. PRO SP/12/212, 80; Laughton, *State Papers*, I, p. 288.
43. Not to be identified with the ship, partly owned by John Hawkins, that Frobisher briefly commanded in the campaign of 1592 and again in a privately financed voyage during 1593.

EIGHTEEN: THE 'WARRE OF 21 JULIE': THE ARMADA CAMPAIGN

1. The instructions are reproduced in Duro, *La Armada invencible*, docs. 18–24, and discussed more recently in Parker, *Philip II*, pp. 196–7, and Pierson, *Armada*, pp. 108–11.
2. Parker, *Philip II*, p. 196.
3. Pierson, *Armada*, p. 113. In fact, this figure, given by Parma in March, was pessimistic. By July, he had a total of 26,000 men allocated to the English campaign, grouped in four *tercios* cantoned in Artois and southern Flanders (O'Donnell, 'Army of Flanders', in Rodriguez-Salgado and Adams, *Gran Armada*, pp. 231–2).
4. Thompson, 'Spanish Armada Guns', p. 370 (c.f. Corbett, *Drake*, II, pp. 194–201). Thompson's work, based upon material from the Simancas archives, has superseded the earlier work of Lewis ('Armada guns', *MM*, vols xxxviii, xxxix), which concluded that the English and Spanish fleets had enjoyed a broad parity in armament.
5. Loades, *Tudor Navy*, p. 244.
6. Rodger ('Broadside gunnery') provides an excellent de-bunking of myths regarding contemporary tactical skills. It should be noted that the contemporary use of the term 'broadside' is not significant in proving the existence of the tactic; this had been a generic reference to a ship's flank armament for much of the sixteenth century.
7. See, for example, Martin and Parker, *Spanish Armada*, pp. 165–6.
8. Frobisher's own record during the campaign, particularly in the fight off Gravelines, offers much evidence of this method of ship-fighting.
9. There is only one contemporary battle – or, rather, skirmish – in which English gunnery appears to have proved unequivocally fatal to an enemy: that of San Juan de Ulua in 1568, where Hawkins's ships destroyed two Spanish galleons in little more than an hour. However, the Spanish ships were under peculiar disadvantages from the first. Their officers were not, apparently, present during the fight (Williamson, *Hawkins of Plymouth*, p. 143); also, 'lucky' shots from the English ships blew up one of the galleons and fired the other, which, without a coordinated or supervised effort to extinguish the flames, subsequently burned down to the water-line. Neither ship, therefore, may be said to have been sunk by the weight or efficacy of English gunfire alone.
10. PRO SP/84/26/57; Laughton, *State Papers*, II, p. 259.

11. The estimate was that of Alonso de Vanegas, an artillery captain on the *San Martin* (Duro, *La Armada invencible*, doc. 185). Arguments on the reason for this massive disparity have exercised naval historians for years. Most recently, Martin and Parker (*Spanish Armada*, pp. 200–2) have examined the issue in great depth; they point out that shortage of ammunition was not a factor here: that most of the Spanish ships' stocks of heavy shot were not fired during the campaign. Contemporary Spanish tactics of dispersing their gun-crews to boarding parties, and inherent flaws in their technology (particularly with respect to gun-carriage design) seem to have made the repeated reloading and firing of their larger guns a much more difficult process than for their English opponents.

12. Casado Soto ('Atlantic Shipping in sixteenth-century Spain and the 1588 Armada' in Rodriguez-Salgado and Adams *Gran Armada*, pp. 95–133) disagrees. His piece is well argued, yet the present author regards the continuing controversy on the accurate measurement of contemporary tonnage as too open to allow such assured conclusions.

13. On the quality of Spanish seamanship during the campaign, see Duro, *La Armada invencible*, II, pp. 102–5.

14. Mattingly, *Armada*, p. 280.

15. As Martin and Parker have shown (*Spanish Armada*, pp. 29–32), the Spanish 'squadrons' were administrative, rather than operational, entities. From the first phase of the battle, the most weatherly and well armed vessels in the Armada (among them the squadron flagships) were despatched to wherever they were most needed in the mêlée – a tactic which, inevitably, resulted in the greatest degree of battle attrition upon the best Spanish ships.

16. PRO SP/12/212, 82; BL Cotton MSS Otho E IX, f. 185v; Laughton, *State Papers*, I, pp. 289–90, 299.

17. PRO SP/12/212, 69; Seymour to Walsingham, 20 July 1588; Laughton, *State Papers*, I, pp. 285–6.

18. Parker, *Philip II*, p. 227.

19. BL Cotton MSS Julius F X, f. 113; Laughton, *State Papers*, I, p. 10. The 'Relation of the Proceedings', the only semi-official English description of the fighting, was neither signed nor attributed. However, its perspective and circumspection make it probable that the document was set down, if not in Howard's own words, then at his instigation. Corbett (*Drake*, ii, p. 443) had no doubt that this was Howard's *apologia*; but his evidence, based upon an Italian translation of the original, is hardly definitive.

20. Account of Emanuel van Meteran; Hakluyt, *PN* 1598–1600, iv, p. 200; see also Pierson, *Armada*, p. 238; Martin and Parker, *Spanish Armada*, p. 38.

21. Oppenheim, *Monson*, II, p. 163 (modernized spelling).

22. The gallease portrayed in the foreground of the anonymous 'Greenwich Cartoon' (National Maritime Museum, A6715) has its principal broadside armament sited immediately above the rowing deck.

23. This was the vessel commanded by Francis Burnell, with a crew of seventy men (Laughton, *State Papers*, II, p. 325); it should not of course be confused with the Queen's ship of the same name, commanded by Edward Fenton during the battle.

24. The captain of musketeers in the *San Lorenzo* apparently believed the battle was winnable, and later claimed that he urged Moncada to increase speed to come up to the *Triumph* (see Martin and Parker, *Spanish Armada* (1999 edn) p. 155). However, this seems to be a case of retrospective bravado. He also admitted the accuracy and 'extraordinary speed' of the *Triumph*'s guns, and Moncada's reluctance to draw closer to the English vessel indicates that he concurred with only the latter opinion.

25. Mattingly, *Armada*, p. 298.
26. Laughton, *State Papers*, II, p. 269 (modernized spelling). The 'isle' to which Howard referred was Wight.
27. Mattingly (*Armada*, p. 307) was the first to identify the relevance of the pattern of currents off Dunnose to this day's fighting.
28. According to a Spanish eye-witness, Pedro Coco Calderon, '. . . she [the *Triumph*] got out so quickly that the galleon San Juan and another fast-sailing ship – the two fastest in the Armada – seemed in comparison with her to be standing still' (quoted in Howarth, *Voyage of the Armada*, p. 146).
29. Stow, *Annales*, p. 1255.
30. See Martin and Parker (*Spanish Armada*, p. 287, n.3) on the enduring confusion regarding the time that Parma claimed he would require to embark.
31. Corbett, *Drake*, ii, p. 279. Corbett consistently portrays the Armada campaign as a personal triumph for Drake, with his compatriots – including the Lord Admiral himself – as supporting actors in the drama. The overwhelming evidence of contemporary records, and the very nature of a series of confused engagements in which some 300 ships participated, make this a highly improbable interpretation.
32. PRO SP/12/214, 63–4. The quotations are from the testimony of Matthew Starke of the *Revenge*, present when Frobisher made his accusations.
33. PRO E351/2225.
34. The claim is that of McFee, *Sir Martin Frobisher*, p. 237.
35. PRO E351/2227, 2229, 2231; AO1 1687/28.
36. PRO SP/12/230, 113.
37. *CSPS*, 1587–1603; 26 November, 1588
38. *APC*, xvi, 4 August 1588.
39. PRO SP/12/215, 41; Laughton, *State Papers*, II, p. 139.
40. PRO SP/12/215, 1; Laughton, *State Papers*, II, p. 108.
41. When Sheffield, listening to Frobisher's protracted rant against Drake, discovered Matthew Starke's identity – and therefore, his probable loyalties – he dismissed him from their presence with a curt 'I have no more to say unto you; you may depart' (PRO SP/12/214, 64: Laughton, *State Papers*, II, p. 103).
42. PRO SP/12/214, 70; 11 August 1588; Laughton, *State Papers*, II, p. 101.

NINETEEN: NARROW SEAS AND TREASURE FLEETS

1. BL Cotton MSS Otho EIX, f. 266.
2. PRO SP/12/215, 6.
3. PRO E351/2225; SP/12/215, 58–9, 66: Laughton, *State Papers*, II, pp. 162, 167, 184.
4. PRO E351/2225.
5. BL Lansdowne MS 62/11.
6. PRO E351/2226.
7. *CSPS*, 1587–1603: 12 January, 3 April 1589. The event that kept this rumour alive may have been Frobisher's further transfer, from the *Vanguard* to the *Rainbow*, on 1 April (PRO E351/2226).
8. BL Add. MS 5664 is a compendium of correspondence from the French Ambassador to Sir Julius Caesar, complaining of English depredations upon French shipping. Frobisher's name appears *ad finem* therein.
9. In fact, the commission authorizing letters of marque against 'Leaguer' vessels was not

issued until November of that year (PRO HCA 14126, 51; reproduced in Marsden, *Law and Custom*, I, pp. 252–3).

10. The various correspondences relating to the case of the *Gerosme* are contained in PRO SP/78/271, 274, 281, 290, 330, 342.

11. PRO SP/12/233, 113, 117, 119; SP/12/234, 1, 37.

12. PRO SP/84/34, 98; *APC*, xvii, 27 April 1589, 8 May, 1589.

13. PRO SP/105/91, 6.

14. BL Lansdowne MS 62/21.

15. The cost of their transportation is given in the declared accounts of the navy, PRO E351/2226.

16. PRO SP/12/224, 12.

17. *CSPF*, 1 May 1589; mentioned in a letter from the Council to Sir John Conway at Ostend. Many of the English soldiers in the Netherlands had been ear-marked for the expedition to Spain and Portugal, though in the event, Drake and Norreys had departed with only six of thirteen footbands promised from this resource (Wernham, *Norris and Drake*, pp. xxiv–xxvi).

18. PRO SP/12/224, 26.

19. PRO SP/12/225, 32; 19 July 1589; *APC*, xvii, 27 July 1589.

20. Cummins, *Drake*, p. 226.

21. Details from the accounts of Edward Wright and Johann Huighen van Linschoten, in Hakluyt, *PN* 1598–1600, vii, pp. 1–31, 62–6.

22. PRO SP/12/225, 74.

23. PRO E351/2226.

24. Ibid.

25. PRO SP/78/20, 62.

26. PRO SP/12/225, 32.

27. The number was provided by Linschoten (Hakluyt, *PN*, 1598–1600, vii, p. 66), though he mistakenly assumed twelve of these ships to have been captured by Frobisher subsequently.

28. PRO SP/94/3, 4; testimony given to Pedro de Valdes, 21 December 1589.

29. Account of Edward Wright: Hakluyt, *PN* 1598–1600, vii, p. 30. Wright (who had only third-hand information on the incident) may have misidentified these Spanish ships. According to Linschoten, the flagship of the *flota* was not captured, but sank with all hands in a storm between Angra and Lisbon, whilst the vice-admiral was grounded at Setubal (ibid., p. 69). Wernham (*After the Armada*, p. 237) accepts Wright's version, and places the sinking of the flagship off Eddystone, though with the recovery of all of her crew. Absent further information, the precise identity of Frobisher's prizes remains ambiguous.

30. Oppenheim, *Monson*, i, p. 239. The prizes, unloaded at Plymouth, carried cargoes of blockwood, silks, hides, cochineal, ginger and sugar, which were sold off in January for a total of £15,050 (BL Lansdowne MS 62/11, 65/30); the cost of setting out Frobisher's ships had been £11,320.

31. PRO SP/94/3, 34: Testimony of Porta to the Privy Council, 13 April 1590.

32. Oppenheim, *Monson*, i, 141. In the midst of war, Ralegh had offered both his services and a ship to Philip – for a suitable price.

33. PRO E351/2227.

34. *APC*, xix; 2 January 1590.

35. See MacCaffrey, *Elizabeth I: War and Politics*, pp. 137–42, and Wernham, *After the Armada*, pp. 174–9 for Willoughby's disastrous (and unauthorized) expedition.

36. *CSPF*, 6 February 1590.

37. *CSPS* 1587–1603, 4 March 1590.

38. PRO SP/12/229, 2; SP/12/230, 66.

39. PRO SP/12/230, 80.

40. PRO E351/2227: '. . . beinge sent by Specyall order from the Lordes of her Ma(ies)ties moste honorable previe Councell . . . for the better discoverie of the pretence and landinge of a spanishe fleete that was notised then to be abroade at Seas . . .'.

41. *APC*, xix; 11 June 1590.

42. Klarwill, *The Fugger Newsletters*, pp. 142–3 (Fugger newsletter from Venice, 12 January 1590): '. . . this delay in the arrival of the first ships is the fact that they took their course several degrees higher than is their wont in order to escape the English cruisers who were waiting for them in the usual degree.'

43. PRO E351/2227.

44. PRO SP/12/233, 4.

45. Oppenheim, *Monson*, i, p. 249.

46. PRO E351/2226. The only source for the Fayal episode, which seems to reveal an uncharacteristic degree of circumspection in Frobisher's character, was Linschoten (Hakluyt, *PN* 1598–1600, vii, pp. 74–5); Oppenheim (*Monson*, i, p. 249) considers the story to have been Spanish propaganda, innocently repeated.

47. PRO SP/12/234, 75; Oppenheim, *Monson*, i, p. 250.

48. PRO SP/12/232, 13; reproduced in Jones, *Sir Martin Frobisher*, pp. 294–6 (modernized spelling). The missing words proposed here are those of the present author.

49. Wright, *Further English Voyages*, pp. lxxv–lxxix.

50. Hakluyt, *PN* 1598–1600, vii, p. 74.

51. This was not an isolated complaint. Howard was obliged to write to Caesar on 24 September, requiring him to assemble all English captains known or suspected to be dropping off their prizes in Ireland and elsewhere in order to avoid payment of the French King's fifth (and, of course, Howard's tenth), 'and compell them to make satisfactione unto the saied Ambassador of the saied dewties' (PRO HCA 13/27, 133).

52. PRO SP/78/21, 1; SP84/38, 21, 31, 50, 76, 105, 111; *APC*, xix, 25 July 1590, 20 November 1590.

53. *APC*, xix; 12 October 1590.

54. PRO SP/12/234, 13.

55. Somerset Record Office: Phellips family papers, 1590.

56. PRO SP/84/42, 504; HCA 24/66, 124; 24/68, 177.

57. PRO SP/12/234, 43.

58. Scammell, 'Sinews of War', pp. 353–7.

59. Writing to the Grand Duke of Tuscany in 1600, Howard (now earl of Nottingham) confirmed that 'all food, warlike and shipping stores' carried by any vessel, neutral or otherwise, and intended for Spain, had been good prize for English privateers since the 'proclamation' (actually, an order in council) of 1589 (PRO HCA 14/34, 96).

60. PRO SP/78/19, 18.

61. Martin junior's immediate patrimony is not clear, and it is possible that either John or Davy Frobisher was his father. However, it seems move likely that he was the son of a privateer, not of a merchant-tailor who had no known connection with his brothers' darker trade.

62. He is named as captain of the *Dreadnought* during the 1592 cruise in the declared accounts of the navy (PRO E351/2227), upon wages of 2sh. 6d. per day.

63. Somerset Record Office: Phellips family papers, 1590.

64. PRO SP/78/22, 110.

65. PRO SP/12/238, 1; SP/84/34, 98. Julius Caesar had written to the Privy Council on 9
    September 1589, asking them to order Frobisher to pay this amount: perhaps an indica-
    tion that the judge of the Court of Admiralty no longer believed that he had the effec-
    tive authority to do so. Moucheron may have been Balthazar de Moucheron, merchant
    of Antwerp (Geyl, *Revolt of the Netherlands*, p. 238).

66. PRO SP/12/238, 61.

67. PRO SP/12/238, 171.

68. PRO SP/12/240, 66.

69. BL Harleian MS 4630, f. 190v.

70. BL Add. MS 39852, f.4: release by Martin and Dorothy Frobisher, executrix of
    Withypool's will, of all claims thereon to Bassingborne and Philip Gawdy of Norfolk,
    19 October 1590.

TWENTY: THE *MADRE DE DIOS*

1. Williamson (*Hawkins of Plymouth*, p. 323) suggests that had the Queen set out more
   ships into the Atlantic in 1592–4, Philip's empire may well have been plunged into enduring bankruptcy (the actual numbers of royal ships attached to raiding expeditions in
   these years were, respectively, two, two and zero). However, given the poor results of the
   1589/90 campaigns, and the increasingly dispersed voyages undertaken by the returning
   Spanish plate fleets, this is by no means certain.

2. Oppenheim, *Monson*, i, pp. 226–37; Andrews, *Elizabethan Privateering*, p. 72.

3. Flicke had missed Howard but not the Spaniards; he had taken prizes with cargoes worth
   £18,000, of which his merchant backers retained £6,000 (Andrews, *Elizabethan Privateering*, p. 248). Flicke's own report of his voyage was reproduced by Hakluyt, *PN*
   1598–1600, vii, pp. 56–62.

4. Oppenheim (*Royal Navy*, p. 166) points out that the *Foresight* had been variously rated
   as low as 250 tons and as high – as she now was – as 450 tons, depending on where the
   Queen's advantage lay under the rules of consortship that determined the split of prize
   monies between ships. Oppenheim gives her true tonnage as marginally more than 300
   (ibid., p. 124).

5. Notwithstanding Oppenheim's claim to the contrary (*Monson*, i, p. 283), surviving financial accounts for the voyage (National Library of Wales (hereafter NLW), Chirk Castle
   MS 12629, ff. 8–37) make it clear that Ralegh had the paramount responsibility for outfitting the fleet, despite the early initiative of the London 'element'.

6. BL Harleian MS 168/57.

7. Murdin, *Burghley Papers*, p. 663; quoted in Oppenheim, *Monson*, i, p. 284 (modernized
   spelling).

8. Williamson, *Hawkins of Plymouth*, p. 325.

9. This may have been William Monson, though he is not specifically identified in any
   extant account (see n. 22 below).

10. The inference, made by several modern commentators, appears to draw provenance from
    the account of the taking of the *Madre de Dios* published by Hakluyt (*PN* 1598–1600,
    vii, p. 107), which claimed that it was Ralegh who directed the dispositions of the fleet.
    Frobisher may well have accepted certain of his suggestions, but having entirely super-
    seded him upon the Queen's authority, he was hardly obliged to do so.

11. Hatfield House, Salisbury MSS, 23 May 1592.

12. Oppenheim, *Monson*, i, p. 286.

13. This was the same Crosse who had made the assault upon the blockhouse at Cartagena with Frobisher some six years earlier.
14. Hakluyt, *PN* 1598–1600, vii, p. 113.
15. BL Lansdowne MS 70, f. 82.
16. Hakluyt, *PN* 1598–1600, vii, p. 114.
17. Statement of John Hampton, master of the *Foresight*; BL Lansdowne MS 70, f. 192.
18. Though subsequently culpable of a degree of misappropriation of the carrack's riches himself, Burgh took care to place the principal blame squarely elsewhere: 'As for the ship, she is very rich, but much spoiled by the soldiers, being entered by force, and to which it was not possible for me to give order not [sic] of a long time, for that the Earl of Cumberland's men stood upon their lord's commission, and thereby challenged as great a commandment as I, notwithstanding that I made it known to the chief of them that I was joined in Her Majesty's commission with Sir Martin Frobiser' (Lethbridge Kingsford, 'Madre de Dios', pp. 113–14; modernized spelling).
19. BL Lansdowne MS 70, f. 41 (Frobisher to Burghley, 13 September 1592): '. . . accordinge to my last letters I comanded my L(ord) of Cumberland(e)s shipps and the greene dragon to staie by me and the Daintie of Sir John Hawkins but I was disobeyed as your honour shall understand . . .'.
20. BL Lansdowne MS 67, f. 192.
21. Hatfield House, Salisbury MS 97/78; BL Lansdowne MS 70, f. 48.
22. Monson's ship had been set upon by six Spanish galleys and taken after 'a long and bloody flight'. Remarkably, the victorious Spaniards had then reclothed and released the common mariners, detaining only Monson himself and five others – possibly the ship's officers (Oppenheim, *Monson*, i, pp. 270, 275).
23. BL Lansdowne MS 70, f. 68.
24. Oppenheim, *Monson*, i, p. 288.
25. BL Lansdowne MS 70, f. 68.
26. Ibid.
27. Ibid.
28. BL Sloane MS 3289, f. 74.
29. Oppenheim, *Royal Navy*, p. 167. The most detailed modern account of the aftermath of the capture of the *Madre de Dios* is that of Bovill, 'Madre de Dios'.
30. Williamson, *Earl of Cumberland*, p. 87.
31. Oppenheim, *Monson*, i, p. 292.
32. BL Lansdowne MS 70, f. 183.
33. Oppenheim, *Monson*, i, p. 293.
34. *APC*, xxiii, p. 269; 27 October 1592.
35. All consortship divisions calculated by Oppenheim, *Royal Navy*, p. 166; *Monson*, i, p. 295.
36. PRO E351/2229.
37. NLW, Chirk Castle MS F12540, f. 139; Frobisher had sent the prize back to England that same day, escorted by the *Galleon Ralegh* (BL Lansdowne MS 70, f. 30).
38. There is some evidence that he also held on to some small portion of the carrack's goods which he had managed to recover; on 22 November, George Barne wrote once more to Burghley, complaining thereof: '. . . the w(h)ich Sir Marten Frobusher and his Companie detayned and will by no means deliver, notwithstanding your hon(or)s l(ett)res com(m)andinge the same' (BL Lansdowne MS 70, f. 205).
39. BL Lansdowne MS 53, f. 38. As early as 1587, during the first few weeks of outright hostilities, a Spanish merchant had observed of his overseas business 'at this present I do not find any that will asure at any price' (Oppenheim, *Royal Navy*, p. 165).

40. Klarwill, *The Fugger Newsletters*, pp. 246–7.
41. *APC*, xxiv, p. 78.
42. Ibid., p. 82; 9 March 1593.
43. Bovill, 'Madre de Dios', pp. 143–4; Evans, 'Sir Thomas Myddelton', p. 85.
44. Andrews, *Elizabethan Privateering*, p. 235.
45. The evidence for this voyage is ambiguous. Myddelton was also involved in arrangements to pay off the 1592 Azores expedition, and several of his account entries in respect of Frobisher (NLW, Chirk Castle MS F12540, ff. 139–40) clearly refer to this. For example: 'Item. For goods w(hi)ch he had out of the Carack I awnswer in acc(ount) for him' is clearly a reference to spoils from the *Madre de Dios* which Frobisher secured following his return to England. However, the protracted period to which most of the individual accounts relate indicates that these are composite entries in Myddelton's ledger (probably summarized from his memorial book), and did not necessarily refer to a single voyage. The dates given for other transactions, particularly the period for which Frobisher's wages were due (as opposed to their payment, which was always long in arrears), and the period for which he was responsible for the victualling of the *Disdain* (not his command for most of the 1592 expedition) strongly suggest that he was set out again in 1593.
46. NLW, Chirk Castle MS F12540, f. 139.
47. Ibid., f. 140.
48. Strictly speaking, Frobisher was involved in the seizure of at least one further prize, taken during the 1594 Brest campaign. A vessel owned by merchants of St Malo, returning from Tripoli, was detained by elements of Frobisher's fleet in Coquet Roads. Henry IV, petitioned by his subjects, asked Elizabeth to intervene to release her (PRO SP/78/34, 609). On 5 November 1584, Frobisher reported that the ship had sunk a week earlier, being damaged during the fight to take her; though having run aground thereafter, a proportion of her cargo had been saved (ibid., 632). However, not only did Frobisher not comply with the French King's wishes, but he and Sir John Norreys, suspecting the vessel to be engaged in carrying materials to the enemy, also took the precaution of obtaining bonds from the St Malo merchants, committing them to paying the Queen £12,000 if the ship could be shown to be good prize. As the seizure was an official one, made during a military operation, it is hardly appropriate to append it to Frobisher's privateering record.
49. *APC*, xxii, pp. 322–3; 8 March 1592.
50. PRO Prerogative Court of Canterbury (PCC), 2 Scott; the will has been reproduced in full by Jones, *Sir Martin Frobisher*, pp. 342–60.
51. BL Harleian MS 4630, f. 191r.
52. Richard Jackson, though only fourth in the line of inheritance, appears to have enjoyed his uncle's particular favour; whether or not he inherited the bulk of the estate, he was to have the rents from Frobisher's manor at Haughton, from which he was to provide also for his younger brother, William.
53. Hawke was to experience great difficulty in securing any part of this from Peter Frobisher, whom he was suing as late as 1601 in the Court of Requests (PRO REQ/2/221/25).

TWENTY-ONE: THE CROZON PENINSULA: *EL LEON*, 1594

1. Williamson, *Sir John Hawkins*, p. 459.
2. Wernham, *List and Analysis*, v, pp. 267, 270–2.

3. The most comprehensive modern analyses of the campaign are those of Wernham, *After the Armada*, chapters xxiii and xxiv, and Nolan, 'English Operations'.

4. Nolan, 'English Operations', p. 265.

5. PRO E351/2231; SP/12/250, 13 (costs of the five ships' total complement – 1,190 men – at 7d. per day). Vice-admiral of the fleet was George Fenner, who had commanded the *Galleon Leicester* during the Armada campaign: according to Emanuel van Meteran, 'a man that had bene conversant in many Sea-fights' (Hakluyt, *PN* 1598–1600, iv, p. 216).

6. BL Cotton MSS Otho E IX, f. 266.

7. Wernham, *List and Analysis*, v, p. 298.

8. PRO SP/78/34, 601.

9. PRO SP/78/34, 611.

10. PRO SP/78/34, 632.

11. Note the description contained in fig. 7, p. 409: '37 foot thick in the topp'.

12. Oppenheim, *Monson*, i, p. 308. Oppenheim claims that as many as nine Spaniards had survived the assault; Frobisher 'five or six', and Norreys, in his report, gave the number as seven (Wernham, *List and Analysis*, v, p. 310).

13. BL Stowe MSS, 166, ff. 157, 159.

14. Crozon.

15. BL Cotton MSS Caligula E IX, i, f. 211.

16. Fuller, *Worthies*, iii, pp. 419–20.

17. During both visitations of the plague, St Giles had one of the highest rates of mortality of any London parish (Slack, *Impact of Plague*, pp. 155–6). The first known memorial to Frobisher was commissioned in 1888, the tricentenary of the Armada campaign. In 1960, during a general restoration of the church (which had lain in ruins since the fire-bomb raids of 1940/1), a plaque recalling the principal episodes in Frobisher's life was placed on the wall of the south aisle.

18. Fuller, *Worthies*, iii, p. 420. In fact, Peter survived until 1616 at least. In that year, he brought an action in Chancery against the estate of Ralegh, claiming that his uncle Martin had been an adventurer in the 1592 voyage, and that he had been due (but was never paid) some £1,600 from the proceeds of the sale of the *Madre de Dios* (French, 'Raleigh, Frobisher and the Great Carack of Spain', pp. 327–8).

19. BL Harleian MS 4630, f. 191v.

20. Ibid., f. 191r. Was that 'old officer' William Hawke? Few others serving at sea with Frobisher would have had such intimate knowledge of his kin and their prospects, or dared the familiarity to air it in so forthright a manner.

21. PRO SP/12/119, 29.

22. For the persistence of Lok's vision, see McDermott, 'Michael Lok', p. 138.

23. PRO Exchequer Decrees & Orders, E124/21/331.

24. For the bequests of three of Lok's sons, see McDermott, 'Michael Lok', p. 145, n.107.

TWENTY-TWO: THY BRUTE AND NAME

1. Arber, *Company of the Stationers*, ii, p. 666.

2. Blundeville, *Exercises*, f. 244.

3. Holland, *Herolwogia*, pp. 96–100.

4. Camden, *History*, p. 487.

5. Fuller, *Worthies*, iii, p. 419. Fuller's opinion was lifted almost verbatim from Stow (*Annals*, p. 808): '. . . he was very valiant, yet harsh and violent.'

6. See figure 2, p. 155. Hakluyt included Lok's map in his 1582 *Divers Voyages* (for which it was commissioned). It was not subsequently reproduced in the successive editions of the *Principal Navigations*. See Hair and Alsop (ed. Quinn), *Richard Hakluyt, Editor*, pp. 11, 19, 22–4.

7. For the evolution of Frobisher's cartographical legacy, see Ruggles, 'Frobisher Voyages', pp. 179–256.

8. The connection was John Frobisher's marriage to Joan, daughter of Sir William Scargill.

9. BL Lansdowne MS 100/1, f. 7v.

10. In 1577, classified as a 'soldier' in Lok's accounts, he received £8 10sh., as opposed to a more usual rate of £5–£7 (PRO EKR E164/35, pp. 27, 142). Though he was admitted as a £25 adventurer *gratis* in 1578 in respect of his former service (PRO SP/12/123, 50), and received money on Frobisher's behalf following the return of the 1578 voyage (PRO EKR E164/35, p. 256: 'for his m(aste)r, marten frobizer'), there is no evidence, either in Lok's wage-lists or the various accounts of the voyage, that Brakenberry actually sailed in 1578.

11. PRO EKR E164/35, p. 287. No beneficiary of Frobisher's will is named Thomas. Hogarth (*Frobisher Voyages*, p. 16) suggests that he was a kinsman from nearby Wakefield. This is possible – George Frobisher identifies a distant cousin of that name via Martin's great-grandfather John – but it cannot be verified from extant evidence.

12. The lodgings were situated in Beech Street, off Aldersgate; immediately to the north of the modern Barbican.

13. The honourable exception of Stefansson and McCaskill should be noted (*Frobisher*, i, p. cxxix), who at least admitted the problem: 'Frobisher's character, in spite of its apparent simplicity, is not altogether easy to estimate.'

14. These are, respectively, the assessments of Morrison, *European Discovery of America*, p. 549; Lacey, *Ralegh*, p. 166; and Rundall, *Narrative of Voyages*, p. 7.

15. BL Lansdowne MS 100/1, f. 13r.

16. The verse is Abraham Fleming's, from his *A rythme decasyllabical, comparative, and congratulatorie*; the second of his florid contributions to Settle's *True Reporte*.

TWENTY-THREE: POSTSCRIPT

1. Hall, *Arctic Researches*, i, p. 303.

2. Ibid., p. 445.

3. Rowley, 'Inuit Oral History', p. 217.

Bibliography

A. ARCHIVAL SOURCES

Public Record Office, London:
—Customs Accounts E87/4, E167/1; Port Books E4/2.
—Exchequer King's Remembrancer E164/35, 36: Michael Lok and others, financial accounts
for the north-west enterprise. These documents, comprising some 700 pages of memorial
book entries, were preserved as evidence presented during several lawsuits brought against
Lok following the demise of the enterprise. With the related material held in the Henry E.
Huntington Library, they comprise the most comprehensive body of financial data relating
to the outfitting of sixteenth-century English voyages.
—Exchequer Decrees & Orders E124/21.
—E351/2195, 2215, 2216, 2224–9; AO1 1687/28: Declared accounts of the Treasurer of the Navy.
—High Court of Admiralty HCA Oyer and Terminer 1/37; Acts 3/13, 14; Examinations
13/13–27; Exemplars 14/6–34; Libels 24/39, 41, 43; Warrant Books 38/6, 7.
—Patent Rolls 12/2604, 2886; 66/1126.
—Prerogative Court of Canterbury wills: 27 Bolein, 26 Carew, 20 Coode, 34 Hayes, 14 Holney,
46 Scott, 72 Wood.
—Proceedings in the Court of Requests. REQ 2: 165/76; 205/50; 207/64, 65; 210/83; 221/25.
—State Papers, domestic, Elizabeth (SP/12): Too numerous to list in full here (see footnotes),
these contain the bulk of correspondence and Privy Council orders relating to the north-
west enterprise and the later naval career of Frobisher. Jones (*Sir Martin Frobisher*) repro-
duced approximately fifty per cent of these (and also assembled the then-known British
Library papers); his SP/12 sources for 1574–79 were later presented, with some additions, by
Collinson (*Martin Frobisher*), and, subsequently, by Stefansson and McCaskill (*Frobisher*).
—State Papers, foreign; SP 70/32; 78/4, 19, 21, 34, 271, 274, 281, 290, 330, 342; 84/34, 38; 94/3
105/91; Colonial CO1/93, 156.
British Library:
—Additional MSS: 5664; 35831; 43827.
—Cotton MSS: Otho E VIII, 40–57, 98, 239; E IX, 267. Caligula E IX, i, 206. Galba D II,
59. Julius F X, 113. Vespasian C VIII, 12.

—Harleian MSS: 167/40, 41, 42 (respectively, Edward Selman's account of the 1578 voyage, Charles Jackman's 1578 ship's log for the *Judith* (fragment) and Christopher Hall's ship's 1578 log for the *Thomas Allen* and – on the return passage – *Ayde*); 168; 541; 4630.

—Lansdowne MSS: 67; 70; 71; 100/1 ('The doynges of Captayne Furbusher Amongest the Companyes busynes': Michael Lok's detailed and damning critique of Frobisher's activities during the course of the north-west enterprise), 100/4, 100/98; 107; 139; 149.

—Sloane MSS: 2442; 3289.

Magdalene College, Cambridge; Pepys MSS 2133: Edward Fenton's 1578 ship's log of the ship *Judith*.

Mercers' Hall, Ironmonger Lane, London: *List of Members of the Mercers Company from 1347*: card index containing biographical data.

Somerset Record Office: Phellips family papers, 1590.

Hatfield House: Salisbury MSS 97.

National Library of Wales, Aberystwyth: Chirk Castle MSS 12540; 12629.

Henry E. Huntington Library, San Marino: HM MS 715 (Lok's accounts for the outfitting of the 1578 voyage. These pages were separated from the main body of accounts sometime before 1821, when Craven Ord acquired and paginated the material now preserved in the PRO).

B. PRIMARY PRINTED SOURCES

(place of publication London unless stated otherwise)

Andrews, K.R. (ed.), 'Appraisements of Elizabethan Privateers-men', *Mariner's Mirror*, xxxvii (1951) pp. 76–9.

—*English Privateering Voyages to the West Indies, 1588–1595* (Cambridge, Hakluyt Society,1959).

—*The Last Voyage of Drake and Hawkins* (Hakluyt Society, 2nd series, 1972).

Anon, *A prayse, and reporte of Maister Martyne Forboishers voyage to Meta Incognita* (1578).

Arber, E. (ed.), *A Transcript of the Registers of the Company of the Stationers of London, 1554–1660* (2 vols, 1875).

Best, G., *A True Discourse of the Late Voyages of Discoverie . . . under the Conduct of Martin Frobisher General* (1578).

Billingsley, H., *The Elements of Geometrie of the most auncient Philosopher Euclide* (1570).

Blake, J.W., *Europeans in West Africa, 1450–1560* (2 vols, Hakluyt Society, 1942).

Blundeville, T., *T. Blundevile His Exercises, Contayning sixe Treatises, etc* (1594).

Bourne, W. (ed. Taylor), *A Regiment for the Sea* (Hakluyt Society, 1963).

Calendar of Letter Books of the City of London (1899).

Calendar of Letters & Papers (Foreign and Domestic) Henry VIII (1862–1932).

Calendar of Patent Rolls, Elizabeth I (1939–60).

Calendar of State Papers, Colonial Series, 1513–1616 (1862).

Calendar of State Papers, Foreign Series, Elizabeth, 1581–2 (1907); *1583* (1913).

Calendar of State Papers, Spanish, 1544–1558 (7 vols, 1890–1954).

Calendar of State Papers, Venetian, 1581–1591, (1894), *1592–1603* (1897).

Calendar of State Papers relating to English affairs . . . in the archives of Simancas (4 vols, 1892–9).

Calendar of State Papers relating to Ireland . . . reign of Elizabeth (11 vols, 1860–1912).

Camden, W. (ed.), *History of the Most Renowned and Victorious Princess Elizabeth, Late Queen of England* (1688).

Churchyard, T., *A prayse, and reporte of Maister Martyne Forboisher's Voyage* (1578).

Collingwood, W., *Elizabethan Keswick: Extracts from the Original Account Books, 1564–1577, of the German Miners, in the Archives of Augsburg* (Whitehaven, 1987).

Collins, A. (ed.), *Letters and Memorials of state . . . by Sir Henry Sidney etc* (2 vols, 1746).

Collinson, R., *The Three Voyages of Martin Frobisher* (Hakluyt Society, 1867).

Cooper, C.P., *Recueil des dépêches, rapports, instructions et mémoires des ambassadeurs de France en Angleterre et en Ecosse pendant le XVIe siècle, etc.* (6 vols, Paris, 1838–40).

Corbett, J.S., *Papers Relating to the Navy during the Spanish War, 1585–1587* (Navy Records Society, 1898).

Croft, P., *The Spanish Company* (London Record Society, vol. ix, 1973).

Culpepper, N., *The Physicall Directory, or a Translation of the London Dispensatory* (1649).

Dasent, J.R. (ed.), *Acts of the Privy Council of England* (new series, 1890–1902).

Donno, E.S. (ed.), *An Elizabethan in 1582. The Diary of Richard Madox, Fellow of All Souls* (Hakluyt Society, 1976).

Duro, C.F. (ed.), *La Armada invencible* (2 vols, Madrid, 1884–5).

Eden, R., *The decades of the Newe world or west India* (1555).

— *History of Travayle in the West and East Indies* (1577).

Ellis, T., *A true report of the third and last voyage into Meta Incognita atchieved by the worthie Capteine M. Martine Frobisher, Esquire. Anno 1578* (1578).

French, J.M., 'Raleigh, Frobisher and the Great Carack of Spain', *Notes and Queries*, 174 (1938), pp. 327–30.

Fry, G.S. (ed.), *Inquisitiones Post Mortem Relating to the City of London, Tudor Period*, vols i and ii (Index Library, 1896, 1898).

Hair, P.E.H. and Alsop, J.D. (eds), *English Seamen and Traders in Guinea, 1553–1565: The New Evidence of their Wills* (*Studies in British History*, 31 (1992)).

Hakluyt, R., *The Principal Navigations, Voyages, Traffiques & Discoveries of the English Nation, etc.* (12 vols, Glasgow, 1903–5).

— *The principall navigations, voiages and discoveries of the English nation by Richard Hakluyt* (eds, R.A. Skelton and D.B. and A.M. Quinn, facsimile edn, 2 vols, Hakluyt Society, extra series, 1965).

— (ed. Quinn), *Richard Hakluyt, Editor: A Study Introductory to the Facsimile Edition of Richard Hakluyt's Divers Voyages, 1582* (2 vols, Amsterdam, 1967).

— *Discourse of Western Planting* (eds, D.B. and A.M. Quinn, Hakluyt Society, extra series, 1993).

Halliwell, J.O., *The Private Diary of John Dee* (Camden Society, 1842).

Heath, J.B., 'An account of materials furnished for the use of Queen Anne Boleyn and the Princess Elizabeth, by William Loke, the King's Mercer', *Miscellanies of the Philobiblon Society*, vii, 1862–3, pp. 1–22.

Holland, P., *Heroωlogia* (1620).

Hughes, P.L. and Larkin, J.F. (eds), *Tudor Royal Proclamations* (vols ii and iii, New Haven, 1964–9).

Keeler, M.F. (ed.), *Sir Francis Drake's West Indian Voyage, 1585–86* (Hakluyt Society, 1981).

Kervyn De Lettenhove, J.M.B.C. and Gilliodts Van Severen, L. (eds), *Relations politiques des Pays-Bas de l'Angleterre, sous le règne de Philippe II* (11 vols, Brussels, 1888–1900).

Kinder, A.G., 'The Protestant Pastor as Intelligencer: Casiodoro de Reina's Letters to Wilhelm IV, Landgrave of Hesse-Cassel (1577–1582)', *Bibliothèque d'Humanisme et Renaissance*, lviii, i (1996), pp. 105–18.

Klarwill, V. von (ed.), *The Fugger news letters. Being a selection of unpublished letters from the correspondents of the House of Fugger* (1924).

Laughton, J.K., *State Papers relating to the defeat of the Spanish Armada* (2 vols, Navy Records Society, 1896).

Lethbridge Kingsford, C. (ed.), 'The taking of the Madre de Dios, Anno 1592', in J.K. Laughton, (ed.), *The Naval Miscellany*, ii (Navy Records Society, 1912), pp. 85–121.

Lyell, L. (ed.), *Acts of Court of the Mercers' Company, 1453–1527* (Cambridge, 1936).

McDermott, J., 'The account books of Michael Lok, relating to the north-west voyages of Martin Frobisher, 1576–1578: text and analysis' (with transcriptions of PRO E164/35, 36 & HM 715); unpublished M.Phil. thesis, University of Hull (1984).

Madden, F., *Privy Purse Expenses of the Princess Mary, Daughter of King Henry the Eighth* (1881).

Marsden, R.G. (ed.), *Select Pleas in the Court of Admiralty* (vols vi (1894), xi (1897), Selden Society).

—*Documents Relating to the Law and Custom of the Sea* (vol. i, Navy Records Society, 1915).

Martin, C.T., 'The Diary of Francis Walsingham, 1570–83', *Camden Society Miscellanies*, iv (1871), pp. ii, 140.

Morley, H. (ed.), *Ireland under Elizabeth and James I* (1890).

Murdin, W. (ed.), *Collection of State Papers . . . of Lord Burghley* (2 vols, 1740, 1759).

Nichols, J.G. (ed.), *The Diary of Henry Machyn* (Camden Society, old series, 1848).

Oppenheim, M. (ed.), *The Naval Tracts of Sir William Monson* (Navy Records Society, 5 vols, 1902–1914).

Purchas, S., *Hakluytus Posthumus, or Purchas his Pilgrims, etc* (London, 1625–6).

—*The Voyages and Colonising Enterprises of Sir Humphrey Gilbert* (2 vols, Hakluyt Society, 1940).

—*The Roanoke Voyages 1584–1590* (2 vols, Hakluyt Society, 1955).

Quinn, D.B. (ed.), *The Hakluyt Handbook* (2 vols, Hakluyt Society, 1974).

—*New American World* (5 vols, New York, 1979).

Ramsay, G.D. (ed.), *The Accounts of John Isham, Mercer and Merchant Adventurer* (Durham, 1962).

Read, C., 'Despatches of Castelnau de la Mauvissière, 1577–81', *American Historical Review*, 31 (1926), pp. 285–96.

Rundall, T., *Narrative of Voyages towards the North-west in Search of a Passage to Cathay and India, 1496 to 1631* (Hakluyt Society, 1849).

Stefansson, V. and McCaskill, E., *The Three Voyages of Martin Frobisher* (2 vols, 1938).

Stow, J. (ed.), *Annales, or, a Generall Chronicle of England, etc* (1615).

Tawney, R.H., *Tudor Economic Documents* (3 vols, 1924).

Taylor, E.G.R. (ed.), *The Original Writings and Correspondence of the two Richard Hakluyts* (2 vols, Hakluyt Society, 1935).

—*The Troublesome Voyage of Captain Edward Fenton, 1582–3* (Hakluyt Society, 1959).

Wernham, R.B., *The Expedition of Sir John Norris and Sir Francis Drake to Spain and Portugal, 1589* (Navy Records Society, 1988).

—*List and Analysis of State Papers, Foreign Series, Elizabeth I* (5 vols, 1964–89).

Williamson, J.A. (ed.), *The Voyages of the Cabots and the Discovery of North America* (Amsterdam, 1971).

Wright, I.A., *Further English Voyages to Spanish America* (Cambridge, Hakluyt Society, 1951).

C. SECONDARY WORKS

Adams, S., 'The Outbreak of the Elizabethan Naval War against the Spanish Empire: The Embargo of May 1585 and Sir Francis Drake's West Indies Voyage' in Rodriguez-Salgado and Adams, *Gran Armada*, pp. 45–69.

Allaire, B., 'French reactions to the north-west voyages and the assays of the Frobisher ore by Geoffrey le Brumen, 1576–1584', in Symons (ed.), *Meta Incognita*, ii, pp. 589–606.

—'Martin Frobisher, the Spaniards and a sixteenth-century northern spy', in Symons (ed.), *Meta Incognita*, ii, pp. 575–88.

Anderson, R.C., *List of English men-of-war, 1509–1664* (Society for Nautical Research Occasional Publications no. 7, 1959).

Andrews, K.R., *Elizabethan Privateering* (Cambridge, 1964).

—*Drake's Voyages: a re-assessment of their place in Elizabethan maritime expansion* (New York, 1967).

—*The Spanish Caribbean: Trade and Plunder 1530–1630* (New Haven and London, 1978).

—'The Elizabethan Seaman', *Mariner's Mirror*, lxviii (1982), pp. 245–62.

—*Trade, Plunder and Settlement: Maritime Enterprise and the Genesis of the British Empire, 1480–1630* (Cambridge, 1984).

—'Elizabethan Privateering', in Youings, *Raleigh in Exeter*, pp. 1–20.

Baldwin, R., 'Speculative ambitions and the reputations of Frobisher's metallurgists', in Symons (ed.), *Meta Incognita*, ii, pp. 401–76.

Beaven, A.B., *The Aldermen of the City of London* (2 vols, 1908–13).

Beckingham, C.F., 'The Near East, North and North-east Africa', in Quinn (ed.), *Hakluyt Handbook*, i, pp. 176–89.

Beer, B.L., 'London and the Rebellions of 1548-9', *Journal of British Studies*, xii (1972), pp. 15–38.

—*Northumberland: The Political Career of John Dudley, Earl of Warwick and Duke of Northumberland* (Kent State University Press, 1973).

Boas, F.S., *Sir Philip Sidney: Representative Elizabethan* (Rochester, 1955).

Bovill, E.W., 'Queen Elizabeth's Gunpowder', *Mariner's Mirror*, xxxiii (1947), pp. 179–86.

—'The Madre de Dios', *Mariner's Mirror*, liv (1968), pp. 129–52.

Bramston, J., *The autobiography of Sir John Bramston* (Camden Society, 1845).

Brigden, S., *London and the Reformation* (Oxford, 1989).

Burwash, M., *English Merchant Shipping 1460–1540* (Toronto, 1947).

Carus-Wilson, E.M., *Medieval Merchant Venturers* (1954).

Challis, C.E., *The Tudor Coinage* (Manchester, 1978).

Cheshire, N., Waldron, T., Quinn, A. and Quinn, D.B., 'Frobisher's Eskimos in England', *Archivaria*, 10 (1980), pp. 23–50.

Cipolla, C.M., *Guns and Sails in the Early Phase of European Expansion, 1400–1700* (1965).

Clay, C.G.A., *Economic Expansion and Social Change: England 1500–1700* (2 vols, Cambridge, 1984).

Collinson, P., 'The Role of Women in the English Reformation, illustrated by the Life and Friendships of Anne Locke', in G. Cumming (ed.), *Studies in Church History* (vol. 2, 1965), pp. 258–72.

—*The Elizabethan Puritan Movement* (1967).

Connell-Smith, G., *Forerunners of Drake* (Plymouth, 1954).

Corbett, J.S., *Drake and the Tudor Navy* (2 vols, 1898).

Cummins, J., *Francis Drake* (1995).

Davis, R., *The Rise of the English Shipping Industry* (1962).

Dickens, A.G., *The English Reformation* (1964).

Dictionary of National Biography (1895–1900).

Donaldson, M.B., 'Burchard Kranich', *Annals of Science*, vi (1950), pp. 308–22.

—*Elizabethan Copper: The History of the Company of the Mines Royal, 1565–1603* (Whitehaven, 1955).

Elliot, J.H., *Europe Divided, 1559–1598* (1968).

—*The Old World and the New: 1492–1650* (Cambridge, 1970).

Elliot, K.M., 'The First Voyages of Martin Frobisher', *English Historical Review*, 32 (1917), pp. 89–92.

L'Estrange-Ewen, C., 'Organized piracy round England in the sixteenth-century', *Mariner's Mirror*, xxxv (1949), pp. 29–42.

Falls, C., *Elizabeth's Irish Wars* (London, 1950).

Fernandez-Armesto, F., *The Spanish Armada: The experience of war in 1588* (Oxford, 1988).

Fitzhugh, W.W. and Olin, J.S. (eds), *Archeology of the Frobisher Voyages* (Smithsonian Institution, 1993).

Foster, F.F., *The Politics of Stability: A Portrait of the Rulers in Elizabethan London* (1977).

Friel, I., *The Good Ship: Ships, Shipbuilding and Technology in England, 1200–1520* (1995).

— 'Frobisher's Ships: the Ships of the North-West Atlantic Voyages, 1576–1578', in Symons (ed.), *Meta Incognita*, ii, pp. 299–352.

Fuller, T. (ed.), *The History of the Worthies of England* (3 vols, 1840).

Fury, C.A., 'Training and Education in the Elizabethan Maritime Community, 1585–1603', *Mariner's Mirror*, lxxxv (1999), pp. 147–61.

Gad, F., *History of Greenland*, i (Montreal, 1971).

Geyl, P. *The Revolt of the Netherlands 1555–1609* (1958 edn).

Glasgow, T., 'Elizabethan ships pictured on Smerwick map, 1580. Background, authentication and evaluation', *Mariner's Mirror*, lii (1966), pp. 157–62.

— 'The Navy in Philip and Mary's War, 1557–1558', *Mariner's Mirror*, liii (1967), pp. 321–43.

Hall, C.F., *Arctic Researches and Life among the Esquimaux* (2 vols, New York, 1865).

Herbert, W., *The History of the Twelve Great Livery Companies of London* (2 vols, 1834–7).

Hill, C., *Intellectual Origins of the English Revolution* (Oxford, 1965).

Hogarth, D.D., 'The Ships' Company in the Frobisher Voyages', in Fitzhugh, *Archeology of the Frobisher Voyages*, pp. 15–16.

Hogarth, D.D., Boreham, P.W. and Mitchell, J.G., *Mines, Minerals, Metallurgy: Martin Frobisher's North-west Venture, 1576–1581* (Canadian Museum of Civilization, Mercury Series, Directorate Paper no. 7, 1994).

Howarth, D., *The Voyage of the Armada: The Spanish Story* (1981).

Hutchinson, G., *Medieval Ships and Shipping* (Leicester, 1994).

Izon, J., *Sir Thomas Stucley c. 1515–1578: Traitor Extraordinary* (1956).

Jones, E.D., 'An account book of Sir Thomas Myddelton for the years 1583–1603', *National Library of Wales Journal*, i, no. 2, pp. 84–8.

Jones, F., *The Life of Sir Martin Frobisher, knight, containing a narrative of the Spanish Armada* (1878).

Kamen, H., *Philip of Spain* (New Haven and London, 1997).

Kelsey, H., *Sir Francis Drake: The Queen's Pirate* (New Haven and London, 1998).

Lacey, R., *Sir Walter Ralegh* (New York, 1974).

Levy, F.J., 'The Strange Life and Death of Captain Henry Stranguishe', *Mariner's Mirror*, xlviii (1962), pp. 133–7.

Lewis, M., 'Armada guns; a comparative study of English and Spanish armaments', *Mariner's Mirror*, xxviii (pp. 41–73, 104–47, 231–45, 259–90) and xxix (pp. 3–39, 100–21, 163–78, 203–31), (1942–3).

Lloyd, R., *Dorset Elizabethans at Home and Abroad* (1967).

Loades, D., *The Tudor Navy* (Cambridge, 1992).

MacCaffrey, W.T., *Queen Elizabeth and the Making of Policy, 1572–1588* (Princeton, 1981).

— *Elizabeth I: War and Politics, 1588–1603* (Princeton, 1992).

McDermott, J., 'Frobisher's 1578 voyage: early eyewitness accounts of English ships in Arctic seas', *Polar Record*, 32: 183 (1996), pp. 325–34.

—'Humphrey Cole and the Frobisher Voyages', in S. Ackermann (ed.), *Humphrey Cole: Mint, Measurement and Maps in Elizabethan England* (British Museum Occasional Paper no. 126, 1998), pp. 15–19.

—'The Company of Cathay: the financing and organization of the Frobisher voyages', in Symons (ed.), *Meta Incognita*, i, pp. 147–78.

—'Michael Lok, mercer and merchant adventurer', in Symons (ed.), *Meta Incognita*, i, pp. 119–46.

—'A right Heroicall Heart: the life of Sir Martin Frobisher', in Symons (ed.), *Meta Incognita*, i, pp. 55–118.

—'The construction of the Dartford furnaces', in Symons (ed.), *Meta Incognita*, ii, pp. 505–22.

McDermott, J. and Waters, D.W., 'Cathay and the Way Thither: the Navigation of the Frobisher Voyages', in Symons (ed.), *Meta Incognita*, ii, pp. 353–400.

McFee, W., *The Life of Sir Martin Frobisher* (New York, 1928).

Maltby, W.S., *The Black Legend in England: The development of anti-Spanish sentiment, 1558–1660* (Durham, North Carolina, 1968).

Manhart, G.B., 'The English search for a north-west passage in the time of Queen Elizabeth', in A.L. Rowland and G.B. Manhart, *Studies in English commerce and exploration in the reign of Elizabeth* (University of Philadelphia, 1924), pp. 1–240.

Marcus, G.J., 'The First English Voyages to Iceland', *Mariner's Mirror*, xlii (1956), pp. 313–18.

Marsden, R.G., 'The High Court of Admiralty in relation to National History, Commerce and the Colonisation of America', *Transactions of the Royal Historical Society*, xvi (1902), pp. 69–96.

—'Early Career of Sir Martin Frobisher', *English Historical Review*, xxi (1906), pp. 538–44.

Martin, C. and Parker, G., *The Spanish Armada* (1st edn 1988, 2nd edn 1999).

Mathew, D., 'The Cornish and Welsh Pirates in the Reign of Elizabeth', *English Historical Review*, xxxix (1924), pp. 337–48.

Mattingly, G., *The Armada* (Boston, 1959).

Maxwell, S., 'Henry Seckford: sixteenth-century merchant, courtier and privateer', *Mariner's Mirror*, lxxxii (1996), pp. 387–97.

Morrison, S.E., *The European Discovery of America: The Northern Voyages A.D. 500–1600* (New York, 1971).

Nolan, J.S., 'English Operations around Brest, 1594', *Mariner's Mirror*, lxxxi (1995), pp. 259–74.

O'Donnell, H., 'The Army of Flanders and the Invasion of England, 1586–8', in Rodriguez-Salgado and Adams, *Gran Armada*, pp. 216–35.

Oppenheim, M., *A History of the Administration of the Royal Navy, and of merchant shipping in relation to the Navy from 1509 to 1660* (1896).

Parker, G., *The Grand Strategy of Philip II* (New Haven and London, 1998).

—'The Dreadnought Revolution in Tudor England', *Mariner's Mirror*, vol. 82 (1996), pp. 269–300.

Parker, J., *Books to Build an Empire* (Amsterdam, 1965).

Pierson, P., *Commander of the Armada: The Seventh Duke of Medina Sidonia* (New Haven and London, 1989).

Pollen, J.H., *Mary Queen of Scots and the Babington Plot* (Edinburgh, 1922).

Prior, M., 'Reviled and Crucified Marriages: the Position of Tudor Bishops' Wives', in Prior (ed.), *Women in English Society 1500–1800* (1985).

Pulman, M.B., *The Elizabethan Privy Council in the Fifteen-Seventies* (Berkeley, 1971).

Quinn, D.B., 'Renaissance Influences in English Colonization', *Royal Historical Society Transactions*, 5th series, 26 (1976), pp. 73–93.

—*The Lost Colonists: Their Fortune and Probable Fate* (Raleigh, 1984).

—*Sebastian Cabot and Bristol Exploration* (Bristol, 1993).

— 'The Context of English North-west Exploration', in Symons (ed.), *Meta Incognita*, i, pp. 7–18.

Quinn, D.B. and Ryan, A.N., *England's Sea Empire* (1983).

Rabb, T., *Enterprise and Empire, Merchant and Gentry Investment in the Expansion of England, 1575–1630* (Cambridge, Mass., 1967).

Ramsay, G.D., *English Overseas Trade during the Centuries of Emergence* (1957).

— *The City of London in international politics at the accession of Elizabeth Tudor* (Manchester, 1975).

— *The Queen's Merchants and the Revolt of the Netherlands* (Manchester, 1986).

Read, C., *Mr Secretary Cecil and Queen Elizabeth* (London, 1955).

— *Bibliography of British History, Tudor period* (Oxford, 1959).

— *Lord Burghley and Queen Elizabeth* (New York, 1960).

Rodger, N.A.M., 'The development of broadside gunnery, 1450–1650', *Mariner's Mirror*, lxxxii (1996), pp. 301–24.

— *The Safeguard of the Sea* (vol. i, 1997).

Rodriguez-Salgado, M.J. and Adams, S., *England, Spain and the Gran Armada: Essays from the Anglo-Spanish Conference, London and Madrid, 1988* (Savage, Maryland, 1991).

Rowley, S., 'Inuit Oral History: The Voyages of Sir Martin Frobisher, 1576–1578', in S. Alsford, (ed.), *The Meta Incognita Project: Contributions to Field Studies* (Canadian Museum of Civilization, Mercury Series, Directorate Paper no. 6, 1993), pp. 211–19.

Rowse, A.L., *Sir Richard Grenville of the Revenge* (1940).

— *Tudor Cornwall* (1941).

Ruddock, A.A., 'John Day of Bristol and the English voyages across the Atlantic before 1497', *Geographical Journal*, 132 (1966), pp. 225–33.

Ruggles, R.I., 'The Cartography of the Frobisher Voyages', Symons (ed.), *Meta Incognita*, i, pp. 179–256.

Scammell, G.V., 'The English in the Atlantic Islands 1450–1650', *Mariner's Mirror*, lxxii (1986), pp. 294–316.

— 'The Sinews of War: Manning and Provisioning English Fighting Ships', *Mariner's Mirror*, lxxiii (1987), pp. 351–67.

Scott, W.R., *The Constitution and Finance of English, Scottish and Irish Joint-Stock Companies to 1720* (3 vols, Cambridge, 1910).

Senior, W., 'Judges of the High Court of Admiralty', *Mariner's Mirror*, xiii (1927), pp. 334–7.

Shammas, C., 'The "Invisible Merchant" and property rights', *Business History*, 17 (1975), pp. 95–108.

Sherman, W.H., 'John Dee's Role in Martin Frobisher's North-west Enterprise', in Symons (ed.), *Meta Incognita*, i, pp. 283–98.

Shillington, V.M. and Wallis Chapman, A.B. (eds), *The Commercial Relations of England and Portugal* (New York, 1970).

Shirley, R.W., *The Mapping of the World: Early Printed World Maps, 1472–1700* (1984).

Slack, P., *The Impact of Plague in Tudor and Stuart England* (Oxford, 1985).

Smith, J.C.C. (ed.), *Index of Wills proved in the Prerogative Court of Canterbury, 1383–1558*, ii (1895).

Spence, R.T., *The Privateering Earl: George Clifford, third Earl of Cumberland, 1558–1605* (Bodmin, 1995).

Sturtevant, W.C. and Quinn, D.B., 'This New Prey: Eskimos in Europe in 1567, 1576 and 1577', in, C. Feest (ed.), *Indians and Europe: an Interdisciplinary Collection of Essays* (Aachen, 1987), pp. 61–140.

Symons, T.H.B. (ed.), *Meta Incognita: A Discourse of Discovery. Martin Frobisher's Arctic Expe-
    ditions, 1576–1578* (2 vols, Canadian Museum of Civilization, Mercury Series, Directorate
    Paper no. 10, 1999).
Taylor, E.G.R., *Tudor Geography, 1485–1583* (1930).
—*Late Tudor and early Stuart Geography* (1934).
— 'Voyages of Martin Frobisher', *Geographical Journal*, 91 (1938), pp. 360–3.
— *The Haven-Finding Art* (1956).
Thomas, D.A., *The Illustrated Armada Handbook* (1988).
Thompson, I.A.A., 'Spanish Armada Guns', *Mariner's Mirror*, lxi (1975), pp. 355–71.
Tillyard, E.M.W., *The Elizabethan World Picture* (1943).
Unwin, G., *The Gilds and Companies of London* (1908).
Waters, D.W., 'The Elizabethan Navy and the Armada Campaign', *Mariner's Mirror*, xxxv
    (1949), pp. 90–137.
— *The Art of Navigation in England in Elizabethan and Early Stuart Times* (1958).
Watt, J., 'The Medical Climate of Frobisher's England: Maritime Influences', in Symons (ed.),
    Meta Incognita, i, pp. 257–82.
— 'The Frobisher Voyages of 1576, 1577 and 1578: The Medical Record', in Symons (ed.), *Meta
    Incognita*, ii, pp. 607–32.
Watt, J. and Savours, A., 'The captured "Countrey People": Their depiction and medical
    history', in Symons (ed.), *Meta Incognita*, ii, pp. 553–62.
Wernham, R.B., *Before the Armada: the growth of English foreign policy, 1485–1588* (1966).
—*After the Armada: Elizabethan England and the Struggle for Western Europe* (Oxford, 1984).
Wheater, W., 'The Ancestry of Sir Martin Frobisher', *Gentleman's Magazine* (November, 1868),
    pp. 852–8.
White, J.G., *History of the Ward of Walbrook in the City of London* (1904).
Willan, T.S., 'Trade between England and Russia in the second half of the Sixteenth Century',
    English Historical Review, lxiii (1948), pp. 307–21.
— *The Muscovy Merchants of 1555* (Manchester, 1953).
— 'Some aspects of English trade with the Levant in the sixteenth century', *English Historical
    Review*, lxx (1955), pp. 399–410.
— *The Early History of the Russia Company* (Manchester, 1956).
—*Studies in Elizabethan Foreign Trade* (Manchester, 1959).
Williamson, G.C., *George, Third Earl of Cumberland, 1558–1605* (1920).
Williamson, J.A., 'Michael Lok', *Blackwoods Magazine*, cxcvi (1914), pp. 58–72.
—*Sir John Hawkins, the time and the man* (Oxford, 1927).
—*Hawkins of Plymouth* (1949).
Wood, A.C., *A History of the Levant Company* (1935).
Youings, J. (ed.), *Raleigh in Exeter 1985: Privateering and Colonisation in the reign of Elizabeth
    I* (Exeter, 1985).
Zins, H., *England and the Baltic* (Manchester, 1972).

Index